T0303856

Biomedical Informatics

An Introduction to Information Systems and Software in Medicine and Health

Biomedical Informatics

An Introduction to Information Systems and Software in Medicine and Health

David J. Lubliner

New Jersey Institute of Technology, Newark, USA

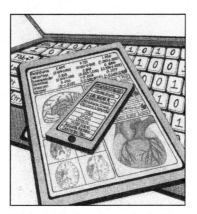

Illustration by Amy Cassandra Lubliner

CRC Press
Taylor & Francis Group
Boca Raton   London   New York

CRC Press is an imprint of the
Taylor & Francis Group, an **Informa** business
AN AUERBACH BOOK

CRC Press
Taylor & Francis Group
6000 Broken Sound Parkway NW, Suite 300
Boca Raton, FL 33487-2742

© 2016 by Taylor & Francis Group, LLC
CRC Press is an imprint of Taylor & Francis Group, an Informa business

No claim to original U.S. Government works

Printed on acid-free paper
Version Date: 20150831

International Standard Book Number-13: 978-1-4665-9620-7 (Hardback)

Visit the Taylor & Francis Web site at
http://www.taylorandfrancis.com

and the CRC Press Web site at
http://www.crcpress.com

Contents

Preface

The inspiration for writing this textbook was fourfold: First, to create a cohesive narrative of the multi-disciplinary concepts linking the Biomedical Informatics field; second, to introduce an improved textbook organizational structure so students will have a clear demarcation between essential and optional materials; third, to provide a primer on the theoretical concepts that underpin the science in this field including an Anatomy & Physiology essentials guide; and lastly, to provide a tutorial on application development so students can understand the tools that can be applied to provide improved user interfaces for EHRs on mobile platforms. I believe that the current spate of textbooks could be improved. Most textbooks in either health, medical, or biomedical informatics are usually a compendium of disparate facts cobbled together from distinct concepts, albeit appropriate for this field, lacking the narrative and content that ties together concepts.

Most books in this field are written by 20–30 individual authors; although experts in their field, their narrow charge and scope limit the cohesive connection between concepts. This textbook attempts to build a cohesive narrative beginning with the forces and government mandates that facilitated this exponential rise in the universal acceptance of the structure and standards that created this new discipline. Later, the science behind these technologies is explored, including a necessary basic primer on anatomy and physiology and in later chapters feedback from nursing experts and managers who have implemented and used electronic health records. The last chapter attempts to define a series of parameters for predictive biomedical informatics so professionals can extrapolate forces that may expand or impede future desired advances. Technological forces are only one factor that leads to innovation; often financial, governmental, and intangible public perceptions need to be factored into the equations for predictive analysis. Appendices A through D are a basic primer on writing applications for portable devices. These devices will play a more important role in healthcare delivery and monitoring in the future.

The second motivation to writing this textbook was to create a structure that facilitated learning. Most books introduce concepts but are not easily structured for the reader or instructor. In a typical 40-page chapter, how do you determine which concepts are essential facts, which are applied concepts, and which ideas fall into the advanced topic realm? The book attempts to create a clear delineation between Level I, basic concepts every biomedical informatics professional should master, Level II, applied concepts and examples, and Level III, advanced topics. Undergraduate and graduate instructors and professionals in the field can quickly focus on the essential topics but if interested can delve in Level III advanced topics. I appreciate feedback from the readers regarding unintentional errors or suggestions for enhancing future editions.

The journey of writing this or any book is transformative. The authors believe they are experts in their fields, but then after, for example, reading 10,000 pages of the DICOM medical imaging standards Parts 1–20, their perceptions evolve and they begin to appreciate the complexities and in-depth interoperability that underlie these standards that they were not privy to before. It also leads readers to explore and hopefully extrapolate meaning that allows them to begin their own journey of exploration and learning. "When you reach that point in life where you realize how little you actually know, that's the first step in your journey to learning." This concept has been echoed from the teaching of the Buddha to the fictional character Don Juan by Tirso de Molina in 1630. There is always more to learn, and I hope this book motivates a few to continue this journey. I have tried to include links to all documents and standards sources so students can explore, in detail, each idea described in this book.

The research process for the book took several years. It was challenging, or agonizing, depending on your perspective. The web provides virtually infinite resources, but extracting the wheat from the chaff is often difficult. Exploring tenuous linkages between concepts, falling deep into the rabbit hole and then trying to extract myself was a challenge. Where do you stop? You could write an entire book on MRIs or HL7 standards, but extracting the essential meaning of concepts so students can begin their own exploration is difficult. The goal was to create a textbook that would provide a teacher or a student with clear, engaging, in-depth explanations and links to resources to explore concepts in more detail if desired.

The book was written to be read in sequential order but allows students the ability to explore topics in detail. The structure of the book allows that mode of exploration. Level I of every chapter is recommended. In addition, Chapter 10, "A Critical Care Nurse's Perspective of EHRs," should be read. How we use technology is as important as the technology itself. Enjoy the journey; this is an exciting, evolving field that will transform healthcare.

David J. Lubliner, PhD

MATLAB® is a registered trademark of The MathWorks, Inc. For product information, please contact:

The MathWorks, Inc.
3 Apple Hill Drive
Natick, MA 01760-2098 USA
Tel: 508-647-7000
Fax: 508-647-7001
E-mail: info@mathworks.com
Web: www.mathworks.com

Author

David J. Lubliner is a member of the faculty at a northeastern university where he runs a medical informatics program that he developed a decade earlier. He earned his PhD in information systems and has graduate degrees in biomedical engineering and computer science. He is currently part of a team developing a handheld medical scanner. Prior to teaching, he worked for 10 years at a Fortune 500 company as a divisional vice president of an architecture–computer security group and before that worked as an engineer on the Patriot missile system.

Dr. Lubliner believes we are at the dawn of a new age of medicine, where instant access to data will change the current top-down model of healthcare to a more user-centric system. At the beginning of the twentieth century, technological advances doubled life spans, and we are poised to recreate that with the exponential growth of medical research and real-time access to information, creating a truly universal medical principia of all human knowledge: "Live long and prosper."

Contributors

Philomena M. DiQuollo is a working health-care IT professional who began her career in nursing and transitioned to IT&S 12 years later. Since 1985, she has been working in acute care facilities, implementing clinical and business technology solutions as well as directing day-to-day operations and supporting strategic goals at a major urban teaching medical center in New Jersey. Currently, her position is system director of analytics within a multifacility health-care system. Philomena DiQuollo is an adjunct faculty at New Jersey Institute of Technology, Newark, New Jersey, teaching in the medical informatics program. She received her BSN from Seton Hall University, South Orange, New Jersey and MA in nursing from New York University, New York, New York. In addition, she is a certified professional in health information management systems and is American Society for Quality Six Sigma Green Belt certified. She resides in New Jersey and is pursuing a master's in analytics at Villanova University, Villanova, Pennsylvania.

Cathy Lubliner is a critical care clinical nurse specialist at an academic teaching hospital. She has more than 30 years experience in the care of patients with end-stage heart failure, cardiogenic and septic shock, pre- and posttransplant procedures, and ventricular assist devices. During the implementation of the EHR, she served as one of the "super users" to facilitate the transition of the nursing staff to the computer-based documentation system.

Daniel Nasello is an experienced mobile and web application developer and project manager, who currently resides in Nutley New Jersey. Having developed some highly successful applications (including multiple applications for various singers and actors) and having worked in multiple industries allow Daniel to bring the experience into the software he develops. Seeing the rapid growth of mobile application development, Daniel has created groundbreaking and innovative applications that will be used in tomorrow's market, and he is also developing mobile and web application opportunities in industries where they are nonexistent. Daniel currently holds a bachelor's degree in computer technology a master's degree in information system from the New Jersey Institute of Technology, Newark, New Jersey. He is also a part-time instructor at NJIT, where he spearheaded the mobile application development class, which is rapidly growing in popularity.

1

Introduction to
Biomedical Informatics

Level I: Core Concepts

1.1 Introduction

Biomedical Informatics (BMI) lies at the intersection of information technology (IT) and healthcare/ medicine. Integrating complex data, linking medical professionals and patients, staying abreast of the lightning changes in both fields, and providing real-time secure data make this field simultaneously exciting and challenging.

The BMI professionals are well versed in IT since they will be working with hospitals' IT staffs and radiologists to ensure seamless integration of digital imaging and communications, working with structured data and protocols; integrating all forms of wired and wireless data, facilitating secure communication protocols, and interfacing with medical professionals and patients will require a broad knowledge of interrelated fields. Electronic health records (EHRs) may be the most visible of technologies the BMI professional facilitates, incredibly complex in their own right, integrating data from a myriad of sources both internal and external and providing expertise in developing user interfaces and facilitating data capture from medical sensors/ monitors. Working with medical staff, their role is to customize user interfaces, which requires a knowledge of medical terminology and standards such as ICD10 and SNOMED and knowledge of best practices meaningful use regulations. They will be at the forefront of the transition to "medical records 2," creating user-friendly and efficient interfaces via mobile devices tailored to the needs of individual professionals. *A nurse should not be a data entry specialist*, but EHR tools and interfaces should facilitate not hinder their profession, so a knowledge of application development and user interfaces is a critical core knowledge.

We are in the infancy of EHR technology, at the awkward stage of barely being able to walk and talk, and certainly not user-friendly, spitting up all over users. The baby was born with the help of HIPAA, the Stimulus Act, and the Affordable Care Act (ACA). BMI professionals have to guide and support the evolution of this infant to stage 2, toddler, walking, talking, and potty training them to be productive members of society. Buckle up, there will be all-night feeding sessions, changing dirty diapers, and ensuring the child becomes a productive member of society.

1.2 Nomenclature

There are a number of medical/biological/health/research informatics fields with sometimes overlapping nomenclatures: Defined as "a set or system of names or terms used in a particular science or art, by an individual or community." The intent of this section is to provide precise definitions needed by the Biomedical Informatics (BMI) professional. The second goal is to explain the evolution of the term "Biomedical" as a more inclusive term rather than the older designation of Medical Informatics. Lastly, a brief description of the many related informatics subfields are provided (Figure 1.1).

This new definition adds two concepts that I believe should enhance the descriptions of the science of BMI, i.e. the terms *meaning* and *intuitive user interfaces*, essential in the evolution of the science. Meaning refers to correlating the growing flood of medical data into an overall systems holistic view rather than simply displaying individual data points. The analogy would be between information and knowledge. The current EHR's have not been tailored for the unique requirements of diverse healthcare providers and often hinder rather than facilitate care. There are a number of chapters in this text describing the nursing perspective and challenges of current EHR implementations and an additional appendices that describe developing EHR applications (apps) for mobile devices.

Definition

Informatics creates meaning out of chaos; Biomedical Informatics extrapolates meaning from diverse biological, medical, nursing, health, and clinical research sources and structures that data via intuitive interfaces to enhance healthcare and delivery (Lubliner 2015).

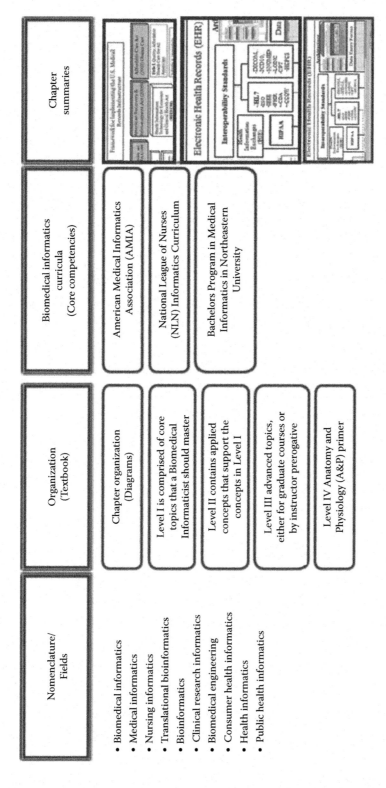

FIGURE 1.1 Organization of topics covered in Chapter 1.

Biomedical informatics syntax

Before listing the current accepted nomenclatures for this field, which are sometimes confusing, an explanation of the derivations of the terms will be introduced. The term *medicine* is derived from the Latin word *medicina*, meaning art of healing. Asclepius was the Greek god of medicine. A physician "practices medicine" through diagnosis, treatment, and prevention of disease. Physicians broadly are categorized as medical or surgical. Medicine refers to the practice of nonoperative medicine. The American Medical Association's (AMA) mission is to "to promote the art and science of medicine and the betterment of public health."

Bio is the Greek word for life. It also is defined as "indicating or involving living organisms." Originally, this informatics field was referred to as *Medical Informatics*, but since *medical* refers to a subset of the health field, a more expansive term *Biomedical Informatics* was used. Other health professionals, nurses also use EHRs so "medical" alone would have been exclusionary. Nursing is defined by the American Nursing Association as "the protection, promotion, and optimization of health and abilities, prevention of illness and injury, alleviation of suffering through the diagnosis and treatment of human response, and advocacy in the care of individuals, families, communities, and populations." In order not to have a discipline's name with a hundred subfields, a compromise was reached that incorporates *bio*, life and living organisms, and *medicine*, which incorporates diagnosis, treatment, and prevention into BMI.

Current informatics descriptors

The following are widely accepted definitions of the various informatics fields related to medicine and healthcare.

Informatics is "a field of study to apply information technology to another field—from healthcare to journalism to biology to economics" (Indiana University).

Two additional BMI definitions:

Biomedical Informatics is "the interdisciplinary field that studies and pursues the effective uses of biomedical data, information, and knowledge for scientific inquiry, problem solving, and decision making, driven by efforts to improve human health" (AMIA Definition) (http://jamia.bmj.com/content/early/2012/06/07/amiajnl-2012–001053.full) (Table 1.1).

Biomedical Informatics is "the core scientific discipline that supports applied research and practice in several biomedical disciplines, including health informatics, which is composed of *clinical informatics* (including subfields such as medical, nursing, and dental informatics) and public health informatics" (American Medical Informatics Association [AMIA]).

Nursing Informatics is the "science and practice (that) integrates nursing and implementation of communication and information technology" (AMIA).

Translational Bioinformatics is the development of analytic methods to optimize the transformation of biomedical data and genomic data, into proactive, predictive, preventive, and participatory health.

The field of *Bioinformatics* has a research focus, analyzes datasets for genomics, proteins, etc. The branch of information science concerned with large databases of biochemical and pharmaceutical information (world English dictionary) intersects with the field of computational biology.

TABLE 1.1   Biomedical Informatics Association/Organization

Name	Link
American Medical Informatics Associations	www.AMIA.org
American College of Medical Informatics	http://www.amia.org/programs/acmi-fellowship
Public Health Informatics	http://www.amia.org/applications-informatics/public-health-informatics
International Medical Interpreters Association	http://www.imiaweb.org/
American Nurses Association—Nursing Informatics	http://www.nursecredentialing.org/InformaticsNursing
Medical Informatics Association Medical Library Association	http://www.medinfo.mlanet.org/
Association for Computing Machinery Human Computer Interfaces SIGCHI	www.acm.org

Clinical Research Informatics is the discovery and management of new knowledge relating to health and disease. It includes management of information related to clinical trials.

Biomedical Engineering is defined as a field dealing with the application of engineering principles to medical practice. It also lies at the intersection of electrical engineering and the biological sciences.

Medical Informatics (often used interchangeably with BMI but the term biomedical is currently the preferred term used by the leading informatics body in this field the AMIA) is "the science and art of modeling and recording real-world clinical concepts and events into computable data used to derive actionable information, based on expertise in medicine, information science, information technology, and the scholarly study of issues that impact upon the productive use of information systems by clinical personnel" (S. Silverstein, MD).

Consumer Health Informatics is the field "devoted to informatics from multiple consumer or patient views. These include patient-focused informatics, health literacy, and consumer education." The focus is on information structures and processes that empower consumers to manage their own health; for example, health information literacy, consumer-friendly language, personal health records, and Internet-based strategies and resources. The shift in this view of informatics analyzes consumers' needs for easier to understand information.

Health Informatics is "the interdisciplinary study of the design, development, adoption, and application of IT-based innovations in healthcare services delivery, management, and planning."

1.3 Textbook Organization

The textbook is structured for both BMI undergraduate and graduate courses. It is sequenced to introduce topics that build on each other. Most chapters have three levels of complexity. Level I is comprised of core topics that a BMI professional should master. Level II contains applied concepts that support the concepts in Level I. Level III has advanced topics that should be included in graduate courses but can be used for undergraduates in selected topic areas. Chapter 7, Medical Sensors, includes a Level IV section on Anatomy and Physiology (A&P) primer. All BMI students should have a basic A&P understanding, especially when working with physicians and nurses. Understanding the underlying medical concepts is the difference between a technologist and a professional. An BMI professional should aspire to the latter.

This primer on BMI offers unique perspectives and core foundational materials not found in other textbooks in this field. In-depth examples of concepts introduced are linked to theoretical concepts with included real-world examples. In Chapter 3, *Electronic Health Records*, specific examples of EHRs are included. Medical nomenclatures, described in Chapter 4 *Data Interoperability*, specific HL7 and ICD10 coded messages and source tables are included so professions can understand the exact message structure exchanged between systems. In Chapter 10, a clinical nurse specialist and CERNER EHR expert discusses a current EHR implementation, its specific benefits and limitations, and specific recommendations necessary to evolve into the next generation of user-friendly interfaces and improved process flow. In Chapter 7, *Medical Sensors*, an in-depth explanation of electro-chemistry provides students with an understanding of the chemistry, physics, and electrical foundations needed for capturing and analyzing medical sensor data. Finally, a primer on the coding of medical apps, Appendices A through D, introduce a skill set that is essential for the evolution of the next generation of medical records; user-friendly interfaces for mobile devices that reduce the IT burden to essential data tailored for individual's medical environments. In 2015, once the core EHR systems are in place for most, not all. A significant group of medical professionals dentists, optometrist, mental healthcare professionals, and a few others are still in the process of implementing EHR's implementation. The next phase, will be "EHR 2" enhancing the user interfaces for more user-friendly and efficient process flow.

Three chapters have been written by experts in their field to provide complementary perspectives and expertise. Two are mastered, prepared nurses who are experts in EHRs from users' and implementers' points of view. The first is a clinical nurse specialist (MSN, CCRN) and CERNER super user. The second is an IT director who implemented a new EHR system in a large medical center. The third is an expert in application development for wireless devices. He has taught several courses at a university in application development and is pursuing a PhD in Information Systems specializing in user interfaces.

Bios

Philomena M. DiQuollo is a working healthcare IT professional who began her career in nursing and transitioned to IT&S 12 years later. Since 1985, she has worked in acute care facilities implementing clinical and business technology solutions as well as directing day-to-day operations and supporting strategic goals at a major urban teaching medical center in New Jersey. Currently, her position is system director of analytics within a multifacility healthcare system. Philomena DiQuollo is an adjunct faculty at New Jersey Institute of Technology teaching in the medical informatics program. She received her BSN from Seton Hall University and MA in Nursing from New York University. In addition, Philomena DiQuollo is a certified professional in Health Information Management Systems and is American Society for Quality Six Sigma Green Belt certified. She resides in New Jersey and is pursuing a master's in analytics at Villanova University.

Cathy Lubliner is a critical care clinical nurse specialist at an academic teaching hospital. She has over 30 years experience in the care of patients with end stage heart failure, cardiogenic and septic shock, pre-and post transplant procedures, and ventricular assist devices. During the implementation of the hospital based EHR, she served as one of the "super users" to facilitate the transition of the nursing staff to the computer-based documentation/data entry system.

Daniel Nasello is an experienced mobile and web application developer and project manager who currently resides New Jersey. Having developed some highly successful applications (including multiple applications for various singers and actors), Daniel's variety of experience allows him to bring the experience of multiple industries into the software he develops.

Seeing the rapid growth of mobile application development, Daniel has created groundbreaking and innovating applications that will be used in tomorrow's markets and is developing mobile and web application opportunities in industries where they are nonexistent.

Daniel currently holds a bachelor's of science in computer technology and a master's degree from the New Jersey Institute of Technology in Information Systems. He is also a part-time instructor at NJIT where he spearheaded the mobile application development class, which is rapidly growing in popularity.

1.4 Biomedical Informatics Challenges

BMI initially focused on transitioning from paper to EHRs. The discipline has evolved to incorporate clinical research, interoperability standards and enhanced user interfaces. The EHR endeavor is by itself extremely complex—creating on-line equivalents for the pharmacy, intake and discharge forms, manual and automated data capture of real-time monitoring, status notes, etc., all tied into billing and inventory, changing documentation processes and education, developing secure, HIPAA Title II requirements and IT infrastructure for zero downtime and emergency procedures for system outages. This complex EHR conversion would be the equivalent of converting a paper-based corporation to all electronic systems in a few years, develop strategies, training, debug the system, etc. These processes, in corporations, have evolved over many decades and still require a great deal of improvement and monitoring.

The major difference is that in a hospital, medical staffs, especially nurses, are taking care of critically ill patients, life and death situations, and then pausing care to enter data into a EHR system. They then have to find the correct dropdown menu, enter the data, and review new medications and directives from doctors, and ensure there are no data entry errors, since the wrong dosage or incorrect data entry is not just a typo, it can be life threatening—and then move to another patient who is having a code. Prior to EHRs, medical staff filled out a tri-fold two-sided form and entered the data, and the process of reviewing a patient status was simply flipping over a paper-based form to see a comprehensive view of a patient's medical status. Medical professionals did not have to go into an often non-user-friendly system to quickly (in reality not so quickly) review a patient status. Can you imagine this scenario with any other discipline—let's say a pilot who not only is responsible for flying the plane but has to then document passenger data, inventory all the food, fuel, and document passenger issues, and they stop and go back to flying? Try doing this during takeoff and landing or an in-flight emergency. Currently, 8–10 hour shifts become 12 hour with added documentation or patient care suffers since time has to be devoted to data entry. Nonhospital EHRs have different issues where additional staff are often required to manage EHR systems.

The positive benefits, in the long run, will be substantial: preventing duplicate tests, sharing data between multiple medical practitioners, automatic drug interaction warnings. An evolved EHR system can cross-check patient IDs, medications, and procedures to reduce errors that are currently the cause of many deaths every year. A report in September 2013 by the *Journal of Patient Safety* estimates up to 98,000 deaths a year are caused by hospital mistakes. Preventable adverse effects add an additional 200,000 injuries http://journals.lww.com/journalpatientsafety/Fulltext/2013/09000/A_New,_Evidence_based_Estimate_of_Patient_Harms.2.aspx.

A seamless system will take a while to evolve. The deadline for the implementation of most EHRs is 2015. This involves some of the most basic functionality defined by meaningful use standards, which rate the functionality of EHRs discussed in Chapter 3. The next phase of EHR implementation, 2015+, will not only include specialties that were not in the initial mandates—dentists, optometrists, mental health workers, etc.—but enhancing automatic data entry from monitors, radio frequency (RF) tags on blood products, supplies and equipment, and user-friendly interfaces to simplify data entry and visualization of medical trends.

1.5 Biomedical Informatics Curriculum

Whether a college freshman or an experienced practitioner transitioning to this field—information technologist, nurse, radiologist, physicians assistant, etc.—guidelines for a course of study need to be quantified. Three perspectives will be introduced regarding possible Biomedical Informatics curricula. First are guidelines from an from an American Medical Informatics Association (AMIA) whitepaper. The second is from the National League for Nursing (NLN) which is comprised of nursing educators. Lastly, a current Biomedical Informatics bachelor's degree program in place for 7 years will be described. The intent is to assist other programs in creating a curriculum for this new breed of professional.

The AMIA suggested competencies are comprehensive and ambitious. They recommend that "one can select a subset that best complements an individual's prior experience and future directions." The AMIA curricula list virtually all computer science and IT courses taught at a university, without highlighting a recommended subset for BMI programs. The last example is a current BS curriculum in medical informatics that illustrates a subset specifically selected to compliment BMI professions with a few targeted optional courses. The question arises, should BMI professionals have all these skills and in what depth? In the technological AMIA skills list, networking, security, databases are listed; each in its own right is a separate field of study; they suggest machine learning, data mining, and simulation and modeling. Very few computer scientists or information technologists are well versed in all those fields. Then, the BMI student needs some expertise in A&P, ethics, human computer interfaces. So, in part three, the BS in medical informatics/BMI will outline an existing bachelor's program with optional concentrations so students can pursue their specific interests. One example is a database concentration that suggests three available courses including database administration if the BMI student wants to focus on backend support systems. General requirements and optional concentration needs to be clearly delineated.

Following are three perspectives for curriculum guidelines

1. The AMIA created a document listing core competencies for graduate BMI training in June 17, 2010, voted and approved by its members. [link to all academic forum documents 2007–2014, http://www.amia.org/programs/academic-forum/annual-conference]
2. The NLN informatics curriculum
3. A bachelor's program in medical informatics, in place for the past 7 years at a Northeastern University, which provides flexibility for students pursing one of the many informatics subfields designed to accommodate the evolving areas of expertise that will be required as this field evolves.

1.5.1 AMIA Core Biomedical Competencies

The AMIA, in June 2010, created a framework primarily of core BMI competencies for graduate students acknowledging the diverse backgrounds of individuals transitioning to this field.

1.5.1.1 AMIA Introductory Course Outline

The AMIA, a branch of the AMA, has recommended a 10 × 10 single 12-week *introductory course* of study. This outline provides a structure of representative topics that can be a starting point for this curriculum (Table 1.2).

1.5.1.2 General Framework AMIA: Core Competencies

Four Key Areas (*Source: AMIA Board White Paper*)

It defines BMI and specifies core competencies for graduate education in the following disciplines (http://jamia.bmj.com/content/early/2012/06/20/amiajnl-2012–001053.full) (Figure 1.2):

1. *Scope and breadth of discipline*: BMI investigates and supports reasoning, modeling, simulation, experimentation, and translation across the spectrum from molecules to individuals and to populations and from biological to social systems, bridging basic and clinical research and practice and the healthcare enterprise.
2. *Theory and methodology*: BMI develops, studies, and applies theories, methods, and processes for the generation, storage, retrieval, use, management, and sharing of biomedical data, information, and knowledge.
3. *Technological approach*: BMI builds on and contributes to computer, telecommunication, and information sciences and technologies, emphasizing their application in biomedicine.
4. *Human and social context*: BMI, recognizing that people are the ultimate users of biomedical information, draws upon the social and behavioral sciences to inform the design and evaluation of technical solutions, policies, and the evolution of economic, ethical, social, educational, and organizational systems.

1.5.1.3 Specific Core Competencies

1.5.1.3.1 Technological Approach

BMI builds on and contributes to computer telecommunication and information sciences and technologies, emphasizing their applications in biomedicine (Table 1.3).

TABLE 1.2   AMIA 10 × 10 Course Outline

AMIA: The 12 units of the on-line portion of the 10 × 10 course	
1.	Overview of discipline and its history
2.	Biomedical computing
3.	Electronic health records and health information exchange
4.	Decision support: evolution and current approaches
5.	Standards: privacy, confidentiality, and security
6.	Evidence-based medicine and medical decision making
7.	Information retrieval and digital libraries
8.	Bioinformatics
9.	Imaging informatics and telemedicine
10.	Consumer health, nursing, public health informatics
11.	Organization and management issues in informatics
12.	Career and professional development

Source: AMIA Curriculum. http://skynet.ohsu.edu/~hersh/ijmi-07–10x10.pdf.

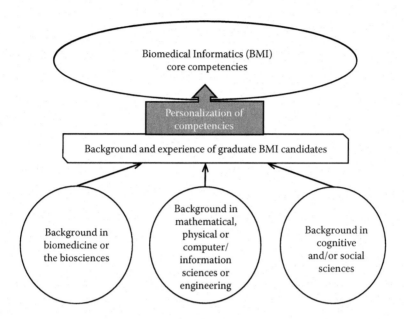

FIGURE 1.2 AMIA biomedical informatics core competencies. (From http://jamia.bmj.com/content/early/2012/06/07/amiajnl-2012–001053.full.)

TABLE 1.3 Information Technology

Technological: Prerequisite knowledge and skills. Assumes familiarity with data structures, algorithms, programming, mathematics, and statistics

Goals: Fundamental knowledge. Understand and apply technological approaches in the context of biomedical problems

1. Networking, security, databases
2. Information documentation, storage, and retrieval
3. Imaging and signal analysis
4. Machine learning, including data mining
5. Simulation and modeling
6. Representation of logical and probabilistic knowledge and reasoning
7. Natural language processing, semantic technologies
8. Software engineering

1.5.1.3.2 Biological Foundations

Population health: detection, prevention, screening, education, stratification, spatiotemporal patterns, ecologies of health, and wellness (Table 1.4).

1.5.1.3.3 Human and Social Context

Human and social context: Prerequisite knowledge and skills—familiarity with fundamentals of social, organizational, cognitive, and decision sciences (Table 1.5).

1.5.1.3.4 Procedural Knowledge

Procedural knowledge and skills: Apply, analyze, evaluate, and create systems approaches to the solution of substantive problems in BMI (Table 1.6).

The AMIA realizes that students will come from a number of diverse backgrounds and realizes these suggested competencies are ambitious and recommends "one can select a subset that best complements an individual's prior experience and future directions."

TABLE 1.4   Biological Competencies

Biological: Prerequisite knowledge and skills. Students must be familiar with biological, biomedical, and population health concepts and problems including common research problems

Goals: Fundamental knowledge. Understand the fundamentals of the field in the context of the effective use of biomedical data, information, and knowledge. For example

1.   Biology: molecule, sequence, protein, structure, function, cell, tissue, organ, organism, phenotype, populations
2.   Translational and clinical research: genotype, phenotype, pathways, mechanisms, sample, protocol, study, subject, evidence, evaluation
3.   Healthcare: screening, diagnosis (diagnoses, test results), prognosis, treatment (medications, procedures), prevention, billing, healthcare teams, quality assurance, safety, error reduction, comparative effectiveness, medical records, personalized medicine health economics, information security, and privacy
4.   Personal health: patient, consumer, provider, families, health promotion, and personal health records
5.   Population health: detection, prevention, screening, education, stratification, spatiotemporal patterns, ecologies of health, and wellness

TABLE 1.5   Human and Social Contexts

Human and Social Context: Prerequisite knowledge and skills. BMI, recognizing that people are the ultimate users of biomedical information, draws upon the social and behavioral sciences to inform the design and evaluation of technical solutions, policies, and evolution of economic, ethical, social, educational, and organizational systems.

Familiarity with fundamentals of social, organizational, cognitive, and decision sciences.

Goals: Fundamental knowledge. Understand and apply knowledge in the following areas:

1.   Design: human-centered design (HCI), usability, human factors, cognitive, and ergonomic sciences and engineering
2.   Evaluation: study design, controlled trials, observational studies, hypothesis testing, ethnographic methods, field observational methods, qualitative methods, mixed methods
3.   Social, behavioral, communication, and organizational sciences: for example, computer-supported cooperative work, social networks, change management, human factors engineering, cognitive task analysis, project management.
4.   Ethical, legal, social issues: for example, human subjects, HIPAA, informed consent, secondary use of data, confidentiality, privacy
5.   Economic, social, and organizational context of biomedical research, pharmaceutical and biotechnology industries, medical instrumentation, healthcare, and public health

TABLE 1.6   Procedural Knowledge and Skills

Procedural knowledge and skills: Apply, analyze, evaluate, and create systems approaches to the solution of substantive problems in Biomedical Informatics

1.   Analyze complex biomedical informatics problems in terms of people, organizations, and sociotechnical systems
2.   Understand the challenges and limitations of technological solutions
3.   Design and implement systems approaches to Biomedical Informatics applications and interventions
4.   Evaluate the impact of Biomedical Informatics applications and interventions in terms of people, organizations, and sociotechnical systems
5.   Relate solutions to other problems within and across levels of the biomedical spectrum

1.5.2 National League for Nursing Informatics

The NLN has 33,000 individual and 1,200 institutional members. They have defined a core framework for Nursing Informatics into four curricular threads: IT, communication, issues, and nursing collaboration.

There is a NLN white paper *Preparing the Next Generation of Nurses to Practice in a Technology-Rich Environment: An Informatics Agenda* introduced in May 2008 whose stated goal is "to prepare the next generation of nurses to practice in a technology-rich environment" that outlines its recommendations to nursing faculty and administration (see recommendations in the following text) http://www.nln.org/aboutnln/PositionStatements/informatics_052808.pdf.

TABLE 1.7   NLN: Information Technology Curriculum

Health IT Tools (Suggest the Curriculum Include Lectures on These Topics)
1. *Computerized order entry*: Clinical application that allows clinicians to order and process lab tests, medications, clinical procedures, and other services electronically.
2. *Health information exchange* enables clinical staff to access *more* information about a patient when it is needed.
3. *Electronic prescribing*: The use of computing devices to enter, modify, review, and output or communicate drug prescriptions.
4. *Electronic medical record systems*: A basic component of a health IT system, *electronic medical record* systems have the potential to provide substantial benefits.
5. *Telehealth*: Geographic disparities in access to care can be addressed partially using technologies that allow for remote audio, visual, and haptic communication between caregivers and specialists or patients.
6. *Clinical decision support*: Given the exponential growth in our knowledge of medicine, it is impossible for any clinician to know everything he or she needs to know.

Source: http://www.nln.org/facultyprograms/facultyresources/facultyresources.htm.

Definition

"Nursing informatics is defined as combining nursing science, information management science, and computer science to manage and process nursing data, information, and knowledge to deliver quality care to the public" (HRSA, 2008). Nursing informatics facilitates the integration of data, information, and knowledge to support patients, nurses, and other providers in their decision making in all roles and settings. (http://www.nln.org/facultyprograms/facultyresources/informatics.htm)

1. Use of health IT to augment/support the nursing care process includes concepts such as safety, care improvement, decision assistance/support, outcome analysis and data analysis.
2. Communication includes EHR personal health records, standardized languages, and terminology.
3. Issues including legal, ethical, social, security, advocacy, and public policy.
4. Nursing involvement through teamwork/collaboration, covering nurses' role in determining usability, workflow analysis, and systems selection/evaluation.

1.5.2.1 NLN Health IT Tools

The NLN IT component lists a skill set of tools they suggest will have to be utilized as indicated by nursing practice (Table 1.7).

Since the rest of the guidelines are generic nursing recommendations, such as ethics and teamwork that are not unique to biomedical informatics curriculum, the included links will provide that additional content.

1.5.3 Bachelor's in Medical/Biomedical Informatics Curriculum

This section is structured around a 4-year bachelor's degree specifically focused on educating Biomedical/Medical Informatics professionals.

The challenge of training professionals, from their first encounter within this field provides an unprecedented opportunity to shape the future of the discipline. There are only a handful of BS programs in this field and even fewer associates degrees. But the employment opportunities are stellar for new graduates, not only evidenced by Department of Labor, but due to the change in demographics, i.e. the U.S. Census Bureau projects one-fifth of the U.S. population will be over 65 by 2030, and with the expanded Affordable Care Act (ACA), this expanded healthcare demand will necessitate more trained professionals to handle the millions of new individuals with healthcare coverage. New wearable wireless technologies, feeding data into EHRs, will also necessitate the need for more professionals in this field.

The BS degree is structured into core areas that allow flexibility, so programs or students can develop additional expertise in areas of interest.

Core medical/biomedical areas are as follows:

1. IT
2. Biological/medical
3. Medical informatics
4. Ethics/management/economics

1.5.3.1 Future Employment Prospects for BS Degrees in Medical/Biomedical Informatics

1. The U.S. Bureau of Labor Statistics has projected that the fastest-growing professions are in the computer and heathcare industries specifically in the medical records/informatics areas (http://www.bls.gov/ooh/healthcare/medical-records-and-health-information-technicians.htm).
   a. They indicate in 2012, the last full-year statistics are available, that there were 186,300 individuals employed in this profession and projections call for 41,000 additional hires the next year. They project a 22% growth rate from 2102 to 2022.
   b. The U.S. Department of Labor 2012–2022 has projected that for the next decade 2012–2022 projections call, the medical records and health information technicians occupation will grow 22%. http://www.bls.gov/ooh/healthcare/medical-records-and-health-information-technicians (htm#tab-6).
2. The projected doubling of the over 65 population in the next 2 decades one-fifth will be over 65 by 2030 indicated by the U.S. Census Bureau. Baby boomers, in the next 20 years, will necessitate the need for medical informatics professionals to upgrade the tens of thousands of medical practices across the United States. Subfields of medical informatics, i.e., wireless medical devices, will necessitate the need for additional trained personnel to integrate data from these devices.
3. Forty percent of all medical costs are related to medical documentation, billing, and administrative overhead, costs that will necessitate the need of reducing the overhead by automated medical records systems.
4. The large population in the New York metropolitan area indicates the need for a large number of medical/biomedical informatics professionals. As per the 2012 U.S. census in the New York metropolitan area, tri-state area has 19.8 million people. It is the most populous metropolitan area in the United States defined by the Office of Management and Budget as the *New York-Northern New Jersey-Long Island, NY-NJ-PA Metropolitan Statistical Area*.

1.5.3.2 BS Medical/Biomedical Curriculum

The Medical/Biomedical Informatics bachelor's degree includes the traditional curriculum core courses: English I, II, and III (technical writing), and history/sociology/psychology, capstone core courses. The math courses are statistics, precalculus, calculus (business calculus is an alternative), several core computer and database courses. Management and (medical) economics courses round out the first 64 credits with a few electives. Some students can choose a management track, taking additional accounting, business, and cost-analysis courses. Others choices include additional biology and chemistry courses for their electives.

Bachelor's degree 128 credits are broken down into these general categories:

- 64 credits common core courses
- 64 medical/biomedical informatics and information technology
- The curriculum for a 2/year associates degree in Medical Informatics is provided in Table 1.8.

1.6 Chapter Summaries

The chapters in this book are designed to be covered in sequential order. Concepts build on preceding chapters. Chapter 7 on medical sensors is the exception where Level IV provides four optional sections on A&P basics. Some instructors add between 10 and 30 minutes of selected A&P lectures at the end of their lectures. The rationale is to create a basic core A&P knowledge base where students develop a balanced technological

TABLE 1.8   Medical/Biomedical Informatics Curriculum 64 Credits

Core Area(s)	Required	Electives	Credits
Bachelor's Curriculum in Medical Informatics/Biomedical Informatics (64) (optional courses depend on program and student interests)			
Information Technology	Intro Information/Computer Technology[a]		3
15 credits required 15 credits recommended	Intro to Programming (object oriented Python, VB)[a]	Advanced Programming (C++, JAVA) (Recommended) (3 credits)	3
	Intro to Database Design I[a]	Advanced Database design II (3 credits)	3
		Database Administration III (3 credits)	
	Intro Computer Security	Wireless Networks Security (Recommend) (3 credits)	3
	Web Design (optional in first 2 years[a])	App Design for Mobile Devices (recommend) (3 credits)	3
		Human Computer Interface (HCI) Design (3 credits)	
Biological–Medical	Anatomy and Physiology I[a]	Biology I	4
14 credits required 8 credits recommended	Anatomy and Physiology I	Chemistry I	4
	Medical Terminology[a]		3
	Pharmacology[a]		3
Ethics/Management/Economics	Medical Ethics (optional in first 2 years[a])		3
9 credits required 6 credits recommended			
	Economics (Medical)[a]	Cost Analysis (3 credits)	3
	Intro Management	Management in Healthcare environments (3 credits)	3
(Bio)medical Informatics	Medical Informatics I (survey of the field)[a]	Internship I: 75 hours (2 credits)	3
-9 credits required -6 credits recommended	Medical Informatics II Advan: management, case studies	Internship II: 75 hours (2 credits)	3
	Medical Informatics III EHR's hands on exercises	Internship III: 75 hours (2 credits)	3
Totals (64 should be taken)	47 Credits	At least 17 credits selected/35	

[a] Courses taken at community colleges.

and biological underpinning. The two chapters at the end of the book, written from the perspective of nurses utilizing EHRs and a managers perspective implementing EHRs, can be added at any point in the semester. Some instructors believe that right after Chapter 3 on EHRs is the time to introduce the real world perspectives by professionals utilizing EHRs. Lastly, the appendices on application (app) development for EHRs either can be instructor led or provided as exercises for students to pursue for a final class project. All EHRs will eventually evolve to provide user friendly intuitive interfaces simplifying user input and providing long-term trend analysis of medical conditions (Table 1.9).

Most chapters include an illustration that summarizes the content of each chapter.

TABLE 1.9 Textbook Synopsis of Each Chapter

Chapter Summary	Illustration Summarizing the Content of Most Chapters			
	Nomenclature/ Fields	Organixzaton (Textbook)	Biomedical Informatics curricula (Core competencies)	Chapter summaries
1. Introduction to Biomedical Informatics: This chapter frames the challenges addressed by Biomedical Informatics (BMI). A discussion on BMI curricula introduces AMIA, NLN, and an evolving BS program curriculum that was introduced in 2007.	• Biomedical informatics • Medical informatics • Nursing informatics • Translational bioinformatics • Bioinformatics • Clinical research informatics • Biomedical engineering • Consumer health informatics • Health informatics • Public health informatics	Chapter Organization (Diagrams) Level I is comprised of core topics that a Biomedical informaticist should master Level II contains applied concepts that support the concepts in Level I Level III advanced topics, either for graduate courses or by instructor prerogative Level IV Anatomy and Physiology (A&P) primer	American Medical Informatics Association (AMIA) National League of Nurses (NLN) Informatics Curriculum Bachelors Program in Medical Informatics in Northeastern University	

(Continued)

TABLE 1.9 (*Continued*) Textbook Synopsis of Each Chapter

Chapter Summary	Illustration Summarizing the Content of Most Chapters
2. The U.S. legislation that has spurred the explosion of electronic health records (EHR) adoption.	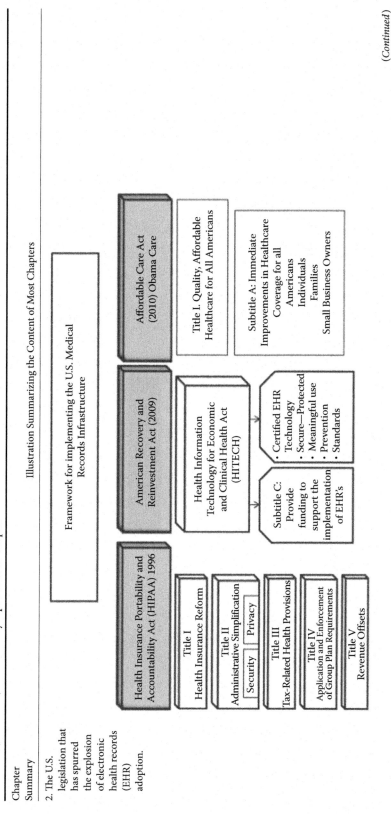

(*Continued*)

TABLE 1.9 (*Continued*)   Textbook Synopsis of Each Chapter

Chapter Summary	Illustration Summarizing the Content of Most Chapters
3. EHR are a collection of data accumulated from various sources that document a patient's journey through the healthcare system.	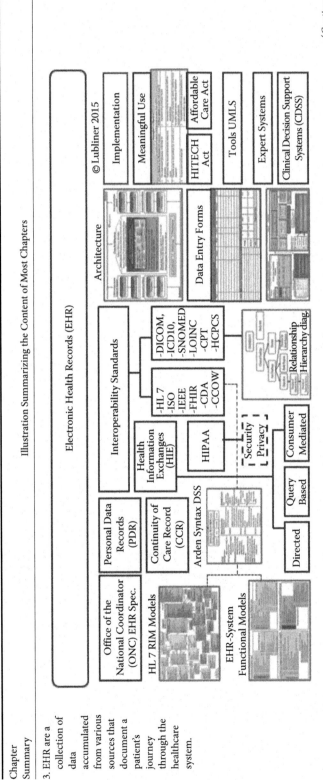

(*Continued*)

TABLE 1.9 (*Continued*)   Textbook Synopsis of Each Chapter

Chapter Summary	Illustration Summarizing the Content of Most Chapters
4. Data interoperability focuses on electronic medical communication and data sharing. EHR, medical devices, laboratories data, imaging studies, etc., have to agree on *common protocols to exchange data.*	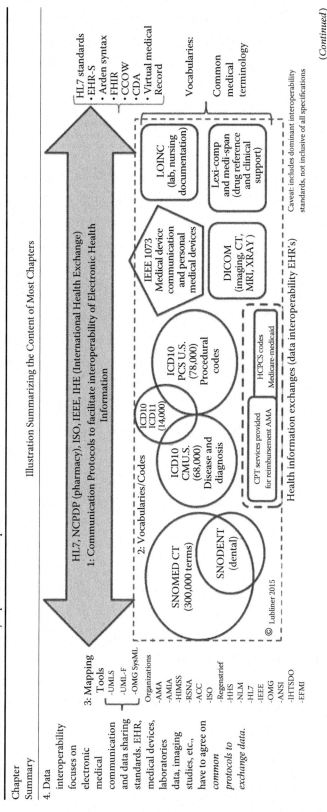

(*Continued*)

TABLE 1.9 (*Continued*) Textbook Synopsis of Each Chapter

Chapter Summary	Illustration Summarizing the Content of Most Chapters
5. Privacy and Security: HIPAA Title II describes *security* as the safeguards that must be in place to ensure appropriate protection of electronic protected health information (ePHI). A security primer introduces basic security techniques.	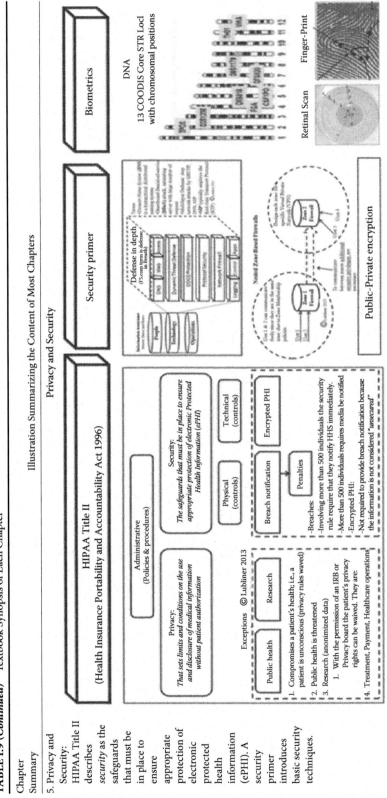

(Continued)

TABLE 1.9 (*Continued*)   Textbook Synopsis of Each Chapter

Chapter Summary	Illustration Summarizing the Content of Most Chapters
6. Telehealth– Telemedicine is the practice of medicine or analyzing medical data remotely. mHealth refers to medical practice using mobile monitoring devices. Teleradiology, telesurgery, and certifications are also discussed.	*(see illustration below)*

Telehealth

Telemedicine (Delivery of services and diagnosis)

Communications	M-health (Mobile Wireless Medical Devices And Software)	Tele-surgery	Tele-radiology and medical consults	CCRN-E AACN cert.	Cost/Need
WaveLan • IEEE 802.11n 600 Mbit/s • IEEE 802.11ac 6.93 Gbit/s Wireless-Personal-Networks • Bluetooth4 24 Mbits/s • IrDA-UFIR 96 Mbits/s • WUSB 480 Mbits/s • IrDA-GigaIR 1024 Mbits/s	M-Health • First generation wireless medical devices 2013 • Second generation 2014 iHealth, Fitbit, iWatch	• FDA Approved • da Vinci System • 1.5 million perf.	-90% radiologists are in large remote groups -In 2013 the top 100 firms have 5000 radiologists -Specialists provide expert opinions 24/day	-Monitor critically ill patients remotely -Consultation	10,000 baby Boomers reach 65 every day
Electronic health records	Implantable medical devices	Telemental health	Tele-education	Nurse working in tele-ICU or eCCU	Affordable Care Act focus on prevention
SNOMED, ICD11, HL7, DICOM	Home monitoring of patients and devices: EKG, implantable assist devices	Crisis response		Qualifications: RN 5 years with critically ill patients	-Reduce inpatient costs -Reduce cost of large facilities outpatient ER

Some Apps deliver services: fall under telemedicine

1. Doctors-on-demand app 2. RingaDoc.com 3. 3GDoctor.com England	-Reimbursement by Medicare -Rural Areas	Mini clinics (will require remote consults)

© Lubliner 2013

(Continued)

TABLE 1.9 (*Continued*) Textbook Synopsis of Each Chapter

Chapter Summary	Illustration Summarizing the Content of Most Chapters

7. Medical Sensors. This chapter focuses on the exponential growth of medical sensors. It introduces foundations of chemistry, biology, physics, and electronics to ensure the BMI professionals are well grounded in their field. It also includes an anatomy and physiology primer.

Wireless medical monitoring

Body sensor networks (BNSs)c

Data mining and big data in healthcare

Medical Sensors and Measurements

Blood pressure

Pulse oximetry

Lambert-Bouguer Lawl

$I = Io \, e^{-(ad)}$

Beer's Law $C_i = \dfrac{n_i}{V}$

Beer Lambert law

Absorbance (ad) = $\varepsilon c d$

Medical sensors

Data Acquisition: basic theory

Electrical conduction

Heart

Action potential

(ATP) Adenosine triphosphate

Electrical and chemical conduction basics

Valence electrons

Subatomic particles

Current flow

$Ohm's\ Law$

Inductive charging

Battery chemistry

Cods

Primary core

Secondary core

L_1

L_2

Magnetic field

Anatomy and Physiology Primer

Part I: Neurons and nervous system, brain, spinal cord, muscles, heart, eye

Part II: Cells, ATP, hearing, kidneys, pancreas, liver, digestive system

Part III: Lungs, immune system, strokes, blood flow, prostate

Part IV: Heart disease, cancer

(*Continued*)

TABLE 1.9 (*Continued*) Textbook Synopsis of Each Chapter

Chapter Summary	Illustration Summarizing the Content of Most Chapters
8. Imaging: This chapter, first, discusses imaging devices and the complex physics and algorithms involved in analyzing this data; second, the standards used for transmitting and visualizing these images; and third, the system for storage and retrieval of images picture archiving and communication system.	Medical imaging (DICOM) Digital communications and communications in medicine (framework supports communication, storage and handling of medical images) Medical imaging hardware, physics and algorithms Picture archiving and retrieval system (PACS) Radio pharmacology Image analysis Principal component analysis DICOM Standards • Object definitions • Data classes • Data structures • Data dictionary • Message service • Presentation • Storage media and file service • Media storage • Media formats • Gray scale standards • Security and System Management • Web Access • Content mapping • Transformations • Handling • Storing • Printing • Communications

(*Continued*)

TABLE 1.9 (*Continued*) Textbook Synopsis of Each Chapter

Chapter Summary	Illustration Summarizing the Content of Most Chapters
9. Ethics: This chapter discusses the American Medical Association, the American Nurses Association, and case studies relating to medical ethics.	Medical Ethics — Hippocratic oath (original and revised); American Medical Association (AMA) ethics groups; American Nurses Association (ANA) ethics group; Ethical case studies
10. Nursing Documentation and the Electronic Health Records	The focus of this chapter is to explain the complexity of critical care nursing in the context of the data that are generated and the process of recording that data. Documenting patient care activities during emergency situations, which occur often in the critical care setting, is particularly challenging because many activities are occurring simultaneously.
11. Nursing Management	In this chapter, the focus will be on what it takes to support a healthcare organization's IT infrastructure and to understand the complexity of a heavily regulated, highly technical, and safety conscious environment.

(*Continued*)

TABLE 1.9 (*Continued*) Textbook Synopsis of Each Chapter

Chapter Summary	Illustration Summarizing the Content of Most Chapters
12. The future directions of biomedical informatics	Future directions of Biomedical Informatics

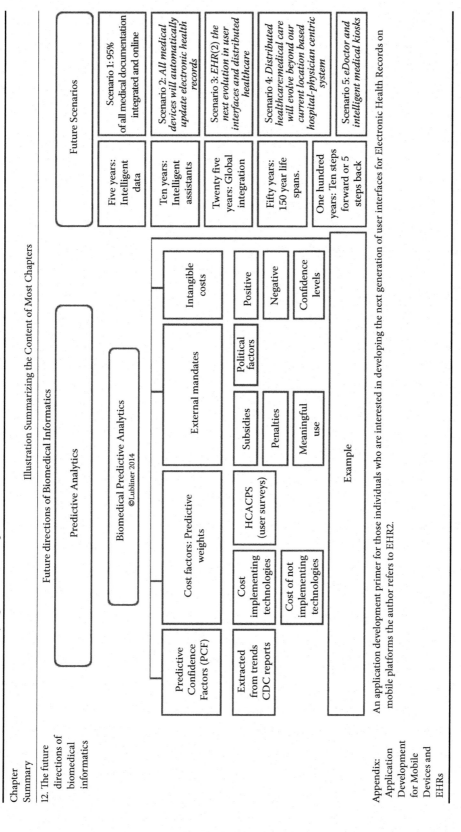

An application development primer for those individuals who are interested in developing the next generation of user interfaces for Electronic Health Records on mobile platforms the author refers to EHR2.

Appendix: Application Development for Mobile Devices and EHRs	

Glossary

Bioinformatics, research focus, analyzes datasets for genomics, proteins etc. "The branch of information science concerned with large databases of biochemical and pharmaceutical information" *(World English Dictionary)*, it intersects with the field of computational biology.

Biomedical engineering is defined as a field dealing with the application of engineering principles to medical practice. It also lies at the intersection of electrical engineering and the biological sciences.

Biomedical informatics extrapolates meaning from diverse biological, medical, nursing, health, and clinical research sources and structures data via intuitive interfaces to enhance healthcare and delivery (Lubliner 2014).

Clinical research informatics is the discovery and management of new knowledge relating to health and disease. It includes management of information related to clinical trials.

Consumer health informatics is the field "devoted to informatics from multiple consumer or patient views. These include patient-focused informatics, health literacy, and consumer education." The focus is on information structures and processes that empower consumers to manage their own health; for example, health information literacy, consumer-friendly language, personal health records, and Internet-based strategies and resources. The shift in this view of informatics analyzes consumers' needs for information.

Health informatics is "the interdisciplinary study of the design, development, adoption, and application of IT-based innovations in healthcare services delivery, management, and planning."

Informatics is "a field of study to apply IT to another field, from healthcare to journalism to biology to economics" (Indiana University).

Medical informatics (often used interchangeably with biomedical informatics, but the term biomedical is currently the preferred term used by the leading informatics body in this field, the AMIA). It is "the science and art of modeling and recording real-world clinical concepts and events into computable data used to derive actionable information, based on expertise in medicine, information science, IT, and the scholarly study of issues that impact upon the productive use of information systems by clinical personnel" (S. Silverstein, MD).

Nursing informatics is the "science and practice (that) integrates nursing and implementation of communication and IT" (AMIA).

Translational bioinformatics is the development, analytic methods to optimize the transformation of biomedical data, and genomic data, into proactive, predictive, preventive, and participatory health.

1.A Appendix

Curricula for existing medical informatics associates degree programs
1: This is an information technology–centric 2-year medical informatics associates degree program. (IT–centric refers implies that it was created by the IT department with additional courses focusing on the medical informatics curriculum.)

General Education Requirements		
Communication		
	EN 101 Composition I	3
	EN 102 Composition II	3
Mathematics Electives		
	MA 108 College Algebra	3

(Continued)

Science Electives

	BS 103 Anatomy and Physiology I	4
	BS 104 Anatomy and Physiology II	4
Technology Competency or Information Literacy		
	CIS 107 Information Technology Fundamentals and Applications	3
	CIS 125 Microcomputer Software I	3
Social Science	EC 101 Economics I	3
	PS 101 Introduction to Psychology	3
Humanities Elective	Choose 3 credits from General Education Humanities course list	3
Total general education credits		32
Major Requirements	CIS 106 Linux Fundamentals	1
	CIS 108 Programming Fundamentals	3
	CIS 165 Fundamentals of C++ Programming	4
	CIS 180 Networking Essentials	3
	CIS 202 Systems Analysis and Design	3
	CIS 286 Network Security Fundamentals	3
	CIS 290 Database Fundamentals	3
	CIS 294 CIS Internship or CIS 295 Capstone Project	2
	HIT 111 Culture of Healthcare	3
	HIT 112 Introduction to Medical & Healthcare Terminology	1
	HIT 212 Computer Applications in Healthcare	3
Total major credits		29
Total degree credits		61

2: This is a health-centric associates degree program in medical informatics since the program evolved from a health curriculum with added information technology courses.

Semester 1	
WRT101 English Composition I	3
BIO109 Anatomy and Physiology I	4
MOA140 Medical Terminology	3
INF101 Introduction to Information Technology	3
INF... Programming Language Fundamentals	3
Total	16
Semester 2	
WRT201 English Composition II	3
BIO209 Anatomy and Physiology II	4
MOA201 Diagnostic and Procedural Coding	4
INF... Advanced Programming Languages	3
Humanities Elective*	3
Total	17

(Continued)

Semester 3

MOA141 Introduction to Medical Assistant	3
MOA218 Medical Economics	2
INF217 Database for Business Applications (note: curriculum request to change name to Database for Applications)	3
Humanities Elective*	3
MAT... Mathematics Elective**	3–4
WEX101 Dynamics of Health and Fitness	2
Total	16–17

Semester 4

MOA200 Pharmacology for Medical Office Assistants	2
INF218 Database Programming	3
INF219 Database Administration	3
BUS101 Introduction to Business	3
Social Science Elective***	3
WEX... Wellness and Exercise Elective	1
Total	15
Total Degree Credits	64–65

2

Framework for Implementing the U.S. Medical Records Infrastructure

Level I: Core Concepts

2.1 Introduction

In the United States in the early 1960s, a number of public and private initiatives began the exploration of EHRs (see Section 3.2 on the history of EHRs in 1960 to 1996 that led up to the HIPAA of 1996). The Veterans Administration in 1971, the largest medical provider in the United States, started developing an EHR and rolled out a working system worldwide in 1987, originally called the Veterans Health Information Systems and Technology Architecture (VistA) (http://www.ehealth. va.gov/VistA.asp) and currently renamed HealthVet, the next generation of VistA. This chapter focuses on initiatives that spurred the development of the EHRs in the United States: HIPAA [3], the Affordable Care Act (ACA) [1], and the stimulus bill. Government documents, many of which can be found at www.HHS.gov, are used to outline important provisions contained in these acts focusing on the evolution and implementation of EHRs. For a complete list of all provisions of HIPAA, ACA, and the stimulus bill, links are provided.

The beginnings of a quantified approach to healthcare first began in 1996 with the HIPAA under President Clinton, Public Law 104–191. A number of incremental modifications in the ensuing decade were made culminating in the Final Rule in 2013 (see Figure 2.1). The evolution and adoption of EHRs continued with the American Reinvestment and Recovery Act(ARRA)[2] Feb.17,2009 [stimulus bill] with a Health IT funding component the HITECH ACT[4], 19.7 billion of which was earmarked to subsidize EHR implementation, and later with the ACA of 2010. These three major government initiatives spanning 1996 and 2010 laid the foundations for the evolution of the electronic medical infrastructure in the United States whose goals were to enhance healthcare delivery and accessibility, reduce errors, eliminate duplicate diagnostic procedures, and create integrated research and clinical databases with patient confidentiality specified by HIPAA Title II, which brought healthcare efficiencies in par with other industries. The rationale was that unless the government subsidized the considerable costs inherent in the transition, most physicians and hospitals would be unwilling or unable to convert to EHRs. Punitive measures were added so that e-prescriptions, issued by physicians, after 2013 and Medicare and Medicaid reimbursement costs after 2015, would receive reduced compensation if they breached that deadline.

HIPAA, a core component of the evolution of U.S. EHRs, was not created in a vacuum. The modern need for standard medical vocabularies was started in 1948 by the World Health Organization by creating the International Classification of Diseases (ICD) (see Chapter 4). The need for classifying disease began much earlier at the dawn of written text, papyrus, where ancient Egyptians and Babylonians around 3300 BC began to quantify a system of medicine. Technology has evolved with the emergence of medical texts. In 1450, Johannes Gutenberg developed the first practical screw printing press, but these presses were not widely available till the early 1500s. Soon after in 1542, the first wide-scale pharmaceutical text *Antidotarium Florentine* was published by the Florence College of Medicine, quantifying medicines and treatments.

EHRs became possible with the evolution of mainframes in the 1950s, personal computers in 1980s and the Internet in the 1990s. The emergence of HIPAA in 1996 logically followed the ability to connect medical data worldwide. Since then, the growth has been exponential. The limiting factor was cost, and also political factors can't be discounted, so the American Resources and Recovery Act in 2009 with the HITECH Act included amendments providing resources to subsidize hospitals and physicians to defer the initial start-up costs (see Chapter 3). The next logical step was the ACA, that is, ObamaCare, which made healthcare universally accessible and affordable in the U.S. A caveat, universal dental care still lags behind. Only 50% of U.S. citizens have dental insurance, which is the next challenge to be addressed.

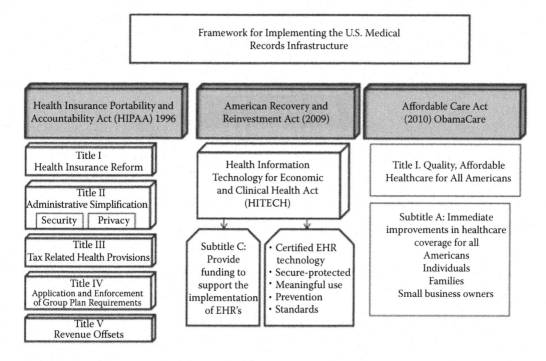

FIGURE 2.1 Implementation dates of critical components to healthcare infrastructure.

Three core U.S. healthcare initiatives (Figure 2.1):

1. The HIPAA of 1996, under President Clinton (http://www.hhs.gov/ocr/privacy/hipaa/administrative/)
2. The $787 billion economic stimulus bill passed under President Obama on February 19, 2009, of which 19.7 billion was targeted at Health IT (HITECH Act U.S. news, http://news.cnet.com/8301–13578_3–10161233–38.html)
3. The ACA of 2010, passed under President Obama, often referred to as ObamaCare (http://www.hhs.gov/healthcare/facts/timeline/)

2.2 HIPAA

The HIPAA was enacted in 1996 and had several goals: portability of insurance when moving between jobs, security and privacy of personal medical data, setting guidelines and penalties for fraud and abuse of health information relating to unauthorized access to patient data, and creating a framework of standards that could ensure accurate communication and coding schemas so practitioners could reliably communicate. For example when describing heart attack, you might use angina or angina pectoris (temporary inadequate blood supply to the heart muscle), variant angina (caused by a spasm), or Prinzmetal's angina (pain caused in clusters). Clear precise terms agreed upon by all are essential in medical diagnosis and treatment. Figure 2.2 summarizes the components of HIPAA and the first paragraph of law 104–191 that clearly espouses its objectives.

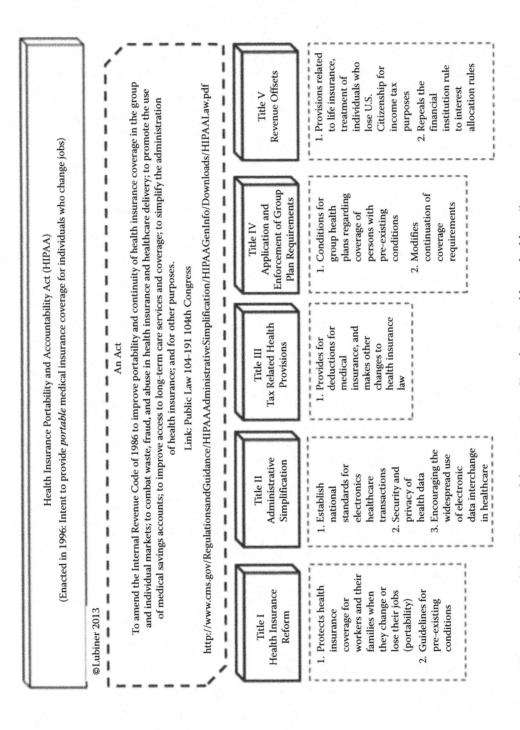

Health Insurance Portability and Accountability Act (HIPAA)

(Enacted in 1996: Intent to provide *portable* medical insurance coverage for individuals who change jobs)

©Lubiner 2013

An Act

To amend the Internal Revenue Code of 1986 to improve portability and continuity of health insurance coverage in the group and individual markets; to combat waste, fraud, and abuse in health insurance and healthcare delivery; to promote the use of medical savings accounts; to improve access to long-term care services and coverage; to simplify the administration of health insurance; and for other purposes.

Link: Public Law 104-191 104th Congress

http://www.cms.gov/RegulationsandGuidance/HIPAAAdministrativeSimplification/HIPAAGenInfo/Downloads/HIPAALaw.pdf

Title I
Health Insurance Reform

1. Protects health insurance coverage for workers and their families when they change or lose their jobs (portability)
2. Guidelines for pre-existing conditions

Title II
Administrative Simplification

1. Establish national standards for electronics healthcare transactions
2. Security and privacy of health data
3. Encouraging the widespread use of electronic data interchange in healthcare

Title III
Tax Related Health Provisions

1. Provides for deductions for medical insurance, and makes other changes to health insurance law

Title IV
Application and Enforcement of Group Plan Requirements

1. Conditions for group health plans regarding coverage of persons with pre-existing conditions
2. Modifies continuation of coverage requirements

Title V
Revenue Offsets

1. Provisions related to life insurance, treatment of individuals who lose U.S. Citizenship for income tax purposes
2. Repeals the financial institution rule to interest allocation rules

FIGURE 2.2 Health Insurance Portability and Accountability Act provisions. (From http://www.hhs.gov.healthcare/.)

2.2.1 Title I: Health Insurance Reform

Title I sets guidelines and expands access to medical coverage. There were a number of inequities that Title I addresses. First, health plans, specifically group plans, can't deny access to coverage based on previous conditions, referred to as pre-existing conditions, and premiums of fellow plan participants would remain at similar levels. Second, HIPAA guarantees that when you move between jobs, a comparable level of insurance will be available. Third, when moving from a group to an individual health plan, you also can't be denied for a preexisting condition but premiums can rise:

A. Increased portability (limiting the use of pre-existing conditions in group health plans)
B. Special enrollment plans for dependents
C. Health insurance that must be renewable in small (0–50) and large markets
   (http://www.ssa.gov/policy/docs/ssb/v60n4/v60n4p18.pdf)

2.2.2 Title II: Privacy, Security, Standards, Administrative Simplification

Privacy, Security, Fraud and Abuse, Medical Simplification, Transactions (see Chapter 5 for more details).

Most of this discussion of HIPAA focuses on Title II since it specifically applies to EHRs. *Administrative simplification* specifies standards for information transactions, privacy guidelines and penalties for unauthorized access, and security measures, such as electronic Protected Health Information (ePHI) guidelines to ensure patient confidentiality. A National Patient Identifier, a 10-digit identifier recommendation, has yet to be implemented. Title II also outlines exceptions where anonymous medical data, where all identifying information is removed, can be used for public healthcare emergencies and sanctioned researches.

Title II contains a number of components that fall into three categories (see Figure 2.3):

1. Healthcare fraud and abuse prevention
2. Medical liability reform

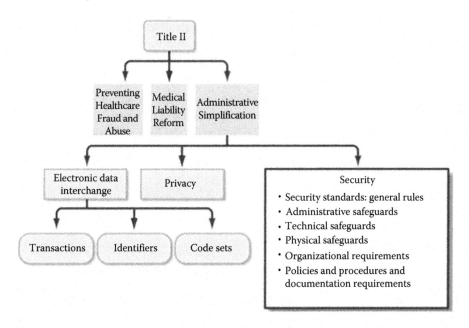

FIGURE 2.3 Title II, Health and Human Services (HHS). (From http://www.hhs.gov/ocr/privacy/hipaa/administrative/securityrule/nist80066.pdf.)

3. Administrative simplification
   a. Privacy
   b. Security
   c. Electronic data exchange

2.2.2.1 Fraud and Abuse Prevention

This section of Title II was amended in 2000 and is enforced by the Health and Human Services (HHS) Office for Civil Rights (www.hhs.gov/ocr/office/news/2000/prprifl.doc).

There are five components of this section:

1. Consumer control
   a. Procedures to ensure patients have access to their medical records, to correct mistakes, and to advance consent for release of their information, except for public health emergencies, and documentation outlining their privacy rights.
2. Boundaries
   a. Hospitals and healthcare organizations may not release or use data for nonhealth-related activities such as hiring and firing, promotions, or determining premiums for commercial products such as life insurance. Data should be used for patient medical care.
   b. Exceptions can be made, with proper authorization, for research with safeguards for removing patients' identifying information.
3. Accountability
   a. There are outlined penalties if an individual's privacy rights are violated; these include disclosure by error, $100 per violation up to limit of $25,000/year; knowingly disclosing information, up to $50,000 and up to 1 year in prison; and finally, obtaining information fraudulently, up to $250,000 and up to 5 years in prison.
4. Public responsibility
   a. There are guidelines to ensure access of medical data for public health emergencies such as infectious disease outbreaks; all efforts should be made to obscure individuals' identity.
5. Security
   a. Organizations must do everything possible to secure patient information and establish procedures and training or face penalties (see accountability for fines).

2.2.2.2 Medical Liability Reform

Medical liability refers to both the patient's rights to be compensated for malpractice, i.e., medical injury during a procedure or under medical care, and the physician's costs and responsibilities regarding medical liability insurance and possible penalties for nurses and doctors. HIPAA suggests guidelines, but specific regulations are currently being dealt with at the state level. Some of the issues are whether patients have unlimited rights to sue for pain and suffering contrasted with the cost of physicians to pay for insurance. Some specialty' malpractice insurance may run between $100,000 and $200,000 per year, driving many doctors to switch from high-risk specialties. This is an evolving dilemma that will not be resolved soon.

2.2.2.3 Title II Privacy Rule

The HIPAA Privacy Rule intent is to safeguard individuals' health information while traversing the myriad of systems that require access to these data. The scope of the privacy rule includes patient records referred to as electronic protected health information (ePHI) dealing with covered entities, i.e., healthcare organizations. The privacy rule tenets continue to be amended to address changes in technology and our understanding of the complexity of sharing medical data to ensure effective healthcare delivery.

Congress created a committee to advise the HHS to provide guidelines on health data and statistics to guide national policies; that is, the National Committee on Vital and Health Statistics (NCVHS) (http://www.ncvhs.hhs.gov/intro.htm). It originally was created in the 1960s to provide health statistics, disease classification, and other medical data standards but was significantly expanded in the 1990s to support HIPAA. Its charter was expanded to "form standards for the confidentiality of health information required to assure the safety of the shared information."

HIPAA Privacy Rule (http://www.hhs.gov/ocr/privacy/hipaa/administrative/privacyrule/index.html).

The HIPAA Privacy Rule establishes national standards to protect individuals' medical records and other personal health information and applies to health plans, healthcare clearinghouses, and those healthcare providers that conduct certain healthcare transactions electronically. The Rule requires appropriate safeguards to protect the privacy of personal health information, and sets limits and conditions on the uses and disclosures that may be made of such information without patient authorization. The Rule also gives patients rights over their health information, including rights to examine and obtain a copy of their health records, and to request corrections.

A subcommittee of NCVHS on privacy, confidentiality, and security report "Recommendations Regarding Sensitive Health Information" can be found at http://www.ncvhs.hhs.gov/101110lt.pdf. Figure 2.4 illustrates NCVHS guidelines on privacy for medical records containing genetic information, psychotherapy notes, and substance abuse treatments.

2.2.2.4 HIPAA Security Rule

The HIPAA Security Rule focuses on ePHI. It is broken down into (1) administrative, (2) technical, and (3) physical components:

The HIPAA Security Rule establishes national standards to protect individuals' electronic protected health information (ePHI) that is created, received, used, or maintained by a covered entity. The Security Rule requires appropriate administrative, physical and technical safeguards to ensure the confidentiality, integrity, and security of electronic protected health information.

Level II Applications: Implementing HIPAA Title II (Sections 2.2.2.4.1 through 2.2.5)

2.2.2.4.1 Administrative Safeguards

The administrative safeguards involve management procedures to analyze an organization's procedures to ensure patient data security as well as analyze potential risk, that is, risk analysis.

The Security Rule defines administrative safeguards as, "administrative actions, and policies and procedures, to manage the selection, development, implementation, and maintenance of security measures to protect electronic protected health information and to manage the conduct of the covered entity's workforce in relation to the protection of that information."

(www.hhs.gov/ocr/privacy/hipaa/administrative/securityrule/index.html)

2.2.2.4.1.1 Security Management Process
1. *Risk analysis*: The process of identifying potential security risks
   a. Identifying potential security risks and vulnerabilities
      i. How does ePHI flow throughout the organization? This includes ePHI that is created, received, maintained, or transmitted by the covered entity.
      ii. What are the less obvious sources of ePHI? Has the organization considered portable devices like PDAs?

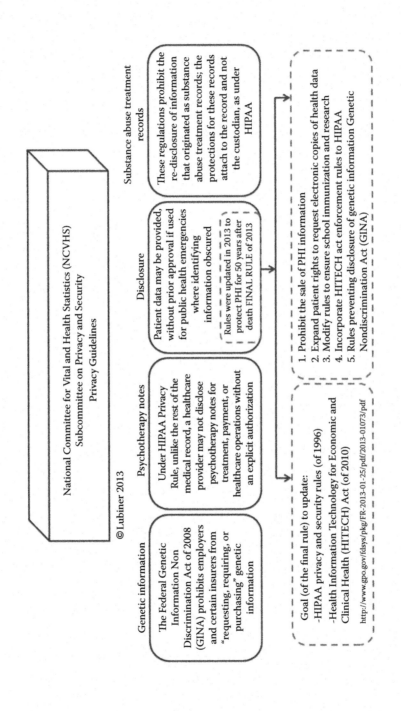

FIGURE 2.4 Privacy guidelines (sample) from the National Committee on Vital and Health Statistics source. (From http://www.ncvhs.hhs.gov/101110lt.pdf.)

      iii. What are the external sources of ePHI? For example, do vendors or consultants create, receive, maintain, or transmit ePHI?

      iv. What are the human, natural, and environmental threats to information systems that contain ePHI?

  b. Determining the probability of occurrence and magnitude of risks

2. *Risk management*

  a. Is executive leadership and/or management involved in risk management and mitigation decisions?

  b. Are security processes being communicated throughout the organization?

  c. Does the covered entity need to engage other resources to assist in risk management?

3. *Sanction policy*

Apply appropriate sanctions against workforce members who fail to comply with the security policies and procedures of the covered entity.

  a. Does the organization require employees to sign a statement of adherence to security policy and procedures (e.g., as part of the employee handbook or confidentiality statement) as a prerequisite to employment?

  b. Does the statement of adherence to security policies and procedures state that the workforce member acknowledges that violations of security policies and procedures may lead to disciplinary action, for example, up to and including termination?

4. *Information system activity review*

Implement procedures to regularly review records of information system activity, such as audit logs, access reports, and security incident tracking reports.

  a. What are the audit and activity review functions of the current information systems?

  b. Are the information system functions adequately used and monitored to promote continual awareness of information system activity?

  c. What logs or reports are generated by the information systems?

  d. Is there a policy that establishes what reviews will be conducted?

  e. Is there a procedure that describes specifics of the reviews?

2.2.2.4.1.2 Assigned Security Responsibility   The intent is to determine who in an organization is responsible to monitor and guarantee that the employees comply with the security rules:

Identify the security official who is responsible for the development and implementation of the policies and procedures required by this subpart (the Security Rule) for the entity.

1. This requires all covered entities to designate a privacy official.

2. The security official and privacy official can be the same person, but necessarily applicable in all cases.

  a. Has the organization agreed upon, and clearly identified and documented, the responsibilities of the security official?

  b. How are the roles and responsibilities of the security official crafted to reflect the size, complexity, and technical capabilities of the organization?

3. While one individual must be designated as having overall responsibility, other individuals in the covered entity may be assigned with specific security responsibilities (e.g., facility security or network security).

2.2.2.4.1.3 Workforce Security   The organization must assign individuals who have access to ePHI. This will include the determination of the levels of access and which computer terminals and systems are to be used. This includes auxiliary devices such as flash drives that should contain encryption software and security access keys:

> Implement policies and procedures to ensure that all members of its workforce have appropriate access to electronic protected health information, as provided under the Information Access Management standard and to prevent those workforce members who do not have access under the Information Access Management standard from obtaining access to protected electronic health information.

In workforce security, there are three subspecifications:

1. Authorization and/or supervision
   a. Implement procedures for the authorization and/or supervision of workforce members who work with electronic protected health information or in locations where it might be accessed.
      i. Are detailed job descriptions used to determine what level of access to ePHI the person holding the position should have?
      ii. Who has or should have the authority to determine who can access ePHI, e.g., supervisors or managers?
      iii. Are there similar existing processes used for paper records that could be used as an example for the ePHI?
2. Workforce clearance procedure
   a. Implement procedures to determine that the access of a workforce member to electronic protected health information is appropriate.
      i. Are there existing procedures for determining that the appropriate workforce members have access to the necessary information?
      ii. Are the procedures used consistently within the organization when determining access of related workforce job functions?
3. Termination procedures
   a. Implement procedures for terminating access to electronic protected health information when the employment of a workforce member ends or as required by determinations made as specified in paragraph (a3)(ii)(B) (the Workforce Clearance Procedure).

(http://www.hhs.gov/ocr/privacy/hipaa/administrative/securityrule/adminsafeguards.pdf)

      i. Do the termination policies and procedures assign responsibility for removing information system and/or physical access?
      ii. Do the policies and procedures include timely communication of termination actions to insure that the termination procedures are appropriately followed?

2.2.2.4.2 Technical Safeguards

Access should only be made for individuals who have a need, to complete their job responsibilities, to access ePHI.

1. Isolating healthcare clearinghouse functions
   a. If a healthcare clearinghouse is part of a larger organization, the clearinghouse must implement policies and procedures that protect the electronic protected health information.
      i. Does the larger organization perform healthcare clearinghouse functions?
      ii. If healthcare clearinghouse functions are performed, are policies and procedures implemented to protect ePHI from the other functions of the larger organization?
      iii. Are additional technical safeguards needed to separate ePHI in information systems, used by the healthcare clearinghouse, to protect against unauthorized access by the larger organization?

2. Access authorization
  a. Implement policies and procedures for granting access to electronic protected health information, for example, through access to a workstation, transaction, program, process, or other mechanism.
    i. How is authorization documented? How can it be used to grant access?
    ii. Are the policies and procedures for granting access consistent with applicable requirements of the privacy rule?
    iii. Have appropriate authorization and clearance procedures, as specified in workforce security, been performed prior to granting access?
    iv. Are access rules specific to applications and business requirements? For example, do different workforce members require different levels of access based on job function?
    v. Is there a technical process in place, such as creating unique user name and an authentication process, when granting access to a workforce member?
3. Access establishment and modification

The organization should create access procedures not only for individuals but for all downstream equipment used to access electronic personal health information (ePHI).

1. Implement policies and procedures that, based upon the entity's access authorization policies, establish, document, review, and modify a user's right of access to a workstation, transaction, program, or process.
  a. Are policies and procedures in place for establishing access and modifying access?
  b. Are system access policies and procedures documented and updated as necessary?
  c. Do members of management or other workforce members periodically review the list of persons with access to ePHI to ensure they are valid and consistent with those authorized?

2.2.3 Title III: Tax Simplification Rule

Tax code changes to generate more revenue to pay for the increased costs of HIPAA implementation.

Title III discusses financial tax incentives that fall into three categories. Tax deductions for medical insurance, medical savings accounts that use pretax dollars, and long-term medical insurance guidelines.

2.2.4 Title IV: Group Healthcare Guidelines and Enforcement

Title IV provides more details regarding enforcement for group medical plans to prevent exclusion based on pre-existing conditions and continuation of coverage when moving between jobs.

2.2.5 Title V: Application and Enforcement of Group Health Plans

Title V includes provisions related to company-owned life insurance and treatment of individuals who lose U.S. citizenship for income tax purposes and repeals the financial institution rule to interest allocation rules.

Company-Owned Life Insurance
Deductions are prohibited for interest on loans with respect to company-owned life insurance, including company-owned endowment or annuity contracts.

Treatment of Individuals Who Lose U.S. Citizenship
Provisions were revised concerning expatriation to avoid taxes, including the following changes: (1) applying the provisions to certain long-term residents, (2) permitting the Treasury Secretary to expand the 10-year taxation period to 15 years, (3) increasing the categories of income treated as U.S. source income, (4) crediting foreign taxes imposed on U.S. source income, and (5) requiring the filing of certain information by expatriates.

Level I: Core Concepts (Continued)

2.3 American Recovery and Reinvestment Act of 2009

The American Reinvestment and Recovery Act (ARRA) passed by Congress in 2009 contained $782 billion to jumpstart the economy. The ARRA provided $31 billion for healthcare initiatives, of which $19.7 billion was earmarked to facilitate the adoption of electronic medical records (EMRs) by the healthcare community. It includes the Health Information Technology for Economic and Clinical Health (HITECH) Act, which incorporated meaningful use (MU) specifications that became guidelines for reimbursement and categorization of the effectiveness of integration of EHRs into their processes (http://www.gpo.gov/fdsys/pkg/BILLS-111hr1enr/pdf/BILLS-111hr1enr.pdf).

2.3.1 Health Information Technology for Economic and Clinical Health Act

In 2009, the HITECH Act, part of the ARRA, was adopted and provided almost $20 billion in funding to help hospitals and physicians make the transition to EHRs and provided $44,000 to $64,000 per physician to offset the cost of EHR implementation (Figure 2.5). Hospitals received millions per implementation. As part of that effort, MU standards levels 1 to 7 required medical practitioners to document the effectiveness of their implementation efforts, and their reimbursement was conditional on these levels of compliance of these standards. Further regulations required all medical practitioners to implement electronic prescription technologies by 2012 and most hospital and physicians to apply EHRs by 2015. A number of healthcare providers such as dentists, optometrists, and mental health physicians have more time to implement EHRs. Financial penalties, for example, 1%, 2%, and 3% of reimbursements, would be withheld if these deadlines were not met.

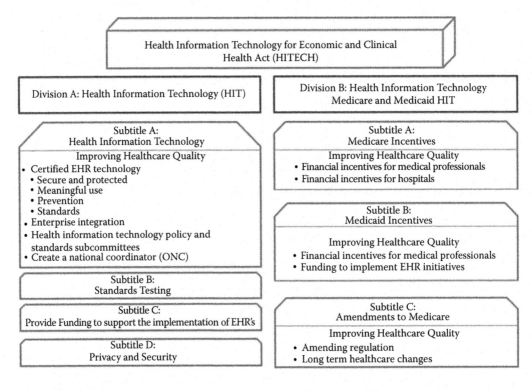

FIGURE 2.5   Health Information Technology for Economic and Clinical Health provisions.

2.4 Affordable Care Act

The ACA was passed in March 2010 and upheld by the Supreme Court in June 2012, often referred to as ObamaCare (Table 2.1).

The following are some key conditions:

1. Establish marketplace to compare healthcare plans (2014).
2. Acquire lower costs, depending on income, subsidized up to $88,000.
3. Obtain access to Medicaid or the Children's Health Insurance Program.
4. Preexisting conditions will be covered.
5. Remove lifetime medical limits.

TABLE 2.1 Affordable Care Act Provisions

Ten Sections of the ACA	
Title I: Quality, Affordable Healthcare for All Americans (http://www.hhs.gov/healthcare/rights/law/title/i-quality-affordable-healthcare.pdf)	Subtitle A—Immediate Improvements in Healthcare Coverage for All Americans
	Individuals
	Families
	Small business owners
	Subtitle B—Immediate Actions to Preserve and Expand Coverage
	Immediate access to insurance for uninsured individuals with a preexisting condition
	Subtitle C—Quality Health Insurance Coverage for All Americans
	Health Insurance Market Reforms
	Preservation of right to maintain existing coverage
	Subtitle D—Available Coverage Choices for All Americans
	Establishment of Qualified Health Plans
	Consumer choice
	State flexibility in operation and enforcement of Exchanges and related requirements
	Federal program to assist establishment and operation of nonprofit, member-run health insurance issuers
	Subtitle E—Affordable Coverage Choices for All Americans
	Premium Tax Credits and Cost-Sharing Reductions
	Eligibility Determinations
	Subtitle F—Shared Responsibility for Healthcare
	Requirement to maintain minimum essential coverage
Title II: The Role of Public Programs	
Title III: Improving the Quality and Efficiency of Healthcare	
Title IV: Prevention of Chronic Disease and Improving Public Health	
Title V: Healthcare Workforce	
Title VI: Transparency and Program Integrity	
Title VII: Improving Access to Innovative Medical Therapies	
Title VIII: Community Living Assistance Services and Supports Act (CLASS Act)	
Title IX: Revenue Provisions	
Title X: Reauthorization of the Indian Healthcare Improvement Act	

Source: http://www.hhs.gov/healthcare/rights/law/.

6. Require coverage for dependents up to 26 years of age.
7. Create uniform coverage standards.
8. Require coverage of preventive services and immunization.
9. Provide assistance for the uninsured.
    a. Tax credits for individuals with 100% to 400% of the poverty line (up to $88,000)
    b. Medicaid expansion for those individuals with 130% of the federal poverty line
10. Everyone is required to have healthcare coverage by 2014 or pay a small fee.
11. Employers with greater than 200 employees must enroll new hires.
12. $20 billion in funding to help hospitals and physicians make the transition to EHRs is needed and $44,000 to $64,000 is provided per physician to offset the cost of HER implementation.
13. MU standards levels 1 to 7 required medical practitioners to document the effectiveness of their implementation efforts.
    (http://www.dpc.senate.gov/healthreformbill/healthbill52.pdf)

2.4.1 Meaningful Use

The term "meaningful use" was defined by the Centers for Medicare and Medicaid Services (CMS) as a series of standards and incentive programs used as criteria for physician reimbursement wherein physicians are funded between $44,000 and $64,000 and hospitals between $3,000,000 and $5,000,000 to offset the costs of implementing EHRs: "The goal of meaningful use was to promote the spread of EHRs to improve healthcare in the United States" (www.healthit.gov).

CMS specified four general benefits of implementing EHRs:

1. Complete and accurate information and history of their patients. Paper patient records were dispersed among many providers and tests were often duplicated unnecessarily.
2. Better access to information.
3. Patient empowerment.
4. Patients are allowed access to all their medical records and can be part of the decision-making process. Personal data records allow individuals to maintain their own personal copy of their medical information.

The Office of the National Coordinator (ONC) for Health Information Technology, part of the U.S. Department of HHS, created a nonprofit Certification Commission for Healthcare Information Technology (http://www.cchit.org/) to certify that organizations met meaningful standards (Table 2.2).

TABLE 2.2 Meaningful Use Timetable by the Centers for Medicare and Medicaid Services

Stage 1: Data Capture of Medical Information and Sharing among Multiple Providers 2011–2012	Stage 2: Advance Clinical Processes 2014	Stage 3: Improved Outcomes 2016
Electronically capturing health information in a standardized format	More rigorous health information exchange (HIE)	Improving quality, safety, and efficiency, leading to improved health outcomes
Using that information to track key clinical conditions	Increased requirements for e-prescribing and incorporating lab results	Decision support for national high-priority conditions
Communicating that information for care coordination processes	Electronic transmission of patient care summaries across multiple settings	Patient access to self-management tools
Initiating the reporting of clinical quality measures and public health information	More patient-controlled data	Access to comprehensive patient data through patient-centered HIE
Using information to engage patients and their families		Improving population health

Source: CMS.gov.

TABLE 2.3 Objectives, of Which 19 Have to Be Satisfied to Receive Meaningful Use Funding

Meaningful Use Objectives (to Qualify for Incentive Reimbursement Program from ARRA)	
14 Core Objectives for Physicians (All Required)	10 Menu Options (Comply with at Least 5)
1. Use computerized physician order entry for physicians.	1. Implement drug formulary checks.
2. Implement drug–drug and drug–allergy interaction checks.	2. Incorporate clinical lab test results into EHR as structured data.
3. Maintain an up-to-date problem list of current active diagnoses.	3. Generate lists of patients by specific conditions to use for quality improvement, reduction of disparities, research, and outreach.
4. Keep an active medication list.	4. Send patient reminders per patient preference for preventive follow-up care.
5. Maintain an active medication allergy list.	5. Provide patients with timely electronic access to their health information (including lab results, problem list, medication lists, and allergies) within 4 business days of the information being available.
6. Record specified demographics on patients.	6. Use certified EHR technology to identify patient-specific education resources and provide those resources to the patient if possible.
7. Record and chart changes in specific vital signs.	7. The physician who receives a patient from another setting of care or provider or believes an encounter is relevant should perform medication reconciliation.
8. Document whether patients age 13 and older are smokers.	8. The physician who transitions patients to another setting of care or refers patients should provide a summary of care record for each transition.
9. Report clinical quality measures.	9. Capability to submit electronic data to immunization registries or immunization information systems and submission to applicable law and practice.
10. Implement one clinical decision support rule related to a high-priority hospital condition.	10. Capability to submit electronic syndrome surveillance data to public health agencies and actual submission according to applicable law and practice.
11. Offer patients an electronic copy of their health information upon request.	
12. Give patients an electronic copy of their discharge instructions upon request.	
13. Have the capability to exchange key clinical information.	
14. Protect electronic health information.	

MU has two sets of standards: one for physicians and another for hospitals. Physicians have 24 objectives, of which 19 have to be met to qualify for EHR reimbursement of implementation costs. Hospitals have 23 MU objectives, 18 of which have to be satisfied. These are further broken down into core objectives and a second set of 10 subobjectives from which you have to complete 50% (Table 2.3).

2.5 Summary

In 1985, the Veterans Administration implemented an EHRs system, under development for a decade. This was a rudimentary system by modern standards, but marked the beginning of the U.S. Government's support and funding for this concept. With the emergence of the Internet, that is, the World Wide Web in the 1990s, the stage was set via HIPAA to set guidelines for the modern EHR infrastructure. This was not a single event; a series of modifications over the next decade culminating with the Final Rule of 2013 set specific rational implementable standards for transactions between systems including privacy and security. In parallel, the ARRA, including the HITECH Act funding, directed $19.7 billion to subsidize this effort. Then in 2010, the ACA set guidelines to ensure all citizens had access.

This is an ever-evolving endeavor but we have established a firm foundation on which to build.

Note: With the Supreme Court Decisions the fate of the ACA appears to be secure: June 2012. National Federation of Independent Business V. Sebelius: Upholds Medicaid expansion and individual mandates. June 25, 2015, King et al. V. Burwell: Upholds health insurance subsidies.

Questions

Level I

1. What is HIPAA and what in general was it supposed to accomplish?
    a. What are the five components/titles of HIPAA? Briefly summarize their objectives (some information is in Level II sections of this chapter).
    b. What led up to HIPAA prior to 1996 (research on the web)?
2. What is ARRA? Explain its objectives relative to EHRs.
    a. What is the HITECH Act?
3. Explain the ACA.
    a. List at least five key components that you believe are relevant to EHRs. Why?
4. Explain the function of MU standards. Why was it created?
    a. What are the differences between hospital and physician MU standards, and why are they not the same objectives?
    b. What are the penalties of not reaching MU standards (research on web)?
5. How do HIPAA and NCVHS overlap in their objectives?

Level II

6. Why is HIPAA Title II the most detailed of the five components of HIPAA?
    a. Explain the function of HIPAA Title II Privacy Rule in detail.
    b. Explain the function of HIPAA Title II Security Rule in detail.
7. HIPAA describes detailed security management procedures to protect personal health information (PHI). Explain these management guidelines and why they were implemented.
    a. Risk analysis
    b. Risk management
    c. Sanctions: Be specific on the sanctions and penalties. The details can be found in Chapter 5.
    d. Technical safeguards

Glossary

Affordable Care Act (ACA): Passed in March 2010 and upheld by the Supreme Court in June 2012, which is often referred to as ObamaCare.
American Reinvestment and Recovery Act (ARRA): Passed by Congress in 2009, containing $782 billion to jump-start the economy and 20 billion targeted at promoting EHRs.
Electronic health record (EHR)*: A collection of health data from multiple sources. This is a *more expansive term* than electronic medical record and refers to all information of the health of the body. It is designed to share information among providers and includes all laboratory information and specialist data (used almost exclusively by the Office of the National Coordinator [ONC] for health information).

Electronic medical record (EMR): Used for diagnosis and treatment, which refers to medical treatment and history and is a digital form of a medical chart and often refers to information gathered in a local practice (it is often used but electronic health record is the preferred term).

Electronic protected health information (ePHI): Guidelines to ensure patient confidentiality.

Health Insurance Portability and Accountability Act (HIPAA) of 1996, Required HHS to develop standards for electronic health records (EHRs), data interchange, security, and unique EHR.

HIPAA Privacy Rule: Establishes national standards to protect individuals' medical records and other personal health information and applies to health plans, healthcare clearinghouses, and those healthcare providers that conduct certain healthcare transactions electronically.

HIPAA Security Rule: Establishes national standards to protect individuals' electronic protected health information that is created, received, used, or maintained by a covered entity.

Health Information Technology for Economic and Clinical Health Act (HITECH): In 2009, the HITECH Act, part of the ARRA, was adopted and provided almost $20 billion in funding to help hospitals and physicians make the transition to EHRs.

Meaningful use: Defined by the CMS as a series of standards and incentive programs used as criteria for physician reimbursement.

References

1. Affordable Care Act, http://www.hhs.gov/healthcare/facts/timeline/, 2010.
2. American Recovery and Reinvestment Act, http://www.treasury.gov/initiatives/recovery/Pages/recovery-act.aspx, 2009.
3. HIPAA, http://www.hhs.gov/ocr/privacy/hipaa/administrative/.
4. HITECH ACT, http://www.healthit.gov/policy-researchers-implementers/hitech-act, 2009.
5. Veterans Health Information Systems and Technology Architecture (VistA), http://www.ehealth.va.gov/VistA.asp, 1985.

3

Electronic Health Records

Level I: Core Concepts

3.1 Introduction

Electronic health records (EHRs) began as an aggregate of discrete data accumulated from various sources which were integrated into a seamless narrative that documented a patient's journey through the healthcare system. The newer generation of EHRs incorporate real-time dynamic data from mobile sensors, telehealth, external and implanted sensors. Prototype watches and medical sensors woven into clothing began to appear in 2013 and are becoming more mainstream and this data will begin to be incorporated into EHRs. System analysis techniques utilized in other engineering disciplines will add to the dynamic predictive analysis in medical records providing probabilities of potential acute conditions such as a stroke or heart attack and possible immune responses that may be affected by stress and pollution in the environment. The field of epigenomics will also benefit from the additional data provided from dynamic medical data, where external factors can affect gene expression and regulation, i.e., the probability of developing a specific cancer. Inheriting a trait from DNA is only one of many factors that determine susceptibility to developing serious diseases. We are on the cusp of a revolution that will bring healthcare parity with other engineering advances by creating a systems approach to healthcare (Figure 3.1).

3.2 History

In the 1960s when large mainframe computers began to proliferate, a number of EHR pilots appeared (Figure 3.2). Physician Lawrence Weed developed an EHR framework, the University of Vermont PROMISE project, a joint effort by Akron Children's Hospital and International Business Machines Corporation (IBM) utilizing an IBM 305 tube-based mainframe with a 5 mb storage capacity.

In the mid-1960s, the National Library of Medicine began providing an online indexing of biomedical literature originally called Medicus and later Medline. By the early 1970s, the Veterans Affairs (VA) began investing in an EHR system called VistaA. Ten years later, the system went public and was used at VA facilities worldwide. An open-source version of VistaA is available to hospitals; details can be found at www.WorldVistA.org.[9]. In the 1970s, the Regenstreif Institute [7], affiliated with the Indiana University School of Medicine, developed one of the first EHRs, but at this early stage, few physicians adopted the technology. With the two major technological advances, namely; the emergence of the PCs in 1981 and the web/Internet in 1990, Tim Berners-Lee created the first practical implementation of the web, at the Conseil Européen pour la Recherche Nucléaire (CERN) [1] at the super collider facility, which spurred the ability to share data ubiquitously, the scene was set for the emergence of EHRs. A number of commercial systems appeared in the mid-1990s such as Eclipsys, Clinitec, and others. In 1996, a turning point for the U.S. medical records efforts began with the Health Insurance Portability and Accountability Act (HIPAA). It was initially created to provide standards for submitting online medical claims, but later evolved incorporating the HIPAA Title II security framework and guidelines for a national EHR system. In 2009, the Health Information Technology for Economic and Clinical Health (HITECH) Act was adopted, part of the ARRA, which provided $19.7 billion in funding to help hospitals and physicians make the transition to EHRs. The HITECH Act provided $44,000 to $64,000 per physician to offset the costs of EHR implementation for millions for hospitals for EHR implementation. As part of that effort, meaningful use standards levels 1 to 7 required medical practitioners to document the effectiveness of their implementation efforts, and their reimbursement was conditional on these levels of compliance of these standards. Further regulations required all medical practitioners to implement electronic prescription technologies by 2012 and most hospital and physicians to utilize EHRs by 2015. A number of healthcare providers, dentists, optometrists, and providers of mental health services have more time to implement EHRs. Financial penalties of between 1%–3% of Medicare and Medicaid reimbursements would be withheld if these deadlines were not met.

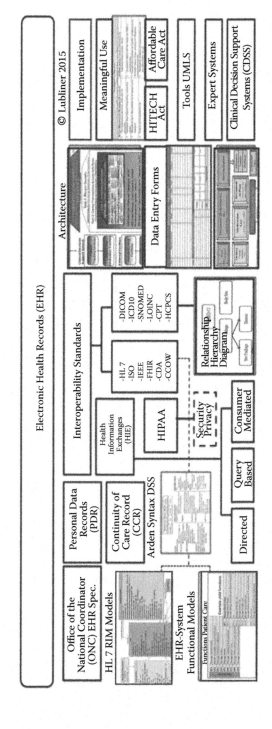

FIGURE 3.1 (See color insert.) Electronic health records.

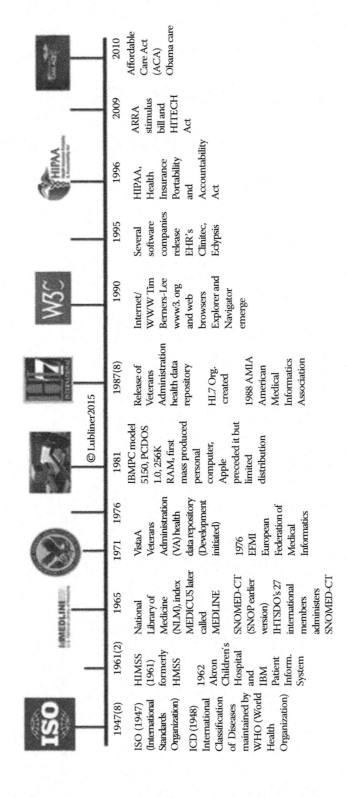

FIGURE 3.2 Timeline of electronic medical records.

3.3 Electronic Health Records

An EHR is a collection of health data from multiple sources. This is a more expansive term than an electronic medical record (EMR) and refers to all patient information acquired. It is designed to share information among medical providers and has the ability to track populations and potential spread of infectious diseases. It includes all laboratory information and specialist data. The EHR term is used almost exclusively by the Office of the National Coordinator (ONC) for Health Information.

An EHR is an integrated medical view of a patient that accesses modules available in Integrated Health Information System (Figure 3.5). These modules may be located either in a central repository, hospital or Cloud-based, or more likely in a number of databases geographically dispersed. This fragmented patient record in theory can be accessed by health information exchanges (HIEs), Section 3.3, which are government-supported systems, at least one per state, that eventually will have the ability to convert EHR data from multiple vendors. In 2010, the ONC for Health Information awarded grants to 56 states and territories to support first regional and later an integrated national HIE network. Grants ranged from $600,000 for American Samoa to $28 million to Texas Health and Human Services (HHS) Commission. (A complete grant list is available at http://www.healthit.gov/policy-researchers-implementers/state-healthinformation-exchange.)

EHRs are a synthesis of static data acquired during medical visits and procedures integrated with more dynamic data from wireless and mobile medical devices. A new generation of mobile wearable sensors that can track the stimuli and stresses in daily life connected into Smart phones and tablets will provide valuable insights into triggers that might create acute responses, providing a more comprehensive view of patients that were never available in printed medical records. In many engineering disciplines, we study forces and loads of systems under min/max conditions. Heart attacks and stroke prediction will benefit from real-time analysis of data. Drug absorption and effectiveness may also be dependent of dynamic metabolic effects during daily activities.

EHRs will continue to evolve incorporating lifestyle choices, i.e., data that may add to a better picture of the overall human system. Data collected during personal encounters, work interactions, eating habits, environmental exposures commuting to work, sun exposure, etc., will add to a dynamic view of patient health. National Science Foundation–funded studies are currently under way to evaluate the effectiveness and preventive benefits of wireless medical devices. A national center for wireless health at University of California, Los Angeles (http://www.wirelesshealth.ucla.edu/) is a good source of current research, and in addition, a global nonprofit organization, the Wireless-Life Sciences Alliance, connects innovators, globally relevant companies, scientists, physicians, and policy makers (www.wirelesslifesciences.org). Better methods of visualizing medical data will also enable both healthcare professionals and individuals, utilizing personal data records, a better view of changes over time contributing to illness.

A universal national patient ID has yet to be realized, but EHRs associated with a particular hospital/medical software vendor assigns a tracking ID. Sometimes, it's an algorithm based on Social Security, birth date, age, hospital system, or possibly it's simply the next in sequence. Other key searchable fields are secondary identifiers such as Social Security, birth date, and age.

3.3.1 EHR Taxonomy

There are three general categories; EHRs, Continuity of Care Records (CCRs), and Personal Health Records (PHR). Each provides unique data relevant for different medical situations. The key to these EHRs is interoperability, the ability to share and exchange data. They incorporate features that benefit individuals, healthcare organizations, and governmental agencies, such as the Centers for Disease Control and Prevention (CDC), to ensure the health of the population at large. The enactment of laws such as HIPAA in 1996 and funding initiatives of the American Recovery and Reinvestment Act (ARRA) in 2009 were designed to ensure these interoperability, privacy, and security objectives.

The term EMR is used primarily for diagnosis and treatment. It refers to medical treatment and history and is a digital form of a medical chart and often refers to information gathered in a local practice.

(EHR is the preferred and the more expansive term.) CCR refers to a subset of medical information focused on timely care of an individual either in an emergency situation or provided to another physician focusing on current health status, medications, and treatment.

3.3.1.1 Personal Health Record

A PHR is medical information in possession of an individual patient or a patient's nonprofessional caregiver, such as a home aid. The format may be either paper documents, electronic media, or a combination. The sources of the information include patient-generated lists, copies of reports from physicians, hospitals and labs, legal documents such as living wills and healthcare proxy forms, and insurance statements. Organizations such as the American Health Information Management Association (AHIMA) encourage individuals to keep their own complete PHR, including any information that a doctor may not have, such as exercise routines, dietary habits, herbal or nonprescription medications, or results of home testing such as home blood pressure or sugar readings. Consumers can purchase PHRs software for their PC or in the Cloud. According to AHIMA, 42% of U.S. adults surveyed said they keep some form of a PHR. PHR is also available free of cost from several Internet sites (Figure 3.3).

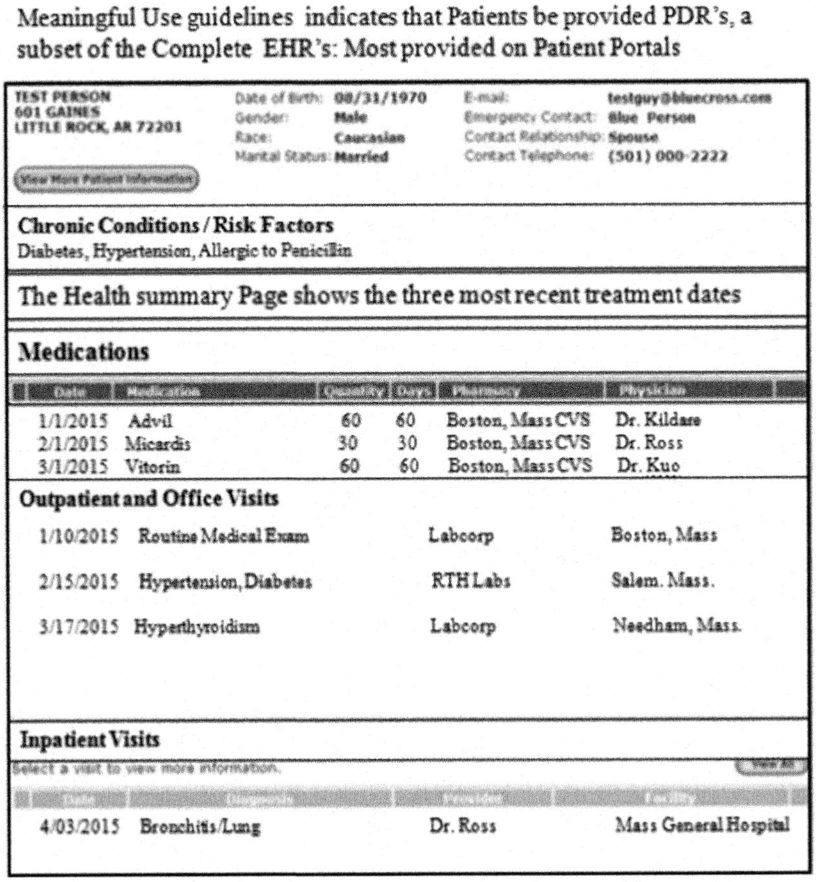

FIGURE 3.3 Provider dispute resolutions example provided by Blue Cross and Blue Shield contains conditions, medications, and in- and outpatient visits.

Definition:

(HHS.gov) "A PHR is an electronic record of an individual's health information by which the individual controls access to the information and may have the ability to manage, track, and participate in his or her own healthcare."

  http://www.hhs.gov/ocr/privacy/hipaa/understanding/special/healthit/phrs.pdf.
PHR usually includes

1. Longitudinal health history
2. Medical diagnoses
3. Medications
4. Test results
5. Location to keep family medical histories
6. Emergency contact numbers
7. Keep track of appointments
8. Location to track other family members for whom they are responsible

Benefits:

1. Manage their own health records
2. Control who has access to this information
3. Able to monitor medical records and correct errors
4. Facilitate treatment for emergencies away from the healthcare providers
5. Data sharing: Most provider dispute resolutions (PDRs) have an option of adding or deleting users' access

Types of PHRs:

1. Provided by healthcare provider fall under HIPAA *Privacy Rule* (provided by covered entities: known as protected health information [PHI]). The privacy rule allows individuals to view and obtain a copy of their health information including billing, medical records, claims, and other information used for treatment decisions (Table 3.1).
   a. Provided by healthcare plans or providers
   b. Usually a subset of their larger health record
   c. Read only, can't update information
   d. Control of access, family members, etc.
   e. Not always complete but users have the right to request information from other providers to be added to this PHR
   f. Disclosure requires users written consent except in the case where it is used to provide medical services

TABLE 3.1   HIPAA Privacy Rule Entities

Healthcare Providers	Health Plans	Healthcare Clearinghouses
Clinics	Company health plans	Billing services
Chiropractors	Health maintenance organizations	Community health management
Doctors	Long-term care insurers	Repricing companies
Dentists	Medical, dental, vision plans	Value-added networks
Nursing homes	Medicare and Medicaid	
Pharmacies	Medicare choice and supplement	
Psychologists	Veterans' health plans	

2. Third-party PHR software not covered under HIPAA
   a.   Third-party company, not a health plan, clearinghouse, or provider, is not bound by HIPAA requirement.
   b.   A few third-party providers who say they are HIPAA compliant are legally required to follow privacy rules.

Definition:

Covered entity (under HIPAA privacy rule) "refers to three specific groups, including health plans, healthcare clearinghouses, and healthcare providers that transmit health information electronically" (http://www.hrsa.gov/healthit/toolbox/HealthITAdoptiontoolbox/PrivacyandSecurity/entityhipaa.html).

A sample PDR is provided by Blue Cross and Blue Shield (http://www.bcbs.com/healthcare-partners/personal-health-records/consumer-personal-health-record.html).

3.3.1.2 Continuity of Care Record

The CCR is a core data set of the most relevant and timely facts about a patient's healthcare. It is to be prepared by a practitioner at the conclusion of a healthcare encounter in order to enable the next practitioner to readily access such information. It includes a summary of the patient's health status (e.g., problems, medications, allergies) and basic information about insurance, advance directives, care documentation, and care plan recommendations. It also includes identifying information and the purpose of the CCR. The CCR may be prepared, displayed, and transmitted on paper or electronically, provided the information required by this standard specification is included. However, for maximum utility, the CCR should be prepared in a structured electronic format that is interchangeable among EHR systems. To ensure interchangeability of electronic CCRs, this standard specifies that XML coding is required when the CCR is created in a structured electronic format. XML coding provides flexibility that will allow users to prepare, transmit, and view the CCR in multiple ways, e.g., in a browser, as an element in an Health Level 7 (HL7) message or Clinical Document Architecture (CDA) compliant document, in a secure email, as a PDF file, as an HTML file, or as a word processing document. It will further permit users to display the fields of the CCR in multiple formats. Equally important, it will allow the interchange of the CCR data between otherwise incompatible EHR systems.

Definition:

"The Continuity of Care Record (CCR) was developed in order to facilitate the transfer of health information among healthcare providers when patients transition from one healthcare setting to the next" (http://www.hrsa.gov/healthit/toolbox/HealthITAdoptiontoolbox/PersonalHealthRecords/aboutccr.html).

CCR features

1. Clinical summary of a patient's healthcare status (XML based)
   a.   Advanced directives
   b.   Care plan
   c.   Care documentation
      1.   Vital signs
      2.   Problems
      3.   Medications, immunizations, allergies
      4.   Procedures
      5.   Family history
      6.   Medical encounters

     d. Insurance information (payers)
     e. Identifying data
     f. Improve healthcare interoperability
  2. Used for transferring care between multiple healthcare providers

Standards

In 2007, American National Standard Institute (ANSI) (www.ansi.org) created a standard for Continuity of Care Documents using HL7 (www.HL7.org) (see Chapter 4). It utilizes the Clinical Architecture (CDA) and data defined by ASTM CCR and is compatible with the Integrating Healthcare Environment (IHE) designed to share information between systems.

The HL7 Reference Information Model (RIM) is an object model that provides a visual representation of HL7 clinical data domains. It identifies the life cycle of message groups that are moved between domains of the model. The blocks for patient encounter, observation, procedure, etc., include fields that indicate relationships between domains (Figure 3.4).

3.3.2 EHR Architecture

There are a number of U.S. and international guidelines for the EHR architectures. The goals are not simply the comprehensiveness of the patient information, the categories are clinical, ethical, legal, secure, and allow for data analysis, but conform to international standards; International Classification of Diseases (ICD10), Digital Imaging and Communications in Medicine (DICOM), Systemized Nomenclature of Medicine Clinical Terms (SNOMED CT), etc., which allow for communication between multiple EHR vendors both nationally and internationally and HL7 for standard communications protocols (Chapter 4).

The principal purpose of EHRs is the clinical care of patients. It's a central repository of information from not only medical personnel but data from labs, medical scans, personal histories, etc., that can create a holistic view of the patient and can prevent duplicate unnecessary tests. Once all other practitioners have transitioned to EHRs such as dentists, optometrists, and mental healthcare workers, the interrelated complex medical factors contributing to a disease can be fully appreciated. Correlations can be missed by an incomplete medical record, an example of which is periodontal disease that has been shown to be a factor in heart disease, specifically inflammation in the gums and arteriosclerosis and its relationship to the inflammatory process in arteries. Intelligent software can correlate these diverse factors and can suggest treatments that might be missed. Finally, errors due to incomplete data and patients' misidentification create thousands of patient injuries a year that can be reduced using EHRs. The benefits far outweigh cost and additional labor entering patient data.

The International Organization for Standardization (ISO) (http://www.iso.org/iso/home.html) is a federated group of organizational standards for organization management, environment, energy, food, and healthcare. The ISO standard 18308:2011 (EN) defines the architecture, services, and communication standards for EHRs and their term "shared health records." It also follows the Open Distributed Processing Model ISO/International Electrotechnical Commission (IEC) 10746–1. The IEC is a French nonprofit standards organization. Its definition summary states that (https://www.iso.org/obp/ui/#iso:std:iso:18308:ed-1:v1:en) "one or more repositories, physically or virtually integrated, of information in computer processable form, relevant to the wellness, health and healthcare of an individual, capable of being stored and communicated securely and of being accessible by multiple authorized users, represented according to a standardized or commonly agreed logical information model. Its primary purpose is the support of life-long, effective, high quality and safe integrated healthcare."

The ISO standards do not simply discuss technical guidelines but include a broader definition of wellness and complimentary services, "alternative medicine." This includes herbal remedies and other nonwestern medicine.

Another organization that began in the United States in 1987 but quickly expanded to a global reach was HL7 (http://www.hl7.org/). The term HL7 came from the ISO seven-layer communication model for

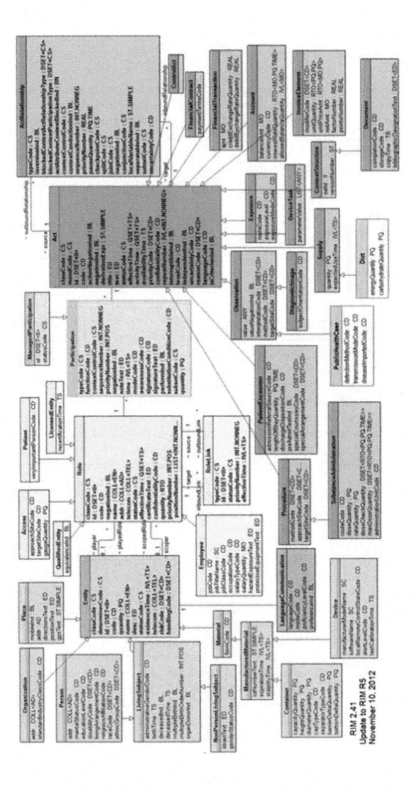

FIGURE 3.4 (See color insert.) Health Level 7 Reference Information Model models a visual representation of domains and messages exchanged. (From http://www.hl7standards.com/blog/2011/05/31/hl7-v3-rim-is-it-really-that-intimidating/.)

Open System Interconnection. It's an international organization for the interoperability of health information technology (HIT). The organization includes thousands of medical practitioners and over 500 major healthcare companies who regularly meet to discuss HIT standards and ensure these standards are integrated into their products. Their website is an excellent source of database and architectural models. A joint medical record specification is ISO/HL7 10781, a synthesis of the work of both these standards organizations.

3.3.2.1 EHR Model

The core of any EHR system is built around interoperability standards, i.e., a series of terms, data structures, and libraries all protected by a security layer. So the EHR model (Figure 3.5) begins with a privacy/security layer defined by HIPAA Title II. The next core layer are the libraries that incorporate international naming conventions such as ICD10 and DICOM that allow interoperability of EHRs, i.e., to allow multiple vendors and systems to seamlessly communicate.

The next core component is documentation by medical practitioners—inpatient hospital services such as doctors, nurses, and external providers specialists in medical practices and medications. An intelligent layer of software, clinical decision support systems (CDSS), provides intelligence to help the medical practitioner. It can be as simple as workflow analysis, for example, steps that have to be completed during discharge of patients. Others involve medication tracking, alerts to ensure dosage, and allergies and drug interactions to provide patient safety.

All these layers are connected, via a network, to internal and external EHR components such as radiology, pharmacies, and laboratories. This complex system of interconnected medical records provide a single point of care record, very different from the past where very few doctors had a complete integrated view of patient care. Since these systems may be part of different EHR systems, Health Information Exchanges (HIEs) are being developed, funded by the federal government, to convert data between multiple EHR vendors so systems and databases can exchange data (Figure 3.5).

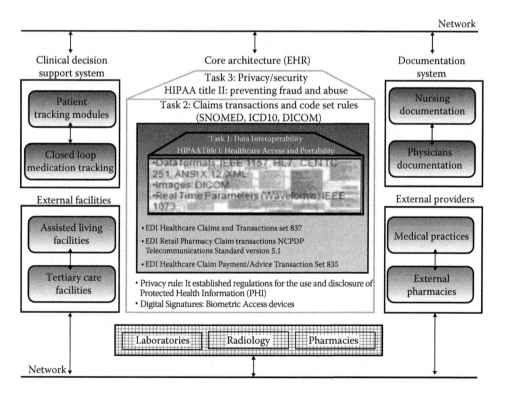

FIGURE 3.5   Electronic health record architecture.

3.3.2.2 EHR System Specifications

EHRs are an integrated system of information sources that tie together patient information as they travel through the healthcare system. Diagnostic testing, medical specialists, medications, in- and outpatient services that span a lifetime are aggregated. The challenge is to present and visualize these data as a continuum rather than discrete events. A graph that tracks similar vital signs, for example, blood pressure, cholesterol, and glucose, over the years overlaid with medications can simplify diagnoses. An integrated EHR specification linking diverse data resources is critical to provide an integrated medical record.

In 2014, the ONC for Health Information Technology (http://www.healthit.gov/newsroom/about-onc) released the "ONC Fact Sheet: 2014 Edition Standards & Certification Criteria (S&CC) Final Rule" for standards for implementing EHRs. It is in conjunction with the Center for Medicare and Medicaid Services (CMS) incentive programs. The ONC-stated goals for this specification was to "promote patient safety and patient engagement; enhance EHR technology's interoperability, electronic HIE capacity, public health reporting, and security; enable clinical quality measure data capture, calculation, and electronic submission to CMS or States; and introduce greater transparency and efficiency to the certification process" (https://www.federalregister.gov/articles/2012/09/04/2012–20982/health-information-technology-standards-implementation-specifications-and-certification-criteria-for).

This 2014 ONC specification provides enhanced privacy–security, interoperability, and data interoperability between systems (Table 3.2).

EHR Systems (EHR-S) Functional Model Release 2 (2014) "outlines important features and functions that should be contained in an EHR system. Through the creation of functional profiles, this model provides a standard description and common understanding of functions for healthcare settings. To date,

TABLE 3.2 Office of the National Coordinator for Health Information Technology Electronic Health Record Standards Final Rule 2014

Privacy and Security	Adopted a certification criterion that focuses on the encryption of health information if it is stored on end-user devices.
	Adopted a new certification criterion that would require EHR technology to be able to support corrections and amendments to a patient record.
	A new certification criterion that enables secure messaging between a provider and a patient.
	Adopted a new certification criterion that permits a patient to securely view, download, and electronically transmit his or her health information, including the ability to track the use of these patient capabilities.
Interoperability	In many instances, certification criteria reference single vocabulary and context exchange standards for recording and representing clinical health information for use during electronic health information exchange.
	Adopted transport standards for the exchange of transitions of care/referral summaries as well as the transmission of patient summaries as part of the view, download, and transmit to a third-party certification criterion.
	The "transitions of care" certification criterion focused on receipt was revised to include the display of previously adopted summary care record standards, Continuity of Care Document/C32 and Continuity of Care Record, providing a form of backward compatibility.
	The test procedure for the transitions of care/referral certification criteria is expected to ascertain electronic health record (EHR) technology's ability to engage in standard-based exchange with any other EHR technology that has also implemented the adopted transport standards.
Data Portability	Adopted a new certification criterion that will enable providers to create a set of "patient summaries." In the event provider switches EHR technology, this capability will help prevent the need to manually reenter basic patient information into the new EHR.
Safety and Usability	Adopted two new certification criteria related to patient safety—one that focuses on the application of user-centered design to medication-related certification criteria and another that focuses on the quality management system used during the EHR technology design.

Source: ONC Specification, http://www.healthit.gov/sites/default/files/pdf/ONC_FS_EHR_Stage_2_Final_082312.pdf.

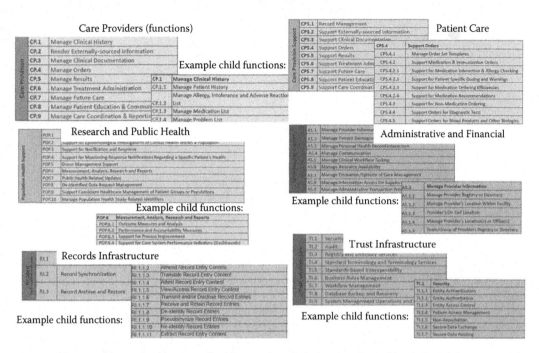

FIGURE 3.6 Health Level 7 electronic health record system Functional Model standards. (http://www.hl7. org/documentcenter/public_temp_1A89AEE6–1C23-BA17–0CBBF529101474E6/calendarofevents/himss/2012/ Electronic%20Health%20Record%20System%20Functional%20Model%20R2.pdf.)

HL7 has developed or is developing profiles for areas such as child health, emergency care, long-term care, behavioral health and vital statistic reporting" (HL7.org definition).

A number of standards organizations, HL7, the ISO, and Healthcare Information Management Systems Society (HIMSS), in 2012 issued the "HL7 EHR System Functional Model and Standard (ISO/ HL7 10781), Release 2" specifications for EHR-S (Figure 3.6). Its goal was to create a standard framework for EHR design (http://www.hl7.org/documentcenter/public_temp_1A89AEE6–1C23-BA17– 0CBBF529101474E6/calendarofevents/himss/2012/Electronic%20 Health%20Record%20System%20 Functional%20Model%20R2.pdf.).

HL7's primary focus are standards for communication of medical data between systems but they also provide modeling standards such as EHR-S and a decision support framework Arden. (See Chapter 4 on interoperability.) *Definition*: HL7 refers to a set of international standards for transfer of clinical and administrative data between hospital information systems (www.HL7.org).

3.3.3 EHR Adoption Statistics

The growth rate of EHRs, as reported by the CDC in January 2014, was 78% of office physicians that had incorporated some level of basic EHR systems (CDC data; Figure 3.7). That is dramatic growth from 2010 when the number stood at 51%. The major cause of this acceleration in implementation was the passage of the ARRA's (HITECH Act) in 2009 that allocated $19.7 billion to subsidize EHR costs and new added mandates that enacted penalties for Medicare and Medicaid reimbursement beginning in 2015 if bills and treatment records were not electronically submitted (http://www.himss.org/News/NewsDetail. aspx?ItemNumber=27596).

As of January 2015, there were approximately 600 EHR vendors. Larger vendors, in the hospital arena, accounted for 90% of the market. The top three, Epic, Meditech, and Computer Programs and Systems' Inpatient (CPSI), hold just over 50% of the market. In the smaller market, physicians, and small practices, Epic is also the leader, but the rest of the market is more fragmented (Figure 3.8).

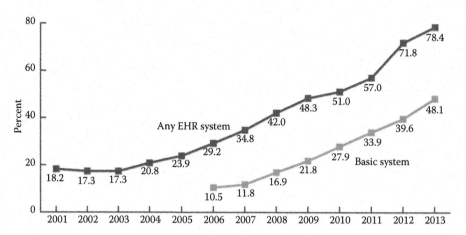

FIGURE 3.7 Electronic health record implementation statistics as of January 2014 source CDC. *Note*: EHR is electronic health record. "Any EHR system" is a medical or health record system that is either all or partially electronic (excluding systems solely for billing). Data for 2001–2007 are from in-person National Ambulatory Medical Care Survey (NAMCS) interviews. Data for 2008–2010 are from combined files (in-person NAMCS and mail survey). Estimates for 2011–2013 data are based on the mail survey only. Estimates for a basic system prior to 2006 could not be computed because some items were not collected in the survey. Data include nonfederal, office-based physicians and exclude radiologists, anesthesiologists, and pathologists. (From CDC/NCHS, National Ambulatory Medical Care Survey and National Ambulatory Medical Care Survey, Electronic Health Records Survey. https://www.google.com/url?sa=i&rct=j&q=&e src=s&source=images&cd=&cad=rja&uact=8&docid=-Wg5J-nGEhQ6nM&tbnid=ZL5cFGMGhYbfKM:&ved=0CA UQjRw&url=http%3A%2F%2Fwww.cdc.gov%2Fnchs%2Fdata%2Fdatabriefs%2Fdb143.htm&ei=RwaeU9iYNq7jsATU yYDYCw&bvm=bv.68911936,d.cWc&psig=AFQjCNErUDWAq0Ky5ZuQKfNXsFQCleaoeg&ust=1402951600266245.)

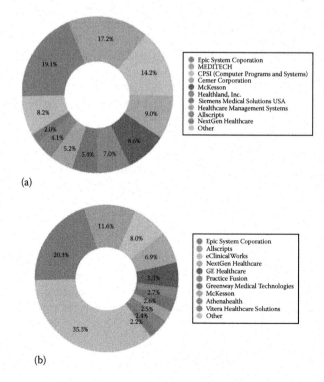

FIGURE 3.8 Electronic medical record. (a) Hospitals and (b) smaller practices. (Adoption by Vendorhttp://www. policymed.com/2014/05/2014-electronic-health-records-market-share.html.)

3.4 Data

The challenge is to efficiently populate EHRs and extract summary information tailored to different medical environments. The optimum goal is to minimize manual data input and to maximize automatic data feeds so practitioners can focus on patient care. Automated medical monitors, wireless medical devices, and data feeds from various sources such as labs, pharmacies, medical scans, and integrated medicated records through HIEs, will continue to increase over time. Phase I EHR mandate was to convert all medical data to an e-health format, Phase II is an ubiquitous exchange of data from multiple EHRs and integrated medical monitoring equipment and wireless sources, internal and implanted, this effort in underway. Phase III goal is to develop better user interfaces (see Appendix on APPs development for EHRs) tailored for each medical environment; this effort has barely begun.

Medical units previously utilized manual flow sheets (Figure 3.9), which have all the information nurses needed to capture in a concise format that was easy to enter and visually evaluate. The first generation EHRs requires nurses to navigate from screen to screen and sit in front of a computer console, which is not very efficient and reduces patient contact time. The next phases of EHR development will involve customizing apps on touch screen tablets to recreate these flow sheets with the added benefits that EHRs provide such as integrating data from labs and scans, displaying graphs and summaries over longer periods of time, sharing data instantly with multiple healthcare providers, and soon integrating clinical support systems that can provide diagnosis or at least prompt users of possible errors or concerns.

3.4.1 EHR Data Entry

The challenge of entering medical data into an online system is developing intuitive user interfaces to provide quick, concise, accurate, and intuitive methods of data entry that will allow the caregiver to focus on patient care and reduce medication and documentation errors. EHRs, medical errors accounted for more deaths, approximately 100,000/year, than car accidents in 2001 (http://www.medicalnewstoday.com/releases/11856.php). When possible, automated transfer of lab and vital signs should be integrated into data entry. The following is an actual data entry challenge in a hospital. A nurse from a major medical center explained that during a routine patient care interaction, EHRs had just been introduced 4 months earlier into their hospital, the process of entering the data on a pint of blood was as follows. Even though bar code scanners are available at some hospitals, bar codes are available on most blood products, a bar code scanner link between the EHR was not available at this particular

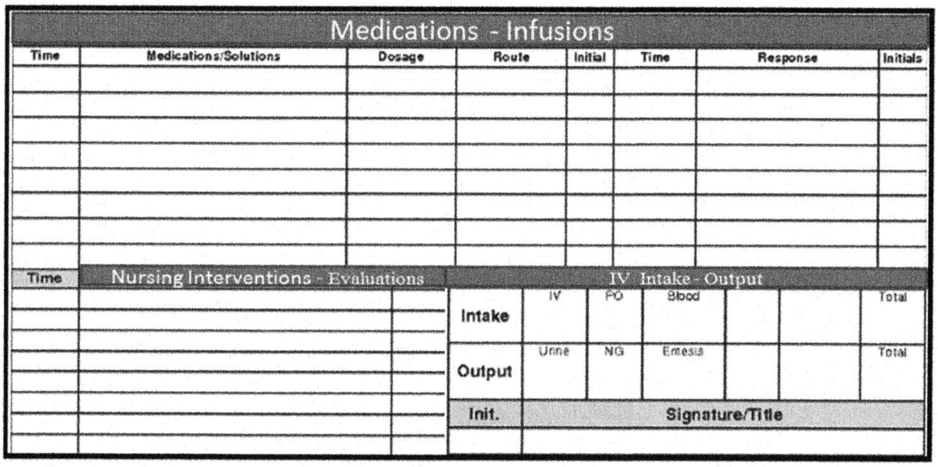

FIGURE 3.9 Manual flow sheets used in hospitals prior to electronic health records.

hospital. Two nurses are typically required for this process, one to read the label and the other to check the patient ID and both sign and verify that the correct blood was administered. When this was manual, a paper form was filled out and sometimes an extra barcode sticker was attached and both nurses signed to ensure accuracy. In this case, this all had to be done while entering the data into an EHR computer console rolled to the bed. The codes were multiple 20 digit codes, where there is, of course, opportunities for errors. Rather than take a couple of minutes, it was exacerbated by the fact that the patient started having pain issues and a third nurse came in to enter the data to speed up the process. It took three times as long as the manual process. The purpose of this true story was that EHR data entry processes have to be constantly reevaluated and nurses involved in the feedback process to change procedures that don't work efficiently. Sometimes, EHRs can be worse in terms of nursing processes, and installing an EHR without constant process improvement can be detrimental to patient care, patient satisfaction, and nursing morale.

Entering data in EHRs can be from user input or from external sources. Human-Centered input data can be free-form, codes, drop-down lists, voice input, transcription, bar code scanners, or as yet-to-be-designed input devices. Automatic form entry can be from direct transmission from medical devices, bar code scanners, pulled from databases, or from external record feeds through remote EHRs filtered through HIEs.

When possible, the free-form data entry should be limited since generating summaries, graphs, and reporting data to external reporting agencies becomes more difficult. If you enter "a patient is experiencing right lower quadrant pain" and explain the symptoms, as opposed to a drop-down list for pain, the symptoms can be selected from the ICD10 where as you type in a field, it autocompletes the terms: The ICD10 code for right lower quadrant pain is R10.31. Many EHR systems are including this autocomplete option. SNOMED is also used to define medical terms, diseases, microorganisms, etc.

SNOMED CT, provides a granular, detailed, level description of conditions and the subsequent associated symptoms versus using ICD10. The term "multiple granularities" (mg) refer to the level of detail; SNOMED has 20 levels versus ICD10 4. In contextual representations, SNOMED CT is stronger, provides more contextual details, than ICD10.

Figures 3.10a and 3.10b represent some of the coding schemes and a relationship—hierarchy diagram from SNOMED CT shows levels of description of a disease.

Some new EHR systems allow you to define relationships and the complexity of a particular medical condition beyond just a simple code. After you enter the initial symptom-associated granularities such as right lower quadrant pain and other descriptive options, following the preceding text, entity–relationship diagram that illustrates increasing levels of detail available will appear with the associated codes. These autofill suggestions can be very sophisticated, are further described in Level II CDSS, and can guide you through terminologies and even check recommended medications and treatment.

Other coding schemes for data entry are Logical Observation Identifiers Names and Codes (LOINC), which is a database and universal standard for identifying medical laboratory observations. It was developed in 1994 and is maintained by the Regenstrief Institute, a U.S. nonprofit medical research organization. LOINC was created in response to the demand for an electronic database for clinical care and management and is publicly available at no cost.

It is endorsed by the American Clinical Laboratory Association and the College of American Pathologists. Since its inception, the database has been expanded to include not just medical and laboratory code names, but also nursing diagnoses, nursing interventions, outcomes classifications, and patient care data set.

3.5 U.S. Initiatives

In 1996, HIPAA and the ARRA in 2009 created the foundation for EHRs development in the United States. ARRA included financial incentives, $19.7 billion, to modernize the U.S. medical infrastructure, a component of ARRA was the HITECH Act. One feature of HITECH was to define the guidelines to determine the effectiveness of the EHR implementation and reimbursement documentation. This was referred to as meaningful use, which was categorized by how EHRs and their implementation in a particular setting contribute to the quality, safety, efficiency of patients, and reduce health disparities.

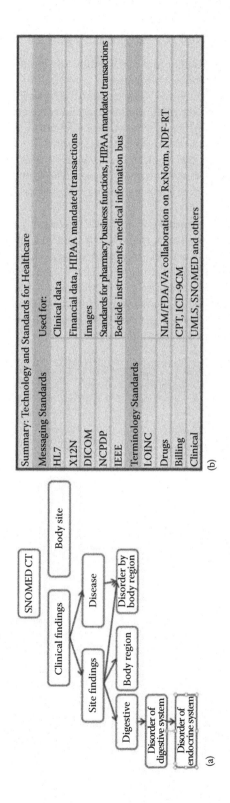

The following table appears within the figure:

Summary: Technology and Standards for Healthcare

Messaging Standards	Used for:
HL7	Clinical data
X12N	Financial data, HIPAA mandated transactions
DICOM	Images
NCPDP	Standards for pharmacy business functions, HIPAA mandated transactions
IEEE	Bedside instruments, medical infomation bus
Terminology Standards	
LOINC	
Drugs	NLM/FDA/VA collaboration on RxNorm, NDF-RT
Billing	CPT, ICD-9CM
Clinical	UMLS, SNOMED and others

(b)

(a)

FIGURE 3.10 (a, b) Systematized Nomenclature of Medicine Clinical Terms entity–relationship diagram and various coding schemes from HHS.gov.

3.5.1 HIPAA

The HIPAA of 1966 was comprised of two main components (Figure 3.11).

1. Title I: Healthcare access, portability, and renewability. This protected individuals from losing their health insurance when they lose their jobs.
2. Title II: Preventing healthcare fraud and abuse, administrative simplification, and medical liability reform. It also included privacy rules, transactions and code sets rules, security rule, unique identifiers rule, and an enforcement rule. It provided guidelines for privacy and security and provides national standards for medical records and transactions.
   a. The HIPAA Title II privacy rule regulates the disclosure and use PHI. It refers to any portion of the EHR and medical payments. Any violations can be reported to HHS, but it has a poor enforcement record. In 2013, the law was amended to restrict disclosure to 50 years after death called the omnibus rule.
      i. Specifications for anonymizers, i.e. methods to remove patient identifiers from EHRs (Social Security number, names, etc.) to ensure patient confidentiality. Anonymizers are used when large medical data sets are shared to track outbreaks.
   b. The administrative simplification portion of Title II specifies documentation standards such as ICD and ICD10 for reimbursement of Medicare and Medicaid services. ICD10 is a comprehensive list developed by the World Health Organization of diseases, symptoms, etc. Examples of some of the categories are A00–B99 infectious and parasitic diseases, F00–F99 mental and behavioral disorders, and I00–I99 diseases of the circulatory system.

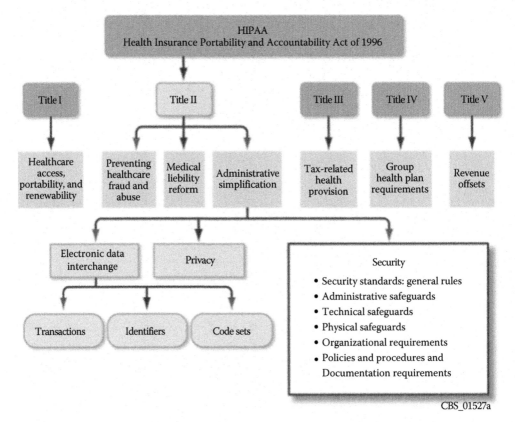

FIGURE 3.11 HIPAA standards created by the U.S. Government in 1996. (From HHS, http://www.hhs.gov/ocr/privacy/hipaa/administrative/securityrule/nist80066.pdf.)

3.5.2 American Recovery and Reinvestment Act

The ARRA passed by Congress in 2009 contained $782 billion to jumpstart the economy. The ARRA provided $31 billion for healthcare initiatives of which $19.7 billion were earmarked to facilitate the adoption of EMRs by the healthcare community. It includes the HITECH Act, which incorporated meaningful use specifications that became guidelines for reimbursement and categorization of the effectiveness of integration of EHRs into their processes (http://www.gpo.gov/fdsys/pkg/BILLS-111hr1enr/pdf/BILLS-111hr1enr.pdf).

3.5.3 Meaningful Use

The term "meaningful use" was defined by the CMS as a series of standards and incentive programs used as criteria for physician reimbursement for physicians that were to be funded between $44,000–$64,000 and for hospitals $3,000,000–$5,000,000 to offset the costs of implementing EHRs. "The goal of meaningful use was to promote the spread of EHRs to improve healthcare in the United States" (www.healthit.gov).

CMS specified three general benefits of implementing EHRs: (1) Complete and accurate information and history of their patients. Paper patient records were dispersed among many providers, and tests were often duplicated unnecessarily. (2) Better access to information. (3) Patient empowerment. Patients are allowed access to all their medical records and can be part of the decision-making process. Personal data records allow individuals to maintain their own person copy of their medical information.

The ONC for Health Information Technology part of the U.S. Department of HHS created a nonprofit Certification Commission for Healthcare Information Technology (http://www.cchit.org/) to certify that organizations met meaningful standards (Table 3.3).

Meaningful use has two sets of standards, one for physicians another for hospitals. Physicians have 24 objectives of which 19 have to be met to qualify for EHR reimbursement of implementation costs. Hospitals have 23 meaningful use objectives, 18 of which have to be satisfied. These are further broken down into core objectives and a second set of 10 subobjectives from which you have to complete 50% (Table 3.2).

3.5.3.1 Meaningful Use Stage 2 Final Rule

An important feature of meaningful use Stage 2 is for data interoperability that will enable the HIEs (see Section 3.6) ability to exchange data between EHRs (http://www.gpo.gov/fdsys/pkg/FR-2012-09-04/pdf/2012-21050.pdf) from different vendors. The meaningful use Stage 2 final rule specifies data sets and structured coded data to be transmitted between systems.

TABLE 3.3 Meaningful Use Timetable by Center for Medicaid and Medicare Services (CMS.gov)

Stage 1: Data Capture of Medical Information and Sharing among Multiple Providers 2011–2012	Stage 2: Advance Clinical Processes 2014	Stage 3: Improved Outcomes 2016
Electronically capturing health information in a standardized format	More rigorous health information exchange (HIE)	Improving quality, safety, and efficiency, leading to improved health outcomes
Using that information to track key clinical conditions	Increased requirements for e-prescribing and incorporating lab results	Decision support for national high-priority conditions
Communicating that information for care coordination processes	Electronic transmission of patient care summaries across multiple settings	Patient access to self-management tools
Initiating the reporting of clinical quality measures and public health information	More patient-controlled data	Access to comprehensive patient data through patient-centered HIE
Using information to engage patients and their families		Improving population health

Some specific Stage 2 specifications are (see Chapter 4)

1. Procedures (SNOMED CT)
2. Laboratory test results (LOINC)
3. Medications and allergies (RxNorm) (normalized names for clinical drugs)
4. Encounter diagnosis (SNOMED CT or ICD10-Clinical Modification)
5. Immunizations (CVX) (CDC vaccine codes) (Table 3.4)
6. Vital signs including height, weight, blood pressure, and smoking status (SNOMED CT)
7. Patient name and demographic information: preferred language (ISO 639–2 alpha-3), sex, race/ethnicity (OMB Ethnicity), and date of birth
8. Functional status including activities of daily living, cognitive, and disability status
9. Care plan field including goals and instructions
10. Discharge instructions (for hospitals)

Sample of CDC vaccine codes (CVX): http://www2a.cdc.gov/vaccines/iis/iisstandards/vaccines.asp?rpt=vg.

Table 3.5 lists the meaningful use objectives for laid out in the ARRA of 2009 that will determine the level of reimbursement for EHR implementation.

3.5.4 E-Prescribing

Electronic prescribing (e-prescribing) refers to the electronic submission of prescriptions from a physician directly to a pharmacy. The goal was to reduce medication errors created by hand-writing ambiguities and improve patient care by integrating online error checking that evaluates drug interaction and allergies. It also enhances oversight by funding agencies to evaluate overprescribing of controlled substances and track treatment protocols.

E-prescribing was mandated in the Medicare Modernization Act (MMA) of 2003. In 2005, MMA published standards under the Medicare Prescription Drug Benefit called Medicare part D. Medicare

TABLE 3.4   CVX Vaccine Reference Tables

Short Description	CVX Code	Vaccine Status	Vaccine Group Name	Uncertain Formulation CVX
Adenovirus types 4 and 7	143	Active	ADENO	82
Adenovirus, type 4	54	Inactive	ADENO	82
Adenovirus, type 7	55	Inactive	ADENO	82
Adenovirus, unspecified formulation	82	Inactive	ADENO	82
Anthrax	24	Active	ANTHRAX	
BCG	19	Active	BCG	
Botulinum antitoxin	27	Active		
Cholera	26	Inactive	Cholera	26
CMVIG	29	Active	IG	14
Dengue fever	56	Never active		
Diphtheria antitoxin	12	Active		
DT (pediatric)	28	Active	DTAP	107
DTaP	20	Active	DTAP	107
DTaP, 5 pertussis antigens	106	Active	DTAP	107
DTaP, unspecified formulation	107	Inactive	DTAP	107
DTaP, IPV, Hib, HepB	146	Pending	DTAP	107

TABLE 3.5 Meaningful Use, 24 Objectives, of which 19 Have to Be Satisfied, to Receive Meaningful Use Funding

Meaningful Use Objectives (to Qualify for Incentive Reimbursement Program from the American Recovery and Reinvestment Act)	
14 Core Objectives for Physicians (All Required)	10 Menu Options (Comply with at Least 5)
Use computerized physician order entry for physicians.	Implement drug formulary checks.
Implement drug–drug and drug–allergy interaction checks.	Incorporate clinical lab-test results into electronic health record (EHR) as structured data.
Maintain an up-to-date problem list of current active diagnoses.	Generate list of patients by specific conditions to use for quality improvement, reduction of disparities, research, and outreach.
Keep an active medication list.	Send patient reminders per patient preference for preventive follow-up care.
Maintain an active medication allergy list.	Provide patients with timely electronic access to their health information (including lab results, problem list, medication lists, and allergies) within 4 business days of the information being available.
Record specified demographics on patients.	Use certified EHR technology to identify patient specific education resources and provide those resources to the patient if possible.
Record and chart changes in specific vital signs.	The physician who receives a patient from another setting of care or provider or believes an encounter is relevant should perform medication reconciliation.
Document whether patients age 13 and older are smokers.	The physicians who transition their patients to another setting of care or refer their patients should provide a summary of care record for each transition.
Report clinical quality measures.	Capability to submit electronic data to immunization registries or immunization information systems and applicable law and practice.
Implement one clinical decision support rule related to a high-priority hospital condition.	Capability to submit electronic syndrome surveillance data to public health agencies and actual submission according to applicable law and practice.
Offer patients an electronic copy of their health information upon request.	
Give patients an electronic copy of their discharge instructions upon request.	
Have the capability to exchange key clinical information.	
Protect electronic health Information.	

part D (http://www.medicare.gov/part-d/) is a program to subsidize prescription drugs under the Medicare program enacted in 2006. The initial plan covered the first $2970 cost of prescriptions. Then, the *donut hole* kicked in where coverage resumed after exceeding $4750. So, for this $2000 gap, patients received no coverage. The affordable healthcare plan, ObamaCare, eliminated this *donut hole* gap in prescription drug coverage.

The CMS (www.cms.gov) mandated that all physicians convert to e-prescribing by January 1, 2013, and register before that date with CMS. There are reimbursement penalties increasing every year initially 1% then 2% year then finally 3%. There are hardship exemptions that can be applied for and which can be found at http://www.ama-assn.org/resources/doc/hit/avoid-erx-penalty-tip.pdf (Figure 3.12).

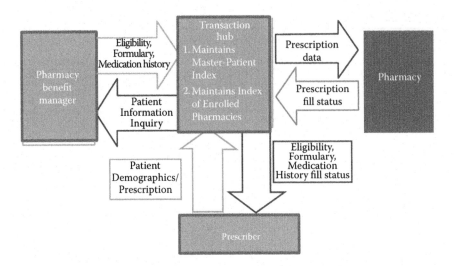

FIGURE 3.12   E-prescribing defined by the Center for Medicare and Medicaid Services.

3.6 Health Information Exchanges

The term "health information exchange" (HIE) refers to the sharing of information among multiple providers and organizations that have different EHR systems (Figure 3.13). There are 56 funded HIEs, link to all state and territory HIEs (http://statehieresources.org/state-plans/). In 2011, $548 million from the ARRA created the State Health Information Exchange Cooperative Agreement Program to promote and fund HIEs across the U.S. healthcare system. The grants ranged from $600 thousand to American Samoa to $28 Million to Texas HHS. Its goal was to create interoperability of all medical records. The goal of HIEs is to provide transparency among EHR providers, where a medical record is created in a particular hospital/physician's office using an EHR such as Cerner, and that medical data are accessible from another hospital utilizing another EHR, for example, EPIC. All EHR/medical records are required by HIPAA to be designed around data storage standards such as HL7, DICOM, SNOMED, and ICD9–10. Unfortunately, there is enough variation in internal data structures that require an HIE to ensure smooth communication between systems built by different vendors.

An added benefit was the ability to gather patient demographics data and potential outbreaks and report them to the CDC. The goal of the CDC is to protect public health and safety. One of the key meaningful use objectives is to "submit electronic syndrome surveillance data to public health agencies."

The ONC for Health Information Technology has set guidelines to (1) standardize the structure of the data with formats such as HL7, www.hl7.org; (2) standard medical vocabularies such as SNOMED and ICD10, www.cdc.gov/nchc/icd/icd10.htm; (3) standard application programming interface (API); and (4) security and encryption as outlined by the National Institute of Standards and Technology (NIST) security architecture (www.nist.gov/healthcare/security/hiesecurity.cfm). The Nationwide Health and Information Network (NHIN) from the ONC details those standards in the document NIST Interagency Report 7497 "Security Architecture Design Process for Health Information Exchanges" by Kenneth Lin and Daniel Steinberg, September 2010 (http://csrc.nist.gov/publications/nistir/ir7497/nistir-7497.pdf).

3.6.1 Three Types of Health Information Exchange

1. Directed exchange—ability to send and receive secure information electronically between care providers to support coordinated care
   a. Directed, often called point-to-point, uses a secure messaging protocol called Direct Project services offered by the ONC's state HIE program (http://www.healthit.gov/providers-professionals/state-health-information-exchange), one of the meaningful use

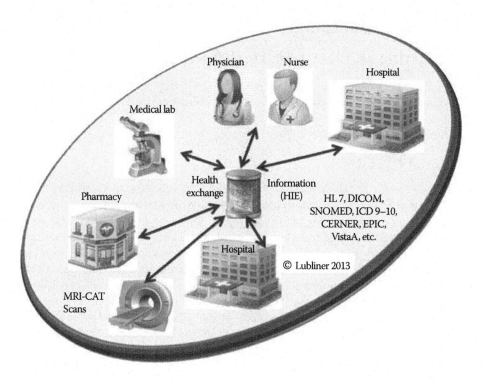

FIGURE 3.13 Health information exchange.

certification requirements. It will allow medical providers to share patient records utilizing a process as simple as e-mail but securely encoded.

2. Query-based exchange—ability for providers to find, search, and/or request information on a patient from other providers, often used for unplanned care (http://www.healthit.gov/sites/default/files/query_based_exchange_final.pdf)

   a. Key challenge is converting medical records between data formats allowing queries.

   b. Defined by five rights: right information, right person, right format, right channel, and right time.

3. Consumer-mediated exchange—ability for patients to aggregate, get personal copies, and control the use of their health information among providers.

   a. Allows patients to correct wrong or missing information and correct billing errors.

   b. Allows them to track their own health information, which can be stored in personal data records.

A regional health information organization brings together medical organizations in a particular region, which includes public health organization and certified laboratories; it is often used to assist the development of HIEs. The goals are similar to HIEs; it is a group of companies, hospitals, or organizations that have developed a system to provide a seamless exchange of health information.

NHIN also called an eHealth Exchange developed by the U.S. ONC for Health Information Technology is a series of specifications to securely exchange health data. The goal of the ONC is to tie together HIEs to create a nationwide network. Some of the organizations that are currently part of the NHIN are (1) Social Security Administration, (2) VA, (3) CDC, (4) CMS, and (5) Department of Defense.

http://www.healthit.gov/sites/default/files/pdf/fact-sheets/nationwide-health-information-network-exchange.pdf.

Level II: EHR Applications

3.7 Navigating an Electronic Health Record

This section illustrates components of typical examples EHRs and the common sections/tabs that are typically available. They include a central navigation console, patient lists, orders, lab/medications, and a discharge screen that usually acts as a checklist by multiple care providers to ensure all medications and signatures have been completed.

3.7.1 Central Console

All EHRs have a central navigation console (Figure 3.14). It provides you with access to a subset of the EHR database i.e., display a patient's medications in a Medication Administration Record (MAR). A list of your patients appears when you log on that are automatically categorized into folders based on their needs. If a new medication request is made, i.e., a patient has requested additional pain medication, the nurse will check a priority field, and those requests, when you log on, will be placed in your urgent/priority folder. If a patient is scheduled for discharge and requires your signature, electronic, that request also will be filtered into a separate folder. The potential for efficiency is impressive and potentially transformational in improving healthcare and reducing errors, but the process of customizing your inbox environment takes time and requires a good support staff. That support component is often underfunded in most healthcare systems. Three to six months after an EHR system is implemented is the time to reevaluate the processes and effectiveness of its daily use. Morale can also be enhanced significantly if it is treated as an evolutionary process.

3.7.2 Patient List

Starting from a central navigation screen, you begin by selecting a patient list that has been assigned to one of the medical providers, physician, nurse, etc. (Figure 3.15). Next, select a specific patient, and his or her history, medication, diagnosis, and treatment can be reviewed.

3.7.3 Demographics

1. Name, age, allergies, date of birth, sex, attending, discharge date.
2. Drill down: Many of these items can be selected for further details.
   a. Click on, for example, allergies. A detailed list appears and then right click on a specific allergy to add more information. They are usually listed from most severe at top.

3.7.4 Navigator

1. Navigator bar: Select features of the patient records.
2. Results: Usually the first option is a general summary of patient information.
3. Diagnosis: Will usually show diagnosis and problems for the patient.
4. Notes: Used to document patient encounters. There is usually an option to included other scanned forms into this patient record.
5. Forms: Will be any charted information (Figure 3.16).

3.7.5 Medication Administration Record

Orders: Medication Administration Record (MAR) place, view, modify, cancel, or work with any type of orders (Figure 3.17 a and b)

1. Drug references: Usually used by pharmacist and clinicians
2. ICU summary: Available for patient treatment just in the ICU

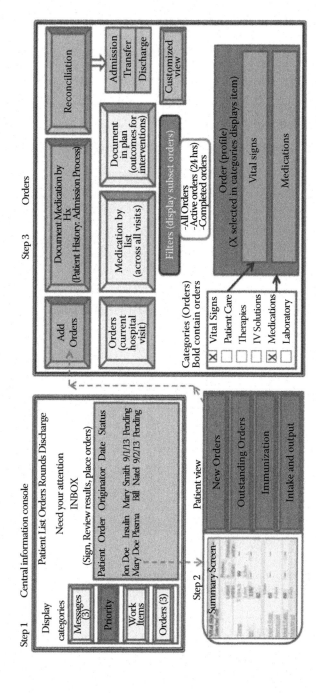

FIGURE 3.14 Navigation in an electronic health record, central console inbox, patient view, and medication orders.

Patient List (active) When a Nurse/Doctor/Specialist logs on the patients assigned to them are Displayed

Name	Room	Bed	Age (years)	Sex	MRN	Length of Stay	Admitting Phy	Note
John Doe	0601	A	80	M	0123456789	10 Days	Arthur	Physician
Jane Doe	0602	A	65	F	1234567890	12 Days	Arthur	Physician
John Smith	0603	B	42	M	2345678901	05 Days	Ross	Physician
Jane Smith	0604	A	81	F	3456789012	02 Days	Arthur	Physician
John Rand	0605	B	77	M	4567890123	12 Days	Kiel	Physician
Jane Rand	0606	A	48	F	5678901234	10 Days	Arthur	Physician
Bill Doe	0607	B	73	M	6789012345	05 Days	Ross	Physician
Alice Doe	0608	A	60	F	7890123456	15 Days	Arthur	Physician
Bill Rand	0609	B	70	M	8901234567	03 Days	Patel	Physician

FIGURE 3.15   Patient list associated with a healthcare provider.

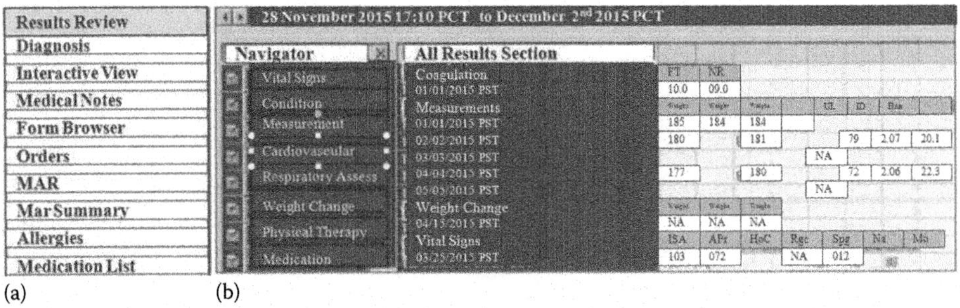

(a)   (b)

FIGURE 3.16   **(See color insert.)** (a, b) Navigator on left; patient status view on right.

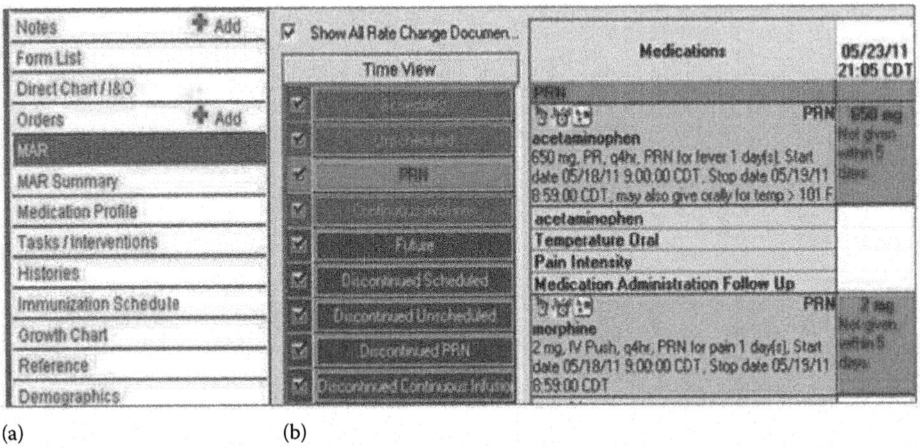

(a)   (b)

FIGURE 3.17   **(See color insert.)** (a, b) Medication Administration Record (MAR) delivery timetable, MAR drug summary table. (From http://www.pearsonhighered.com/realehprep/learn-about/what-is.html.)

3.7.6 Orders

Inpatient summary: screen for therapeutic results: Vitals after medications are administered (Figure 3.18).

3.7.7 Discharge Orders

Discharge: Allows you to manage the process of documenting and planning the patient discharge process (Figure 3.19). There are usually workflow tabs to select if each of the required steps have been completed, and once all steps are done, the physician electronically signs the discharge.

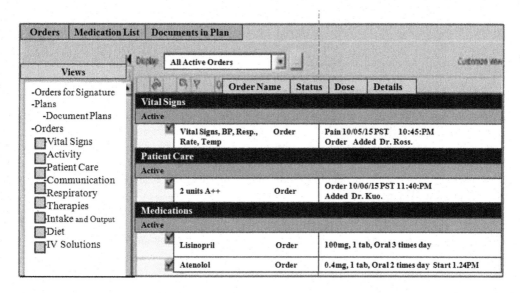

FIGURE 3.18 Patient orders from physicians are summarized.

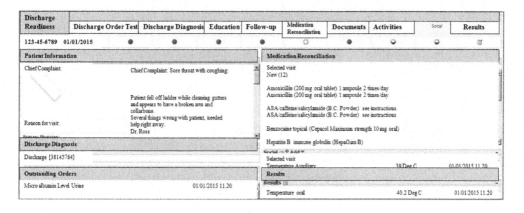

FIGURE 3.19 Patient discharge checklist. (From https://store.cerner.com/.)

Level III: Advanced Topics: Decision Support Systems, Expert Systems

3.8 Clinical Decision Support System

A CDSS is a software that assists healthcare professionals in making diagnosis, treatment decisions, and workflow decisions. A number of synonyms have been used for CDSS such as knowledge management, artificial intelligence (AI)-neural networks, inference engines, and diagnosis support system. The adoption of CDSS is sketchy in clinical diagnoses since there is concern about incorrect or medical recommendations based on incomplete information. Does the knowledge base take into account all the factors, such as patient history, genetics, symptoms, and even geographical data, which might contribute to root causes of illness? As EHRs proliferate and a larger more inclusive database evolves, research will evaluate symptoms and treatments and produce reliable probabilities to aid healthcare workers. It's only a matter of time till they become more widely accepted based on larger studies of patient outcomes.

Meaningful use guidelines mandate that at least one clinical decision support system component, diagnostic test ordering, be integrated in their EHR system. Prescription and billing systems also are required to submit electronically their reimbursement requests and many systems currently include CDSS to ensure all components required for Medicare and Medicaid are completed before submission.

3.8.1 HL7 Decision Support Services

HL7 "is a not-for-profit, ANSI-accredited standards developing organization dedicated to providing a comprehensive framework and related standards for the exchange, integration, sharing, and retrieval of electronic health information that supports clinical practice and the management, delivery and evaluation of health services" (www.hl7.org). A Decision Support Service inputs patient data and provides specific assessment and recommendations on diagnosis and treatment to aid medical personnel based on an evolving knowledge base.

3.8.1.1 Arden Syntax for Medical Logic Modules

The Arden syntax for medical logic systems, from HL7, encodes procedural medical knowledge. Its function is to help clinicians make better decisions based on prior patient treatment knowledge. The health databases, in HL7, consist of medical logic modules (MLMs), each containing knowledge for a single decision (Figure 3.20).

Features the MLM provides (wiki.hl7.org/images/a/aa/Arden_Syntax_2.10_draft_2014–03–18.docx) are as follows:

1. MLM, contains sufficient knowledge to make a single decision.
2. Contraindication alerts.
3. Management suggestions.
4. Data interpretations.
5. Diagnosis scores.

3.8.1.2 Fuzzy Data Sets

Fuzzy sets allow you to define data sets or classes with unsharp boundaries to calculate degrees of truth or if they fall if values fall in borderline range. Examples such as small or large, cold or warm, normal and elevated, enlarged and symmetric, diabetic and hypoxic are inherently a set, or class, with unsharp boundaries. An example with a sharp/crisp data set with clear boundaries between concepts are normal and pathological.

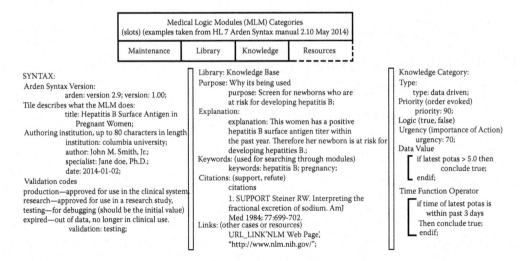

FIGURE 3.20 Medical logic modules coding syntax.

Fuzzy number

The data type fuzzy number is dedicated to fuzzy sets over the reals. A fuzzy number partitions the reals into a finite number of (possibly unbounded) intervals, on each of which the fuzzy set is linear and continuous.

Formally, a fuzzy set $\mathbf{u: R} \rightarrow \mathbf{[0, 1]}$ can be stored into a variable of the type fuzzy number, if the following condition is met: There are $\mathbf{a_1 < a_2 < \ldots < a_k}$ with $\mathbf{k >= 1}$, such that $\mathbf{u}$ is linear on each open interval $(\mathbf{a_1; a_2}), \ldots, (\mathbf{a_{k-1}; a_k})$, $\mathbf{u}$ is constant on $(-\infty; \mathbf{a_1})$ and $(\mathbf{a_k}; +\infty)$, and for each $\mathbf{x}$ in $\mathbf{R}$, $\mathbf{u(x)}$ coincides either with the left limit or the right limit of $\mathbf{u}$ at $\mathbf{x}$. If $\mathbf{u}$ is continuous, we then define

Fuzzy set u = fuzzy set (a_1, t_1), $(a_2, t_2), \ldots, (a_k, t_k)$,

where $\mathbf{t_i} = \mathbf{u(a_i)}$ for $\mathbf{i = 1}, \ldots, \mathbf{k}$ and $\mathbf{u(x)}$ is called the characteristic function of the fuzzy set.

In MLMs discontinuity points, data are undefined or unknown in those regions, which means that approaching 2 from the left side, the membership value is 0, while approaching 2 from the right side, the membership value is 1. An example is

Two to three = **fuzzy set** (2, truth value 0), (2, truth value 1), (2, truth value 1), (3, truth value 1), (3, truth value 0)

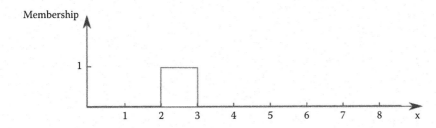

Example of MLM-coded logic

logic:

```
        if last_pulse_rate is greater than 60 and
            low_dose_beta_use then
            if angina_frequency is greater than 4 then
                let msg be
                        "Increased dose of beta blockers may be " ||
                        "needed to control angina.";
                conclude true;
        else
            if premature_beat_frequency is greater than 5 then
                let msg be
                        "Increased dose of beta blockers may " ||
                        "be needed to control PVC's.";
                conclude true;
            endif;
        endif;
    endif;
    conclude false;
    ;;
action:
    write msg;;
end:
```

3.8.2 Pharmacy Decision Support Systems

In the pharmacy, CDSSs are in widespread use and are usually integrated with e-prescription systems. They check drug interactions, contraindications, allergies, and dosage levels and report possible side effects and are linked in e-prescribing systems. They also cross-check guidelines and recommendations. Federal regulations for prescribing medications and controlled substances can be found under the U.S. Food and Drug Administration under Title 21, which is revised every year (http://www.fda.gov/Drugs/default.htm). Title 21 is a more inclusive series of guidelines that includes, besides drugs, medical devices, medical scanners, and cosmetics. These drug indexes can be linked to pharmacy CDSSs, for example, to check for prescribing controlled substances 21 CFR 1306.04. These controlled substance guidelines are broken down into five categories; schedule 1, has a high potential for abuse, down to schedule 5, which has a low abuse potential. All these drugs are automatically reported back to the Drug Enforcement Administration (DEA) and these reports have resulted in investigation for overprescribing. The DEA also has a pharmacist manual that will be linked by the CDSS when certain substances are prescribed for quick reference (Table 3.6).

Research studies on pharmacy CDSSs have confirmed the effectiveness and reduction of medication errors when linked in EHRs. On the U.S. National Library of Medicine website (http://www.ncbi.nlm.nih.gov/pubmed), a large number of studies validate the safety benefits of pharmacy CDSSs. In 2012, a study funded by the U.S. Agency for Healthcare Research and Quality on the effectiveness of medication management information technology by McKibbon K.A. et al. titled "The effectiveness of integrated Health Information Technologies across the phases of medication management: a systematic review of randomized controlled trials http://www.ncbi.nlm.nih.gov/pubmed/21852412." The results indicated an improvement in the process of care of 50% of the institutions studied. Clinical data on medical outcomes were not available. Since the Affordable Care Act will be in common use by 2015, more clinical studies will be available in the near future.

TABLE 3.6 Clinical Decision Support Systems

Clinical Decision Support Systems (CDSS) (Representative List of Vendors)	
Name	Link
Agfa HealthCare (Belgium)	http://www.agfahealthcare.com/he/global/en/internet/main/
Athenahealth, Inc. (United States)	http://www.agfahealthcare.com/he/global/en/internet/main/
Allscripts Healthcare Solutions, Inc.	http://www.allscripts.com/
Carestream Health, Inc. (United States)	http://www.carestream.com/
Cerner Corporation (United States)	http://www.cerner.com/
Epic (United States)	http://www.epic.com/
GE Healthcare (United Kingdom)	http://www.gehealthcare.co.uk/
McKesson Corporation (United States)	http://www.mckesson.com/
NextGen Healthcare Information System, LLC (United States)	https://www.nextgen.com/
Novarad Corporation (United States)	http://www.novarad.net/
Philips Healthcare (Netherlands)	http://www.medical.philips.com/
Siemens Healthcare (Germany)	http://www.healthcare.siemens.com/
Zynx Health (United States)	http://www.zynxhealth.com/
CDSS Primary Software Product	
The Archimedes Model	http://archimedesmodel.com/archimedes-model/
Elsevier Clinical Decision Support	http://www.clinicaldecisionsupport.com/
The Isabel system	http://www.isabelhealthcare.com/home/default
PKC (which stands for problem–knowledge coupling)	http://www.pkc.com/
Micromedex point-of-care clinical decision support suite	http://micromedex.com/
Wolters Kluwer Health	http://www.wolterskluwerhealth.com/pages/welcome.aspx/

3.9 Expert Systems

"Expert Systems are computerized applications that combine computer hardware, software and specialized information to imitate expert human reasoning and advice." [5] The core components of expert systems are a knowledge base composed of rules and facts and an inference engine supplied with data from a user that selects the appropriate rules based on the data and calculates probabilities that the rules apply to a particular situation. An additional component is feedback from clinical data that cross-checks the validity of the rule/diagnosis that then adds to the refinement of the expert system knowledge base (Figure 3.20).

Once a basis framework has been selected, the inference engine asks a series of targeted questions proposed by the expert system to refine matches to the existing knowledge base. A list of probabilities are then generated, i.e., an example of a system used for determining heart arrhythmias states to the medical professional that 62% of arrhythmias are due to hypokalemia, a low potassium level, and 75% due to hypomagnesaemia, low magnesium, that might be making the patient more prone to arrhythmias. The system asks the individual to enter potassium and magnesium results from blood test to validate or refute the hypothesis. This type of feedback mechanism provides more accurate diagnosis where additional data increases the probability of an accurate diagnosis. This is an example of a rule-based expert system (Figure 3.21).

3.9.1 Inference Engine

Inference engines determine which rules match those of the supplied data and match those with the highest probabilities. There are forward-chaining inference (FCI) engines that analyze the facts to some conclusion or disease. These systems are used to predict outcomes, an example of an FCI systems is EMYCIN, written in lisp, was used to identify bacteria-causing infections, which was developed at Stanford University [2]. It provided a 69% success rate, which was higher than practitioners at the time. A backward-chaining inference engine is from hypothesis to the facts used primarily for diagnosis; an example is the knowledge engineering environment.

Other paradigms for medical expert systems are Case-Based Reasoning (CBR), cognitive systems, and crowd-based expert systems. The CBR utilizes a library, an evolving library of cases where matches are made to the current case, rather than utilizing a standard rule-based engine; this is similar to the process of how doctors make a diagnosis. The process involves these three steps; retrieve similar cases,

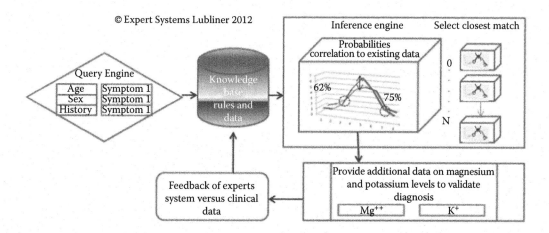

FIGURE 3.21 Expert system architecture.

reuse the case to solve similar problems, revise and modify the case, and finally, retain the new case with updates for the case library (4 Rs).

Cognitive systems [3] are a series of AI paradigms with "the ability to engage in abstract thought that goes beyond immediate perceptions and actions." Originally, comprehensive AI systems attempted to model human consciousness but, due to their lack of success, were modified for a more narrow expertise in specific domains of knowledge. An example is chess programs that are the equal of the best master level chess players. Cognitive systems utilize structured representations and probabilistic models to support problem solving utilizing concepts from psychology, logic, and linguistics.

Crowd sourced, wisdom of the crowds, provides a new method to extract large amounts of relevant data from the web on the assumption that large data sets may be more accurate than limited clinical data from the web. An example is IBM's "Watson" [4] famous for beating experts on the Jeopardy game show, based on a crowd-sourcing paradigm. So far, this approach has yet to be validated in the medical arena. This crowd-based approach has showed some success on social networking sites, where specific diseases are targeted and individuals supply anecdotal data.

3.10 Summary

Computer databases have been the foundation of computer systems since the dawn of technology in the 1950s. Aggregating medical data, dispersed among numerous databases and stored into standard nomenclatures that can be accessed and shared in a secure environment, is the goal of EHRs. There are a number of reasons why online medical data lagged behind, such as data privacy, changing mindsets of practitioners, cost, technology, will of government agencies to set standards and financing. The innumerable advantages of data sharing to prevent duplicate tests, mining data to determine the best outcomes of drugs and procedures, tracking excellence or lack thereof in particular medical institutions, preventing disease outbreaks in the early stages, and implantable or wearable medical devices that can detect life-threatening conditions before they become acute. We are in the early stages of creating a seamless data sharing network similar to ubiquitous cell phones, which can communicate and share information seamlessly. The real short-term challenge is to create better user interfaces and minimize tedious data entry. We are on an exciting roller coaster of change with wearable medical devices and clothes with embedded medical devices that will change medicine by providing proactive rather than reactive medicine.

Questions

Level I

1. What are the different types of EHR?
   a. Explain three unique features of each type of record.
   b. What benefits do you see in maintaining these records?
2. What sources/organizations provide standards for EHR development?
   a. What key areas do EHRs need to address?
   b. Explain key components of these core EHR components.
3. When entering EHR data, what standard nomenclatures are used to ensure all parties understand the clear meaning of the information entered?
   a. Explain what an entity–relationship diagram is.
   b. What is a CDSS?
   c. What role does an entity–relationship diagram play in a CDSS?
4. Explain, in general, what HIPAA is
   a. Explain what Tile I and Tile II of HIPAA provides.
5. What is the ARRA?

6. Explain the role of meaningful use criteria in EHR implementation
    a. Explain the general (meaningful use) features of Stage 1, 2, and 3.
    b. What are the top three deliverable features (meaningful use) of Stage 2?
    c. Explain your reasoning.
7. What is the purpose of HIEs?
    a. Name the three types of HIEs.

Level II

8. As you navigate an EHR explain the levels of subrecords such as MAR and discharge orders and how you perceive a typical interaction might take place, i.e., what sequence of data entry you would follow.
    a. Draw a diagram of how you think a data entry session might progress.
    b. Explain your reasoning with details.

Level III

9. What is the purpose of a CDSS?
    a. Explain how the HL7 Arden syntax is used in the development of a CDSS.
    b. Using the embedded MLM, use the specific format terms provided in Figure 3.20 and write a simple CDSS code interaction to define a patient with some authoring, patient information, citations, a priority level, and if then, block(s) to suggest treatment option based on a patient with moderate blood pressure (systolic/diastolic) 90/130 and high blood pressure above 100/150.
    c. For extra credit, write a working program as a web page using HTML and some scripting language (JavaScript, PHP, etc.) and provide the working link to the teacher (this can be done in a group if more complex diagnostic choices are added).
10. What is a fuzzy data set used in a CDSS?
    a. Explain what a discontinuity in that data set is.
    b. Give a specific example different from the textbook example defining the truth values.
    c. Extra credit: Using the link to Arden HL7 syntax manual, find the section on fuzzy sets and use another discontinuity example, nonrectangular, from that manual and explain in detail what that would mean in a real-world CDSS example.
    d. Link wiki.hl7.org/images/a/aa/Arden_Syntax_2.10_draft_2014–03–18.docx.
11. What is an expert system?
    a. What is an inference engine?
    b. How do an expert system and CDSS differ? Give details.
    c. Extra credit: Research an expert system, developed after 2010, for a specific medical disease or condition. Provide some level of details.

Glossary

A clinical decision support system is software that assists healthcare professionals in making diagnoses, treatment decisions, and workflow decisions.

Continuity of Care Record is designed as a subset of information focused on timely care of an individual either in an emergency situation or provided to another physician focusing on current health status, medications, and treatment.

Cognitive systems are a series of artificial intelligence paradigms with "the ability to engage in abstract thought that goes beyond immediate perceptions and actions."

Electronic health record* is a collection of health data from multiple sources. This is a more expansive term, versus electronic medical record, and refers to all information of the health of the body.

It is designed to share information among providers and includes all laboratory information and specialist data (used almost exclusively by the Office of the National Coordinator for Health Information Technology).

Electronic medical record is used for diagnosis and treatment, refers to medical treatment and history, and is a digital form of a medical chart and often refers to information gathered in a local practice. (It is often used but electronic health record is the preferred term.)

Expert systems are computerized applications that combine computer hardware, software, and specialized information to imitate expert human reasoning and advice.

Health information exchange is the ability to share/exchange medical information across different medical records systems (http://www.healthit.gov/HIE).

Healthcare Information and Management Systems Society is a global nonprofit organization focused on health information technology.

Health Level 7 International (HL7) is a standards organization that provides a framework for medical data exchange and sharing and standards that software organizations use to ensure data interoperability. It's a nonprofit organization with members that represent a large percentage of all electronic health records development organizations. HL7 is an American National Standards Institute accredited standard for healthcare. The level 7 refers to the ISO seventh level, the highest achievement of software integration and usability of the ISO seven-layer models.

Health Insurance Portability and Accountability Act of 1996 required that required Health and Human Services develop standards for electronic health records (EHR), data interchange, security, and unique EHR identifies for records.

Inference engines determine which rules match those of the supplied data and match those with the highest probabilities.

International Statistical Classification of Diseases and Related Health Problems (ICD9–10) is a comprehensive list by the World Health Organization of diseases, symptoms, etc. Example of some of the categories is A00-B99 Infectious and Parasitic Diseases, F00-F99 Mental and Behavioral Disorders, I00-I99 Diseases of the Circulatory System.

International Classification of Diseases and Related Health Problems (ICD10) is created by the World Health Organization. It provides a list of codes, symptoms, diseases, and social issues related to disease. It has over 14,000 codes to ensure that medical documents clearly refer to similar medical conditions to later be cross-referenced to track epidemics and treatment.

Medical logic modules contain knowledge for a single medical diagnosis decision.

The Office of the National Coordinator (ONC) for Health Information Technology is at the forefront of the administration's health information technology efforts and is a resource to the entire health system to support the adoption of health information technology and the promotion of nationwide health information exchange to improve healthcare. ONC is organizationally located within the Office of the Secretary for the U.S. Department of Health and Human Services.

Personal health record is a personal copy of a patient's health information so the patient can track, maintain, and make informed medical decisions. All doctors are required to provide this information upon request. It's a subset of the electronic health record and usually contains personal information, medical tests, diagnoses, medications, allergies, and family history.

Pharmacy clinical decision support systems are in widespread use and are usually integrated with e-prescription systems. They check drug interactions, contraindications, allergies, dosage levels, and report possible side effects and are linked in e-prescribing systems.

Nationwide Health Information Network also called eHealth Exchange developed by the U.S. Office of the National Coordinator (ONC) for Health Information Technology is a series of specifications to securely exchange health data. The goal of the ONC is to tie together health information exchanges to create a nationwide network.

Regional Health Information Organization, often used interchangeably with a health information exchange, is a group of companies, hospitals, or organizations that have developed a system to seamless exchange of health information.

HL7 Reference Information Model is an object model that provides a pictorial representation of HL7 clinical data domains. It identifies the life cycle of message groups that are moved between domains of the model.

References

1. Berners-Lee, T. (1991). Conseil Européen pour la Recherche Nucleaire, and now the European Particle Physics Laboratory, http://www.livinginternet.com/w/wi_lee.htm
2. Englebardt, S.P. and Nelson, R. (July 14, 2015). The role of expert systems in nursing and medicine. *Anti Essays*. From the World Wide Web, http://www.antiessays.com/free-essays/185731.htmlp. P. 137.
3. Heckerman, D. and Shortliffe, E. (1992). From certainty factors to belief networks. *Artificial Intelligence in Medicine* 4(1), 35–52. doi:10.1016/0933–3657(92)90036-O. http://research.microsoft.com/en-us/um/people/heckerman/HS91aim.pdf.
4. Mahn, T. (2010). Wireless medical technologies: Navigating government regulation in the new medical age, http://www.fr.com/files/uploads/attachments/FinalRegulatoryWhitePaperWireless MedicalTechnologies.pdf
5. Langley, P. (2012). The cognitive systems paradigm, CogSys.org
6. Morris, G., Silberman, S., and Covich-Bordenick, J. (2011). Report on health information exchange: The Changing Landscape. Washington, DC. http://www.cfrhio.org/images/2_2011_Report_on_Health_Information_Exchange_-_Sustainability_Report.pdf
7. Regenstreif Institute: Indiania School of Medicine. https://www.regenstrief.org/
8. Why these doctors love their RHIO. Medical Economics, http://www.memag.com/memag/article/articleDetail.jsp?id=182803
9. Veterans Administration. (1987). http://www.WorldVistA.org.

4

Data Interoperability

Level I: Core Concepts

4.1 Introduction

The term interoperability implies ubiquitous communication and a clear, precise language where the meanings of terms and ideas leave no room for doubt or interpretation. We, as human beings, have yet to accomplish this task successfully in our communications. Mathematics is the closest we have come to precisely describe some aspects of the universe, but this too is imprecise till we understand the entire complexity of space-time, dark energy, and dark matter that comprises approximately 90% of our universe, but we still have few clues on its composition. How can we describe the universe precisely if we are unsure of its underlying composition? A grand unified field theory that unites strong and weak interactions of particles and electromagnetic and gravitational forces into a single series of formulas even eluded Einstein. Medical science is evolving, so too is our schema for describing it.

The medical community, industry, and government have jointly developed a series of standards, namely, the International Statistical Classification of Diseases and Health Related Problems (ICD10), Systematized Nomenclature of Medicine (SNOMED, medical terminologies), Digital Imaging and Communications in Medicine (DICOM, images), Health Level 7 (HL7, communications), National Council for Prescription Drug Programs (NCPDP, pharmacy communications), and Institute of Electrical and Electronics Engineers (IEEE, electronics), but we rely on an individual's perception to enter those data. Is their diagnosis correct, are their tests conclusive, or is there an unknown disease that we approximate with one that fits it best? We can define precise terms but the underlying medical science is evolving; so too is interoperability. These standards are incorporated into electronic health records (EHRs), data definitions of diseases and medications, medical transmission protocols, etc. There are currently 600 EHR vendors as of 2014 (http://www.emrandhipaa.com/emr-and-hipaa/2012/04/11/over-600-ehr-vendors/). Imagine if there were 600 languages spoken, a tower of Babel of medical terminology. Under the best of circumstances, there would be some ambiguity. This chapter will describe the current state of the art, as of 2015, in generating medical standards for communicating information and links to the standards organization so you can keep abreast of the latest evolution of the science, with the caveat that this is a work in progress.

Here is the definition of interoperability by the Healthcare Information and Management Systems Society (HIMSS):

Interoperability means the ability of health information systems to work together within and across organizational boundaries in order to advance the effective delivery of healthcare for individuals and communities.

http://www.himss.org/files/HIMSSorg/content/files/AUXILIOHIMSSInteroperability Defined.pdf.

4.2 Interoperability

The term interoperability refers to the seamless exchange of information and consistent language and meaning. It implies both communications standards such as HL7 and medical vocabularies such as the SNOMED and ICD10 and ICD11 that will be released in 2017, so all facets of the healthcare system can exchange data with comparable meaning intact (Figure 4.1). Interoperable development tools that create the cross terminology mapping between concepts, such as the Unified Medical Language System (UMLS), simplify the development process.

The term interoperability can be broken down into three general categories:

1. *Communications* refer to the message structure of information transmitted between systems. HL7, a communications standards organization, defines its charter as "dedicated to provide a comprehensive framework and related standards for the exchange, integration, sharing and retrieval of

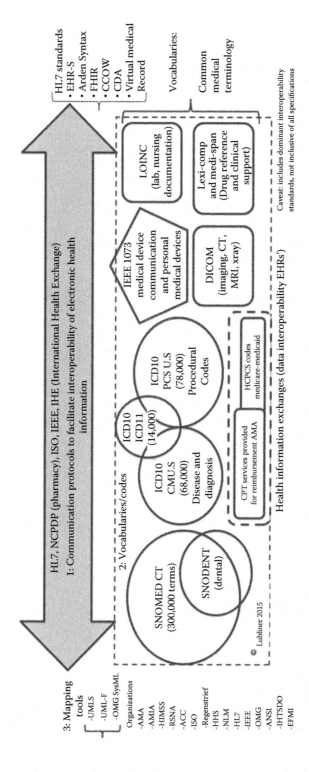

FIGURE 4.1 Interoperability: communication, terminology, and mapping standards.

electronic health information that supports clinical practice and the management, delivery and evaluation of health services" (www.HL7.org).

a. The additional medical communications standards are International Organization for Standardization (ISO), Technical Committee (TC) 215 and IEEE 1073.

2. *Vocabularies* refer to a set of generally accepted naming standards for disease, symptoms, procedures, epidemiology, etc., to facilitate accurate communications between medical practitioners worldwide. SNOMED Clinical Terms (SNOMED CT) is administered by the International Health Terminology Standards Development Organisation (IHTSDO), which, owned and governed by 27 international members, is "the most comprehensive clinical vocabulary available, in any language, with a concept oriented structure that meets the criteria for a well-formed, machine-readable terminology. HL7 and SNOMED organizations signed an agreement, renewed every two years," to "drive harmonization between HL7, SNOMED and the HL7 Reference Information Model (RIM)" (http://www.ihtsdo.org). (Reference Information Model [RIM] is an object model that displays the HL7 domains as a pictorial representation.)

a. There are some additional vocabularies: ICD10, DICOM (imaging), Logical Observation Identifiers Names and Codes (LOINC, nursing), and Lexicomp (pharma).

3. *Mapping tools* are used to link different medical vocabularies and concepts. It is used by medical informatics developers to generate categories of terms and their relationships. The relationships between terms are usually parent–child that form a broader category to a narrower one or one with more granularities. Terms are also grouped into broad categories/classifications. Semantic categories assist in extracting context and meaning. The *UMLS* contains approximately five million concepts–names and one million concepts–relationships between names and terms. The U.S. National Library of Medicine (NLM, UMLS), the largest medical library, uses UMLS to link to PubMed, which has publications of 23 million journals and reference articles. The UMLS defines its charter "to promote the creation of more effective and interoperable biomedical information systems and services, including electronic health records" (http://www.nlm.nih.gov/databases/umls.html).

4.2.1 Interoperability: Communications

This section will focus on electronic medical communications standards between EHRs, medical devices, laboratory data, and imaging studies, which have to agree on *common protocols to exchange data*. The message header and content fields, specified by communication protocols such as HL7 (Figure 4.2),

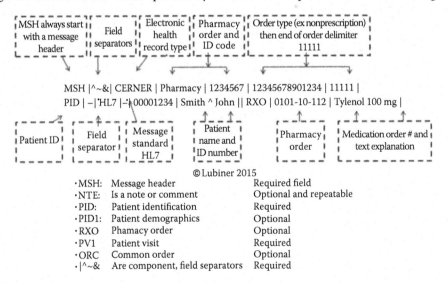

FIGURE 4.2   Health Level 7 (HL7) sample pharmacy, HL7 *communications message* between systems.

ensure that both sending and receiving systems maintain the precise meaning of information. This example shows a typical HL7 message structure with some of the fields identifying the EHR vendor CERNER and the type of message such as pharmacy order (RXO) and patient identification (PID) [00001234 Smith John] and medication order [0101-10-112 Tylenol].

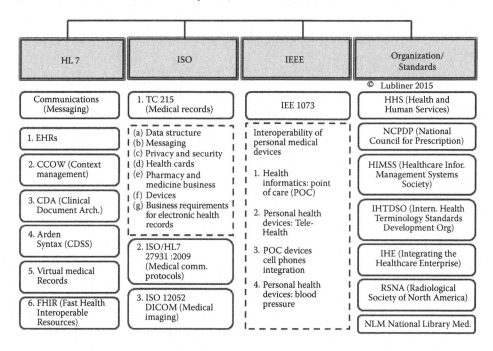

4.2.1.1 HL7

HL7 started in 1987 (www.HL7.org). Its charter is to define communication protocols for the seamless exchange of electronic health information. HL7 is an open standard, i.e., free and publicly available (e.g., in the pharmacy industry, the NCPDP is used to ensure communications interoperability between pharmacy orders [NCPDP.org]). It's a nonprofit organization whose members include most of the healthcare vendors worldwide. The standards categories that are maintained by HL7 are listed in Table 4.1. The original name aptly borrowed the concept from the ISO seven-layer communications standards (Figure 4.3). Layer 7, the highest level, is the application communications exchange protocols, as opposed to the other ISO lower hardware communications specifications such as layer 1, physical connections between computers; layer 2, data link frames for packaging messages with error checking; and layer 3, network that focuses on addressing issues such as IPV6 and routing packets to their correct destinations.

HL7 standards nomenclatures: HL7, a nonprofit organization that started in 1987 and is comprised of corporate and medical professionals, sets primarily a communications standard for messaging clinical data between systems, but it provides other functional standards for EHRs, decision support systems (DSS), etc. (www.HL7.org).

This link is the HL7 Master Index of all standards, versions, and documentations (http://www.hl7.org/implement/standards/product_matrix.cfm?ref=nav):

1. *EHR-S* Functional Model (FM), Release 2, 2014: "Outlines important features and *functions that should be contained in an EHR system*. Through the creation of functional profiles, this model provides a standard description and common understanding of functions for healthcare settings. To date, HL7 has developed or is developing profiles for areas such as child health, emergency care, long term care, behavioral health and vital statistic reporting" (HL7.org definition).

TABLE 4.1 HL7 Communications Standards Categories

HL7[a]	
1. Primary standards (used most often)	Structure and semantics of clinical documents to communicate between healthcare providers
	Point of use CCOW
	Messaging for data exchange
	Specification based on RIM V3
	Document markup standard based on structure product labeling specification that is attached to any medicine
	Continuity of care fosters interoperability of data by physicians
2. Foundational standards	Arden syntax for procedural clinical knowledge to share health knowledge databases
	DSS that recommends possible treatments; its AI software with embedded rules (see DSS in Chapter 3)
	Control data for the contents of each data field
	Service-oriented architecture
3. Clinical and administrative domains	Messaging standards
	Claims and reimbursements
	Genomics
	Drug stability reporting
4. EHR profiles	Child health profiles
	Clinical research profiles
	Medication
	Behavioral Health Functional Profile
5. Implementation guides	ANSI orders and observations
	Clinical oncology
	Questionnaire assessment
6. Rules and references	Arden syntax reference V1.6
	GELLO version 3
	DSS release 1
7. Education and awareness	Books and guides
	Data access rules/consent
	Quality reporting documents

[a] Core standards categories (http://www.hl7.org/implement/standards/product_matrix.cfm?ref=nav).

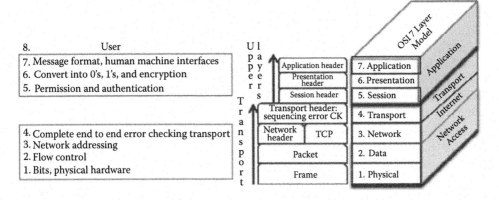

FIGURE 4.3 **(See color insert.)** ISO seven-layer model.

2. *Context Management Specification (CCOW):* "CCOW is a standard for *allowing independent systems to synchronize context* on a single workstation, providing a seamless interface for the user of that workstation (e.g., ensuring consistent user authentication, display of the same patient, display of the same order, etc.). In theory, FHIR resources could be used as an alternative CCOW implementation technology; however, the business case for doing this is not clear. CCOW profiles

include V2 mappings. These mappings can be used to help identify the equivalent FHIR data elements when establishing CCOW linkages in FHIR-based systems" (HL7.org definition).

3. *Clinical Document Architecture (CDA)*: "The HL7 Version 3 Clinical Document Architecture (CDA') is a document markup standard that *specifies the structure and semantics of 'clinical documents'* for the purpose of exchange between healthcare providers and patients. It defines a clinical document as having the following six characteristics: 1) persistence, 2) stewardship, 3) potential for authentication, 4) context, 5) wholeness, and 6) human readability. A CDA can contain any type of clinical content—*typical CDA documents would be a Discharge Summary, Imaging Report, Admission and Physical, Pathology Report* and more. The most popular use is for inter-enterprise information exchange, such as is envisioned for a U.S. Health Information Exchange (HIE)" (HL7. org definition).

4. *Arden syntax (2.9)*: This "is a language for *defining decision support rules*. These rules make reference to data elements that are used as part of the decision-making process. However, the specification does not define how these data elements are identified. FHIR element and extension identifiers would provide one mechanism for identifying the relevant data elements" *(HL7.org definition)*.

   a. *GELLO*: GELLO is "part of the HL7 Version 3 Normative Edition and is a standard *query and expression language* that provides a framework for manipulation of clinical data for *decision support* in healthcare. The GELLO language can be used to build queries to extract and manipulate data from medical records and construct decision criteria by building expressions to correlate particular data properties and values. These properties and values can then be used in decision-support knowledge bases that are designed to provide alerts and reminders, guidelines, or other decision rules."

5. *Virtual Medical Records*: "The Virtual Medical Record is a draft specification under development by HL7 that also *serves the decision support space*. It defines a logical medical record that decision support rules can be constructed against. At present, this model is a custom model created specifically for VMR. However, the Decision Support work group is evaluating the possibility of using FHIR as a structure for future versions of the specification."

6. *Fast Healthcare Interoperability Resources (FHIR)*: This "is a next generation standards framework created by HL7. FHIR combines the best features of HL7's Version 2, Version 3, and CDA' product lines while leveraging the latest web standards and applying a tight focus on implementability. FHIR solutions are built from a set of modular components called 'Resources.' These resources can easily be assembled into working systems that solve real world clinical and administrative problems at a fraction of the price of existing alternatives. *FHIR is suitable for use in a wide variety of contexts – mobile phone apps, Cloud communications, EHR-based data sharing, server communication* in large institutional healthcare providers, and much more" (hl7.org/fhir).

4.2.1.1.1 Reference Information Model

The HL7 RIM is an *information model for healthcare* development. It's a graphical representation of HL7 clinical data and describes the life cycle of messages moving through an EHR. It constitutes a series of classes composed of entities, roles, participants, relationships, and actions. It is derived based on the Unified Modeling Language (UML). (An entity–relationship [ER] diagram is a visual [graphic] tool that represents the entities and the relationships between them in a database.)

An information model is a way of representing relationships, rules, and constraints for a particular domain, for instance, its healthcare delivery. It provides an organized structure of information and knowledge. In data modeling, an information model refers to the properties and operations performed on those entities; in this instance, an entity is a patient or service performed. *It provides a formal way of describing a domain, healthcare, mapped to a specific implementation of EHR software.* Languages to implement informational models are ER graphic notations, Integrated Definition Language, UML, etc. (Section 4.5).

This RIM was introduced to insure *consistent and best practices in software development and software engineering in the EHR design process.* Some of the classifications in the RIM are as follows: An act is any procedure, medication, etc. Acts are related through an act relationship. Entities are persons, organizations, places, devices, etc. The RIM has four main classes: (1) entity, (2) role, (3) participation, (4) act (some definitions include two more main classes: role relationship and act relationship). For example, subclasses of act are observations and procedures.

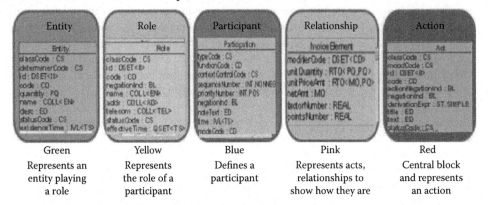

Entity	Role	Participant	Relationship	Action
Green	Yellow	Blue	Pink	Red
Represents an entity playing a role	Represents the role of a participant	Defines a participant	Represents acts, relationships to show how they are	Central block and represents an action

The following are the general concepts when creating an ER class diagram:

- An entity is something you want to describe or track, for example, any patient or service.
- A class describes an entity that includes its attributes and behavior, for example, patient treatment.
- An object is one instance of a class with unique data, for example, John Smith.
- A property is a descriptor of a class or entity, for example, age and last name.
- A method is a function executed by a class, for example, add a new patient to the EHR.
- An association is a relationship between two or more classes.

The following are examples of identifiers used in a RIM: *DEF*, a definition of an act; *INT*, an intention to perform an act; *RQO*, a request or order for a service; *CNF*, confirmation by an order; and *EVN*, an event that happens. A more complete description can be found at https://www.hl7.org/document-center/public_temp_B669E2A2-1C23-BA17-0C7A999023268366/calendarofevents/himss/2011/HL7%20 Reference%20Information%20Model.pdf.

The RIM diagram is color coded based on the entity, role, act relationship key provided earlier (Figure 4.4).

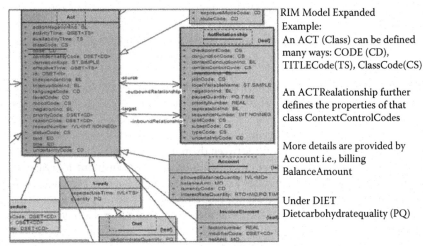

RIM Model Expanded Example:
An ACT (Class) can be defined many ways: CODE (CD), TITLECode(TS), ClassCode(CS)

An ACTRealationship further defines the properties of that class ContextControlCodes

More details are provided by Account i.e., billing BalanceAmount

Under DIET Dietcarbohydrateequality (PQ)

A high-resolution link to RIM can be found in the website http://www.healthintersections.com.au/wp-content/uploads/2011/05/RIM.png.

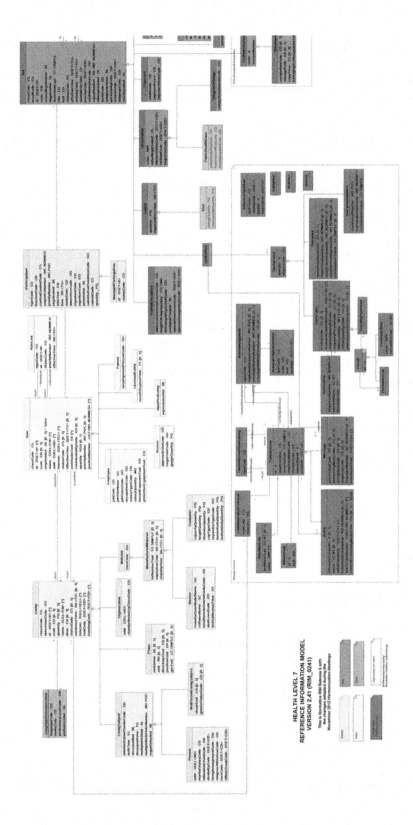

FIGURE 4.4 Reference Information Model diagram. (From https://www.hl7.org/documentcenter/public_temp_B669E2A2-1C23-BA17-0C7A99902326366/calendarofevents/himss/2011/HL7%20Reference%20Information%20Model.pdf.)

4.2.1.2 ISO

The International Organization for Standardization (ISO) is a standards organization from 130 countries established in 1947. "The mission of ISO is to promote the development of standardization and related activities in the world with a view to facilitating the international exchange of goods and services, and to developing cooperation in the spheres of intellectual, scientific, technological and economic activity" (http://www.iso.org/iso/home.html).

The Open Systems Interconnection (OSI) project, at ISO, is the source of the seven-layer communications model, a theoretical 30-year-old standard mainly used in classes, describes networking standards, where layer 1 is the simplest (physical) hardware level, for moving binary data across networks–wires. Layer 7 is the highest layer, which is the application layer, such as SFTP, for secure file transfers. The Transmission Control Protocol/Internet Protocol, which is an actual series of protocols, is used and is equivalent to the OSI levels 3 and 4. To gain more insight, refer to the paper by Hettick [2].

ISO is an international organization that covers standards ranging from quality management, ISO 9000, to food safety, ISO 22000 (Table 4.2). This table lays out a representative list of the ISO standards categories and subcategories. The two categories that specifically relate to medical records are ISO TC 215, which specifies communications standards for the seven categories (messaging, privacy, medical devices, etc.), and ISO/HL7 27931:2009, which coordinates interoperability standards between the most used medical communications protocols ISO and HL7.

TABLE 4.2   ISO Standards: Some Representative Examples of ISO Standards

Standards	Description
ISO TC 215	*Technical Committee on Health Informatics*
(a) Working Group 1	*(a) Data structure*
(b) Working Group 2	*(b) Messaging*
(c) Working Group 4	*(c) Privacy and security*
(d) Working Group 5	*(d) Health cards*
(e) Working Group 6	*(e) Pharmacy and medicine business*
(f) Working Group 7	*(f) Devices*
(g) Working Group 8	*(g) Business requirements for electronic health records*
ISO 631	Language codes
ISO 3166	Country codes
ISO 4217	Currency codes
ISO 9000/9001	Quality management
(a) ISO 9126	(a) Software engineering (functionality, reliability, usability,
(b) ISO 9451	efficiency, maintainability, portability)
(c) ISO 9592	(b) Information technology
	(c) Computer graphics
ISO 12052	*DICOM medical imaging* (see Chapter 8)
ISO 14000	Environmental management
ISO 22000	Food safety management
ISO/HL7 27931:2009	*Data exchange standards HL7*
(a) 27809: 2007	*(a) Health informatics: patient safety*
(b) 27799: 2008	*(b) Health informatics: information security*
(c) 21549–7:2007	*(c) Patient healthcard data: medication*
(d) 21549–5: 2007	*(d) Patient healthcard data: identification cards*
(e) 21730: 2007	*(e) Use of wireless communication in healthcare setting*
ISO 31000	Risk management
ISO 50001	Energy management

Note: Subset of all ISO categories (http://www.iso.org/iso/home.html).
Italics are medical standards.

4.2.1.2.1 ISO TC 215 on Health Informatics

The ISO TC 215 was set up to focus on EHR communications standards. The HL7 organization works closely with the ISO to coordinate efforts.

Coordination between communications standards organizations ensures standards are interoperable across organizations and borders. In 2008, the Joint International (Initiative) Council, which includes the European Standards Organization (CEN) TC 251 (www.cen.edu), HL7, ISO group TC 215 (http://www.iso.org/iso/iso_technical_committee?commid=54960), IHTSDO (www.IHTSDO.org), and Clinical Data Interchange Standards Consortium (www.CDISC.org) which all regularly meet to ensure coordination between communications standards.

ISO TC 215 on Health Informatics Categories

1. Messaging and communications
   a. Architecture
   b. Device interfaces
      i. Clinical messaging
      ii. Device communication
   c. Methodology
   d. DICOM objects (medical imaging)
2. Health records and modeling
   a. Transmitting and receiving medical records
   b. Country identifier
   c. Modeling a and b
3. Health concept representation
   a. Clinical terminologies
   b. Concept mapping between diverse EHR systems
4. Security
   a. Secure communications
      i. Confidentiality
      ii. Security management
   b. Public key infrastructure
   c. Archiving and backup

Table 4.3 lists the nine ISO TC 215 EHR working groups. Various organizations are working on similar EHR standards, such as HL7, and they coordinate their effort to ensure interoperability.

4.2.1.3 IEEE 11073 Health Device Communications Standards

The IEEE Standards Association (SA) develops standards for the interoperability electronic of devices (http://standards.ieee.org/). An area of IEEE standards focuses on health IT standards referred to as

TABLE 4.3 ISO TC 215 Working Groups for EHR Communications

WG 1	Data structures
WG 2	Messaging and communications
WG 3	Health concept representation
WG 4	Privacy and security
WG 5	Health cards
WG 6	Pharmacy and medicine
WG 7	Devices
WG 8	Business requirement for EHRs
WG 9	Standards Development Organization harmonized workgroup for devices

TABLE 4.4   IEEE 1073 Medical Device Communications Standards[a]

Standard (Last 4 Digits, Year Enacted)	Description	Link	Layer (ISO Communications Model)
11073–00101–2008	Health informatics, POC medical device communication	http://standards.ieee.org/findstds/ standard/11073–00101–2008. html	Lower layers
1073–00103–2012	Health informatics, personal health device communication for personal *telehealth devices*	http://standards.ieee.org/findstds/ standard/11073–00101–2008. html	Layers 3 and 4
1073–10404–2010	Health informatics, personal health device communication (cell phones, PCs), *pulse oximeter*	http://standards.ieee.org/findstds/ standard/11073–00101–2008. html	Lower layers
1073–10407–2008	Health informatics, personal health device, *blood pressure monitor*	http://standards.ieee.org/findstds/ standard/11073–10407–2008. html	Lower layers

[a] These standards statuses are all *active* as of 2014 (examples) (http://standards.ieee.org/findstds/standard/healthcare_it.html).

11073 Medical Device Communications Standards, i.e., interoperability of personal medical devices. These standards evolve over time (check the IEEE site for the latest active version). They fall into several categories: (1) health informatics, point of care (POC); (2) personal health devices, telehealth; (3) POC devices, cell phone integration; and (4) personal health devices, blood pressure (Table 4.4).

4.2.1.4 Integrating the Healthcare Enterprise

Integrating the Healthcare Enterprise (IHE) (http://ihe.net/) is a nonprofit organization created by the U.S. *Healthcare Industry* and the Radiology Group of North America and supported by the HIMSS. It originally focused on the interoperability of health and IT systems and DICOM, which is the standard for medical imaging storage such as CT, MRI, and PET scans, and later expanded to incorporate the LOINC used to identify medical laboratory observations. IHE, HL7, and LOINC are standards used to transmit data between external systems. In order to accurately specify a disease, it's necessary to describe the proper domain: imaging, pharmacy, etc.

The IHE mission is "to bring together information technology stakeholders and healthcare professionals to implement standards for communicating patient information efficiently throughout healthcare facilities, large and small" (http://ihe.net).

The Healthcare Industry regularly holds seminars to ensure that medical devices and systems are interoperable, i.e., able to seamlessly share data. The current standards incorporated into the IHE standards are given in Table 4.5:

An example of IHE laboratory data sharing message is illustrated as follows. They include Laboratory Code Set Distribution (LCSD) for testing and observation codes. For example, LAB-51 code set, based on HL7, such as MFN.M10, includes standard batteries of tests used in standard clinical environments.

A message might look like this: a battery of tests requested in the emergency room (department)

MFN^M10/[OM5]/MSH|^~\&|OF|LabSystem|OP||20050205094510||MFN^M08|2106|2.5|||NLD|MFI| OMA|OF_OMA_NL_20050205|REP|||ER|

with the codes

OM1–2 producer's service/test/observation ID
OM1–4 specimen required
OM1–5 producer ID/OM5, battery of tests
OM1–18 nature of service/test/observation

TABLE 4.5 IHE Standards Categories[a]

Categories	Description	Link
Anatomic pathology	Anatomic pathology laboratory data and imaging systems.	http://ihe.net/Anatomic_Pathology/
Cardiology	Sharing information in cardiology clinical domain. The test includes cath labs, echocardiography, ECG, stress tests, and implantable cardiac devices.	http://ihe.net/Cardiology/
Dental	Secure exchange of dental images.	http://ihe.net/Dental/
Eye care	Eye evaluations, cataract surgery.	http://ihe.net/Eye_Care/
IT infrastructure	Working group started by the HIMSS specifying an IT integration framework for implement systems to support EHRs and communications.	http://ihe.net/IT_Infrastructure/ The It infrastructure White Paper http://www.ihe.net/Technical_Framework/upload/IHE_ITI_White-Paper_Enabling-doc-sharing-through-IHE-Profiles_Rev1-0_2012–01–24.pdf
Laboratory	Specific laboratory test codes supported by HL7 such as the LCSD.	http://ihe.net/Laboratory/
Patient care coordination	Patient care across providers, document sharing, order processing.	http://ihe.net/Patient_Care_Coordination/
Patient care devices	Integrating patient care devices into electronic medical records.	http://ihe.net/Patient_Care_Devices/
Pharmacy	Codes for transmitting pharmacy data; PRE pharmacy prescriptions, DIS pharmacy dispensing, HMW hospital medication workflow, PADA pharmacy advice.	http://ihe.net/Pharmacy/
Radiology Radiation oncology	Nuclear medicine images. Mammography (MAMMO), XDS1 (cross image document sharing etc.).	http://ihe.net/Radiology/ http://ihe.net/Radiation_Oncology/

[a] Improve information sharing.

The IHE utilizes healthcare and industry participation to improve communications and interoperability between systems. They work with the HL7, DICOM, NCPDP (pharmacy), and other standards organizations to improve EHR communications. The IHE has a four-step development methodology: (1) Experts define use cases for data sharing. (2) They optimize the process creating standards. (3) They work with EHR companies to implement these standards. (4) They evaluate the effectivity of these protocols under IHE supervision (Figure 4.5).

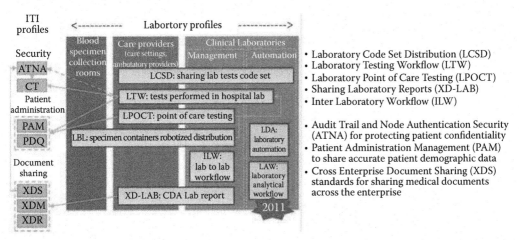

FIGURE 4.5 Integrating the Healthcare Enterprise laboratory data sharing guidelines. (From http://wiki.ihe.net/index.php?title=Laboratory.)

TABLE 4.6 NCPDP Pharmacy Transmission Header, to Standardize Communications

			NCPDP prescription Message Header					
Sender ID	Segment Identifier	Segment Identification	Version	Batch No.	Transaction Ref. Number	Group Indicator		

			Explanation of NCPDP Message Header Fields					

			Batch Header Record					
NCPDP Data Dictionary Name	Field Number	Definition of Field	Format	Valid Values	Copybook	Starting Position	Ending Position	
Sender ID*	880-K1	Identification number assigned to the sender of the data by the processor of the data.	X(24)		NCPKFLAT	1	24	
Segment Identifier*	701	Unique record type required on Batch Transaction Standard.	X(02)	00 =File Header	NCPKFLAT	25	26	
Segment Identification*	111-AM	Identifies the segment in the request record. This field is only populated on records with Segment Identifier G1.	X(02)	Spaces	NCPKFLAT	27	28	
Version*[1]	N/A	Represents the current version of VIPs NCPDP software that is being used.	X(01)	A	NCPKFLAT	29	29	
Batch Number*	806-5C	Number assigned by processor. Matches trailer record	9(07)		NCPKFLAT	30	36	
Transaction Reference Number*	880-KS	Number assigned by provider to each transaction record. This number is unique to each set of flat file records that represent a single claim. This field is only populated on records with Segment Identifier G1.	X(10)	Spaces	NCPKFLAT	37	46	
Group Indicator*[1]	N/A	This field is used to indicate a group of related segments. These segments together represent the equivalent of 1 claim per line. This field is only populated on records with Segment Identification '07' (claim segment).	X(01)	N	NCPKFLAT	47	47	

4.2.1.5 NCPDP (Pharmacies)

The NCPDP has created templates for pharmacy telecommunications regarding what should be shared between pharmacies and payers (http://www.ncpdp.org/pdf/200903HIPAA_Implementation_v2.pdf). The Health Insurance Portability and Accountability Act (HIPAA), document 5010, through the Department of Health and Human Services has certified pharmaceutical transaction version D.0, effective January 2012, which coincides with the mandates that physicians should use e-prescriptions, i.e., all scripts should be sent electronically to pharmacies to reduce errors (Table 4.6).

The HIPAA of 1996 specified that a single standard be used to submit pharmacy claims in NCPDP format (http://www.cms.gov/Medicare/Billing/ElectronicBillingEDITrans/downloads/NCPDPflatfile.pdf).

4.2.2 Medical Classification Systems: Medical Vocabularies

In order for two medical practitioners to accurate communicate, they have to agree on similar terms to describe a disease, procedure, or patient observation. Even with that level of synchronization, slight variations in wording may obscure meaning. Medical vocabularies/classification systems incorporate thesauri referred to as metathesauri, similar to those available in Microsoft Word, which take those potential wording variations and replace it with a universally accepted term. In addition, the commonly used classification systems, such as SNOMED and ICD10, collaborate to produce cross system equivalencies.

Another important aspect to document is the context of the condition. These can be provided by attribute relationship hierarchy diagrams (see Figure 4.6). If a bacterium is found, what is the site of the infection and what is the specific strain? No single code may reflect this information. So the documentation system may provide a series of targeted questions; SNOMED CT has that feature to provide a graphical display of the context:

SNOMED context → Body structure → Lung → Bacterial pneumonia → Bacteria

New medical relationships between causative agents can be constructed with the UMLS tools (Section 4.5), which provide not only cause–effect relationships but linkages between different medical classification systems.

Interoperability 2: Vocabularies/Codes

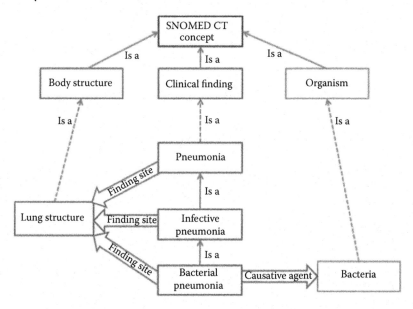

FIGURE 4.6 Systematized Nomenclature of Medicine attribute relationship hierarchy. International Health Terminology Standards Development Organisation SNOMED CT User Guide. (From http://ihtsdo.org/fileadmin/user_upload/doc/download/doc_UserGuide_Current-en-US_INT_20130731.pdf.)

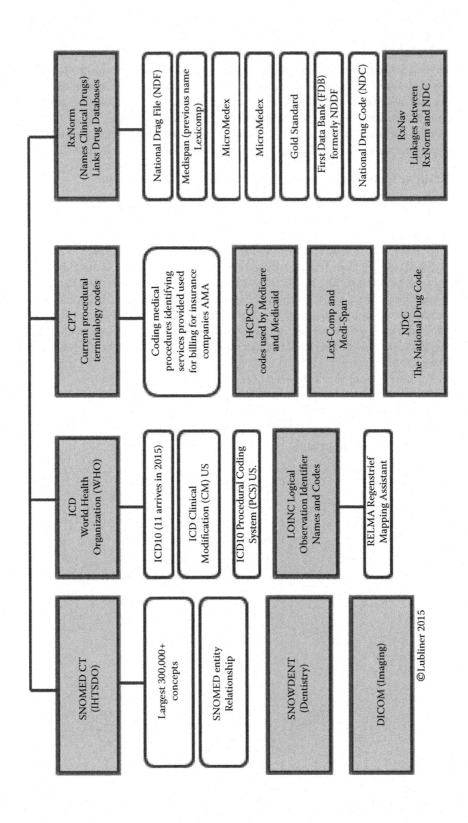

©Lubliner 2015

4.2.2.1 SNOMED CT

The *SNOMED CT* is the most comprehensive international medical classification available as of 2013; it had 300,000 medical codes to support medical documentations. It began in 1965 as Systematized Nomenclature of Pathology, which evolved beyond just pathology into SNOMED Reference Terminology (RT). In 1999 SNOMED RT maintained by the College of American Pathologists merged with the United Kingdom's Clinical Terms Version 3, formerly known as Read Codes, to create SNOMED CT. The current version is now administered by the IHTSDO, a multinational effort. These codes map to other classification systems such as ICD10, HL7, LOINC, DICOM, and ANSI and are available in numerous languages.

SNOMED Data Architecture

1. Concept identifier, a unique medical code
2. Hierarchies from general to specific
3. Human readable terms → concepts with synonyms
   a. 1 million English terms linked to foreign language descriptions
   b. 300,00+ concepts
4. Relationships, link concepts
   a. *Relationship*, link concept to a more general concept
   b. Type of relationship that has causative agents, *viral pneumonia → virus → lung*
   c. 1+ million relationships

SNOMED CT codes are affected by the context. For example, the breast cancer codes indicate potential sources: either from a family history, a cancer in remission, or a new diagnosis. Each code indicates the context in which it is described. These contexts have different SNOMED codes. Similar to context modifiers, axis modifiers are modifiers that can change the meaning or type of a procedure or clinical finding. An example of a modifier is (needle) biopsy for a procedure. Other types of biopsy modifier codes specify alternate biopsy techniques (Table 4.7).

SNOMED CT creates hierarchies between medical concepts to illustrate attribute relationships where causative agents relate to physical structures, symptoms, and diseases (see Figure 4.6).

4.2.2.1.1 International Health Terminology Standards Development Organization

The IHTSDO is a nonprofit organization in Denmark. It owns SNOMED CT (http://www.ihtsdo.org/).

The following is the IHTDSO charter:

The IHTSDO seeks to improve the health of humankind by fostering the development and use of suitable standardized clinical terminologies, notably SNOMED CT, in order to support safe, accurate, and

TABLE 4.7 SNOMED CT ER Attributes

Attribute Values	Example
Clinical finding | 404684003	Seizure disorder had definitional manifestation, seizure finding
	Hypertensive disorder | systemic arterial disorder
	Has definitional manifestation, finding of increased blood pressure
Clinical finding | 404684003	*Family history* of stroke
Event | 272379006	Associated finding cerebrovascular accident (disorder)
Procedure | 71388002	
Anatomical or acquired body structure | 442083009	Procedure on colon, procedure site colon structure
Substance | 105590001	Protein measurement procedure
Observable entity | 363787002	Component | protein (substance)
Cell structure | 4421005	
Organism | 410607006	

effective exchange of clinical and related health information. The focus is on enabling the implementation of semantically accurate health records that are interoperable. Support to association members and licensees is provided on a global basis allowing the pooling of resources to achieve shared benefits.

4.2.2.1.2 *Systematized Nomenclature of Dentistry*

A U.S. government mandate for universal EHR implementation by 2015 will require that all of a patient's medical and *dental records* be available in an electronic format *if the provider is a participant in a Medicare or Medicaid incentive program.* Eventually, the EHR mandate may be extended to all providers (https://www.aaoinfo.org/news/2014/01/electronic-health-records-implementation-aao-representatives-ensure-orthodontic).

Dentists and orthodontists who either have a small number of patients or have no Medicare and Medicaid patients are currently not affected by the reimbursement penalties for not submitting bills in electronic format. These rules are evolving but as of 2014, no dental requirement for EHR or electronic dental record (EDR) has been specified.

The American Dental Association (ADA) has been working, since 2007, on the Systematized Nomenclature of Dentistry (SNODENT) to standardize terminology in the dental field, similar to SNOMED *(http://www.ada.org/en/member-center/member-benefits/practice-resources/dental-informatics/snodent).*

1. Provides standardized terms for describing dental disease
2. Captures clinical detail and patient characteristics
3. Permits analysis of patient care services and outcomes
4. Is to be interoperable with EHRs and EDRs
5. Updates added in 2014
   a. Eliminated the "Not Otherwise Specified" (NOS) designation.
   b. Identified "frequently used terms" and added terms from the ADA health history form.
   c. The ADA has also developed a new numeric codes.
   d. Assigned concepts to hierarchies.
   e. Reviewed descriptions that were assigned to the concepts.
   f. Reviewed synonyms for the concepts.
   g. Developed a crosswalk from SNODENT to ICD9 and ICD Clinical Modification (CM) version 10 (ICD10 CM).

4.2.2.2 ICD10 and ICD11 in 2015

ICD10 version 10, schema circa 2013, which has 14,000+ codes and subcategories, is a medical classification list of diseases, symptoms, diagnoses, health management, and epidemiologies created by the World Health Organization (WHO). The WHO constitution mandates "the production of international classifications on health so that there is a consensual, meaningful and useful framework which governments, providers and consumers can use as a common language." An internationally agreed-upon standard aids in the interpretation and comparison of medical data (see Section 4.4 for more details). This list can be expanded by using subcodes related to other disease categories. The online browser is available in 43 languages (http://apps.who.int/classifications/icd10/browse/2010/en). For example, most countries use International Classification of Diseases (ICD) to report mortality rates, i.e., maternal mortality rates per 100,000 live births (Figure 4.7), which is an indicator of general health conditions in that region. SNOMED CT and UMLS integrate ICD10 libraries to ensure compatibility.

4.2.2.2.1 *ICD11*

ICD11 is currently under development, based on user inputs and needs, and the first version will be available in 2017 (http://www.who.int/classifications/icd/revision/icd11faq/en/index.html).

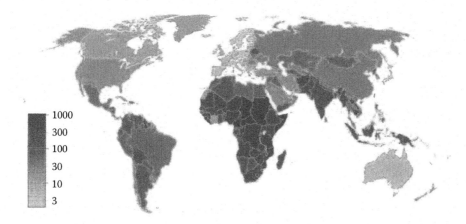

FIGURE 4.7 International Statistical Classification of Diseases and Health Related Problems report: infant mortality rates per 100,000 as of 2010. (Maternal mortality: Fact sheet N°348. World Health Organization.)

The following are the new features of ICD11 (WHO):

1. ICD11 revision process allows for collaborative web-based editing that is open to all interested parties. To assure quality, it will be peer reviewed for accuracy and relevance.
2. It will be free to download online for personal use (and in print form for a fee).
3. It will be available in multiple languages.
4. Definitions, signs and symptoms, and other contents related to diseases will be defined in a structured way so it can be recorded more accurately.
5. It is compatible with electronic health applications and information systems.

4.2.2.2.2 U.S. ICD Clinical Modification

ICD10 CM is maintained by the Centers for Medicare and Medicaid Services (CMS) and is a U.S. national code that provides more detail than the WHO's ICD10, with 68,000 codes. It provides a disease and diagnosis code set that lists the causes for hospital or medical interventions. The codes are in the form of 3–7 digits, wherein the seventh digit provides detail not available in ICD10 (Table 4.8):

- ICD10 CM: U.S. National Code provides more detail with 68,000 codes.
- ICD10 PCS (ICD10 Procedural Coding System): U.S. (exclusively) procedural code has 76,000 codes.

TABLE 4.8 ICD10 CM U.S. Coding System Example

Classification	First Three Characters (1,2,3)	Second Three Characters (4,5,6)	Seventh Character (Example D or G)
External causes of morbidity	• V00-X58, accidents • V10-V19, pedal cyclist injured in transport accident • *V20-V29,* motorcycle rider injured in transport accident	• 79.0, 79.1 A fracture designated as closed • *82.0* open fractures	• *D* subsequent encounter for fracture with *routine healing* • G subsequent encounter for fracture with *delayed healing*
Example, seven-digit code	V20	82.0	D

4.2.2.2.3 U.S. ICD10 Procedure Coding System

The U.S. PCS is maintained by the Center for Medicaid and Medicare Services (CMS) which provides a procedure classification system with 78,000 codes that is not included in ICD10 CM (http://www.cms.gov/Medicare/Coding/ICD10/Downloads/pcs-slides-2013.pdf) (Table 4.9).

It provides

1. Standardized terminologies
2. Multiaxial definitions in which each character has the same meaning within and across sections
3. No diagnostic information; that is, the information is in ICD10 CM
4. Terms not classified that are used for new devices and substances
5. Definitions for all substantially different procedures
6. Codes in the form of seven digits, that is, in letters A–Z and numbers 0–9

(Letters O and I excluded so as not to be confused with numbers 0 and 1)

TABLE 4.9 ICD10 PCS Terms and Coding Example

ICD10 PCS System Structure (16 Sections)[a]	
1. Medical and surgical (*Section* O)	9. Other procedures
31 body systems (med-surg.)	
Central nervous	Subcutaneous tissue and fascia
Peripheral nervous	Muscles
Heart and great vessels	Tendons
Upper arteries	Bursae and ligaments
Lower arteries	Head and facial bones
Upper veins	Upper bones
Lower veins	Lower bones
Lymphatic and hemic	Upper joints
Eye	Lower joints
Ear, nose, sinus	Urinary
Respiratory	Female reproductive
Mouth and throat	Male reproductive
Gastrointestinal (*body system* D)	Anatomical regions, general
Body part Approach Device Qualifier	
F large intestine O open Z no device X diagnostic	
Hepatobiliary and pancreas	Anatomical regions, upper extremities
Endocrine	Anatomical regions, lower extremities
Skin and breast	
2. Obstetrics	10. Chiropractic
3. Placement	11. Imaging
4. Administration	12. Nuclear medicine
5. Measurement and monitoring	13. Radiation oncology
6. Extracorporeal assistance and performance	14. Physical rehabilitation and diagnostic audiology
7. Extracorporeal therapies	15. Mental health
8. Osteopathic	16. Substance abuse treatment

[a] http://www.cms.gov/Medicare/Coding/ICD10/Downloads/pcs-slides-2013.pdf.

4.2.2.3 LOINC

LOINC is a coding scheme used in laboratories for *clinical observations* and in *nursing* for *diagnosis, interventions, outcomes, and patient care* that facilitates interoperability of clinical observations between EHR systems (http://loinc.org/). It creates different codes for each test, measurement, or observation that has a clinically different meaning. As of 1999, LOINC has been recommended for transmitting laboratory and clinical observations in HL7 messages. A free license is available at http:loinc.org/terms-of-use.

The LOINC codes distinguish a given observation (test ordered/reported, survey question, clinical document) across six dimensions called "parts":

1. Component
2. Property
3. Time
4. System (specimen)
5. Scale
6. Method (manual count)

LOINC provides the question and SNOMED CT provides the answers. LOINIC provides nursing observations that lead to the final classification provided in the SNOMED or ICD10 code. It also provides a more detailed series of events that lead to the eventual diagnosis creating a trail of clues that can be reviewed later.

The following are examples from observations/discrete measurements/collections from a lab test:

1. Lab tests such as glucose in urine (mg/dl) and complete blood count
2. Measurements of a patient, for example, weight and height
3. Questions on a form: can you move your arm/range
4. Clinical measurements such as temperature
5. Documents, that is, intake or discharge summary

The *OBX-4* slot, in a HL7 message, allows two sets of triplets: one for your local concept and the other for the concept from the vocabulary standard (LN indicates a LOINC coding system).

4.2.2.3.1 Regenstrief LOINC Mapping Assistant

The Regenstrief LOINC Mapping Assistant (RELMA) is a search tool for the LOINC clinical database (*http://search.loinc.org*). It provides utilities to map codes between LOINC and other clinical libraries. It provides a ranked list of terms.

To search for specific LOINC codes, go to http://search.loinc.org

Example: If you entered *HEMOTOCRIT* at the aforementioned search site: Search Results:

LOINC	LongName
4544	3 Hematocrit (volume fraction) of blood by automated count
20670	8 Hematocrit (volume fraction) of blood
31100	1 Hematocrit (volume fraction) of blood by impedance

4.2.2.4 RxNorm

RxNorm provides standardized names for clinical drugs by referencing a number of pharmaceutical libraries produced by the NLM (http://www.nlm.nih.gov/research/umls/rxnorm/). It is similar to the Metathesaurus in the UMLS that references numerous drug-naming conventions and creates an agreed-upon naming convention (Table 4.10).

4.2.2.5 NDC

The National Drug Code (NDC) is maintained by the Food and Drug Administration (FDA) and was mandated by the U.S. Federal Government in 1972 by the Drug Listing Act. It requires the FDA "list

TABLE 4.10 Drug Databases That Are Referenced by RxNorm

RxNorm Clinical Drug Library (Repository Linking Numerous Pharmaceutical Databases Listed)		
Database	Description	Link
National Drug File	Provides standard nomenclatures for drugs for the Department of Veterans Affairs	http://www.va.gov/vdl/documents/ Clinical/Pharm-National_Drug_File_ (NDF)/psn_4_tm_r0206.pdf
Medi-Span (previous name Lexicomp)	Drug reference guide that provides prescription drug information and adverse effects to medical professionals	http://www.medispan.com/
Micromedex	Provide reference information on symptoms and treatments of diseases	http://www.micromedex.com/
Multum	Provides consumer drug information and side effects and provides a drug insert in prescriptions (sources CDC and WHO)	http://www.drugs.com/mtm/
Gold Standard	Drug reference and patient information and alternative therapies	http://www.goldstandard.com/product/ drug-reference-patient-education/
First Data Bank (FDB), formerly NDDF	Drug information designed to integrate with EHRs	http://www.fdbhealth.com/ fdb-medknowledge/
NDC	FDA list of drugs that include the manufacturer and packaging codes	http://www.accessdata.fda.gov/scripts/ cder/ndc/default.cfm

of all drugs manufactured, prepared, propagated, compounded, or processed by it for commercial distribution. All drug products are identified and reported using a unique, three-segment number, called the National Drug Code (NDC), which serves as a universal product identifier for drugs" (http://www.fda.gov/Drugs/InformationOnDrugs/ucm142438.htm). The NDC is a 10-segment code for all drugs (Figure 4.8).

4.2.2.6 RxNorm versus NDC

The NDC numbers are more complex to read than RxNorm, which creates a standardized name from multiple databases, i.e., a thesaurus of names referencing the same data. NDC contains the manufacturer labeler, product code, and packing information in a 10–11-digit code (manufacturer's name), which is essential as part of the required labeling on medicine containers. Two manufacturers will have different codes for the same medication. Also, packaging information for the same medication creates additional code variation.

When EHRs reference a medication, the RxNorm value provides a standard reference term with no duplicate entries that may be available with the NDC numbers. But RxNorm, after generating a generic reference term with them, contains linkages to the multiple NDC codes (Figure 4.9).

RxNorm: acetaminophen 500 MG oral tablet

The National Institutes of Health (NIH) states the following:

RxNorm's standard names for clinical drugs and drug delivery devices are connected to the varying names of drugs present in many different controlled vocabularies within the Unified Medical Language System (UMLS) Metathesaurus, including those in commercially available drug information sources. These connections are *intended to facilitate interoperability among the computerized systems* that record or process data dealing with clinical drugs.

4.2.2.7 Current Procedural Terminology Codes

Current Procedural Terminology (CPT) codes are used for coding medical procedures and identifying services provided that are used for billing by insurance companies. It is a U.S. code created by the American Medical Association. (In contrast, ICD10 codes focus on the diagnosis of diseases)

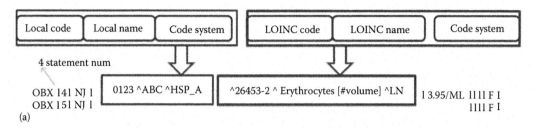

(a)

Row # US Version 1.1	Row # SI Version 1.1	Lonic	Long common name	Description of change
1443	1457	38390-1	Cryptococcus neoformans Ag (presence) in Cerebral spinal fluid	Deprecated term. LOINC 38390-1 replaced with 31788-3, *Cryptococcus* sp Ag (presence) in cerebral spinal fluid
742	745	40844-3	Immunoglobulin light chains.kappa.free/immunoglobulin light chains.lambda (mass rstio) in serum	Deprecated term. LOINC 40844-3 replaced with 48378-4, Immunogolobulin light chains.kappa.free/immunoglobulin light chains.lambda.free (mass ratio) in serum
1846	1860	48577-1	HFE gene p.G845A (presence) in blood or tissue by molecular genetics method	Deprecated term. LOINC 48577-1 replaced with 21695-2, HFE gene p.C282y (presence) in blood or tissue by molecular genetics method
1444	1458	5119-3	Cryptococcus neoformans Ag (titer) in serum by latex agglutination	Deprecated term. LOINC 5119-3 replaced with 9820-2, *Cryptococcus* sp Ag (titer) in serum by Latex agglutination
1801	1815	9785-7	Microscopic observation (identifier) in stool by ova and parasite preparation	Deprecated term. LOINC 9785-7 replaced with 10704-5, Ova and parasites identified in stool by light microscopy

(b)

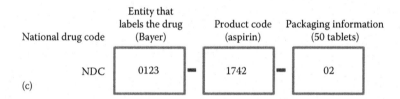

(c)

FIGURE 4.8 (a) Logical Observation Identifiers Names and Codes (LOINC) code imbedded in a Health Level 7 message. (From https://loinc.org/get-started/02.html.) (b) LOINC codes. (From http://loinc.org/usage/obs/introduction-to-the-mappers-guide-for-the-top-2000-plus-loinc-laboratory-observations.pdf.) (c) Food and Drug Administration National Drug Code, 10–11-digit, three-segment code for drugs.

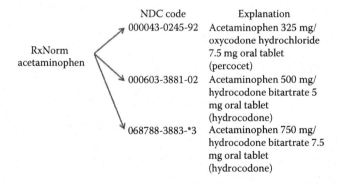

FIGURE 4.9 RxNorm linkages to the numerous National Drug Code product codes.

provided   (http://www.ama-assn.org/ama/pub/physician-resources/solutions-managing-your-prac-tice/coding-billing-insurance/cpt.page).

Single and "pseudo" single bill data for CPT code 78492	CY 2011 final rule data	CY 2012 proposed rule data	CY 2012 final rule data
Median line item CCR	0.1708	0.1350	0.1272
Median line item charge	3,858.75	4,051.70	4,051.70
Median line item cost ($)	649.85	539.07	492.02
Median packaged cost ($)	391.06	327.69	273.43
Hospitals reporting	48	60	64
Single bills	3,910	8,617	9,727
Total frequency	5,922	10,531	11,912

In the table three significant observations are noted for CPT code 78492, which is the myocardial PET imaging service (https://www.federalregister.gov/articles/2011/11/30/2011–28612/medicare-andmedicaid-programs-hospital-outpatient-prospective-payment-ambulatory-surgical-center):

- A bill from a doctor will have CPT codes.
- If you use Medicare, you will receive Healthcare Common Procedure Coding System (HCPCS) codes.
- Codes with letters and numbers most likely will be ICD9–ICD10 codes.

The CPT codes are broken down into three categories:

1. Category I is for vaccines:
   a. Updates released twice a year (in January and July).
   b. Emergency releases, to respond to crises, which can be made available any time
2. Category 2 is for performance measurement, the purpose of which is to minimize the administrative burden on physicians and other healthcare professionals, hospitals, and entities seeking to measure the quality of patient care.
3. Category III is for
   a. Services
   b. Procedures
   c. Emerging technologies

4.2.2.7.1 Healthcare Common Procedure Coding System Codes

HCPCS codes are the billing codes used by Medicare and monitored by CMS. They are based on the CPT codes.

CY 2011 HCPCS code	CY 2012 HCPCS code	CY 2012 long descriptor	Final CY 2012 status indicator	Final CY 2012 APC
C9280	J9179	Injection, eribulin mesylate, 0.1 mg	G	1426
C9281	J2507	Injection, pegloticase, 1 mg	G	9281
C9282	J0712	Injection, ceftarolin fosamil, 10 mg	G	9282
C9729	0275T	Percutaneous laminotomy/laminectomy (intralaminar approach) for decompression of neural elements. (with or without ligamentous resection, discectomy, facetectomy and/or foraminotomy) any method under indirect image guidance (e.g., fluoroscopic, CT), with or without the use of an endoscope, single or multiple levels, unilateral or bilateral; lumbar	T	0208
Q2040*	J0588	Injection, incobotulinumtoxin A, 1 unit	G	9278

Examples of HCPCS codes can be found at https://www.federalregister.gov/articles/2011/11/30/2011–28612/medicare-and-medicaid-programs-hospital-outpatient-prospective-payment-ambulatory-surgical-center.

4.2.3 Interoperability: Mapping Tools

4.2.3.1 UMLS

UMLS is a mapping system and toolset used to coordinate between different medical vocabularies (http://www.nlm.nih.gov/research/umls/). It is used by medical informatics developers. It contains approximately five million concepts–names and one million concepts–relationships between names and terms (Figure 4.10). The U.S. NLM, the largest medical library linked to PubMed (23 million journal and reference articles), maintains these tools with free licensing (http://www.ncbi.nlm.nih.gov/pubmed). The UMLS defines its charter as "to promote the creation of more effective and interoperable biomedical information systems and services, including electronic health records."

The architecture of UMLS contains resources to allow interoperability and health information exchange (HIE) and designs the tools to create linkages between diverse medical libraries and EHR systems. There are three knowledge databases accessed by UMLS: Metathesaurus, Semantic Network, and Lexical Tools (see Section 4.5 in Level III for more details on UMLS).

4.2.4 Medical Databases

4.2.4.1 MEDLINE/PubMed

Medical Literature Analysis and Retrieval System (MEDLINE) is the preeminent life science and medical database whose content is selected by a NIH panel of experts (i.e., Literature Selection Technical Review Committee) that contains approximately 20 million articles and reference materials (http://pubmed.gov). Ninety percent are in English, but articles are available in 60 languages. Most of the databases are journals but a smaller percentage are magazines, news articles, etc. Abstract and searchable keyword access is free but some content is protected by copyright and those protected articles can be obtained from the LoansomeDoc (https://docline.gov/loansome/login.cfm). This website is supported by the NIH.

A more generic consumer access portal, MedlinePlus (http://medlineplus.gov/), contains more focused and fewer technical resources. An example selected from MedlinePlus is shown in Figure 4.11. It is maintained by the NIH. It contains approximately 1,000 topics including medications available, treatments, and

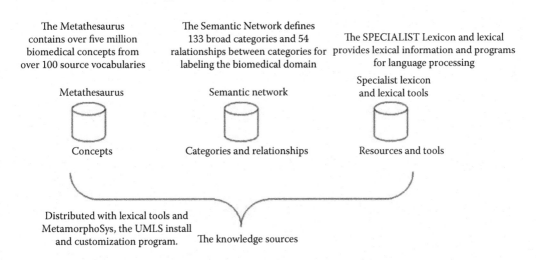

FIGURE 4.10 Unified Medical Language System architecture.

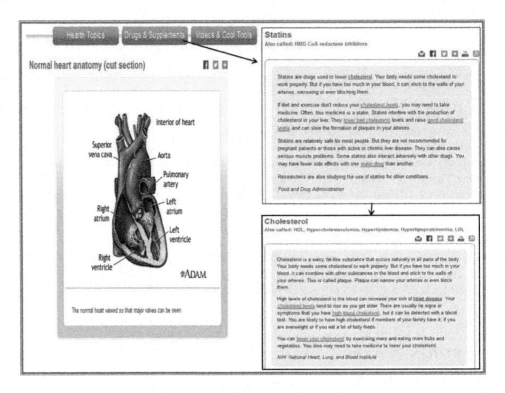

FIGURE 4.11 MedlinePlus consumer information portal: information on the heart and statin drugs available.

educational videos and links into your EHRs (http://www.nlm.nih.gov/medlineplus/connect/overview. html). The specific medical codes used in your EHR taken from one of the standards medical vocabularies such as ICD10 or SNOMED embedded in your EHR can be linked directly to MedlinePlus for patient education resources and a drug reference guide for interactions and possible side effects linked to RxNorm.

MedlinePlus also contains abstracts and journal articles on biological and medical sciences and is available online for free and is maintained by the NLM (http://www.ncbi.nlm.nih.gov/pubmed).

4.2.4.2 Medical Subject Headings

Medical Subject Headings (MesH) is a thesaurus/vocabulary for accessing either specific medical resources related to the search topic such as medical journal articles through PubMed database or terms/related concepts through a hierarchy of related terms. It is maintained by the U.S. NLM and used by the MEDLINE or MEDLARS (online).

The main MeSH search page provides multiple views and related concepts (Figure 4.12) (https://www. nlm.nih.gov/mesh/MBrowser.html).

The most basic MeSH search parameters under basic headings provide general and then narrower terms and subheadings in the field. Searching cardiology results in a display of related terms such as cardiovascular disease, vascular medicine, and angiology and related ICD codes illustrated (Figure 4.13).

Also, you can refine your search by selecting cardiovascular diseases and then selecting subheadings displaying a hierarchical tree structure including cardiovascular abnormalities, heart defects congenital, and heart septal defects with four subcategories (Figure 4.14):

1. Aortopulmonary septal defect
2. Endocardial cushion defects
3. Heart septal defects atrial
4. Heart septal defects ventricular

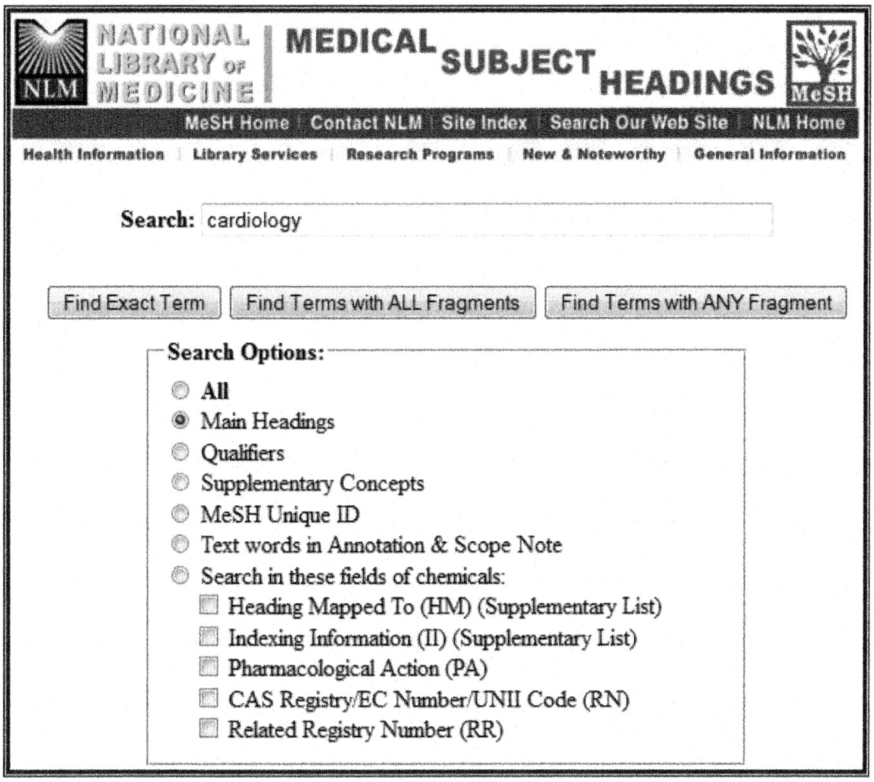

FIGURE 4.12 Medical Subject Headings search page. (From nih.gov.)

4.2.4.3 Document-Type Definition

A document-type definition (DTD) is used by PubMed to index articles. It's a list of markup declarations used to describe the elements and context to enhance searching articles. It is consistent with the Standard Generalized Markup Language, which is an ISO standard that describes the article's structure and content.

Example (Structure)

<!DOCTYPE html Public "-//W3C//DTD XHTML 1.0 //EN" "http//www.w3.org ...."">

<HTML> BODY of document **</HTML>**

- It starts with a Document Type (DOCTYPE identifier) **<!DOCTYPE html…..**
- It conforms to World Wide Web (W3C) standards conformance **//W3C//**
  - **http//www.w3.org**
- It also conforms to DTD and XHTML **/DTD XHTML**
  - Or simply HTML version number 5.0 /DTD HTML 5.0/
- Language (English) **//EN**
- Then the Document Body enclosed in <HTML>..document… </HTML>

Example (Content)

- Specific searchable information using the ENTITY tag with identifiers can accelerate locating the article
- **<!ENTITY** followed by a specific tag
  - **%author** "authors name">
  - **%title** "Cancer Interventions for Lymphomas">
  - **%date** "1/1/2013">

MeSH Heading	Cardiology	
Tree Number	H02.403.429.163	
Annotation	use for the discipline (education, history, etc) only; corresponding disease term is <u>CARDIOVASCULAR DISEASES</u> or specifics	
Concept 1 (Preferred)	Cardiology	
	Concept UI	M0003461
	Scope Note	The study of the heart, its physiology, and its functions.
	Semantic Type	T091 (Biomedical Occupation or Discipline)
	Term (Preferred)	Cardiology
	Term UI	T006634
	Date	01-JAN-1999
	Lexical Tag	NON
	Thesaurus	NLM (1966)
Concept 2 (Narrower)	Cardiovascular Disease Specialty	
	Concept UI	M0554084
	Semantic Type	T091 (Biomedical Occupation or Discipline)
	Term (Preferred)	Cardiovascular Disease Specialty
	Term UI	T785887
	Date	18-FEB-2011
	Lexical Tag	NON
	Thesaurus	NLM (2012)
Concept 3 (Narrower)	Vascular Medicine	
	Concept UI	M0554085
	Scope Note	The study, diagnosis, and treatment of diseases of the blood vessels (<u>VASCULAR DISEASES</u>) and vessels of lymphatic system (<u>LYMPHATIC DISEASES</u>).
	Semantic Type	T091 (Biomedical Occupation or Discipline)
	Term (Preferred)	Vascular Medicine
	Term UI	T784727
	Date	28-JAN-2011
	Lexical Tag	NON
	Thesaurus	NLM (2012)
	Term	Angiology
	Term UI	T784728

FIGURE 4.13 Medical Subject Headings basic search results.

Level II: Application and Theory: Messaging HL7 with Embedded SNOMED

4.3 Introduction

This section illustrates *specific* communications protocols, formats, and coding schema for the transfer of medical data (SNOMED) embedded in a message between EHRs. The HL7 message structure is illustrated in Figure 4.15. Embedded into the HL7 communications wrapper is the SNOMED content, i.e., the actual medical data that will be communicated and exchanged between EHRs (Figure 4.15).

4.3.1 HL7 Message Architecture

HL7 communications protocols define standards for the seamless exchange of electronic health information (www.hl7.org). Interoperability is defined as the seamless exchange of data between EHRs. There are currently 600 plus EHR vendors.

4.3.2 HL7 Message Structure

The following example describes a typical HL7 message. HL7 is the transport structure of the message with fields for PID, medications (RXO), notes or comments field abbreviation (NTE), etc. (Figure 4.16).

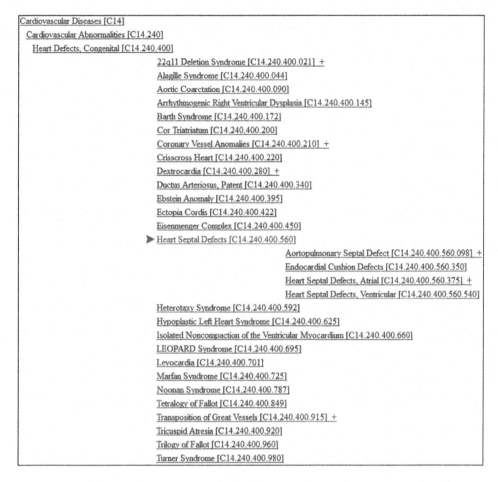

FIGURE 4.14 Medical Subject Headings cardiovascular disease and hierarchical diagram of related concepts.

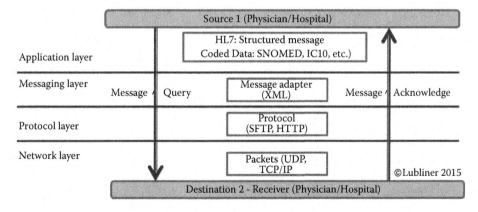

FIGURE 4.15 Messaging architecture between medical systems/electronic health records: Health Level 7 is the communications protocol.

```
MSH |^~&|CERNER|Pharmacy |1234567 |12345678901234
| 11111|
PID |  _   | HL7 |  _  | 00001234 | Smith ^ John ||  RXO|
0101-10-112 | Tylenol 100mg |
```

FIGURE 4.16 Example of a Health Level 7 message from a CERNER electronic health record system for John Smith.

Category	Example Message Code
1. Message starts with:	*MSH* (message header)
2. Group:	EVN (event type)
3. Segment:	*PID*
4. Data type:	PVI (patient visit information)
5: Component: Group	AL1 (patient allergy information)
6. Components:	DG1 (diagnosis), PR1 (procedures), *RXO* (pharmacy)

4.3.3 HL7 Codes in Tables

In the aforementioned sample message, components such as PID and pharmacy orders (RXO) are sub-field identifiers for the HL7 code set. Tables 4.11 through 4.13 illustrate some of the possible subcodes with a link to the complete set of possible messages available.

4.3.4 HL7 with Embedded SNOMED CT

The *SNOMED CT*, the most comprehensive international medical classification available with 300,000 plus medical codes/concepts, is used to support medical documentation. Each concept has a unique

TABLE 4.11 HL7 Message Codes (HL7 Table 9999)[a]

Value	Description	Value	Description
ACC	Accident	NTE	Notes and comments
AL1	Patient allergy Information	ODS	Dietary orders
BLG	Billing	*PID*	*Patient identification*
DG1	Diagnosis	PR1	Procedures
IN1	Insurance	PV1	Patient visit
MSH	*Message header*	*RX0*	*Pharmacy prescription order*

[a] Subset of HL7 messages available, complete list (http://amisha.pragmaticdata.com/~gunther/oldhtml/tables.html).

TABLE 4.12 HL7 Medical Record Transaction Codes (HL7 Tables 178 and 180)[a]

MAC	Reactivate deactivated record.
MAD	Add record to master file.
MDC	Discontinue record in master file.
MDL	Delete record from master file.
MUP	Update record for master file.
REP	Replace current version of this master file with version contained in this message.
UPD	Change file records.

[a] Subset of codes available.

TABLE 4.13 HL7 Physiology: Administrative Descriptors (HL7 Table 163)[a]

CT	Chest tube	RACF	Right antecubital fossa
LA	Left arm	RPC	Right posterior chest
LPC	Left posterior chest	RSC	Right subclavian
LSC	Left subclavian	RUA	Right subclavian
LVL	Left vastus lateralis	RVG	Right upper arm
RAC	Right anterior chest	RVK	Right vastus lateralis

[a] Subset of physiological messages.

identifier term. They are available in English, Spanish, and German. There are approximately a million relationships defined between terms (statistics as of January 2014).

The SNOMED CT concepts are arranged in hierarchies to provide embedded context to the terms (Table 4.14). In Table 4.14, a procedure will have subcomponents/contexts that document when, where, and how the procedure took place.

TABLE 4.14 SNOMED Hierarchies[a]

SNOMED Training Videos[b]		
Hierarchies	Explanation	Example
Clinical finding/disorder	Results from a clinical observation	Appendicitis
Procedure/intervention • Component • Direct morphology • Substance • Focus • Intent • Specimen • Measurement method	Activities performed in healthcare environment	Surgery, MRI, dressing change
Observable entity	Action that results in observable data	Blood pressure, heart rate, temperature
Body structure	Normal or abnormal physiological descriptions	Heart valves operating normally, 90% blockage of coronary artery
Organism	Organisms responsible for disease	Bacteria, viruses
Substance	Chemical in drugs, allergens, toxicity, etc.	Acetaminophen, insulin, etc.
Pharmaceutical/biologic product	Upper-level root hierarchy, indicates substance categories	Product categories
Specimen	Analysis of specimens from patients	Urine, etc.
Physical forces	Forces that can create injury	Electric current
Event	External events that can cause injury	Earthquakes, bioterrorism
Environments and geographical locations	New Jersey, surgery	ICU, emergency room
Social context	Social environments that affect health	Occupation, economic status, religion, family history
Staging and scales	Assessment scales	Stage 4 cancer
Attributes	Relate two SNOMED concepts	

Cancept A — Attribute Relationship — Concept B

Pneumonia → Site → Lung

[a] http://www.ihtsdo.org/snomed-ct/snomed-ct0/snomed-ct-hierarchies/.
[b] http://www.youtube.com/playlist?list=PL4DE2FA9DA297015F.

TABLE 4.15   Sample SNOMED CT Codes[a]

SNOMED CID Code	Description
195967001	Asthma (disorder)
21522001	Abdominal pain (symptom)
29857009	Chest pain (finding)
53741008	Coronary arteriosclerosis (disorder)
44054006	Diabetes mellitus type 2 (disorder)
233604007	Pneumonia (disorder)
54150009	Upper respiratory infection (disorder)

[a] Sample of 300,000 codes available: http://www.clinicalarchitecture.com/blog/clinical-architecture-healthcare-it-blog/july-2009/snomed-ct-core-subset-quick-overview-and-impressio/.

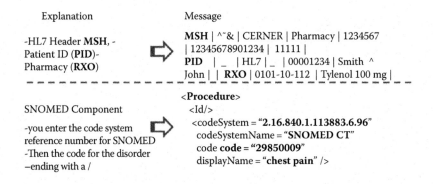

Explanation	Message
-HL7 Header **MSH**, - Patient ID (**PID**)- Pharmacy (**RXO**)	**MSH** | ^~& | CERNER | Pharmacy | 1234567 | 12345678901234 | 11111 | **PID** | _ | HL7 | _ | 00001234 | Smith ^ John | | **RXO** | 0101-10-112 | Tylenol 100 mg |

<Procedure>
  <Id/>

SNOMED Component	
-you enter the code system reference number for SNOMED -Then the code for the disorder —ending with a /	<codeSystem = "**2.16.840.1.113883.6.96**" codeSystemName = "**SNOMED CT**" code **code = "29850009"** displayName = "**chest pain**" />

FIGURE 4.17   A Health Level 7 header with embedded Systematized Nomenclature of Medicine content message.

SNOMED tables have 300,000 plus codes that will be used to populate data fields embedded in the HL7 wrapper communications message. Table 4.15 lists a few of those codes that are available.

Embedded in the HL7 message will be the specific SNOMED codes to describe a particular symptom/disorder/finding that can be exchanged between health record systems (Figure 4.17).

Building on the aforementioned first HL7 example that contains the start of the message (MSH) and the EHR software CERNER, PID, and the pharmacy order (RXO). The SNOMED component starts with the word "Procedure" and the code for the SNOMED medical vocabulary system is "2.16.840.1.113883.6.96". The parsing software, which analyzes the message, then pulls the codes from the appropriate vocabulary coding tables. The SNOMED procedure ends with "/". If ICD10 were used, instead of SNOMED, we would use a different code, i.e., 2.16.840.1.113883.5.4 for ICD10 version 3.

4.4 ICD10

International Statistical Classification of Diseases and Related Health Problems (ICD10), is a medical vocabulary and classification system maintained by the WHO (ICD11 2017). It contains codes for diseases, symptoms, findings, and social circumstances contributing to a disease. ICD10 codes are appended to HL7 header messages, some of which are listed in subcategories in Table 4.16 (http:// apps.who.int/classifications/icd10/browse/2010/en). Example A02.2 for Localized *Salmonella* infectors.

ICD10 version 10, schema circa 2013, which has 14,000+ codes and subcategories, also includes health management and epidemiologies created by the WHO. Table 4.16 illustrates the 20 general ICD categories from infectious and parasitic diseases to external causes of morbidity and portability and an example of the subcategories A00–A99 from intestinal infections to arthropod-borne viral fevers.

TABLE 4.16 ICD10 Classification Categories (WHO)[a]

1. Infectious and parasitic diseases

	A00–A09	Intestinal infectious diseases (sample)
		A02, salmonella infection, infection or food-borne intoxication due to any *Salmonella* species other than *S. typhi* and *S. paratyphi*
		A02.0 *Salmonella enteritidis, salmonellosis*
		A02.1 *Salmonella septicemia*
		A02.2 *Localized salmonella infections:* Arthritis+ (*M01.3**) Meningitis+ (*G01**) Osteomyelitis+ (*M90.2**) Pneumonia+ (*J17.0**) Renal tubulointerstitial disease+ (*N16.0**)
		A02.8 *Other specified Salmonella infections*
		A02.9 *Salmonella infection, unspecified*
	A15–A19	Tuberculosis
	A20–A28	Certain zoonotic bacterial diseases
	A30–A49	Other bacterial diseases
	A50–A64	Infections with a predominantly sexual mode of transmission
	A65–A69	Other spirochaetal diseases
	A70–A74	Other diseases caused by chlamydiae
	A75–A79	Rickettsioses
	A80–A89	Viral infections of the central nervous system
	A90–A99	Arthropod-borne viral fevers and viral hemorrhagic fevers
	B0–B99	Viral infections; viral hepatitis; HIV; mycoses; protozoal diseases; helminthiases; pediculosis, acariasis, and other infestations; sequelae of infectious and parasitic diseases; bacterial, viral, and other infectious agents; other infectious diseases

2. Neoplasms
3. Diseases of the blood and blood-forming organs, the immune mechanism
4. Endocrine, nutritional, and metabolic diseases
5. Mental and behavioral disorders
6. Diseases of the nervous system
7. Diseases of the eye and adnexa
8. Diseases of the ear and mastoid process
9. Diseases of the circulatory system
10. Diseases of the respiratory system
11. Diseases of the digestive system

(Continued)

TABLE 4.16 (*Continued*)   ICD10 Classification Categories (WHO)[a]

12. Diseases of the skin, subcutaneous tissue
13. Diseases of the musculoskeletal system and
    connective tissue
14. Diseases of the genitourinary system
15. Pregnancy, childbirth
16. Conditions originating in the perinatal period
17. Congenital malformations, deformations, and
    chromosomal abnormalities
18. Symptoms, signs, and abnormal clinical and
    laboratory findings, not elsewhere classified
19. Injury, poisoning, and certain other
    consequences of external causes
20. External causes of morbidity and mortality

[a] http://apps.who.int/classifications/icd10/browse/2008/en#/I.

Level III: Advanced Topics: Mapping Tools

4.5 Unified Medical Language System

The *UMLS*, provided by the U.S. NLM, provides tools to visualize and integrate medical vocabularies, publications, electronic medical records, etc. (http://www.nlm.nih.gov/research/umls/about_umls. html). The three core components in the UMLS toolset are the Metathesaurus, Semantic Network, and Specialist Lexicon. The *Metathesaurus* contains a number of databases, such as SNOMED and ICD10, whose goal is to resolve multiple naming conventions into a single representative medical term. The Semantic Network displays relationships, i.e., parent–child or hierarchical relationships between concepts (Figure 4.18). The Specialist Lexicon interprets common natural language terms embedded, for example, in PubMed publications, and resolves that different natural language variations. The Specialist Lexicon has a natural language processing component for commonly used English words (Figure 4.19). Its overall goal is to enhance the interoperability of EHRs and support HIEs.

The UMLS defines its charter as "to promote the creation of more effective and interoperable biomedical information systems and services, including electronic health records."

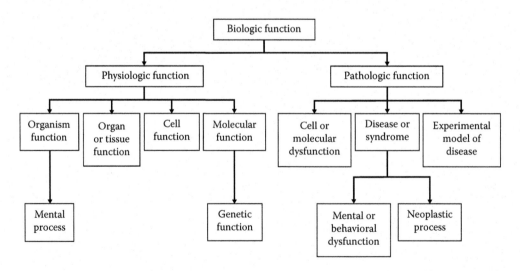

FIGURE 4.18   Semantic categories.

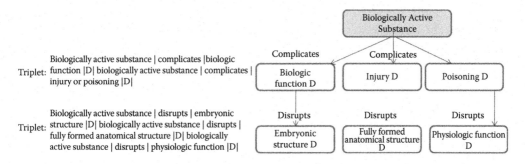

FIGURE 4.19 Semantic mapping example from a series of triplet relationships.

4.5.1 UMLS Metathesaurus

1. The Metathesaurus is a multilingual database that contains medical concepts and relationships between them. The thesaurus tool contains synonyms of terms entered into the EHRs and recommends a preferred term used across databases (Table 4.17).

Metathesaurus databases contain

1. Diagnoses, LOINC
2. Procedures, current procedural technology
3. Diseases, ICD10
4. Vocabularies and thesauri, *SNOMED CT*
5. Additional categories
   i.   Nursing
   ii. Drugs
   iii. Anatomy
   iv. Genetics

TABLE 4.17 Metathesaurus of Medical Terms Entered into the EHR and It Selects a Preferred Term

Collection of Terms in the Concept	Preferred Term
disease; Hodgkin	Hodgkin Disease
Hodgkins disease	
Hodgkin Disease	
Hodgkin's disease, unspecified	
Hodgkin's disease, unspecified type	
Hodgkin's disease (clinical)	
Hodgkin's disease NOS, unspecified site	
Hodgkin's disease NOS (disorder)	
Hodgkin's sarcoma (clinical)	
Hodgkin's sarcoma NOS	
Hodgkin's sarcoma of unspecified site	
Hodgkin's sarcoma of unspecified site (disorder)	
Hodgkin's sarcoma-unspec. site	
Hodgkin lymphoma	
Lymphogranuloma, Malignant	
Lymphogranulomatosis	
Lymphogranulomatosis, malignant	
Lymphomas Hodgkin's disease	

Table 4.17 illustrates the possible ways on how the term "Hodgkin's disease" could be entered into an EHR and how the Metathesaurus database is used to determine a common term used in a series of medical vocabularies such as SNOMED and ICD10 to ensure interoperability between systems.

4.5.2 UMLS Semantic Network

Semantic types are used to generate categories of terms and their relationships used in the Metathesaurus. The relationships between terms are usually parent–child, from a broader category to a narrower one or one with more granularities. Terms are also grouped into broad categories/classifications (Figure 4.18). Semantic categories assist in extracting context and meaning.

Visualizing the relationships between terms, functions, and causalities, UMLS provides mapping of tools to not only aid in the development of the triplet relationships (i.e., A is related to B) but also to provide another method for medical practitioners to visualize the chain of causative elements in the disease process (Figure 4.19).

4.5.3 Lexical Tools (Dictionary)

The UMLS *Specialist Lexicon* contains 200,000+ terms that can be used to create new features or add new functionality to a medical classification system. It also contains natural language terms to help in the parsing of data input by the medical practitioner. This dictionary draws from several standardized sources such as MEDLINE, which contains 23 million medical citations from PubMed; Dorland's Illustrated Medical Dictionary, which is currently published by Elsevier in its 32nd edition that originally began in 1890; and several other English dictionaries.

The Specialist Lexicon contains the following (NLM, www.nlm.nih.gov):

a. The lexical tools that provide the entry of nonformatted data presented in sentences. Language parsing tools that can determine verbs, nouns, adjectives, etc., can extrapolate meaning from free-form data entry.
b. Embedded lexical computer software tools such as a lexical variant generator, normalized string generator (Norm), and word index generator (WordIndex) analyzes variations in terminology to extract meaning. A number of free UMLS tools can be found at uts.nlm.nih.gov.

4.6 RxNav

RxNav, a pharmaceutical database that is provided by the NIH, provides linkages between RxNorm names and the various generic and brand name medications, including the NDC FDA codes http://rxnav.nlm.nih.gov/RxNavViews.html. This tool provides multiple formats for viewing the relationships between medications and manufacturers, both generic and brand names. Multiple graphical and physical views of the drugs including the color, numeric labeling codes, and manufacturers' copyrighted symbols available to cross-reference medications are shown in Figure 4.20.

4.7 Summary

Creating a common medical vocabulary and coding schema that can be used planetwide is a daunting task. Many organizations are pursuing those lofty goals. The added challenge is to synchronize those various databases to ensure exact meaning is maintained when communicating between systems. International organizations regularly meet to create equivalencies. It's unlikely in the near future that one system will prevail, though SNOMED CT and ICD10 and ICD (CM & PCS) come close to the goal of a universal medical vocabulary. Communications protocols, such as HL7,

Pill images of the same drug **Diclofenac Sodium 100MG** produced by different manufacturers

Property	Image 1	Image 2	Image 3
Image			
Acq Date	12-02-2009	02-07-2011	12-19-2012
Manufacturer	Actavis Elizabeth LLC	Watson Laboratories, Inc.	Teva Pharmaceuticals USA Inc
SplSetId	NONE	Link to DailyMed	Link to DailyMed
NDC	00228-2717-11	00591-0676-01	00093-1041-01
Shape	ROUND	ROUND	ROUND
Size	9	10	9
Color	YELLOW	RED	PINK
Imprint	R;717	DX41	93;1041
ImprintType	DEBOSSED	DEBOSSED	DEBOSSED

RxNorm thesaurus to multiple data sources and codes for the same medication

Category	Property	Value
NAMES	RxNorm Name	venlafaxine 100 MG Oral Tablet [Effexor]
	RxNorm Synonym	Effexor 100 MG Oral Tablet
	RxNorm Synonym	Effexor 100 MG (as venlafaxine hydrochloride) Oral Tablet
CODES	RxCUI	208848
	UMLSCUI	C0710468
	NDA	NDA020151
	SPL SET ID	cf2d9bee-f8e3-477a-e4b4-f0e82657b7d2
ATTRIBUTES	TTY	SBD
	HUMAN_DRUG	US
	PRESCRIBABLE	Y
	AVAILABLE_STRENGTH	100 MG
SOURCES	Source	Gold Standard Alchemy
	Source	Multum MediSource Lexicon
	Source	Micromedex RED BOOK
	Source	Metathesaurus FDA National Drug Code Directory
	Source	Metathesaurus FDA Structured Product Labels

FIGURE 4.20 **(See color insert.)** RxNav visualization engine visualizing the same drug from multiple manufacturers.

provide the communications envelope to encase those specific medical messages into a common format with 90% using those standards.

We have embarked on a journey to add EHRs to the instantaneous communications revolution. The next phase is to add interoperability between all systems; that effort is taking place in the United States under the Health Information Exchanges (HIEs) funded by the NIH. Once interconnected, disease outbreaks, such as a new strain of flu virus, can be identified and contained quickly. This exponential interoperability trajectory is bright!

Questions

Level I

1. What is data interoperability?
   a. What are the three general categories? Explain each.
   b. List a few key standards in each of those three interoperability categories.
2. What is the main functionality of HL7? Explain its purpose.
   a. What standards are specified (categories)? Briefly explain each.
   b. Explain some of the details from the HL7 communications message shown in Figure 4.2.
   c. Explain the relationship between the OSI model and HL7.
   d. What is HL7 RIM? Explain its purpose.
3. What is ISO?
   a. Explain ISO TC 215.
4. Describe the need for IEEE 11073 Health Device Communications Standards.
   a. Select one of the IEEE 11073 standards links from Table 4.4 and explain some details of specific communications standards.

5. What is the role of the *NCPDP*?
   a. Explain the e-prescription mandates and penalties.
6. What role do medical classification systems play in interoperability? Briefly explain the following:
   a. SNOMED CT
   b. SNODENT
   c. ICD10–11
   d. LOINC
   e. RxNorm
7. What is *UMLS*?
   a. Explain the three knowledge databases incorporated in UMLS.

Level II

8. In the HL7 message sent between clinical systems, modify the message to include patient allergy, diagnosis data, and insurance: be creative and make up some allergies and diagnoses (Figure 4.16 and Tables 4.11 through 4.13).
9. For the HL7 message incorporating SNOMED CT, add some fields and update the procedure in Figure 4.17.
   a. Do the same for the HL7 message but use ICD10 (use the data from Table 4.16).

Level III

10. Using the UMLS thesaurus framework, create your own set of interchangeable terms for some real mythical conditions; be creative (Table 4.17).
11. Utilizing the UMLS Semantic Network framework, create a specific mapping sample, choose some diseases, and create your own semantic mapping sample: use Figure 4.19 as a template.

Glossary

Context Management Specification (CCOW): CCOW is a standard for allowing independent systems to synchronize context on a single workstation, providing a seamless interface for the user of that workstation (e.g., ensuring consistent user authentication, display of *the same patient, display of the same order, etc.*).

Clinical Document Architecture (CDA): The HL7 Version 3 Clinical Document Architecture (CDA') is a document markup standard that specifies the structure and semantics of 'clinical documents' for the purpose of exchange between healthcare providers and patients.

EHR-S Functional Model (FM) Release 2 2014: The model that outlines important features and functions that should be contained in an EHR system. Through the creation of functional profiles, this model provides a standard description and common understanding of functions for healthcare settings.

Fast Healthcare Interoperability Resources (FHIR) (hl7.org/fhir): FHIR is a next generation standards framework (2014) created by HL7. It combines the features of HL7's version 2 and version 3 and CDA product lines while leveraging the latest web standards and applying a tight focus on implementability for mobile phone apps, Cloud communications, EHR-based data sharing, and server communications.

International Statistical Classification of Diseases and Health Related Problems (ICD10): Version 10, schema circa 2013, which has 14,000+ codes and subcategories, is a medical classification list of diseases, symptoms, diagnoses, health management and epidemiology created by the World Health Organization.

ICD Clinical Modification (CM) version 10 (ICD10 CM): Maintained by the Center for Medicaid and Medicare Services (CMS), it is a U.S. National Code, which provides more detail than the WHO's ICD10, with 68,000 codes.

Institute of Electrical and Electronics Engineers (IEEE) Standards Association (SA): Develops standards for the interoperability electronic of devices.

International Health Terminology Standards Development Organisation (IHTSDO): Nonprofit organization in Denmark. It owns SNOMED CT (http://www.ihtsdo.org/).

Integrating the Healthcare Enterprise (IHE): Nonprofit organization created by the U.S. *Healthcare Industry* and the Radiology Group of North America and supported by the Health Information Management Systems Society (HIMSS) (http://ihe.net/).

Logical Observation Identifiers Names and Codes (LOINC): Used to identify medical laboratory observations.

Reference Information Model (RIM): Provides software developers with architecture for information exchange between electronic health records in accordance with HL7 standards.

Regenstrief LOINC Mapping Assistant (RELMA): Search tool for the LOINC clinical database.

Systematized Nomenclature of Medicine Clinical Terms (SNOMED CT): The most comprehensive international medical classification available, as of 2013; it had 300,000 medical codes to support medical documentation.

Unified Medical Language System (UMLS): Mapping system and toolset used to convert between different medical vocabularies. It is used by medical informatics developers. It contains approximately 5 million concepts–names and 1 million concepts–relationships between names and terms.

References

1. Health Information Exchange (HIE) Technical Guidelines (2011) HIMSS. http://www.himss.org/files/HIMSSorg/content/files/HIMSSHIETechnicalOverview.pdf. (Generated by HIE committees).
2. Hettick, L. (2013). Data networking basics. *Networking World*, Feb 2013. (Generated by HIE committees).
3. HL7 Message types, http://www.hl7.org/special/committees/vocab/v26_appendix_a.pdf. (Generated by HIE committees).
4. *International classification of Diseases 10th revision*. World Health Organization. February 26, 2010, http://apps.who.int/classifications/icd10/browse/2010/en
5. Dolin, R. (2004) Introduction to SNOMED clinical terms and its use with HL7, http://www.park-streetsolutions. com/documents/SNOMED_Overview.Acapulco.pdf.
6. Durkin, S. and Just, B. *An IT primer for health information exchange*, AHIMA http://library.ahima.org/xpedio/groups/public/documents/ahima/bok1_036239.hcsp?dDocName=bok1_03629
7. SNOMED Clinical Term (CT), Reference Manual, http://ihtsdo.org/fileadmin/user_upload/doc/download/doc_UserGuide_Current-en-US_INT_20130731.pdf. (Generated by HIE committees).

5

Security

Level I: Core Concepts

5.1 Introduction

Information security is an ever-evolving endeavor. We are regularly bombarded by large-scale security breaches. In 2014, the Department of Health and Human Services (HHS) under the Health Insurance Portability and Accountability Act (HIPAA) Title II fined two New York City (NYC) hospitals $4.8 million for a security breach [3] of Electronic Protected Health Information (ePHI). The hospital systems were secure but a physician's personal computer/server was at fault. In another security breach target, one of the largest retailers in the United States reported that 70 million customer data had potentially been compromised [9]. *The Wall Street Journal* reported that "Target attackers were able to gain access to the retailer's system by way of stolen credentials from a third-party vendor." Target's systems may have been secure, but a third-party vendor's security was lax, so they gained access through a backdoor. Security breaches often occur through innocuous lapses in security in tertiary systems. Simple, easily hacked passwords such as *12345*, leaving a system unattended, and phishing, a form of social engineering where an individual is fraudulently contacted to reset his or her password and provide confidential information, are some of the many techniques used to breach a system's security. "They lunge, we parry" is a fencing analogy, a continual dance of attack/defense, that will probably always be with us. The benefits of electronic health records (EHRs) far outweigh any potential security breaches. Healthcare professionals sharing data and evaluating the effectiveness of treatments and real-time consults are moving medical practices exponentially forward. This chapter discusses medical computer security best practices that will evolve over time (Figure 5.1).

> HIPAA fines for ePHI 2014 for two NYC hospitals (http://www.hhs.gov/news/press/2014pres/05/20140507b.html).
>
> Target security breach (http://www.washingtonpost.com/business/economy/target-says-70-million-customers-were-hit-by-dec-data-breach-more-than-first-reported/2014/01/10/0ada1026-79fe-11e3-8963-b4b654bcc9b2_story.html).

5.2 HIPAA Title II Security and Privacy

This text focuses on medical informatics, i.e., software, hardware, operational, and ethical components of the healthcare environment that support efficient, effective, and *secure* information exchange. The goal of HIPAA, created in 1996, was to "improve the health, safety, and well being of America population" and to create a framework for the EHR infrastructure (Figure 5.2).

HIPAA Title II describes *security* as "the safeguards that must be in place to ensure appropriate protection of electronic Protected Health Information (ePHI), and *privacy*, that sets limits and conditions on the use and disclosure of medical information without patient authorization."

These security goals are also described in Section 13402 of the Health Information Technology for Economic and Clinical Health Act, part of the American Recovery and Reinvestment Act of 2009 (http://www.gpo.gov/fdsys/pkg/FR-2009-08-24/pdf/E9-20169.pdf).

5.2.1 Privacy Rule

The HIPAA Privacy Rule sets federal standards to protect individuals' personal health information (PHI) and describes limits to disclosure of medical information without patient authorization. The exceptions listed in Figure 5.2 focus on balancing the patient's privacy with providing efficient health delivery. Possible scenarios: a patient is unconscious, or transferred to a tertiary medical facility, or a

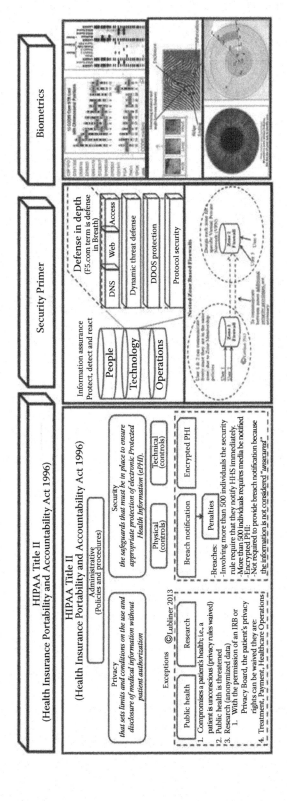

FIGURE 5.1 **(See color insert.)** Security and privacy.

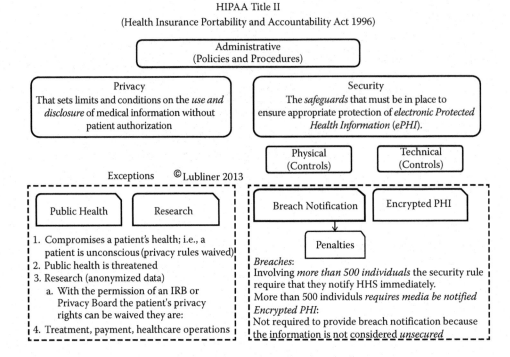

FIGURE 5.2 HIPAA Title II security and privacy rules.

public health emergency, anonymized data, i.e. patient's name, Social Security number, etc. are removed from the medical record, so it can be shared under strict HIPAA Title II guidelines. These regulations are enforced by the HHS Office of Civil Rights (OCR) (http://www.hhs. gov/ocr/privacy/hipaa/understanding/coveredentities/usesanddisclosuresfortpo.html).

1. The privacy rule restricts the use of ePHI without patient consent unless the following are given:

Exceptions

a. It compromises a patient's health such that a patient is unconscious and can't provide consent or the speed of lifesaving treatment would be compromised.
b. Public health is threatened wherein data are anonymized, and patient's identifying information is removed, so by this exception, we can track national disease outbreaks.
c. Research and anonymized data can be used to study the effectiveness of the treatment.
d. Treatment, payment, healthcare operations, and legal system efficiency uses are authorized under very limited guidelines.
    i. Treatment: coordination of services among practitioners or third-party referral services.
    ii. Payment: providers have the right to be reimbursed for their services.

    Exception areas

    1. Determining eligibility or coverage
    2. Billing and collection activities
    3. Reviewing healthcare services for medical necessity, coverage, and justification of charges
    4. Utilization review

5.   Disclosures to consumer reporting agencies that are limited to payment history and identifying information about the covered entity
6.   Risk adjustments

  iii. Healthcare operations: administrative, legal, and efficiencies of operations

1.   Quality assessment and improvement activities, improving health or reducing healthcare costs and case management and care coordination
2.   Evaluating the competence or qualifications of healthcare professionals, plan performance, training healthcare and nonhealthcare professionals, accreditation, certification, licensing, or credentialing activities
3.   Activities relating to the creation, renewal, or replacement of a contract of health insurance or health benefits
4.   Medical review, legal, and auditing services, including fraud and abuse detection and compliance programs
5.   Business planning and development, such as cost-management and planning analyses
6.   Business management and general administrative activities, including those related to implementing and complying with the privacy rule and other administrative simplification rules

2. Individuals have right to view and get copied all medical records.
3. The scope of protected information covers the following:

  a. All information doctors, nurses, and other healthcare providers put in the patient's medical records
  b. Conversations doctor has about the patient's care or treatment with nurses and others
  c. Information about the patient's in the patient's health insurer's computer system
  d. Billing information

5.2.1.1 Public Health

Protecting public health, that *the needs of the many outweigh the needs of the few or the one* (quote for science fiction enthusiasts) provides exceptions of disclosure of ePHI. If an imminent disease outbreak can be detected and treated quickly, many lives can be saved. In 1918, the flu epidemic, later identified as H1N1 influenza virus, infected 500 million out of a worldwide population of less than 2 billion; essentially 1 in 3 people were infected and 50 to 100 million died, about 4% of the planet's population. It is estimated that during World War I, the movements of troops and refugees and malnutrition due to the conflict added to the deadly transmission. The variants that later occurred were H1N2 and H3N2. In 1976, a H1N1 virus was detected in Fort Dix and never left the facility due to enhanced reporting procedures. In the next year, roughly 48 million people were vaccinated and very few died that year. One side effect of rushing out a vaccine was the occurrence of the 500 additional cases of the Guillain–Barré syndrome, a nervous system disease that causes paralysis, or an increased occurrence of the syndrome for 1 in 100,000 vaccinations. Hundreds, as opposed to millions, were potentially spared infection by early detection and treatment. In today's global village, airline travel has the potential of spreading disease quickly, so early detection is even more urgent.

The privacy rules permit covered entities to disclose PHI for public health purposes:

The term "covered entity" under the HIPAA Privacy Rule refers to three specific groups: including *health plans, healthcare clearinghouses*, and *healthcare providers* that transmit health information electronically. Covered entities under the HIPAA Privacy Rule must comply with the Rule's requirements for safeguarding the privacy of protected health information. (http://www.hhs.gov/ocr/privacy/hipaa/understanding/special/index.html).

5.2.1.2 Research

Medical research, using deidentified information, is allowed but under strict guidelines. In general, as in all medical research, if deidentified information is required, i.e., any information that can be used to identify subjects must be removed to ensure privacy. Certain privacy provisions listed below may be waived.

1. Institutional review board (IRB) or privacy board approval. With the permission of an IRB or privacy board, the patient privacy rights can be waived:

   Exclusions and required documentation:

   a. A statement that the IRB or privacy board has determined that the alteration or waiver of authorization, in whole or in part, satisfies the three criteria in the rule:
      i. A description of the PHI that explains why access has been determined to be necessary
      ii. A statement that waiver has been reviewed and approved under either normal or expedited review procedures
      iii. The signature of the chair or other designated member of the IRB is affixed
2. The criteria of patient privacy waiver include
   a. A plan to protect identifying information from improper use and disclosure.
   b. A plan to destroy the identifier's consistent with the conduct of the research, unless there is a health or research justification for retaining the identifiers or such retention is otherwise required by the law.
   c. Written assurances that the PHI will not be reused or disclosed to any other person or entity, except as required by law, for authorized oversight of the research project.
3. Preparatory to research, the PHI being sought is used to prepare a research protocol, to determine the feasibility of the research.
4. Research on protected health information of decedents: in order to study deceased individuals, release of PHI may be granted.
5. Limited data sets with a data use agreement: limited data on sex, age, and demographics may be released as long as they don't contain PHI of an individual, relatives, or household members.

   This data use agreement should contain the following information:

   1. Establish the permitted uses and disclosures of the limited data set by the recipient, consistent with the purposes of the research, which may not include any use or disclosure that would violate the rule if done by the covered entity.
   2. Limit who can use or receive the data.
   3. Require the recipient to agree to the following:
      i. Do not use or disclose the information other than that as permitted by the data use agreement or indicated by law.
      ii. Use appropriate safeguards to prevent the use or disclosure of the information.
      iii. Report any use or disclosure of the information not provided for by the data use agreement of which the recipient becomes aware.
      iv. Ensure agents and subcontractors, to whom the recipient provides the limited data set, agree to the same restrictions not to identify the information or contact the individual.
6. Research use/disclosure with individual authorization.
   a. Authorization for a research purpose may state that the authorization does not expire till the end of the research.
   b. Can be coupled with multiple research activities, such as clinical trials.
   c. For future research, the authorization can indicate that it can be used for future trials so long as the authorization describes the nature of those future trials.
7. In accounting for research disclosures, the individual has the right to request a detailed accounting of all research uses of his or her PHI.

5.2.2 Security

The HIPAA Security Rule requires "administrative, physical and technical safeguards to ensure the confidentiality, integrity, and security of electronic protected health information." The original documentation was created in 1996 but the Final Security Rules were published in 2003 (http://www.hhs.gov/ocr/privacy/hipaa/administrative/securityrule/securityrulepdf.pdf).

The security rule applies to all healthcare providers, clearing houses, and third-party vendors who maintain EHRs.

5.2.2.1 Administrative Controls and Safeguards

A covered entity must periodically assess security and risks to electronic PHIs (ePHIs) and reduce risks to a minimum. The organization must appoint a security officer responsible for security policy and implementation. Role-based access should be implemented where only individuals who have a need to access that data have security privileges. Finally, periodic training and assessment are required to ensure policies are being met.

The *security administrative controls* fall into three categories:

1. Practices

   Company practices

   a. Education
   b. Security practices
   c. Privacy practices

   Technical practices

   d. Physical security
   e. Disaster recovery
   f. Access controls
   g. Authentication
   h. Secure communications: internal and external
   i. Software best practices
2. Procedures
   a. Designating an information security officer
   b. Auditing and implementing periodic evaluations of systems
   c. Instituting sanctions for infractions
   d. Informing patients of privacy rights
   e. Educating patients in their rights to obtain a copy of their medical records
   f. Controlling access of PHIs to a minimum needed by third parties
3. Policies
   a. A covered entity must adhere to HIPAA security and privacy policies.
   b. A covered entity must retain for 6 years written policies, procedures, actions, and assessments.
   c. A covered entity must periodically update its rules and procedures related to security practices.

The term "covered entity" under the HIPAA Privacy Rule refers to three specific groups, including *health plans*, healthcare *clearinghouses*, and healthcare *providers* that transmit health information electronically. Covered entities under the HIPAA Privacy Rule must comply with the Rule's requirements for safeguarding the privacy of protected health information (http://www.hrsa.gov/healthit/toolbox/HealthITAdoptiontoolbox/PrivacyandSecurity/entityhipaa.html).

Physical controls: Facility access must be limited to authorized users. Computers and electronic media, such as flash drives and DVDs, must be monitored and procedures in place to limit access and policies for wiping unused hard drives and disposal of retired systems.

Technical controls: Access controls must be implemented to ensure only authorized personnel have privileges. Audits must periodically access procedures and track changes in records, i.e., improper changes or deletion of records. Transmission of data must be monitored for unauthorized access.

5.2.2.2 Breach Notification Rule

This rule requires that all HIPAA organizations must notify the Federal Trade Commission of any unauthorized access of ePHIs. The HIPAA rules define electronic protected health information (ePHI) "as the individually identifiable health information held or transmitted in any form or medium by these HIPAA covered entities and business associates, subject to certain limited exceptions." In all cases, the security rule requires all individuals whose information has been accessed be notified.

1. In breaches involving more than 500 individuals, the security rule requires that they notify the secretary of the HHS immediately (Section 164.408).
    a. In this category that involves greater than 500 individuals, the rule requires media organizations be notified (Section 164.406 implements section 13402(e)(2) of the act).
    b. The law also requires, in this category, that covered entities and business associates be notified.
2. In breaches including fewer than 500 individuals, the organization can retail a log and submit it to the secretary of the HHS at the end of the year during which the breaches have occurred.

In 2007, according to the HHS, a state mental health agency reported the loss of 2.9 million records, which was the highest for that year, followed by 375,000, which was the next highest. Table 5.1 illustrates that the costs were approximately $17 million to remediate this breach (Table 5.1).

5.2.2.3 Encrypted PHI

If one of the covered entities chooses to encrypt the individual's medical information and there is unauthorized access, "they will not be required to provide breach notification because the information is not considered 'unsecured protected health information' as it has been rendered unusable, unreadable, or indecipherable to unauthorized individuals."

5.2.2.4 Penalties

Noncompliance of HIPAA Title II results in civil and criminal penalties. It is enforced by the HHS OCR. The maximum penalty of $250,000 and 10 years in prison is imposed for obtaining PHI for commercial, malicious intent or personal gain. Table 5.2 lists the penalties, maximum prison terms, and guidelines.

TABLE 5.1 HHS Provided Data of a Single Breach of 2.8 Million Health Records in 2007

Cost Elements	Number of Breaches	Number of Affected Individuals	Cost/Breach	Cost/Affected Individuals	Cost
E-mail and 1st class mail	106	2,888,804	$12,986	$0.477	1,376,528
Alternative notices media notice	70	2,888,804	487	0.012	34,080
Toll-free number	70	2,888,804	117,676	2.851	8,237,309
Imput cost to affected individuals	70	2,888,804	103,172	2.500	7,222,010
Notice to media breach 500+	56	2,887,032	75	0.001	4,200
Report to the secretary	56	2,887,032	75	0.001	4,200
Investigation costs:					
Under 500	50	1,772	400	11	20,000
Over 500	56	2,887,032	2,211	0.043	123,800
Annual report to the secretary	106	2,888,804	30	0.001	3, 180
Total cost			160,616	5.89	17,025,306

Source: Privacy Rights Clearinghouse, a California Nonprofit Corporation, http://www/datalossdb.org.

TABLE 5.2   HIPAA Title II Penalties

Fines (%)	Maximum Prison Terms	Guidelines
250,000	10 years	Obtaining PHI for commercial, malicious intent or personal gain
100,000	5 years	Getting PHI under false pretenses.
50,000	1 year	Knowingly and wrongfully using PHI data
25,000 per year	For each violation	For noncompliance, it is determined that the infraction was not intentional and remediation, once found, was corrected in 30 days

TABLE 5.3   Administrative Transaction Codes

Eligibility for benefits	270
Eligibility response by insurance	271
Claim status inquiry	276
Referrals	278
Claim status response	277
Claim submission	835
Claim payment	837

5.2.2.5 Transaction Codes (Title II)

Under Title II that describes privacy and security are certain transactions to support administrative functions such as eligibility for reimbursement, treatment, and referrals. This will be coordinated by the Center for Medicare and Medicaid Services and include Employer Identification Numbers (Table 5.3).

Level II: Computer Security Best Practices

5.3 Defense in Depth

The concept of defense in depth involves layers of security, similar to an onion, to ensure that if any breach occurs, it can be detected and repulsed before it can access the next level where sensitive information is obtained. An analogy would be a bank, wherein there are gates, cameras, and security guards at the entrance. If any suspicious individual enters, they are stopped or an alarm is triggered. If they pass through this first level and approach the teller, that individual could also sound an alarm. There are additional layers of locked drawers, daily audits of finances and tellers, and finally a vault with extreme levels of security and access controls for a limited set of individuals. Cameras and security code access, audits, and forensics allow them to reconstruct events. If all these failed, there are extreme federal penalties for robbing banks (Figure 5.3).

The following defense-in-depth strategies were described in a National Securities Agency (NSA) white paper (http://www.nsa.gov/ia/_files/support/defenseindepth.pdf). The term "information assurance" (IA) is used in the context of guaranteeing the safety and validity of data. It can be achieved by applying the following security services: *availability, integrity, authentication, confidentiality,* and *nonrepudiation.*

(*Nonrepudiation* legally refers to signatures or contracts where their validity is being *repudiated* or questioned. The term "nonrepudiated" means it cannot be questioned; it is definitely valid. In computer terms, it often refers to the proof of the integrity and origin of data or a digital signature, the goal being that the validity is so secure that it can't be questioned or can't be repudiated.)

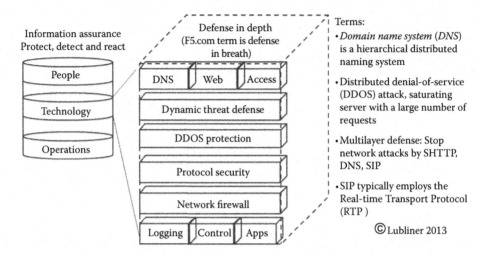

FIGURE 5.3   Defense-in-depth strategies.

5.3.1 Achieving Information Assurance

1. People
   a. Process begins with a chief security officer
   b. Policies and Procedures: Assigning roles and responsibilities
   c. Training and Awareness: System administrators and accountability
   d. System security administration
   e. Physical security: Control
   f. Personnel security monitor facilities
2. Technology
   a. Architectures for IA validated by a third party
      i. Defense in depth (can be attacked internally or externally)
         1. Defend the network from denial-of-service attacks or distributed denial-of-service attack, saturating the server with a large number of requests.
         2. Defend the computer systems infrastructure boundaries: firewalls, intrusion detection, and access controls (Figure 5.4).
         3. For layered defenses, any defense can be broken, but if one layer is breached and detected, that provides time for a response (www.NSA.gov).

Examples of layered defenses		
Class of attack	*First line of defense*	*Second line of defense*
Passive	Link and Network Layer Encryption and Traffic Flow Security	Security Enabled Applications
Active	Defend the Enclave Boundaries	Defend the Computing Environment
Insider	Physical and Personnel Security	Authenticated Access Controls, Audit
Close-In	Physical and Personnel Security	Technical Surveillance Countermeasures
Distribution	Trusted Software Development and Distribution	Run Time Integrity Controls

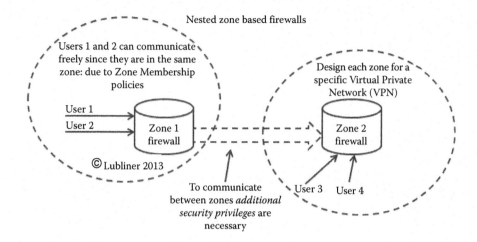

FIGURE 5.4 Nested security zones increase protection.

providing nested firewalls, each with a layer of detection and protection: a good resource is from Cisco Systems (http://www.cisco.com/c/en/us/td/docs/security/security_management/cisco_security_manager/security_manager/3-3-1/configuration/example/ZBF_ConfigExample.html).

4. Use strong key message encryption such as public key encryption (PKE).
5. Use infrastructure monitoring software to aid in intrusion detection. The National Institute of Standards and Technology (NIST) has a guide for intrusion detection best practices (http://csrc.nist.gov/publications/nistpubs/800-94/SP800-94.pdf).

3. Operations
   a. Security policies
   b. Security management
      i. Timely security patches and virus updates
   c. Certification and accreditation
   d. Key management
   e. System assessments
      i. Providing regular security readiness assessments and vulnerability assessments including independent third parties.
      ii. The National Information Assurance Partnership between NSA and NIST along with the International Organization for Standardization (ISO) sets standards for IA (http://niap.nist.gov) and also lists recommended IA software.
   f. Disaster recovery
      i. Risk assessment
      ii. Impact analysis
         1. Take inventory of assets.
         2. Assign roles.
         3. Sell plan to management.
         4. Identify possible solutions.
         5. Choose solution.
         6. Create a recovery manual.
      iii. Disaster recovery testing and planning
         1. Test recovery plan.
         2. Train, maintain, and document.

The following sections describe specific strategies and technologies to enhance system security. This is not an exhaustive list, rather it is a reprehensive compendium of defense-in-depth technologies.

5.3.2 Access Controls

Physical

5.3.2.1 Biometrics

Biometrics refer to a some physiological characteristic, such as fingerprints, that can be input and converted into digital format and can be used to verify an individual's identity. Instead of using something physical in your possession, a key or a password, biometrics uses who you are to identify you. Biometrics can use physical characteristics, like your face, fingerprints, irises or veins, or behavioral characteristics like your voice, handwriting, or typing rhythm. Most systems don't store the complete image or recording. They instead analyze your trait and translate it into a code or graph. Then they compare the trait to the information on file.

5.3.2.1.1 Iris Scanners

Iris scanners capture a series of 2D Gabor wavelets, which are linear filters used in edge detection that capture frequency and orientation, to extract features that are represented as phasors, i.e., vectors in a plane. This process is so compact that the iris pattern can be stored in a few hundred bytes. A link to an iris scanning code example in MATLAB®, or Matrix Laboratory that is a programing language environment created by MathWorks, illustrates the matrix multiplications. An example of IRIS scanning software algorithms is shown in Figure 5.5.

Multiple authentication layers, similar to defense in depth, increase the level of security. A *layered system* combines a biometric input with a secondary source such as a pin number. Multimodal systems combine multiple biometric systems.

5.3.2.1.2 Fingerprint Scanner

Ridges on fingers evolved as beneficial evolutionary trait that enabled individual to better grip objects. The actual pattern is created in the womb and is caused by a series of random events and by the

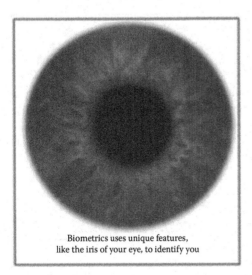
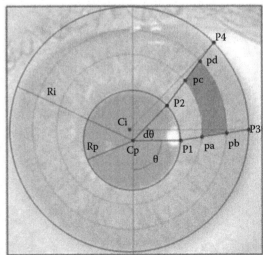

FIGURE 5.5 (See color insert.) Biometric input and retinal analysis, using phasors (vectors in a plane). (From MATLAB® http://matlabsproj.blogspot.com/2012/06/iris-detection-matlab.html; Photo courtesy of Iridian Technologies.)

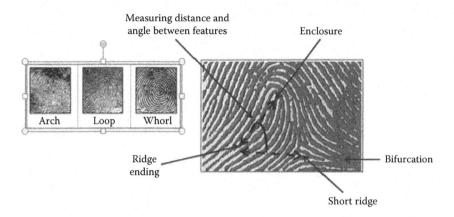

FIGURE 5.6 Fingerprint analysis.

composition and density of the surrounding amniotic fluid. A fingerprint scanner compares features of the fingerprint referred to as *minutiae*. The software focuses on points where ridge lines end or where a ridge splits into two bifurcations or two lines. Collectively, these unique features are referred to as typica (every time a ridge line splits or end its called a typica) (Figure 5.6).

5.3.2.1.3 DNA Scanner

The Federal DNA Identification Act in 1994 established a National DNA Indexing System (NDIS) that contains DNA profiles, which is part of the larger FBI DNA indexing System (CODIS) that includes the software and infrastructure to support this endeavor. The NDIS System is a nationwide database containing the DNA profiles contributed by federal, state, and local participating forensic laboratories. CODIS matching algorithm searches a number of indexes, following strict rules that protect personal privacy. The CODIS algorithm produces a list of *candidate matches* that they referred to a DNA specialist.

Source: (http://www.nature.com/scitable/topicpage/forensics-dna-fingerprinting-and-codis-736).

There are 13 DNA core STR Loci, points in the DNA that are used for matching purposes. An STR contains repeating units of a short, three- to four-nucleotide DNA sequence. The number of repeats within an STR is referred to as an allele. the STR known as D7S820, found on chromosome 7, contains between 5 and 16 repeats of GATA. Therefore, there are 12 different alleles possible for the D7S820 STR.

The FBI established the frequency with which each allele of each of the 13 core STRs naturally occurs in people of different ethnic backgrounds. the FBI-determined STR allele frequencies reveals that the probability of two unrelated Caucasians having identical STR profiles, or so-called "DNA fingerprints," is approximately 1 in 575 trillion [9] (Reilly, 2001) (Figure 5.7).

The CODIS database as of 2013 had 10 million offenders and 1.5 million arrestees, not convicted.

You can extract DNA from almost any tissue, including hair, fingernails, bones, teeth, and bodily fluids. The most commonly used database in the United States is CODIS. CODIS is maintained by the FBI. By law, authorities in all 50 states must collect DNA samples from convicted sex offenders for inclusion in CODIS. Some states also require all convicted felons to submit DNA. The FBI's CODIS database uses samples that have undergone STR analysis examining 13 loci.

5.3.2.1.4 Biometric Architecture

Biometric systems are comprised of three components: sensors that capture the trait, digital processors that capture and store the data, and analytical software that processes and analyzes the image. The environment and the quality of the reading, for example, in fingerprinting, may be damaged by some physical activity. Another example is voice prints that can be affected by colds. The measurement accuracy will determine

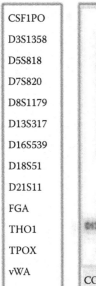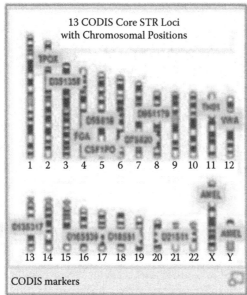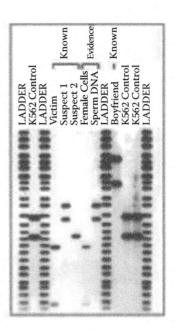

FIGURE 5.7 **(See color insert.)** There are 13 genetic markers that searched in DNA samples.

the probability of a correct match. False acceptance rate refers to the percentage of incorrect individuals the system recognizes. The false rejection rate refers to the percentage of correct individuals the system refuses. The failure-to-enroll rate refers to the percentage of individuals the system will not enroll due to the quality of a unique biometric reading, i.e., the fingerprints are so scarred individual features are not distinct enough. Finally, the failure-to-acquire rate refers to the number of times it takes before the system recognizes them.

Authentication refers to determining the validity of a user's identity by a username, password, biometrics, smart card, or some yet-to-be-determined technologies.

5.3.2.2 Encryption: Cryptography

The science of analyzing and encrypting data is called "cryptography." "Encryption" is defined as encoding messages or information so that only authorized parties can read them.

5.3.2.2.1 Symmetric Key Encryption

Two popular encryption techniques are symmetric key encryption (SKE) and PKE. SKE *uses the same keys to encrypt and decrypt messages.* The major drawback is that both systems need to have the key; this flaw is not true with PKE. The SKE ciphers are prone to attack using a plaintext attack if you have both sides of the message. The term was coined in Bletchley Park, England, during World War II when the technique was used to break German codes.

If the keys are sufficiently random, the code can be very difficult to crack. The Data Encryption Standard, a symmetric cipher, was used by the NIST and later replaced by the Advanced Encryption Standard in 2002.

5.3.2.2.2 Asymmetric Public Key Encryption

Public key encryption (PKE) systems use asymmetric keys, i.e., different keys at both ends to encrypt and decrypt. It is virtually impossible and computationally infeasible to determine the private key from the original message and public key. The public key is published and the private key is only known to the receiver. The message can't be decrypted by anyone but the owner of the private key (Figure 5.8).

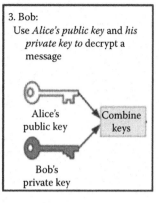

FIGURE 5.8   Public key encryption system.

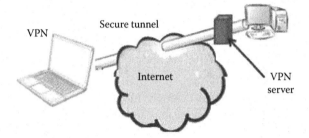

FIGURE 5.9   Virtual private network creates a secure connection utilizing tunneling.

5.3.2.3 Virtual Private Networks

A virtual private network (VPN) allows you to send information securely over the Internet as if it were your own private network. It sets up a virtual point-to-point connection, i.e., a permanent link between two users, using either dedicated connections, encrypting the traffic or virtual tunneling protocols that appear as public messages. Here are some examples: Microsoft's point-to-point tunneling protocol, Cisco's Generic Routing Encapsulation, Transport Layer Security (TLS/SSL), Secure Shell VPN, and Internet Protocol Security for IPv6, which uses a 128 bit address space.

There are some advantages of VPNs:

1. Message integrity, tampering can be detected.
2. Messages are authenticated.
3. Encryption ensures confidentiality of messages.

Before the tunnel can be established, both ends of the connection are authenticated with passwords, biometrics, etc. VPNs can also be used for mobile devices by permanently connecting to a fixed IP address, which are referred to as mobile VPNs (mVPNs). An mVPN maintains a virtual connection even when the endpoint changes and seamlessly handles the network log-ins (Figure 5.9).

Level III: Advanced Topics

5.4 Cyber Security for Medical Devices

Medical devices are increasingly connected to the network to seamlessly exchange data with EHRs and to send remote alarms. Some systems/monitors are configured to send diagnostics to manufacturer and provide periodic software updates. The imbedded security on medical devices is often limited and susceptible to malware. The Federal Drug Administration (FDA) has published some lists of concerns and vulnerabilities for medical devices (http://www.fda.gov/medicaldevices/safety/alertsandnotices/ucm356423.htm).

Here are FDA warnings published on June 13, 2013:

- Network-connected/network-configured medical devices *infected or disabled by malware*
- The presence of *malware on hospital computers*, smartphones, and tablets, targeting mobile devices using wireless technology to *access patient data, monitoring systems, and implanted patient devices*
- *Uncontrolled distribution of passwords*, disabled passwords, hard-coded passwords for software *intended for privileged device access* (e.g., to administrative, technical, and maintenance personnel)
- *Failure to provide timely security software updates and patches to medical devices* and networks and to address-related vulnerabilities in older medical device models (legacy devices)
- *Security vulnerabilities in off-the-shelf software* designed to prevent unauthorized device or network access, such as plaintext or no authentication, hard-coded passwords, documented service accounts in service manuals, and poor coding/SQL injection

For healthcare facilities, the FDA is recommending that you take steps to evaluate your network security and protect your hospital system. In evaluating network security, hospitals and healthcare facilities should consider

- Restricting unauthorized access to the network and networked medical devices
- Making certain appropriate antivirus software and firewalls up to date
- Monitoring network activity for unauthorized use
- Protecting individual network components through routine and periodic evaluation, including updating security patches and disabling all unnecessary ports and services
- Contacting the specific device manufacturer if you think you may have a cybersecurity problem related to a medical device; that is, if you are unable to determine the manufacturer or cannot contact the manufacturer, the FDA and DHS ICS-CERT may be able to assist in vulnerability reporting and resolution
- Developing and evaluating strategies to maintain critical functionality during adverse conditions

5.4.1 Future Medical Security Risks for Medical Devices

Can implantable devices such as a pacemakers or medical delivery systems be hacked? Maybe. As more devices are networked to provide real-time monitoring, the potential exists. Medical devices are microprocessors, with software, connected to dedicated hardware potentially linked wirelessly through Bluetooth connected to a smartphone or tablet to transmit medical data, monitor battery life, and have the ability for periodic software updates. These systems have rudimentary security protection, at the moment. In 2012 on the TV series *Homeland*, a scenario was used to kill the vice president by attacking the software on his or her pacemaker. Six months earlier in 2012, the FDA listed guidelines to assess medical security risks on medical equipment. Risk assessment of potential security threats seems prudent if not actually imminent.

Risk management, as defined by the ISO 31000 (http://www.iso.org/iso/home/standards/iso31000.htm), refers to a coordinated set of activities and methods that is used to direct an organization and to control the many risks that can affect its ability to achieve objectives. According to the *Introduction to ISO 31000 2009*, the term "risk management" also refers to the architecture that is used to manage risk. This architecture includes risk management principles, a risk management framework, and a risk management process.

In a recent publication, in April 2014 by the Healthcare IT Systems, a group of cyber security experts were given access to a number of Midwest healthcare facilities. Over a 2-year period, they found numerous vulnerabilities in devices: the "team found that drug infusion pumps used for morphine drips and chemotherapy could be remotely accessed to change dosages. An another example, they found bluetooth enabled defibrillators that could be manipulated to deliver random shocks and prevent shocks from happening" (http://healthcareitsystems.com/2014/04/hacking-medical-devices-is-easier-than-you-think/).

5.5 Summary

The HIPAA in 1996 began the process of quantifying privacy and security standards for patients' protected health information (PHIs). Since then, computer security, in all aspects of our daily lives, has risen to a higher state of concern. As more of our infrastructures are mobile and linked and electronic transfers and payments and even watching entertainment on mobile devices have linked our planet into a global communications web, the security of information will be an ever-increasing concern. Will there ever be an absolute solution? No. An apt analogy would be bank robbers. As we became more urban, more centralized banks evolved and became more attractive targets. The technology evolved at the same pace to prevent theft. That has made physically robbing banks less likely or at least reducing the loss per incident. Electronically hacking banks and credit card companies has increased. Can we stop using credit cards or electronic funds transfer? The benefits clearly outweigh the risks. As one technology is secure, other new technologies and vulnerabilities arise. So too is the issue of medical security, the benefits of EHRs, and the networked medical devices that far outweigh the risks.

Questions

Level I

1. Explain the scope of HIPAA Title II Security and Privacy. How do they differ?

   Privacy rule component:

   a. Explain at least three provisions of the privacy rule; be specific.
   b. Describe the public health exceptions to the privacy rule, and explain in what context do they apply?
   c. Describe the privacy rule exclusions for medical research.

   Security rule component:

   d. Describe the administrative safeguards used in implementing the security rule.
   e. Explain the security rule safeguards.
2. When there is unauthorized access to patient data, what are the hospital's or covered entity's required notification obligations? Be specific.
   a. What are the potential penalties?

Level II

3. Explain the concept of defense in depth.
   a. What is IA? Explain steps to achieve IA: people, technology, operations, disaster recovery, and system architecture.
4. What are access controls? Provide a few examples and specific details.
5. Explain the need for encryption to enhance HIPAA Title II.

Level III

6. Explain cyber security for medical devices.
   a. Explain the potential security concerns for medical devices.
7. Research articles on examples of potential security breaches on medical devices.

Glossary

CODIS: The program that was established by the Federal DNA Identification Act in 1994 as a national identification index of DNA records.

Defense in depth: The concept that involves layers, similar to an onion, of security to ensure that if any breach occurs, it can be detected and repulsed.

Privacy rule: This sets federal standards to protect individuals' PHI and limits to disclosure without patient authorization: *electronic protected health information (ePHI)*.

HIPAA Title II: The law that describes *security* and *privacy*, and sets limits and conditions on the use and disclosure of medical information without patient authorization.

Institutional review board (IRB): Or privacy board.

Public key encryption (PKE): A system that uses asymmetric keys, i.e., different keys at both ends to encrypt and decrypt.

Symmetric key encryption (SKE): The technique that uses the same keys to encrypt and decrypt messages.

Virtual Private Network (VPN): The network that allows you to send information securely over the Internet as if it were your own private network. It sets up a virtual point-to-point connection, i.e., a permanent link between two users, using either dedicated connections, encrypting the traffic or virtual tunneling protocols that appear as public messages.

References

1. http://www.fda.gov/medicaldevices/safety/alertsandnotices/ucm356423.htm
2. http://www.deloitte.com/assets/DcomUnitedStates/Local%20Assets/Documents/Center%20 for%20health%20solutions/us_chs_networkedmedicaldevice_091913.pdf
3. HIPAA fines for ePHI (2014) for two NYC hospitals, http://www.hhs.gov/news/press/2014pres/ 05/20140507b.html. HHS News Release.
4. http://matlabsproj.blogspot.com/2012/06/iris-detection-matlab.html
5. http://www.nature.com/scitable/topicpage/forensics-dna-fingerprinting-and-codis-736
6. http://www.hhs.gov/ocr/privacy/hipaa/understanding/coveredentities/usesanddisclosuresfortpo. html
7. http://www.hhs.gov/ocr/privacy/hipaa/administrative/securityrule/securityrulepdf.pdf
8. http://www.hrsa.gov/healthit/toolbox/HealthITAdoptiontoolbox/PrivacyandSecurity/ entity hipaa.html
9. Reilly, P. (2001), http://www.nature.com/nrg/journal/v2/n4/full/nrg0401_313a.html.
10. Yang, J. and Jayakumar, A. (2014). Target security breach. http://www.washingtonpost.com/ business/economy/target-says-70-million-customers-were-hit-by-dec-data-breach-more-than- first-reported/2014/01/10/0ada1026–79fe–11e3–8963–b4b654bcc9b2_story.html.
11. MATLAB®, http://matlabsproj.blogspot.com/2012/06/iris-detection-matlab.html

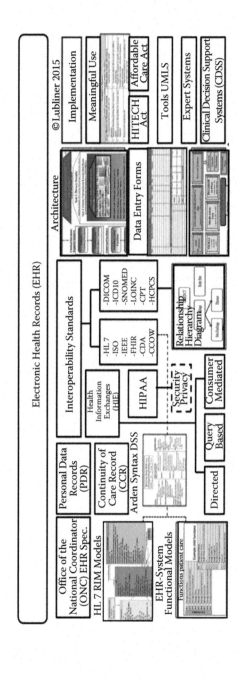

FIGURE 3.1 Electronic health records.

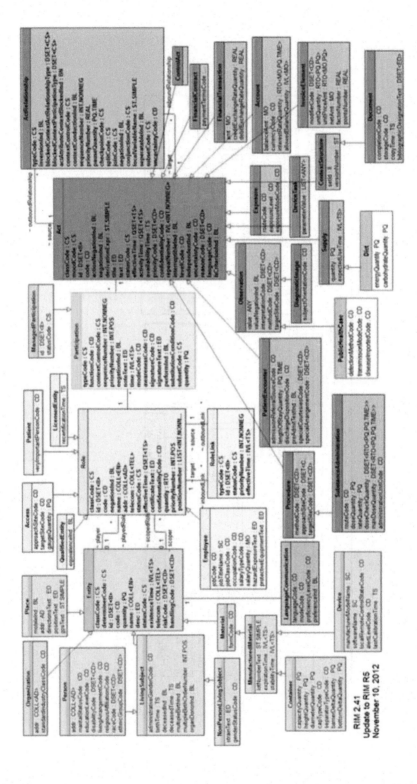

FIGURE 3.4 Health Level 7 Reference Information Model models a visual representation of domains and messages exchanged. (From http://www.hl7standards.com/blog/2011/05/31/hl7-v3-rim-is-it-really-that-intimidating/.)

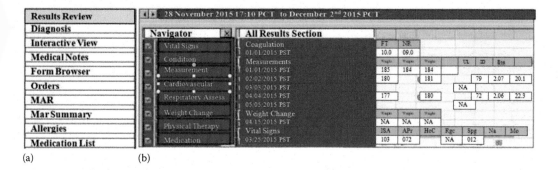

(a)   (b)

FIGURE 3.16   (a, b) Navigator on left; patient status view on right.

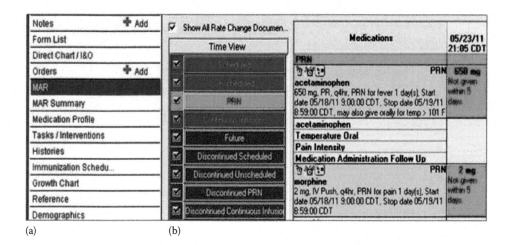

(a)   (b)

FIGURE 3.17   (a, b) Medication Administration Record (MAR) delivery timetable, MAR drug summary table. (From http://www.pearsonhighered.com/realehprep/learn-about/what-is.html.)

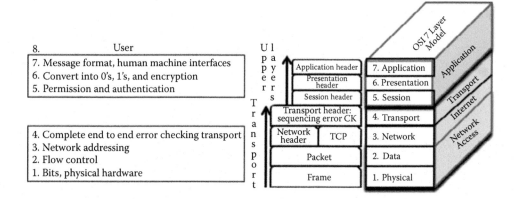

FIGURE 4.3   ISO seven-layer model.

Pill images of the same drug **Diciofenac Sodium 100MG** produced by different manufacturers

Property	Image 1	Image 2	Image 3
Acq Date	12-02-2009	02-07-2011	12-19-2012
Manufacturer	Actavis Elizabeth LLC	Watson Laboratories, Inc.	Teva Pharmaceuticals USA Inc
SplSetId	NONE	Link to DailyMed	Link to DailyMed
NDC	00228-2717-11	00591-0676-01	00093-1041-01
Shape	ROUND	ROUND	ROUND
Size	9	10	9
Color	YELLOW	RED	PINK
Imprint	R;717	DX41	93;1041
ImprintType	DEBOSSED	DEBOSSED	DEBOSSED

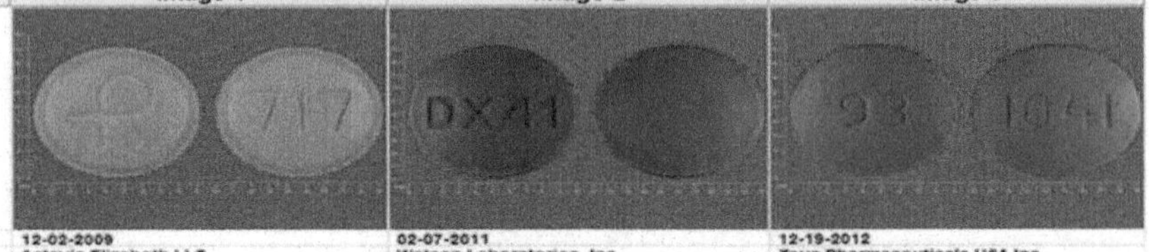

RxNorm thesaurus to multiple data sources and codes for the same medication

Category	Property	Value
NAMES	RxNorm Name	venlafaxine 100 MG Oral Tablet [Effexor]
	RxNorm Synonym	Effexor 100 MG Oral Tablet
	RxNorm Synonym	Effexor 100 MG (as venlafaxine hydrochloride) Oral Tablet
CODES	RxCUI	208848
	UMLSCUI	C0710468
	NDA	NDA020151
	SPL SET ID	cf2d9bee-f8e3-477a-e4b4-f0e82657b7d2
ATTRIBUTES	TTY	SBD
	HUMAN_DRUG	US
	PRESCRIBABLE	Y
	AVAILABLE_STRENGTH	100 MG
SOURCES	Source	Gold Standard Alchemy
	Source	Multum MediSource Lexicon
	Source	Micromedex RED BOOK
	Source	Metathesaurus FDA National Drug Code Directory
	Source	Metathesaurus FDA Structured Product Labels

FIGURE 4.20 RxNav visualization engine visualizing the same drug from multiple manufacturers.

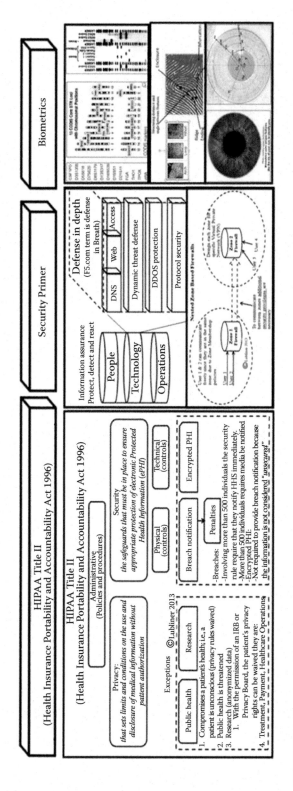

FIGURE 5.1 Security and privacy.

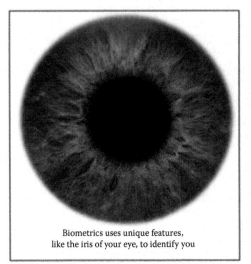
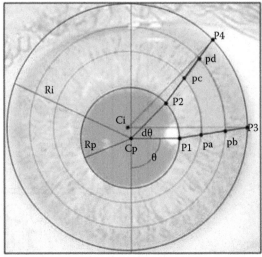

FIGURE 5.5 Biometric input and retinal analysis, using phasors (vectors in a plane). (From MATLAB® http://matlabsproj.blogspot.com/2012/06/iris-detection-matlab.html; Photo courtesy of Iridian Technologies.)

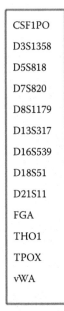
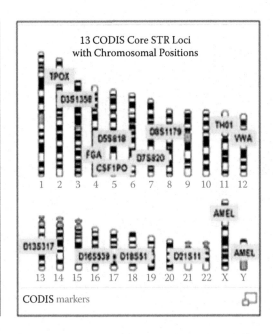
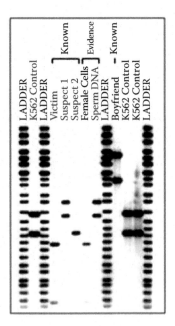

FIGURE 5.7 There are 13 genetic markers that searched in DNA samples.

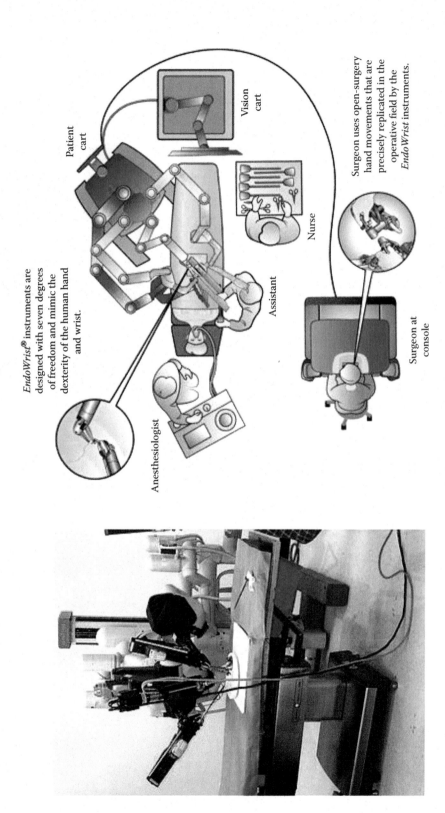

EndoWrist® instruments are designed with seven degrees of freedom and mimic the dexterity of the human hand and wrist.

Patient cart

Vision cart

Nurse

Assistant

Anesthesiologist

Surgeon uses open-surgery hand movements that are precisely replicated in the operative field by the *EndoWrist* instruments.

Surgeon at console

FIGURE 6.2 da Vinci telesurgery system. (From IntuitiveSurgical.com, parent company.)

TABLE 6.4   Examples of On-Demand Medical Consultation Apps

Medical Apps—On-Demand Doctors' Visits (Live Video Consultations and Text Chat Health Inquiries)

Ringadoc http://www.ringadoc.com/	1. 1000 physicians in 40 states 2. Different from other systems that select a doctor from an available online pool for a consult; options include the following: a. Connect with a single primary care physician. b. Leave a text message with the urgency of situation. c. Choice of a larger network of physicians.	$69/month or $868/year

Doctor on Demand http://www.doctorondemand.com/	1. Licensed physicians 2. Nonemergency medical issue 3. Pediatric questions 4. Prescriptions 5. Specialist referral Examples	$40 per call

Short-term prescriptions and Rx refills	Cold, flu, cough, fever, allergies
Urinary tract infections	Pediatric fever, advice, or other issues
Vomiting/ diarrhea	STDs
Rashes/bites/ skin problems	Sports injuries, athlete's foot

3G Doctor (United Kingdom and Ireland) http://www.3gdoctor.com/	1. 24 hours day. 2. Live video chat with a licensed doctor. 3. On-demand doctors are available to diagnose and address minor medical problems such as rashes, aches, or pains. 4. Doctors can recommend treatments and answer health-related questions. 5. Real-time access to your medical records.	£35 per session

(Continued)

TABLE 6.4 (*Continued*) Examples of On-Demand Medical Consultation Apps

Medical Apps—On-Demand Doctors' Visits (Live Video Consultations and Text Chat Health Inquiries)		
Live Chat (consult) Live Person https://www.liveperson.com/experts/ health-medicine	1. A text chat 2. Consult a live medical practitioner 3. Doctor, nurse, oncologist, dentist, physical therapist, nurse, allergist, optometrist, chiropractor, pharmacologist, pregnancy/childbirth specialist, or sex therapist 4. A detailed list of verified professionals to select from 5. Other specialties, education, programming	$1.50/min 
ConsultADoctor http://www.consultadr.com/	1. A service provided for health plans that can be tailored for employers to service the health needs of their employees 2. Nonemergency, preventive, and routine health issues 3. Provides EHRs through the company	
Health book/Health Kit (Apple) https://developer.apple.com/ healthkit/ 	1. System for integrating health and fitness data across Apple's product lines, including charting and long-term trending and individual's health and fitness progress. 2. It is a part of IOS 8. 3. The iWatch will provide additional biometric sensors that will pool all these data into a single location.	

TABLE 6.6 Productivity Apps for Physicians

Mobile MIM
Radiology Visualization Software
http://www.mimsoftware.com/about/news-center/

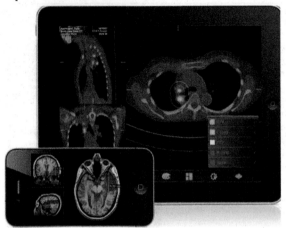

Allows physicians to make diagnosis remotely after analyzing CT and MRI scans
- Approved by the FDA
- Primarily targeted at radiologists
- Take notes; share information
- Tools to measure and highlight features of the scan
- Zoom in on details of the image
  - Voxel-based analysis
  - Region-based analysis
  - SUVR computation
  - Cluster analysis
  - Surface projection analysis
  - Quantitative functional neuroimaging software

Merge iConnect Access System
Radiology imaging
http://mobihealthnews.com/15782/
  merge-healthcare-focuses-on-mobile-access-not-apps-for-remote-medical-
  imaging/

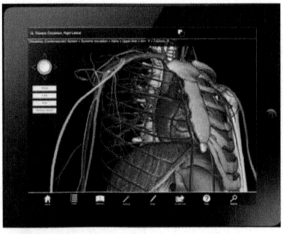

- Sliding one finger across the iPad screen changes the contrast and grayscale of a radiological image.
- Buttons on the screen allow for additional image manipulation.
- A patient history fly-out menu on the edge of the patient screen allows viewers to bring up as many as three studies simultaneously for side-by-side comparison.

drawMD
http://www.drawmd.com/

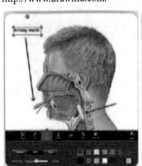
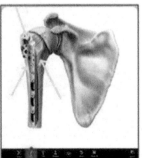

- Allows physicians to show details of what a surgery entails.

(Continued)

TABLE 6.6 (*Continued*)   Productivity Apps for Physicians

Visible Body
http://www.visiblebody.com/ap/ipad/

- 3D human anatomy allows doctors to describe issues to patients.
- Medical students have detailed anatomical models.
- Diagnosis and treatments.
- Allows doctors to hold video conference with patients.

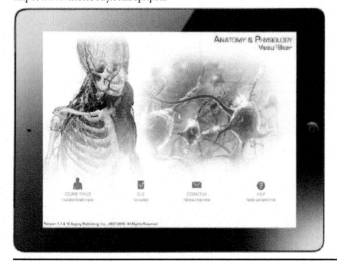

Source: Mobile Medical Productivity Tools. http://www.mednet-tech.com/newsletter/mobile-marketing/top-mobile-apps-for-doctors.

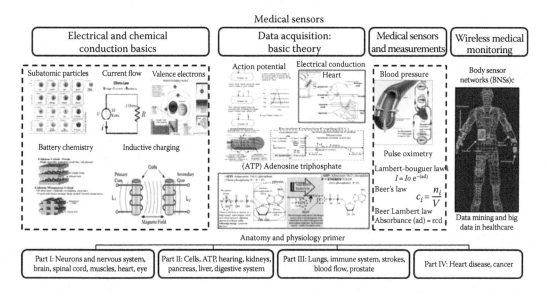

FIGURE 7.1   Medical sensor primer.

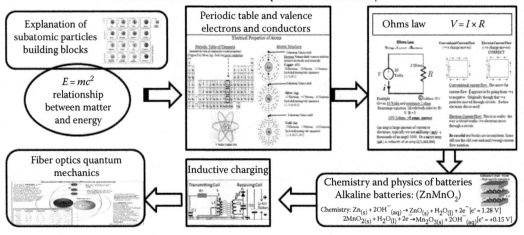

FIGURE 7.2 Linkages between topics covered in the first section.

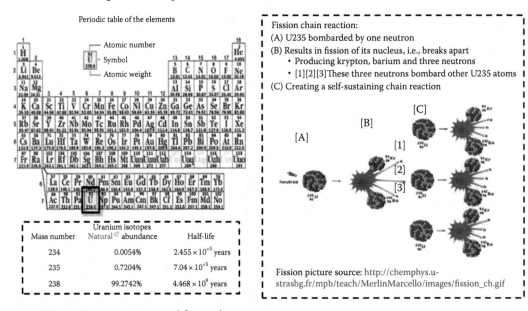

Periodic table of the elements

Fission chain reaction:
(A) U235 bombarded by one neutron
(B) Results in fission of its nucleus, i.e., breaks apart
  • Producing krypton, barium and three neutrons
  • [1][2][3] These three neutrons bombard other U235 atoms
(C) Creating a self-sustaining chain reaction

| Uranium isotopes | | |
Mass number	Natural ⬚ abundance	Half-life
234	0.0054%	$2.455 \times 10^{+5}$ years
235	0.7204%	$7.04 \times 10^{+5}$ years
238	99.2742%	4.468×10^{9} years

Fission picture source: http://chemphys.u-strasbg.fr/mpb/teach/MerlinMarcello/images/fission_ch.gif

FIGURE 7.3 Uranium isotopes and fission chain reaction.

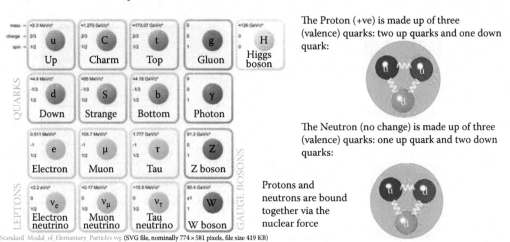

The Proton (+ve) is made up of three (valence) quarks: two up quarks and one down quark:

The Neutron (no change) is made up of three (valence) quarks: one up quark and two down quarks:

Protons and neutrons are bound together via the nuclear force

Standard_Modal_of_Elemantary_Particles.svg (SVG file, nominally 774 × 581 pixels, file size 419 KB)

FIGURE 7.4 Standard model of elementary particles inside a nucleus. (From Creative Commons, http://home.web.cern.ch/about/physics/standard-model).

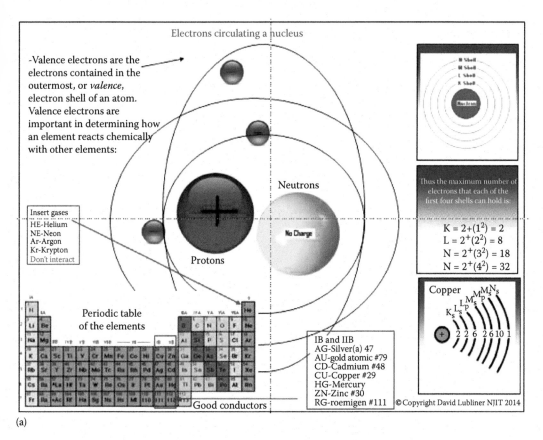

(a)

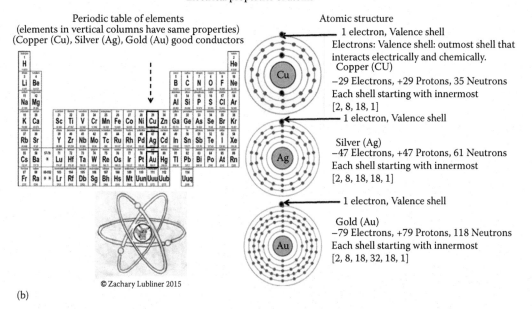

(b)

FIGURE 7.6 Valence electrons, in an atom's outer shell, conduct current (I). (a) Copper (Cu), silver (Ag), and gold (Au) valence electrons. (b) Conductors in the periodic table group 11, all have 1 electron in their valence shell.

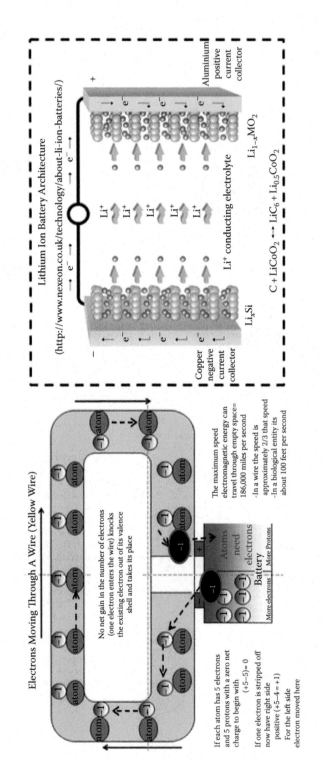

FIGURE 7.7 Battery and electrons (valence shell) moving through a wire and lithium ion battery.

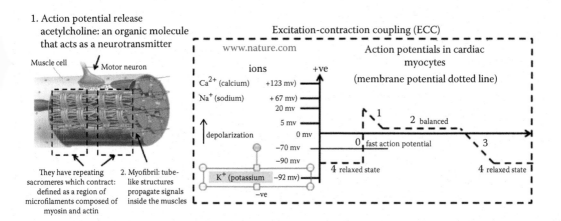

1. Action potential release acetylcholine: an organic molecule that acts as a neurotrophtransmitter

Muscle cell   Motor neuron

They have repeating sacromeres which contract: defined as a region of microfilaments composed of myosin and actin

2. Myofibril: tube-like structures propagate signals inside the muscles

Excitation-contraction coupling (ECC)

www.nature.com

Action potentials in cardiac myocytes
(membrane potential dotted line)

ions   +ve

Ca^{2+} (calcium)   +123 mv

Na$^+$ (sodium)   +67 mv
                  20 mv
depolarization   5 mv
                  0 mv
                  −70 mv
                  −90 mv

K$^+$ (potassium)   −92 mv)
                  −ve

1
2 balanced
0 fast action potential
3
4 relaxed state   4 relaxed state

FIGURE 7.15 Cardiac myocytes and the ECC action potential triggered by sodium, calcium, and potassium ions.

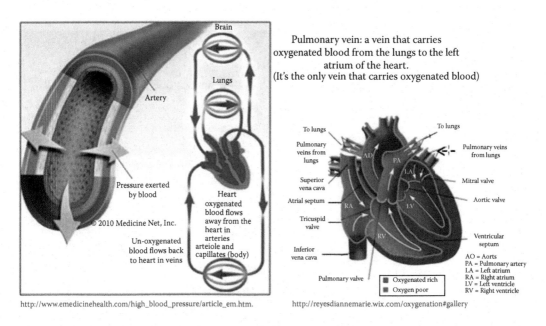

Brain

Lungs

Artery

Pressure exerted by blood

© 2010 Medicine Net, Inc.

Heart oxygenated blood flows away from the heart in arteries arteiole and capillates (body)

Un-oxygenated blood flows back to heart in veins

Pulmonary vein: a vein that carries oxygenated blood from the lungs to the left atrium of the heart.
(It's the only vein that carries oxygenated blood)

To lungs   To lungs
Pulmonary veins from lungs   Pulmonary veins from lungs
Superior vena cava   Mitral valve
Atrial septum   Aortic valve
Tricuspid valve
                                  Ventricular septum
Inferior vena cava
                                  AO = Aorts
                                  PA = Pulmonary artery
Pulmonary valve   ▪ Oxygenated rich   LA = Left atrium
                   ▪ Oxygen poor   RA = Right atrium
                                       LV = Left ventricle
                                       RV = Right ventricle

http://www.emedicinehealth.com/high_blood_pressure/article_em.htm.   http://reyesdiannemarie.wix.com/oxygenation#gallery

FIGURE 7.19 Blood pressure exerted on the artery walls.

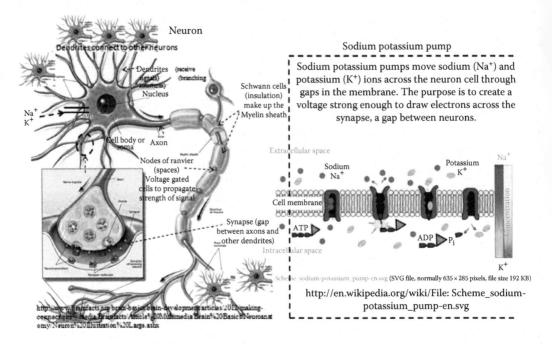

FIGURE 7.20 Neurons and signal transmission across synapses.

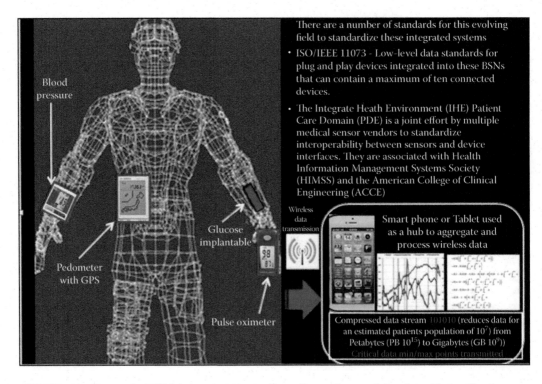

FIGURE 7.25 Case study: BSN data capture integrated into a Smart phone and then forwarded to Cloud storage.

Neurons and the Central Nervous System

The Central Nervous System (CNS) contains two major types of cells, Neurons and Glia. They are responsible for transmitting information. Neurons make up our brains, information processing system, and communicate signals throughout our body. (movement, sensory and healing). Neurons are electrically excitable cells that communicate information through electrical and chemical signals. Neurons are connected via synapses, a gap between neurons, that allows a neuron to pass an electrical or chemical signal to another neuron. (refer to: Chapter 7, Neurons/Action Potential).

Sodium(Na^+)–Potassium(K^+) pumps move positive ions (Na^+ and K^+) across the synapse to make one side more positive (voltage / potential difference) so current flows (electrons) from negative to positive.

Glial cells surround the neurons and provide support and insulation between neurons (composed of Schwann, microglia, astrocytes, satellite and ependymal cells).

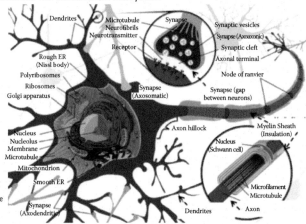

Dendrites: Are thin protrusions from the cell body of a neuron that collect chemical and electrical signals from other neurons. Axons: Are the projection of a neuron that conducts electrical impulses away from the cell body to the axon terminals

Brain

The Cerebrum, it's the evolved part of the brain, the largest part of the human brain, which comprises 4/5 of its weight. It consists of about two-thirds of the brain mass and lies over and around most of the structures of the brain. The outer portion ranges in thickness between 1.5 and 5 mm, and is covered by a thin layer of gray tissue called the cerebral cortex. It is divided into right and left hemispheres that are connected by the corpus callosum.

Cerebrum includes the hippocampus, olfactory bulb and basal ganglia
-Hippocampus, part of the limbic system involved in the integration from short-term to long-term memory
  -Limbic System: emotion, behavior long term memory
  -Olfactory bulb: sense of smell
  -Basal Ganglia: voluntary movements, learning, eye movements, emotion

The Cerebral Cortex surface, folded in large mamals. Two thirds of the surface is embedded groves (valleys) called the "sulci". The ridges are called "gyri".
  • Frontal lobe: voluntary movement, planning. Though
  • Parietal lobe: includes the somatosensory cortex: touch
  • Temporal lobe: hearing and comprehending speech
  • Occipital lobe: visual processing center   © Lubliner 2015

The Cerebellum involved in motor control. The functions include balance, voluntary movements, motor learning, and some congnitive functions (language); (10% volume, but contains 50% of neurons brain.

The Brain Stem includes the midbrain, Pons and medulla oblongata. Functions include the cardiac, respiratory and autonomic (involuntary functions), blood pressure and heart rate.

Cerebral Cortex

Left brain
Analytical thought
language

Right brain
Creativity
Art and Music

Frontal lobe   Parietal lobe
Occipital lobe
Temporal lobe

Brainstem

Cerebellum
(Older part brain)

en.Wikipedia: public domain

Olfactory bulb

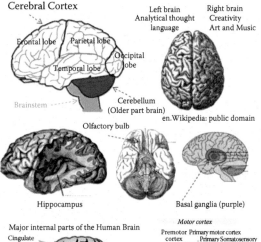

Hippocampus

Basal ganglia (purple)

Major internal parts of the Human Brain

Cingulate
Sulcus
Corpus
Callosum
Dioncophalon
Anterior
Commissure
Temporal
Lobe
Midbrain
Pons

Mid Brain
Pons
Medulla

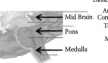

Medulla

Cerebellum

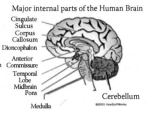

Motor cortex
Premotor Primary motor cortex
cortex   Primary Somatosensory
    SMA cortex   Posterior
                  parietal
                  cortex

The Motor Cortex
involved in control of
voluntary actions

Eye

The Eye detects electromagnetic radiation (light) and converts it into electro-chemical impulses in neurons.

Light enters through the cornea and passes through the pupil. The pupil is surrounded by the Iris, that controls the size and diameter of the pupil. Behind the pupil is the lens that focuses light onto the retina that has photoreceptor cells.

The Retina is a light sensitive layer of tissue made up of photoreceptor cells located at the back of the eye. It's made up of Rods which are used in peripheral vision, and Cones, responsible for color vision.

The actual image is portrayed upside down on the retina. The process of reinventing the image is a combination of brain architecture and processing of the image. (*It starts at the optic nerve where there is a crossing of axons in the optic chiasm to the lateral geniculate nucleus and then to the primary visual cortex.*)

Anatomy of Human Eye

Pupil
Iris
Cornea
Posterior chamber
Anterior chamber (aqueous humour)
Zonular fibres
Lens
Ciliary muscle
Suspensory ligament
Retina
Vitreous humour
Choroid
Sciera
Hyaloid canal
Optic disc
Optic nerve
Fovea
Retinal blood vessels

Image inverted by the eye

Focal point

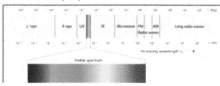

Visible light has a wavelength in the range of 400 nanometers (nm), or 400×10^{-9} m, to 700 nm

Level IV: Anatomy and Physiology Primer

Photosynthesis

- Process by which green plants and certain other organisms transform light into chemical energy.

In green plants, light energy is captured by chlorophyll in the chloroplasts of the leaves and used to convert water, carbon dioxide, and minerals into oxygen and energy-rich organic compounds (simple and complex sugars) that are the basis of both plant and animal life.

- During the light-dependent stage (light reaction), chlorophyll absorbs light energy, which excites some electrons in the pigment molecules to higher energy levels; these leave the chlorophyll and pass along a series of molecules, generating formation of NADPH (an enzyme) and high-energy ATP molecules.
- The NADPH oxidase (nicotinamide adenine dinucleotide phosphate-oxidase) complex is an enzyme complex.
- It generates superoxide by transferring electrons from NADPH inside the cell across the membrane and coupling these to molecular oxygen to produce the superoxide, which is a highly reactive free radical.

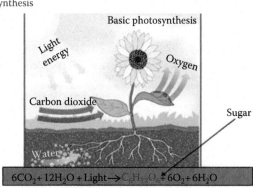

Basic photosynthesis

Light energy

Oxygen

Carbon dioxide

Sugar

Water

$$6CO_2 + 12H_2O + Light \rightarrow C_6H_{12}O_6 + 6O_2 + 6H_2O$$

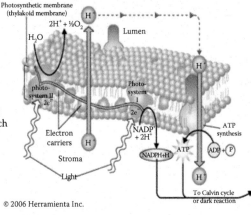

Photosynthetic membrane (thylakoid membrane)

Level IV: Anatomy and Physiology Primer

Kidneys

- Your kidneys are two bean-shaped organs, each about the size of your fist. They are located in the middle of your back, just below your rib cage, on either side of your spine. Your kidneys weigh about 0.5% of your total body weight.
  - Although the kidneys are small organs by weight, they receive a huge amount—20%—of the blood pumped by the heart.
    The large blood supply to your kidneys enables them to do the following tasks:
- Regulate the composition of your blood
  - keep the concentrations of various ions and other important substances constant
  - keep the volume of water in your body constant
  - remove wastes from your body (urea, ammonia, drugs, toxic substances)
  - keep the acid/base concentration of your blood constant
- Help regulate your blood pressure
- Stimulate the making of red blood cells
- Maintain your body's calcium levels

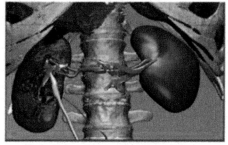

Right Kidney Sectioned in Several Planes

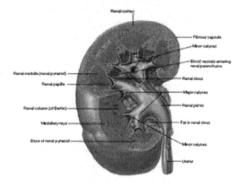

Level IV: Anatomy and Physiology Primer

Liver (continued)

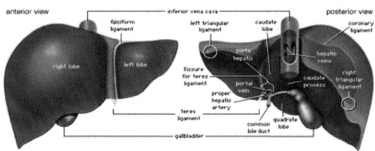

Anterior and posterior views of the liver.

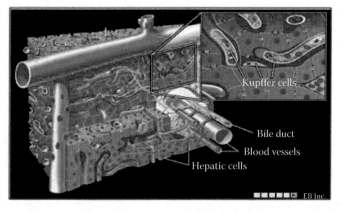

Level IV: Anatomy and Physiology Primer

Lungs

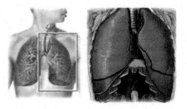

- They take in oxygen, a gas that your body needs, and gets rid of waste carbon dioxide made by your cells.
- You breathe in and out anywhere from 15 to 25 times per minute.
- They also help in regulating the concentration of hydrogen ion (pH) in your blood.
- You don't have to think about breathing because your body's autonomic nervous system controls it.
- The respiratory centers that control your rate of breathing are in the brainstem or medulla. The nerve cells that live within these centers automatically send signals to the diaphragm and intercostal muscles to contract and relax at regular intervals.

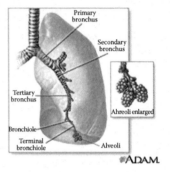

*ADAM.

Level IV: Anatomy and Physiology Primer

Immune System

AIDS

- AIDS (Acquired Immune Deficiency Syndrome) is a disease caused by HIV (the Human Immunodeficiency Virus). This is a particularly problematic disease for the immune system because the virus actually attacks immune system cells.

  - In particular, it reproduces inside Helper T cells and kills them in the process.
  - Without Helper T cells to orchestrate things, the immune system eventually collapses and the victim dies of some other infection that the immune system would normally be able to handle.
  - HIV invades the cells of our immune system and reprograms the cells to become HIV-producing factories.

- Viruses, like HIV, don't have cell walls or a nucleus. Basically, viruses are made up of genetic instructions wrapped inside a protective shell. An HIV virus particle, called a virion, is spherical in shape and has a diameter of about one 1/10,000th of a millimeter.

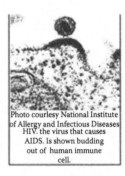

Photo courlesy National Institute of Allergy and Infectious Diseases HIV. the virus that causes AIDS. Is shown budding out of human immune cell.

HIV Replication Animation

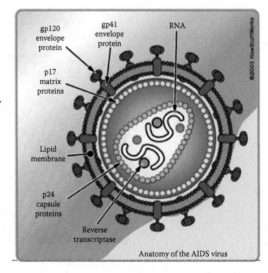

Anatomy of the AIDS virus

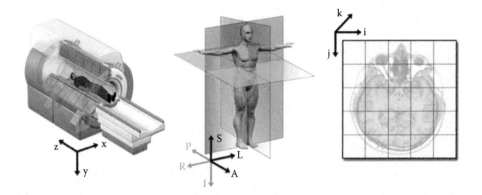

FIGURE 8.6 Reference coordinate system diagrams relating scanners and individual 2D slices. (*Source*: Image from http://www.slicer.org/slicerWiki/index.php/Coordinate_systems)

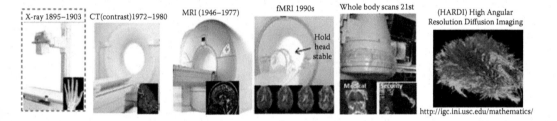

FIGURE 8.11 Evolution in medical imaging technology.

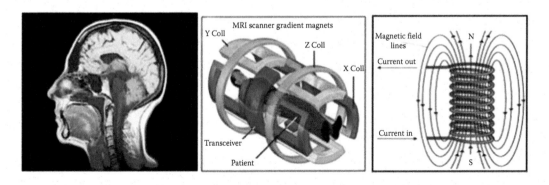

FIGURE 8.16 MRI scan, schematic of scanner gradient magnets, and magnetic fields generated. (*Source*: Images from the National High Magnetic Field Magnetic Lab., at the Florida State University, http://www.magnet.fsu.edu/education/tutorials/magnetacademy/mri/fullarticle.html)

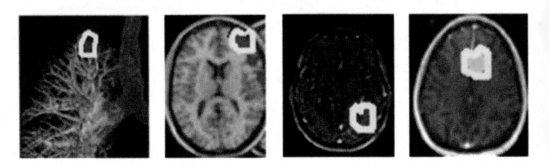

FIGURE 8.25 Indexing images, ImageCLEF tools by shape, color, or texture.

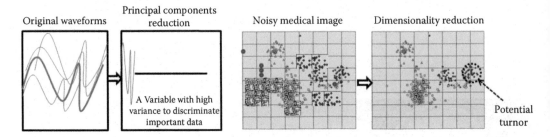

Original waveforms

Principal components reduction

A Variable with high variance to discriminate important data

Noisy medical image

Dimensionality reduction

Potential turnor

FIGURE 8.26 Digital image processing architecture. (*Source*: From http://www.ncbi.nlm.nih.gov/pmc/articles/PMC3701154/figure/F1/)

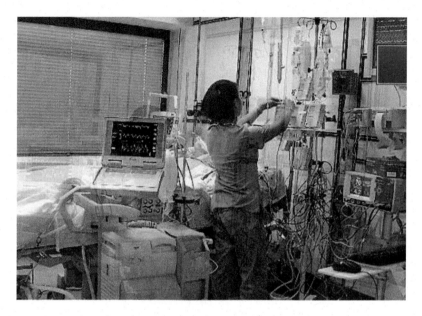

FIGURE 10.1 A critical care nurse provides care for a patient in the immediate postoperative period after cardiac surgery.

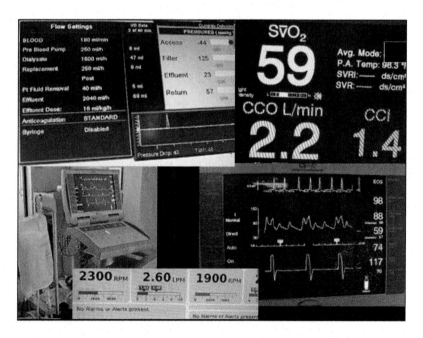

FIGURE 10.2 The data that are generated on a critically ill patient often include far more than just vital signs. Pictured are the screens from a continuous cardiac output monitor, an intra-aortic balloon pump, a continuous renal replacement therapy device, and a ventricular assist device. All of the aforementioned parameters and numbers are recorded every hour.

FIGURE 10.11 *Smart* medication infusion pumps and cardiac monitors are capable of communicating directly with the electronic health record (EHR) to download the dose and rate. If this capability is not enabled by the system, the nurse is responsible for typing every number into the EHR, usually every hour.

6

Telehealth

Level I: Core Concepts

6.1 Introduction

Telemedicine is the practice of medicine or analyzing medical data remotely. Communications technology has reached the singularity point, often referred to as a transformational event. In artificial intelligence, the singularity is the creation of intelligent machines, or in astronomy it's a property with infinite mass such as the center of a black hole or the universe before the "Big Bang," not the TV show, my personal favorite. Instant communications is ubiquitous, which is the first essential part of telemedicine. The second is quality wireless medical monitoring device-software, and some are currently available: iHealth, Fitbit®, Flex™, and the iWatch. All have medical monitoring technology, this is just the beginning. The term "mHealth" is linked to this second step; it refers to medical practice using mobile monitoring devices, a subset of the larger telehealth field. The last is the overwhelming need to pivot to telemedicine. In the United States, 10,000 baby boomers hit 65 every day. Healthcare companies are trying to reduce hospital stays and the Affordable Care Act (ACA) is focused on prevention strategies. Telehealth [9] fits the bill for prevention, i.e., responding in a timely fashion before conditions become acute and require hospitalization or monitoring recently released inpatients. Telemedicine should become mainstream (Figure 6.1).

> Telemedicine is the use of medical information exchanged from one site to another via electronic communications to improve a patient's clinical health status and delivery of remote clinical services using technology [1].

American Telemedicine Association (http://www.americantelemed.org)

6.2 Telehealth

Telehealth is an all-inclusive term encompassing remote healthcare and all its support services that are delivered utilizing the Internet and wireless/wired communications. Telemedicine is a more narrow definition that refers to the delivery of treatment or diagnoses remotely (Figure 6.1). The following is an example of the distinction between the two terms: Telemedicine would include the remote diagnosis by radiologists, using teleradiology tools, but the transmission infrastructure of Digital Imaging and Communications in Medicine (DICOM), the standards for encoding and transmitting medical images (see Chapter 8), would fall under the larger definition of telehealth.

Medicine anywhere is becoming the new norm with the proliferation of smartphones, tablets, and high-speed Internet, fixed and wireless; it has removed many of the previous limitations. Real-time video is common and wireless medical devices provide physiologic data. Access to a patient's medical records, one of the last missing components, is almost universally available. Electronic health records (EHRs) now tie everything together. A patient walks into an urgent care center or a less acute miniclinic and his or her complete patient records can be accessed immediately. Once the last missing piece, the incompatability of EHRs, is completely addressed through health information exchanges (HIEs) that integrate different systems into a coherent view which are currently under way, distance will no longer be an issue in most situations. Trauma, heart attacks, etc. that require immediate attention are the exceptions. Even these life threatening conditions are being addressed with implantable defibrillators [10].

New technologies, e.g., apps for remote healthcare, such as Doctor on Demand and Ringadoc, pull on a large pool of verified professionals, who can provide simple diagnosis and treatments, or at least triage a condition immediately and recommend a course of action. The old house calls can be replicated, in most cases, by these new technologies. Prevention, a key mandate from the Affordable Care Act (ACA), can be more effectively delivered if illnesses can be diagnosed and treated before they become acute. Catching outbreaks can be more expeditiously discovered using remote health technology. This chapter discusses those technologies, part of the panoply of skills, needed by informatics professionals, the complex interplay of systems and software that create the web of healthcare.

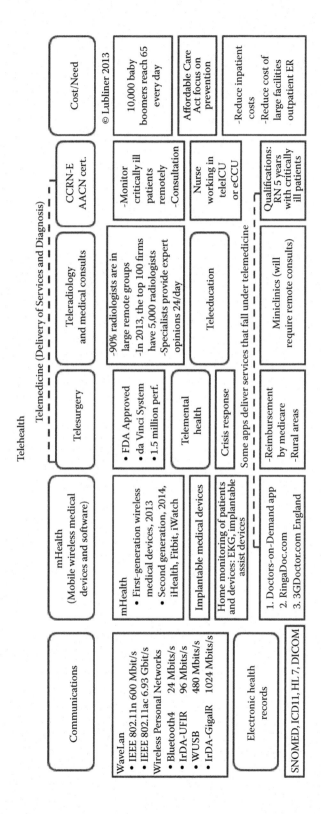

FIGURE 6.1 Telemedicine field.

6.2.1 Telemedicine

Telemedicine is the delivery of medicine and the diagnosis of medical conditions remotely. It is not a separate discipline; it is simply an extension of existing medical services using remote technology due to the inaccessibility of these services in rural areas or the need for in-home care or a robust real-time monitoring capability, for example, an implantable ventricular assist device (VAD) used as an outpatient device but requiring enhanced monitoring, as opposed to the conventional necessity of patients to periodically visit a fixed healthcare site.

The American Telemedicine Association (ATA) defines telemedicine as follows (http://www.americantelemed.org/):

Telemedicine is the use of medical information exchanged from one site to another via electronic communications to improve a patient's clinical health status. Telemedicine includes a growing variety of applications and services using two-way video, email, Smart phones, *wireless tools* and other forms of telecommunications technology.

An excellent resource is the *Journal of Telemedicine and Telecare* (http://jtt.sagepub.com/).

There have been a number of studies comparing the cost-effectiveness of telemedicine versus conventional care. In a paper evaluating 80 studies spanning 20 years (1990–2010 titled *"Systematic review of studies of the cost-effectiveness of telemedicine and tableware; Changes in the economic evidence over twenty years"*), the results showed conclusive evidence that the cost and access provided by telehealth provided substantial benefits, especially those individuals who, due to a remote location, would have received poorer care (link: http://jtt.sagepub.com/content/18/1/1.short; *Health Economics Unit, University of Birmingham, U.K.*).

The following are common telemedicine applications:

1. Telesurgery
2. Remote psychotherapy
3. Virtual home visits to manage chronic medical problems have all been demonstrated, although deployment remains limited
4. Remote monitoring of chronic medical conditions using networked medical devices such as blood pressure cuffs or blood glucose monitors
5. Multiple websites describe these and other innovative uses of telemedicine for interested clinicians to explore
6. Remote monitoring of ICU patients by intensivists
7. Remote dermatologic, pathologic, or radiographic consultations
8. Monitoring compliance with home drug dispensers
9. Home fetal monitoring during complicated pregnancies

Interstate practice of medicine is still limited.

Liability and malpractice are thorny issues, such as the practice of telemedicine; it presents a new form of the patient–caregiver relationship and creates potential hazards, such as technical failures leading to altered or suboptimal data. An accurate diagnosis depends on reliable data.

The practices of the healthcare insurers/payers are also lagging behind the technology. Medicare and other insurers will reimburse telemedicine interactions that *meet a restrictive set of criteria* (Table 6.1). Table 6.1 lists conditions and situations that fulfill the Medicare reimbursement criteria for telehealth with its associated billing codes. The last two entries added in 2014 refer to monitoring of patients recently discharged from a hospital—"Transitional Care Management Services with the following required elements: Communication (direct contact, telephone, electronic) with the patient and/or caregiver within 2 business days of discharge." This makes a great deal of sense, with the aid of wireless monitoring devices

TABLE 6.1 Medicare Telehealth Services and Billing Codes

Service (Telehealth Consultations, Emergency Department, or Initial Inpatient)	Healthcare Common Procedure Coding System (HCPCS)/CPT
1. *Follow-up inpatient telehealth consultations* furnished to beneficiaries in hospitals or SNFs	HCPCS codes G0406–G0408
2. Office or other *outpatient visits*	CPT codes 99201–99215
3. Subsequent *hospital care services*, with the limitation of 1 telehealth visit every 3 days	CPT codes 99231–99233
4. Subsequent *nursing facility care services*, with the limitation of 1 telehealth visit *every 30 days*	CPT codes 99307–99310
5. Telehealth visit *every 30 days*	CPT codes 99307–99310
6. Individual and group *kidney disease education* services	HCPCS codes G0420 and G0421
7. Individual and group *diabetes self-management training services*, with a minimum of 1 h of in-person instruction to be furnished in the initial year training period to ensure effective injection training	HCPCS codes G0108 and G0109
8. Individual and group health and *behavior assessment* and intervention	CPT codes 96150–96154
9. *Individual psychotherapy* (services furnished after January 1, 2013)	CPT codes 90832–90834; 90836, 90838
10. *Psychiatric diagnostic interview examination* (after January 1, 2013)	CPT codes 90791 and 90792
11. *End-stage renal disease* (*ESRD*)-related services included in the monthly capitation payment	CPT codes 90951, 90952, 90954, 90955, 90957, 90958, 90960, and 90961
12. Individual and group medical *nutrition therapy*	HCPCS code G0270 and CPT codes 97802–97804
13. *Neurological behavioral status* examination	CPT code 96116
14. *Smoking cessation services*	HCPCS codes G0436 and G0437 CPT codes 99406 and 99407
15. *Alcohol and/or substance* (*other than tobacco*) *abuse structured assessment* and intervention services (services furnished after January 1, 2013)	HCPCS codes G0396 and G0397
16. *Annual alcohol misuse screening*, 15 min (after January 1, 2013)	HCPCS code G0442
17. Brief face-to-face behavioral *counseling for alcohol misuse*, 15 min (services furnished after January 1, 2013)	HCPCS code G0443
18. *Annual depression screening*, 15 min (after January 1, 2013)	HCPCS code G0444
19. High-intensity *behavioral counseling to prevent sexually transmitted infection*, face-to-face, individual, includes education, skills training, and guidance on how to change sexual behavior; performed semi-annually, 30 min (services furnished after January 1, 2013)	HCPCS code G0445
20. Annual, face-to-face intensive behavioral therapy for cardiovascular disease, individual, 15 min (services furnished after January 1, 2013)	HCPCS code G0446
21. Face-to-face *behavioral* counseling for obesity, 15 min (January 1, 2013)	HCPCS code G0447
22. *Transitional care management services* with the following required elements: communication (direct contact, telephone, electronic) with the patient and/or caregiver within 2 business days of discharge. *Medical decision making of at least moderate complexity*	CPT code 99495 (*new 2014*)
23. *Transitional care management services* with the following required elements: communication (direct contact, telephone, electronic) with the patient and/or caregiver within 2 business days of discharge. *Medical decision making of high complexity*	CPT Code 99496 (*new 2014*)

Source: https://www.cms.gov/Outreach-and-Education/Medicare-Learning-NetworkMLN/MLNProducts/downloads/TelehealthSrvcsfctsht.pdf.

that can provide precise physiological readings. Often, current care standards suggest patients return in a week, two weeks, etc., which creates an added burden on the patient who may have limited resources; it may be physically taxing just after a procedure or the hospital may be a great distance away.

6.2.1.1 Telesurgery

Telesurgery is a robotic system that can perform surgeries remotely, also referred to as telepresence, with higher accuracy and smaller incisions that reduce postoperative recovery. Most current robotic operations are performed by surgeons in the same location. The Federal Drug Administration (FDA) approved both the ZEUS telesurgery system and da Vinci Surgical System in 2000. The most recent model, the da Vinci Xi System, was FDA approved in April 2014.

6.2.1.1.1 da Vinci Telesurgery System

The da Vinci telesurgery system is currently the only FDA-approved system in the United States. There have been approximately 1.5 million surgeries performed since 2000. In minimally invasive operations, the da Vinci system is the most commonly used surgical device in hysterectomies and prostatectomies. There were 2000 systems in use in 2014. The da Vinci system utilizes a 3D HD camera with a 10 times magnification so that extremely small details can be visualized (Figure 6.2). There are feedback mechanisms, called haptic feedback and tactile feedback, that are under development. A third-party company VerroTouch is providing haptic feedback for the da Vinci system. The following is a recent case study, in 2014, describing the technology and process involved in that research.

6.2.1.1.2 Case Study: Adding Haptic Force Feedback to the da Vinci Telesurgery System

Description: Accelerometers that measure tool vibrations are mounted to the patient-side manipulators of a da Vinci S robotic surgical system. These sensors lie within the sterile drapes, avoiding the need for sterilization. The measured right and left tool vibrations are processed and relayed to speakers on the surgeon's console and to voice coil actuators attached to the console handles. Previously, 11 surgeons used a VerroTouch-augmented da Vinci S to perform three in vitro manipulation tasks under four feedback conditions: with visual feedback, visual–audio feedback, visual–haptic feedback, and visual–audio–haptic feedback. Additionally, two transperitoneal nephrectomies and two midureteral dissections with ureteroureterostomy were performed by two urologists on a porcine model using a da Vinci S augmented with VerroTouch for in vivo validation.

Results: Surgeons who participated in the manipulation task study significantly preferred some form of tool vibration feedback over visual feedback alone. Survey ratings and written comments also indicate that the additional feedback significantly improved subjects' concentration. No significant differences in root mean square (RMS) force, RMS acceleration, or task completion time were found across feedback conditions. In the porcine model, human review of a 30 minute operation excerpt resulted in the identification of 1404 manipulation events; subsequent analysis demonstrated that 82% of identified events resulted in significant vibrations that were measured by VerroTouch.

Conclusion/Future Directions: VerroTouch has been successfully implemented both in vitro and in vivo and proved reliable in detecting technically relevant instrument manipulation events. VerroTouch is currently being modified for compatibility with the da Vinci Standard and Si models. While surgeons tend to prefer the presence of its feedback, further quantitative studies of the cognitive ergonomic effects of VerroTouch are required. We hypothesize that the presence of tool vibration feedback may lead to improved control of the surgical instruments, particularly for novices. Studies to test the utility of VerroTouch as an assessment tool for surgical skill and a prospective study of the effects of vibrotactile feedback on training novice surgeons are planned.

Case Study Link: http://www.sages.org/meetings/annual-meeting/abstracts-archive/verrotouch-detection-of-instrument-vibrations-for-haptic-feedback-and-skill-assessment-in-robotic-surgery/

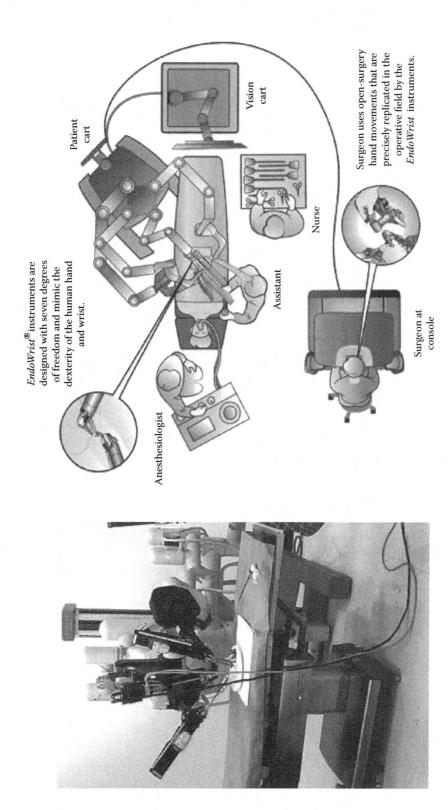

EndoWrist® instruments are designed with seven degrees of freedom and mimic the dexterity of the human hand and wrist.

Surgeon uses open-surgery hand movements that are precisely replicated in the operative field by the *EndoWrist* instruments.

Patient cart

Vision cart

Nurse

Assistant

Anesthesiologist

Surgeon at console

FIGURE 6.2 **(See color insert.)** da Vinci telesurgery system. (From IntuitiveSurgical.com, parent company.)

Telesurgery advantages are as follows:

1. Greater surgical precision
   a. Improved access to narrow anatomic spaces
2. Increased range of motion
   a. The instruments provide seven degrees of freedom (three for translation, three for rotation, and one for grasping).
3. Improved dexterity
4. Enhanced visualization
   a. The 3D stereoscopic display provides a detailed rendition of anatomic features, even in compact spaces.
5. Less time under anesthesia (depends on the procedure, but closing sutures usually reduces surgical time)
6. Less nerve damage and pain among patients

The procedures most commonly performed (Figure 6.3) are as follows:

1. Urologic surgery
2. General surgery performed through the abdominal wall
3. Gynecologic surgery
4. Head and neck surgery performed through the mouth restricted to benign (noncancer) and malignant tumors (cancer) classified as T1 and T2 (early-stage cancer)
5. Thoracic surgery performed through the rib cage on structures like the lungs
6. Heart surgery performed through the rib cage

In 2013, the FDA reported an increase in adverse effects, including injuries; an FDA warning was enacted in July 2013, and in May 2014, the FDA indicated in a letter to the company dated April 25, 2014, "that based on the FDA's evaluation, it appears that the Intuitive Surgical has addressed the violations contained in the July 16, 2013 warning letter" (Figure 6.4; http://www.intuitivesurgical.com/company/media/statements/#sthash.evhNWpYE.dpuf).

6.2.1.2 CCRN-E

Telehealth requires new skills and training especially in remote critically ill patient monitoring. A new certification for registered nurses (RNs), CCRN-E [2], extends the Critical Care Registered Nurse (CCRN) certification for RNs who monitor crucially ill patients remotely in a tele-ICU or an e-ICU. They both monitor patients visually and receive data feeds remotely from all the monitors. They also have access to the EHRs. Small rural intensive care units (ICUs) may not always have the range of expertise in house. CCRNs fill that gap by providing additional expertise from a remote location.

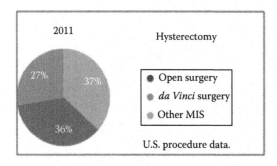
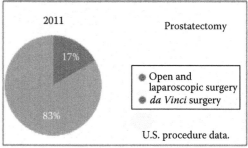

FIGURE 6.3 Percentages of hysterectomies and pros performed by telesurgery.

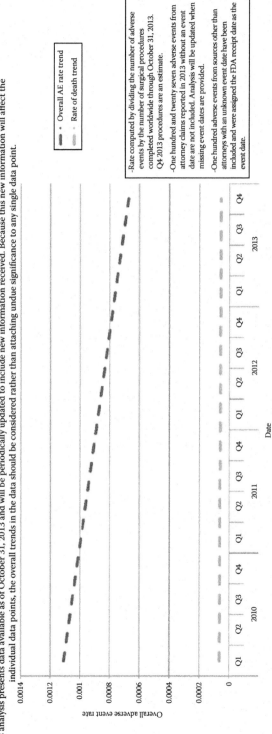

FIGURE 6.4   da Vinci Surgical System adverse effect decline.

The following eligibility criteria necessary to take the CCRN-E exam are listed as follows* (CCRN-E handbook: http://www.aacn.org/wd/certifications/docs/ccrn-eexamhandbook.pdf):

1. Possession of a current, unencumbered U.S. RN license
2. Meets one of the following clinical practice requirement options:
    a. *Option 1*: Practice as an RN or APRN for 1750 h in the care of acutely and/or critically ill adult patients in a tele-ICU or in a combination of tele-ICU and direct bedside care during the previous 2 years, with 875 of those hours accrued in the most recent year preceding application.
    b. *Option 2*: Practice as an RN or APRN for at least 5 years with a minimum of 2000 h in the care of acutely and/or critically ill adult patients in a tele-ICU or in a combination of tele-ICU and direct bedside care, with 144 of those hours accrued in the most recent year preceding application.
3. Eligible clinical practice hours are those completed in a U.S.-based facility or in a facility determined to be comparable to the U.S. standard of acute/critical care tele-ICU nursing practice. (http://www.aacn.org/wd/certifications/content/ccrnefaqs.pcms?menu=certification#What_are_the_CCRN-E_initial_exam_eligibility_requirements_)

6.2.1.3 Telemental Health

Telemental health is similar to the other tele definitions; it is defined as providing behavioral/mental health services, substance abuse, crisis intervention, and education, remotely. Originally used in remote crisis situations, in 2014, Medicare [3,4,5] provided guidelines on reimbursement. They still require that the coverage area be rural or areas outside a metropolitan area without sufficient available services. States individually decide eligibility for Medicaid reimbursement. Currently, 42 states allow some form of telehealth services (see Table 6.1, codes 8–10, 15–20).

Medicare also sets additional restrictions:

- *Category 1*: Services that are similar to professional consultations, office visits, and office psychiatry services that are currently on the list of telehealth services. The request is evaluated based on the similarities between the services already eligible for reimbursement and that of the requested service.
- *Category 2*: Services that are not similar to the current list of telehealth services. The assessment will be based on whether the service is accurately described by the corresponding code when delivered via telehealth and whether the use of a telecommunications system to deliver the services produces a demonstrated clinical benefit to the patient. Supporting documentation should be included.

The ATA has taken the leadership in defining guidelines for telehealth services. The following section is taken from those guidelines.

The telehealth services fall under these general categories:

1. Services
    a. Prehospitalization assessment
    b. Posthospital follow-up care
    c. Scheduled and urgent outpatient visits
    d. Medication management
    e. Psychotherapy and consultation
2. Clinical interviews
    a. Telemental health interviews may be conducted between physicians in consultation or between a physician and another healthcare provider (e.g., a case manager, clinical nurse practitioner, or physician assistant [PA]).
    b. Telemental health interviews may be conducted between mental health professionals and a patient.

---

* *Source*: AACN website.

c. Telemental health interview may be an adjunct to periodic face-to-face contact or may be the only contact.

3. Emergency evaluation

   a. Emergency evaluations for psychiatric hospitalization can be conducted via telemedicine and usually will require additional personnel to provide physical control of the environment and possibly the patient, for patient safety.

   b. Situations such as a patient who is suicidal, homicidal, or suffering from dementia or acute psychosis may require additional personnel in the room in addition to family members.

   c. In general, adequate support staff or responsible family members shall be present at the remote site in order to safely care for the patient.

   d. Special attention shall be paid to the enhanced need for privacy and confidentiality and every attempt made to preserve the patient's right to privacy.

4. Case management

   a. In large distributed systems where multiprovider case management is needed, videoconferencing allows collaboration between all the involved clinical participants regardless of distance.

   b. Clinical treatment plans can be developed with input from experts who would not otherwise be available.

5. Clinical supervision

   a. Supervision of trainees (residents or interns) at a distant site can facilitate both training and patient care.

   b. Supervision may be done either in real time with the supervisor present via videoconferencing or, when appropriate, by the use of store and forward technology.

   (http://www.americantelemed.org/docs/default-source/standards/practice-guidelines-for-videoconferencing-based-telemental-health.pdf?sfvrsn=6)

6.2.2 mHealth

The term "mHealth" stands for mobile health. It is remote medical care supported by mobile devices. It usually refers to using mobile devices such as smartphones, tablets, and other remote technologies for medical services and education. It also refers to connecting wireless medical devices, like pulse oximeters, blood pressure and glucose monitors, and health fitness and a range of cardiac monitoring devices, to these smartphones or tablets and extracting useful information and providing that data to medical personnel. This market is expanding so rapidly that there is now an international health summit for this field such as the "mHealth Summit" (http://www.mhealthsummit.org/). There are also numerous organizations appearing to focus in this area; the influential mHealth Alliance (http://mhealthalliance.org) "advocates for standardization and interoperability of mHealth platform." It is hosted by the United Nations Foundation and funded by the Rockefeller Foundation. Its stated goal is to "harness the power of wireless technologies to improve health outcomes in low and middle income countries." (I recommend Robin Cook's "CELL" sci-fi novel on cell phones role in mHealth).

6.2.2.1 Health and Human Services

Health and Human Services (HHS) has announced several initiatives to set standards for mHealth. Several task forces have been initiated for tele-education, telehealth security, and standards for this rapidly expanding field (Table 6.2) (http://www.hhs.gov/open/initiatives/mhealth/).

6.2.2.2 National Institutes of Health and National Science Foundation mHealth Initiatives

The NIH mHealth training initiatives provide investigators with an introduction to mHealth methodologies that may be used to study behavioral and social dimensions of public health. They work

TABLE 6.2   HHS mHealth Initiatives and Recommendations

1   Facilitating health text messaging development: *The task force recommends that HHS develops and hosts evidenced-informed health text message libraries to leverage HHS' rich and scientifically based information.* This information should be open access and free to the public. Areas prime for development include smoking cessation, emergency response/preparedness, early childhood health, maternal/child health, heart disease, diabetes, mental health, oral health, and obesity.

2   Research and evaluation: *The task force recommends that HHS develops further evidence on the effectiveness of health text messaging programs.* HHS is currently conducting a formal evaluation of the text4baby program, a public–private partnership that is the first free-to-end-user health text messaging program available nationwide. Future health text messaging programs by HHS, or in which HHS is a partner, should also include a scientific evaluation component. To keep pace with the dynamic nature of mobile technology, robust and periodic (e.g., quarterly or annually) assessments of funding opportunities and the development of new/emerging technologies are also recommended.

3   Partnerships among federal government agencies and with nonfederal organizations: *The task force recommends that HHS explores and develops partnerships to create, implement, and disseminate health text messaging and mobile health (mHealth) programs. It is further recommended that in FY2012 specific HHS staff persons (e.g., HHS mHealth lead) serve as main points of contacts to represent HHS in discussions of collaborations or partnerships with other stakeholders in the mHealth ecosystem.* Because health text messaging and mHealth utilize consumer-facing technologies and are relevant to many stakeholders, partnerships among HHS, other governmental agencies, and nonfederal organizations often are needed to develop successful projects. Identifying specific HHS representatives would facilitate the development and coordination of partnerships and should work closely with the HHS chief technology officer.

6   Delineating privacy/security issues: *The task force recommends that HHS conducts further research into the privacy and security risks associated with text messaging of health information and establish guidelines for managing such privacy/security issues. Furthermore, mHealth issues should be discussed within the HHS Inter-Division Health IT Policy and Security Task Force.* The exchange of health information via text messages raises privacy and security issues specific to this medium. Text messaging programs may be subject to numerous privacy and security laws, including the Health Insurance Portability and Accountability Act of 1996 (HIPAA) privacy and security rules.

7   Regulatory issues: *The task force recommends that relevant HHS agencies (FDA, NIH, AHRQ, ONC, etc.) conduct research on future trends of text messaging technologies and establish regulatory guidelines for these interactive systems that can be used in treating, curing, mitigating, or preventing diseases or conditions.* Future developments in health text messaging and mHealth technology will likely create and extend beyond its current capabilities to create interactive systems that will enable active treatment and prevention of diseases or conditions in humans. Applying medical device and clinical research principles to evaluate interactive text messaging programs must take into account the safety and effectiveness of SMS technology while also facilitating innovation.

Source: http://www.hhs.gov/open/initiatives/mhealth/recommendations.html.

with expert mentors to create their own interdisciplinary mHealth projects. The use of mobile technology affords methodological advantages over traditional approaches, including reduced memory bias, the ability to capture time-intensive longitudinal data, date- and time-stamped data, and the potential for personalizing information in real time. (http://obssr.od.nih.gov/training_and_education/mhealth/index.aspx)

> "mHealth"—has the potential to be a transformative force. mHealth has the potential to change when, where, and how healthcare is provided; to ensure that important social, behavioral, and environmental data are used to understand the determinants of health; and to improve health outcomes.

> **http://obssr.od.nih.gov/scientific_areas/methodology/mhealth/**

Some of the current National Science Foundation (NSF) and National Institutes of Health (NIH) grants for mHealth that were funded in 2013–2014 provide an indication of the future directions of the mHealth field (Table 6.3). They are as follows: improving the tracking and communication

TABLE 6.3 NSF and NIH Projects for mHealth

	Title	Description
(R01)PA-14–180 http://grants.nih.gov/ grants/guide/pa-files/ PA-14-180.html Posted: April 18, 2014	NSF: mHealth Tools for Individuals with Chronic Conditions to Promote Effective Patient– Provider Communication, Adherence to Treatment and Self-Management (R01)	The purpose of this initiative is to stimulate research utilizing mobile health (mHealth) tools aimed at the improvement of effective patient–provider communication, adherence to treatment, and self-management of chronic diseases in underserved populations.
(R21)(PAR-14–028) http://www.fic.nih. gov/Programs/Pages/ mhealth.aspx Application due date: February 19, 2015	NIH: Mobile Health: Technology and Outcomes in Low- and Middle-Income Countries (mHealth)	*Mobile Health: Technology and Outcomes in Low- and Middle-Income Countries* will support research on the development or adaptation of mHealth technology specifically suited for low- and middle-income countries (LMICs) and the health-related outcomes associated with the implementation of the technology.
Funded 2013	*Large: Collaborative research: Computational Jewelry for Mobile Health*	The vision is that computational jewelry, in a form like a bracelet or pendant, will provide the properties essential for successful body-area mHealth networks. These devices coordinate the activity of the body-area network and provide a discreet means for communicating with their wearer. Such devices complement the capabilities of a smartphone, bridging the gap between the type of pervasive computing possible with a mobile phone and that enabled by wearable computing.
Funded 2012	NSF-funded project looks to mHealth to improve preoperative services	The National Science Foundation has awarded $797,066 to three university professors to research how mobile technology can improve coordination in preoperative services.

between doctors and patients for chronic disease follow-up care, remote area access to low-income groups, and preoperative education.

Level II: Distributed Healthcare

6.3 Introduction

This section describes facilities, services, and software that lie outside of traditional inpatient systems such as hospitals, emergency rooms (ERs) in hospitals, or a physician's office. With the advent of telehealth, medical services can draw upon external resources that can supplement the infrastructure that was previously only available in either larger organizations, such as hospitals that required all support services centralized to ensure they were prepared for every eventuality. The same is true for urgent care facilities that can replace traditional ERs in most, not all, situations. The line is blurred here since many urgent care facilities are extremely well staffed with a comprehensive suite of equipment, especially those that are certified by the Urgent Care Association of America (UCAOA). These triage trade-offs are often due to either rural locations where a large facility is a distance away or the severity of the injury may not require the complex support facilities of a hospital ER sometimes referred to as emergency department [ED]. A number of hospitals have closed in the last few decades, due to cost–benefit trade-offs of maintaining full care facilities, but often the ER remains open to provide local emergency outpatient services, especially in distressed communities where transportation or other options are severely limited.

With the limited number of physicians and often simple, nonacute treatments that are required such as cold, flu remedies, immunization shots, etc., another external facility referred to as miniclinics—the largest system is CVS Minute Clinic with currently 800 locations and growing—can provide care cost-effectively and more conveniently utilizing RNs and PAs, again also supported remotely by telehealth technology.

Last, software on smart devices provides another instant response system available to communicate with medical professionals. With the addition of mHealth devices such as wireless pulse oximetry and blood pressure and glucose monitors, detailed data can augment the remote diagnosis and treatment.

6.4 Medical Apps for Remote Healthcare

This new generation of on-demand medical virtual doctor visits will change the current medical paradigm, They provide the following benefits: its ability to instantly contact a pool of licensed medical practitioners at a low cost starting at $39, who can triage situations immediately, no arranging for appointments, traveling to a location, and no waiting. Just select an app on your phone, fill in a few fields, and you're talking to a professional in minutes. This low-cost option may still be out of reach for many individuals; $39 may be the cost of food for the family for 1 or more days. We have to have a subsidized plan similar to food stamps to ensure access to all; healthcare is a basic human need. But since the cost of a single ER visit averages $500–$1,000 or waiting till a situation becomes acute escalates the cost, the overall cost of providing subsidies for early diagnostic services pays for itself and may actually lower overall healthcare costs. In the United States, we pay twice/per capita the cost of every country with single-payer systems and our outcomes, life expectancy, infant mortality rates, etc., are well below the average of other countries.

In the *nonacute category*, a cold, mild pain, fever, or any early-stage medical issue, the question that arises, is whether intervention by a medical practitioner is necessary? Can over-the-counter medications and/or bed rest suffice? Do I have to travel to some location, make an appointment, keep my child out of school, take time out of work when in a low-income or rural environment simply getting to that location may be a significant burden? Often in all of these situations, no action is taken; the rationale usually is that it will pass or because of financial or transportation limitations. Miniclinics, in places like CVS stores, are one solution if they are close and operate on 24 hour schedules. Medical apps are another solution for nonacute care where individuals can get diagnoses and prescriptions remotely from a large pool of medical practitioners that have been certified by the site for a relatively small fee (Table 6.4).

6.5 Urgent Care Centers

In the acute care category: Urgent care is a broad term that is defined as follows: "Urgent Care Medicine (UCM) is the provision of immediate medical service offering outpatient care for the *treatment of acute and chronic illness and injury*. It requires a broad and comprehensive fund of knowledge to provide such care" (https://aaucm.org/about/urgentcare/default.aspx). There are approximately 9,000 centers in the United States, with 3 million plus visits/week and 160 million visits/year, and 85% are open 7 days/week (Table 6.5).

Urgent care associations

UCAOA: http://www.ucaoa.org/.

National Association for Ambulatory Urgent Care (NAFAC): http://www.urgentcare.org/.

American Academy of Urgent Care Medicine (AAUCM): *Urgent care medicine (UCM) is the provision of immediate medical service offering outpatient care for the treatment of acute and chronic illness and injury. It requires a broad and comprehensive fund of knowledge to provide such care* (https://aaucm.org/about/urgentcare/default.aspx).

Certifications: The UCAOA provides certifications for these facilities. Since these urgent care centers are more acute facilities, providing outpatient services, and 94% of the time have physicians on-site, a certified site provides a degree of assurance that basic care standards are met.

TABLE 6.4   (See color insert.) Examples of On-Demand Medical Consultation Apps

Medical Apps—On-Demand Doctors' Visits (Live Video Consultations and Text Chat Health Inquiries)		

Ringadoc
http://www.ringadoc.com/
	1. 1,000 physicians in 40 states
	2. Different from other systems that select a doctor from an available online pool for a consult; options include the following:
	  a. Connect with a single primary care physician.
	  b. Leave a text message with the urgency of situation.
	  c. Choice of a larger network of physicians.
		$69/month or $868/year

Doctor on Demand http://www.doctorondemand.com/	1. Licensed physicians 2. Nonemergency medical issue 3. Pediatric questions 4. Prescriptions 5. Specialist referral Examples | Short-term prescriptions and Rx refills	Cold, flu, cough, fever, allergies
Urinary tract infections	Pediatric fever, advice, or other issues
Vomiting/diarrhea	STDs
Rashes/bites/skin problems	Sports injuries, athlete's foot		$40 per call 
3G Doctor (United Kingdom and Ireland) http://www.3gdoctor.com/	1. 24 hours/day. 2. Live video chat with a licensed doctor. 3. On-demand doctors are available to diagnose and address minor medical problems such as rashes, aches, or pains. 4. Doctors can recommend treatments and answer health-related questions. 5. Real-time access to your medical records.	£35 per session

(Continued)

TABLE 6.4 (*Continued*)   Examples of On-Demand Medical Consultation Apps

Medical Apps—On-Demand Doctors' Visits (Live Video Consultations and Text Chat Health Inquiries)		
Live Chat (consult) Live Person https://www.liveperson.com/experts/ health-medicine	1. A text chat 2. Consult a live medical practitioner 3. Doctor, nurse, oncologist, dentist, physical therapist, nurse, allergist, optometrist, chiropractor, pharmacologist, pregnancy/childbirth specialist, or sex therapist 4. A detailed list of verified professionals to select from 5. Other specialties, education, programming	$1.50/min 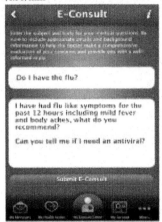
ConsultADoctor http://www.consultadr.com/	1. A service provided for health plans that can be tailored for employers to service the health needs of their employees 2. Nonemergency, preventive, and routine health issues 3. Provides EHRs through the company	
Health book/Health Kit (Apple) https://developer.apple.com/ healthkit/ 	1. System for integrating health and fitness data across Apple's product lines, including charting and long-term trending and individual's health and fitness progress. 2. It is a part of IOS 8. 3. The iWatch will provide additional biometric sensors that will pool all these data into a single location.	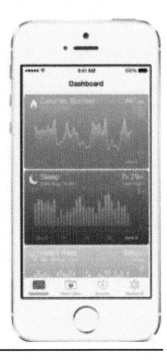

TABLE 6.5   Urgent Care Facilities Statistics

Urgent Centers		
• 94.1% of centers have at least one full-time employed physician on staff.		
• At the end of 2012, there were 108,000 employees in the United States (revenue 16 billion dollars).		
Schedule	70% open at 8 am or earlier	95% close after 8 pm	
Wait times	69% wait <20 min	28% between 21 and 40 min	3% >40 min
Location	75% suburban	15% urban	10% rural
Ownership	35% physician or group physicians	30.5% corporation	25% hospital
Specialties	47.7% family medicine	30% emergency	9.9% more than one specialty
Visits	3 million/week	160 million/year	9,000 centers

Source: 2012. http://www.ucaoa.org/docs/UrgentCareMediaKit_2013.pdf; http://www.ibisworld.com/industry/urgent-care-centers.html.

The certifications fall into two categories*:

Facilities receive a certification of Category 1 or Category 2 depending on their staffing model:

Category 1 = licensed physicians (MD/DO) on-site during all posted hours of operation
Category 2 = licensed providers (MD/DO or NP/PA) on-site during all posted hours of operation (mixed models)

6.5.1 Urgent Care Certification Criteria

1. Facility must accept and advertise that walk-in patients of all ages are accepted for a broad spectrum of illness, injury, and disease during all hours the facility is open to see patients.
   a. Pediatric specialty centers are exempt from above age requirement *if* pediatric-only specialization is included in the name of the facility.
2. The following must be available during all posted hours of operation for the facility:
   a. X-ray on-site
   b. Phlebotomy services on-site
   c. Licensed provider on-site with the appropriate state
   d. Licenses and resources to
      i. Obtain and read an EKG and x-ray on-site
      ii. Administer PO, IM, and IV medications/fluids on-site
      iii. Perform minor procedures (e.g., sutures, cyst removal, incision and drainage, splinting) on-site
      iv. The following equipment and staff trained in its use: portable defibrillator, portable oxygen, and Ambu bag/oral airway, portable drug cart stocked appropriately for all ages of patient population (as determined by the facility)
      v. Working phone to dial 911 and at least two exam rooms, separate waiting area, and restricted-access patient restrooms
3. Minimum hours of operation (must meet all three criteria)
   a. 7 days/week (not including national holidays; see www.ucaoa.org/certification)
   b. 4+ hours each day
   c. 3000 hours/year
   d. Note: Alternatively, special circumstances will be considered for a facility if all of the following are met:
      i. Facility is part of a multicenter system.
      ii. Facility is open 5+ days/week (not including national holidays).
      iii. Another facility that is part of the same system meets standard minimum hours of operation criteria *and* is ≤5 miles away.

---

* *Source:* http://www.ucaoa.org/docs/CUC_brochure.pdf.

4. Facility must have a physician designated as medical director for the facility (with an active, unrestricted license for the state where the facility is located) who is responsible for overall clinical quality.
5. Facility must provide clinical care and perform business activities in an ethical manner.

6.6 Miniclinics

Miniclinics are walk-in clinics usually staffed by Physician Assistants (PAs) or Registered Nurses (RNs) to treat nonacute medical conditions, i.e., not serious enough to require ER care. In March of 2014, there were 5,275 clinics with a revenue of $16 billion with an annual growth rate of 8.2%.* The ACA has spurred growth in urgent care centers due to the expansion of individuals covered under private and government-supported healthcare plans. The ACA, specifically under title IV subsection D and title V subtitle A sec 5001, promotes the expansions of preventive and chronic care services. The HHS, in 2012, also funded $730 million to support and expand access via outpatient clinics.

1. Hospitals and health insurers are investing in these clinics to reduce costs.
2. With the advent of the ACA and more insured individuals, up to 13 million by March 31, 2014 (8 million signees and 5 million additional Medicare recipients), the current providers may be unable to provide timely appointments without the aid of miniclinics.
   a. Prevention, one of the ACA directives, involves providing funding for additional clinics. In May 2012, the HHS announced $730 million in grants to support community health centers. Its estimated 900,000 new patients will be serviced by these new and expanded centers (http://www.hhs.gov/healthcare/facts/blog/2012/05/healthcenters050112.html):
      i. *The healthcare law has already supported 190 health centers' construction and renovation projects and the creation of 67 new health center sites across the country.*
      ii. *Since the beginning of 2009, employment at health centers nationwide has increased by 15%.*
      iii. *Due to primarily the ACA and the Recovery Act, community health centers are serving nearly three million more patients.*
   b. The ACA plans are to continue to supply future funding for miniclinics specifically addressing the problems of access in inner cities and rural areas:
      i. Over the next few years, the healthcare law will support more than 485 new health center construction and renovation projects and the creation of 245 new community health center sites, estimating an additional 6,000 jobs and access for 1.3 million new patients.
      ii. The ACA Title IV Subsection D relating to "chronically ill patients" mandates the expanded availability of preventive and follow-up care for critically ill patients. A major expense and cause of death are discharged critically ill patients who don't follow their medication regimen or follow-up care. This can be resolved with either miniclinics or telehealth (http://www.hhs.gov/healthcare/rights/law/title/iv-amendments.pdf).
      iii. The ACA title V subtitle A sec 5001 "Healthcare Workforce":

The purpose of the ACA is to improve access to and the delivery of healthcare services for all individuals, particularly low-income, uninsured, minority, and rural populations by[†]:

1. *Gathering and assessing comprehensive data in order for the healthcare workforce to meet the healthcare needs of individuals, including research on the supply, demand, distribution, diversity, and skills.*

---

* *Source*: http://www.ibisworld.com/industry/urgent-care-centers.html.
† Text from HHS.gov.

2. *Increasing the supply of a qualified healthcare workforce to improve access to and the delivery of healthcare services for all individuals.*
3. *Enhancing healthcare workforce education and training to improve access to and the delivery of healthcare services for all individuals.*
4. *Providing support to the existing healthcare workforce to improve access to and the delivery of healthcare services for all individuals*
   http://www.hhs.gov/healthcare/rights/law/title/v-healthcare-workforce.pdf

6.6.1 U.S. Miniclinics

Most miniclinics will have increased telehealth options for remote consultations. With the exponential growth, currently expanding at 8% a year, it is estimated that most people will use these clinics more often than conventional doctor visits:

- CVS Minute Clinic, with 800 clinics by the end of 2013, is expanding its miniclinics, has planned for expansion of 150 clinics/year, and is developing apps for telehealth.
  - In Massachusetts, Blue Cross and Blue Shield have partnered with miniclinics (http://www.bluecrossma.com/bluelinks-for-employers/whats-new/special-announcements/cvs-minute-clinic.html).
  - In Vermont, with the closing of North Adams Regional Medical Center, in 2014, Blue Cross has increased access to miniclinics (https://www.bluecrossma.com/bluelinks-for-employers/whats-new/special-announcements/index.html).
- Walgreen miniclinics (largest drugstore chain in the United States) announced in 2013 "that its 370+ *Take Care Clinics* will be the first retail store clinics to both diagnose and manage chronic conditions like asthma, diabetes, high blood pressure, and high cholesterol. The Nurse Practitioners (NPs) and Physician Assistants (PAs) who staff these clinics will provide an entry point into treatment for some of these conditions" (http://thehealthcareblog.com/blog/2013/04/12/chronic-care-at-walgreens-why-not/).
- Walmart miniclinics have not been as aggressive as other vendors with drugstores.
- Rite Aid NowClinic miniclinics, as of the end of 2013, have clinics in Michigan, Maryland, and Pennsylvania (https://www.mynowclinic.com/riteaid/locations/).
- Target: Target Clinics have miniclinics, as of the end of 2013, in Florida, Illinois, Maryland, Minnesota, North Carolina, and Virginia (http://www.target.com/store-locator/find-clinic).
- MedExpress Urgent Care is the dominant clinic operator in Western Pennsylvania (http://medcitynews.com/2013/08/affordable-care-act-could-lead-to-increase-in-walk-in-clinics/#ixzz31WUC3neD).
  - At the end of 2012, there were 115 clinics in 9 states (double from the previous year).
- Concentra has 342 miniclinics in 42 states as of 2013, owned by Humana Healthcare.

6.6.2 Miniclinic Certification Criteria

The Joint Commission, formerly JCAHO, is the national evaluation and certifying agency for nearly 15,000 healthcare organizations and programs in the United States, including hospitals, nursing homes, laboratories, rehabilitation centers, and behavioral healthcare organizations. The Joint Commission's standards focus on patient safety and quality of care and are updated regularly to reflect the rapid advances in healthcare and medicine (http://www.jointcommission.org/).

The certification standards include (subset of the 180 certification standards) the following:

1. Review and verification of education of the clinics' personnel
2. Licensure and certifications
   a. A copy of their DEA license
   b. A copy of their state license
   c. A copy of their CPR certification
   d. A copy of their national certification
3. On-site surveys
   a. "Tracing" the patient's experience—looking at services provided by various care providers
   b. Departments within the organization, as well as "hand-offs" between them
   c. On-site observations and interviews with surveyors
   d. Review of documents provided by the organization
   e. Assessment of the physical facility
4. Medication management
   a. Addresses the stages of medication use, including selection, storage, and safe management of medications; ordering, preparing and dispensing, administration, and monitoring of effect; and evaluation of the processes
5. Performance improvement
6. *Record of care*: handling and security of patient records (EHRs)

The Minute Clinics (CVS) are JCAHO certified, which signifies that they comply with more than 180 national standards in the implementation of established clinical practice guidelines, as well as more than 500 performance measurements.

The Health Resources and Services Administration (HRSA) certifies rural clinics. The criteria by which they are certified are listed in the document "Starting a Rural Clinic," which include a rural healthcare (RHC) certification and policy manuals that conform to individual state laws (http://www.hrsa.gov/ruralhealth/pdf/rhcmanual1.pdf).

Level III: Advanced Topics

6.7 Mobile Tools to Support Physicians

EHRs provide access to a patient's medical records but they are still in their early phases of implementation. We are in the early flip-phone phase, reference to the rudimentary early mobile phones, of EHRs where ease of use and functionality are still lacking. A number of third-party companies have stepped in to fill the gap. It is likely that start-up companies will be purchased by larger EHRs such as Epic and Cerner, which is what happened when YouTube was purchased by Google in 2006 for $1.65 billion only a few years after its creation, to incorporate cutting edge user interfaces. This field is ripe for future entrepreneurs. That is why I have included appendices on app development for EHRs, since all Phase I medical records will need to be upgraded and we need to train or at least inform informatics practitioners of the direction we're moving toward. Also the chapter written on EHR implementation, by a practicing clinical nurse specialist, highlights the need to enhance the current nurse/physician interface for usability and efficiency.

There are currently about 5,000 apps on ITunes and Android devices and a few for Blackberry (Mobile Health News: http://mobihealthnews.com/).

There are apps to allow physicians to remotely visualize, enhance, or compare CT/MRIs side by side to compare changes over time. Some examples are Mobile MIM or Merge iConnect. Other app softwares allow physicians to illustrate surgeries with patients or hold remote video conferences to communicate with patients. There are apps to allow surgeons to communicate with families in waiting rooms so they can get instant updates after surgery (MDconnectME). Many of these apps tie into EHRs and soon to HIEs to share data seamlessly between different vendors (http://www.mdconnectme.com/) (Table 6.6).

TABLE 6.6 **(See color insert.)** Productivity Apps for Physicians

Mobile MIM
Radiology Visualization Software
http://www.mimsoftware.com/about/news-center/

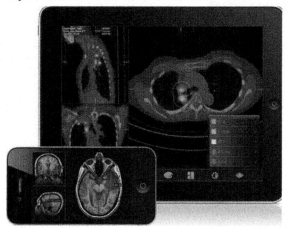

Allows physicians to make diagnosis remotely after analyzing CT and MRI scans
- Approved by the FDA
- Primarily targeted at radiologists
- Take notes; share information
- Tools to measure and highlight features of the scan
- Zoom in on details of the image
  - Voxel-based analysis
  - Region-based analysis
  - SUVR computation
  - Cluster analysis
  - Surface projection analysis
  - Quantitative functional neuroimaging software

Merge iConnect Access System
Radiology imaging
http://mobihealthnews.com/15782/
merge-healthcare-focuses-on-mobile-access-not-apps-for-remote-medical-imaging/

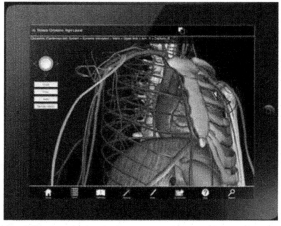

- Sliding one finger across the iPad screen changes the contrast and grayscale of a radiological image.
- Buttons on the screen allow for additional image manipulation.
- A patient history fly-out menu on the edge of the patient screen allows viewers to bring up as many as three studies simultaneously for side-by-side comparison.

drawMD
http://www.drawmd.com/

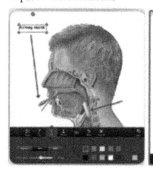
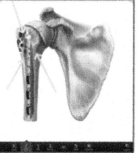

- Allows physicians to show details of what a surgery entails.

(Continued)

TABLE 6.6 (*Continued*)   Productivity Apps for Physicians

Visible Body http://www.visiblebody.com/ap/ipad/ 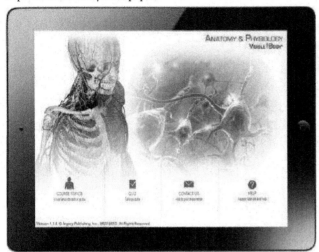	• 3D human anatomy allows doctors to describe issues to patients. • Medical students have detailed anatomical models. • Diagnosis and treatments. • Allows doctors to hold video conference with patients.

Source: Mobile Medical Productivity Tools. http://www.mednet-tech.com/newsletter/mobile-marketing/top-mobile-apps-for-doctors.

Examples of medical productivity tools include Apple's Research Kit (2015), a tool to allow researchers to turn the iPhone into a diagnostics tool, drawing data from mobile devices. The system can potentially collect large amounts of data from millions of consenting iPhone users, thus showing correlations and trends. https://www.apple.com/researchkit/.

6.8 Summary

Telehealth is a broad term that refers to providing services, diagnoses, education, and data remotely. Everything today is connected and healthcare is quickly following. The quality of medical services soon will not be dependent on location and, hopefully, personal finances. Once wireless medical devices become common, or at least accessible in public venues, we can quickly assess an individual's medical state, not waiting for the traditional doctor's or ER visit, thus enhancing preventive medicine. Integrated with EHRs, tied into the Cloud, healthcare will become a basic service and right accessible anywhere and costs may decline significantly.

Questions

Level I

1. Explain the difference between telehealth and telemedicine; provide details.
    a. Describe telemedicine applications.
2. What are some of the issues in practicing telemedicine across state lines?
3. What is Medicare's position on the reimbursement for telehealth services?
    a. Provide details on specific reimbursed activities.
4. What is telesurgery?
    a. What specific advantages does it provide?
    b. What surgical procedures is it most commonly used for?
    c. Summarize the da Vinci telesurgery case study in Section 6.2.1.

5. What is the CCRN-E?
   a. In what situations are CCRNs used in telemedicine?
6. What is mHealth?
   a. Explain some examples where mHealth has provided health services not available by any other means.
   b. Explain the NIH mHealth initiatives.

Level II

7. What is distributed healthcare?
   a. Explain the role of stand-alone emergency departments (EDs), urgent care, and miniclinic centers.
   b. What are the unique regulatory requirements for urgent care and miniclinics?
8. What are medical apps?
   a. Research a medical app and provide details of the service and statistics and speculate on the potential benefits over conventional paradigms.

Level III

9. Describe some of the remote productivity tools available for physicians to visualize and diagnose CT/MRIs.
   a. Research a remote productivity tool, not mentioned in the textbook, to aid physicians in practicing telemedicine.

Glossary

CCRN-E extends the Critical Care Registered Nurse (CCRN) certification for registered nurses (RNs) who monitor crucially ill patients remotely in a teleICU or an eICU.

The term "mHealth" stands for mobile health. It is remote medical care supported by mobile devices.

Miniclinics are walk-in clinics usually staffed by physician assistants or registered nurses to treat non-acute medical conditions.

Telehealth is an all-inclusive term encompassing remote healthcare and all its support.

Telemedicine is the use of medical information exchanged from one site to another via electronic communications to improve a patient's clinical health status and delivery of remote clinical services using technology.

Telemental health is similar to the other tele definitions; it is defined as providing behavioral/mental health services, substance abuse, crisis intervention, and education, remotely delivered utilizing the Internet and wireless communications.

Telesurgery is a robotic system that can perform surgeries remotely, also referred to as telepresence, with higher accuracy and smaller incisions that reduce postoperative recovery.

Urgent care medicine is a broad term that is defined as follows: "Urgent Care Medicine (UCM) is the provision of immediate medical service offering outpatient care for the treatment of acute and chronic illness and injury."

References

1. American Telemedicine Association. http://www.americantelemed.org/docs/default-source/standards/a-lexicon-of-assessment-and-outcome-measurements-for-telemental-health.pdf?sfvrsn=2
2. CCRN-E handbook. http://www.aacn.org/wd/certifications/docs/ccrn-eexamhandbook.pdf.

3. HHS. http://www.cms.gov/Outreach-and-Education/Medicare-Learning-Network-MLN/MLN MattersArticles/downloads/MM8553.pdf.

4. HHS 2. https://www.cms.gov/Outreach-and-Education/Medicare-Learning-Network-MLN/MLN Products/downloads/TelehealthSrvcsfctsht.pdf.

5. Medicare Telehealth Services. https://www.cms.gov/Outreach-and-Education/Medicare-Learning-Network-MLN/MLNProducts/downloads/TelehealthSrvcsfctsht.pdf.

6. What is mHealth, www.himss.org/library/mhealth.

7. Public Policy TeleHealth. http://www.ihealthbeat.org/perspectives/2013/public-policy-for-telehealth-in-2013-its-time-for-government-to-lead-or-get-out-of-the-way.

8. PubMed Telemedicine. http://www.ncbi.nlm.nih.gov/pubmed/21119593.

9. Telehealth prospects by IHealthBeat. http://www.ihealthbeat.org/perspectives/2013/public-policy-for-telehealth-in-2013-its-time-for-government-to-lead-or-get-out-of-the-way.

10. What Is an Implantable Cardioverter Defibrillator. http://www.nhlbi.nih.gov/health/health-topics/topics/ic.

7

Medical Sensors

Level I: Core Concepts

7.1 Introduction

Biological organisms developed sensory capabilities to enhance their survival. Identifying foods sources, evading predators, enhanced communications, and finding mates are all augmented with more sophisticated methods of perceiving their environment. In the last two centuries, we have developed our own enhanced sensory technologies—x-rays, 3D computer tomography (CT), magnetic resonance imaging (MRI), EEGs, EKGs, high-resolution electron microscopes, genomic sequencers, etc.—to augment our senses to improve healthcare. These diagnostic technologies along with antibiotics, gene therapy, and modern pharmaceuticals have doubled life expectancy in the past century increasing our survival by utilizing our intellects. Modern *Homo sapiens* emerged approximately 200,000 years ago and only in the last few centuries, utilizing the scientific method, have we begun to be masters of our own fates.

This chapter will focus on the exponential growth of sensor technology and the science underpinning this growing discipline. Linked to high-speed communications with chip-sized microprocessors that can process terabytes (1,012 bytes) of data and mining these large data sets for gems, correlations linking diverse diseases and drug therapies, we can provide greater insights into treatments. Linking sensory data, from wearable and embedded sensors, body sensor networks (BSNs) etc., a group of sensors can provide a holistic analysis of an individual's medical status. All this data can then be fed, not only into electronic health records, but also stored in the Cloud providing larger analytics on the effectiveness of medical interventions that further accelerate medical science and possibly doubling, or greater, life spans again in the next century (Figure 7.1).

7.2 Electrical and Chemical Conduction Basics

Before delving into medical sensors, it's critical to understand the underlying physics, chemistry, and electronics principles underpinning medical sensors. A Biomedical Informatics professional needs to understand how and why it works and with this basic knowledge contribute to the advancement of the science and provide input to the next generation of sensors.

The intent of this first section is to ensure you are well grounded in the basic concepts of the relationship between atomic structure, the periodic table and its organization, the role valence electrons play in

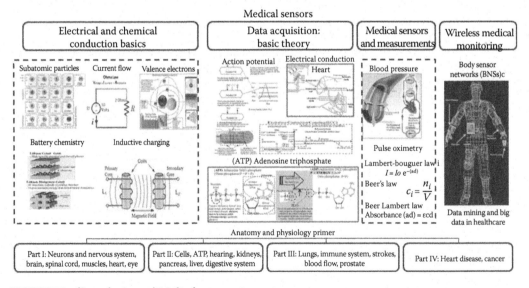

FIGURE 7.1 (See color insert.) Medical sensor primer.

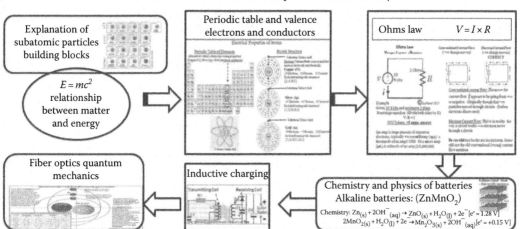

Electrical and chemical conduction primer: electrochemistry

FIGURE 7.2 (**See color insert.**) Linkages between topics covered in the first section.

electrical conduction, Ohm's law and basic circuit theory, the chemistry of batteries that power many medical sensors, and inductive charging used to charge batteries especially in the case of implantable medical devices. Figure 7.2 encapsulates the core concepts covered in this first section.

7.2.1 Subatomic Particles

Electrons are negatively charged subatomic particles. Subatomic means part of a larger atom. Atoms, at the most fundamental level, are compressed of energy. If you release the energy in a group of uranium or plutonium isotopes, isotopes are relatively unstable atoms that can be more readily broken apart to release their internal energy. Isotopes also refer to the fact that the same element such as uranium has forms with different numbers of neutrons. So uranium 235 is fissile, which means it can sustain a fission chain reaction, leading to the release of its inherent energy used for an atomic bomb. Uranium 235 has 143 neutrons and 92 protons and makes up 0.72% of all uranium atoms; the rest is primarily uranium 238 (99.2752%), which has 146 neutrons and 92 protons. U238 can't be used to support a chain reaction due to the fact that it has inelastic scattering where the kinetic energies essentially dissipate on collisions. Uranium 235 is different since it allows for elastic chain reactions, i.e., which cause additional reactions, i.e., positive feedback, which results in an amplifying effect. Those extra neutrons in 235 strike the other nucleus and the chain reaction continues creating a critical mass, i.e., sustained nuclear reaction. Just to be complete, there are a number of other uranium isotopes with different numbers of neutrons that make up <1% of the remaining family of uranium atoms (U217 to U243; Figure 7.3).

Fission equation: U235 plus *one neutron* results in krypton, barium, and *three neutrons* + energy:

$$_{92}U^{235} + {}_0n^1 \rightarrow {}_{55}Cs^{140} + {}_{37}Rb^{93} + 3\ {}_0n^1 + \textbf{energy}$$

$E = mc^2$ developed by Einstein states that "mass and energy are the same physical entity and can be changed into each other." Physical atoms, at a basic level excluding all the subcomponents or elementary particles like quarks, leptons, bosons, and gluons (i.e., there are six types of quarks—up, down, strange, charm, bottom, and top—that make up neutrons and protons), have a nucleus with protons (positive charge) and neutrons (no charge) with orbiting electrons (negative charge) that all make up the standard model of elementary particles. The Higgs boson, postulated in 1964, was recently confirmed by the Large Hadron Collider in 2012; it explains why particles have mass generating the Higgs field (particles gain matter by passing through the Higgs field) and is an important piece used to explain the standard model of elementary particles (Figure 7.4).

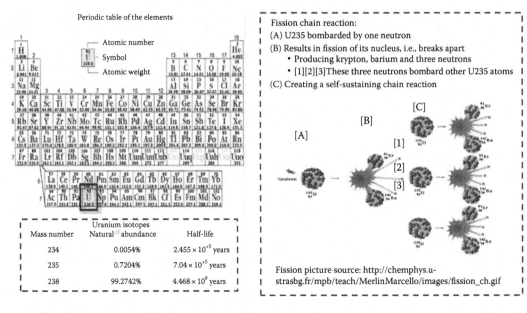

FIGURE 7.3 **(See color insert.)** Uranium isotopes and fission chain reaction.

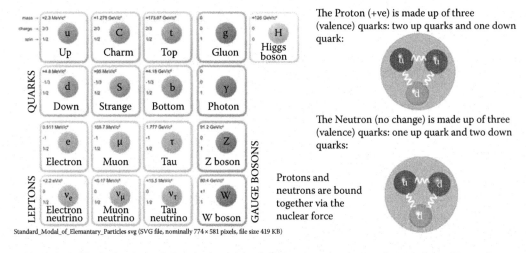

FIGURE 7.4 **(See color insert.)** Standard model of elementary particles inside a nucleus. (From Creative Commons, http://home.web.cern.ch/about/physics/standard-model).

Atoms are more complex than the simple +ve proton, neutral neutron, and −ve electron models we are familiar with. They contain 17 subcomponents (see Figure 7.4) including the now confirmed Higgs boson and Higgs field that gives mass to particles. Atoms have an overall zero net charge. That means the number of −ve negative electrons equals the number of +ve positive protons.

The succeeding text is a brief description of the standard model of particle physics (Conseil Européen pour la Recherche Nucléaire CERN http://home.web.cern.ch/about/physics/standard-model):

1. All matter around us is made of elementary particles, the building blocks of matter. These particles occur in two basic types called quarks and leptons. Each group consists of six particles, which are related in pairs.

2. The six leptons are similarly arranged in three generations—the *electron* and the *electron neutrino*, the *muon* and the *muon neutrino*, and the *tau* and the *tau neutrino*. The electron, the muon,

and the tau all have an electric charge and a sizeable mass, whereas the neutrinos are electrically neutral and have very little mass.

3. There are four fundamental forces at work in the universe: the strong force, the weak force, the electromagnetic force, and the gravitational force. They work over different ranges and have different strengths. Gravity is the weakest but it has an infinite range. The electromagnetic force also has infinite range but it is many times stronger than gravity. The weak and strong forces are effective only over a very short range and dominate only at the level of subatomic particles. Despite its name, the weak force is much stronger than gravity but it is the weakest of the other three. The strong force, as the name suggests, is the strongest of all four fundamental interactions.

4. Three of the fundamental forces result from the exchange of force-carrier particles, which belong to a broader group called "bosons." Particles of matter transfer discrete amounts of energy by exchanging bosons with each other. Each fundamental force has its own corresponding boson— the strong force is carried by the "gluon," the electromagnetic force is carried by the "photon," and the "W and Z bosons" are responsible for the weak force.

5. On October 8, 2013, the Nobel Prize in Physics was awarded jointly to François Englert and Peter Higgs "for the theoretical discovery of a mechanism that contributes to our understanding of the origin of mass of subatomic particles, and which recently was confirmed through the discovery of the predicted fundamental particle, by the ATLAS and CMS experiments at CERN's Large Hadron Collider."

7.2.2 Current and Ohm's Law

The flow of electrons in electronic devices and biological systems is essentially the flow of electrons, −ve charged particles. **Ohm's law $V = I \times R$** (Voltage = Current[I] [times] Resistance) describes the relationship between voltage (V), also called potential difference, which is the force that moves, or pulls, electrons through a wire; current (I), which is the measurement or amount of current flowing; and resistance (R), which regulates the amount of current. There are many ways to explain voltage. One side of the circuit has to be more positive than the other side. It pulls, or attracts, the −ve electrons through the wire. The *only moving component is these electrons, called current (I)*, which is measured in amps, and the electrons (−ve) are attracted to the positive (+ve) side, i.e., called potential difference between two sides of the wire. Resistance is a method of slowing down the electrons to control the amount of current, or electrons. Resistance is measured in ohms. Another analogy is water flowing in a pipe. The water is the current (electrons); turning on the faucet changes the water pressure, which is the voltage; and if you put rocks in the pipe, that would be equivalent to resistance slowing the movement of the water.

Example 7.1: If volts = 10 and resistance is **2 ohms**, then we can calculate the current through the circuit as $V/R = I$ or 10 V/**2 ohms** = *5 amps* (amps are a large amount of current).

Example 7.2: If you increase the resistance to **5 ohms**, then 10 V/**5 ohms** = *2 amps* (Figure 7.5).
Increasing resistance will reduce the current, or number of electrons, moving through the wire.

7.2.2.1 Circuit Diagrams

Conventional current flow: The arrow for current flow, shows the direction of electron movement, *I* as it goes from +ve to negative. Originally, it was thought that +ve particles moved through circuits (before electrons were discovered). This is incorrect but still used in many textbooks.

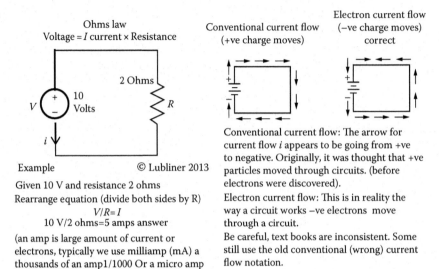

Conventional current flow: The arrow for current flow *i* appears to be going from +ve to negative. Originally, it was thought that +ve particles moved through circuits. (before electrons were discovered).

Electron current flow: This is in reality the way a circuit works −ve electrons move through a circuit.

Be careful, text books are inconsistent. Some still use the old conventional (wrong) current flow notation.

Ohms law
Voltage = *I* current × Resistance

2 Ohms

V (+ 10 Volts −) *R*

i

Example   © Lubliner 2013

Given 10 V and resistance 2 ohms
Rearrange equation (divide both sides by R)
$$V/R = I$$
10 V/2 ohms=5 amps answer

(an amp is large amount of current or electrons, typically we use milliamp (mA) a thousands of an amp1/1000 Or a micro amp (μA) A millionth of an amp (1/1,000,000)

FIGURE 7.5   Ohm's law. For example, $V = I \times R$.

Electron current flow: This is in reality the way a circuit works; −ve electrons move through a circuit, from −ve to positive. Correct representation of current flow.

Be careful, textbooks are inconsistent. Some still use the old conventional (wrong) current flow notation.

7.2.3 Electrochemistry

This section focuses on the linkages between chemistry, physics, and electrical conductors. Understanding the molecular connection of *valence electrons*, current flow, or a voltage caused by a chemical reaction in a battery is critical to understanding the underlying principles of medical sensors. Quantum mechanics addresses physics at the atomic level. When energy is applied to an atom, an electron can jump from a lower energy shell to a higher one in a discrete quantum. Once it returns back to its stable state, a photon is given off. This principle used is medical imaging. Adenosine triphosphate (ATP), chemical energy, utilizes the same quantum process, which is responsible for the energy released when ATP is hydrolyzed; add H_2O, and it is converted to ADP (diphosphate); a phosphate is broken off and the energy is released. This section introduces some of those concepts linking chemistry, physics, and electronics.

Definition:

Electrochemistry is "a science that deals with the relationship of electricity to chemical changes and the interconversion of chemical and electrical energy."*

7.2.3.1 Conductors

Wires or conductors are made of materials that have valence electrons in their outer shells that can be easily stripped off. In the periodic table, metals such as copper (Cu), silver (Ag), and gold (Au) are all in the same vertical column (group), which indicates similar electrical properties (Figure 7.6).

Batteries have zero voltage, no charge; they are composed of chemical solutions that can be charged by moving electrons from one side to another. If the chemical solution on the *positive* side has +5 protons and −4 electrons (+5 − 4 = +1), it has a net charge or voltage of +1. The electrons were moved to the *negative* side, which now has +5 protons and −6 electrons (+5−6 = −1). Then if a wire was placed between

---
* *Source:* Merriam Webster.

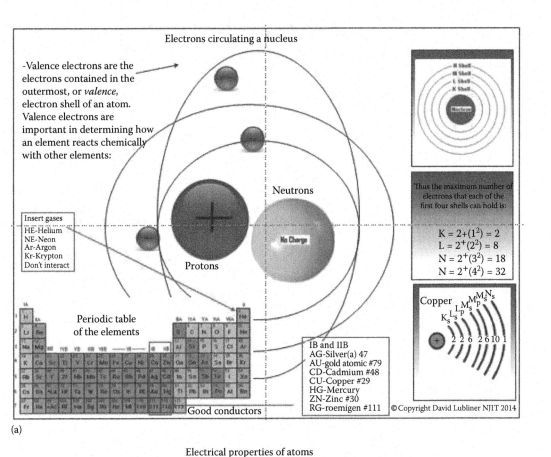

(a)

(b)

FIGURE 7.6 (See color insert.) Valence electrons, in an atom's outer shell, conduct current (I). (a) Copper (Cu), silver (Ag), and gold (Au) valence electrons. (b) Conductors in the periodic table group 11, all have 1 electron in their valence shell.

both sides of a battery, you would need to place some resistance in the wire or the electron flow would be so high the wires would melt; electrons will flow from the negative to positive side till they are balanced, i.e., net charge of zero (Figure 7.7).

Lithium ion batteries are common in electrical devices. They contain a negative electrode made of carbon (graphite), the positive electrode is a metal oxide (lithium cobalt oxide), and the electrolyte is a lithium salt in an organic solvent.

7.2.3.2 Batteries

Batteries provide electrical energy from chemical reactions. They incorporate electrochemical cells, which allow the flow of ions. Ions are atoms with an imbalance of electrons and protons, i.e., are positively and negatively charged (negative charge refers to molecules that have more −ve electrons than +ve protons). Alessandro Volta designed the first battery in 1800, but the general concept was discussed by Benjamin Franklin in 1748. The first practical battery cells appeared in the 1830s.

Batteries are classified by chemistry, voltage, specific energy, energy density, specific power, C rates, and load (measured in watts [w], volt-amps [VA], and power factor [pf] where 1 is optimum):

1. *Chemistry*: Most common are nickel and lithium (different chargers are recommended).
2. *Voltage*: Potential difference between two points (one side has more charge, +ve or −ve).
   a. Open-circuit voltage.
   b. Closed-circuit voltage (underload).
3. *Capacity*: Measured in ampere-hours (AH) at a given discharge rate (for example, 20 amps delivered for 10 h = 20 × 10 = *200 AH*) (it is usually less than the max capacity rating).
4. *Specific energy*: Is energy per unit mass. It is measured in watt-hours/kilogram (also called gravimetric energy density).
5. *Energy density*: Is energy stored in a given unit of space. It is measured in watt-hour/L (liter of volume) (also called volumetric energy density).
6. *Specific power*: Is the load density, how much current can it draw.
7. *C rates*: Charge and discharge rates.
8. *Load*: Drawing energy from the battery with reduced charge and resistance drops over time.

Convention compares battery ratings over a 20 hours period at 68°F. A 50 AH battery releases 2.5amps over 20 h (50 AH = 2.5 amps × 20). Battery ratings are quantified by the relationship between capacity, current, and discharge time described by *Peukert's law*, developed originally for lead–acid batteries. Another perspective is the efficiency factor for discharging a battery. In a lead–acid battery that has 180 amp rating, you would expect 180 amps for 1 hour and 90 amps for 2 hours, but that is not the case. In reality you would get 180 amps for 37 minutes, a *63% loss* due to the inherent limitations of batteries. The rule is the smaller the current draw, the closer it gets to the maximum rating of the battery. Finally, the Peukert value increases with age, which also limits the total current available.

7.2.3.2.1 Peukert Equation for Battery Efficiency

Peukert's law determines battery efficiency, which is the relationship between what is put in and what is removed. Lead–acid batteries have a 75% efficiency, so only three-fourths of what's put in can be utilized (i.e., this is affected by discharge rates and temperature). Battery capacity is the useable amount of energy in a battery. In general, a manufacturers' listed capacity, in AH, is only 80% available for use. For example, if a battery has 1,000 AH, only 800 amps are actually available. An AH is the total amount of electrical charge transferred when a current of 1 amp flows for 1 hour. A Peukert value of 1 indicates a well-performing battery with good efficiency and minimal loss (Figure 7.8).

Peukert values for common batteries are as follows:

- Lithium ion batteries: 1.08
- Nickel based: 1.1–1.5
- Lead–acid batteries of 1.3–1.4 used for k in the succeeding formula I^k

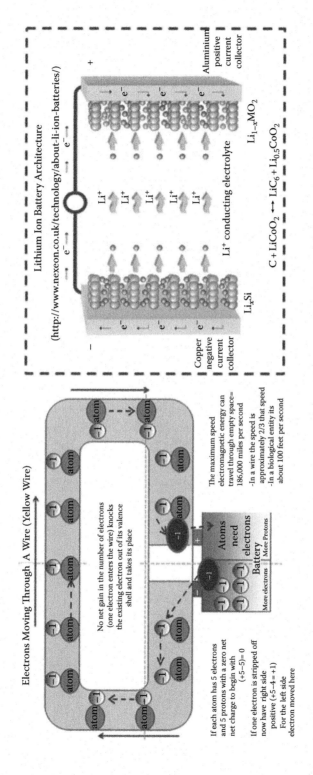

FIGURE 7.7 (See color insert.) Battery and electrons (valence shell) moving through a wire and lithium ion battery.

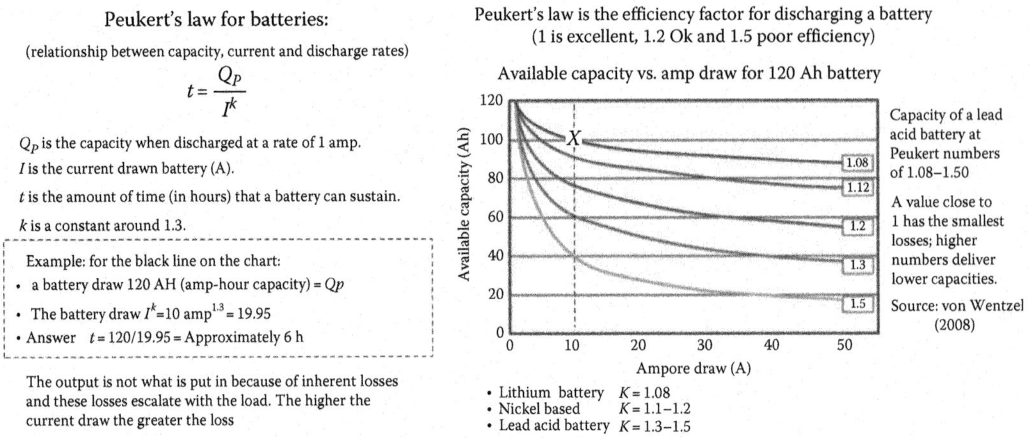
Peukert's law for batteries:
(relationship between capacity, current and discharge rates)
t = Qp / I^k
Qp is the capacity when discharged at a rate of 1 amp.
I is the current drawn battery (A).
t is the amount of time (in hours) that a battery can sustain.
k is a constant around 1.3.
Example: for the black line on the chart:
• a battery draw 120 AH (amp-hour capacity) = Qp
• The battery draw I^k=10 amp^1.3 = 19.95
• Answer t = 120/19.95 = Approximately 6 h
The output is not what is put in because of inherent losses and these losses escalate with the load. The higher the current draw the greater the loss
Peukert's law is the efficiency factor for discharging a battery
(1 is excellent, 1.2 Ok and 1.5 poor efficiency)
Available capacity vs. amp draw for 120 Ah battery
Available capacity (Ah)
120
100
80
60
40
20
0
X
1.08
1.12
1.2
1.3
1.5
0
10
20
30
40
50
Ampore draw (A)
Capacity of a lead acid battery at Peukert numbers of 1.08–1.50
A value close to 1 has the smallest losses; higher numbers deliver lower capacities.
Source: von Wentzel (2008)
• Lithium battery K = 1.08
• Nickel based K = 1.1–1.2
• Lead acid battery K = 1.3–1.5

FIGURE 7.8 Peukert equation for calculation battery efficiency.

The term "battery memory effect" refers to batteries that hold less charge if they are charged and discharged at less than full power, found in rechargeable batteries made from nickel–cadmium and nickel–metal hydride. The environmental impact is that batteries with lead and cadmium in lead–acid and nickel–cadmium batteries have to be treated as *hazardous materials.*

7.2.3.3 Battery Classification

The following is a list of characteristics of popular batteries. Batteries are classified by their performance characteristics. For example, are high-surge currents needed when starting cars (lead–acid provides high-surge current)?

1. *Lead–acid batteries* (invented in 1859; are the oldest rechargeable battery)
   a. Ability to provide high-surge currents, used in automobiles.
   b. Inexpensive.
   c. Low energy-to-weight ratio.
   d. Used as backup for cell towers.
   e. Chemistry: (negative plate) $Pb(s) + HSO_4^-(aq) \rightarrow PbSO_4(s) + H + (aq) + 2e^-$.
   f. Advantage over other chemistries. It is relatively simple to determine the state of charge by measuring the specific gravity of the electrolyte.
   g. Excessive overcharging can result in gassing, releasing hydrogen and oxygen, which can result in an explosion if not properly vented.
   h. Environmental concerns: Some of the lead products are very toxic and have to be properly handled when discarding. Toxins dangerous to children.
2. *Nickel–iron rechargeable batteries* (*NiFe*) (invented in 1899)
   a. Have nickel-ion-hydroxide and iron plates.
   b. Used in backup systems but have poor charge retention.
   c. Chemistry: $2NiOOH + 2H_2O + 2e^- \leftrightarrow 2Ni(OH)_2 + 2OH^-$.
   d. The charging and discharging transfer of oxygen from one electrode to the other.
   e. Environmental impact: Do not have to be treated as hazardous materials.
3. *Nickel–zinc rechargeable battery* (*NiZn*) (In 1901, Edison received a patent [#684,204])
   a. Often used in AA and AAA batteries.
   b. Higher discharge ratio, up to 75%, compared to lead–acid batteries.
   c. After 30 charges, batteries tend to self-discharge more quickly.
   d. Chemistry: $2H_2O + Zn + 2NiOOH \leftrightarrow Zn(OH)_2 + 2Ni(OH)_2$.
   e. Usually expensive.

4. *Alkaline batteries (ZnMnO₂)* (developed in 1899)
   a. Contain zinc and manganese dioxide.
   b. Higher energy density than zinc–carbon batteries.
   c. Largest percentage of batteries made in the United States.
   d. Chemistry: $Zn_{(s)} + 2OH^-_{(aq)} \rightarrow ZnO_{(s)} + H_2O_{(l)} + 2e^-$ [e° = 1.28 V].
   e. $2MnO_{2(s)} + H_2O_{(l)} + 2e^- \rightarrow Mn_2O_{3(s)} + 2OH^-_{(aq)}$ [e° = +0.15 V].
   f. Most are not designed for recharging, though some are.
   g. Newer alkaline batteries are allowed to be disposed of as regular domestic waste.
5. *Lithium ion batteries (Li-ion)*
   a. There are environmental benefits with reduced toxins compared to conventional batteries.
   b. Lightweight: They have higher capacity/weight ration than convention batteries.
   c. Low discharge rate 1.5% per month.
   d. Safety issues if overcharged or overheated.
   e. Do not suffer from memory charging effect.

7.2.3.3.1 Battery Energy Density Levels

Energy density is defined as "the amount of energy stored in a given system or region per unit volume."*

The succeeding chart illustrates the energy density comparison ranging from lead–acid to lithium–cobalt batteries (Figures 7.9 and 7.10). Lead–acid has 50% of the energy capacity of lithium oxide.

7.2.3.4 Inductive Charging

Charging devices without a physical connection can be an important feature of implanted or wireless medical devices. Any opening in the skin is a pathway for infection. So the optimal configuration is wireless inductive charging. Inductive charging involves two coils separated by a small distance. Current going through a coil produces a magnetic field. A second coil utilizes that magnetic field to create current flow in the second device, thus charging the implanted battery.

Lithium cobalt batteries, or more specifically Lithium Nickel Cobalt Aluminum Oxide (LiNiCoA1O₂), are able to store the highest capacity, or specific energy per unit size.

A. High specific energy and power densities
B. Long life span
C. Used in electric vehicles
D. Negatives: high cost and safety issues

Lithium manganese or more specifically Lithium Nickel Manganese Cobalt Oxide (LiNiMnCoO₂), and lithium phosphate, Lithium Iron Phosphate (LiFePO₄), have higher load, power draw capabilities.

A. Nickel is known for its high specific energy, but low stability
B. Manganese has low internal resistance and low specific energies

Lithium cobalt oxide
-High specific energies used for cell phones

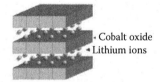

· Cobalt oxide
◄ Lithium ions

Lithium manganese cobalt
-3D structure: cathode crystalline structure
-50% more energy than nickle-based chemistries.

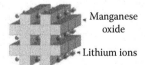

◄ Manganese
 oxide

◄ Lithium ions

http://batteryuniversity.com/leam/article/types_of_lithium_ion

FIGURE 7.9   Comparison of high-energy lithium cob lot versus high-energy lithium manganese.

---

* *Source*: Dictionary.com.

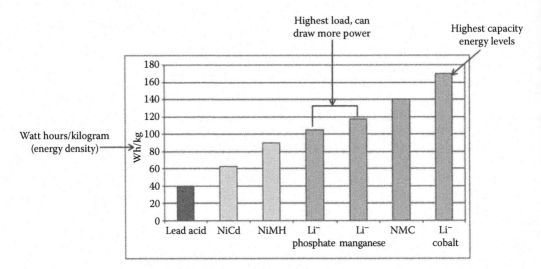

FIGURE 7.10 Comparison of battery energy densities. (From http://batteryuniversity.com/learn/article/types_of_lithium_ion.)

> Definition: *Inductive charging* is a method by which a magnetic field transfers electricity from an external source to a mobile device without the use of standard wiring. It does this by generating a magnetic field and creating a current in the receiving device. Electricity can move through the air and recharge your device's battery.

> **(http://wireless-charger-review.toptenreviews.com/wireless-chargers-inductive-charging-explained.html.)**

When transferring energy between coils and the transformer equation in the succeeding text, transformers are used to step up or down current. When you plug in a charger for your phone, a transformer, which has two coils, reduces voltage from 110 ac to 9 V dc.

The transformer equation relates to the turns of wire on the coil, i.e., a coil is wire wrapped around a metal post a few thousand times. The equation relates the voltage between the first, primary coil to the secondary coil. Transformers work with alternating current that creates a changing magnetic field. So in the secondary coil, you then convert the ac to dc (Figure 7.11):

$$Vp/Vs = Np/Ns$$

where
   Vp is the voltage in the primary core
   Np is the turns of wire in the primary core
   Vs is the voltage in the secondary core
   Ns is the turns in the secondary core

7.2.4 Fiber Optics

Electrons are not the only way information can flow through wires. Photons, packets of energy, can flow through fiber-optic cables, pure glass materials, with almost no resistance. Photons are generated when energy is applied to an atom. An electron moves from a lower energy shell to a higher one. Quantum mechanics states that electrons are in fixed orbits and can only exist at discrete shells or energy levels. When that moved electron returns to its preferred low shell or lower-energy state, one packet of energy or photon is given off (Figure 7.12).

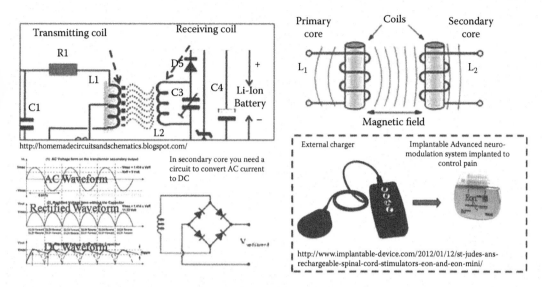

FIGURE 7.11 Inductive current circuit and coils, conversion from ac to dc, and implantable neuromodulation system with 10-year life span charged externally using inductive charging device.

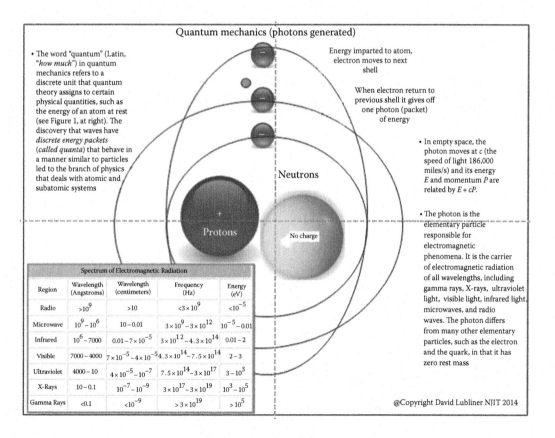

FIGURE 7.12 Quantum mechanics, photons created when electrons return to their original shells.

7.3 Data Acquisition: Medical Sensors

Medical data acquisition falls into a number of categories: electrical (EEG/EKG), electromagnetic, imaging (MRI, PET), chemical, biological, and genomic data sequencing. This section describes the theory behind some of those data acquisition technologies and explains various medical sensors and scanners. A prerequisite for mining data and extracting meaning is a basic understanding of those technologies that generate this information.

7.3.1 Sensors

Electrical current in nerve cells, at the highest level of abstraction, current flows (electrons –ve) move toward a positive potential, i.e., one side of a wire or nerve is positive. In a battery, you have two chemical solutions, initially both neutral; let's say, for argument, that the atoms on each side of the battery have 10 protons and 10 electrons. When charging a battery, you move electrons from one side to the other, i.e., one side has 9 electrons and the other 11 electrons (Figure 7.13). This provides a positive potential difference between the two sides of the battery, i.e., one side is more positive than the other. When connecting a wire between terminals of the battery, the electrons, negative, move to the positive side. Once both sides are neutral, both have 10 protons, positive, and 10 electrons, the potential difference disappears, and no current flows.

The same is true for electron flow in the body. In order for current to flow, a potential difference must be created from one synapse, the space between neurons, to the next. This is achieved by pumping positive ions across that gap between nerves. This sodium (NA^+)–potassium (K^+) pump (Figure 7.13).

7.3.2 Electrical Conduction System of the Heart

7.3.2.1 Action Potential

EKG measures the electrical activity of the cardiac muscle of the heart. When the sinoatrial (SA) node, the pacemaker of the heart located in the right atrium, initiates signals, it then sends signals to the atrioventricular (AV) node, then the bundle of His, and the right and left bundle branches and then to the Purkinje fibers that propagate the signals to the ventricles.

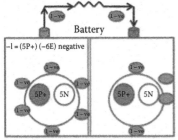

Resistance to regulate current flow
$V = IR$ Voltage = current*resistance

Potential difference, or voltage, between the two electrodes; i.e. one side is more positive than the other. We move –ve eletrons, charge the battery, from one side to the other.
© Potential difference Lubliner 2012

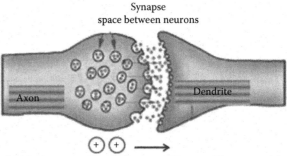

Synapse
space between neurons

Positive ions moved across the gap making one side more positive, potential difference

FIGURE 7.13 Potential difference in a battery and 4b potential generated in synapse.

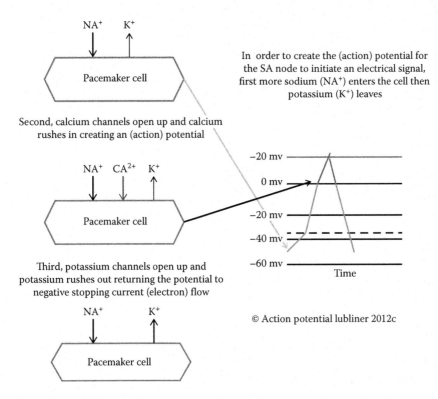

In order to create the (action) potential for the SA node to initiate an electrical signal, first more sodium (NA⁺) enters the cell then potassium (K⁺) leaves

Second, calcium channels open up and calcium rushes in creating an (action) potential

Third, potassium channels open up and potassium rushes out returning the potential to negative stopping current (electron) flow

© Action potential lubliner 2012c

FIGURE 7.14   Action potential in cardiac nerves.

In the SA node/pacemaker step 1, a large number of sodium ions (NA⁺) and a small number of potassium ions (K⁺) are migrating through the cell. Then in step 2, calcium (CA²⁺) channels open up, creating an (action) potential, i.e., cells become more positive generating a current (flow of electrons) in millivolts, a thousandth of a volt (Figure 7.6). In step 3, a potassium channel opens up so more potassium ions flow out and the potential difference returns to negative, stopping the flow of current.

The action potential in cardiac muscle cells is initiated by a sodium spike that generates a calcium spike, which then produces muscle contraction (Figure 7.14). The voltage of a cell is usually measured in millivolts (mv), a thousandth of a volt.

7.3.2.1.1 Excitation–Contraction Coupling

This section is intended to provide more detail than the previous action potential section specifically focusing on electrical properties. The cardiac myocyte is a muscle cell that is 100 μ in length. It is composed of bundles of myofibrils that contain filaments. The myofibril, tubelike structures, propagates signals inside the muscles. They have repeating *sarcomeres*, which contract and have regions of microfilaments composed of myosin and actin. Excitation–contraction coupling (ECC) is the process whereby an action potential triggers a myocyte to contract [4].

ECC: The action potential in cardiac myocytes (Figure 7.15).

The interior of the muscle cells have a negative charge, so moving positive ions in and out of the cells produce action potential, a fast positive spike that triggers the cell to contract. The positive ions are Ca²⁺ (calcium +123 mv), Na⁺ (sodium +67 mv), and K⁺ (potassium −92 mv); the ions move into and out of cells, via voltage-gated cells, that change the polarity inducing muscle contraction.

1. Begins with a baseline negative state (−90 mv)—**stage 4**
2. Threshold (70 mv): Ca²⁺ and Na⁺ enter the cell and become more positive—**stage 0**

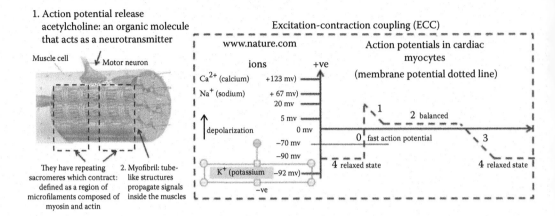

1. Action potential release acetylcholine: an organic molecule that acts as a neurotransmitter

Muscle cell

Motor neuron

They have repeating sacromeres which contract: defined as a region of microfilaments composed of myosin and actin

2. Myofibril: tube-like structures propagate signals inside the muscles

Excitation-contraction coupling (ECC)

www.nature.com

Action potentials in cardiac myocytes (membrane potential dotted line)

ions   +ve

Ca²⁺ (calcium)   +123 mv

Na⁺ (sodium)   + 67 mv

                            20 mv

                             5 mv

depolarization   0 mv

                           −70 mv

                           −90 mv

K⁺ (potassium) −92 mv

                             −ve

1

2 balanced

0 fast action potential

3

4 relaxed state

4 relaxed state

FIGURE 7.15   **(See color insert.)** Cardiac myocytes and the ECC action potential triggered by sodium, calcium, and potassium ions.

3. Fast Na^+ channels open, Na^+ enters the cell, and voltage-gated cells close when it reaches 20 mv— **stage 1**
4. K^+ channels open and move to negative, and Ca^{2+} enters and stabilizes (flat line 5 mv)—**stage 2**
5. Ca^{2+} channels close and it goes negative—**stage 3**

7.3.2.2 Cardiac Conduction System

The heart takes deoxygenated blood from the veins, entering through the right side of the heart; blood passes through the right atrium and right ventricle and then moves to the lungs to oxygenate the blood (and releases CO_2); it then returns to the left atrium and left ventricle and passes out of the aorta to the arteries and to the rest of the body.

7.3.2.2.1 Definition

- The *SA node* is located in the right atrium where the superior vena cava joins the atrial tissue; the SA node acts as the main pacemaker in the heart.
- *Automaticity*: AV cells can depolarize by themselves.
- *Depolarization*: Muscle cells, cardiac myocytes, are made up of negatively charged cells; when positive ions are pumped into the cell, calcium (Ca^{2+}), sodium (Na^+), and potassium (K^+), the polarity of the cell becomes positive and the cell contracts (negative to positive membrane potential).

7.3.2.2.2 Electrical Conduction in the Heart

Step 1: The SA node is composed of negatively charged cells that can depolarize by themselves called automaticity. They send out depolarization signals, to start other muscles cells to contract (from the SA node, the impulse travels through the right and left atrium along three internodal tracts) (Figures 7.16 and 7.17).

Step 2: This depolarization signal goes simultaneously to the left atrium, called Bachman's bundle, and to the AV node. It travels along three internodal tracks: anterior, Wenckebach's, and Thorel's.

Step 3: The AV node creates a 0.1 second delay (explanation: the atria contracts, the signal is sent from the first SA node to the atria, then the depolarization signal travels to the AV node and delays, and then the ventricles contract; the purpose is to move the blood first from the atria and then

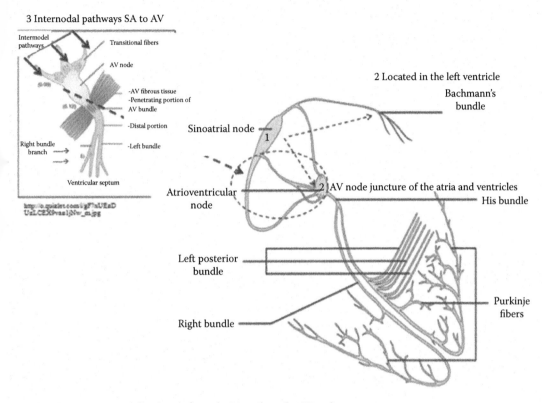

FIGURE 7.16 Intermodal pathways from the SA node to the AV node.

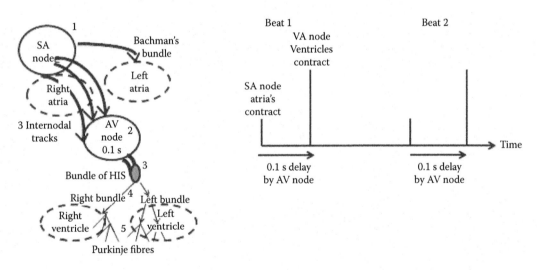

FIGURE 7.17 Electrical conduction system of the heart.

they contract and push the blood to the ventricles, which then also contract; timing needs to be properly sequenced).

Step 4: The AV node sends the signal to the bundle of His.

Step 5: From there, it splits to the right bundle wires (nerves) and left bundle (the left bundle broken into left posterior fascicle and right anterior fascicle).

Step 6: The signal spreads out to smaller nerves in the ventricles called the Purkinje fibers.

7.3.2.3 Adenosine Triphosphate

ATP is a molecule that provides energy to power biological systems, i.e., intercellular energy transfer or chemical energy in cells for metabolism, an enzyme-catalyzed reaction. ATP is made up of three phosphate groups, each having a phosphate atom with three oxygen atoms, and an adenosine molecule that's composed of adenine (subcomponent of DNA: adenine, guanine, cytosine, and thymine) and ribose, a subcomponent of RNA.

When ATP is hydrolyzed and H_2O is added, it breaks into a phosphate and ADP and *releases energy* that can be used for intercellular energy. One hydrogen atom bonds to the diphosphate molecule, the other to the phosphate, creating a resonance state, a stable state for the molecules (Figure 7.18). As we discussed earlier, when describing quantum mechanics, electrons want to return to their stable states. So in ATP, the third phosphate shares an electron in a higher energy state with another phosphate group, i.e., an electron in a higher orbit, but when hydrolyzed, it releases energy and returns to its original lower stable electron state, orbit (Figure 7.18).

7.3.3 Blood Pressure

Blood pressure is the pressure on the walls of blood vessels that is exerted by circulating blood and is measured by the force per unit area. Blood pressure is the brachial arterial pressure usually measured in the upper arm as blood moves away from the heart.

1. When the heart muscle *contracts*, called *systole*, it pumps blood *out of the heart through* the arteries to the rest of the body. This blood pressure on the arteries is systole. Normal blood pressure is 120 or lower. Hypertension, or high blood pressure, is 140 or above. A systolic pressure of 120–139 is prehypertension, meaning there is an elevated risk of heart disease.
    a. The heart contracts in two stages.
        i. In the first stage, the right and left atria contract at the same time, pumping blood to the right and left ventricles.
        ii. Then the ventricles contract together to propel blood out of the heart.
2. Then the *heart muscle relaxes*, called *diastole*, before the next heartbeat. This allows blood to fill up in the heart again. This is the lower reading in blood pressure that indicates the pressure on the arteries when the heart rests between beats. Normal values are 80 or below. A diastolic pressure of 90 or above is hypertension and 80 to 89 is prehypertension.

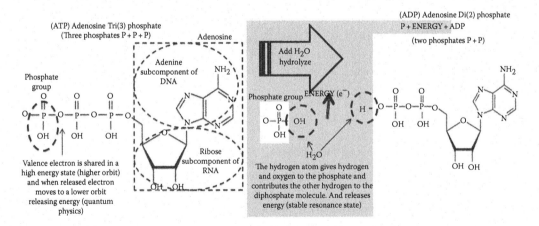

FIGURE 7.18 ATP molecule, which hydrolyzes released energy, results in ADP. (From http://en.wikipedia.org/wiki/File:Adenosintriphosphat_protoniert.svg.)

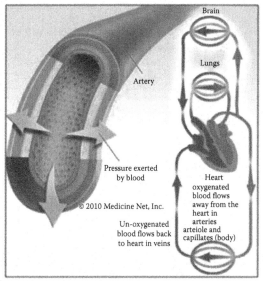

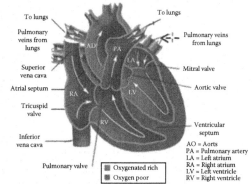

Pulmonary vein: a vein that carries oxygenated blood from the lungs to the left atrium of the heart.
(It's the only vein that carries oxygenated blood)

http://www.emedicinehealth.com/high_blood_pressure/article_em.htm.

http://reyesdiannemarie.wix.com/oxygenation#gallery

FIGURE 7.19   **(See color insert.)** Blood pressure exerted on the artery walls.

The conventional device used to measure blood pressure is called the sphygmomanometer. It has a pressure gauge, and when the cuff is inflated to a pressure higher than your systolic pressure, it stops blood flow. The pressure is slowly released and, through a stethoscope, a hearing device, a whooshing sound is heard, and at this point, the systolic pressure is measured; when this sound goes away, the diastolic pressure is measured (Figure 7.19). A number of wearable (watch) blood pressure devices are available that conform to the same process (accuracy of wearable devices is within 5% of manual devices).

7.3.4 Pulse Oximetry

Pulse oximetry is a noninvasive method of monitoring oxygen saturation of a patient's hemoglobin, the protein in blood that carries oxygen. Pulse oximetry can alternatively be measured invasively by arterial blood gas (ABG) analysis. Individuals without coronary disease have a pulse oximetry reading of 90% to 95%. In transmissive pulse oximetry, the process uses a pair of light-emitting diodes on one side of a finger and a photoreceptor on the other. There are two LEDs, one red at 660 nm wavelength and a second at 905 to 940 nm in the infrared range. The absorption at these wavelengths differs between its oxygenated hemoglobin and deoxygenated state. The ratio of the two can be calculated using the two frequencies. The absorption is calculated from the minimum versus peak values of the pulsing arterial blood flow, which makes simultaneous monitoring of the pulse critical. Reflective pulse oximetry can be used in more areas of the body but can lead to inaccurate readings in cyanotic tissues close to the surface having low oxygenation, or areas where arterial and venous pulsations mask readings.

Limits of pulse oximetry

- *Hypoperfusion*: Inaccurate low readings may be caused by vasoconstriction, i.e., narrowing of the blood vessels that results from contraction of the muscular walls of the vessels or poor circulation in the extremity.
- Calloused skin.
- Movement (shivering).

7.3.4.1 Physics of Pulse Oximetry

The two wavelengths of light used in pulse oximetry are red at 660 nm and infrared at 905 to 940 nm. Radiation absorption is governed by two laws, Beer's law and the Lambert–Bouguer law.

1. Lambert–Bouguer law involves
   a. A solution of thickness (*d*)
   b. The solution is transilluminated by monochromatic light (*I*)
      i. Definition: Transilluminate refers to passing a strong light through an organ or part of the body in order to detect disease or abnormality.
   c. Incident light (*Io*): The direct light that falls on a surface:

$$I = Io\ e^{-(ad)}$$

2. Beer's law
   The absorbance is a linear function of the molar concentration.
   Definition: The molar concentration, C_i, is defined as the amount of a constituent n_i measured in moles divided by the volume of the mixture V:

$$C_i = \frac{n_i}{V}$$

3. Beer–Lambert law
   Definition: Attenuation of light by a material passing through a substance. A photon is absorbed by matter, the electrons, and transformed into internal energy or thermal energy. The reduction in intensity of the light wave is referred to as absorption.
   a. ε is the molar extinction coefficient:
      i. The greater ε is, the greater the absorption, which means less light is transmitted.
      ii. Oxygenated hemoglobin (HbO_2) at 660 nm has a lesser extinction coefficient than hemoglobin (Hb) and therefore absorbs less red light.
   b. *c* is the molar concentration.
   c. *d* is the thickness of the layer.
   Absorbance (ad) = εcd
   Definitions:
1. *Oxyhemoglobin (oxygenated hemoglobin [HbO_2]) saturation is the ratio*, expressed as a percentage of the amount of oxygen relative to the total amount of hemoglobin in the blood.
2. *Hemoglobin* is an iron-containing protein bound to red blood cells and makes up nearly all the oxygen presence: except there is a small amount dissolved in the plasma. It's a metalloprotein, a generic term for a protein that contains a metal ion cofactor.
   a. Hemoglobin is responsible for transporting oxygen from lungs to other parts of the body. Oxyhemoglobin (HbO_2) is the red hemoglobin that is a combination of hemoglobin and oxygen from the lungs.
   b. A hemoglobin molecule can carry a maximum of four oxygen molecules. For example, 100 hemoglobin molecules could carry a maximum of 400 oxygen molecules (100 × 4); if it only carried 360 oxygen molecules, (360/400) × 100% = *90% saturation rate*.
   c. The protein makes up about 96% of the red blood cells' dry content (by weight) and around 35% of the total content (including water) in mammals.
      i. It carries a portion of the body's respiratory CO_2, about 10% of the total, and the regulatory molecule nitric oxide.

7.3.4.2 Arterial Blood Gasses

ABG requires drawing blood from an artery, often taken from the radial artery at the wrist or the femoral artery in the groin, but a number of other sites are used. ABG provides more comprehensive information than simply pulse oximetry information, which is vital for critically ill patients in intensive care units.

ABG measurements

1. pH of the blood.
2. Partial pressure of carbon dioxide and oxygen.
3. Transcutaneous carbon dioxide measurement is an alternative method of obtaining similar information as well.
4. An ABG test measures the arterial oxygen tension (**PaO_2**).
5. Carbon dioxide tension (**$PaCO_2$**).
6. Arterial oxygen saturation is (**SpO_2**) in the range of 95% to 100%.
   a. Defined as the ratio of oxygen to the total concentration of hemoglobin present in the blood.
7. Venous Oxygen Saturation (SvO_2) (Range 65%–75%)
   b. Percentage of oxygen bound to hemoglobin in blood returning to the right side of the heart. This is the oxygen remaining after the tissues remove what they need. It is used to determine when a patient's body is extracting more oxygen than normal. It's taken from the tip of the pulmonary artery catheter

$$\text{Oxygen delivery (}DO_2\text{)} = \text{cardiac output (HR} \times \text{stroke volume)} \times \text{oxygen content (Hb} \times SaO_2)$$

   c. *Rationale*: If SvO_2 *decreases*, it indicates that the tissues are extracting a higher percentage of oxygen from the blood than normal.
      i. It may imply that the cardiac output is not high enough to meet tissue oxygen needs.
      ii. Another explanation is that the patient has resorted to anaerobic metabolism. (Anaerobic metabolism is the creation of energy through the combustion of carbohydrates in the absence of oxygen.) It indicates that the tissues are unable to extract enough oxygen. It can be seen in late septic shock or poisoning such as cyanide.
      iii. Measuring SvO_2 before and after a change can determine if the therapy was beneficial.
      iv. It's also helpful when evaluating changes to ventilator therapy.

7.3.5 Neurons

Neurons are electrically excitable cells that communicate information through electrical and chemical signals. Neurons are connected via synapses, a structure that allows a neuron to pass an electrical or chemical signal to another neuron (Figure 7.20). Na^+ ions, from other neurons, are attached to the neuron via the dendrites, synapse in between the connection, thin filaments. When enough of these dendrites send a sufficient amount of Na^+ ions, the action potential of the cell is triggered and a signal is sent along the neuron. As the charge dissipates along the length of the neuron, electrotonic spread, voltage-gated channels open up to add more Na^+ ions amplifying the signal.

The architecture of a neuron starts with a nucleus surrounded by a cell body or soma. They have a number of branching structures called dendrites that receive signals. Dendrites are connected to other neurons. If multiple signals on different dendrites reach a threshold, they are added up to generate a composite signal. They trigger an action potential, and a signal is sent along the axon. This signal might trigger muscles or other neurons. Neurons are connected through axons, long conductors, that are covered with Schwann cells covered in an insulating myelin sheath. The myelin sheath creates an insulated wire that allows signals to flow faster than action potentials. There are gaps between these insulators; myelin sheaths are called nodes of Ranvier. The rationale, reiterating concept from earlier, of the nodes of Ranvier is that since current dissipates along the neuron, called electrotonic spread, at these

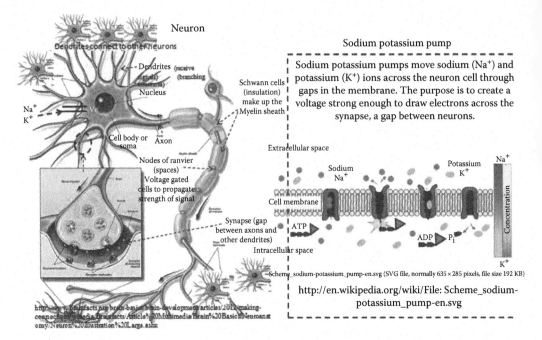

Neuron

Dendrites connect to other neurons

Dendrites (receive inputs) (branching)

Nucleus

Na$^+$
K$^+$

Cell body or soma   Axon

Schwann cells (insulation) make up the Myelin sheath

Nodes of ranvier (spaces)

Voltage gated cells to propagate strength of signal

Synapse (gap between axons and other dendrites)

Sodium potassium pump

Sodium potassium pumps move sodium (Na$^+$) and potassium (K$^+$) ions across the neuron cell through gaps in the membrane. The purpose is to create a voltage strong enough to draw electrons across the synapse, a gap between neurons.

Extracellular space

Sodium Na$^+$

Potassium K$^+$

Na$^+$

Cell membrane

ATP

ADP   P$_i$

Intracellular space

Concentration

K$^+$

Scheme_sodium-potassium_pump-en.svg (SVG file, normally 635 × 285 pixels, file size 192 KB)

http://en.wikipedia.org/wiki/File: Scheme_sodium-potassium_pump-en.svg

FIGURE 7.20   (See color insert.) Neurons and signal transmission across synapses.

junctures, voltage-gated channels open up to allow in more Na$^+$ ions in to propagate the signal down the length of the neuron, essentially amplifying the signal (Figure 7.20).

Sodium–potassium pumps move sodium (Na$^+$) and potassium (K$^+$) ions across the neuron cell through gaps in the membrane. The purpose is to create a voltage strong enough to draw electrons across the synapse, a gap between neurons; it's a structure that permits a neuron (or nerve cell) to pass an electrical or chemical signal to another cell and create current flow. It uses ATP cellular energy to bind the Na$^+$ and K$^+$ to proteins to the surface of the pump to draw in or expel ions. The neuron cells are negative inside and positive outside creating a voltage (potential) difference. There are positive sodium and potassium ions outside the neuron and the cell is negative inside. As we discussed earlier, a resting balance −ve 70 mv is maintained by channels in the neuron cell membrane that allows Na$^+$ and K$^+$ to move in and out of the neuron to maintain this resting balance. Finally, the channels maintain the negative potential difference inside due to the fact that these channels are less permeable to Na$^+$ flowing in and more permeable to K$^+$ flowing out.

When signals propagate along neurons, Na$^+$ ions flow in channels into the neuron membrane, creating a current, and over distances in the neuron, these Na$^+$ ions dissipate (called electrotonic spread, meaning the concentration per unit area is less; voltage-gated channels open up further down the neuron to add more Na$^+$ ions in to propagate the signal [Figure 7.21]).

Definition:

Electrotonic spread. A change in membrane potential (e.g., a receptor potential or synaptic potential) originating in one region of a cell (ΔV_0) is associated with local transmembrane currents that distribute and flow intracellularly and extracellularly to adjacent membrane regions (at distance d), where they in turn cause changes in membrane potential ($\Delta V(d)$). However, the underlying currents get progressively smaller with distance because fractions of them are diverted through transmembrane ion leak channels. Thereby, the elicited adjacent membrane potential changes ($\Delta V(d)$) are reduced in size and altered in shape (electrotonic decrement), http://www.springerreference.com/docs/html/chapterdbid/116505.html.

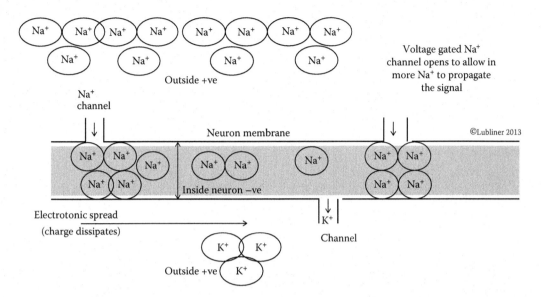

FIGURE 7.21 Electrotonic spread: charge dissipates over the length of the neuron so additional voltage-gated channels open up to allow in more Na⁺ ions to propagate the signal.

Level II: Wireless Medical Monitoring

7.4 Wireless Medical Devices

Wireless medical devices are defined as "any medical monitoring technology, worn or implanted, that gather physiological information [14]." These devices can contain local data storage for subsequent download or to transmit data in real time via various wireless technologies such as Bluetooth or protected wireless spectrums designated by the Federal Communications Commission (FCC) as indicated by 802.11b specifications.

These sensors are classified as either stand-alone devices or integrated in a sensor network where all devices share a common microprocessor controller that sends information as an integrated package. Both hospitals and individuals now currently utilize these devices. Research has indicated that these real-time data have reduced follow-up admissions. A new field is emerging where BSNs, an integrated suite of mobile medical monitors, are often integrated into clothing that can be a significant aid to prevent more serious conditions.

As wireless medical devices or body sensor webs become common, large real-time data streams from millions of devices are creating a new challenge in real-time data mining/big data, defined as extremely large data sets [11]. To analyze this data in near real time, or to respond to possible life-threatening conditions in a timely matter by locally intelligent processing, tablet or PC, can display trends in an easily decipherable format. Filtering this data at the transmission source to transmit just summary information; and any anomalous readings; i.e., high blood pressure or high glucose levels, can be used to reduce large data sets to manageable levels. Life expectancy has doubled in the last 100 years; the potential to match this rate of improvement utilizing real-time wireless sensors integrated with smart devices/phones has the potential to be transformational.

7.4.1 Bluetooth Wireless Communications

Bluetooth is one of the most accepted international wireless standards for wireless medical devices. It's characterized at short range and recently in low-power variants with well-defined security protocols. It also contains specifications for personal area networks, piconets, of up to eight integrated devices.

There is an international organization/special interest working group (SIG) (https://www.bluetooth.org/apps/content/) that includes representatives from most medical equipment manufacturers and publishes standards and holds regular seminars. The group also certifies testing laboratories to ensure Bluetooth standards meet local regulations. Health Level 7, another international working group (www.HL7.org) that establishes electronic medical record (EMR) standards, closely works with this and other standards organizations such as the Health Information Management Systems Security (HIMSS). HIMSS "focused on providing global leadership for the optimal use of information technology (IT) and management systems for the betterment of healthcare" (www.HIMSS.org).

7.4.2 Body Sensor Networks

A BSN (Figure 7.22) is a series of medical devices, either external or implanted, worn by patients. The concept is linking a series of devices, using Bluetooth, short-range communications with a computer or smart device into an integrated packaged signal. Bluetooth IEEE 802.15.4 standard up to this point has been a relatively inefficient system with higher transmission power required for communications. A new low-power Bluetooth called Wibree may provide longer battery life for these BSNs [10].

There are a number of standards for this evolving field to standardize these integrated systems:

- *ISO/IEEE 11073*: Low-level data standards for plug-and-play devices integrated into these BSNs that can contain a maximum of 10 connected devices.
- *The Integrate Health Environment*: Is a joint effort by multiple medical sensor vendors to standardize interoperability between sensors and device interfaces. They are associated with HIMSS and the American College of Clinical Engineering.

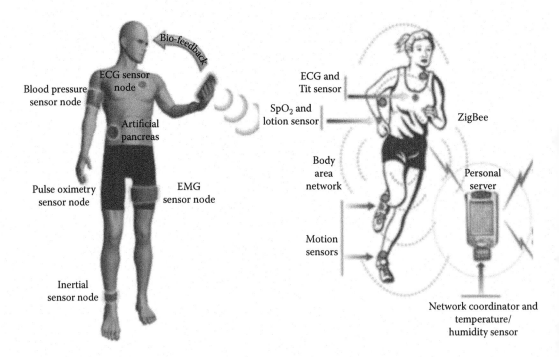

FIGURE 7.22 BSNs. (Images from Robust Low Power VLSI Group; http://rlpvlsi.ece.virginia.edu/category/projects/body-sensor-networks.)

7.4.3 Wireless Medical Device Protected Spectrum

In May 2012, the FCC set aside part of the spectrum, 2,360 to 2,400 MHz, for use by low-power medical devices. The term for these low-power medical networks, typically used in hospital environments, is medical body area networks. This spectrum was selected to prevent interference from Wi-Fi devices. Initially, this spectrum will be used by medical device manufacturers in relatively structured environments but will evolve for all wireless medical devices.

7.4.4 Integrated Data Capture Modeling for Wireless Medical Devices

There are sea changes evolving in structured, fixed medical facilities and nonstructured private emergency care delivery and loosely structured technology–mediated monitoring (Figure 7.23). This includes transport, ambulances, triage environments, disaster, and military and personal healthcare. This new model involves integrating multiple data sources into EMRs, personal data records, and continuity of care records and providing intelligent software to correlate data.

In structured environments, the need to correlate patient data, common physiological monitoring parameters, blood pressure, heart rate, pulse oximetry, blood gases, etc., requires integration into a larger data repository, EMRs that include medications, lab tests, MRI/CT scans, and feedback from medical practitioners. Expert systems [5] are evolving to manage and report on potential adverse scenarios.

In nonstructured environments, a disaster scenario involves a number of patients (N) with various levels of acuity and the need to coordinate response and transport based on acuity triage models. This can be divided into several subcategories: professional, trained personnel entering the environment, FEMA, Red Cross, or city or federal services; volunteers, local respondents responding to assist family or neighbors; and possible automated devices, either dropped in methods to utilize the large base of wireless smart cell devices.

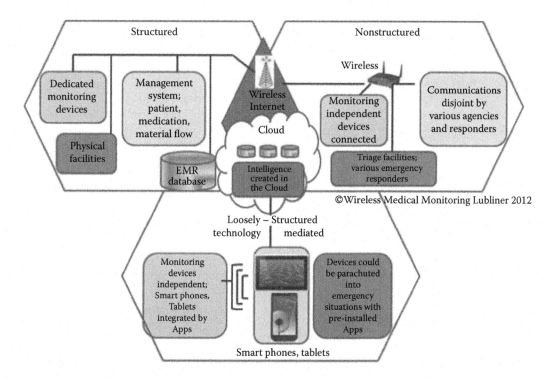

FIGURE 7.23 Structured, nonstructured, and loosely structured medical monitoring.

This typically involves personnel finding and deploying monitoring equipment. Since wireless devices are relatively short range, some temporary wireless network/monitoring structure need to be linked into longer-range systems for coordination, point-to-point versus wide-area response. GPS and establishing patient ID also augment these systems.

Level III: Advanced Data Analysis

7.5 Expert Systems: Utilized to Evaluate Medical Data

"Expert Systems are computerized applications that combine computer hardware, software and specialized information to imitate expert human reasoning and advice" [4]. The core components of an expert system are a *knowledge base,* composed of rules and facts, and an *inference engine,* supplied with data from a user, that selects the appropriate rules based on the data and calculates probabilities that the rules apply to a particular situation. An additional component is feedback from clinical data that cross checks the validity of the rule/ diagnosis that then adds to the refinement of the expert system knowledge base (Figure 7.24).

Once a basis framework has been selected, the inference engine asks a series of targeted questions proposed by the expert system to refine matches to the existing knowledge base. A list of probabilities are then generated, i.e., an example of a system used for determining heart arrhythmias states to the medical professional that 62% of arrhythmias are due to hypokalemia, a low potassium level, and 75% due to hypomagnesaemia, low magnesium, that might be making the patient more prone to arrhythmias. The system asks the individual to enter potassium and magnesium results from blood tests to validate or refute the hypothesis. This type of feedback mechanism provides more accurate diagnosis where additional data increase the probability of an accurate diagnosis. This is an example of a rule-based expert system.

Inference engines determine which rules match those of the supplied data and match those with the highest probabilities. There are forward-chaining inference (FCI) engines that analyze the facts to some conclusion or disease. These systems are used to predict outcomes; an example of an FCI system is E-mycin, written in lisp, which was used to identify bacteria causing infections developed at Stanford University [7]. It provided a 69% success rate, which was higher than practitioners at the time. A backward-chaining inference engine is from hypothesis to the facts used primarily for diagnosis; an example is the knowledge engineering environment.

Other paradigms for medical expert systems are case-based reasoning (CBR), cognitive systems, and crowd-based expert systems. The CBR utilizes an evolving library of cases where matches are made to

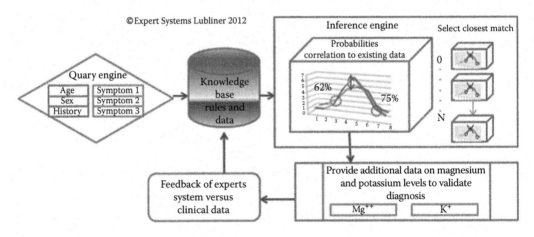

FIGURE 7.24   Expert system architecture.

the current case, rather than utilizing a standard rule-based engine; this is similar to the process of how doctors make a diagnosis. The process involves these three steps: retrieve similar cases, reuse the case to solve similar problems, revise and modify the case, and retain the new case with updates for the case library (4Rs).

Cognitive systems [13] are a series of artificial intelligence paradigms with "the ability to engage in abstract thought that goes beyond immediate perceptions and actions." Originally, comprehensive artificial intelligence systems attempted to model human consciousness but due to their lack of success were modified for a more narrow expertise in specific domains of knowledge. Examples are chess programs that are the equal of the best master level chess players. Cognitive systems utilize structured representations and probabilistic models to support problem solving utilizing concepts from psychology, logic, and linguistics.

Crowd source, wisdom of the crowds, provides a new method to extract large amounts of relevant data from the web on the assumption that large data sets may be more accurate than limited clinical data from the web. An example is IBM's "Watson," famous for beating experts on the Jeopardy game show, based on a crowd-sourcing paradigm. So far, this approach has yet to be validated in the medical arena. This crowd source–based approach has shown some success on social networking sites, where specific diseases are targeted and individuals supply anecdotal data.

7.6 Data Mining and Big Data in Healthcare

Data mining can be defined as the process of finding previously unknown patterns and trends in databases and using that information to build predictive models. In healthcare, data mining focuses on detailed questions and outcomes. What symptoms, quantitative data, and clinical outcomes in combination lead to specific diagnosis and treatments. As discussed in the previous expert systems section, a combination of probabilistic and human-directed diagnosis evolves into an evolving knowledge base. This works well with a finite data set but with big data defined as "a collection of data sets so large and complex that it becomes difficult to process using on-hand database management tools [12]." Imagine millions of individuals with real-time wearable or implanted medical sensors sending data through Smart phones. The data stream would certainly be in the terabyte range, but as these devices became ubiquitous, petabyte levels of data are not unreasonable. Information can be summarized and evaluated locally on ever-evolving Smart phones, but additional analysis and correlation, on a regional or global level, would require new stochastic techniques, i.e., algorithms to analyze random events. This seems like a contradiction in terms. Markov chains, random events, quantified as a time series events or limited by a field space, or a finite geographical area or subpopulation can provide a deterministic function used to correlate or classify seemingly random events. Examples are plumes of breast cancer patients that appear to be random but with large enough data sets can create correlations, i.e., the butterfly effect, the concept that a butterfly flapping its wings in on one area can create small finite effects over larger distances. Tracking the cause back to that original butterfly or a random mutation of flu virus anywhere in the world could predict and prevent epidemics.

7.6.1 Body Sensor Network Research and Big Data

Big data is usually defined as "data sets with sizes beyond the ability of common software tools to capture, curate and process within a tolerable elapsed time" [16]. Data sizes range from terabytes (10^{12}) to petabytes (10^{15}).

Another looming big data challenge is the real-time processing and analysis of BSN data. As millions of individuals begin to use mobile health monitoring equipment, external and implanted sensors, it's estimated that, at the minimum, terabytes (10^{12}) and at the high-end petabytes (10^{15}) of data will be generated daily [3].

7.6.1.1 Body Sensor Network Research

A research project at New Jersey Institute of Technology is currently under way to reduce the data generated by BSNs by a factor of 1,000 by preprocessing the information into summaries that just highlight anomalies. For example, if your blood pressure stays consistent 20 hours of the day, rather than transmitting all the individual data points, a brief summary describing the range and duration and the anomalies outside of this range is forwarded to a medical practitioner.

7.6.1.2 Case Study: Body Sensor Network Research, Mining Large Data Set

Title: Body Sensor Networks and Big Data Algorithms to Reduce Real Time Data Streams from Petabytes to Gigabytes (Lubliner, D., Endo, T., and Gregoriev, E.)

This *research* explores algorithms, data compression techniques, and sociological cues that narrow the scale of raw data transmissions and provides techniques to categorize and summarize root cause medical triggers, i.e., physiological events that indicate the precursors of more serious life-threatening medical conditions.

7.6.1.2.1 Introduction

The medical challenge of the twenty-first century is to exploit the evolving field of wireless medical sensors to proactively treat medical conditions reducing emergency room visits and treating chronic diseases before they become acute, significantly reducing healthcare costs. The evolving field of body sensor networks (BSNs) provides a framework to integrate external and internal sensors into a single coherent data stream. The challenge with the ubiquitous use of BSNs is to reduce the scope of daily data streams, estimated in the petabyte (PB) 10^{15} range, which could double current wireless data traffic overwhelming our wireless data infrastructure.

A BSN is a series of medical devices, either external or implanted, worn by patients linked together to form a coherent picture of an individual's medical state. BSNs link a series of devices, using Bluetooth or short-range RF communications with a computer or smart device into an integrated packaged signal.

In this research project, creating an integrated network of external and implantable sensors was solved by utilizing Bluetooth and a software application embedded into a Smart phone. These raw data were then sent to a central server for processing and analysis (Figure 7.25).

7.6.1.2.2 Research Methodology

Phase I:

1. Develop a methodology to categorize structured versus nonstructured wireless medical data.
2. Analyze data streams from various mobile devices.
3. Determine optimum frequency of data capture.
4. Develop algorithms/expert systems to extract critical data.
5. Develop software to provide both detailed and event-oriented visualization.
6. Determine efficiencies of raw data versus compressed data streams on overall traffic.

Phase II: Clinical Trials

7. Compare wireless medical devices/BSN raw data versus compressed data traffic.
8. Analyze outcomes of compressed data versus raw data.

7.6.1.2.3 Testing Methodology

Three environments/frameworks were utilized for integrating wireless data.

Structured: Used in conventional hospital settings

1. Nonstructured worn as mobile devices at home/work
2. Loosely structured, technology mediated; fires, hurricanes, disaster scenarios, etc., where fixed and personal devices are integrated to create dynamic ad hoc networks

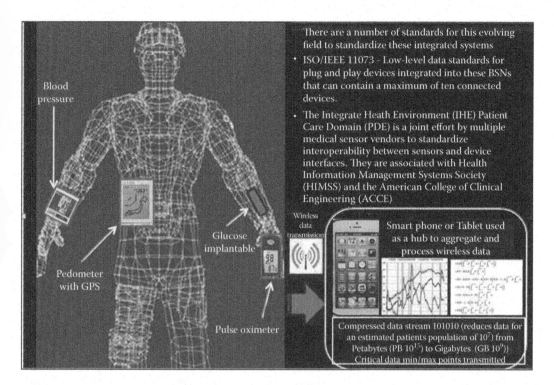

The following text appears within the figure:

There are a number of standards for this evolving field to standardize these integrated systems

• ISO/IEEE 11073 - Low-level data standards for plug and play devices integrated into these BSNs that can contain a maximum of ten connected devices.

• The Integrate Heath Environment (IHE) Patient Care Domain (PDE) is a joint effort by multiple medical sensor vendors to standardize interoperability between sensors and device interfaces. They are associated with Health Information Management Systems Society (HIMSS) and the American College of Clinical Engineering (ACCE)

Blood pressure

Glucose implantable

Wireless data transmission

Smart phone or Tablet used as a hub to aggregate and process wireless data

Pedometer with GPS

Pulse oximeter

Compressed data stream 101010 (reduces data for an estimated patients population of 10^7) from Petabytes (PB 10^{15}) to Gigabytes (GB 10^9)) Critical data min/max points transmitted

FIGURE 7.25 **(See color insert.)** Case study: BSN data capture integrated into a Smart phone and then forwarded to Cloud storage.

The testing methodology varied significantly depending on the environment. In a well-structured hospital environment, all environmental factors were controlled: diet, controlled stimulus (i.e., no unexpected stress), and nursing reports to fill in any other factors that might influence wireless data readings. In a nonstructured environment, individuals wearing sensors at home or work, the research relied on an application embedded on their Smart phones for individual to record events, diet, etc., to provide context to the data. Sociological data are a key to provide context to the medical readings.

7.6.1.2.4 Data Analysis

Wireless medical data were recorded from two out of the three environments, i.e., (1) structured and (2) nonstructured environments. (3) Loosely structured, i.e., analyzing wireless medical sensors in a disaster, will be explored in future research. The chart as shown in Figure 7.26 is an example of wireless blood pressure data captured from 62 individuals, where suspect readings were flagged and plotted to provide a graphic display to practitioners. Working with medical staff at a local hospital, they indicated that they were interested in a visual presentation of the data that quickly indicate steady-state readings, i.e., consistent values, and those anomalies that diverged from the norm. We both presented a graphic representation where values exceeded some threshold, diastolic above 80 in the graph for a number of patients. Then if they wanted to delve deeper, a table would show precise readings, again highlighting anomalies in red.

7.6.1.2.5 Results

By aggregating data, i.e., summarized events that remained stable over periods of time, and flagged anomalies that appeared outside of normal measurement ranges, values highlighted in red (Figure 7.27), we were able to reduce a patient's daily data into a concise summary. An example is a patient's systolic/diastolic for 10/24/12 that was in the range of 131–121/85–93 and providing a graph. Individual anomalies were removed from the report if they didn't persist for several sequential reading but were available in a

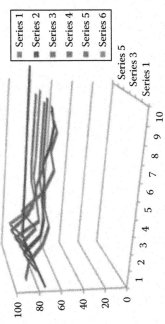

Sample Blood Pressure Data, where suspect reading flagged and plotted to provide a graphic display to practitioners

Patient	Systolic/Diastolic	Data Sets					Low/High Readings(%)
	10/1/13	10/2/13	10/3/13	10/4/13	10/5/13	10/6/13	
1000	91/131	79/133	78/119	77/118	79/115	77/117	2/33
1001	89/128	91/131	92/135	94/138	94/137	94/141	6/100
1002	78/110	77/115	78/120	72/112	79/118	72/109	0/0
1003	74/107	75/112	92/118	75/118	74/116	70/110	1/16
1004	79/114	78/119	75/118	77/113	78/117	73/114	0/0
1005	80/119	77/115	78/120	72/112	79/118	72/109	0/0
1006	73/115	79/118	78/120	72/112	79/118	72/109	0/0
1007	77/117	74/111	78/120	72/112	79/118	72/109	0/0
1008	73/109	72/110	78/120	72/112	79/118	72/109	0/0
1009	79/118	75/114	78/120	72/112	79 127	72/109	1/16
							Transmitted 10/60 16%

Linear regression model: this method minimizes the sum of squared vertical distances between the observed responses in the dataset and the responses predicted by the linear approximation.

Data consist of n observtions $\{y_i, x_i\}_{i=1}^{n}$. Each observation includes a scalar response y_i and a vector of p predictors (or regressors) x_i. In a linear regression model, the response variable is a linear function of the regressors: $y_i = x_i^T\beta + c_i$, where B is a vector of unknown parameters and x are scalar variables.

FIGURE 7.26　Case study: data generated with red indicating anomalies in readings.

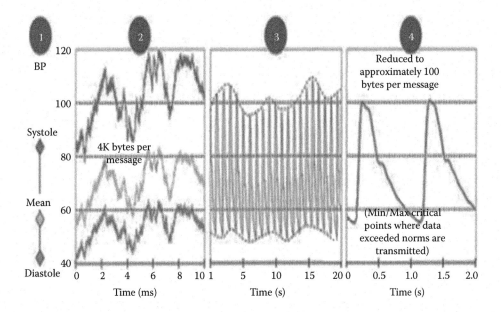

FIGURE 7.27 Case study diagram: data analyzed and compressed to transmit summary and anomalies.

tabular form from the Cloud server if requested. Individual anomalies were determined to most likely due to shifting of sensors. The devices were able to take additional readings when anomalies occurred to validate if they were caused by sensor movement during some activity. In addition, an audible signal on the Smart phone asked the patient, during the anomaly, to describe his or her activity at that point in time in a brief drop-down list of choices that were easy to analyze and annotate on the patient's records.

7.6.1.2.6 Data Analysis (Figure 7.27)

1. Blood pressure absolute.
2. Blood pressure changes in order to detect hemodynamic instabilities.
3. Physiological rhythms that deliver insight into the hemodynamic control function and/or fluid management.
4. Further pulse wave analysis provides additional cardiovascular parameters.
5. Results in data transmission *reduction to 2.5% of original data stream.*

By aggregating data in a single integrated record that summarizes information into a continuity of care record, essential information can be transmitted without loss of critical medical information. The reduction in data transmitted is about 1/100 the original size. Extrapolated over millions of patients simultaneously wearing BSN daily, transmitted data would be reduced from petabytes to terabytes in a population of 1 million. We believe this can be further reduced by transmitting delta information, i.e., comparing previous daily readings to current values and just transmitting delta changes over a period of time, i.e., blood pressure increases 3% over a 30-day period. That may be the only information a medical practitioner may need.

7.6.2 Future Directions: Mining Large Data Sets: NSF and NIH Research Initiatives

The following section describes initiatives underway to analyze the growing field of big data including initiative underway by the National Science Foundation (NSF), National Institutes of Health (NIH), and Department of Defense (DOD) to provide significant research funds to enhance analysis of medical data, geological, and defense research. The hope is that these new methodologies may be extrapolated to other disciplines. NSF and NIH research is often a predictive indicator for future medical innovations, similar to previous Defense Advanced Research Projects Agency (DARPA) investments that were responsible for many of today's internet and computer advancements [1].

This field of big data is the focus of support by several U.S. research agencies, NSF, DOD, and NIH committing $200 million in 2012 to this "Big Data Initiative."

To gain an understanding of these initiatives, the following was a solicitation on an NSF page to researchers to submit big data research grant proposals [8].

The Obama Administration announced a "Big Data Research and Development Initiative." By improving our ability to extract knowledge and insights from large and complex collections of digital data, the initiative promises to help solve some the nation's most pressing challenges.

To launch the initiative, six Federal departments and agencies today, March 29th, 2012 announced more than $200 million in new commitments that, together, promise to greatly improve the tools and techniques needed to access, organize, and glean discoveries from huge volumes of digital data.

The NIH also has dedicated significant funds to the analysis of larger data sets, specifically focused on genomic research. The NIH announced in 2012 that the world's largest set of data on human genetic variation, produced by the International 1000 Genomes Project, was available on the Amazon Web Services (AWS) Cloud. Two hundred terabytes is the equivalent of 16 million file cabinets filled with text. The source of the data, the 1000 Genomes Project data set, is a prime example of big data where data sets become so massive that few researchers have the computing power to make the best use of them. AWS is storing the 1000 Genomes Project as a publicly available data set for free and researchers will only pay for the computing services that they use.

Large data sets are also currently being generated by researchers in other fields, which are the focus of a number of research initiatives:

- "EarthCube"—a system that will allow geoscientists to access, analyze, and share information about our planet.
- The DARPA is an XDATA program, established to develop computational techniques and software tools for analyzing large volumes of data, both semistructured (e.g., tabular, relational, categorical, metadata) and unstructured (e.g., text documents, message traffic). Also to harness and utilize massive data in new ways and bring together sensing, perception, and decision support to make truly autonomous systems that can maneuver and make decisions on their own.
- A project that will integrate three powerful approaches for turning data into information—machine learning, Cloud computing, and crowd sourcing.
- The Smart Health and Wellbeing program of the NSF whose goal is the "transformation of healthcare from reactive and hospital-centered to preventive, proactive, evidence-based, person-centered and focused on wellbeing rather than disease." The categories of this effort include wireless medical sensors, networking, machine learning, and integrating social and economic issues that affect medical outcomes.

The following is a representative funded research grant in the field of wireless medical devices. These of bleeding edge research initials have the potential to shape advancements in medical data mining. This research proposal was selected by experts in the field assembled at the NSF.

"NSF award to utilize Wireless Medical Sensors to Manage and Proactively Treat Chronic Illnesses. Forty percent of all medical costs are associated with treating patients with chronic illnesses in the last two years of their lives."

Telemedicine technologies offer the opportunity to frequently monitor patients' health and optimize management of chronic illnesses. Given the diversity of home telemedicine technologies, it is essential to compose heterogeneous telemedicine components and systems for a much larger patient population. The objective of this research is to thoroughly investigate the heterogeneity in large-scale telemedicine systems for cardiology patients. To accomplish this task, this research seeks to develop (i) a novel open source platform medical device interface adapter that can seamlessly interconnect medical devices that conform to interoperability standards, such as IEEE 11703, to Smart phones for real-time data processing and delivery; (ii) a set of novel supporting technologies for wireless networking, data storage, and data integrity checking, and (iii) a learning-based early warning system that adaptively changes patient and disease models based on medical device readings and context.

The challenge of the aforementioned grant is to not just collect data but to build in sociological components, stress, economic conditions, etc., that might generate transient results and to proactively treat patients with early conditions thus reducing costly hospital stays and increasing their quality of life. Results from previous studies have shown that filtering out unusual readings may result in more reliable data. Also integrating smoking, drinking, etc., helps quantify the results. So apps allow users to input data regarding their frame of mind or habits; while the data are being monitored on the wireless medical devices, we can provide invaluable information for analysis of causal effects to physiological readings (Figure. 7.28).

Assuming wireless mobile medical devices become common, estimates of data generated daily, with only a million users, range from 1 terabyte to 1 petabyte/day (Figure 7.28). To put this in perspective, the

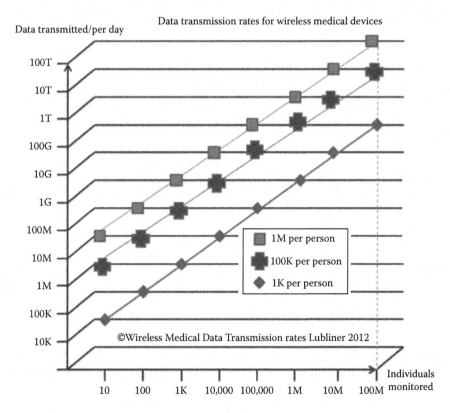

FIGURE 7.28 Smart health data transmission projections as wireless medical sensors become commonplace.

digital storage for the Library of Congress is 200 terabytes. The population in 2012 is 300 million in the United States and 7 billion worldwide, and 50% of Americans have some type of Smart phone or tablet. In the next 25 years, 20% of the U.S. population will be over 65 making either wearable smart medical devices or those abilities directly embedded in smart devices are likely to expand rapidly. This flood of potential data dwarfs all other applications. Data mining of this treasure trove of medical data will be the challenge of the ensuing decades to come.

Level IV: Anatomy and Physiology Primer

This last section, segmented into four parts, is a basic Anatomy & Physiology (A&P) Primer geared toward the BMI practitioner. BMI professionals should be encouraged to take A&P I and II courses, but if they haven't, this section is presented in a format that can be easily used in PowerPoint presentations.*

7.7 Part I: Neurons and Nervous System, Brain, Spinal Cord, Muscles, Heart, Eye

Human physiology I

1. Neurons and nervous system
2. Brain
3. Spinal chord
4. Muscles
5. Heart
6. Eye

Neurons and the Central Nervous System (**See color insert.**)

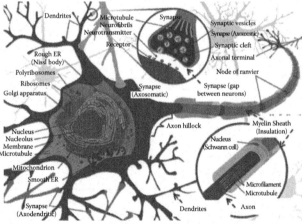

The Central Nervous System (CNS) contains two major types of cells, Neurons and Glia. They are responsible for transmitting information. Neurons make up our brains, information processing system, and communicate signals throughout our body. (movement, sensory and healing). Neurons are electrically excitable cells that communicate information through electrical and chemical signals. Neurons are connected via synapses, a gap between neurons, that allows a neuron to pass an electrical or chemical signal to another neuron. (refer to: Chapter 7, Neurons/Action Potential).

Sodium(Na^+)–Potassium(K^+) pumps move positive ions (Na^+ and K^+) across the synapse to make one side more positive (voltage / potential difference) so current flows (electrons) from negative to positive.

Glial cells surround the neurons and provide support and insulation between neurons (composed of Schwann, microglia, astrocytes, satellite and ependymal cells).

Dendrites: Are thin protrusions from the cell body of a neuron that collect chemical and electrical signals from other neurons. Axons: Are the projection of a neuron that conducts electrical impulses away from the cell body to the axon terminals

---

* Illustrations taken from Creative Commons A&P resources.

Brain (See color insert.)

The Cerebrum, it's the evolved part of the brain, the largest part of the human brain, which comprises 4/5 of its weight. It consists of about two-thirds of the brain mass and lies over and around most of the structures of the brain. The outer portion ranges in thickness between 1.5 and 5 mm, and is covered by a thin layer of gray tissue called the cerebral cortex. It is divided into right and left hemispheres that are connected by the corpus callosum.

Cerebrum includes the hippocampus, olfactory bulb and basal ganglia
-Hippocampus, part of the limbic system involved in the integration from short-term to long-term memory
-Limbic System: emotion, behavior long term memory
-Olfactory bulb: sense of smell
-Basal Ganglia: voluntary movements, learning, eye movements, emotion

The Cerebral Cortex surface, folded in large mamals. Two thirds of the surface is embedded groves (valleys) called the "sulci". The ridges are called "gyri".
• Frontal lobe: voluntary movement, planning. Though
• Parietal lobe: includes the somatosensory cortex: touch
• Temporal lobe: hearing and comprehending speech
• Occipital lobe: visual processing center　　© Lubliner 2015

The Cerebellum involved in motor control. The functions include balance, voluntary movements, motor learning, and some congnitive functions (language); (10% volume, but contains 50% of neurons brain).

The Brain Stem includes the midbrain, Pons and medulla oblongata. Functions include the cardiac, respiratory and autonomic (involuntary functions), blood pressure and heart rate.

Cerebral Cortex

Frontal lobe　Parietal lobe
Occipital lobe
Temporal lobe
Brainstem
Cerebellum (Older part brain)

Left brain
Analytical thought
language
Right brain
Creativity
Art and Music

en.Wikipedia: public domain

Olfactory bulb

Hippocampus　　　　Basal ganglia (purple)

Major internal parts of the Human Brain
Cingulate
Sulcus
Corpus
Callosum
Diencephalon
Anterior
Commissure
Temporal
Lobe
Midbrain
Pons
Medulla
Mid Brain
Pons
Medulla
Cerebellum

Motor cortex
Premotor Primary motor cortex
cortex　Primary somatosensory
SMA　cortex　Posterior parietal cortex

The Motor Cortex involved in control of voluntary actions

Brain (cont.)

Motor cortex is the region of the cerebral cortex involved in the planning, control, and execution of voluntary movements
• Primary motor cortex generates neural impulses sent to the spinal cord that control the execution of movement
• The supplementary motor area (SMA), involved in the planning of movement, planning of sequences of movement, and the coordination of the two sides of the body

Motor cortex
Premotor cortex　Primary motor cortex
Primary Somatosensory
SMA　cortex
Posterior parietal cortex

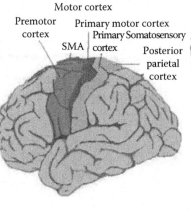

• The motor areas are located in both hemispheres
• The right half controls the left side and left half the right side

Spinal chord

The Vertebral column is divided into the cervical, thoracic, and lumbar regions. The spinal nerves that branch out are called Lower Motor neurons. They exit at each vertebral level and contain sensory and motor segments.

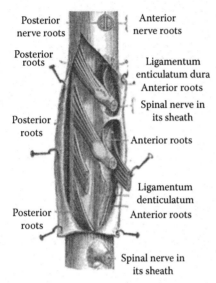

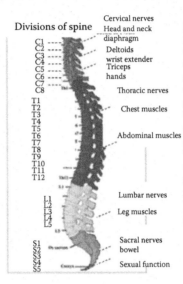

Posterior nerve roots — Anterior nerve roots

Posterior roots

Ligamentum enticulatum dura
Anterior roots

Spinal nerve in its sheath

Posterior roots — Anterior roots

Ligamentum denticulatum
Anterior roots

Posterior roots

Spinal nerve in its sheath

Divisions of spine

Cervical nerves
Head and neck
C1 diaphragm
C2 Deltoids
C3
C4 wrist extender
C5 Triceps
C6 hands
C7
C8
T1 Thoracic nerves
T2 Chest muscles
T3
T4
T5 Abdominal muscles
T6
T7
T8
T9
T10
T11
T12
L1 Lumbar nerves
L2
L3 Leg muscles
L4
L5
S1 Sacral nerves
S2 bowel
S3
S4 Sexual function
S5

It is surrounded by rings of bone called vertebra. The eight vertebra in the neck are referred to as Cervical nerves. The next twelve are Thoracic and control the chest and abdominal muscles. The Lumbar vertebra control the leg muscles and Sacral nerves control the bowel and affect sexual function.

Overhead (axial)view

Costal facet (costovertebral joint)

Spinous process
Costotransverse facet (costovertebral joint)

Transverse costal facet
Superior articular Process and facet
Body
Superior costal facet
Spinous process

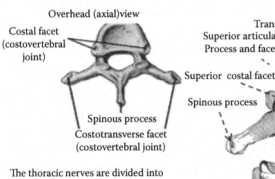

Cervical vertebra C1–C7 [and 8 cervical nerves (c1–c8)] C1 is the suboccipital nerve. They have the greatest range of motion, of the vertebrae, so as to support the head and its movements

The thoracic nerves are divided into anterior and posterior branches called the dorsal ramus and ventral ramus. They connect to upper body deep tissue and skin and muscles.

The vertebra are stronger than the cervical bones, which allows them to absorb greater force on the mid back and prevent injury.

Thoracic vertebra T1–T12 (attached to the thoracic cage, they protect the organs in the chest and have a more limited range of motion). The thoracic nerves T1 and T2 connect to the shoulder and arms, T3, T4, T5, T6, connect to the chest, the last five connect to the chest and abdomen.

http://en.wikipedia.org/wiki/Thoracic_vertebrae

Muscles

Muscles perform four essential functions: They maintain body posture, stabilize joints, produce movement, and generate heat we need to survive. This illustrates what different muscles do and how muscles work together.

Skeletal Muscles ────────────────────►

Skeletal muscle, or striated muscle, is the type of muscle you can see and feel. Learn about skeletal muscle and its complex structure.

Skeletal muscle is also called striated muscle, because when it is viewed under polarized light or stained with an indicator, you can see alternating striations.

Cardiac and smooth muscles ──────────►

Smooth muscle and cardiac muscle contract involuntarily. While most of the processes are similar, there are some notable differences between the actions of skeletal, cardiac, and smooth muscle.

- Skeletal muscle is a well-organized body tissue. During muscle contractions, sections of muscle fiber fit together like pieces of a puzzle.

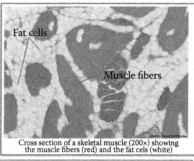

Cross section of a skeletal muscle (200×) showing the muscle fibers (red) and the fat cels (white)

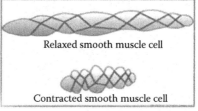

Relaxed smooth muscle cell

Contracted smooth muscle cell

Heart

- The Right side of the heart collects oxygen-poor blood from the body (veins) and pumps it to the lungs where it picks up oxygen and releases carbon dioxide.

- The Left side of the heart collects oxygen rich blood from the lungs and pumps it to the body (arteries) (*the pulmonary veins [4] are one of the few veins that carry oxygen: from the lungs to the aorta*).

- Blood enters the heart through the Atria (smaller chambers) which collect the blood and pass it on to the ventricles. Its role is as a holding chamber and pump.

- The ventricles (larger chambers) pump blood: Right ventricle to the lungs, left ventricle to the Aorta.

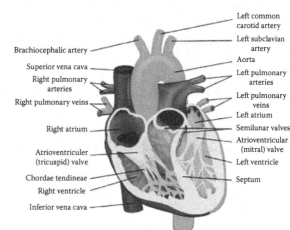

Brachiocephalic artery
Superior vena cava
Right pulmonary arteries
Right pulmonary veins
Right atrium
Atrioventriculer (tricuspid) valve
Chordae tendineae
Right ventricle
Inferior vena cava

Left common carotid artery
Left subclavian artery
Aorta
Left pulmonary arteries
Left pulmonary veins
Left atrium
Semilunar valves
Atrioventricular (mitral) valve
Left ventricle
Septum

- The valves are flaps of tissue that prevent backward flow of blood (one way transport)

1. Mitral Valve
2. Tricuspid Valve
3. Aortic Valve
4. Pulmonary Valve

Atria ventricular (between upper atria and lower ventricles)

Semi lunar valves (in the arteries leaving the heart)

Heart (blood pressure)

Systole is the period of contraction of the ventricles of the heart. In a single heartbeat Systole causes the ejection of blood into the aorta (left) and lungs (right). During systole, arterial blood pressure reaches its peak, which is normally about 90 – 120 mm of mercury in humans.

Diastole is the relaxation of the heart muscle, accompanied by the filling of the chambers with blood. Initially both atria and ventricles are in diastole, and there is a period of rapid filling of the ventricles followed by a brief atrial systole. At the same time, there is a corresponding decrease in arterial blood pressure to its minimum, normally about 80 mm of Mercury in humans.

Korotkoff sounds are the sounds that medical personnel listen for when they are taking blood pressure using a non-invasive procedure. There are five Korotkoff only two are primarily used for blood pressure: systolic (first) and diastolic (fourth: within 10 mmHg above the diastolic blood pressure). Some devices are also using the fifth. The other three used to detect heart disease. (*As the cuff relaxes, and blood flow returns to the arm. The first sound heard is the Korotkoff sound—indicates systolic pressure.*)

Pressure waveform (different from EKG which is electrical)

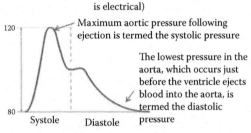

Maximum aortic pressure following ejection is termed the systolic pressure

The lowest pressure in the aorta, which occurs just before the ventricle ejects blood into the aorta, is termed the diastolic pressure

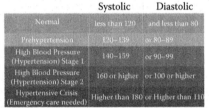

	Systolic	Diastolic
Normal	less than 120	and less than 80
Prehypertension	120–139	or 80–89
High Blood Pressure (Hypertension) Stage 1	140–159	or 90–99
High Blood Pressure (Hypertension) Stage 2	160 or higher	or 100 or higher
Hypertensive Crisis (Emergency care needed)	Higher than 180	or Higher than 110

Heart (continued)

Electrical system:

• A special group of cells that have the ability to generate electrical activity on their own are responsible for the heart beating.

• The natural pacemaker of the heart is called the sinoatrial node (SA node). It is located in the right atrium. The heart also contains specialized fibers that conduct the electrical impulse from the pacemaker (SA node) to the rest of the heart.

• The electrical impulse leaves the SA node (1) and travels to the right and left atria, causing them to contract together. This takes 0.04 s. There is now a natural delay to allow the atria to contract and the ventricles to fill up with blood. The electrical impulse has now traveled to the atrioventricular node (AV node) (2). The electrical impulse now goes to the Bundle of His (3), then it divides into the right and left bundle branches (4) where it rapidly spreads using Purkinje fibers (5) to the muscles of the right and left ventricle, causing them to contract at the same time.

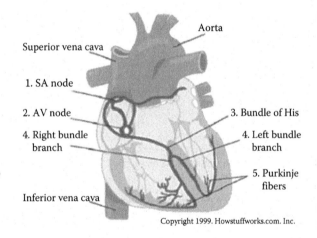

Aorta

Superior vena cava

1. SA node

2. AV node

3. Bundle of His

4. Right bundle branch

4. Left bundle branch

5. Purkinje fibers

Inferior vena cava

Copyright 1999. Howstuffworks.com. Inc.

Heart (continued)

Although the pacemaker cells create the electrical impulse that causes the heart to beat, other nerves can change the rate at which the pacemaker cells fire and how strongly the heart contracts. These nerves are part of the autonomic nervous system. The autonomic nervous system has two parts—The sympathetic nervous system and the parasympathetic nervous system. The sympathetic nerves increase the heart rate and increase the force of contraction. The parasympathetic nerves do the opposite.

All this activity produces electrial waves we can measure. The measurement is typically represented as a graph called an electrocardiogram (EKG). Here is an example of three heartbeats from an EKG

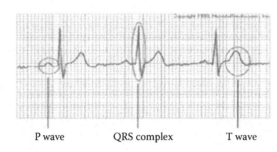

P wave   QRS complex   T wave

Each part of the tracing has a lettered name:
- *P wave*: coincides with the spread of electrical activity over the atria and the beginning of its contraction
- *QRS complex*: coincides with the spread of electrical activity over the ventricles and the beginning of its contraction.
- *T wave*: coincides with the recovery phase of the ventricles.

Arrhythmia

- An irregular heartbeat, or arrhythmia, can result from a change in the heart's standard electrical conduction system.
- A serious variety of arrhythmia is known as fibrillation. The muscle cells of the heart normally function together, creating a single contraction when stimulated. Fibrillation occurs when the heart muscle begins a quivering motion due to a disunity in contractile cell function. Fibrillation can affect the atrium (atrial fibrillation) or the ventricle (ventricular fibrillation); ventricular fibrillation is imminently life-threatening.
- *Atrial fibrillation* is the quivering, chaotic motion in the upper chambers of the heart, known as the atria.
- *Ventricular fibrillation* occurs in the ventricles (lower chambers) of the heart; it is always a medical emergency. If left untreated, ventricular fibrillation (VF, or V-fib) can lead to death within minutes. When a heart goes into V-fib, effective pumping of the blood stops. V-fib is considered a form of cardiac arrest, and an individual suffering from it will not survive unless cardiopulmonary resuscitation (CPR) and defibrillation are provided immediately.
- CPR can prolong the survival of the brian in the lack of a normal pulse, but defibrillation is the intervention which is most likely to restore a more healthy heart rhythm. It does this by applying an electric shock to the heart, after which sometimes the heart will revert to a rhythm that can once again pump blood.

Almost every person goes into ventricular fibrillation in the last few minutes of life as the heart muscle reacts to diminished oxygen or general blood flow, trauma, irritants, or depression of electrical impulses themselves from the brain.

Eye (**See color insert.**)   Anatomy of Human Eye

The Eye detects electromagnetic radiation (light) and converts it into electro-chemical impulses in neurons.

Light enters through the cornea and passes through the pupil. The pupil is surrounded by the Iris, that controls the size and diameter of the pupil. Behind the pupil is the lens that focuses light onto the retina that has photoreceptor cells.

The Retina is a light sensitive layer of tissue made up of photoreceptor cells located at the back of the eye. It's made up of Rods which are used in peripheral vision, and Cones, responsible for color vision.

The actual image is portrayed upside down on the retina. The process of reinventing the image is a combination of brain architecture and processing of the image. (*It starts at the optic nerve where there is a crossing of axons in the optic chiasm to the lateral geniculate nucleus and then to the primary visual cortex.*)

Image inverted by the eye

Focal point

Visible light has a wavelength in the range of 400 nanometers (nm), or 400×10^{-9} m, to 700 nm

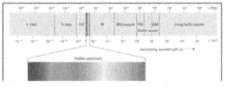

7.8 Part II: Cells, ATP, Hearing, Kidneys, Pancreas, Liver, Digestive System

1. Cells
   a. DNA
   b. RNA
   c. Proteins
2. ATP
   a. Photosynthesis
3. Hearing
4. Kidneys
5. Pancreas
6. Liver
   a. Gallbladder
7. Digestive system

Cell

Cells are the basic functional unit of living organisms. They are smallest unit that can replicate. Humans contain approximately 100 trillion cells. Plants and animals are made up of eukaryote cells which contain compartmentalized areas, organelles, where metabolic activities take place. The cell's nucleus contains its DNA, a blueprint which is organized as linear molecules of 23 pairs of chromosomes that carry all the information that help a cell grow, survive and reproduce. RNA (Ribonucleic acid) is involved in coding, decoding and expression of genes. It plays a role in catalyzing biological reactions. One of these is protein synthesis where mRNA directs the assembly of ribosomes. Proteins are required for the structure, function, and regulation of the body's tissues and organs.

Animal eukaryotic cell   DNA (Deoxyribonucleic acid)

- Hydrogen
- Oxygen
- Nitrogen
- Carbon
- Phosphorus

Genome

Chromosomes

genes

Cell

Genes contain instructions for making proteins

DNA

Protein myoglobin

ATP (adenosine triphosphate)

For your muscles—in fact, for every cell in your body— the source of energy that keeps everything going is called ATP. ATP is the biochemical way to store and use energy.

Adenosine 5′-triphosphate (ATP) is a multifunctional nucleotide that is most important as a "molecular currency" of intracellular energy transfer. In this role ATP transports chemical energy within cells for metabolism.

- It is produced as an energy source during the processes of photosynthesis and cellular respiration and consumed by many enzymes and a multitude of cellular processes including biosynthetic reactions, motility and cell division.

- ATP consists of adenosine—itself composed of an adenine ring and a ribose sugar—and three phosphate groups (triphosphate).

Adenosine 5′-triphosphate	
Chemical name	5-(6-aminopurin-9-yl)-3,4-dihydroxy-oxolan-2-yl methoxy-hydroxy-phosphoryl oxy-hydroxy-phosphoryl oxphosphonic acid
Abbreviations	ATP
Chemical formula	$C_{10}H_{16}N_5O_{13}P_3$

Photosynthesis (**See color insert.**)

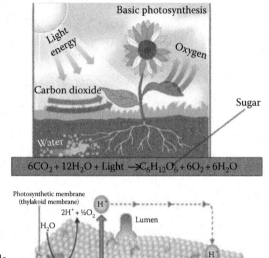

- Process by which green plants and certain other organisms transform light into chemical energy.

  In green plants, light energy is captured by chlorophyll in the chloroplasts of the leaves and used to convert water, carbon dioxide, and minerals into oxygen and energy-rich organic compounds (simple and complex sugars) that are the basis of both plant and animal life.
- During the light-dependent stage (light reaction), chlorophyll absorbs light energy, which excites some electrons in the pigment molecules to higher energy levels; these leave the chlorophyll and pass along a series of molecules, generating formation of NADPH (an enzyme) and high-energy ATP molecules.
- The NADPH oxidase (nicotinamide adenine dinucleotide phosphate-oxidase) complex is an enzyme complex.
- It generates superoxide by transferring electrons from NADPH inside the cell across the membrane and coupling these to molecular oxygen to produce the superoxide, which is a highly reactive free radical.

© 2006 Herramienta Inc.

Hearing

- The ear has three major regions: the outer ear, the middle ear and the inner ear.
  - The process of hearing begins when sound waves make it to the middle ear, causing the ear drum to vibrate.
- *The human ear is the anatomical structure responsible for hearing and balance.*

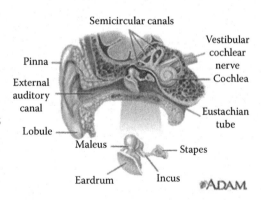

- The second part of the outer ear, the external auditory canal, is a passageway in the temporal lobe of the skull, which leads from the outside of the head and extends inward and slightly upwards. In the adult human, it is lined with skin and hairs and is approximately 1 inch (2.5 cm) long.
- The third part of the outer ear, the tympanic membrane or eardrum, is a thin, concave membrane stretched across the inner end of the external auditory canal much like the skin covering the top of a drum. The eardrum transmits sound to the middle ear by vibrating in response to sounds traveling down the external auditory canal.

Kidneys **(See color insert.)**

- Your kidneys are two bean-shaped organs, each about the size of your fist. They are located in the middle of your back, just below your rib cage, on either side of your spine. Your kidneys weigh about 0.5% of your total body weight.

  - Although the kidneys are small organs by weight, they receive a huge amount—20%—of the blood pumped by the heart. The large blood supply to your kidneys enables them to do the following tasks:
- Regulate the composition of your blood
  - keep the concentrations of various ions and other important substances constant
  - keep the volume of water in your body constant
  - remove wastes from your body (urea, ammonia, drugs, toxic substances)
  - keep the acid/base concentration of your blood constant
- Help regulate your blood pressure
- Stimulate the making of red blood cells
- Maintain your body's calcium levels

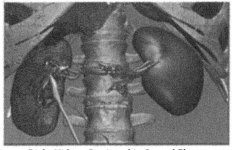

Right Kidney Sectioned in Several Planes

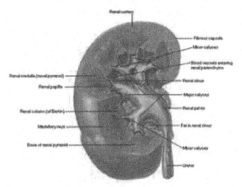

Pancreas/diabetes

- The Pancreas is located behind the liver and stomach. In addition to secreting digestive enzymes, the pancreas secretes the hormones insulin and glucagon into the bloodstream. The release of insulin into the blood lowers the level of blood glucose (simple sugars from food) by enhancing glucose to enter the body cells, where it is metabolized. If blood glucose levels get too low, the pancreas secretes glucagon to stimulate the release of glucose from the liver.

The pancreas secretes insulin in response to glucose levels in the blood.

- Type 2 diabetes means that your body doesn't make enough insulin, or doesn't properly use the insulin your body makes. Insulin, which is made in your pancreas, helps your body's cells use sugar from your bloodstream, which comes from foods and drinks. Sugar is a source of energy for cells. Type 2 diabetes,is rising fast in the United States. It accounts for most diabetes cases.Typically, with type 2 diabetes, the body still makes insulin, but its cells can't use it. This is called insulin resistance. Over time, high levels of sugar build up in the bloodstream. Being overweight and inactive increase the chances of developing type 2 diabetes.

- Type 1 diabetes. This form often affects children, but adults can develop it, too. In this form of diabetes, the body can't make insulin. The immune system by mistake attacks the cells in the pancreas that make and release insulin. As these cells die, blood sugar levels rise. People with type 1 diabetes need insulin shots.

Liver **(See color insert.)**

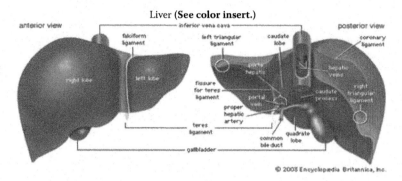

Anterior and posterior views of the liver.

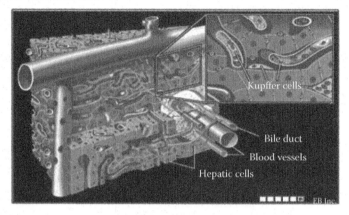

Liver (continued)

- The Liver is in the right upper abdomen. The liver serves many functions, including the detoxification of substances delivered from the intestines, and the synthesis of many proteins.
- The largest gland in the body, a spongy mass of wedge-shaped lobes that has many metabolic and secretory functions. The liver secretes bile, a digestive fluid; metabolizes proteins, carbohydrates, and fats; stores glycogen, vitamins, and other substances; synthesizes blood-clotting factors; removes wastes and toxic matter from the blood
- A liver transplant may be recommended for: liver damage due to:
  - alcoholism (Alcoholic cirrhosis)
  - end-stage liver disease (primary biliary cirrhosis)
  - long-term (chronic) active infection (hepatitis)
  - liver (hepatic) vein clot (thrombosis)
  - birth defects of the liver or bile ducts (biliary atresia)
  - metabolic disorders associated with liver failure (e.g., Wilson's disease)

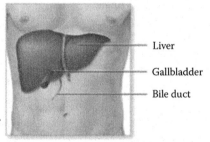

Arteries/Veins/Capillaries inside Liver

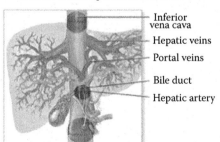

Gallbladder

The Gallbladder is a muscular sac located under the liver. It stores and concentrates the bile produced in the liver that is not immediately needed for digestion. Bile is released from the gallbladder into the small intestine.

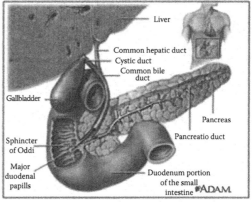

The Digestive System

- Digestion is the process by which the body converts food into basic substances that can either be absorbed in the bloodstream as nutrients or passed out of the body as waste.

  - This process of breakdown and assimilation occurs within the digestive tract, a convoluted tube more than 30 feet long that is lined with a mucous membrane.

- Other digestive juices required by the small intestine to digest and absorb food, particularly fats and starches, come from the pancreas, an organ located just behind the stomach.

- Whatever substances are not assimilated into the bloodstream through the small intestine move into the large intestine. Within the large intestine, waste material is processed into stool (feces), and water and certain chemicals are absorbed into the bloodstream to preserve the body's fluid balance.

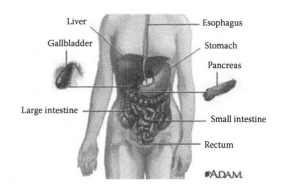

The digestive track includes the: mouth, esophagus, stomach, small intestine and large intestine. Each has a function in the digestive process. The muscles in these organs move food through the digestive system and mucus lubricates the tract. The liver, gallbladder and pancreas are also part of this digestive process.

The small intestine is where most of the digestion and absorption of food occurs. It is composed of three parts:

1: Duodenum: It's the shortest part, where most of the chemical digestion takes place; iron absorption takes place here.

2: Jejunum: In this section sugars, amino acids, and fatty acids are absorbed into the bloodstream. (It's approximately 7 feet long).

3: Ileum: It absorbs vitamin B12 and bile acids and any other remaining nutrients. (approximately 9 feet long). B12 is an essential nutrient for the brain, nervous system and blood formation.

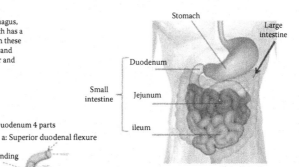

Duodenum 4 parts
  a: Superior duodenal flexure
  b: Descending
  c: Horizontal
  d: Ascending part

The Large Intestine: primary role is to remove water from the body. The secondary function via bacteria, break down undigested sugars and fibers into fatty acids. The bacteria has a side affect that produces methane, hydrogen sulfide and CO_2. A by product of the bacteria produces vitamin K and biotin that is reabsorbed back into the body. (5 feet)

7.9 Part III: Lungs, Immune System, Stroke, Blood Flow, Prostate

1. Lungs
2. Immune system
   a. Bacteria and viruses
   b. Epidermis (skin)
   c. Lymph system
   d. Thymus
   e. Antibodies
   f. White blood cells
   g. Leukocytes
3. Stroke
4. Blood flow
   a. Arteries
   b. Veins
   c. Capillaries
5. Prostate

Lungs **(See color insert.)**

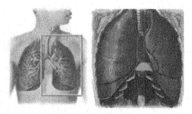

- They take in oxygen, a gas that your body needs, and gets rid of waste carbon dioxide made by your cells.
- You breathe in and out anywhere from 15 to 25 times per minute.
- They also help in regulating the concentration of hydrogen ion (pH) in your blood.
- You don't have to think about breathing because your body's autonomic nervous system controls it.
- The respiratory centers that control your rate of breathing are in the brainstem or medulla. The nerve cells that live within these centers automatically send signals to the diaphragm and intercostal muscles to contract and relax at regular intervals.

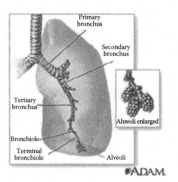

Lungs (continued)

- When you inhale, the diaphragm and intercostal muscles (those are the muscles between your ribs) contract and expand the chest cavity.

- This expansion lowers the pressure in the chest cavity below the outside air pressure. Air then flows in through the airways (from high pressure to low pressure) and inflates the lungs.

- When you exhale, the diaphragm and intercostal muscles relax and the chest cavity gets smaller.

- The decrease in volume of the cavity increases the pressure in the chest cavity above the outside air pressure. Air from the lungs (high pressure) then flows out of the airways to the outside air (low pressure). The cycle then repeats with each breath.

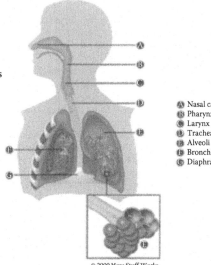

Ⓐ Nasal cavity
Ⓑ Pharynx
Ⓒ Larynx
Ⓓ Trachea
Ⓔ Alveoli
Ⓕ Bronchlai tree
Ⓖ Diaphragm

© 2000 How Stuff Works

As you breathe air in through your nose or mouth, it goes past the epiglottis and into the trachea. It continues down the trachea through your vocal cords in the larynx until it reaches the bronchi. From the bronchi, air passes into each lung. The air then follows narrower and narrower bronchioles until it reaches the alveoli.

- There within each air sac, the oxygen concentration is high, so oxygen passes or diffuses across the alveolar membrane into the pulmonary capillary.

- At the beginning of the pulmonary capillary, the hemoglobin in the red blood cells has carbon dioxide bound to it and very little oxygen.

  - The oxygen binds to hemoglobin and the carbon dioxide is released. Carbon dioxide is also released from sodium bicarbonate dissolved in the blood of the pulmonary capillary. The concentration of carbon dioxide is high in the pulmonary capillary, so carbon dioxide leaves the blood and passes across the alveolar membrane into the air sac. This exchange of gases occurs rapidly (fractions of a second). The carbon dioxide then leaves the alveolus when you exhale and the oxygen-enriched blood returns to the heart

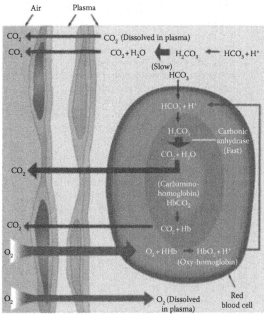

© 2000 How Stuff Works

Lungs (continued)

Anatomy of the Lung

- Alveolus—tiny, thin-walled air sac at the end of the bronchiole branches where gas exchange occurs (plural-alveoli).
- Bronchioles—numerous small tubes that branch from each bronchus into the lungs. They get smaller and smaller.
- Bronchus—a branch of the trachea that goes from the trachea into the lung (plural-bronchi).
- Diaphragm—muscle at the base of the chest cavity that contracts and relaxes during breathing.
- Epiglottis—a flap of tissue that closes over the trachea when you swallow so that food does not enter your airway.
- Intercostal muscles—muscles along the rid cage that assist in breathing.
- Larynx—voice box where the vocal cords are located.
  nasal cavity—chamber in from the nose where air is moistened and warmed.
- Pleural membranes—thin, membranes that cover the lungs, separate them from other organs and form a fluid—filled chest cavity.
- Pulmonary capillaries—small blood vessels that surround each alveolus.
- Trachea—rigid tube that connects the mouth with the bronchi (windpipe).

Immune System (**See color insert.**)

AIDS
- AIDS (Acquired Immune Deficiency Syndrome) is a disease caused by HIV (the Human Immunodeficiency Virus). This is a particularly problematic disease for the immune system because the virus actually attacks immune system cells.

  - In particular, it reproduces inside Helper T cells and kills them in the process.
  - Without Helper T cells to orchestrate things, the immune system eventually collapses and the victim dies of some other infection that the immune system would normally be able to handle.
  - HIV invades the cells of our immune system and reprograms the cells to become HIV-producing factories.

- Viruses, like HIV, don't have cell walls or a nucleus. Basically, viruses are made up of genetic instructions wrapped inside a protective shell. An HIV virus particle, called a virion, is spherical in shape and has a diameter of about one 10,000th of a millimeter.

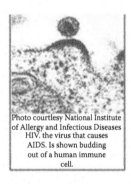

Photo courtlesy National Institute of Allergy and Infectious Diseases HIV. the virus that causes AIDS. Is shown budding out of a human immune cell.

HIV Replication Animation

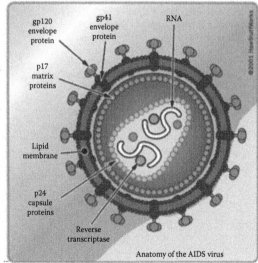

gp120 envelope protein

gp41 envelope protein

RNA

p17 matrix proteins

Lipid membrane

p24 capsule proteins

Reverse transcriptase

Anatomy of the AIDS virus

Immune System (continued)

The immune system is a network of cells, tissues, and organs that work together to protect the body from infection. (NIH)

http://www.niaid.nih.gov/topics/immunesystem/Pages/default.aspx

1. There are a number of triggers called Danger-Associated Molecular Patterns (DAMPs) that can differentiate between health and unhealthy cells.

   - The innate immune system recognizes molecules via the innate immune system by pattern recognition receptors triggered by cell death or injury.

   - DAMPS are often derived from the plasma membrane, nucleus, endoplasmic reticulum and cytosol and mitochondria.

2. Pathogen-associated molecular patterns (PAMPs) another set of triggers generated by Bacteria and viruses.

   - Delivery of PAMPs to their respective receptors constitute part of the initiated innate immune control.

   - Colds and flu are caused by viruses.
   - A virus must have a host cell (bacteria, plant or animal) to make more viruses.

   - The epidermis (skin) contains special cells called Langerhans cells (mixed in with the melanocytes in the basal layer) that are an important early-warning component in the immune system.

     - The skin also secretes antibacterial substances. These substances explain why you don't wake up in the morning with a layer of mold growing on your skin—most bacteria and spores that land on the skin die quickly.

     - it is made up of two main layers:

     - The epidermis on the outside and the

     - The dermis on the inside.

     - The epidermis is the barrier, while the dermis is the layer containing all the "equipment" – things like nerve endings, sweat glands, hair follicles and so on.

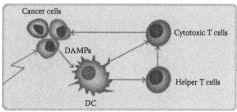

Certain chemotherapeutics agents (anthracyclines) will induce immunogenic apoptosis in cancer cell through induction of (DAMPs).

http://openi.nlm.nih.gov/detailedresult.php?img=2896720 JBB2010-692097.001&reg=4

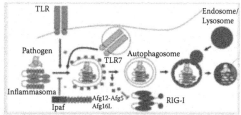

Some PAMP receptors stimulate macroautophagy

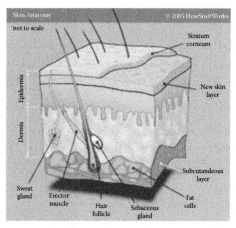

Sunbum animation

Immune System (continued)

Lymph System

- The lymph system, lymph nodes, are just one part of a system that extends throughout your body in much the same way your blood vessels do.
- The main difference between the blood flowing in the circulatory system and the lymph flowing in the lymph system is that blood is pressurized by the heart, while the lymph system is passive.

  - There is no "lymph pump" like there is a "blood pump" (the heart).
  - Instead, *fluids ooze into the lymph system and get pushed by normal body and muscle motion to the lymph nodes.*
  - Lymph is a clearish liquid that bathes the cells with water and nutrients. **Lymph is blood plasma – the liquid that makes up blood minus the red and white cells.** Think about it—each cell does not have its own private blood vessel feeding it, yet it has to get food, water, and oxygen to survive.
  - *Blood transfers these materials* to the *lymph through the capillary walls*, and lymph carries it to the cells.
  - The cells also produce *proteins and waste products* and the **lymph absorbs these products and carries them away.**
  - Any random **bacteria** that enter the body also find their way into this intercell fluid.
  - One job of the lymph system is to *drain and filter these fluids to detect and remove the bacteria.*
  - Small lymph vessels collect the liquid and move it toward larger vessels so that the fluid finally arrives at the lymph nodes for processing.

All immune cells come from precursors in the bone marrow and develop into mature cells through a series of changes that can occur in different parts of the body

Immune Response (white Blood Cells)
(white blood cells, another term for immune cells) http://www.niaid.nih.gov/topics/immuneSystem/Pages/overview.aspx

1. Skin: The skin is usually the first line of defense against microbes. Skin cells produce and secrete important antimicrobial proteins, and immune cells can be found in specific layers of skin.

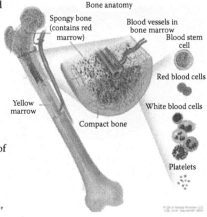

2. Bone marrow: The bone marrow contains stems cells that can develop into a variety of cell types. Ex: neutrophils, eosinophils, basophils, monocytes, dendritic cells, and macrophages

3. Lymphocytes: Adaptive immune cells—B cells and T cells are responsible for mounting responses to specific microbes based on previous encounters (immunological memory).

4. *Thymus*: T cells mature in the thymus, a small organ located in the upper chest.

5. The lymphatic system is a network of vessels and tissues composed of lymph, an extracellular fluid, and lymphoid organs, such as lymph nodes. Immune cells are carried through the lymphatic system and converge in lymph nodes, which are found throughout the body.

6. The spleen: Immune cells are enriched in specific areas of the spleen, and upon recognizing blood-borne pathogens, they will activate.

Immune System (continued)

Antibodies

- Antibodies (also referred to as immunoglobulins and gammaglobulins) are **produced by white blood cells.**
  - They are Y-shaped proteins that each respond to a specific **antigen** (bacteria, virus or toxin).
  - Each antibody has a special section (at the tips of the two branches of the Y) that is sensitive to a specific antigen and binds to it in some way. When an antibody binds to a toxin it is called an antitoxin (if the toxin comes from some form of venom, it is called an antivenin). The binding generally disables the chemical action of the toxin. When an antibody binds to the outer coat of a virus particle or the cell wall of a bacterium it can stop their movement through cell walls.
    - Antibodies come in five classes:

Immunoglobulin A (IgA)
Immunoglobulin D (IgD)
Immunoglobulin E (IgE)
Immunoglobulin G (IgG)
Immunoglobulin M (IgM)

Whenever you see an abbreviation like **IgE** in a medical document it's an antibody

White blood cells work together to destroy viruses and bacteria. They are classified into lymphocytes and myeloid leukocytes. Lymphocytes are B cells, T cells and Killer cells. Myeloid Leukocytes are composed of monocytes, neutrophils, basophils and eosinophils.

White Blood Cells
Leukocytes
Lymphocyte
Monocytes
Granulocytes
B-cells
Plasma cells
T-cells
Helper T-cells
Killer T-cells
Suppressor T-cells
Natural killer cells
Neutrophils
Eosinophils
Basophils
Phagocytes
Macrophages

Neutrophils, are a type of white blood cell which travel to infected tissue and surround bacteria, rendering them harmless to the body.

Lymphocyte (T and B cells):

T cells are especially important in cell-mediated immunity, which is the defense against tumor cells and pathogenic organisms inside body cells. They are also involved in rejection reactions.

B cells, in the presence of an antigen (a substance that stimulates an immune response), secrete large quantities of antibodies

White blood cell distribution chart

White Blood Cell Type	Range%
Neutrophils	50–70
Lymphocytes	15–40
Monocytes	2–8
Eosinophils	1–4
Basophils	0.4–1.0

White blood cell distribution

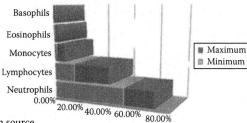

Illustration: Source Wiki books Open source

Leukocytes

- **All white blood cells are known officially as leukocytes.**
- White blood cells are not like normal cells in the body—they actually *act like independent, living single-cell organisms* able to move and capture things on their own.
- White blood cells behave very much like amoeba in their movements and are able to engulf other cells and bacteria. Many white blood cells cannot divide and reproduce on their own, but instead have a factory somewhere in the body that produces them. That factory is the bone marrow.

Leukocytes are divided into three classes:

- **Granulocytes**: Granulocytes make up 50%–60% of all leukocytes. Granulocytes are themselves divided into three classes: neutrophils, eosinophils, and basophils. Granulocytes get their name because they contain granules, and these granules contain different chemicals depending on the type of cell.
- **Lymphocyte**: Lymphocytes make up 30%–40% of all leukocytes. Lymphocytes come in two classes: *B cells (those that mature in bone marrow)* and *T cells (those that mature in the thymus)*.
- **Monocyte**: Monocytes make up 7% or so of all leukocytes. Monocytes evolve into macrophages.

All white blood cells start in bone marrow as stem cells.

7.10 Part IV: Heart Disease, Cancer

1. Heart disease
   a. Coronary balloon angioplasty
   b. Stent placement
   c. Blood types
2. Cancer

Heart disease

Heart disease describes a number of conditions that affect your heart. They include diseases of blood vessel diseases, such as coronary artery disease; heart rhythm problems (arrhythmias); and heart defects (congenital heart defects). Most common references refer to coronary heart disease refer to blocked or narrowing blood vessels.

Arteriosclerosis is where the walls thicken due to inflammation and the accumulation of plaques that reduce the elasticity of the walls. (*Plaque consists of fat, cholesterol, calcium, and other substances found in the blood.*)

The term angina is defined as: blood flow to your heart muscle is reduced or blocked, symptoms are chest pain or discomfort) or a heart attack)

Atherosclerosis is initiated by inflammatory processes in the endothelial cells of the vessel wall

Diagnostic tests

• EKG

ST segment (the line between the QRS complex and the T wave) depression and T wave changes (usually inversion) are the hallmarks of ischemia.

> • However, an EKG in someone with a history of CAD and angina often has a "normal" reading. If an EKG is done during an episode of angina, sometimes the typical ST segment depression can be seen.

Stress Test

Because a resting EKG often results in a "normal" reading for a person with angina, your physician may need to have a stress test to evaluate the presence of CAD. As described earlier, if the characteristic ST segment depression occurs during stress testing, especially if typical chest pain occurs, the test is considered "positive."

Cardiac Catheterization

A cardiac catheterization test can be used to determine if CAD is present, how severe it is and determine if a coronary artery bypass graft is needed. It can definitely exclude CAD if it is not present. This test is performed for many reasons. It is especially important if:

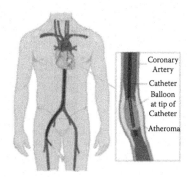

> • During a cardiac catheterization, blockages are treated as a balloon is blown up inside the coronary arteries, thereby opening the passage.
>
> • This procedure is called Percutaneous Transluminal Coronary Angioplasty (PTCA) or just plain angioplasty. Here is an example of how an angioplasty works:

Coronary balloon angioplasty

• The illustration shows a cross-section of a coronary artery with plaque buildup.

• The coronary artery is located on the surface of the heart.

• Figure A shows the deflated balloon catheter inserted into the narrowed coronary artery.

• In Figure B, the balloon is inflated, compressing the plaque and restoring the size of the artery.

• Figure C shows normal blood flow restored in the widened artery.

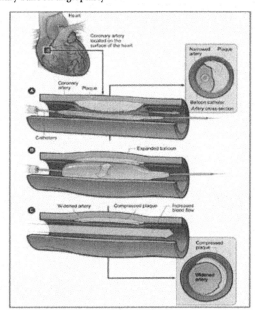

Stent Placement

- The illustration shows the placement of a stent in a coronary artery with plaque buildup.

- The coronary artery is located on the surface of the heart.

- Figure A shows the deflated balloon catheter and closed stent inserted into the narrowed coronary artery.

- In Figure B, the balloon is inflated, expanding the stent and compressing the plaque to restore the size of the artery.

- Figure C, shows normal blood flow restored in the stent-widened artery.

Angioplasty-Stent Animation

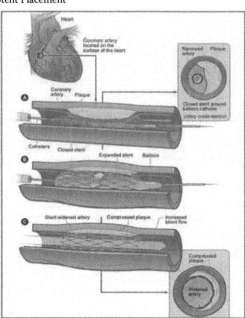

Blood types

Blood carries nutrients and oxygen to the cells and waste products away from the cells. Blood is composed of three types of cells: Red blood cells that carry oxygen via hemoglobin (a protein). White blood cells fight infection and Platelets that clot, stopping bleeding. They are all suspended in blood plasma, a liquid comprising 55% of total blood volume. Plasma is comprised of 92% to 95% of water. The rest is composed of proteins, glucose, clotting factors, electrolytes and CO_2 (Plasma is used to excrete waste: CO_2. urea, lactic acid.)

Blood PH (Potential of Hydrogen) measures the hydrogen concentration in the blood. It's either acidic (0–6) or alkaline (8–14); a PH of 7 is neutral. Normal PH is 7.35–7.45) Acid-Base PH disorders caused by diet and stress leads to Inflammation which is intern linked to cancer, heart disease, and strokes. APH below about 7 or over 7.7) can be fatal. (pH is a logarithmic scale: difference of 1 pH is a 10x difference.)

The blood carries CO_2 away in the lungs, the biggest source of acid elimination in our body. The kidneys provide a secondary protection in urine (but more slowly).

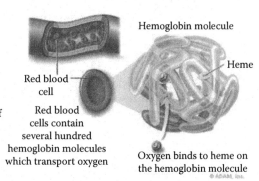

Hemoglobin molecule

Heme

Red blood cell

Red blood cells contain several hundred hemoglobin molecules which transport oxygen

Oxygen binds to heme on the hemoglobin molecule

Red blood cells

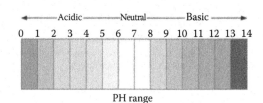

PH range

A blood type(group) is determined by the presence or absence of an inherited antigen, contributed by both parents, on the surface of red blood cells (antigens cause an immune response).
(There are over 30 human blood group systems. The ABO and Rh blood systems are the dominant ones.) (*The International Society of Blood Transfusions officially recognizes 33 groups as of 2012.*)

The four major blood groups are:
Group A – has only the A antigen on red cells (and B antibody in the plasma)
Group B – has only the B antigen on red cells (and A antibody in the plasma)
Group AB – has both A and B antigens on red cells (but neither A nor B antibody in theplasma)
Group O – has neither A nor B antigens on red cells (but both A and B antibody are in the plasma)

Both the ABO and Rh blood group System can affect transfusion compatibility.

Type O– universal donor
Type A– can donate to As and ABs
Type B– can donate to B and ABs
Type AB– donate to ABs but can receive from all

	Group A	Group B	Group AB	Group O
Red blood cell type	A	B	AB	O
Antibodies in plasma	Anti-B	Anti-A	None	Anti-A and Anti-B
Antigens in red blood cell	A antigen	B antigen	A and B antigens	None

ABO blood group antigens present on red blood cells and IgM antibodies present in the serum

ABO blood system

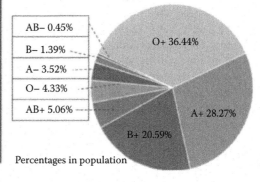

AB– 0.45%
B– 1.39%
A– 3.52%
O– 4.33%
AB+ 5.06%
O+ 36.44%
A+ 28.27%
B+ 20.59%

Percentages in population

Cancer

- Cancer is the uncontrolled growth of abnormal cells in the body. Cancerous cells are also called malignant cells.

  - Alternative Names: Carcinoma; Malignant tumor

- Cancer grows out of normal cells in the body. Normal cells multiply when the body needs them, and die when the body doesn't. Cancer appears to occur when the growth of cells in the body is out of control and cells divide too rapidly.

  There are multiple causes of cancers, including:
  Radiation
  Sunlight
  Tobacco
  Certain viruses
  Benzene

- The three most common cancers in men in the United States are prostate cancer, lung cancer, and colon cancer. In women in the United States, the three most frequently occurring cancers are breast cancer, lung cancer, and colon cancer.

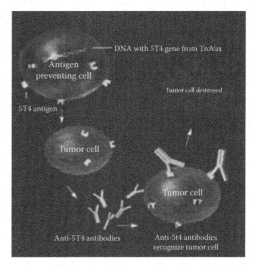

Cancer Animation 1
Cancer Treatment Angiogenesis Animation

7.11 Summary

This chapter focuses on electrochemistry, electrical and chemical properties, needed to understand, capture, and process medical sensor data. Current, electrons, traveling through computer circuitry is essentially the same as signals sent through biological systems except that some of the intermediate propagation mechanisms are electrochemical, i.e., positive ions are moved across cell membranes to create a voltage and then current flows sending or receiving a sensory signal. The propagation speed in electric circuits is much faster, and the theoretical limit is the speed of light 186,000 miles/s (electromagnetic signal light traveling through empty space; space is not empty but close enough), but in reality, the speed is more closer to two-thirds of that due to the limitation of traveling through materials, wires. In biological systems, the max speed is about 100 m/s since there is not just one wire but countless neurons separated by gaps, synapses, where a sodium–potassium pump has to transfer positive ions further slowing conduction speeds. A section on the chemical–electrical batteries was included since medical sensors, especially wireless, need to be powered so the reader can make informed decisions on embedded power sources, plus the internal chemical–electrical properties of batteries complete a student's understanding of voltage and current flow regardless of the source.

Level II introduces wireless medical devices, since wearable medical sensors will be worn or implanted in a large percentage of the population in the next decade when preventive medicine will then come into its own. It will certainly be cost effective, though I don't like to focus on that aspect since we should expand free healthcare for all as a basic right as is the case in most of the industrialized countries, but since prevention will decrease hospitalizations and reduce overall costs, treating a cold is cheaper than pneumonia, and wearable medical devices will be as common as cell phones.

Level III focuses on intelligent expert systems and data mining since the torrent of data from medical sensors will provide the opportunity to accelerate medical research expediting the analysis of drug effectiveness and treatment, a key component of the BMI discipline.

Level IV is a basic anatomy and physiology primer for BMI students.

Questions

Level I

1. What is the role of medical sensors in healthcare?
   a. What role do you believe they have played in improving medical delivery?
2. Why do you believe it's important to understand the basics of electrical and chemical conduction basics while studying biomedical informatics?
   a. What are subatomic particles?
3. What is Ohm's law?
   a. Create your own $V = I \times R$ example similar to Example 7.1.
4. What is electrochemistry?
   a. What role do valence electrons play in electrical conduction?
   b. Explain the similarities of copper, silver, and gold as relates to their conduction characteristics (Figure 7.6a).
5. Explain the general working characteristics of batteries. How do they supply current to an electrical device?
   a. What are the characteristics of a dead battery? Explain the underlying mechanism.
   b. What is the difference between a lithium and lead–acid battery? Explain some of the operating characteristics: current, weight, and safety in medical devices.
   c. Define inductive charging of batteries. When is it useful in medical devices?

6. Explain the difference of electrical conduction in wires versus that in a biological organism: for example, electrons flowing in a nerve synapse.
   a. What is an action potential?
7. Briefly explain the cardiac conduction systems. How do electrical signals coordinate the excitation and contraction of the four chambers of the heart?
   a. Specifically track the signals from the SA node to the AV node and bundle of His.
8. What role does ATP play in chemical/electrical conduction systems?
9. Explain and describe sensors used to measure the following:
   a. Blood pressure
   b. Pulse oximetry
   c. Measuring ABG
10. Explain how neurons conduct electrical signals.
    a. What is the sodium–potassium pump? Why is it important in electrical conduction in biological systems?

Level II

11. What are the advantages of wireless medical monitoring devices?
    a. Explain Bluetooth wireless communications.
12. What are body sensor networks?
    a. In body sensor networks, explain the three types of data capture: structured, nonstructured, and loosely structured data capture.

Level III

13. What is an expert system?
    a. What is a cognitive system?
    b. What are crowd-sourced systems? What advantages do they provide?
14. How is data mining used in large data sets in healthcare?
15. Summarize Case Study 7.6.1.2 on body sensor networks.
16. Research an example of an expert system used in healthcare.

Level IV

Answer the following questions after reviewing this section:

1. Neurons send electrical signals across a _____ by pumping positive ions across.
   a. Axon
   b. Synapse
   c. Voltage
   d. Gap
   e. None of the above
2. This process limits the speed of electrical conduction in humans to ____ ft/s.
   a. Speed of light
   b. 3×10^{10} m/s
   c. 50
   d. 100
   e. 200
3. The part of the brain that _____ integrates pathways, using the constant feedback on body position to fine-tune motor movements (learned-programmed sequences).
   a. Frontal lobe
   b. Pons

   c.   Cerebellum
   d.   Cerebral cortex
   e.   None of the above

4. The _____ motor areas are directly connected to this part of the brain that is connected to the nerves of the spinal cord.
   a.   Somatomotor cortex
   b.   Occipital lobe
   c.   Temporal lobe
   d.   Medulla oblongata
   e.   None of the above

5. The _____receptor cells of the eye that translate colors into electrical signals are
   a.   Rods
   b.   Cones
   c.   Cornea
   d.   Retina
   e.   Lens

6. Link the terms (draw connecting lines) from column one to column two:

a.	DNA	a. Catalyze biochemical reactions
b.	RNA	b. Genetic instructions
c.	Proteins	c. Translate genetic information
d.	Cell	d. Intracellular energy transfer
e.	ATP	e. Structural and function unit

Glossary

Arterial blood gases (ABGs) require drawing blood from an artery, often taken from the radial artery at the wrist or the femoral artery in the groin, but a number of other sites are used. ABG provides more comprehensive information than pulse oximetry information, which is vital for critically ill patients in intensive care units.

Automaticity: AV cells can depolarize by themselves.

Batteries provide electrical energy from chemical reactions; it incorporates electrochemical cells, which allows the flow of ions.

Blood pressure is the pressure on the walls of blood vessels that is exerted by circulating blood and is measured by the force per unit area. Blood pressure is the brachial arterial pressure usually measured in the upper arm as blood moves away from the heart.

The cardiac myocyte is a muscle cell that is 100 μm in length. It is composed of bundles of myofibrils that contain filaments. The myofibril, tubelike structures, propagates signals inside the muscles.

Data mining can be defined as the process of finding previously unknown patterns and trends in databases and using that information to build predictive models.

Depolarization: Muscle cells, cardiac myocytes, are made up of negatively charged cells; when positive ions are pumped into the cell calcium (Ca^{2+}), sodium (Na^+), and potassium (K^+), the polarity of the cell becomes positive and the cell contract (negative to positive membrane potential).

Electrochemistry is "a science that deals with the relation of electricity to chemical changes and with the interconversion of chemical and electrical energy."

Electrocardiogram measures the electrical activity of the cardiac muscle of the heart.

Electrotonic spread: A change in membrane potential (e.g., areceptor potentialor synaptic potential) originating in one region of a cell (ΔV_0) is associated with local transmembrane currents that distribute and flow intracellularly and extracellularly to adjacent membrane regions (at distance d), where they in turn cause changes in membrane potential ($\Delta V(d)$). However, the underlying currents get progressively smaller with distance because fractions of them are diverted through transmembrane ion leak channels. Thereby, the elicited adjacent membrane potential changes ($\Delta V(d)$) are reduced in size and altered in shape (electrotonic decrement) (http://www.springerreference.com/docs/html/chapterdbid/116505.html).

Excitation–contraction coupling (ECC) is the process whereby an action potential triggers a myocyte to contract.

Expert systems are computerized applications that combine computer hardware, software, and specialized information to imitate expert human reasoning and advice.

Hemoglobin is an iron-containing protein bound to red blood cells and makes up nearly all the oxygen presence: except there is a small amount dissolved in the plasma. It's a metalloproteinase, a generic term for a protein that contains a metal ion cofactor.

Inductive charging is a method by which a magnetic field transfers electricity from an external source to a mobile device without the use of standard wiring. It does this by generating a magnetic field and creating a current in the receiving device. Electricity can move through the air and recharge your device's battery.

Beer–Lambert law is the attenuation of light by a material passing through a substance.

Ohm's law $V = I \times R$ (voltage = current[I] [times] resistance) describes the relationship between voltage, also called potential difference, which is the force that moves, or pulls, electrons through the wire.

Oxyhemoglobin (*oxygenated hemoglobin* [HbO_2]) saturation is the ratio, expressed as a percentage, of the amount of oxygen relative to the total amount of hemoglobin in blood.

Peukert's law: It is the efficiency factor for discharging a battery. Battery ratings are quantified by the relationship between capacity, current, and discharge time. Qp = capacity when discharged at 1 amp/h, I = amount of current drawn, and k is a constant around 1.3: $t = \mathbf{Qp/I^k}$

Pulse oximetry is noninvasive method of monitoring oxygen saturation of a patient's hemoglobin, the protein in blood that carries oxygen.

SA node is located in the right atrium where the superior vena cava joins the atrial tissue; the SA node acts as the main pacemaker in the heart.

The transformer equation relates to the turns of wire on the coil, i.e., a coil is wire wrapped around a metal post a few thousand times. The equation relates the voltage between the first, primary coil, to the secondary coil: $Vp/Vs = Np/Ns$.

Venous oxygen saturation (SvO_2): (Range 65%–75%) Percentage of oxygen bound to hemoglobin in blood returning to the right side of the heart.

Wireless medical devices are defined as "any medical monitoring technology, worn or implanted, that gathers physiological information."

References

1. Brachman, R. and Lemnios, Z. (2002). DARPA's cognitive systems vision. *Computing Research News*, 14, 1.
2. Crookshank, E. (1888). The history of the germ theory. *The British Medical Journal*, 1(1415), 312.
3. Dignan, L. (February 1, 2011). Cisco predicts mobile data traffic explosion, http://seekingalpha.com/article/250005-cisco-predicts-mobile-data-traffic-explosion., Editor ZDNet.
4. Klabunde, R. (2007). Excitation contraction coupling, http://www.cvphysiology.com/Cardiac%20Function/CF022.htm.
5. Englebardt, S. P. and Nelson, R. (2002). The role of expert systems. In: *Nursing and Medicine. Anti Essays*. Retrieved: November 18, 2012, from the World Wide Web: http://www.antiessays.com/free-essays/185731.htmlp. p. 137.
6. Geller, M. J. (2010). *Ancient Babylonian Medicine: Theory and Practice*. Chichester, U.K.: Wiley-Blackwell. ISBN 978-1-4051-2652-6.

7. Gopakumar, T. G. (June 2012). Switchable nano magnets may revolutionize data storage: Magnetism of individual molecules switched, http://www.sciencedaily.com/releases/2012/06/120614131049.htm.

8. Master list of Government Funded R&D Centers, Government Publications: IEEE, HHS.gov, House.gov NSF.gov.

9. Heckerman, D. and Shortliffe, E. (1992). From certainty factors to belief networks. *Artificial Intelligence in Medicine*, 4(1), 35–52. doi:10.1016/0933–3657(92)90036-O, http://research.microsoft.com/en-us/um/people/heckerman/HS91aim.pdf.

10. IEEE. (2012). *Medical Interoperability Standards*, http://www.IEEE.org/standards.

11. Kincade, K. (1998). Data mining: Digging for healthcare gold. *Insurance & Technology*, 23(2), IM2–IM7.

12. Kusnetzky, D. What is big data, ZDNet.

13. Langley, P. (2012). The cognitive systems paradigm, CogSys.org., *Advances in Cognitive Systems*, 1(20), 3–13.

14. Mahn, T. (2010). Wireless medical technologies: Navigating government regulation in the new medical age, http://www.fr.com/files/uploads/attachments/FinalRegulatoryWhitePaperWirelessMedicalTechnologies.pdf.

15. Ross, P.E. (December 2004). Managing care through the air, *IEEE Spectrum*, 41(12), 14–19.

16. Matzat, U. and Snijders, C. (2010). Does the online collection of ego-centered network data reduce data quality? An experimental comparison. *Social Networks*, 32(2), 105–111.

8

Imaging

Level I: Core Concepts

8.1 Introduction

Medical imaging is a broad field that encompasses three core components: (1) the imaging devices and the complex physics and algorithms involved in analyzing these data, (2) the standards used for transmitting and visualizing these images in Digital Imaging and Communications in Medicine (DICOM), which is the de facto standard, and (3) the system for storage and retrieval of images in a Picture Archiving and Communication System (PACS). Imaging informatics is more narrowly defined because once the image is captured, it interprets the image and manages all imaging standards such because DICOM. The Society for Imaging Informatics in Medicine (SIIM) defines imaging informatics as:

> image creation and acquisition, image distribution and management, image storage and retrieval, image processing, analysis and understanding, image visualization and data navigation; image interpretation, reporting, and communications. (www.siim.org)

> Medical imaging is one of the top developments that "changed the face of clinical medicine" during the last millennium. (New England Journal of Medicine)

This chapter begins with the de facto imaging standard DICOM used by over 90% of imaging practitioners. The next section describes each of the imaging technologies with its basic underlying operational physics. Level II introduces the PACS used to store and process images, teleradiology, and the Cross Language Evaluation Forum (CLEF), which provides multilingual conversion capabilities. Level III discusses the advanced topics in radio pharmacology, the science of radio isotopes used to enhance images and advanced techniques used for automated image analysis (Figure 8.1).

8.2 Medical Imaging Formats

8.2.1 DICOM

DICOM Standards Organizations
Acronyms

1. *ACR*: American College of Radiology (www.acr.org)
2. *ANSI*: American National Standards Institute
3. *CEN TC251*: Comite Europeen de Normalization Technical Committee 251
4. *DICOM*: Digital Imaging and Communications in Medicine (dicom.nema.org)
5. *HISPP*: Healthcare Informatics Standards Planning Panel —sponsored by the American National Standards Institute
6. NEMA: National Electrical Manufacturers Association (www.nema.org)
   a. MITA: Medical Imaging & Technology Alliance (www.medicalimaging.org)
   b. NEMA documents (http://medical.nema.org/standard.html)
7. *JIRA*: Japan Industries Association of Radiological Systems
8. *MSDS*: Healthcare Message Standard Developers Sub-Committee
9. *NIST*: National Institute of Standards and Technology
10. *TCP/IP*: Transmission Control Protocol/Internet Protocol

A number of preliminary imaging standards were published in 1985 by the American College of Radiology (ACR), that is, ACR-NEMA No.300–1985 ver.1. Several iterations were published in the succeeding years focusing on hardware standards, software, and data formats (http://medical.nema.org/Dicom/2011/11_01pu.doc).

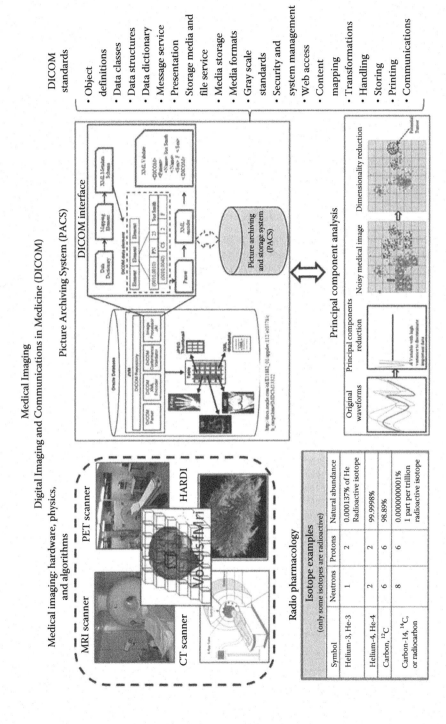

FIGURE 8.1 Medical imaging overview.

DICOM evolved out of these earlier efforts and was officially introduced in 1993 specifying standards for transmitting images, storing images, and finally processing those images. It is an international standard developed in conjunction with the International Organization for Standardization (ISO) 12052 (see ISO, Chapter 4). These standards are maintained by the Medical Imaging & Technology Alliance (MITA), which is part of NEMA (http://www.medicalimaging.org/). MITA also provides standards for radiation therapy for cancer. The National Cancer Institute defines radiation therapy as "Radiation therapy that utilizes high-energy radiation to kill cancer cells by damaging their DNA" (Figure 8.2), http://www.cancer.gov/cancertopics/factsheet/Therapy/radiation.

DICOM Imaging Standards, Parts 1–20

This section summarizes, in a few pages, the thousands of pages of imaging documentation provided by MITA a division of the National Electrical Manufacturers Association (NEMA), which collectively is referred to as DICOM. Not every document is addressed, but the core concepts are summarized so the reader can gain an appreciation of the scope of these imaging standards. At the beginning of each section, a link is provided to the source standards documentation. All items taken directly from the NEMA documents are in *italics*.

8.2.1.1 Part 1: DICOM Introduction and Overview

With the advent of advanced imaging technology, computed tomography (CT), magnetic resonance imaging (MRI) in the 1970s and 1980s, advanced computer processing, that is, the first PC's that arrived in 1980's and the World Wide Web (www), Internet, one of whose creators was Tim Berners-Lee in the early 1990s; it was an opportune time to create industry standards for medical imaging and

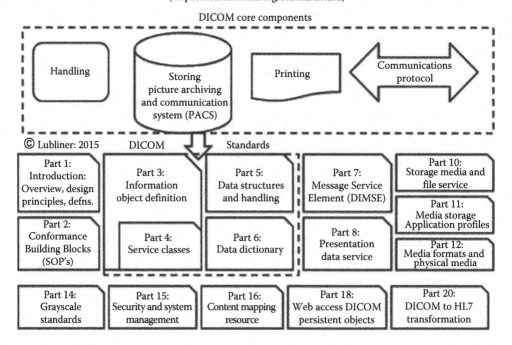

FIGURE 8.2   DICOM architecture.

TABLE 8.1 DICOM Terms

	Definitions (Used throughout the DICOM Documents)
Attribute	A property of an information object. An attribute has a name and a value that are independent of any encoding scheme.
Command	A request to operate on information across a network.
Command element	An encoding of a parameter of a command that conveys this parameter's value.
Command stream	The result of encoding a set of DICOM command elements using the DICOM encoding scheme.
Conformance statement	A formal statement that describes a specific product implementation that uses the DICOM standard. It specifies the service classes, information objects, and communication protocols supported by the implementation.
Data dictionary	A registry of DICOM data elements that assigns a unique tag, a name, value characteristics, and semantics to each data element.
Data element	A unit of information as defined by a single entry in the data dictionary.
Data set	Exchanged information consisting of
Data stream	The result of encoding a data set using the DICOM encoding scheme (data element numbers and representations as specified by the data dictionary).
Information object	An abstraction of a real information entity (e.g., CT image and structured report) that is acted upon by one or more DICOM commands.
Information object class	A formal description of an information object that includes a description of its purpose and the attributes it possesses. It does not include values for these attributes.
Information object instance	A representation of an occurrence of a real-world entity, which includes values for the attributes of the information object class to which the entity belongs.
Message	A data unit of the Message Exchange Protocol exchanged between two cooperating DICOM applications. A message is composed of a command stream followed by an optional data stream.
Service class	A structured description of a service that is supported by cooperating DICOM applications using specific DICOM commands acting on a specific class of information object.

communications, which currently are used by 90% of imaging practitioners and manufacturers. This comprehensive standard is also used by dentists, pathologists, cardiologists, etc., for handling and manipulating medical images (Table 8.1).

The DICOM standard facilitates interoperability of medical imaging equipment by specifying

- *For network communications, a set of protocols to be followed by devices claiming conformance to the standard*
- *The syntax and semantics of commands and associated information that can be exchanged using these protocols*
- *For media communication, a set of media storage services to be followed by devices claiming conformance to the standard, as well as a file format and a medical directory structure to facilitate access to the images and related information stored on interchange media*
- *Information that must be supplied with an implementation for which conformance to the standard is claimed*

8.2.1.2 DICOM Part 2: Conformance

Conformance refers to a set of guidelines and principles that all manufacturers and practitioners should adhere to ensure interoperability, that is, standards which imaging systems would utilize to guarantee accurate communication and transmission of data (Table 8.2).

Data flow diagrams in the document correlate real-world entities to DICOM application entities following data flow diagram conventions (Figure 8.3).

TABLE 8.2 Conforms to the Following Syntaxes and Vocabularies

Conformance (to the ISO and DICOM Standards)				
Reference Model Definitions ISO 7498–1	Presentation Service Definitions ISO 8822	DICOM Introduction and Overview Definitions	DICOM Service Class Specification Definitions	DICOM Data Structure and Encoding Definitions
Application entity	Abstract syntax	Information object	Real-world activity	DICOM defined UID
Application entity title	Abstract syntax name	IOD	Service class	Privately defined UID
Protocol data unit	Presentation context		*Service class user*	Transfer syntax (standard and private)
Transfer syntax	Transfer syntax		*Service class provider*	UID
	Transfer syntax name		*Service object pair* (SOP)	
			Meta SOP class	

Application Data Flow Diagram Conventions (DICOM)

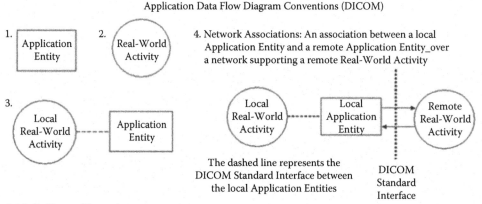

FIGURE 8.3 DICOM application data flow diagram conventions.

8.2.1.3 DICOM Parts 3 and 4: Information Object Definitions and Service Classes

DICOM Part 3 describes object-oriented data models and service classes used to communicate and interface medical images with external systems. An "object" is an instance of class. That means that we define generic computer code called a class. This class might be used to process some part of an image. Generic code means the class is designed to process a number of different images but is without specific form. An example would be a *car class*. It is used to describe certain general attributes of any car class: that is, it has wheels, a motor, steering wheel, etc. We then want to describe a specific car such as a Ford Mustang. Then a second car, a Nissan Altima, would be an another instance of the class that contain details of each car, or in this case various medical images (Figure 8.4).

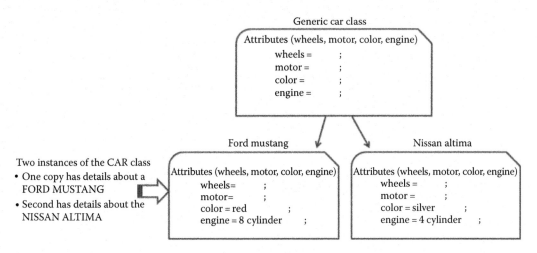

FIGURE 8.4 Generic example of classes and instances of a class.

The DICOM Part 3 document describes various Information Object Definitions (IODs), which describe an object-oriented abstract data model used to specify information about real-world objects. The definitions depict generic classes of real-world objects that share similar properties, just like the car example (Figure 8.4). There are standards group image classes that have the same general properties (Figure 8.5).

The following are IOD object types:

1. An IOD is used to represent a *single class* of real-world objects is called a *normalized* information object.
2. An IOD that includes information about *related* real-world Objects is called a *composite* information object.

The relationship between object models and the other DICOM standards are depicted in (Figure 8.5).

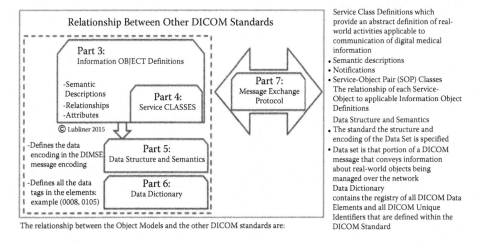

FIGURE 8.5 Relationship between DICOM standards relating to objects and classes.

8.2.1.2.1 *Multidimensional Definitions: Orientation in 3D Space (Sec 3.17 in Part 3)*

- *Reference Coordinate System (RCS): The RCS is the spatial coordinate system in a DICOM frame of reference. It is the chosen origin, orientation, and spatial scale of an image IE in a Cartesian space. The RCS is a right-handed Cartesian coordinate system, that is, the vector cross product of a unit vector along the positive x-axis and a unit vector along the positive y-axis is equal to a unit vector along the positive z-axis. The unit length is 1 mm.*
- *Fiducial: A fiducial is some unique feature or landmark suitable as a spatial reference or correlation between similar objects. The fiducial may contribute to the definition of the origin and orientation of a chosen coordinate system. Identifying fiducials in different data sets is a common means to establish the spatial relationship between similar objects.*
- *Fiducial point: A fiducial point defines a specific location of a fiducial. A fiducial point is relative to an image or to an RCS (Figure 8.6).*

Individual image data elements, described in more detail in Part 7, contain tag, value, value length, and value fields to represent distinct image information. Figure 8.7 lists some of those reference tag numbers. Some of those tags that define image metadata, that is, data that describe the patient's age, weight, etc., are illustrated in Figure 8.7.

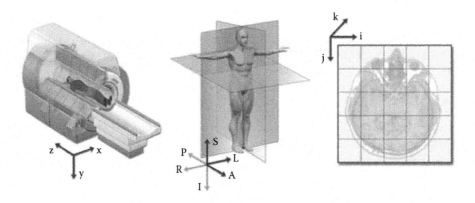

FIGURE 8.6 **(See color insert.)** Reference coordinate system diagrams relating scanners and individual 2D slices. (*Source*: Image from http://www.slicer.org/slicerWiki/index.php/Coordinate_systems)

Description	Tag #
Name of physician(s) reading study	(0008, 1060)
Admitting diagnoses description	(0008, 1080)
Referenced study sequence	(0008, 1110)
>Referenced SOP class UID	(0008, 1150)
>Referenced SOP instance UID	(0008, 1155)
Patient's age	(0010, 1010)
Patient's size	(0010, 1020)
Patient's weight	(0010, 1030)
Occupation	(0010, 2180)
Additional patient history	(0010, 21B0)
Other study numbers	(0020, 1070)
Number of study related series	(0020, 1206)
Number of study related instances	(0020, 1208)

Tag	Value (optional) representation	Value length	Value field

Image descriptors (for each 2D picture slice)		
Type of instances	(0040,E020)	DICOM, CDA
Referenced Frame Number	(0008, 1160)	Required if the referenced SOP instance is a multi-frame image
Referenced Segment Number	(0062, 000B)	Identifies the segment number to which the reference applies.

FIGURE 8.7   Image Metadata

8.2.1.4 DICOM Part 5: Data Structures and Encoding

DICOM Part 5 standard describes the interchange of information between digital imaging systems; it covers the protocols and data sets referred to as "application entities."

These include (http://medical.nema.org/Dicom/2011/11_05pu.doc)

1. *Encoding of values*
2. Structure and usage of a *data set*
3. *Data element* usage and relationships to other elements
4. Construction and usage of *nested data sets*
5. Construction and usage of *data sets containing pixel data*
6. Uniquely *identify information*
7. Specification of the standard DICOM *transfer syntaxes*

Here are the definitions of the aforementioned entities:

1. A *data set* is constructed of data elements.
2. A *data element* is uniquely identified by a data element tag (Figure 8.8).
   a. *Standard data* elements have an even group number that is not (0000,eeee), (0002,eeee), (0004,eeee), or (0006,eeee).
   b. *Private data* elements have an odd group number that is not (0001,eeee), (0003,eeee), (0005,eeee), (0007,eeee), or (FFFF,eeee).

Nested value elements provide an encoding scheme that can be used for structures of repeating sets of data elements or more complex IODs often called folders. Data elements can also be used recursively to contain multilevel nested structures (Figure 8.8).

3. Pixel and overlay data and related data elements
   The pixel data element (7FE0,0010) and overlay data element (60xx,3000) can be used for the exchange of encoded graphical image data.
   Encoded pixel data of various bit depths shall be accommodated. The following three data elements define the pixel structure:
   a. *Bits allocated (0028,0100)*
   b. *Bits stored (0028,0101)*
   c. *High bit (0028,0102)*

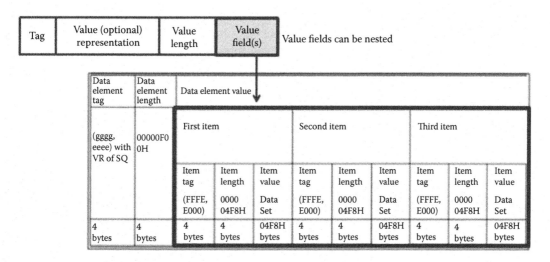

FIGURE 8.8 Nested value filed.

4. Overlay data encoding of related data elements
   Encoded overlay planes always have a bit depth of 1 and are encoded separately from the pixel data in overlay data (60xx,3000). The following two data elements define the overlay plane structure:
   a.   *Overlay bit allocated (60xx,0100)*
   b.   *Overlay bit position (60xx,0102)*

This standards document focuses on specifying data structures and data elements and the tag elements. Complex nested data elements are used to specify layers of each image in a concise hierarchical structure.

8.2.1.5 DICOM Part 6: Data Dictionary

This standard provides definitions for data tags, structured elements, and color palettes used for defining data sets. A representative group is included to illustrate this data dictionary.

Tag: Tag is a unique identifier (UID) for an element of information composed of an ordered pair of numbers (a group number followed by an element number), which is used to identify attributes and corresponding data elements.

- A data element tag is represented as (gggg,eeee), where gggg equates to the group number and eeee equates to the element number within that group. (Table 8.3)

TABLE 8.3   Representative Data Element Examples

Identifying Information

Tag	Name	
(0008,1060)	Name of physician(s) reading the study	
(0008,1070)	Operator's name	
(0008,1080)	Admitting diagnosis description	
Manufacturer and Contrast Dye Information		
(0008,1090)	Manufacturer's model name	
(0008,2259)	*Anatomic Location Of Examining Instrument Code Sequence (Trial)*	
(0008,9209)	Acquisition contrast	
	(0018,1044)	Contrast/bolus total dose
	(0018,1043)	Contrast/bolus start time
	(0018,1043)	Contrast/bolus stop time
Image Coordinate System		
(0014,0023)	CAD file format	
(0014,2208)	Coordinate system, data set mapping	
(0018,0015)	Body part examined	
(0018,0087)	Magnetic field strength	
(0018,1405)	Relative x-ray exposure	
(0018,9325)	CT x-ray detail sequence	
(0018,9732)	PET frame acquisition sequence	
(0028,0040)	*Image format*	
(0046,0012)	Lens description	
	(0046,0014)	Right lens sequence
	(0046,0015)	Left lens sequence
	(0046,0040)	Optical transmittance
(0048,0000)	Imaged volume width	
	(0048,0001)	Imaged volume width
	(0048,0002)	Imaged volume height
	(0048,0003)	Imaged volume depth

8.2.1.6 DICOM Part 7: Message Service Elements (http:// medical.nema.org/Dicom/2011/11_05pu.pdf)

The DICOM Part 7 standards illustrate the transmission of images, using DICOM Message Service Elements (DIMSEs). The tags in the data sets describe categories of information in particular data set fields accompanying the image.

Some of those standards include the following:

1. Data elements and field structures
   a. Data types
   b. *Data elements*
      i. A data element is uniquely represented by a data element tag (Figure 8.9).
      ii. Standard data elements have tags that have even group numbers.
      iii. Private data elements have odd group numbers.
   c. Value representation
   d. Each of these tags has a unique meaning: that is, it explains the context of the subsequent data fields. Some examples are:
      i. (0008,0105) *DCMR = DICOM Content Mapping Resource*
      ii. (0008,2228) Primary Anatomic Structure Sequence
      iii. (0018,0029) Intervention Drug Code Sequence
      iv. (0040,0300) Total duration of x-ray exposure (in seconds)
         I. (0018,1110) distance in mm from source detector (SID)
         II. (0040,0303) dimension of exposed area at the detector plane
         III. (0040,0301) total number of exposures (CT scan multiple slices)

2. Encoding of pixel, overlay, and waveform data
3. UIDs
4. Transfer Syntax (encoding rules for the data set)
   a. Transfer Syntax for Lossless *JPEG Compression*
   b. Transfer Syntax for *Run Length Encoding (RLE)* Compression
   c. Transfer Syntax for *MPEG2* MP@ML Image Compression
   d. Transfer Syntax for MPEG-4 AVC/H.264 Image Compression

8.2.2 NIfTI Data Format

Neuroimaging Informatics Technology Initiative (NIfTI) is an initiative of the National Institute of Health (NIH) and the National Institute of Neurological Disorders and Stroke to spur research into

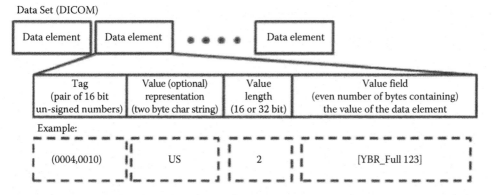

FIGURE 8.9 Data element example.

TABLE 8.4   Neuroimaging Informatics Technology Initiative Charter

Objectives of NIfTI	Operating Principles of NIfTI	Significance of NIfTI
1. Enhancement of existing informatics tools used widely in neuroimaging research	1. Guidance through close and ongoing communication with the tool-user and tool-developer communities	1. More useful and useable neuroimaging informatics tools
2. Dissemination of neuroimaging informatics tools and information about them	2. Intellectual property rights and credit for tools to remain with original authors	2. One-stop resource for neuroimaging informatics tools and information about them
3. Community-based approaches to solving common problems, such as lack of interoperability of tools and data	3. Coordination within NIfTI and across other related programs and activities	3. Environment to facilitate convergence on common solutions to widespread problems
4. Unique training activities and research career development opportunities to those in the tool-user and tool-developer communities	4. Optimal mechanism to be used for each activity, drawing from both intramural and extramural resources	4. Maximize scientific opportunities from neuroimaging research
5. Research and development of the next generation of neuroimaging informatics tools	5. Involvement of multiple institutes at NIH	

Source: NIfTI (http://nifti.nimh.nih.gov/).

neuroimaging tools. This effort has focused initially with the functional MRI (fMRI), that measures brain activity and cerebral blood flow. The organization efforts include standardizing fMRI data formats that vary widely (Table 8.4).

8.2.3 Analyze Data Format

The Analyze-7.5 fMRI imaging format stores imaging data in a volume and pixel (voxel) format (Figure 8.10); its position is defined relative to other 3D elements and is specifically suited to representing elements with empty space that are not uniformly spaced (Table 8.5).

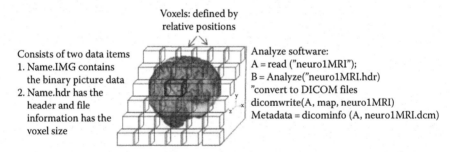

FIGURE 8.10   Voxel fMRI image elements. An individual voxel element is highlighted.

TABLE 8.5   Structure of the Analyze Data Format

Analyze Format	
Header files.**HDR**	Image type, size, and attributes
File.**IMG**	Raw data file
Extension.**lkup**	Color lookup file
Voxel formats	8 bit unassigned
	16 bit signed
	24 bit RGB
	32 bit signed integers or floating point

8.2.4 Additional Data Formats

- Network Common Data Form (NetCDF) supports array-oriented scientific data.
- Hierarchical Data Format (HDF4 or HDF5) stores large numerical data sets.
- Image Cytometry Standard (ICS) is used in microscopy.
- Layered Image File Format (LIFF) is a file format microscope image processing.
- Adobe (PSD) file images with unlimited amount of colors.

8.3 Medical Imaging Technologies

This section describes a number of imaging technologies: x-rays (2D), CT scanner (multiple 2D x-rays merged into 3D view), MRI (soft tissue visualized in 3D that uses a superconducting magnet), fMRI (measures brain activity), and more recent whole body scans for pre-screening and security applications (Figure 8.11).

8.3.1 X-Rays

X-rays, the first noninvasive medical imaging technology, which creates a 2D image, were discovered by Wilhelm Röntgen in 1895 for which he later won the Nobel Prize. W. D. Coolidge created the x-ray tube in 1903 that made x-ray use in medical devices practical. X-rays have a shorter wavelength and higher energy than visible light that makes them capable of passing through soft tissue. X-rays are absorbed by denser structures, such as calcium in the bones (white areas are places X-rays blocked) (Figure 8.12).

8.3.2 Computed Tomography

CT or computed axial tomography (CAT) was invented in 1972 in England by Godfrey Hounsfield who later received the Nobel Prize. Alan Cormack, a South African, is also credited with its CT invention. It uses numerous 2D x-ray slices, to create a 3D view of the body (also referred to as CAT scan) (see Figure 8.12). Most scans are taken with contrast dye to enhance the image such as an iodine-based dye that is injected or a barium sulfate to image the digestive system. Contrast dyes change the magnetic properties of tissues by highlighting soft tissue [1]. The dye absorbs photons and blocks them from being detected by the CT scanner. Ionizing radiation can cause cancer and damage DNA. Since CT scans take numerous 2D x-ray slices to form a 3D image, it subjects a patient to 100 to 5000 times more radiation than standard x-rays, but it is believed that the benefits outweigh the risks. A *Scientific American* article in 2013 estimates from 2007 to 2013 "29,000 future cancers will develop from the 72 million CT scans performed," that is, approximately 1 chance of developing future cancers in every 50,000 CT scans (http://www.scientificamerican.com/article/how-much-ct-scans-increase-risk-cancer/). Manufacturers continue to try to reduce radiation exposures. Magnetic resonance imagers do not produce ionizing radiations, but just strong magnetic fields, which at present don't have similar side effects and appear to be inherently safer (Figure 8.13).

In order to reconstruct or assemble multiple 2D slices, the exact position of the beam must be relative to the isocenter, that is, the center of the beam on the patient; it is essential to the final reconstruction of

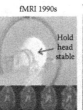

FIGURE 8.11 **(See color insert.)** Evolution in medical imaging technology.

X-rays are 1,000 times smaller than visible light and higher energy that allows them to penetrate soft tissue. Calcium in bones absorbs more x-rays than soft tissue. Photoelectric absorption is the method used by medical x-rays (Compton scattering the other).

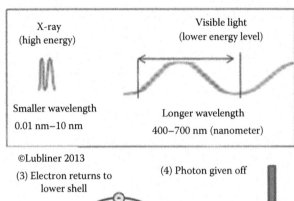

©Lubliner 2013

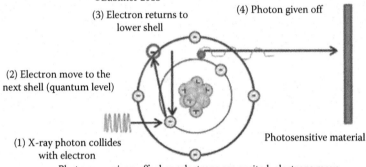

Photons are given off when: electrons are excited, electrons move to the next quantum level, electrons return to their original state they then give off 1 photon of energy

FIGURE 8.12 X-ray imaging and photoelectric absorption.

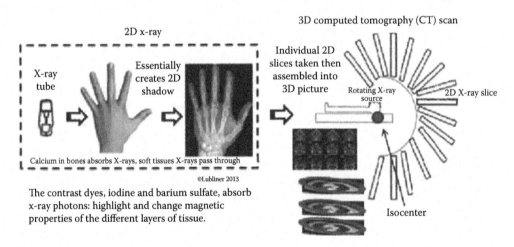

The contrast dyes, iodine and barium sulfate, absorb x-ray photons: highlight and change magnetic properties of the different layers of tissue.

FIGURE 8.13 CT scan and 3D scan created by assembling numerous 2D images.

the 3D image. The DICOM tag, in Section 2.2.1 for the isocenter, is (0018,9402) and the isocenter primary angle tag is (0018,9463) of the X-ray beam (Figure 8.14).

8.3.3 MRI

Magnetic Resonance Imaging (MRI) or nuclear MRI was shortened to address the worries of individuals regarding the term nuclear. In 1946, Edward Purcell and Felix Bloch discovered magnetic resonance of atoms and received the Nobel Prize in 1952. The first commercial machines appeared in the late 1970s.

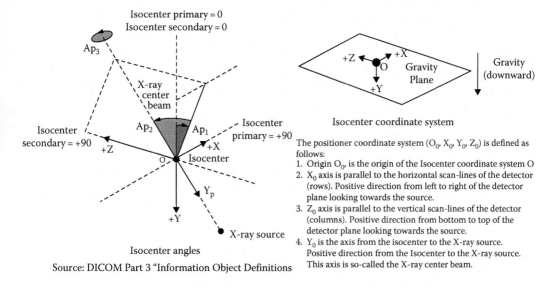

Source: DICOM Part 3 "Information Object Definitions

FIGURE 8.14 Determination of the isocenter of x-ray beam for CT scanner. (*Source*: DICOM whitepaper Part 3.)

The positioner coordinate system (O_0, X_0, Y_0, Z_0) is defined as follows:

1. Origin O_0, is the origin of the Isocenter coordinate system O
2. X_0 axis is parallel to the horizontal scan-lines of the detector (rows). Positive direction from left to right of the detector plane looking towards the source.
3. Z_0 axis is parallel to the vertical scan-lines of the detector (columns). Positive direction from bottom to top of the detector plane looking towards the source.
4. Y_0 is the axis from the isocenter to the X-ray source. Positive direction from the Isocenter to the X-ray source. This axis is so-called the X-ray center beam.

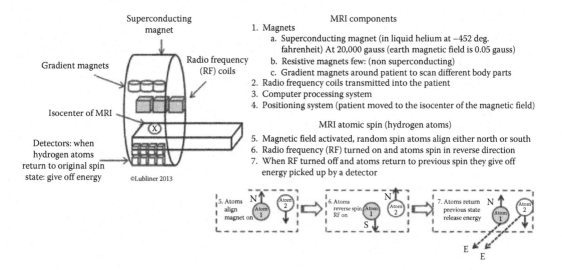

FIGURE 8.15 Magnetic resonance imaging progression.

An MRI produces a magnetic field that excites hydrogen atoms' electrons; that is, electrons are in fixed orbits but when excited, they move to a higher shell. When they return to their original shells, energy is given off. MRIs utilize nonionizing absorption and emission in the radio frequencies and are best suited for noncalcified tissues, that is, soft tissues (Figure 8.15).

In order to reconstruct or assemble multiple 2D slices, the exact position of the beam must be relative to the isocenter, that is, the center of the beam on the patient; it is essential to the final reconstruction of the 3D image.

Magnetic gradients are generated by three orthogonal coils, oriented in the x, y, and z directions of the scanner. These are usually resistive electromagnets powered by amplifiers that permit rapid and precise adjustments to their field strength and direction. The straightness of flux lines within the isocenter of the magnet needs to be almost perfect. In 1983, Ljunggren [8] and Tweig [9] independently introduced

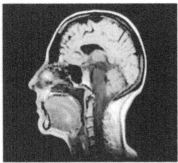 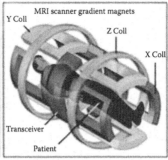 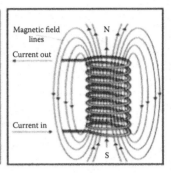

FIGURE 8.16 **(See color insert.)** MRI scan, schematic of scanner gradient magnets, and magnetic fields generated. (*Source*: Images from the National High Magnetic Field Magnetic Lab., at the Florida State University, http://www. magnet.fsu.edu/education/tutorials/magnetacademy/mri/fullarticle.html)

the k-space formalism, a technique to unify different MR imaging techniques. They showed that the demodulated MR signal $S(t)$ generated by freely précising nuclear spins in the presence of a linear magnetic field gradient G equals the Fourier transform of the effective spin density, that is,

$$S(t) = \tilde{\rho}_{effective}(\vec{k}(t)) \equiv \int d^3x \rho(\vec{x}) \cdot e^{2\pi \ell \vec{k}(t) \cdot \vec{x}}$$

MRI is essentially the manipulation of *spins* within a strong magnetic field, which then return to an equilibrium state and give off energy that can be detected. Particle *spin* is a mathematical description of the quantum mechanical state of the atom. A positively charged sphere, the proton, of radius $\sim 10^{-14}$ m, mass $\sim 10^{-27}$ kg, and a net electric charge $\sim 10^{-19}$ C spins and possesses a magnetic dipole moment (Figure 8.16).

8.3.4 Functional MRI

In the 1990s, the fMRI measures brain and neural activities by alterations in blood flow. The core mechanism measures variations in oxygen level in the blood by color coding results over a short period that is usually in seconds. These measurements are taken in parallel with electroencephalography and other various measurement techniques such as near-infrared spectroscopy that dynamically measures hemoglobin levels. It most often used in research settings.

8.3.5 SPECT Imaging

Single-Photon Emission Computed Tomography (SPECT) imaging technique uses ionizing radiation, gamma rays, a radioisotope tracer, and blood flow measuring in capillaries. It is similar to a positron emission tomography (PET) scanner that allows functional studies over time. The radionuclide tracer technetium-99m (^{99m}Tc) tetrofosmin is used to visualize cardiac blood flow over a 10–20 s time period. It is used with an EKG to trigger SPECT imaging: that is, if there were electrical abnormalities, the SPECT could calculate the ejection fraction of the ventricles, that is, the efficiency of the ventricles.

The advantages of SPECT are that it can be used to observe biochemical and physiological processes as well as size and volume of the organ (http://www.nlm.nih.gov/cgi/mesh/2011/MB_cgi?mode=&term=SPECT).

8.3.6 Ultrasound

Ultrasound uses sound waves to visualize soft tissue. The high-frequency waves can track movement in real time by measuring the amplitude and frequency of the returning sound waves utilizing the Doppler effect, that is, the positive frequency shift if the object is moving toward you and the reduction in frequency as the object moves away. The Doppler effect works in other mediums besides sound, light, and water. In light, a blueshift is observed, if an object moves closer, and a redshift is moving away (Figure 8.17):

$$\text{Object moving toward you} \quad f' = \frac{V}{V - Vs} \times f$$

$$\text{Object moving away from you} \quad f' = \frac{V}{V + Vs} \times f$$

where
  V is the velocity of sound
  Vs is the velocity of source
  f is the real frequency
  f' is the apparent frequency

8.3.7 Positron Emission Tomography

PET is a nuclear medicine medical imaging technique that produces a 3D image or map of functional processes or metabolic activities in the body. To conduct the scan, a short-lived *radioactive* tracer *isotope*, which decays by emitting a *positron* which also has been chemically incorporated into a metabolically active molecule, is injected into the living subject (usually into blood circulation) (Figure 8.18). The data set collected in PET has a lower resolution than CT, so reconstruction techniques are more difficult.

8.3.8 Digital Radiography/Computed Radiography

Digital radiography replaces photographic film with x-ray sensors. It is used primarily by dentists but is also used by conventional x-rays and its advantages are fourfold.

1. Less radiation is needed then by a comparable film-based system. Depending on the technology, 50%–90% less radiation is needed than standard analog x-rays. Flat panel detectors (FPDs) using amorphous silicon, primarily, convert images in a digital format. Radiation dose per person from medical x-rays has decreased almost 500% since 1982.

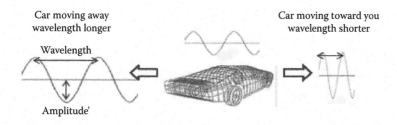

FIGURE 8.17 Example of the Doppler effect.

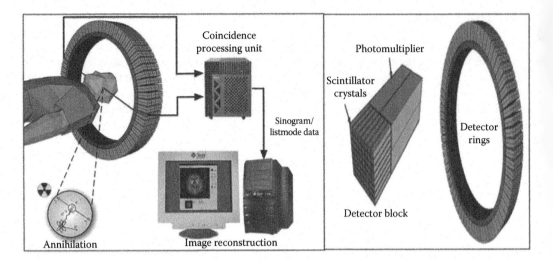

FIGURE 8.18 PET scan. (*Source*: Images from the Max Planck Institute for Neurological Research, http://www.nf.mpg.de/index.php?id=78&L=1; http://en.wikipedia.org/wiki/Position_emission_tomograph#/media/File:PET-schema.png.)

The unit of measurement for an effective radiation dose is the millisievert (mSv). The average person in the United States receives a dose of about 3 mSv per year from naturally occurring radiation. (http://www.webmd.com/fda/reducing-radiation-from-medical-xrays) (digital dental x-ray 0.005 mSv.)

    a. The small risk of cancer depends on several factors (webmd.com):
        i. The lifetime risk of cancer increases as a person undergoes more x-ray exams and the accumulated radiation dose gets higher.
        ii. The lifetime risk is higher for a person who received x-rays at a younger age than for someone who receives them at an older age.
        iii. Women are at a somewhat higher lifetime risk than men for developing cancer from radiation after receiving the same exposures at the same ages.
    b. A typical x-ray produces 2–3 mrem (a millirem is 1/1000 of a rem)
    c. The National Council on Radiation Protection estimates we receive 360 mrem every year from background radiation (Figure 8.19).
  2. Second speed results can be instantly obtained.
  3. For electronic health records (EHRs), once in a digital format, they can be incorporated in EHRs and billing expedited.
  4. In image processing, digital images have a wider range of values and can be dynamically enhanced to visualize disease.

8.3.8.1 Digital Panoramic X-Rays

A digital panoramic x-ray, which is most often used by dentists but is also utilized in security scanners, provides a broad view of teeth and mandible (jaw) in one 120°–180° sweep (.03 mSv) (Figure 8.20). A rotating x-ray camera produces numerous images, from individual 2D slices, similar to a CT scan.

The advantages include a broad view of entire mouth, bones, and teeth, without inserting dental film, which is a diagnostic technique for facial trauma, cancer detection, and pain causality such as temporomandibular joint dysfunction and orthodontic assessment. The disadvantages include poorer resolution, overlapped teeth, and distortions due to changing focal lengths during exposure. It does not provide detailed information about the soft tissues and muscles; a MRI scan would be required.

Radiation doses from imaging technologies (American College of Radiology ACR.org)		
Scales: (milliSievert)	mRem = 1/1000 Rem	mSv = 1/1000 Sievert (Sv)
Conversion	1 Sv = 100Rem 1mSv = 100mRem	©Lubliner 2013
Average Annual Dose (ACR.org) (daily exposure environment)	6.2 mSv	620 mRem/year
X-ray	0.02 mSv	2–3 mRem
CT (multiple 2D x-rays) body	10 mSv	1000 mRem
CT (multiple 2D x-rays) chest	8 mSv	800 mRem
Mammography	0.7 mSv	70 mRem

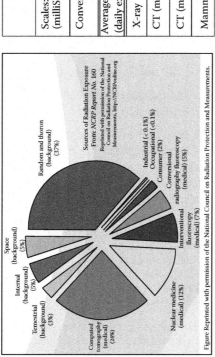

Space (background) (5%)
Internal (background) (5%)
Terrestrial (background) (3%)
Computed tomography (medical) (24%)
Nuclear medicine (medical) (12%)
Interventional fluoroscopy (medical) (7%)
Conventional radiography fluoroscopy (medical) (5%)
Consumer (2%)
Occupational (<0.1%)
Industrial (< 0.1%)
Random and thoron (background) (37%)

Sources of Radiation Exposure From: *NCRP Report No. 160*
Reprinted with permission of the National Council on Radiation Protection and Measurements, http://NCRPonline.org

Figure Reprinted with permission of the National Council on Radiation Protection and Measurements.

FIGURE 8.19 Yearly radiation dosages and a comparison of ionizing radiation dosages from different imaging systems.

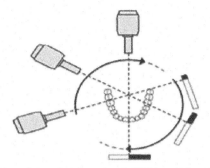
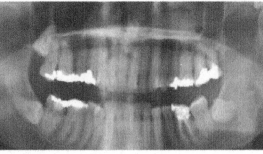

Wikipedia commons

http://www.dentalcare.com/enUS/dentaleducation/continuingedu
cation/ce71/ce71.aspx?ModuleName=coursecontent&PartID=4
&SectionID=0

FIGURE 8.20   Panoramic x-rays, process schematic, and then representative image.

Level II: Implementing and Integrating Imaging Data

8.4 Picture Archiving and Communication System

Picture Archiving and Communication System (PACS) is a storage and retrieval system for medical images. A PACS system is used for transmitting, accessing, and displaying medical images.

DICOM is the standards format for PACS. It defines communications, messaging and data elements, and the data dictionary. Databases such as Oracle and DB2 have embedded translational tables to incorporate DICOM queries and management. The DICOM tags (0010,0011), for example, can be queried via C-Find and C-Move scripts.

An example of an IBM (WebSphere) DB2 query illustrates their find/move commands (Figure 8.21):

- Search parameters are patient name tag (0010,0010) → followed by the element value.
- Access number tag (0008,0050) → followed by the element value.

DB2 Web Sphere DICOM query code taken from http://pic.dhe.ibm.com/infocenter/wmbhelp/v8r0m0/index.jsp?topic=%2Fcom.ibm.healthcare.pattern.DICOM.doc%2Fpattern%2Fexamples.htm

The Oracle architecture utilized the DICOM standards to first create a data dictionary, all standards tag names (xxxx, yyyy), making elements that include values associated with these example tags [(0010,0014),US,2, YBR_Full123] and then converted into the SQL query code for each database (Figure 8.22).

```
example shows an XML query message with two search tags of 00100010
(PatientName) and 00080050 (AccessionNumber), and an additional return tag
configured of 00080054 (RetrieveAETitle):
<DICOM:FindMove xmlns:DICOM="http://com.ibm.healthcare/DICOM">
     <QueryRoot>STUDY</QueryRoot>
     <QueryLevel>STUDY</QueryLevel>
     <Match>
          <Attribute Tag="00100010">FEROVIX</Attribute>
          <Attribute Tag="00080050">1210490</Attribute>
     </Match>
     <Return>
          <Attribute Tag="00080054"/>
     </Return>
</DICOM:FindMove>
```

FIGURE 8.21   XML query code example.

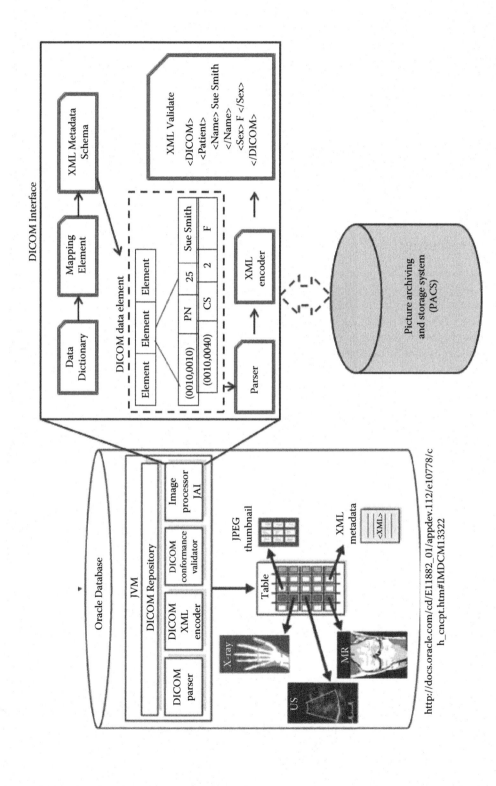

FIGURE 8.22 PACS utilizing an Oracle. (*Source:* From the Oracle DICOM Developer Guide http://docs.oracle.com/cd/E11882_01/appdev.112/e10778/ch_cncpt. htm#IMDCMI3325)

The Health Insurance Portability and Accountability Act (HIPAA) created a PACS standard for insuring the security of PACS images. The standard is independent of an individual PACS system. The HIPAA specification defines an action layer, notification layer, and audit and record layer illustrated in Figure 8.23:

1. *The first layer (the lowest layer) is the record layer, consisting of various logs within PACS components. By logically separating PACS logs from other logs and layers, independence from PACS and portability can be achieved.*
2. *The second layer is the audit layer, which includes a centralized auditing database and other audit data analysis and interpretation tools. HIPAA-compliant audit trails can be generated based on the auditing database. This layer also enables us to automatically monitor the data flow of PACS, which greatly assists PACS management.*
3. *The third layer is the notification layer, which has a notification component sending warning or alert messages of abnormal events to end users, such as PACS administrators.*
4. *In the fourth layer, end users can decide to take certain actions against these abnormal events.*

8.5 Teleradiology

Teleradiology is defined as the process of sharing and analyzing imaging data from a distant location from the original imaging data capture. Medicare and Medicaid require all teleradiology activities be conducted in the United States for reimbursement. The systems that transmit and receive these images must be HIPAA Type II compliant, especially regarding the security of the images. This allows specialists in subfields to provide expert opinions 24 hours a day. Teleradiology spawned a number of radiology consulting groups as a way of outsourcing imaging analysis. These radiology consulting groups are billion dollar businesses. *The Radiology Business Journal* (http://www.desertradiology.com/files/dec_2013. pdf) in December 2013 ranked the top 100 firms containing board certified radiologists totaling over 5,000 just in this top 100 ranking group. There seems to be an effort to consolidate and its estimated groups of 250 radiologists will appear in the near future. The chart (Figure 8.24) lists the top 10 radiology groups as of December 2013.

8.6 CLEF

The Conference and Labs of the Evaluation Forum (CLEF) focuses on how to facilitate systems that can annotate and access imaging data in multiple languages, focusing on European Languages. ImageCLEF (http://imageclef.org/) is a forum that specifically focuses on imaging data cross language and independent contexts. (It was previously named the Cross Language Evaluation Forum).

8.6.1 ImageCLEF Tools

1. The *GNU Image-Finding Tool* is an open framework system. **Gnu's Not Unix**, a UNIX-like operating system, incorporates tools to query images (http://www.gnu.org/software/gift/). It allows you to create your own index of images (Figure 8.25).
   a. It incorporates content-based image retrieval, using a computer vision paradigm that searches for shapes, colors, etc., as opposed to specific tags or text data. It provides a library to facilitate searching parameters. It also has a distance measure tool, that is, how close the image is to some standard image provided. For example, color proportion, shape, or texture can be used. Skin cancer shades and irregularity of borders can be an indicator of a malignant tumor.
2. Lucene Image Retrieval (LIRE) are open-source image retrieval libraries that create an index of medical images based on visual features such as color and texture.

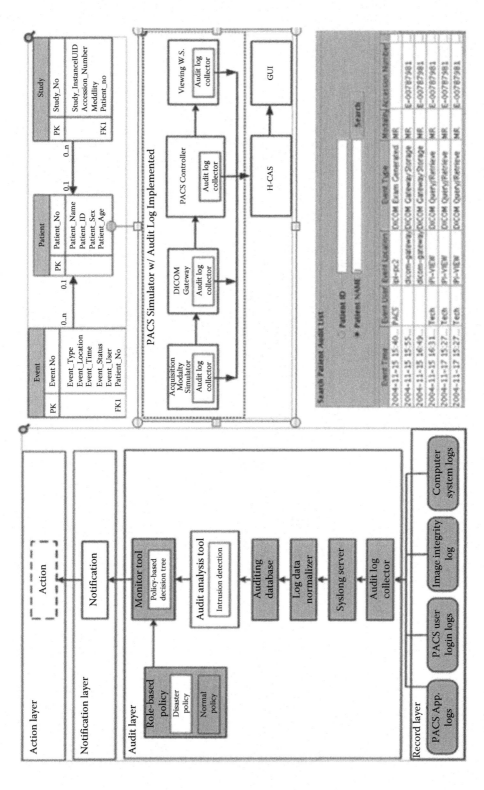

FIGURE 8.23 HIPAA PACS security standard document at link. (http://www.ncbi.nlm.nih.gov/pmc/articles/PMC3045193/)

2013 rank	Practice	Location	CEO	Lead physician	Lead nonphysician	2013 FTE radiologists
1	Radiology Associates of North Texas PA	Fort Worth, TX	Mark J. Kleinschmidt	David Phelps, MD	Mark J. Kleinschmidt	124
2	Advanced Radiology Services PC	Grand Rapids, MI	Richard Moed	Steven Waslawski, MD		111
3	Integra Imaging PS	Spokane, WA	Steve Duvolsin	Jayson Brower and Kristin Manning	Steve Duvolsin	97
4	Radia Medical Imaging	Everett, WA	Bart Keogh, MD, PhD	Bart Keogh, MD, PhD		97
5	Advanced Radiology PA	Baltimore, MD		David Safferman, MD	Kenneth E. Ames	94.25
6	Austin Radiological Association	Austin, TX	Doyle W. Rabe	Gregory C Karnaze, MD	Doyle W. Rabe	86.05
7	Charlotte Radiology	Charlotte, NC	Mark Jensen	Robert Mittl Jr, MD	Mark Jensen	84.5
8	University Radiology Group	East Brunswick, NJ	Thomas Dunlap	Robert E. Epstein, MD	Thomas Dunlap	83
9	Radiology Imaging Consultants SC	Harvey, IL	Jay Bronner, MD	Jay Bronner, MD, and Perry Gilbert, MD	Tara McKennie and Kyle Dwolchak	82
10	Fairfax Radiological Consultants PC	Fairfax, VA		Marshall C. Mintz, MD	Lynn Elliott, MBA, CPA	81

FIGURE 8.24 Top 10 radiological consulting groups as of 2013. (*Source:* The *Radiology Business Journal.*)

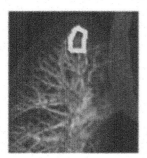 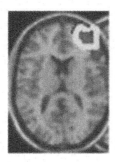 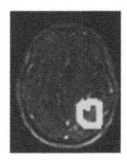 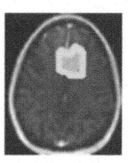

FIGURE 8.25 **(See color insert.)** Indexing images, ImageCLEF tools by shape, color, or texture.

Level III: Advanced Topics

8.7 Radio Pharmacology

Radio pharmacology is the field of study focusing on radio isotopes used in medical imaging. Many radiopharmaceuticals incorporate radioactive isotopes; isotopes have the same number of protons in each atom but they have a different number of neutrons. The atomic number is the number of protons of an atom, which determines the position in the periodic table, so isotopes maintain their same position in the Table 8.6 (i.e., the number of protons and electrons in an atom is equal to maintain a zero net charge). On the other hand, the mass number incorporates neutrons so mass numbers of isotopes vary for elements. Examples are *Helium-3* (He-3) nonradioactive isotope with two protons and one neutron.

Specific radioisotopes are used as tracers to diagnosis [7]. The factors that determine specific radioisotopes are such as adsorption, distribution, metabolism, and excretion of various ^{99m}Tc complexes: "Technetium-99m is the most widely used radioisotope in diagnostic nuclear medicine; it is being estimated that over 80% of the nearly 25 million diagnostic nuclear medicine studies carried out annually are done with this single isotope" (Table 8.7) (http://www.iaea.org/About/Policy/GC/GC51/GC51InfDocuments/English/gc51inf-3-att2_en.pdf).

8.8 Digital Imaging Analysis

Digital medical image processing uses algorithms to analyze and interpret medical images. Newer software is also available to highlight and enhance anomalies, masses, or tumors, which might be too small or difficult to visualize (Figure 8.26).

The term feature extraction is used to extract or highlight anomalous elements of the image. One technique used for feature extraction is the principal component analysis.

a. It uses orthogonal transformations, i.e., orthogonals are square matrices are used to convert correlated variables. A correlation example is a child–parent relationship, into principal components, referred to as linearly uncorrelated variables. This principal component has a large variance, that

TABLE 8.6 Examples of Radioisotopes, Rare Form of Elements

Isotope Examples (only some isotopes are *radioactive*, the process by which atoms loose energy by ionizing radiation)				
Symbol	Neutrons	Protons	Natural Abundance on Earth	
Helium-3, He-3	1	2	0.000137% of He	Radioactive isotope
Helium-4, He-4	2	2	99.9998%	
Carbon, ^{12}C	6	6	98.89%	
Carbon-14, ^{14}C, or radiocarbon	8	6	0.0000000001% 1 part per trillion	Radioactive (used for carbon dating)

TABLE 8.7 Radioisotopes Used for Specific Diagnoses

Bone marrow diseases	1. Sodium chromate
	2. Cr 51 ^{99m}Tc albumin colloid
	3. ^{99m}Tc sulfur colloid
Brain diseases and tumors	1. Fludeoxyglucose F 18
	2. Indium In 111 pentetreotide
	3. Iofetamine I 123
	4. Sodium pertechnetate ^{99m}Tc
	5. ^{99m}Tc exametazime
	6. ^{99m}Tc gluceptate
	7. ^{99m}Tc pentetate
Cancers, tumors	1. Fludeoxyglucose F 18
	2. Gallium citrate Ga 67
	3. Indium In 111 pentetreotide
	4. Methionine C 11
	5. Radioiodinated iobenguane
	6. Sodium fluoride F 18
Colorectal disease	1. ^{99m}Tc arcitumomab
Heart muscle damage (infarct)	2. Ammonia N 13
	3. Fludeoxyglucose F 18
	4. Rubidium Rb 82
	5. ^{99m}Tc pyrophosphate
	6. ^{99m}Tc (pyro and trimeta) phosphates
	7. ^{99m}Tc sestamibi,
	8. ^{99m}Tc teboroxime
	9. ^{99m}Tc tetrofosmin
	10. Thallous chloride Tl 201

Source: http://www.drugs.com/cons/radiopharmaceutical.html.

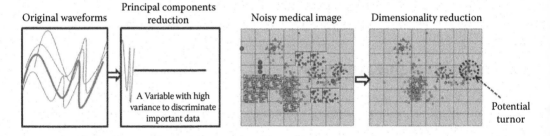

FIGURE 8.26 **(See color insert.)** Digital image processing architecture. (*Source:* From http://www.ncbi.nlm.nih.gov/pmc/articles/PMC3701154/figure/F1/)

is variables are spread out; a variance of zero means all values are identical. This principal component should be responsible for most of the variance in the equation or system.

b. *Dimensionality reduction* maps a vector from a correlated space to an uncorrelated. We keep only those principal component vectors, that is, reduced matrix called dimensionality reduction that is also referred to as a high dimensionality data set with high variance. This data set contains clusters that are spread out, and that are high variance, if plotted. Dimensionality reduction is also useful when there are noisy data and a number of independent variables are removed (Figure 8.27).

c. *Feature extraction*: process by which image features are analyzed to determine unique patterns or features

i. *Corner detection*: a feature or endpoint determined by a curvature, that is, any point where a figure is no longer flat defined by a radius of curvature or curvature vector that determines the change in direction or some arbitrary angle

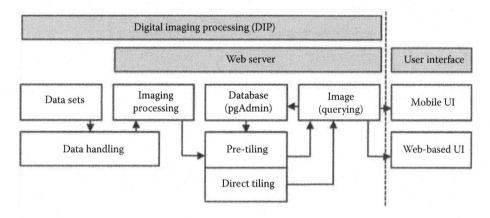

FIGURE 8.27 Example of dimensionality reduction in signals in mapping.

   ii.   *Edge detection:* a point, layer, or boundary between two figures, shades, or gradients
  iii.   *Data mining*: determining patterns in large data sets

8.9 Summary

Medical imaging and Image analysis algorithms are rapidly evolving, the objective is to provide better methods to visualize and extract salient features of images that might not always be caught by radiologists. Cutting edge research has shown that new cancers can form capillaries in fractal patterns that may be a way to detect early cancers. In 2015, 3D printers have created accurate heart models from CT scans. An Israeli company, Zebra Medical Vision, in 2015, created a database of 10 million medical images and new analytical software to compare/contrast this data to new scans, potentially increasing cancer detection, advanced visualization software, EchoPixel, was approved by the FDA in 2015 to create holographic displays of MRI and CT scans. This is a dynamic field that is changing rapidly.

Questions

Level I

1. What is DICOM?
   a. What critical role does it play in medical imaging?
   b. What is DICOM conformance?
   c. What are DICOM IODs?
   d. What are DICOM data structure definitions?
   e. What is a DICOM data dictionary?
   f. What are DIMSEs?
      i. Deconstruct a DIMSE into its four component tags and value fields.
      ii. What role do these tags play in imaging information exchange?
2. What is a 3D RCS?
   a. What role does an RCS play in medical imaging?
3. What is an fMRI?
   a. What is the NIfTI data format?
4. Briefly explain the differences of the different imaging technologies.
   a. Explain technologies such as x-rays, CT, MRI, fMRI, ultrasound, and SPECT.

    b. What are the criteria used to determine which imaging device you would use?

    c. What imaging device(s) would you use for soft tissue? Explain reasoning.

Level II

5. What is a picture archiving system (PACS)?

    a. Relate a PACS to storing and retrieving images using DICOM tags.

6. What is teleradiology?

    a. How has the practice of radiology changed since the adoption of teleradiology?

Level III

7. What is radio pharmacology?

    a. What is the selection criteria for radio isotopes for different medical scans?

8. What imaging analysis techniques are used to final anomalies on medical images?

    a. Explain the principal component analysis used in imaging.

Glossary

Computed tomography (CT or CAT) uses numerous 2D x-rays slices to create a 3D view of the body.

Digital Imaging and Communications in Medicine (DICOM) (dicom.nema.org).

Digital radiography replaces photographic film with x-ray sensors. It is used primarily by dentists, but is also used in conventional x-rays.

The **functional magnetic resonance imager (fMRI)**, in the 1990s, measures brain and neural activities, by alterations in blood flow.

The **GNU Image-Finding Tool** is an open framework system (http://www.gnu.org/software/gift/ GNU). *Gnu's Not Unix*, a UNIX-like operating system, incorporates tools to query images. It allows you to create your own index of images.

Magnetic resonance image (MRI) or nuclear MRI. MRIs utilize nonionizing absorption and emission in the radio frequency and are best suited for noncalcified tissues, that is, soft tissues.

Picture archiving and communication system (PACS) is a storage and retrieval system for medical images.

Positron emission tomography (PET) is a nuclear medicine medical imaging technique that produces a 3D image or map of functional processes or metabolic activities in the body.

Reference coordinate system (RCS) is the spatial coordinate system in a DICOM frame of reference.

References

1. Intro to CT scanning, (2010). http://www.maximintegrated.com/app-notes/index.mvp/id/4682
2. Acharya, R. et al. Biomedical Imaging Modalities, http://www.dtic.upf.edu/~afrangi/ibi/ReviewBiomedicalImaging.pdf.
3. Costa, C. et al. Dicoogle - (2010). An Open Source Peer-to-Peer PACS. DICOM open source tools, http://www.dicoogle.com/4
4. Andriole, K.P. (2006). Overview of medical imaging informatics. In *Advances in Medical Physics*. A.B. Wolbarst and R. Zamenholf, eds. Madison, WI: Medical Physics Publishing, pp. 201–227.
5. The *Journal of Digital Imaging* (JDI) is the official peer-reviewed journal of the Society for Imaging Informatics in Medicine (SIIM).
6. Imaging formats white paper, http://download.springer.com/static/pdf/546/art%253A10.1007%252Fs10278-013-9657-9.pdf?auth66=1396636285_bcfe1d2e96d08ce02b790afdf3d30c95&ext=.pdf
7. The National Isotope Development Center (NIDC). http://isotopes.gov/notice.html
8. Ljunggren, S. (1983). *Journal of Magnetic Resonance* 54, 338–343.
9. Tweig, D. The k-trajectory formulation of the NMR imaging process with applications in analysis and synthesis of imaging methods. *Med Phys*. 1983; 10:610–621.

9

Ethics

Level I: Core Concepts

9.1 Introduction

Ethics defined by the Merriam-Webster dictionary is "A theory or system of moral values" or professional ethics as "the principles of conduct governing an individual or a group." Who decides what is moral: religions, philosophers, general consensus, or a panel of their peers? Is there an absolute truth? Most humans believe it's ethical to help out one's fellow individuals without consideration of social status, ethnicity, or *cost*. The recent supreme court decision *King vs. Burwell 2015* indicates we are moving toward the ethical and moral high-ground of universal medical coverage for all

The U.S. Constitution does not specifically enumerate healthcare coverage, but the Supreme Court decision that upheld the Affordable Care Act (ACA) "National Federation of Independent Business v. Sebelius" (2012) sites the Constitution, Article I, Section 8, clause 1, which states, in part, that "[t]he Congress shall have Power to lay and collect Taxes,..to… provide for the… general Welfare of the United States." I. Even though they focused on the tax collecting portion in the decision, how do we ethically gauge the clause "provide for the general welfare of our citizens"? It seems the founders were grappling with the ethical role of government. Biomedical Informatics professionals need to be not only versed technically but also in how medicine is ethically applied fairly to all individuals (Figure 9.1).

Related decisions include the following:

- The Supreme Court in the 1937 case dealing with the newly enacted Social Security Act. In *Steward Machine Co. v. Davis*, the court sustained a tax imposed on employers to provide unemployment benefits to individual workers.
- *Title VI of the Civil Rights Act of 1964* that prohibits discrimination under federally funded programs affects the manner of delivery of medical services under federal grants.
- Congress enacted the *Consolidated Omnibus Budget Reconciliation Act of 1986 (COBRA)* that directly regulates the healthcare industry by imposing continuing insurance requirements for persons who lose employment-related health insurance benefits (Congressional Research Service: http://www.fas.org/sgp/crs/misc/R40846.pdf).

"Ethical" is used to refer to matters involving moral principles or practices and matters of social policy involving issues of morality in the practice of medicine (AMA Council on Moral Ethics: https://www.ama-assn.org/ama/pub/physician-resources/medical-ethics/code-medical-ethics/opinion101.page?).

9.2 Hippocratic Oath

The Hippocratic Oath dates back to the fifth century BC describing the responsibility of physicians to focus on the well being of their patients. The Hippocratic Oath was included in the Hippocratic Corpus, a compendium of 60 Greek medical texts published in the third century BC that spanned many years and multiple authors. The corpus includes ethical essays, textbooks, and lectures that portrayed opposing points of view.

FIGURE 9.1 Medical ethics chapter contents.

Following World War II, the Hippocratic Oath was rewritten to address the horrors of the war, called the Declaration of Geneva, focusing on the ethical responsibilities of physicians. One of the items was particularly relevant to the aftermath of the war: "I will not use my medical knowledge to violate human rights and civil liberties, even under threat." In 1960, it was amended to remove references to Greek Gods or any deity; it said "utmost respect for human life from its beginning." There are no legal penalties to violating the Hippocratic Oath, but the Department of Justice (DOJ) can level fines for violating Health Insurance Portability and Accountability Act (HIPAA) rules (see Table 5.1 in Chapter 5), and the American Medical Association (AMA) Council on Ethical and Judicial Affairs (CEJA) (Section 8.3) has judicial functions, i.e., appellate jurisdiction over members' appeals of ethics-related decisions made by state and medical societies that are charged with evaluating physicians' fitness for membership in the AMA (Table 9.1).

TABLE 9.1 Hippocratic Oath: Original and Modern Version

Modern Version (Written in 1964 by Louis Lasagna)	Original Version (Fifth Century BC)
I swear to fulfill, to the best of my ability and judgment, this covenant:	I swear by Apollo, the healer, Asclepius, Hygieia and Panacea, and, and I take to witness all the gods, all the goddesses, to keep according to my ability and my judgment, the following Oath and agreement:
I will respect the hard-won scientific gains of those physicians in whose steps I walk, and gladly share such knowledge as is mine with those who are to follow.	To consider dear to me, as my parents, him who taught me this art; to live in common with him and, if necessary, to share my goods with him; To look upon his children as my own brothers, to teach them this art; and that by my teaching, I will impart a knowledge of this art to my own sons, and to my teacher's sons, and to disciples bound by an indenture and oath according to the medical laws, and no others.
I will apply, for the benefit of the sick, all measures [that] are required, avoiding those twin traps of overtreatment and therapeutic nihilism.	
I will remember that there is art to medicine as well as science, and that warmth, sympathy, and understanding may outweigh the surgeon's knife or the chemist's drug.	
I will not be ashamed to say "I know not," nor will I fail to call in my colleagues when the skills of another are needed for a patient's recovery.	I will prescribe regimens for the good of my patients according to my ability and my judgment and **never do harm to anyone**.
I will respect the privacy of my patients, for their problems are not disclosed to me that the world may know. Most especially must I tread with care in matters of life and death. If it is given me to save a life, all thanks. But it may also be within my power to take a life; this awesome responsibility must be faced with great humbleness and awareness of my own frailty. Above all, I must not play at God.	I will give no deadly medicine to any one if asked, nor suggest any such counsel; and similarly I will not give a woman a pessary to cause an abortion. (Rule 2 was changed in 1960) But I will preserve the purity of my life and my arts.
I will remember that I do not treat a fever chart, a cancerous growth, but a sick human being, whose illness may affect the person's family and economic stability. My responsibility includes these related problems, if I am to care adequately for the sick.	I will not cut for stone, even for patients in whom the disease is manifest; I will leave this operation to be performed by practitioners, specialists in this art.
I will prevent disease whenever I can, for prevention is preferable to cure.	In every house where I come I will enter only for the good of my patients, keeping myself far from all intentional ill-doing and all seduction and especially from the pleasures of love with women or men, be they free or slaves.
I will remember that I remain a member of society, with special obligations to all my fellow human beings, those sound of mind and body as well as the infirm.	All that may come to my knowledge in the exercise of my profession or in daily commerce with men, which ought not to be spread abroad, I will keep secret and will never reveal.
If I do not violate this oath, may I enjoy life and art, respected while I live and remembered with affection thereafter. May I always act so as to preserve the finest traditions of my calling and may I long experience the joy of healing those who seek my help.	If I keep this oath faithfully, may I enjoy my life and practice my art, respected by all humanity and in all times; but if I swerve from it or violate it, may the reverse be my life.
	• References in Hippocratic Oath
	– *Apollo* was the god of Greek prophecy and healing.
	– *Asclepius* was a god of medicine and healing in ancient Greek religion.
	– *Hygieia* was the daughter of the god of medicine.
	– *Panacea* was a goddess of universal remedy.

9.3 American Medical Association Ethics Groups

Medical ethics are standards of conduct, not laws, by which medical personnel follow for the benefit of the patients. Its goals are to improve patient care and promote professionalism. The AMA Ethics Group sets guidance for physicians to pursue. The Ethics Group has three parts: the CEJA, Ethics Resource Center, and Institute for Ethics (Figure 9.2).

The AMA publishes the Code of Medical Ethics that is periodically updated, originally published in 1957 and subsequently updated in 1980 and 2001 (Table 9.2).

9.3.1 Council on Ethical and Judicial Affairs

The CEJA focuses on periodic updates of the Code of Medical Ethics and its judicial function, the most recent in 2001 (Table 9.2).

9.3.1.1 Policy Functions

The CEJA policy functions, first started in 1847, are primarily responsible in updating the "Code of Medical Ethics." The second function is to develop policies on how the healthcare system should be organized and how it should function, called the "opinions on the code." It has a search capability called "Policy Finder" for specific areas (the online version can be found at http://www.ama-assn. org/ama/pub/about-ama/our-people/house-delegates/policy-finder-online.page?).

It is divided into three categories:

1. Health and ethics policies
2. Governance policies
3. Directives of the AMA House of Delegates (HOD)
   a. The AMA's HOD meets twice a year (every June and November) to conduct the business of the house. The June meetings are referred to as annual meetings and are referenced as "A-" followed by the year of the meeting (i.e., A-11 means the 2011 annual meeting). November

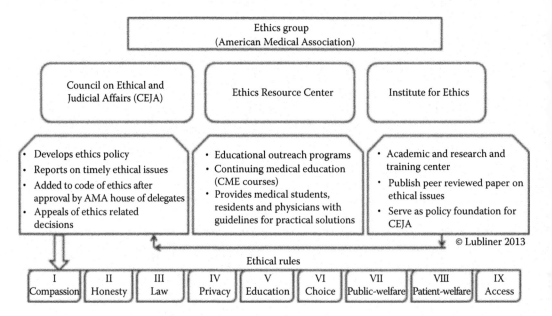

FIGURE 9.2 AMA medical ethics organization.

TABLE 9.2 Principles of Medical Ethics Last Published in 2001 by the American Medical Association (AMA) Ethics Group[a]

	Category	Principles
1	Compassion	A physician shall be dedicated to providing competent medical care, with compassion and respect for human dignity and rights.
2	Honesty	A physician shall uphold the standards of professionalism, be honest in all professional interactions, and strive to report physicians deficient in character or competence, or engaging in fraud or deception, to appropriate entities.
3	Law	A physician shall respect the law and also recognize a responsibility to seek changes in those requirements which are contrary to the best interests of the patient.
4	Privacy	A physician shall respect the rights of patients, colleagues, and other health professionals, and shall safeguard patient confidences and privacy within the constraints of the law.
5	Education	A physician shall continue to study, apply, and advance scientific knowledge, maintain a commitment to medical education, make relevant information available to patients, colleagues, and the public, obtain consultation, and use the talents of other health professionals when indicated.
6	Choice	A physician shall, in the provision of appropriate patient care, except in emergencies, be free to choose whom to serve, with whom to associate, and the environment in which to provide medical care.
7	Public welfare	A physician shall recognize a responsibility to participate in activities contributing to the improvement of the community and the betterment of public health.
8	Patient welfare	A physician shall, while caring for a patient, regard responsibility to the patient as paramount.
9	Access	A physician shall support access to medical care for all people.

[a] https://www.ama-assn.org/ama/pub/physician-resources/medical-ethics.page?

meetings are interim meetings and are referenced as "I-" followed by the year of the meeting (i.e., I-10 means the 2010 interim meeting).
b. The HOD maintains online archives of these meetings (http://www.ama-assn.org/ama/pub/about-ama/our-people/house-delegates/meeting-archives.page?).

9.3.1.2 Judicial Functions

The CEJA evaluates physicians' adherence to ethical standards and has disciplinary action to determine their fitness for membership in the AMA. The CEJA is initially informed as follows:
Case finding

- Statements made in the membership application form
- Reports of disciplinary actions taken by state licensing boards
- Media reports

Determination of reasonable cause for a hearing

- At each of the CEJA meetings, they determine if there is *reasonable cause* for a disciplinary hearing.
- The CEJA reviews up to 100 cases a year.
  - The AMA's Office of General Counsel (OGC) reviews an additional 100 cases a year.

9.3.1.2.1 Litigation Center of the AMA

The Litigation Center of the AMA and State Medical Societies, established in 1995, as part of the AMA physicians' resource center, provides physicians with legal expertise assistance (http://www.ama-assn.org/ama/pub/physician-resources/legal-topics/litigation-center.page?).

AMA Litigation Center Cases

A	E	M	R
Abortions	Economic Credentialing	Managed care payments	Regulatory burdens
Abortion notification	Electronic Medical	Managed care tort liability	Resident physicians
Abusive litigation against	Records	Medicaid	Restrictive covenants
physicians	Emergency services	Medical education	**S**
Access to medical facilities	Employment	Medical society advocacy	Screening Panels
Affidavit of Merit	EMTALA	Medical staff	Scope of Practice
Americans with Disabilities	Environmental protection	Medicare	SLAPP laws
Act	ERISA preemption	Minors' rights	Stark Laws
Anti-tobacco	Ethics	**P**	**T**
Antitrust	Expert witnesses	Patents	Taxation of physicians
Any Willing Provider Laws	**F**	Patient privacy	Termination of employment
Arbitration	False Claims Act	Patient rights	Termination of physician
B	Federal Tort Claims Act	Patient Safety Act	participation in provider
Balanced Billing	Food labeling	Payment issues (for patients)	networks
Blood banks	Fraud and abuse	Payment issues (for physicians)	Tiered and narrowed
C	Freedom of Information Act	Peer review	managed care networks
Certificate of Merit	**G**	Physician Advocacy	Tort reform
Certificate of Need	Gay, Lesbian, Bisexual,	Physician-Patient	**U**
Christian Science	Transsexual Rights	communications	Unions
Civil Rights	**H**	Physician-Patient relationship	Usual customary and
Clinical Trials	Health plan coverage	Physician participation in	reasonable payments
Confidentiality	Hospitals	capital punishment	**V**
Corporate Practice of	**I**	Physician safety	Vaccine Act
Medicine	Independent Review	Physician self-referral	**W**
Criminal Law	Informed consent	Physicians' privacy rights	Workers' Compensation
Criminalization of Medical	Insurance (Liability)	Pregnant Women's Rights	
Judgments	Coverage	Professional liability	
D	**L**	Prompt payment Laws	
Do Not Resuscitate Order	Loss of Chance	Public Health	
Drug Manufacturers		Public Health Service	
Due Process			

FIGURE 9.3 AMA Litigation Center cases by topic.

The Litigation Center provides the following:

1. They ensure physicians' rights are upheld.
2. They protect the integrity of hospital medical staffs.
3. Challenging abusive litigation against physicians, many cases have set important legal precedents and have broad, practical applications for the medical profession and patients.

The Litigation Center provides representation for cases in the following areas (Figure 9.3).

9.4   ANA Code of Ethics

The American Nurses Association (ANA), similar to the AMA, periodically produces a code of ethics; the last was updated in 2001 that certified that nurses have to read, understand, and act upon:

1. The nurse, in all professional relationships, practices with compassion and respect for the inherent dignity, worth, and uniqueness of every individual, unrestricted by considerations of social or economic status, personal attributes, or the nature of health problems.
2. The nurse's primary commitment is to the patient, whether an individual, family, group, or community.

3. The nurse promotes, advocates for, and strives to protect the health, safety, and rights of the patient.
4. The nurse is responsible and accountable for individual nursing practice and determines the appropriate delegation of tasks consistent with the nurse's obligation to provide optimum patient care.
5. The nurse owes the same duties to self as to others, including the responsibility to preserve integrity and safety, to maintain competence, and to continue personal and professional growth.
6. The nurse participates in establishing, maintaining, and improving healthcare environments and conditions of employment conducive to the provision of quality healthcare and consistent with the values of the profession through individual and collective action.
7. The nurse participates in the advancement of the profession through contributions to practice, education, administration, and knowledge development.
8. The nurse collaborates with other health professionals and the public in promoting community, national, and international efforts to meet health needs.
9. The profession of nursing, as represented by associations and their members, is responsible for articulating nursing values, for maintaining the integrity of the profession and its practice, and for shaping social policy.

The American Association of Critical Care Nurses (AACN; www.aacn.org) is the certifying organization for nurses. They publish a series of values that all its members must honor:

- *Ethical accountability and integrity* in relationships, organizational decisions, and stewardship of resources
- *Leadership to enable individuals to make their optimal contribution* through lifelong learning, critical thinking and inquiry
- *Excellence and innovation* at every level of the organization to advance the profession
- *Collaboration* to ensure quality patient- and family-focused care.

Level II: Medical Ethics Scenarios

9.5   Ethical Medical Situations

Sources: AMA Code of Medical Ethics

- Specific practical ethical questions are addressed by the AMA CEJA and in the AMA Journal of Ethics. A virtual tutor is available at http://virtualmentor.ama-assn.org/site/cases.html where you can enter a search parameter.

The following medical ethical scenarios are taken from the previously mentioned sources:

This section describes guidance by the AMA regarding the complex ethical situations that medical professionals may encounter. A useful class interaction that precedes assigning this reading might be to pose these ethical conundrums and engage the class in an interactive debate.

9.5.1   Reporting Impaired Drivers

Summary

- Physicians should use their best judgment when determining when to report impairments that could limit a patient's ability to drive.
- In situations where there is a strong threat to patient and public safety and where the physician's advice to discontinue driving is ignored, it is desirable and ethical to notify the state's Department of Motor Vehicles.

9.5.1.1 AMA Impaired Drivers and Their Physicians Case Study

AMA link: http://virtualmentor.ama-assn.org/2010/12/coet2-1012.html

The National Highway and Transportation and Safety **Reporting laws** for all states link: http://www.nhtsa.gov/people/injury/olddrive/olderdriversbook/pages/Chapter8.html

Question: Impaired Drivers and Their Physicians

Is it the physicians' responsibility to recognize impairments in patients' driving ability that pose a strong threat to public safety and that ultimately may need to be reported to the Department of Motor Vehicles? It does not address the reporting of medical information for the purpose of punishment or criminal prosecution (Figure 9.4).

a. Physicians should assess patients' physical or mental impairments that might adversely affect driving abilities.
b. Each case must be evaluated individually since not all impairments may give rise to an obligation on the part of the physician, nor may all physicians be in a position to evaluate the extent or the effect of an impairment (e.g., physicians who treat patients on a short-term basis).
c. In making evaluations, physicians should consider the following factors:
  i. The physician must be able to identify and document physical or mental impairments that clearly relate to the ability to drive.
  ii. The driver must pose a clear risk to public safety.
d. Before reporting, there are a number of initial steps physicians should take. A tactful but candid discussion with the patient and family about the risks of driving is of primary importance. Efforts made by physicians to inform patients and their families, advise them of their options, and negotiate a workable plan may render reporting unnecessary.
  i. Depending on the patient's medical condition, the physician may suggest to the patient that he or she seek further treatment, such as substance abuse treatment or occupational therapy.
  ii. Physicians also may *encourage* the patient and the family to decide on a *restricted driving schedule.*

Driver licensing agency contact information	New Jersey Motor Vehicle Commission PO BOX 160 Trenton, NJ 08666 www.state.nj.us/mvs	609 292-6500
Licensing Requirement		
Visual acuity	Each eye with/without correction	20/50
	Both eyes with/without correction	20/50
	If one eye blind—other with/without correction	20/50
	Absolute visual acuity mimimum	20/50
	Are bioptic telescope allowed?	Yes, with acuity of 20/50 through telescope
Visual fields	Minimum field requirement	None
color vision requirement	Color vision is tested in new drives, but licenses are not denied based on poor color vision.	
Type of road test	Standardized	
Restricted licenses	Available	

FIGURE 9.4 New Jersey Driver License regulations: typical of state guidelines. (From http://www.nhtsa.gov/people/injury/olddrive/olderdriversbook/pages/NewJersey.html.)

    iii. Efforts made by physicians to inform patients and their families, advise them of their options, and negotiate a workable plan may render reporting unnecessary.

  e. Physicians should use their best judgment when determining when to report impairments that could limit a patient's ability to drive safely. In situations where clear evidence of substantial driving impairment implies a strong threat to patient and public safety and where the physician's advice to discontinue driving privileges is ignored, it is desirable and *ethical* to notify the department of motor vehicles.

  f. The physician's role is to report medical conditions that would impair safe driving as dictated by his or her state's mandatory reporting laws and standards of medical practice. The determination of the inability to drive safely should be made by the state's Department of Motor Vehicles.

  g. Physicians should disclose and explain to their patients this responsibility to report.

  h. Physicians should protect patient confidentiality by ensuring that only a minimal amount of information is reported and that reasonable security measures are used in handling that information.

  i. Physicians should work with their state medical societies to create statutes that uphold the best interests of patients and community and that safeguard physicians from liability when reporting in good faith.

9.5.2 Medical Students Performing Procedures on Fellow Students

Summary

1. Instructors should explain to students how the procedures will be performed, making certain that students are not placed in situations that violate their privacy or sense of propriety.
2. Students should be given the choice of whether to participate prior to entering the classroom.
3. There should be no requirement that the students provide a reason for their unwillingness to participate.
4. Students should not be penalized for refusal to participate.

9.5.3 Surgical Placebo

Summary

Question: Should physicians use surgical "placebo" controls (subjects undergo surgical procedures that have the appearance of therapeutic intervention but during which the essential therapeutic maneuver is omitted) when assessing the efficacy of a surgical intervention?

1. When a new surgical procedure is developed with the prospect of treating a condition for which no known surgical therapy exists, using surgical "placebo" controls may be justified but must be evaluated in light of whether the current standard of care includes a nonsurgical treatment and the benefits, risks, and side effects of that treatment.
2. During the informed consent process, careful explanation of the risks of the operation must be disclosed. Additional safeguards may include using a neutral third party to provide information and obtain consent.
3. The use of placebo control is not justified when testing a surgical technique that represents a minor improvement of an existing surgical procedure.

9.5.3.1 AMA Placebo Case Study

Description

Mr. Marcus is a 70-year-old retiree living on his limited pension. He suffers from advanced osteoarthritis (OA) in his knees and would do anything to be able to walk more easily on his own. He says to Dr. Janus, "My best friend had this surgery last month, and he's already getting around the golf course great. He says this surgery was the best thing he ever did for himself. I sure would love to be able to keep up with him now. What do you say, Doc, can you do this surgery for me?" (http://virtualmentor.ama-assn.org/2012/11/ecas1–1211.html)

Opinion

Once one of the most commonly performed of orthopedic procedures, arthroscopic debridement of the knee has come under scrutiny in recent years with the publication of two major randomized controlled clinical trials that failed to demonstrate benefit to the enrolled patients [2,3]. Even in the current environment, with its emphasis on evidence-based medicine, such level I clinical evidence is hard to come by, particularly in the context of surgery. Nonetheless, a clinical impression endures to support the use of this procedure for OA of the knee, albeit in a more limited, defined subset of patients.

Recommended course of action

Based on current standards of practice, he is obligated to first recommend a comprehensive program of nonsurgical management. Numerous nonoperative treatment options are available to treat patients with OA of the knee. These include activity modification, physical therapy, nonsteroidal anti-inflammatory agents, and intra-articular injections (corticosteroid or hyaluronate). All patients with symptomatic OA of the knee should be treated according to these tenets before more aggressive (surgical) methods are employed. Only for some of those who do not respond should the surgical option be considered: patients with radiographic mild arthritis or near-normal alignment but not patients with valgus configurations or arthritis in both knees.

So what should Dr. Janus recommend to Mr. Marcus and how should he convey it?

Although the risks of this surgery are typically small, available evidence suggests that the benefit of such surgery is likely to be low; indeed clinical experience suggests such intervention may in some instances exacerbate the symptoms and accelerate joint deterioration. Therefore, though for some patients (such as Mr. Marcus' friend) the procedure may prove beneficial, for Mr. Marcus himself, this is unlikely to be the case. Given the low likelihood of success, indeed the potential for making his condition worse, Dr. Janus should advise against surgery and advocate for a more conservative therapeutic strategy. It is critical for Dr. Janus to explain the reasoning and justification for his advice and to ensure that Mr. Marcus comprehends the explanation and, ultimately, finds it satisfactory.

9.5.4   Gifts to Physicians from Industry

Summary

Question: Is it ethically permissible to accept gifts from pharmaceutical representatives?

- Any gift accepted by a physician should primarily entail a benefit to patients and should not be of substantial value.
- Individual gifts of minimal value are permissible as long as they relate to the physician's work.

AMA Opinion 8.061

The AMA *Code of Medical Ethics'* Opinions on Physicians' Relationships with Drug Companies and Duty to Assist in Containing Drug Costs. Link: http://virtualmentor.ama-assn.org/2014/04/coet2–1404.html

9.5.4.1   Opinion 8.061: Gifts to Physicians from Industry

Many gifts given to physicians by companies in the pharmaceutical, device, and medical equipment industries serve an important and socially beneficial function. For example, companies have long provided funds for educational seminars and conferences. However, there has been growing concern about certain gifts from industry to physicians. Some gifts that reflect customary practices of industry may not be consistent with the Principles of Medical Ethics. To avoid the acceptance of inappropriate gifts, physicians should observe the following guidelines:

1. Any gifts accepted by physicians individually should *primarily entail a benefit to patients and should not be of substantial value.* Accordingly, textbooks, modest meals, and other gifts are appropriate if they serve a genuine educational function. Cash payments should not be

accepted. The use of drug samples for personal or family use is permissible as long as these practices do not interfere with patient access to drug samples. It would not be acceptable for nonretired physicians to request free pharmaceuticals for personal use or use by family members.

2. Individual gifts of minimal value are permissible as long as the gifts are related to the physician's work (e.g., pens and notepads).
3. The CEJA defines a legitimate "conference" or "meeting" as any activity, held at an appropriate location, where (a) the gathering is primarily dedicated, in both time and effort, to promoting objective scientific and educational activities and discourse (one or more educational presentation[s] should be the highlight of the gathering) and (b) the main incentive for bringing attendees together is to further their knowledge on the topic(s) being presented. An appropriate disclosure of financial support or conflict of interest should be made.
4. Subsidies to underwrite the costs of continuing medical education conferences or professional meetings can contribute to the improvement of patient care and therefore are permissible. Since the giving of a subsidy directly to a physician by a company's representative may create a relationship that could influence the use of the company's products, any subsidy should be accepted by the conference's sponsor who in turn can use the money to reduce the conference's registration fee. Payments to defray the costs of a conference should not be accepted directly from the company by the physicians attending the conference.
5. Subsidies from industry should not be accepted directly or indirectly to pay for the costs of travel, lodging, or other personal expenses of physicians attending conferences or meetings, nor should subsidies be accepted to compensate for the physicians' time. Subsidies for hospitality should not be accepted outside of modest meals or social events held as a part of a conference or meeting. It is appropriate for faculty at conferences or meetings to accept reasonable honoraria and to accept reimbursement for reasonable travel, lodging, and meal expenses. It is also appropriate for consultants who provide genuine services to receive reasonable compensation and to accept reimbursement for reasonable travel, lodging, and meal expenses. Token consulting or advisory arrangements cannot be used to justify the compensation of physicians for their time or their travel, lodging, and other out-of-pocket expenses.
6. Scholarship or other special funds to permit medical students, residents, and fellows to attend carefully selected educational conferences may be permissible as long as the selection of students, residents, or fellows who will receive the funds is made by the academic or training institution. Carefully selected educational conferences are generally defined as the major educational, scientific, or policy-making meetings of national, regional, or specialty medical associations.
7. No gifts should be accepted if there are strings attached. For example, physicians should not accept gifts given in relation to the physician's prescribing practices. In addition, when companies underwrite medical conferences or lectures other than their own, responsibility for and control over the selection of content, faculty, educational methods, and materials should belong to the organizers of the conferences or lectures.

9.5.5 How to Refer to Medical Students in a Clinical Setting

Summary

Question: Is it appropriate to use terms such as "student doctor" to identify medical students who are caring for patients?

1. Patients should be informed of the training status of individuals involved in their care.
2. Terms that may be confusing when describing the training status of students should not be used.
3. Physicians should relate the benefits of student participation to patients and should ensure that they are willing to permit such participation.

9.5.6   Should Medical Trainees Perform Procedures

Summary

Question: Should medical trainees perform procedures such as endotracheal intubation on the newly deceased patient?

1. In the absence of previously expressed preferences, physicians should request permission from the family before performing procedures.
2. Without such permission, physicians should not perform procedures for training purposes on the newly deceased patient.

9.5.6.1   AMA Patient Care and Student Education

Virtual Mentor. April 2002, Volume 4, Number 4.

Background

Mr. H was admitted yesterday to the general medical service of a teaching hospital. This is his third admission in 8 months. One prior admission was, like this one, due to exacerbation of long-standing chronic obstructive pulmonary disease (COPD). The other admission was prompted by dizziness and fainting brought on by his poorly controlled diabetes. Mr. H is 57 years old African American. Management of his health is complicated by obesity and (as he confessed to Miss Rogers, the third-year medical student who interviewed him when he arrived on the unit) his continued smoking.

Dr. G, the senior resident, decides that a subclavian central line should be placed to gain intravenous access. Then antibiotics, fluids, and other medications, if needed, can be easily and effectively administered without continuing to poke at Mr. H's peripheral veins.

Dr. G is supervising two third-year medical students who are in week 6 of their 8-week internal medicine rotation. The students are Mr. Crane and the previously mentioned Miss Rogers who has interviewed Mr. H. Dr. G has established good working relationships with both students, who are highly motivated and competent. Dr. G takes her role as educator seriously and wants to be confident that students gain the experience and, to the extent possible, the skills they should while under her supervision.

Mr. Crane has successfully placed central lines on several occasions during his rotation. Miss Rogers has been unsuccessful on two attempts with different patients.

Mr. H is a good patient for Miss Rogers' next attempt. His condition is not emergent; he is accustomed to the teaching hospital routine and has taken Miss Rogers' into his confidence. He considers her to be "on his side." On the other hand, his obesity makes the procedure more difficult than usual. Because of his multiple health problems and complications, should Miss Rogers puncture his lung would be life-threatening.

Mr. H is a Medicaid patient, and Dr. G is sensitive to the potential for Medicaid patients to shoulder more than their share of student and intern "practicing." Were she acting solely as clinician and not as educator, Dr. G would ask Mr. Crane to place the line.

Miss Rogers has to succeed at placing a central line before completing her internal medicine rotation, and time is running out. She is on her way in to inform Mr. H about the procedure and its risks and to obtain his consent for it. She identified herself as a student when she first introduced herself and interviewed him. They seem to communicate well. If Dr. G asks her to attempt to place the line, she wonders, how much will she have to tell Mr. H about her past attempts?

Opinion
See One, Do One, Teach One.

Teaching hospitals serve an important function within our society by offering physicians in training the opportunity to learn the skills that they must have to become competent practitioners while attempting to provide an exceptional standard of care to individual patients. Society has an interest and investment in this process.

Naturally, achieving technical competency among physicians is a gradual process marked by several transitions. Medical students begin with lectures and anatomy lab and only after their first years in medical school do they move to the clinical setting where they participate directly in patient care. While the ratio of 1:1:1 is not steadfast, the transitive nature of education that it reflects is noteworthy. Those with less experience first observe a procedure, then perform one, and finally reach a stage of teaching the procedure to the next person with less experience as the cycle begins anew.

Who Is to Attempt Central Line Placement?
Several factors are important for the team to consider as they make this decision:

1. What are the student's and house officer's comfort with the student performing the procedure?
2. How acutely ill is the patient and how quickly is the procedure required?
3. What are the patient's and family's wishes regarding who is to perform the procedure? How technically difficult is the procedure?
4. Finally, what are the likelihood and severity of potential complications and how are these modified by the greater technical experience of more senior physicians?
   a. While perhaps the least quantifiable, the most important global measure that a senior house officer should consider in deciding who is to perform a procedure is his or her own intuition as to the appropriateness of the teaching moment.

What information should Mr. H be told in order to provide an informed consent?

1. Standard components of informed consent, such as the indications, risks, benefits, and alternatives to the procedure, can be discussed.
2. The key question in this setting is how much information Mr. H needs to be provided regarding the identity and technical competency of the person who is to perform the procedure.
3. Not telling Mr. H about who is to perform the procedure would deny him important information that might modify his decision.
4. On the other hand, to tell him who is to perform the procedure while denying him knowledge of that person's technical competency seems inadequate.
5. How then would he use the information regarding this person?

Opinion (Recommendation)
Rather than discuss Miss Rogers' prior experience with central line placement, Mr. H should be informed of the proposal that Miss Rogers, a medical student, will be the person attempting the procedure under the close supervision of Dr. G.

Additionally, any questions that Mr. H may have about Miss Rogers' experience should be addressed honestly and directly.

Bottom Line
Virtually all senior house officers will be challenged during their training to balance the healthcare needs of their patients with the educational needs of their junior colleagues. Sensitivity to the mediators of procedural risk, in conjunction with an adequately thorough informed consent, should be the trainee's primary guide in achieving this balance.

9.5.7 Resident Questions Order of Attending Physician

Summary
Question: A resident has concerns that an attending physician's order is reflective of poor clinical judgment. How should this situation be handled?

1. Trainees may withdraw from the care ordered by the supervisor, provided withdrawal does not itself threaten the patient's immediate welfare.
2. The trainee should communicate his or her concerns to the physician issuing the orders and, if necessary, to the appropriate persons for mediating such disputes.

3. Third-party mediators of such disputes may include the chief of staff of the involved service, the chief resident, a designated member of the institutional grievance committee, or, in large institutions, an institutional ombudsperson largely outside of the hospital staff hierarchy.

4. Retaliatory or punitive actions against trainees who raise complaints are unethical and are a legitimate cause for filing a grievance with the appropriate institutional committee.

Level III: Advanced Topics

9.6 Clinical Decision Support Systems

A clinical decision support system (CDSS) is an expert system, artificial intelligence software, or accumulated medical knowledge used to assist a medical practitioner in diagnosis or treatment. The advantage of a directed knowledge base is the ability to mine large data sets and analyze similarities or more accurately probabilities that a set of factors indicate a particular disorder, especially if it is a rare disease that a medical practitioner might not normally experience.

Typical expert systems use inference engines that make comparisons on a series of logical sequences of events: if a is true, then likely b is the cause, called forward chaining. The following is a classic example: you type in a question to an expert system "is Socrates Mortal?" and then the system finds that Socrates has been defined as human and somewhere else humans have been defined as mortal so it can deduce "Socrates is mortal."

9.6.1 Neural Networks

Neural networks are defined as systems that are modeled after living biological organisms. Complex systems are modeled by simulations.

These systems can be useful but more powerful techniques are under way: Exponential Stability Analysis for Neural Networks and Fuzzy networks. Often if the subject area is more narrowly defined, the system can be more predictive. They are designed to be capable of learning new relationships and are more flexible at recognizing patterns, i.e., pattern recognition.

They are modeled after human neurons that are analog, a continuously variable quantity, similar to data in the real world. The values can take on any value between 0 and 0.999 where the higher values or probabilities indicate that the answer is more likely, i.e. there are no yes and no answers or 0 or 1 responses. Neural networks have adaptive weights and feedback loops that constantly change depending on new inputs, so the strengths, 0–0.999, change as new data come in. If you put your hand near a fire or approach sources of high temperature, the adaptive weight would increase the danger component of the reasoning system. The second component is nonlinear functions, or some close approximation. A nonlinear system is "one that does *not satisfy* the superposition principle," or one whose output is not directly proportional to its input (Figure 9.5).

By narrowly defining the area of diagnosis, the feasibility of narrowing in on effective expert systems increases:

1. An example of computer-aided diagnosis is "Computer-aided diagnosis of human brain tumor through MRI: A survey and a new algorithm" by El-Sayed A. Dahshan et al. "The technique is based on the following computational methods; the feedback pulse-coupled neural network for image segmentation, the discrete wavelet transform for features extraction, the principal component analysis for reducing the dimensionality of the wavelet coefficients, and the feed forward back-propagation neural network to classify inputs into normal or abnormal. The experiments were carried out on 101 images consisting of 14 normal and 87 abnormal (malignant and benign tumors) from a real human brain MRI dataset. The classification accuracy on both training and test images is 99%" (http://www.sciencedirect.com/science/article/pii/S0957417414000426).

The **principle of superposition** simply states that a set of quantities can be added as vectors to determine the net of that quantity at a certain point.

A nonlinear system: whose output is not directly proportional to its input

The Superposition principle suggests that the net response at a given place and time caused by two or more stimuli is the sum of the responses which would have been caused by each stimulus individually.

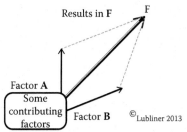

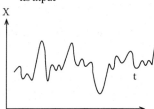

FIGURE 9.5 Superposition theory versus a nonlinear system used in neural networks.

Steps involved in detecting tumor using Boundary Box method are as follows:-
1. Axis of symmetry on an axial MR slice is found which divides brain in two halves left (I) and right (R).
2. One half serves as test Image and the other half supplies as the reference image.
3. Noval score function is used which identify the region of change with two searches — one along the vertical direction and other along the horizontal direction.
4. Noval score function uses Bhattacharya coefficient to detects a rectangle D which represents the region of interest between images I and R.

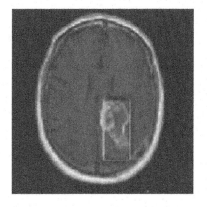 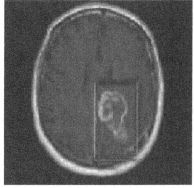

FIGURE 9.6 NIS database. (From http://www.hcup-us.ahrq.gov/nisoverview.jsp#about.)

2. Another example is "An Automated System for Brain Tumor Detection and Segmentation" by Rohan Kandwal et al. It consists of three stages to detect and segment brain tumor. In the first stage, image preprocessing is done to remove any noise and sharpen image. In the second stage, the bounding box method using symmetry is used to automatically detect the location of the tumor in any part of the brain. In the third stage, several postprocessing operations are used to finally segment the tumor portion from the whole image. Several experiments show that our technique in spite of being completely simple detects tumor correctly (http://www.academia. edu/6815417/An_Automated_System_for_Brain_Tumor_Detection_and_Segmentation) (Figure 9.6).

The Nationwide Inpatient Sample (NIS) database is a federal state industry partnership that has currently, as of 2014, 40 million inpatient hospital stays. It was funded by a Health and Human Services (HHS) grant called Agency for Healthcare Research and Quality (AHRQ) (http://www.ahrq.gov/). The NIS can be used to identify, track, and analyze national trends in healthcare utilization, access, charges, quality, and outcomes. NIS data are available from 1988 through 2011, which allow analysis of trends over time. The number of states in the NIS has grown from 8 in the first year to 46 at present.

Key features of the most recent NIS database year (2011) include the following:

- A sampling frame of hospitals that comprises approximately 97% of all hospital discharges in the United States.
- A large sample size, which enables analyses of rare conditions, such as congenital anomalies; uncommon treatments, such as organ transplantation; and special patient populations, such as the uninsured.
- Hospital identifiers for many states that permit linkages to the American Hospital Association (AHA) Annual Survey Database (Health Forum, LLC © 2012) and county identifiers that permit linkages to the Area Resource File.

NIS Data Elements

The NIS contains clinical and resource-use information that is included in a typical discharge abstract, with safeguards to protect the privacy of individual patients, physicians, and hospitals (as required by data sources). It contains more than 100 clinical and nonclinical data elements for each hospital stay, including

- Primary and secondary diagnoses and procedures
- Admission and discharge status
- Patient demographic characteristics (e.g., sex, age, race, and median household income for ZIP code)
- Hospital characteristics (e.g., ownership, size, and teaching status)
- Expected payment source
- Total charges
- Discharge status
- Length of stay
- Severity and comorbidity measures

As a uniform, multistate database, the NIS promotes comparative studies of healthcare services:

- Utilization of health services by special populations
- Hospital stays for rare conditions
- Variations in medical practice
- Healthcare cost inflation
- Regional and national analyses
- Quality of care and patient safety
- Impact of health policy changes
- Access to care

By analyzing data from U.S. hospitals, trends and effectiveness of treatment can be analyzed. An example is "Trends and Outcomes of Hospitalized Patients with Gastrointestinal Bleeds in the US: Data from Nationwide Inpatient Sample Over the Past Decade (2001–2010)" (http://www.eventscribe.com/2012/acg/ajaxcalls/postersinfo.asp?title=6977).

Conclusion: By analyzing US data, results from this large, national database show that hospital admissions for all GIB have increased over the last decade (by almost 5%); this is mainly due to a 45% increase in admissions due to variceal UGIB. However, despite the increased GIB, mortality and length of hospital stay in these patients has significantly decreased over the decade suggesting improved treatment of these patients during their hospital stays (Figure 9.7).

9.7 Summary

Medical ethics is a *system of moral values* and *principles of conduct governing an individual or a group*. In the United States, the AMA Ethics Groups publish a *Code of Ethics* as guidelines for medical personnel. The AMA's CEJA provides for judicial action to sanction medical practitioners who violate the Code of

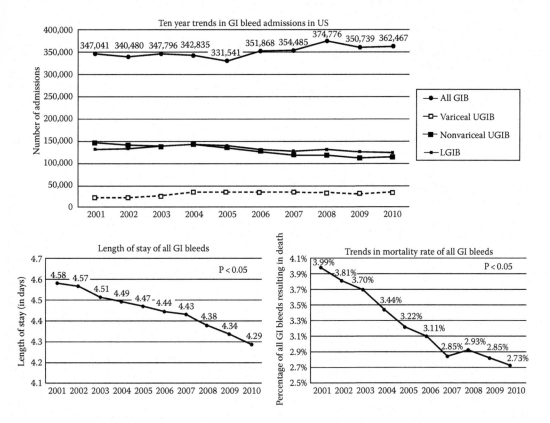

FIGURE 9.7 NIS database analysis of GI bleeds from 2001 to 2010.

Ethics. We aspire to a universal code of ethics that ethically supplies equal medical care for all individuals without any qualifications. On that note equal medical care is often difficult to obtain. New tools are available such as CDSS and the new generation of expert systems, cell phone based, that may level the playing field, i.e., provide equal care regardless of income, a more ethical medical system.

Questions

Level I

1. What is medical ethics?
2. Explain the Hippocratic Oath.
   a. What are the differences between the original (fifth century BC) and the modern version in 1964?
3. The American Medical Association (AMA) periodically updates a code of medical ethics. How is that related to the Hippocratic Oath?
   a. Are there any differences?
4. What is the role of the AMA Council on Ethical and Judicial Affairs?
   a. What areas of medical ethics are they responsible for?
   b. What enforcement capabilities do they have?
   c. What role do they play in judicial functions related to breaches in medical ethics?
5. What is the primary focus of the American Nurses Association (ANA) code of ethics?
   a. How do these differ from the AMA Code of Ethics?

Level II

    6. The AMA provides guidelines and case studies used in medical education. What role do you believe these case studies play in medical education?
      a. Summarize the case study on "Impaired Drivers."
      b. Summarize the case study on "Gifts to Physicians from Industry."

Level III

    7. What is a clinical decision support system (CDSS)?
    8. How are neural networks used to analyze medical data?
      a. Explain the superposition theory versus a nonlinear system used in neural networks.
    9. How is computer-aided diagnosis used to aid physicians in their practice of medicine?
   10. What is the Nationwide Inpatient Sample (NIS) database?
      a. How is the NIS used to aid in diagnosis?
   11. Research a real-world example of a CDSS.

Glossary

The American Medical Association (AMA) Ethics Group sets guidance for physicians to pursue. The Ethics Group has three parts: Council on Ethical and Judicial Affairs, Ethics Resource Center, and Institute for Ethics.

The American Nurses Association (ANA), similar to the AMA, periodically produces a *code of ethics,* which was last updated in 2001, that certified nurses have to read, understand, and act upon.

The Hippocratic Oath dates back to the fifth century BC describing the responsibility of physicians to focus on the well being of their patients.

The Council on Ethical and Judicial Affairs (CEJA) focuses on periodic updates of the Code of Medical Ethics.

A clinical decision support system (CDSS) is an expert system, artificial intelligence software, or accumulated medical knowledge to assist a medical practitioner in diagnosis or treatment.

Ethics defined by the Merriam-Webster dictionary is "A theory or system of moral values" or professional ethics as "the principles of conduct governing an individual or a group."

Hippocratic Oath, dates back to the fifth century BC describing the responsibility of physicians to focus on the well being of their patients.

The Litigation Center of the American Medical Association and State Medical Societies, established in 1995, as part of the AMA physicians' resource center provides physicians with legal expertise assistance.

The National Inpatient Sample (NIS) Database is a federal state industry partnership that has currently, as 2014, 40 million inpatient hospital stays.

Neural networks are defined as systems that are modeled after living biological organisms.

References

1. Swendiman, K. (2012). Health care: Constitutional rights and legislative powers, http://www.fas.org/sgp/crs/misc/R40846.pdf.
2. AMA Medical Ethics, https://www.ama-assn.org/ama/pub/physician-resources/medical-ethics.page.
3. AMA Journal of Ethics virtual tutor, http://virtualmentor.ama-assn.org/site/cases.html.
4. Nationwide Inpatient Sample Database, (2012). https://www.hcupus.ahrq.gov/nisoverview.jsp

10

Critical Care Nursing Perspective on the Electronic Health Record

Cathy Lubliner

10.1 Introduction

The fact that activities relating to nursing care need to be documented is nothing new. From the time that Florence Nightingale brought order and science to the nursing profession, there have been written records. What has changed, however, is the method and means of documenting, evolving from the simple paper and a pen to the sophistication of computer-based systems. The content of the documentation has also evolved with much of it now mandated by regulatory agencies, third-party payers, and government agencies as well as the legal aspect of the record, which is summarized in the adage surrounding malpractice lawsuits that admonishes: "If it wasn't documented, it wasn't done."

Regulatory agencies look to documentation in the medical record to determine if an institution is meeting the standard of care for patient safety. These include bodies such as The Joint Commission (TJC) on Hospital Accreditation and the Departments of Health of varying states. Each year TJC establishes a list of *National Patient Safety Goals (NPSGs)*, and the medical record serves as part of the evidence to document that these have been met. For 2014, the safety goals were as follows: identify patients correctly; improve staff communication; use medications safely; use alarms safely; prevent infections; identify patient safety risks; and prevent mistakes in surgery.

The reimbursement that a facility receives depends on what is documented in the record. Private insurance companies scrutinize the contents of the record to determine whether physician orders for treatment reflect the patient's diagnosis and whether there is documentation that these treatments were actually carried out. The Centers for Medicare and Medicaid Services (CMS) also determine the standard of care that needs to be met for reimbursement. In 2007, CMS implemented a 0% complication rate for a number of clinical diagnoses, including a Stage III and IV pressure ulcer acquired during a hospital stay. These complications are considered to be both serious and preventable and are considered to be "never events." If there is inadequate documentation that a patient was admitted with the wound, CMS will determine that it developed while the patient was hospitalized and reimbursement will be denied. Additional days added to the hospital stay relating to the pressure ulcer may be denied as well. The purpose is to provide a financial incentive for hospitals to provide the best care possible and to avoid complications for patients. The importance of this documentation mandates that entering it correctly should be as easy as possible, with ample reminders of omitted data.

In 1999, the Institute of Medicine (IOM) published *To Err is Human* in which they concluded that there were approximately one million preventable hospital deaths in the United States. As a result of this, The Committee on Quality of Healthcare in America of the IOM proposed wide-ranging strategies that should be implemented to reduce preventable medical errors. One of the prime recommendations of the group was the need to implement a computerized health record system to facilitate improvement in patient safety. In 2003, they defined a basic electronic health record (EHR) as "a longitudinal collection of electronic health information about a person, or healthcare provided; Immediate electronic access to a person or population level information by authorized users; Provision of knowledge and decision-support that enhances the quality, safety, and efficiency of patient care; and Support of efficient processes for healthcare delivery."

The move toward EHRs received a further push forward in February of 2009 when President Barack Obama signed the American Recovery and Reinvestment Act, a $787 billion economic stimulus package that allocated $19 billion as financial incentives for providers to adopt EHR technology. In order to obtain financial incentive payments, facilities had to prove that they have achieved a specific level of *meaningful use* beginning in 2014.

In 2009, EHRs generated $973.2 million in business, and by 2012, this had grown to $6.5 billion as facilities who might otherwise have considered deferring implementation chose to move more quickly in order to meet meaningful use for 2014. With this rapid adoption of EHRs, in many settings, the focus has been primarily on ensuring that those parts of the record that support meaningful use are the focus. While this is a reasonable business decision, it has sometimes been at the expense of not addressing other aspects, such as the ease of entering data by the frontline users of the systems.

The transition to computer-based documentation has affected all members of the healthcare team in all settings, both inpatient and outpatient. However, the documentation requirements for hospital-based nurses present challenges that are not experienced by other disciplines. And in the hospital setting, critical care nurses face the most complex documentation challenges because of the quantity of information and the speed with which it needs to be recorded, combined with the need to instantly access that information to drive patient care decisions.

The focus of this chapter is to explain the complexity of critical care nursing in the context of the data that are generated and the process of recording those data. Documenting patient care activities during emergency situations, which occur often in the critical care setting, is particularly challenging because many activities are occurring simultaneously. An added dimension to the documentation challenge for critical care nurses is that they are typically also providing care for the patient at the same time that they are trying to document. This differs from most other disciplines, including physicians, who document their care activities after the fact. They are able to provide care to the patient and then enter the details about that care into the record. Nurses, on the other hand, not only document the activities that they have performed, but they also document the patient's status through vital signs, systems assessment, medications, and events that occur continuously at over a 24 hour period. The needs of critically ill patients are complex, and they are always at risk for adverse events. Because nursing is the only discipline to provide continuous care over a 24/7 basis, nursing documentation is key to providing a coherent view of the patient's hospital course (Figure 10.1).

The quantity of data to be entered in a critical care unit is enormous and includes multiple vital signs and hemodynamic parameters as well as data about the settings on multiple devices. The data need to be entered not only at frequent intervals but also quickly and accurately and in close proximity to the time that the event occurred. Data retrieval is also a challenge because once entered, it needs to be displayed in a manner that facilitates making sense of the information, so that sound clinical decisions are supported. It is nursing documentation that provides most of the data that are required for meeting the requirements of the regulatory agencies and third-party payers.

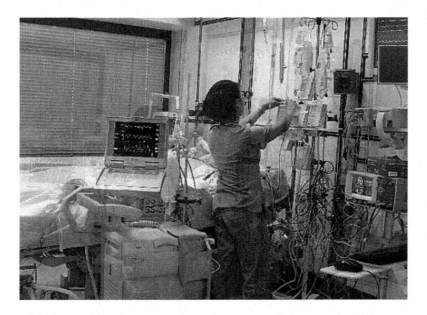

FIGURE 10.1   (See color insert.) A critical care nurse provides care for a patient in the immediate postoperative period after cardiac surgery.

10.2 Episodic versus Dynamic Documentation

Documentation patterns differ according to the setting and workflow in that some is episodic, while other documentation is dynamic. A physician's office or a clinic where a patient is seen intermittently has a different workflow than a critical care unit in a hospital. The office or clinic visit is episodic in nature, whereas the critical care unit has a workflow characterized by continuous ongoing observation and interaction with the patient that will continue over a 24 hour period. The events of the office visit will be recorded, including the patient's current vital signs, complaints, or concerns that brought the patient into the office for that visit and the plan for follow-up. All documentation that is recorded will be a summary of that one visit. There will be no further entries on the patient's record until the next visit, unless it is to record test results or a phone consultation. Trends and changes in the patient's status will reveal themselves over weeks to months depending on the frequency of patient visits.

In contrast, the documentation requirements for a critically ill patient will be dynamic and continuous. The volume of data is copious and needs to be entered quickly and at frequent intervals. An example of this is the documentation that occurs during a code situation. Some EHR vendors have packages for this documentation directly on the computer. Other hospitals have chosen to keep that documentation on the paper *code sheet*, in which case the paper form will become a permanent part of the medical record. Alternatively, in some settings, the code data that have been recorded on the paper form will be transcribed into the EHR after the fact. This practice requires double charting of the same information.

At present, most EHRs function better in documenting static and episodic data than they do in handling dynamic and continuous data. This is not due to an issue of capability, but in decisions that hospitals have made in where to spend their limited dollars to implement the EHR system in time to achieve the meaningful use mandates. The technology exists to support easier documentation for critically ill patients, but it involves an additional financial expenditure to fully utilize the technology that enables cardiac monitors and other biomedical devices to communicate with the EHR and directly download data.

10.3 Critical Care Unit

The current capability of today's intensive care units to support critically ill patients is astounding. There are numerous monitoring and infusion devices, all of which generate data or alarms that require attention. There are biomedical support devices that require close observation and also have settings and readings to interpret and record. Depending on the stability of the patient, the vital signs will be recorded every 1–2 hour. However, the vital signs that are recorded on a critically ill patient will be far more extensive than just the usual *temperature, pulse, and respiration*. A full set of vital signs will often include temperature, heart rate, cardiac rhythm, and blood pressure (systolic/diastolic and mean) obtained via arterial line or via cuff, pulmonary artery pressure (PAP) (systolic/diastolic and mean), central venous pressure (CVP), oxygen saturation via pulse oximetry, cardiac output (CO), cardiac index (CI), and systemic oxygen consumption percent. If the patient is on a ventilator, as is common in someone who is critically ill, the data recorded will also include the airway type (endotracheal tube or tracheostomy), the mode of support from the ventilator, the oxygen concentration, the tidal volume, the respiratory rate from the ventilator and any breaths that the patient is able to generate, continuous positive airway pressure settings, or positive end expiratory pressure (PEEP) levels. A patient who is in cardiogenic shock or heart failure may have an intra-aortic balloon pump (IABP) in place, which will also generate data to record. This will include the frequency of counterpulsation (1:1, 1:2, 1:2) as well as arterial blood pressure reflecting balloon augmentation: systolic, augmented diastolic, end diastolic, and mean arterial pressure (MAP) (Figure 10.2).

Any medications that the patient is receiving via continuous intravenous (IV) infusion are documented hourly to include the dose (e.g., mg/min or mcg/kg/min) as well as the hourly volume that is

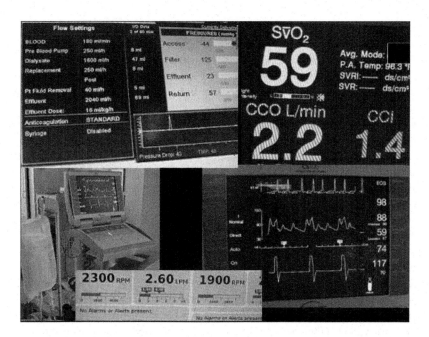

FIGURE 10.2 **(See color insert.)** The data that are generated on a critically ill patient often include far more than just vital signs. Pictured are the screens from a continuous cardiac output monitor, an intra-aortic balloon pump, a continuous renal replacement therapy device, and a ventricular assist device. All of the aforementioned parameters and numbers are recorded every hour.

infused to deliver that dose (mL/h). A patient in a critical care unit might have as many as 9 or 10 continuous IV infusions, delivered via an infusion pump. All IV fluids are recorded each hour for inclusion in the patient's fluid intake. Besides the IV medications, the patient usually requires multiple additional medications to be administered and documented. Some of the medications that the patient requires are titrated according to desired effect, for example, to improve blood pressure. If the blood pressure drops below the specified parameter, the nurse will change the dose and rate of the medication and will document this change.

Administering blood products is considered to be a high-risk process. If the patient requires blood products, it is critical that a patient receives the correct blood that is matched according to blood type and cross matching in the Blood Bank. To ensure that the correct blood transfusion is administered, two nurses check the unit of blood together before it is administered. They will carefully match the patient's name and medical record number on the identification bracelet to the label on the blood product and the accompanying slip. Vital sign monitoring will be more frequent, while the blood is infusing to detect whether a transfusion reaction occurs.

Patients in a critical care unit frequently have a catheter in place for urine drainage and accurate output measurement. The volume is measured every hour. However, it is not uncommon for critically ill patients to experience acute renal failure as a complication of their underlying illness. The treatment is to start acute dialysis utilizing a process known as continuous renal replacement therapy (CRRT) via a large-bore dual-lumen venous catheter. The nurse manages the CRRT device that includes priming the tubing and then monitoring the fluid volume shifts, pressures, and electrolyte changes. The nurse will record the range of pressures hourly that indicate the functioning of this device as well as the volume of the various solutions that are utilized to accomplish this form of dialysis.

Patients in acute or end-stage heart failure may have advanced support devices such as an IABP or a ventricular assist device in use, either as a short-term device used while the heart recovers or as a long-term implanted device that the patient will go home with. Each of these devices requires expert nursing care to ensure that the devices are operating safely and to support and monitor the patient during the use of this therapy. In addition, each device generates data that will be recorded hourly.

However, in any discussion about the environment of a critical care unit, the most important point to understand is that patients who are critically ill are more than just a collection of devices and data. They are people who are at risk for multiple complications and who are under tremendous stress in an alien environment. They require expert medical and nursing care as well as multiple interventions to decrease the risk of developing complications such as pneumonia, bloodstream or urinary tract infections, pressure ulcers, blood clots, and wound infections. They need to have their pain relieved and their fears addressed.

The family members of critically ill patients also need support and explanations about what is happening to their loved one, and they need to have their questions answered. An intensive care unit can be an overwhelming place. The monitoring and biomedical support devices that are in use are foreign to most people, and family members are often devastated at having their loved one in this setting.

It is the nurse at the bedside who is with the patient and the family 24 hours a day, every single day. Many complications and hospital acquired conditions (HACs) can be prevented by attentive nursing care. However, documentation is also extremely important. Data need to be entered correctly in order to be useful and to facilitate making sound decisions about patient care. As EHRs are implemented more widely, it is critical that attention is given to the process of entering data to ensure that it is intuitive, easy to use, and viewable in a format that supports correct interpretation to drive patient care. In looking at the care requirements of a critically ill patient, it is logical to suggest that the best use of a nurse's time is not to be spent typing data into a computer when the technology exists that would allow for most of the monitors, infusion pumps, and devices to download their data directly into the patient's EHR.

10.4 Documentation for the Hospitalized Patient

There are standard elements of documentation that are included for all hospitalized patients. The admission data that are collected during an initial encounter with a patient consist of a detailed history and physical examination, including listing all medications that the patient has been taking at home. This list is reconciled by the physician with medication orders written on admission to ensure that consideration has been given as to whether these medications will be continued or held while the patient is in the hospital. The physician will again reconcile this list on discharge to ensure that home medications that were not ordered while the patient was hospitalized are considered for resumption after the patient has been discharged. The objective is to avoid missing a medication that the patient needs to be taking on a long-term basis.

Based on the results of the diagnosis and admission history and physical exam, the physician writes the initial set of orders for the patient. The admission orders include diet, activity, medications, laboratory, and any other diagnostic tests as indicated. Each day, the physician is also required to write a *progress note* that documents the current status of the patient. This typically includes the current summary of vital signs and lab and other diagnostic test results and concludes with the current impression of the patient's status and the plan for further care.

Besides the attending physician, many other disciplines document in the medical record of a hospitalized patient. This includes physicians who have been called in on consult, fellows, residents, staff nurses assigned to care for the patient, nurses called in on consult such as wound care specialists or nurse practitioners, physician assistants, respiratory therapists, physical therapists, occupational therapists, speech therapists, nutritionists/dieticians, social workers, and case managers. Each discipline documents somewhat differently depending on the nature of their relationship with the patient and the type of care that is rendered.

10.4.1 Time-Sensitive Documentation

Some forms of documentation are *time sensitive*, while others are not. For example, in performing patient or family education, it is not essential to differentiate whether the nurse taught the newly diagnosed diabetic patient to count carbohydrates and administer insulin at 9:30 or 10:30 a.m. Therefore, the documentation does not have to be completed at the exact moment that it was done. The critical information is the education that occurred, the specific content that was included, and the patient's response to the education and plans for follow-up education. It is not extremely relevant that this information be documented at the precise time that it took place.

In contrast to this, vital signs and hemodynamic parameters are extremely time sensitive. It is as important to know precisely when the blood pressure was 74/50 as it is to know that it decreased to that level. It is also important to know what time the previous blood pressure was recorded to determine the span of time that it took for the pressure to fall. In addition, it is also important to know any other events that were happening at that time, for example, ventilator settings, as well as any medications or volume administered.

10.4.2 Documenting Medication Administration

The process of administering medications in the hospital setting bears explaining, in terms of both the process and the required documentation. The process is initiated when the physician orders a particular medication. With an EHR, the physician does not have to be physically present in the unit to write the order. He or she can enter an order from any location. The pharmacist then profiles this medication to cross-check it against documented allergies that the patient has or for any potential interactions between other medications that have been prescribed during this visit. A message is then sent to the dispensing system (often a computer-based automated system) so that it will recognize the request to administer this medication at the scheduled time. If an EHR is in use, the pharmacist will also trigger the medication to appear in the electronic medication administration record (eMAR). Along with the name of the medication, the information on the eMAR will include the dose, the route (by mouth, by injection, etc.), the frequency (once a day, every 6 hours, etc.), and the time that the medication is due to be administered. At this point, the nurse will be able to scan the patient's identification bracelet, scan the medication, and then click to confirm that the medication has been administered (Figure 10.3).

Prior to the transition to a computer-based system, an order for a medication would be generated by the physician by either writing the order or giving the order to the nurse via telephone. Once an order was obtained, two things would happen. The actual order would be transcribed onto a paper medication administration record (MAR) with the type of medication being differentiated according to how it was going to be administered. Options include medications to be administered on a set schedule around the clock, medications that were to be given immediately or STAT as a onetime dose, and medications to be given as needed based on the patient's status, such as an analgesic ordered to be given if the patient had pain. On the MAR, the name of the medication would be transcribed as well as the date and time that it was ordered, the date and time that it would expire and would have to be renewed, the dose, and the frequency, and then the specific times that the medication was to be given would be written in. Each MAR would have space to write the dates across the top. As the nurse administered a particular medication, he or she would initial the space corresponding to the date and time (Figure 10.4).

When administering medications, nurses adhere to the *five rights* in order to avoid a medication error. These five rights are the right patient, the right medication, the right dose, the right route, and the right time. With a paper record, the method of ensuring that these five components were correct included looking at the patient's identification bracelet and asking the patient to state his or her name if possible and to compare that to the name on the MAR where the medication is listed. To confirm that it was the right medication, for the first dose that was administered when a new order was written, the nurse would compare the written order in the chart with the details that had been transcribed onto

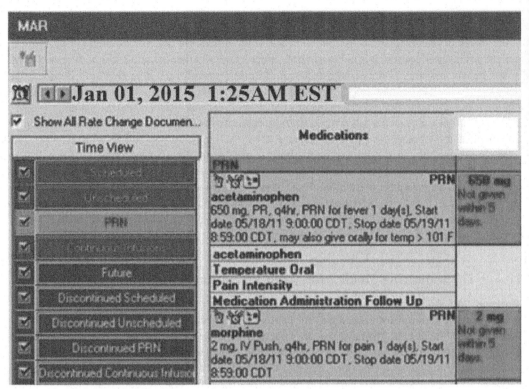

Source: http://www.pearsonhighered.com/realehrprep/learn-about/what-is.html

FIGURE 10.3 An example of an electronic medication administration record. The name of the medication, the dose, route of administration, and frequency are in the left column.

Standing Medication Record

Diagnosis
Allergies

	Date Ordered	Date Expired	Medication Route	Dose Frequency	Time	Date	Date	Date	Date	Date	Date	Date
T												
V												
T												
V												
T												
V												
T												
V												

FIGURE 10.4 An example of a paper medication administration record.

the MAR. This would partially verify the name of the medication, the dose, the route that it was to be administered, and the frequency and times that it was scheduled. To continue checking the five rights, in all instances after the initial administration where the original order would be compared to the MAR, the nurse would use the MAR as the standard for comparison. To verify that it is the correct medication, route, and dose, the nurse would compare the medication in hand to what was written in the MAR. The right time would be verified by comparing the actual time of administration with the scheduled time on the MAR. After completing all of these steps, the nurse would proceed and give the medication and then initial the MAR to complete the documentation.

The process of administering medications using a computer-based system is designed to accomplish all of these safety steps. With an electronic record, the physician enters the order into the computer. The physician can select from a menu of order sets and then modify them with drop-down menus. If there are orders that a physician uses often, he or she can save them as a favorite, so that they are easier to generate in the future. Once the order is electronically generated and signed by the physician, it is visible to the nurses who will electronically sign to acknowledge the order. At the same time, any medications that are included in the order will be visible to the pharmacist who will profile the medication in comparison to the patient's list of allergies and other medications to check for interactions. When this step is complete, the pharmacist will trigger the medication to appear in the electronic MAR. This serves the same purpose as the paper MAR, in that it summarizes all aspects of the order and triggers the nurse when it is time to administer the medication.

At some point, all hospitals using EHRs have introduced or will introduce a method of bar-code scanning for medication administration, as well as for identification with other processes. This is actually using the computer to the fullest extent and it changes radically the way that nurses administer medication. In the previous description of medication administration and the five rights, it was clear that the entire burden for verifying that everything was correct was the nurse's responsibility, in other words, relying totally on human factors. When medication errors occurred, they were often due to human error if someone administering a medication was interrupted or distracted or if there were issues of legibility in reading the handwriting on the MAR. A bar coding system addresses the five rights and supports the process of medication safety.

With a bar coding capable EHR, the nurse will determine that a medication is due at a particular time and will initiate a medication administration window that displays all medications that are due to be given at that time. The nurse will remove the medication from the medication dispensing system and will bring the medications and the computer to the patient's bedside. The first step is to scan the bar code on the patient's identification bracelet and then scan the bar code on the medication that is to be administered. This step verifies that it is the correct patient and confirms that it is the correct medication, dose, route, and time. When the nurse has administered the medications, he or she will confirm and electronically sign the medication.

The previous discussion about the advantages of the electronic record would not be complete without the caveat that everything does not always work as designed. Patients inexplicably disappear entirely, individual medications disappear from the eMAR without explanation, and entries that a nurse is sure that he or she has entered correctly are nowhere to be found.

10.4.3 Interdisciplinary Plan of Care

The interdisciplinary plan of care (IPOC) incorporates the planned activities of all disciplines that are designed to meet the individualized goals for the patient. Besides serving as a template to guide the patient care activities, an appropriate and individualized IPOC is required by most regulatory bodies, including CMS and TJC.

Regulatory agencies require that all members of the healthcare team collaborate on the patient's plan of care; hence, it is usually referred to as the IPOC. The IPOC serves as the roadmap to identify the goals for the current hospital stay, along with the strategies to meet those goals. Even for critically ill patients, this is a form of static rather than dynamic documentation, and it is one form of documentation that is more effective on a computer than on paper. Prior to the EHR, hospitals struggled with the IPOC when it was a paper-based form. In the 1960s to 1970s, the IPOCs were entirely handwritten, if they were done at all. And even if they were written on admission, they were rarely updated. At best, they were not comprehensive, since it simply took too long to write everything out. At worst, they were written in pencil and were discarded when the patient was discharged. To address these deficiencies, a common solution was to create a preprinted *standard IPOC* that was diagnosis based, with predetermined goals and interventions. There was space to customize as needed, but these documents were often not updated. In addition, with a paper format, most patients had only one IPOC generated, despite having multiple problems. It was simply not feasible to add multiple IPOCs for documentation, or to revise them as the needs of the patient changed. During visits from TJC or CMS, surveyors expected the IPOC to be individualized to the specific patient. On paper, this requirement was often cited as being deficient.

Computer-based systems have solved most of these problems. For any given diagnosis of the patient, there are many IPOCs to choose from. Additionally, based on the diagnosis and problem list that has been entered for the patient, the computer will often suggest potential IPOCs. Once an IPOC has been selected, the nurse can review the optional interventions and choose those that are most applicable for the patient and delete those that are not. This results in an IPOC that is truly individualized for the specific patient. As part of daily documentation, the nurse can indicate whether each prescribed intervention to meet the goal was done or not done and can sign off on the goals once they are met.

One aspect of the IPOC that is more problematic in a computer-based system than a paper-based system is the issue of access to different parts of the EHR by different disciplines. To maintain protected health information of individuals, in compliance with the HIPAA requirements, each individual who documents in the patient record has access to only those parts of the record that are required for patient care. This means that different disciplines accessing the record will see different versions of it electronically. Unfortunately, this sometimes includes the IPOC, where each discipline sees only certain IPOCs and documents separately on them, rather than all disciplines seeing the same IPOCs regardless of which discipline initiated it. Ironically, in those instances, the IPOC reflects only one discipline at a time. Undoubtedly, this issue will be resolved as EHRs evolve, but at present, it is a problem that exists in many institutions.

10.4.4 Documenting Physiologic Parameters

Physiologic parameters, such as vital signs, are arguably the most difficult type of data to record because of the frequency with which they need to be recorded. Any monitors that have been designed within the past 10 years have the capability of communicating with computer-based documentation systems. In addition, most of the life-support devices that are used with critically ill patients are already capable of downloading data either directly into the EHR or to the monitoring system, which will then download the data to the EHR. Devices that are designed to communicate with the EHR or with the monitoring system include ventilators, IABPs, hypothermia devices, *smart* infusion pumps, and also CRRT devices. This form of automatic data entry is in use in some hospitals today, but certainly not in the majority. The problem is that this is usually an add-on feature of the EHR vendor and is available at an additional charge. Many hospitals opt not to purchase this feature when they initially go live with their EHR. The lack of this feature has the greatest impact on the critical care nurse.

In the absence of communication capability between the monitor and the EHR, vital signs will be entered manually. In contrast to information such as a system assessment, which will lend itself to a drop-down menu of choices, entering physiologic data does not fall into this category since a patient's vital signs will not conform to a standard set of choices. Vital signs consist of numbers and if those numbers are not downloaded directly from the monitor, they must be typed into the electronic record by the nurse. In addition, there is a significant difference in frequency; assessments will be performed no more frequently than every four hours, but vital signs on a critically ill patient will be recorded at least every hour and at times even more frequently if the patient is particularly unstable. Going forward, as the important milestones of meaningful use benchmarks are successfully achieved, attention will have to turn toward improving the process of data entry.

10.4.5 Evolution from Paper to Computers: Capturing Nursing Activities

The earliest critical care units were created in the late 1960s and into the 1970s. The most sophisticated tools for documenting patient care activities were paper and a pen, and vital signs were documented on a graphic sheet. There was an additional document that was called "Nursing Notes," which was used to record the results of the nurse's assessment of the patient as well as any other noteworthy events that occurred during the shift. The format was unstructured and the notes page had the appearance of a sheet of loose-leaf paper. Because it was unstructured, each nurse used a slightly different format, even in doing a *head-to-toe* assessment. The language and abbreviations might vary from nurse to nurse. In retrieving the information, it was not always clear where to look, since everyone's notes differed slightly. It was also easy to miss documenting something since there were no triggers to remind the nurse of what was missing and still needed to be documented. For newer nurses, there were also no triggers to remind the nurse about the components of the assessment.

In the 1980s, as the care of critically ill patients became more complex with more data available, the paper record began to undergo a change. Vital signs moved to a redesigned flow sheet where all data were aligned across the sheet according to the time that they were recorded. These data included the hourly intake and output, laboratory results, and all medications that were being administered by continuous IV infusion. Most critical care units had some form of a flow sheet at this time. They were often *foldout*-type documents of three or four connected sheets. The flow sheet was efficient because it opened up to be able to view multiple hours together with all parameters as well as events. Every item of data that the nurse was monitoring hourly on a patient was recorded on this sheet, so it was very easy to ascertain, at a glance, how the patient was doing just by looking at this sheet. The flow sheets were typically kept at the bedside on a clipboard. Documentation was very easy because there was a space for everything and the information was arranged in an organized manner. Assessments were organized on the back with a space designated for each system.

With the advent of critical care units, patients who were hospitalized were sicker because newer technologic advances that could support failing body systems allowed them to survive complications that would have previously resulted in death. There were more technologies, treatments, medications, and surgical interventions as well as support devices. Patients unable to breathe on their own had breathing tubes placed and were supported by ventilators—machines that delivered oxygenated breaths to the patient and allowed the patient to exhale passively. Those whose kidneys were failing were treated with hemodialysis or acutely with peritoneal dialysis. Cardiac support devices included the IABP. Medication infusion pumps began to replace the original method of counting the drops as a method of calculating the dose. More sophisticated methods of monitoring the patient's status also became available. Catheters could be placed in an artery to measure blood pressure and in a central vein to measure venous pressure. Procedures that once could be conducted only in specially designated cardiac catheterization units could now be performed at the bedside, thus creating new vital signs such as PAPs, CO, CI, and SVO2 to reflect systemic oxygen consumption.

On the flow sheet, items were typically arranged in the order that they appeared on the monitor so that the data could be easily entered. Time synchronicity occurred across the flow sheet in that events that occurred at the same time were aligned with each other. For example, the vital signs that are recorded at a particular time will align with the ventilator settings, fluid volume intake and output, notable events that have occurred, and the current doses of all medications that are being administered via continuous infusion. Laboratory tests such as arterial blood gas results will also align with the vital signs and ventilator settings for more accurate interpretation. The information to be recorded was prompted by the column headings and blank spaces. In looking at the data spread across the timeline, the patient's status could be assessed at a glance with all events that occurred at the same time aligned. Moving down the sheet, trends were easy to discern by looking at changes in the vital signs and other parameters over time. Visually, it was easy to follow the data because the nurse would enter the exact time that the entry occurred and could choose to skip a line or not, but there was very little distracting space on the sheet (Figure 10.5a and b).

In addition to recording vital signs and assessment parameters, many flow sheets also had a column called "event." An *event* could be something as simple as a patient getting out of bed or as complex as a patient being extubated and able to breathe independently. There was often another column labeled "Stat Medications." The purpose of this column was to record medications that were given emergently as a single dose, often in response to a change in the patient's condition. These medications were documented in the MAR but were recorded in this column on the flow sheet so that the medication could be correlated with the vital signs and other parameters that reflected the patient's status. This allowed for a complete picture of the patient's status to be viewed as a snapshot in time (Figure 10.6).

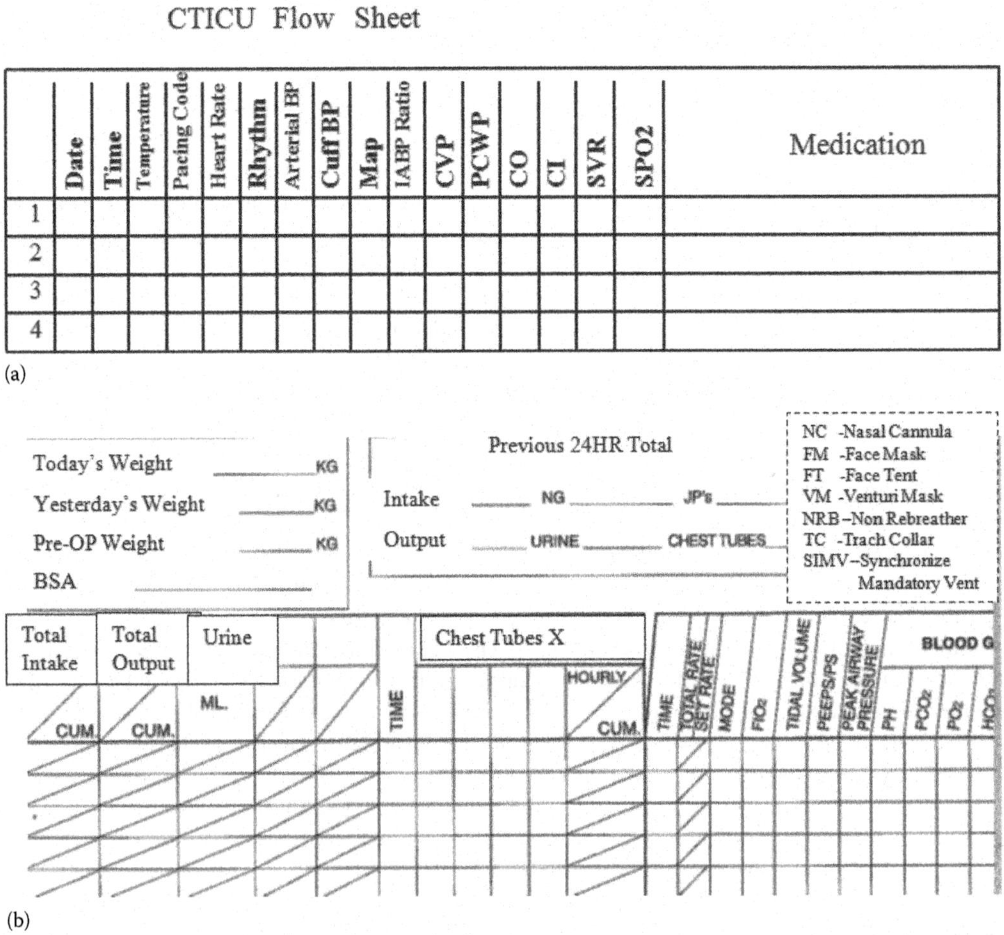

(a)

(b)

FIGURE 10.5 (a) An example of a flow sheet from a cardiothoracic intensive care unit. The vital signs were aligned along according to time. Emergency medications could be correlated with the vital signs to present a full picture of the patient. (b) In addition to vital signs, the typical critical care flow sheet also continued across the time line with space to record intake and output, each hour with a cumulative running total. The preceding example also has space to record the ventilator settings and arterial blood gas values.

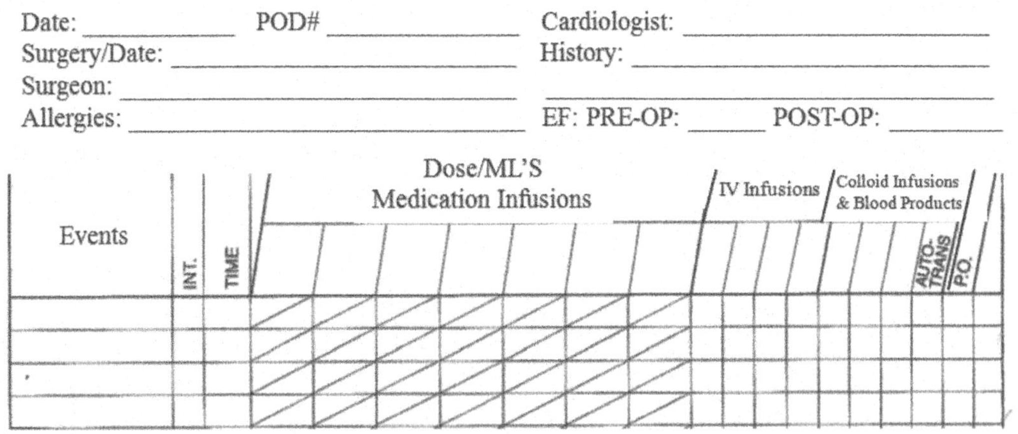

Date: _____ POD# _____   Cardiologist: _____
Surgery/Date: _____   History: _____
Surgeon: _____   _____
Allergies: _____   EF: PRE-OP: _____ POST-OP: _____

FIGURE 10.6 The same page of the flow sheet continued across the timeline with an "Events" column for the nurse to record anything that was unusual or noteworthy. All of the continuous medication infusions that the patient was receiving were also recorded on the flow sheet. With all information aligned according to the time that it occurred, it was easy to get an instant snapshot view of the patient's status.

With the increase in support devices and patient complexity, the physical assessments that were recorded were also more complex. The flow sheets that were designed to handle the vital signs were also utilized to organize the assessment data, typically on the back of the sheet. The free-form Nursing Notes disappeared and were replaced with designated spaces for the assessment results. Since space was limited, the most common solution for documenting assessment data was to create a key of abbreviations listing the most common assessment results. The nurse would select the number that corresponded to the information that he or she wanted to enter and write that number in the designated space. This could be viewed as the precursor to the *drop-down* menu of computer-based documentation (Figure 10.7).

Using the flow sheet, data retrieval was very easy. Information was organized together and had a logical flow. Nurses often refer to the patient's *story* that is the cumulative events that have occurred during the hospital stay. An important component of the patient story is recording the dates and times of all procedures that have been performed including those that are formal surgical procedures, performed in the operating room (OR), as well as minor procedures that are performed in the unit, such as inserting lines or chest tubes. With paper documentation, the story was easy to follow by reviewing the flow sheets to look at the "Events" column or by quickly looking at the boxes where line insertions were recorded (Figure 10.8a through c).

A computer-based system somewhat mimics the advantage of serving as a reminder of assessments to be performed, in that all of the systems are listed with space for the specific components of the assessment and a drop-down menu of choices. However, because the screen has a finite size, the nurse needs to scroll up or down to find the correct space for data entry or needs to click between screens to enter different categories of information. Some computer-based documentation systems have task reminders; however, they sometimes display inconsequential tasks or do not remove a task when it has been completed. This feature should be an advantage with a computer-based system, but there is still work to be done to ensure that the triggered tasks are meaningful and easy to view.

Despite the need to improve on selected aspects, a computer-based system offers definite potential advantages. With paper documentation, the medical record of a patient who had been hospitalized for a prolonged period of time eventually outgrew the physical space of the binder that constituted the chart. In those cases, it would be necessary to *thin* the chart simply because there were just too many pages to fit in the binder. The thinned chart would be housed elsewhere in the unit. There were guidelines as

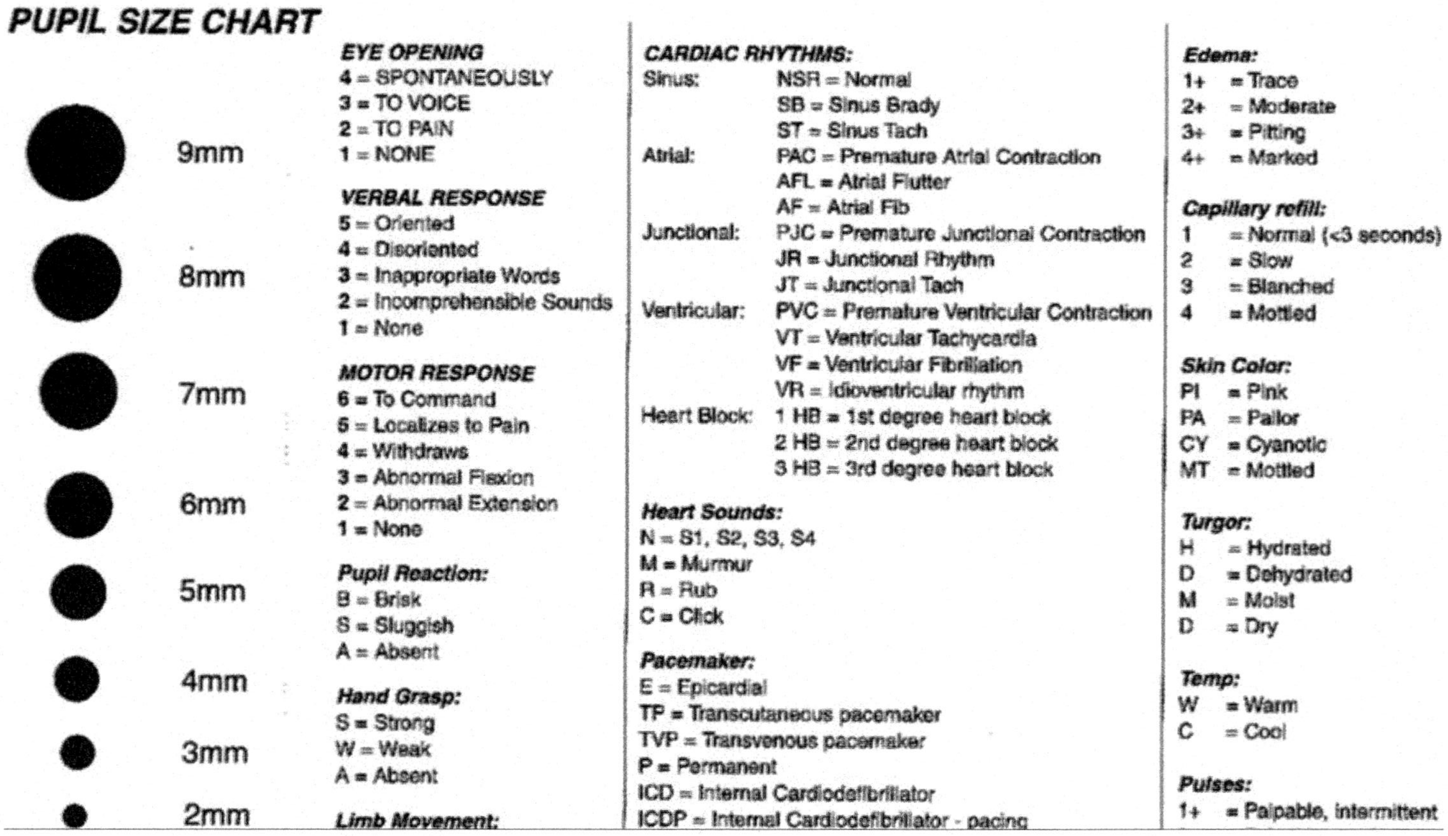

PUPIL SIZE CHART

EYE OPENING
4 = SPONTANEOUSLY
3 = TO VOICE
2 = TO PAIN
1 = NONE

9mm

VERBAL RESPONSE
5 = Oriented
4 = Disoriented
3 = Inappropriate Words
2 = Incomprehensible Sounds
1 = None

8mm

MOTOR RESPONSE
6 = To Command
5 = Localizes to Pain
4 = Withdraws
3 = Abnormal Flexion
2 = Abnormal Extension
1 = None

7mm

Pupil Reaction:
B = Brisk
S = Sluggish
A = Absent

6mm

Hand Grasp:
S = Strong
W = Weak
A = Absent

5mm

4mm

3mm

2mm   **Limb Movement:**

CARDIAC RHYTHMS:

Sinus: NSR = Normal
            SB = Sinus Brady
            ST = Sinus Tach

Atrial: PAC = Premature Atrial Contraction
            AFL = Atrial Flutter
            AF = Atrial Fib

Junctional: PJC = Premature Junctional Contraction
            JR = Junctional Rhythm
            JT = Junctional Tach

Ventricular: PVC = Premature Ventricular Contraction
            VT = Ventricular Tachycardia
            VF = Ventricular Fibrillation
            VR = Idioventricular rhythm

Heart Block: 1 HB = 1st degree heart block
            2 HB = 2nd degree heart block
            3 HB = 3rd degree heart block

Heart Sounds:
N = S1, S2, S3, S4
M = Murmur
R = Rub
C = Click

Pacemaker:
E = Epicardial
TP = Transcutaneous pacemaker
TVP = Transvenous pacemaker
P = Permanent
ICD = Internal Cardiodefibrillator
ICDP = Internal Cardiodefibrillator - pacing

Edema:
1+ = Trace
2+ = Moderate
3+ = Pitting
4+ = Marked

Capillary refill:
1 = Normal (<3 seconds)
2 = Slow
3 = Blanched
4 = Mottled

Skin Color:
Pl = Pink
PA = Pallor
CY = Cyanotic
MT = Mottled

Turgor:
H = Hydrated
D = Dehydrated
M = Moist
D = Dry

Temp:
W = Warm
C = Cool

Pulses:
1+ = Palpable, intermittent

FIGURE 10.7 Since the spaces to document assessment results on the flow sheet were small, the margins typically contained the key words to describe the results of the physical assessment. Each word was represented by an abbreviation that could be entered in the designated space. This is the precursor to the electronic health record drop-down menu of typical choices for patient assessment results.

to which paper forms would be relocated to the thinned chart, but as often happens with human error, there would invariably be important documents accidentally relegated to the thinned chart resulting in time-consuming searches to retrieve these data. An additional aspect of the thinned chart was the hope that the thinned chart did not become misplaced if the patient was transferred from one unit to another during the hospital stay.

All units had a designated space where the paper charts were supposed to be kept. However, because the same paper chart was used by every discipline with contact with that patient, the chart was inevitably never where it was supposed to be. Additionally, if one person was using the chart, it was inaccessible to another who needed to use it. Lost charts or portions of charts are mostly eliminated as a problem with the electronic records. Time is saved looking for misplaced records because one only needs to sign on to a computer and any chart that is needed will be instantly accessible. EHR systems in many facilities are still accompanied by a streamlined version of a paper chart, which will contain records that need a signature from the patient or family, such as consents.

(a)

(b)

FIGURE 10.8   (a) Assessment results were usually documented on the back of the flow sheet. The aforementioned is an example of pain documentation. The spaces are completed using the numbered choices on the bottom and left side of the grid. (b) Skin-assessment documentation on a paper flow sheet. There were sections and spaces on the back of the flow sheet that corresponded to all body systems. All of the results were visible at the same time, so that it was easy to discern the patient's *story*.   (Continued)

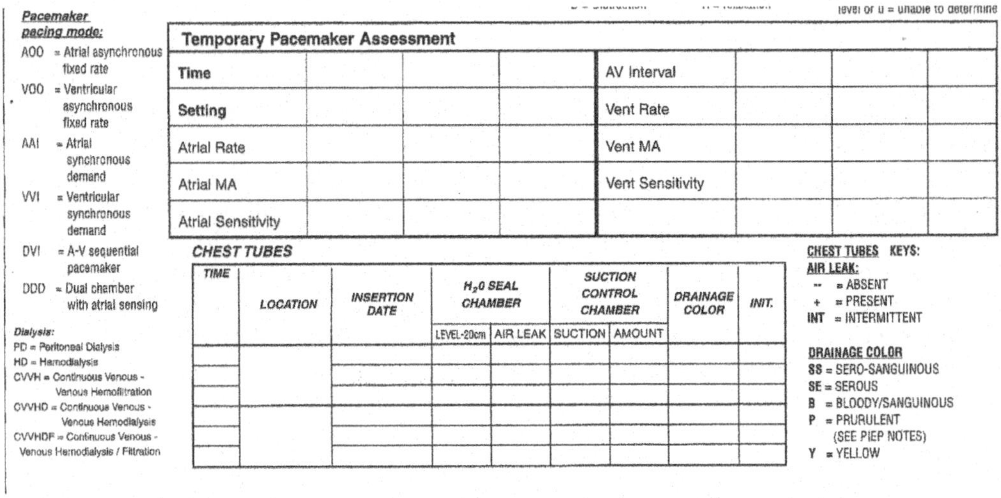

Pacemaker pacing mode:				
AOO = Atrial asynchronous fixed rate				

Temporary Pacemaker Assessment

				AV Interval		
Time				AV Interval		
Setting				Vent Rate		
Atrial Rate				Vent MA		
Atrial MA				Vent Sensitivity		
Atrial Sensitivity						

Pacemaker pacing mode:
AOO = Atrial asynchronous fixed rate
VOO = Ventricular asynchronous fixed rate
AAI = Atrial synchronous demand
VVI = Ventricular synchronous demand
DVI = A-V sequential pacemaker
DDD = Dual chamber with atrial sensing

Dialysis:
PD = Peritoneal Dialysis
HD = Hemodialysis
CVVH = Continuous Venous - Venous Hemofiltration
CVVHD = Continuous Venous - Venous Hemodialysis
CVVHDF = Continuous Venous - Venous Hemodialysis / Filtration

CHEST TUBES

TIME	LOCATION	INSERTION DATE	H₂0 SEAL CHAMBER		SUCTION CONTROL CHAMBER	DRAINAGE COLOR	INIT.
			LEVEL-20cm	AIR LEAK	SUCTION	AMOUNT	

CHEST TUBES KEYS:
AIR LEAK:
-- = ABSENT
+ = PRESENT
INT = INTERMITTENT

DRAINAGE COLOR
SS = SERO-SANGUINOUS
SE = SEROUS
B = BLOODY/SANGUINOUS
P = PRURULENT
(SEE P/EP NOTES)
Y = YELLOW

(c)

FIGURE 10.8 (*Continued*) (c) Pacemaker documentation on a paper flow sheet.

With paper-based records, additional forms for documentation were developed to handle specific pieces of information. Often these forms were designed to meet the documentation requirements of the various regulatory bodies. They were a convenient method of collecting all related information together in one place. Examples of this documentation included restraint forms, skin assessment/pressure ulcer forms, falls risk assessment, and MARs. These additional forms would often be kept on the clipboard with the flow sheet. The presence of the forms at the bedside served as a reminder to the nurse that this documentation needed to be completed.

Another form that was typically employed was a cardstock *Kardex*. A separate form was created for each patient on admission with the basic information of name, date of admission, age, and diagnosis. As diagnostic tests or procedures were ordered and completed, the Kardex would be updated with this information. There was space to record all IV lines that the patient had, including when they were inserted and removed. Likewise, catheters and any devices were recorded as well as any significant events that had occurred. This constituted the patient's story and at a glance it was easy to see the trajectory of the hospital stay. Many EHRs have a screen that serves a similar function.

10.4.6 Elements of Nursing Documentation

Nursing workflow is complex. Nurses get interrupted and have to shift to different tasks. They are recording vital signs, assessment data, and events continuously at the same time that they are providing care for the patient, interacting with the family, communicating with other disciplines, and making sense of trends in vital signs and other parameters to determine if the patient is stable. If asked to design the ideal computer-based documentation system, most nurses would say that the primary requirement is that the system must be very easy to use for inputting large amounts of data frequently and that it is visually friendly to enable quick and accurate interpretation of the vital signs trends and other data that have been entered. It should not be burdensome to enter information and there should be built-in reminders of critical information that has not been documented.

As described elsewhere in this text, the nursing activities involved with caring for a critically ill patient might be compared to the activities of a pilot flying a plane. Both are responsible for lives, whether a patient or passengers and both are exposed to large quantities of ever-changing data displayed on monitors. Trends need to be noted with decisions made about air speed and altitude or blood pressure and CI. Both the pilot and the nurse are functioning in an environment where focus and critical thinking are essential. Given this analogy, it should not be surprising that the nursing expression for a patient who is deteriorating rapidly is "crashing," certainly an aviation term for a very undesirable situation as well. Knowing that it is also important to record the data accurately while understanding the performance level that is expected of the pilot and the nurse, it seems doubtful that anyone would conclude that having either of these professionals frantically typing numbers on a keyboard is a viable solution. At the very least, the passengers on the plane and the desperately ill patient in the bed and their loved ones would want the person in whose hands their well-being rests to be able to focus on the important priorities.

When the nurse admits a new patient, required documentation includes completing a number of screening tools and risk assessments. This includes evaluating the patient's risk of developing a pressure ulcer or of falling. These assessments are performed when the patient is first admitted and will then be repeated every shift for critically ill patients. Additionally, there needs to be documentation that complies with regulatory bundles for a select group of target conditions, including acute coronary syndrome (ACS), stroke bundle, sepsis bundle, heart failure, and venous thromboembolism (VTE) prevention bundle.

The nursing assessment is a physical examination of a patient and includes all body systems. Many nurses organize their assessment as a *head-to-toe* approach. A complete assessment will be performed by the nurse when the patient is first admitted and again at the beginning of every shift. Depending on the stability of the patient and whether the patient is in a critical care unit or a medical-surgical unit, this assessment may be repeated every 4 or 6 hours.

Information entered by nurses into the record contributes to determining whether the evidence-based core measures have been met for patients with stroke, ACS, certain orthopedic procedures, and heart failure. The assessments also include completing standardized tools to determine the patient's risk of developing certain HACs. The Hendricks Tool looks at the patient's risk of falling—and the Braden Scale evaluates the patient's risk of developing a pressure ulcer.

Nursing documentation is different from that of other disciplines in that it is both episodic and dynamic. Similar to physicians and other health professionals, nurses perform initial assessments at the beginning of a shift according to systems. This is an example of where the documentation is episodic in that the nurse will complete the assessment and then record the results. The bigger challenge that nurses face in the critical care setting is the need to record vital signs at a very high frequency on a regular basis as well as intermittently whenever there is a change in the patient's status. Most critical care units traditionally had a paper *flow sheet* of some design. While the actual design would vary from hospital to hospital, there was a consistent similarity. Many hospitals had columns across the top with spaces labeled for the various parameters that were routinely documented as well as blank spaces that can be labeled with specific information that needed to be recorded for a specific patient.

10.4.7 Computer-Based Documentation

All documentation is moving inevitably toward an electronic version, which is a positive evolution. However, the objective needs to design an EHR that is as easy to use and view as a paper-based flow sheet but that utilizes the full capability of a computer-based record. Many of the issues that need to be resolved with computer-based documentation are issues that are inherent to providing safe care to patients regardless of the type of medical record that is in use. These issues and problems were solved in a particular way when the technology only supported a paper record and the only way to communicate from one department to another was telephone, fax, or scanning. The problems have not changed but the options for solving them have changed dramatically with the advent of the EHR.

The greatest challenge in improving the EHR lies in the area of data entry by the frontline professional. Utilizing the full capability of computer technology should result in data entry that is easier and faster and less stressful. However, technology, when used without auto entry of vital sign data, has increased the difficulty of documenting and increased the time spent in completing this task. In addition, the visual appearance of those data once entered needs to be easy to look at. There needs to be a priority placed on replicating the advantage that a flow sheet had in pulling all critical data together into a useable format. Decisions about patient therapy are made based on the results of these data and it is critical that both entry and retrieval are seamless.

Another challenge to address is entering data in an emergency situation, such as a cardiac arrest or *code*. Even in facilities with auto entry of data into the computer from the monitor, all of the data that need to be documented in a code do not originate from the cardiac monitor. As part of the code process, emergency medications are given from the ER Cart, based on protocols of advanced cardiac life support (ACLS) or verbal orders. There will be other activities that occur, such as starting new IV lines. Some EHR systems have code programs available, some of which align with the American Heart Association ACLS protocols. However, other EHR systems do not and a facility needs to decide whether to have staff attempt to enter data electronically or to default to a paper-based code sheet. The subsequent decision then becomes whether to include the paper code sheet as a permanent part of the record or to consider it as an unofficial worksheet and to require the nurse to transfer the data from the code sheet into the EHR. The current status is mixed at present, but this is a huge opportunity to improve on the computer-based capability of keeping up when data entry is rapid and complex and must be accurately timed.

Paper records always presented issues of legibility as well as omissions of recording the date and time with certain entries. On many occasions, hospitals have been cited by regulatory body surveyors for missing dates and times. Conversion to an electronic record instantly eliminates both of these issues because all notes are legible with the date and time is automatically entered by the computer.

One of the current disadvantages of many EHRs is that they do not display the data in a visually friendly manner on the screen. It is sometimes necessary to scroll up or down or to click between screens to find the desired data. What the nurse needs to see is all assessment and labs in one location without having to scroll up or down too excessively or without having to click between screens (Figure 10.9a and b).

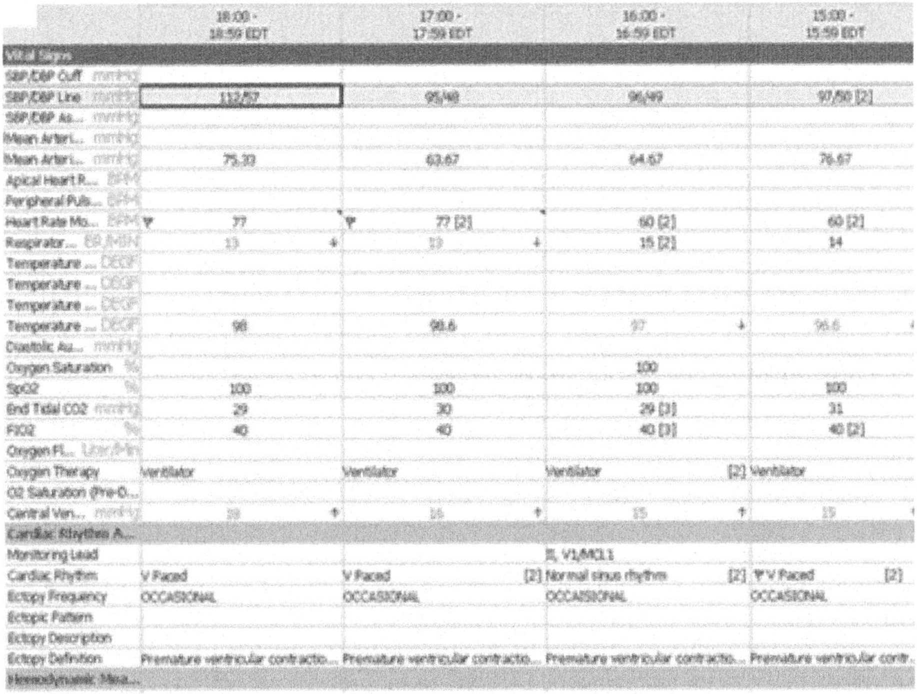

(a)

FIGURE 10.9 (a) Vital signs as displayed in one version of an electronic health record. Although each entry is tagged by the computer with the exact time that it was entered, the data are displayed in a 1 hour window, for example, 10:00–10:59.   (*Continued*)

	18:00 - 18:59 EDT		17:00 - 17:59 EDT		16:00 - 16:59 EDT		15:00 - 15:59 EDT	
ardiac Rhythm A...								
fonitoring Lead					II, V1/MCL1			
ardiac Rhythm	V Paced		V Paced		[2] Normal sinus rhythm		[2] ▼ V Paced	[2]
ctopy Frequency	OCCASIONAL		OCCASIONAL		OCCAISIONAL		OCCASIONAL	
ctopic Pattern								
ctopy Description								
ctopy Definition	Premature ventricular contractio...		Premature ventricular contractio...		Premature ventricular contractio...		Premature ventricular contr...	
lemodynamic Mea...								
entral Ven... mmHg	18	↑	16	↑	15	↑	15	↑
ight Atrial ... mmHg								
VSP/RVDP mmHg								
ASP/PADP mmHg	45/24	↑	43/21	↑	42/18	↑	39/24	↑
ulmonary ... mmHg								
ulmonary ... mmHg								
eft Atrial Pr... mmHg								
/Min/Square Meter	3.9/2.2	↓	3.5/2.0	↓	3.7/2.1	↓	5.0/2.9	
cvO2 %								
ivO2 %	79		74		70		79	
VEDV... mL/mL/m2								
ight Ventricular ... %								
c ka-m/ka-ro/m2|								

(b)

FIGURE 10.9 (*Continued*) (b) The visual appearance of displaying the physiologic data in the EHR is an important factor in being able to quickly ascertain the patient's status. Having to click between screens and scroll up or down to find information makes it difficult to correlate different parameters and events into the same timeframe.

The goal is to create a user-friendly, functional EHR that employs the best features of a computer, while not losing the advantages that worked well with the paper record. It is important to look at the goals of the documentation and the requirements and not necessarily try to mimic the paper chart. However, a sometimes overlooked priority needs to be the ease of entering data by the frontline professionals as well as being able to easily look at that data during real time while the patient is hospitalized.

10.5 Nursing Priorities for an Electronic Health Record

The concern of the critical care nurse, as the frontline user of the electronic medical record, is the ease of entering data as well as the ability to quickly retrieve the data so that it are useful for making decisions in real time about the patient's status. Data entry needs to be easy, with the capability of immediate data viewing in a visually logical format.

With a paper system, data entry was relatively easy. The nurse only had to glance up at the monitor and quickly write the numbers down on the flow sheet, which was typically organized in such a way that the spaces for the numbers followed consecutively in the same order as they appeared on the monitor. Performing the same activity, recording vital signs is very different when using a computer. Every entry has to be typed into the computer. It is often necessary to scroll to a different part of the screen while recording the numbers, because unlike paper, the entire form is not visible at the same time. It is often necessary to not only scroll but also click through different screens. The action of typing is different from the action of writing. Very few people have the ability to easily type numbers without looking at the keyboard. Finding the numbers on the keyboard requires greater attention than finding a space on a flow sheet and filling in a number. Since it takes more attention and effort to type in the numbers, it becomes necessary for the nurse to look away from the monitor for a longer period of time (Figure 10.10a and b).

To again use the analogy of a pilot, requiring the nurse to document vital signs by typing every number would be the equivalent of requiring a pilot to not only fly the plane but record every setting on every instrument, using a keyboard. This would never be acceptable, certainly not to those who are passengers on the plane. It should not be acceptable that a nurse who is taking care of a critically ill patient is required to type every vital sign, while at the same time continuously observing the patient and also providing nursing care.

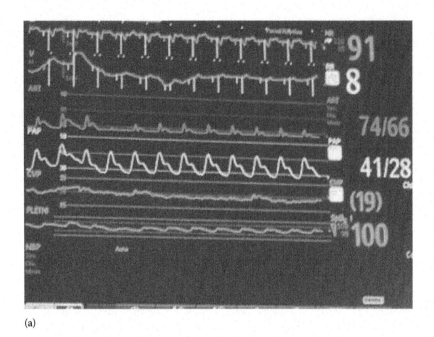

(a)

	18:59 EDT	17:59 EDT	16:59 EDT	15:59 EDT	14:59 EDT	13:59 EDT
Hemodynamic Mea...						
Central Ven... mmHg	18 ↑	16 ↑	15 ↑	15 ↑	15 ↑	12 [2] ↑
Right Atrial ... mmHg						
RVSP/RVDP mmHg						
PASP/PADP mmHg	45/24 ↑	43/21 ↑	42/18 ↑	39/24 ↑	37/28 ↑	36/23 [2] ↑
Pulmonary ... mmHg						
Pulmonary ... mmHg						
Left Atrial Pr... mmHg						
sr/Min/Square Meter	3.9/2.2 ↓	3.5/2.0 ↓	3.7/2.1 ↓	5.0/2.9 ↓	4.4/2.5	4.2/2.4 [2] ↓
ScvO2 %						
SvO2 %	79	74	70	79	100 ↑	100 [2] ?
RVEDV... mL/mL/m2						
Right Ventricular ... %						
RC... kg-m/kg-m/m2						
R g-m/beat/g-m/m2						
P... dynes/sec/cm-5						
LC... kg-m/kg-m/m2						
LVS... g-m/g-m/m2						
K /beat/mL/m2/beat	51/0 ↓	57/0 ↓	80/0 ↓	53/0 ↓	43/0 ↓	42/0 [2] ↓
IS... dynes/sec/cm-5	1,176/2,085	1,090/1,907	1,074/1,892	987/1,701	1,109/1,952	1,041/1,822 [2]
Intra-abdom... mmHg						
SVV %						
Mechanical Ventila...						
◁ Mechanical Ven...						
Ventilator Mode	(PRVC) Pressure Regulated Volu...	(PRVC) Pressure Regulated Volu...	(PRVC) Pressure Regulated ... [3]	(PRVC) Pressure Regulated...	(PRVC) Pressure Regulated Volu...	(PRVC) Pressure Regulated Volume Co...
FIO2 - Ventilator			40	40		
FIO2 %	40	40	40 [3]	40 [2]	70	70 [2]
Breath Type			VC (Volume Control)			
Ventilat... BR/MIN	12	12	12 [3]	12	12	12
Tidal Volume... mL	600	600	600 [3]	600	600	600
Positive ... CMH2O	5	5	5 [3]	5	5	5
Pressure... CMH2O						

(b)

FIGURE 10.10 (a) Data about the patient's hemodynamic status are displayed on the cardiac monitor as waveforms with numeric values. (b) An electronic health record display of a patient's hemodynamic parameters.

The technology for effortless data entry exists. It is reasonable that hospitals, with a finite amount of funds to spend, felt some pressure to go live with the basic computer-based capability to meet the requirements of meaningful use. There was also a time constraint to accomplish this quickly in order to meet the deadlines. But going forward, auto entry of data from monitors and life-sustaining devices directly into the EHR needs to be a priority in the next round of decisions. In the long term, the hospital will benefit from this wise use of resources. The time that will be gained by the nurse not having to type copious amounts of data will help to pull the nurse away from the computer screen and back to the bedside. This will undoubtedly benefit patients and their families, resulting in improved customer satisfaction scores.

Research studies have supported that increased staffing ratios result in fewer HACs and in higher satisfaction scores. This translates directly into dollars of reimbursement for the hospital. Implications for future research include investigating whether the same benefit occurs when staffing ratios are *virtually* increased by decreasing the nonpatient care activities of the nurse by increasing the capability of computer documentation.

10.5.1 Data Entry

Data entry with a flow sheet involved picking up a pen and writing every single vital sign, assessment, or event that occurred with the patient. Recording by hand is a relatively fast and easy way to record information. In a critical situation when a patient is *crashing* and a great deal of information needs to be recorded quickly and at very frequent intervals, handwriting is easy. With a computer, data entry in a critical care setting can be seamless if the data are automatically downloaded from all of the monitors and devices that are in use or it can be a nightmare if the nurse has to type every number of every vital sign and make sure that it is in the correct space and repeat this every hour at least and more frequently if the patient is unstable. To compare typing with writing, undoubtedly typing is faster if one is free-texting information in a narrative form. However, if the data entry involves looking up at a monitor and then down at a computer keyboard for the numbers, writing is faster. Typing in dozens of numbers and scrolling to the next empty box take longer. And while the legibility issues that are present with writing are nonexistent with typing, the flipside is that typographical errors or *typos* can occur quite easily when trying to type on a keyboard. At best, the nurse realizes the error and has to spend extra time backspacing and reentering the numbers, and at worst, the typo will be undetected and the vital sign will be erroneous.

When purchasing decisions are made about the type of EHR to install, hospitals have options as far as documentation packages for the critical care units in the facility. One option is to have the EHR as a freestanding entity devoid of any connection with the monitors and devices in the room. With this disconnected version, all data that are generated must be typed into the computer. The second and far better option is to ensure that the cardiac monitors in the rooms are able to communicate with whatever EHR system has been selected. This method proves far more accurate than handwriting and is faster and includes more data points. A frequency is selected and the monitor sends data to the computer at those intervals. Any information that is needed immediately or *stat* can be sent by the nurse activating a button to send those data to the record in between scheduled downloads. The best systems also allow other equipment in use in the patient's room to be sent to the monitoring system and then sent on to the computer. Current technology for monitors, infusion pumps, and life-support devices almost universally supports being integrated with a variety of different EHR systems. The biggest barrier to implementing a fully integrated EHR system is usually cost. Some of the cost barrier is related to the pressure behind meeting meaningful use targets by the federally mandated deadlines.

Reimbursement of millions of dollars is dependent on meeting these milestones and hospitals cannot afford to lag behind. Other documentation-related reimbursement triggers include documentation by the nurse and physician on measures to prevent VTE, measures to prevent readmission of patients with a diagnosis of heart failure within 30 days of hospital discharge, documentation on the presence or absence of a pressure ulcer on admission, and the measures taken to prevent progression to a reportable stage. Unfortunately, at present, there are no reimbursement bonuses that trigger on the nurse's ease of documenting reams of vital signs. However, it should be considered that malpractice judgments for or against a hospital, costing millions in compensation, might well rest on the correct and timely documentation of vital signs to support the defense that the patient was being adequately monitored. In addition, it can also be argued that the time that the nurse does not have to spend in recording routine physiologic data can be better spent in providing direct care for the patient and family and documenting on the bundles that will directly result in reimbursement.

There are challenges with the visual display of many computer-based systems in that due to the screen size and other demographic data that are continuously displayed typically on bands across the top or sides of the screen, the area of screen available to display the physiologic parameters is limited. The information that is available for viewing at any one time is only a portion of the total data entered. With some systems, moving between dates of service in the hospital is cumbersome, with only the most recent dates immediately available. It is necessary to enter other search parameters in order to find the desired date. Clicking between screens often causes a loss of continuity or train of thought as new data are displayed and trigger a response. Font size is important and must be adjustable. What we see affects what we think.

There are some systems where the new orders that are written by the physician need to be viewed and acknowledged by the nurse, prior to implementation. This is analogous to the actions that were previously required with a paper chart. The physician would write the order and sign it, but the nurse would need to review it and transcribe any medications or order lab tests and would then indicate that this had been completed by marking a line under the order and signing, dating, and timing when this was done.

With the EHR, the nurse also needs to review the order and then electronically *sign* it before it is activated. However, instead of the order remaining together, as soon as the order has been signed off by the nurse, the individual components are reorganized into the categories where they belong. For example, lab tests that are ordered move to the lab test section of the orders and medications move to the medication section of the orders. In some ways, this is very logical because it keeps like information together. However, it can be confusing as well since the nurse cannot always see at a glance the most recent orders in their entirety. Task reminders usually display as a list, but it is not always accurate or up to date.

The possibilities for wireless communication are interesting. One current example is the capability of *smart* infusion pumps. These pumps are preprogrammed with a library of medications and include information about the usual concentration and dose. When the nurse initiates an infusion of a medication, he or she enters the name, concentration, and dose. The pump will confirm that the set parameters are within the normal dosing parameters of the particular medication. However, the pumps have the capability to be even *smarter* than this. They are also designed to communicate with the EHR, which would enable them to download the data about the medication infusion directly into the EHR. At any time that the nurse changes the rate and dose of the medication, this information would also be entered directly into the EHR. However, the capability of many pumps goes even further, in that they can communicate with the pharmacy through bar coding. With this function operational, once the order has been entered into the EHR and communicated to the pharmacy for profiling, prior to administering the medication, the nurse scans the patient's identification bracelet, the bag of medication, and then the particular infusion pump. This will automatically enter the correct dose and rate into the pump, without the nurse entering those data, and the pump will then communicate with the EHR to download the information. When updates are available for the infusion pump library, it is not necessary to program each pump individually. Instead, this information can be transmitted wirelessly to all pumps in the facility. At present, there is varying utilization of the full capability of the smart pumps across different facilities (Figure 10.11).

10.5.2 Reports

The ability to run reports was not possible with a paper chart. Previously, with paper, data had to be obtained manually, by having an actual human being comb through the chart to find the desired information. This was not only laborious, but it also often resulted in missed data items.

With an electronic record, the number and types of reports that can be run are almost limitless in both scope and detail. For example, as new initiatives become active, such as the access to the Patient Portal, things that have to be documented to show *meaningful use* and ensure that reimbursement is forthcoming can be easily assessed. Reports can be run to show whether the required documentation for required initiatives such as the Patient Portal, the VTE prevention bundle, or the heart failure core measures has been correctly documented. It is even possible to run reports on the documentation of specific

FIGURE 10.11 **(See color insert.)** *Smart* medication infusion pumps and cardiac monitors are capable of communicating directly with the electronic health record (EHR) to download the dose and rate. If this capability is not enabled by the system, the nurse is responsible for typing every number into the EHR, usually every hour.

individuals as a form of performance appraisal. Reports can be run that reflect hospital performance as a whole or that reflect a specific unit or even the documentation performance of individual practitioners.

10.5.3 Data Retrieval: We have Entered the Data but Where Did It Go?

Once the information has been documented, the next challenge is how to quickly find the information when it is needed. One advantage of computer-based technology is the ability to pull data that are entered in one screen to populate into another screen, if the same information is applicable to both. An example of this is medications that are administered as continuous IV infusions. The nurse will document the dose per minute or per hour and will also document the rate that it is infusing at in mL/h to deliver that dose. With most systems, when this is documented in the eMAR, the volume will automatically populate into the intake/output section so that it will be included in the hourly volume totals, without the nurse having to manually enter it in that screen. This allows for the dose of the medication that is administered to be documented as a medication but also for the volume that it is diluted in and administered in to cross-populate into the area for documenting intake.

One of the most promising aspects of the EHR is the ability to pull data from multiple patients' charts and assemble it into usable reports. This was not possible with a paper chart without exerting a tremendous amount of effort. To accomplish what takes several keystrokes to complete with a computer-based system would have taken hours of human labor to pull this same information from the paper-based records. It was not feasible to do this with any regularity, and in general, this type of data collection from paper-based systems was usually conducted as part of a research project. With the EHR, it is possible to look at specific quality indicators to determine if the documentation of care being delivered meets the standards specified by the regulatory bodies. Beyond looking at data reflecting groups of patients, reports can be generated to look at a specific nurse's documentation across time. Any quality indicator can be looked at, for example, documenting according to bundles for pressure ulcer prevention or fall risk or whether the nurse has been correctly scanning medications and verifying patient identity with medication administration.

Ordinarily, references to data retrieval refer to data that have been collected in the past and are retrieved at a later point in time. However, in the critical care setting, data retrieval also refers to the immediate need to review related vital sign and physiologic parameters together to detect trends and influence decisions about therapy. An effective EHR needs to be equally capable of recording data and retrieving it in real time as well as looking at trends for root cause analysis at a later point in time.

For a specific patient, data retrieval will be used as a means of piecing together the results of tests and assessments in coming to a diagnosis. It can also be used to determine what happened in the event of an incident. For groups of patients, data retrieval can be used to determine overall compliance with specific documentation requirements such as for the bundles or in meeting the requirements of regulatory agencies. Computerized systems add an interesting possibility to data retrieval in that it is no longer necessary to have direct access to a paper chart to glean information. Instead, patient data can be retrieved from a remote location.

10.6 Literature Review

Many of the research studies on computer-based documentation and EHRs are relatively recent, coinciding with the increased adoption of this technology in response to government incentives. This is new area of study for nurse researchers as well as a lively topic for editorial commentaries in the journals. Several studies have looked at the issue of standardizing nursing terminology and data entries in order to be able to include information documented by nurses in *big data*. Other studies have addressed the role that user acceptance of an EHR plays in the success of implementation. Several studies also looked at whether adopting an EHR would result in improved documentation of content that is required by regulatory agencies.

"Big data" refers to a large complex data set that yields substantially more information when analyzed as compared to the information achieved with smaller sets of the same data that are not integrated. In the *Online Journal of Nursing Informatics*, Keenan (2014) made the point that little to none of the data that nurses currently enter into EHRs can be used in *big data* analysis, due to the fact that nursing data are not standardized and therefore not interoperable. Interoperable data contain data elements that are defined, measured, and retrievable in the exact same format. In contrast, EHRs across different organizations have been assembled and tailored to meet the unique needs of each organization. While there might be good reasons for this in terms of making an EHR work for a particular organization, it compromises the ability to compare data across organizations, which is necessary for big data.

Englebright et al. (2013) also looked at the importance of standardization in order for nursing activities to be available for retrieval and inclusion in big data. They wrote that it is necessary that terminology needs to be standardized and to that end, they looked at developing a definition of basic nursing care for the hospitalized adult patient. They identified nine basic activities that were then incorporated into the EHR. Their conclusion was that this project represents a first step in capturing meaningful data elements that are specific to nursing.

Keenan et al. (2012) tested the hypothesis that Hands-on Automated Nursing Data System, which provides a *big picture summary*, could be implemented uniformly across diverse settings and result in positive plan of care data outcomes across time. They concluded that it is possible to effectively standardize the capture and visualization of useful big picture healthcare information across diverse settings. They identified that there is a lack of plan of care tools, based on standardized terminologies and processes, in today's EHRs. They also stated that a review of eight of the best EHRs in the country showed that individual clinicians spend too much time sifting through raw data getting a true picture of the patient's situation. Their conclusion was that this sifting wastes clinicians' cognitive resources and makes it difficult to see higher-order issues. Completing forms is a burden rather than a useful tool that will result in better patient care.

Scherb et al. (June 2013) have described what EHR meaningful use requirements mean for nursing clinical information system (CIS) development. They discussed that the CIS in many hospitals has a number of critical design inadequacies that constrain the meaningful use of nursing data to ensure quality outcomes for patients and data-based maturing of the nursing profession. They point out that to address this shortcoming, interoperable clinical nursing data must be documented in a properly integrated and operational CIS and must be retrievable and stored in data repositories for analysis and reports. In their opinion, an unintended consequence of the rush to develop, market, and adopt software and CISs that are compliant with meaningful use requirements may actually obstruct the development or refinement of a fully integrated and effective hospital CIS, resulting in less effective systems. The focus on meaningful use underscores that improved healthcare is more than just adopting technology. It is also the adoption of technology for use and sharing of information to support quality clinical decisions and outcomes. In the absence of standardized nursing nomenclature, nursing data that are important for the evaluation of quality and effectiveness will be precluded from analysis by local clinicians and administrators and from inclusion in large national EHR data sets. They conclude by observing that nurses document the implementation of physician orders, actions for which there is a charge to the consumer, and other externally mandated data, while limiting and compromising the documentation of nursing care data. In many settings, nursing electronic documentation does not represent the knowledge-based nursing care that contributes to the quality of healthcare.

A survey was conducted by Estrada and Dunn (2012) to obtain feedback from registered nurses as end users of standardized nursing terminology for care planning in an EHR. Revisions to the care plan terminology were completed as part of an evidence-based project by nurses at one facility. The premise is that the plan of care in the electronic record is expected to offer nurses the ability to communicate the needs of the patient and assess outcomes of care. However, the survey findings indicated weaknesses warranting further exploration to identify changes needed to improve care planning documentation.

In a study published in 2013, Hamad and Cline explored acceptance factors and barriers associated with providers' intentions to adopt EHRs by provider type. Perceived management support, provider involvement, and adequate training were identified by participants as being acceptance facilitators. Perceived lack of usefulness and provider autonomy were seen as barriers.

In a study published in 2014, Don O'Mahony et al. explored South African nurses' knowledge, attitudes, and perceptions regarding information and communication technology (ICT) to inform the future implementation of electronic medical record systems. Their premise was that individual user acceptance is a crucial factor in successful ICT implementation. In this study, the nurses identified many challenges with the current recording methods; however, they were supportive of installing an EMR in the community health setting. They concluded that the nurses' knowledge about EMR, positive attitudes to ICT, and personal use of ICT devices increase the likelihood of successful EMR implementation.

Documenting specific aspects of care, especially relating to mandates from regulatory agencies or to reimbursement issues, such as CMS list of *never events*, has always been a challenge with paper documentation. Li and Korniewicz (2013) tracked the EHR documentation of pressure ulcers on a medical-surgical unit and compared it to the written medical record. They found that documentation of pressure ulcers was incomplete or inaccurate in both the EHR and the written record. They concluded that the actual use of an EHR was more important for improving quality than its presence alone and that adopting an EHR without determining the correct use of it is insufficient to improve quality.

In a 2011 letter to the editor, published in *Critical Care Nurse*, Patricia Kelly commented on whether the EHR could foster better documentation of family history as an inexpensive and often underutilized genetic tool. With paper documentation, this was identified as being a long-standing problem and the hope was that the EHR would facilitate assessment and documentation. However, her observation was that for many health systems, this has not been a reality and that many EHR systems actually interfere with assessments. Her recommendation was that there should be red flags to cue important aspects of documentation.

Fowler et al. (2014) created two tools to achieve the goals of providing physicians with a way to review alternative diagnoses and improve access to relevant evidence-based library resources without disrupting established workflows. One of the tools lifted terms from standard, coded fields in the EHR and then produced a list of possible diagnoses. The physicians chose their diagnosis and were then presented with the "knowledge page," which is a collection of evidence-based library resources, which was automatically populated with search results based on the chosen diagnosis. In this study, the physicians responded positively to having access to the *knowledge page.*

The details of operating within an EHR were raised in the June 2011 issue of *Critical Care Nurse*, where Harrington and associates posed the question of attributing authorship of EHR data by persons other than the actual individual providing the care. This question addresses whether documentation is the sole responsibility of the person who provided the care or whether attestation is an acceptable solution to clinical situations where direct authorship is not possible.

Pasek et al. (2009) utilized the EHR at Children's Hospital of Pittsburgh to address the challenge of describing the role of the advanced practice nurses (APNs), in particular, the clinical nurse specialists (CNSs) in the hospital setting. They identified that evidence is necessary to support the value of the APN and the sustainability of the role and that documentation in the medical record is an important way to capture their contribution to patient care. They also identified that in their institution, virtually all disciplines had a designated space in the EHR except the APNs. They utilized the technology of the EHR to address this gap.

In the July 1, 2011, "Crucial Conversations about Optimal Design" column of the *Online Journal of Nursing Informatics*, Nancy Staggers discussed the details of the April 2011 hearing concerning the usability of EHRs. Nurses generally view EHRs as superior to paper-based systems but consider usability a significant challenge. For example, finding pertinent data in the sea of available electronic information can be a challenge. The questions that clinicians need to be able to answer include the following:

1. *What has changed on this patient over the last 2, 4, 8, 12, 24, or 48 hours?*
2. *Are these patients' vital signs/lab values trending up or down over time?*
3. *How has the change in medication affected the patient's blood pressure or pain scale rating?*
4. *What is the set of combined social, financial, and functional status information that will impact the decision to place a patient into an independent living versus a skilled nursing facility?*

The authors noted that users currently have to flip through screen after screen to find data of interest. Nurses are patient advocates coordinating care activities across the team of providers, but data for this coordination are often assembled via memory or on paper or contained in a separate note within a set of hundreds of other documentation entries in an EHR. This process is not only time consuming but it is also highly prone to error. An interesting quote that the author attributed to a clinician referred to this process as "death by keystroke."

Fleming et al. (February 2014) looked at a commercially available ambulatory EHR's impact on workflow and financial measures. They concluded that expenses increased and productivity decreased following EHR implementation, but it was not as much or as persistently as they had expected. Staffing and practice expenses increased following the EHR implementation. Productivity, volume, and net income decreased initially but recovered to close to preimplementation levels after 12 months. They recommend that longer-term effects still need to be examined.

An interesting study by Penoyer et al. (2014) examined what information is used by clinicians, how this information is used for patient care, and the amount of time clinicians perceive they review and document information in the EHR. A survey administered at a large, multisite healthcare system was used to gather this information. Findings showed that diagnostic results and physician documents are viewed more often than documentation by nurses and ancillary caregivers. Most clinicians use the information in the EHR to understand the patient's overall condition, make clinical decisions, and communicate with other caregivers. The majority of respondents reported they spend 1 to 2 hours per day reviewing information and 2 to 4 hours documenting in the EHR. In contrast to this, bedside nurses spend 4 hours per day documenting, with much of this time spent completing detailed forms seldom viewed by others. The aim of this study was to determine what information from the EHR is viewed and how that information is used by different types of clinicians. They concluded that it is essential to engage clinical practitioners with the designers of these documents to meet clinicians' need as consumers. Creating views of data that are concise, relevant, and meaningful for clinicians may augment their ability to make clinical decisions.

As facilities scramble to demonstrate that they are meeting the key components of meaningful use, an article by Galbraith (2013) questioned the importance of what constitutes meaningful use. As an example, he cited the Patient Portal, which is intended to increase patients' participation in their own care. One core objective of stage 1 meaningful use involves healthcare providers being able to "provide patients with an electronic copy of their health information." But he points out that this doesn't take into account the digital divide between those with and without internet access. The same people caught in this digital divide are the same ones most likely to suffer from limited healthcare access and poor health outcomes. Thus, those populations who would benefit most from learning more about their health are also least likely to have access to that information, at least through the electronic format.

In the "Research with Information Technology" column in the *Online Journal of Nursing Informatics*, Topaz and Bowles (February, 2012) reviewed the mandate that by the end of 2015, healthcare providers across the United States are expected to prove they are meaningful users of certified EHR technology in ways that can be significantly measured in quality and in quantity or else they would be financially penalized when providing services for Medicare and Medicaid clients. This mandate is based on the assumption that EHRs will improve caregivers' decisions and patient outcomes. The editorial reviewed some of the shortcomings in the emerging body of research evaluating the impact of EHRs on the quality of ambulatory care.

Silver and Straub (January, 2014) in *Contemporary OB/GYN* state that it is time to insist that electronic medical records are assiduously created and carefully maintained so that they are more than just expensive versions of their paper ancestors. They suggest that caregivers need to conceptualize data entered on behalf of patients as of the highest value to their current and future health status, making accurate completion of the EHR an act of professionalism.

In an editorial in the November 2013 issue of the *American Journal of Critical Care*, Richard H. Savel and Cindy L. Munro commented on the "Promise and Pitfalls of the Electronic Health Record." They commented that many of the problems facing bedside critical care practitioners who worked with EHRs in the mid-1990s remain largely unchanged today. Their conclusion is that interfaces between systems should be enhanced to decrease the amount of data bedside nurses need to enter into the computer. Bedside monitors should interface directly with EHRs and *smart pumps* should enter data in a similar fashion allowing bedside nurses to do what they do best: provide care to patients. Finally, they make the salient observation that systems whose poor design and flaws are obvious to the bedside nurse may seem to work perfectly from the perspective of hospital leaders.

10.7 Implications for Future Research

Based on the results of current research studies as well as information about challenges that have been observed in the various types of EHRs, several topics seem to lend themselves to requiring further study.

From a critical care perspective, the question of optimum methods of data entry, particularly in situations of patient instability, is of paramount importance. The technology exists to allow for many devices to communicate with the EHR and download data directly into the record. However, since this is a relatively expensive addition to the computer-based system, ease of data entry is often not one of the most obvious priorities to hospital administrators. Therefore, research is needed to determine the impact that data entry options have on other aspects of patient care, especially those that have a positive financial benefit, such as patient satisfaction scores and documentation that reflects compliance with regulatory standards.

Studies looking at data entry options could also tie into the existing research that has demonstrated that documentation relating to content required by regulatory bodies for reimbursement, such as pressure ulcer prevention, has not shown the compliance that was originally expected with EHR implementation. There have always been issues with this documentation on paper, but it was hoped that adherence to the standards would improve with an electronic system of documentation. However, it would be intriguing to look at whether the poor performance in documenting on the standards was related to the style of data entry for vital signs and other physiologic parameters. It would be interesting to see if there is any correlation between manual data entry via keyboard versus auto data entry on the compliance with other aspects of documentation. This would then tie back to looking again at ease of data entry as being a crucial component for all other potentially advantageous pieces of electronic documentation to fall into place.

An informal observation that has been made in many institutions after they have *gone live* with their electronic documentation system is that the nurses are suddenly spending less time interacting directly with their patients and more time staring at the computer screen. The contention is that the computer demands more attention than was necessary with paper-based documentation. It has been stated that the nurse is more likely to continue looking at the screen or the keyboard while talking to the patient as opposed to maintaining eye contact and just glancing briefly at the paper record to make the entry. Anecdotally, many nurses have commented on the fact that they feel that the computer pulls them away from their patients. There is an opportunity here for research studies to determine whether this is actually the case or just a perception. Based on the results, follow-up studies would be indicated to look at the specific barriers and evaluate which methods are the most effective in addressing these issues.

Research studies on nurse–patient ratios have demonstrated that increased staffing ratios result in fewer HACs such as infections or falls and in higher satisfaction scores, all of which translates directly into dollars of reimbursement for the facility. An interesting topic to investigate is whether the same benefit occurs when staffing ratios are *virtually* increased by reducing the nonpatient care–related activities of the nurse. This would also include looking at strategies that improve the user interface capabilities of the EHR to make the data entry easier and less time consuming for the nurse.

As the technology advances and improvements are made in the design of the EHRs, attention needs to be paid to the appearance of the screens and the different ways that data can be displayed. Research is needed to determine the best visual cues for observing and processing information. This research could correlate the way that the brain processes information with the optimum appearance of the computer screen

10.8 Electronic Documentation: The Good, the Bad, and the Potential

Going forward, the potential for computer-based documentation and a truly electronic system are virtually limitless. Creative thinking and an understanding of patient needs and the workflow of the healthcare system can create an EHR that fully uses all of the capabilities that a computer can offer. In much the same way that the use of paper and pen for critical care documentation evolved through many different iterations, from the earliest versions on unstructured loose-leaf-type paper to a flow sheet with choices and an incorporated assessment, computer-based documentation is also evolving. The systems that will be in use 10 years from now will probably look very different from the current systems that are in use today. To use an analogy that relates the current state of electronic documentation to the evolution of phone technology, we have definitely moved beyond the era of a rotary dial telephone but are at best at the level of a *flip* phone with a built-in camera. At the very least, we should be able to anticipate that something as critically important as an EHR will be able to achieve the same level of user-friendly technology as a Smart phone.

In creating a *wish list* for the ideal EHR, the main objective would be to ensure that computer-based technology is utilized to the fullest extent of its capability, so that the EHR can be integrated seamlessly into patient care activities in such a way that it is not a barrier to providing care but, instead, facilitates and enhances this process. The move to the next version of the EHR should emulate the change that occurred when nurses first stopped documenting on loose-leaf paper and moved to a flow sheet that efficiently allowed them to document vital signs and assessments in one place and combined the best features of ease of data entry with meaningful display of data.

The current state of computer-based documentation has been driven, in large measure, by the incentive of obtaining funding for achieving a particular level of *meaningful use* from the federal government. The good news is that this has spurred many hospitals to implement a system of computerized documentation much sooner than they might otherwise have intended. The bad news is that many of the systems that have been implemented, while being successful at achieving meaningful use levels in the mandated areas, have been less developed and in fact have proven to be a barrier to delivery of patient care in other areas. Facilities have chosen different go-live options with implementing their EHR systems. Some hospitals went live with the entire facility at the same time, while others introduced the EHR, department by department. Some hospitals chose the most sophisticated system that would be able to *do everything* including communication between monitors, physiologic devices, and the EHR for automatic downloading of data, while others began only with the bare bones. Some facilities chose commercial products, while others chose to implement their own version. Based on an observation of how other cutting-edge industries evolved, it might be expected that over the next few years, there might be mergers and takeovers with the major computer-based technology providers so that there will emerge only two or three major providers. The advantage of this, overlooking the financial disarray of the companies that will be acquired or taken over, is that it should enhance the ability of EHRs in different settings to communicate more seamlessly with each other than is currently the case.

The wish list for the ideal EHR is long. But it is hard to miss the observation that other industries have applied computer-based technology in present day use that are already far beyond the capability of many of the bare-bones EHR systems in place. For example, many supermarkets have bar-code scanners that customers can use to directly scan products while shopping. On entering the store, the customer scans his or her loyalty card that is then matched to a particular scanner. While shopping, the customer scans each product selected and places it directly in the shopping bag in the cart. When the customer has finished shopping, he or she goes to one of several self-checkout registers and scans a bar code over the register screen and his or her customer card. The order items are displayed on the screen for review and the customer can pay by any means desired: cash, credit, or debit. There is no need to take the items out of the cart, place them on the belt, and then bag the order, because this has already been done while shopping. Meanwhile, the store knows exactly which items were purchased and need to be replenished on the shelves. Undoubtedly, many nurses would appreciate it if the bar-coding system implemented in many hospitals for medication administration worked as well as the system in place for buying baked beans.

An interesting conflict exists between the desire and need to customize an EHR to the needs of a particular facility and the need for at least some degree of standardization so that data can be retrieved. This was a theme of several research studies that concluded that some of the issues with nursing documentation not being available for inclusion into big data are based on the problem that much of the information that nurses document does not use standardized terminology. On the other hand, many facilities also look at the EHR and insist that the data collected and the appearance be customized to meet the needs of that particular facility. Going forward, however, it might be suspected that large-scale collaboration, as well as multisite research studies to identify the ideal components of the EHR, would be indicated to address this issue. And if, as expected, the commercial providers of EHR systems will begin to merge at some point, it would be a step in the direction of promoting some degree of standardization.

The information that is documented in the EHR can be viewed as constituting *raw data*. This includes items such as vital signs, assessment results, and narrative descriptions that the nurse enters into a free-text nursing progress note. The computer needs to be able to organize raw data more effectively so that meaningful reports and compilations of aggregate data can be obtained. It needs to not only be able to search for items that have been documented in the expected location using standardized terminology but also be able to search the entire record for key words and phrases. No areas of the electronic record should be unavailable for retrieval.

If everything on the *wish list* were ranked in order of importance, most critical care nurses would probably request that any feature that makes the EHR easier to use, so that the nurse is able to spend more time doing actual nursing care for patients, would be at the top of the list. To that end, the request for the EHR to communicate with all of the devices that have been designed to do so would be a priority. Not only does this feature decrease the workload and the frustration level of the nurse, but it also increases patient safety—smart pumps for medications, bar coding for medications, and blood products all decrease the potential for errors by adding an extra layer of patient identification and dose verification. Some facilities incorporated the device–EHR communication feature from the very beginning, while other systems did not. The result is that for critical care nurses practicing without the capability of auto entry of vital sign data, the task of entering vital signs is accomplished by typing numbers into the EHR. This is a particularly onerous process in critical care simply because of the volume and frequency of data that needs to be entered. The burden of this cannot be overemphasized. However, recognizing the challenges that currently exist, yet ceding to the temptation to truly look at the possibilities of computer-based technology, most critical care nurses would assume that when the dust settles, device/EHR communication will be a basic minimum level of performance for any computer-based system. And to push the envelope a little further, it would not be surprising if critical care nurses choose to move beyond monitor–device–EHR synchronicity and suggest that voice recognition would not be a bad next step. Based on the impact that meaningful use financial incentives have had on the rapid adoption of computer-based documentation, perhaps the next step would be to choose data entry or issues relating to ease of use as the next target for meaningful use incentives.

Assuming that we will get to a point where data entry in a critical care unit is no longer an issue in that all monitors and life-support devices will communicate directly with the EHR, the next important item on the wish list would be related to the manner of displaying the data that have been entered. To touch back on a paper flow sheet for a moment, the advantage was that it was a very efficient tool for easy entry of data as well as for viewing that data in a logical, easy-to-view format. Currently, with many EHRs, most of the vital sign data are difficult to look at, no matter how it was entered: whether by laborious typing by an irritated critical care nurse or via reasonably effortless entry directly from the monitor and devices in the room. All of this translates into the next objective, that is, the EHR should provide a view of all critically important data, including vital signs, hemodynamic parameters, critical lab values, medications delivered via continuous IV infusion, important events that have occurred lab values, medications delivered via continuous IV infusion, and important events that have occurred and are easy to look at and interpret. Data should be grouped with time synchronicity so that data pertaining to the same time period are displayed together.

A feature that computers are particularly adept at accomplishing is the ability to track required tasks that need to be completed and to identify those that have not been completed by the target deadline. Many EHRs have this feature already, but it is not always as well developed as it could be. The tasks that are displayed are not always accurate or useful and they do not always disappear when the activity has been completed. Sometimes, the same task is listed multiple times. In addition, not all activities are included in the task list. Therefore, added to the wish list would be the requirement that an accurate and useful task list needs to be incorporated into the EHR. This would be a task list that contains appropriate activities that are important and meaningful to the nurse and that disappears appropriately when the task has been completed.

During the era of paper-based documentation, there were additional forms that would be used for high-acuity situations, with one example being the *code sheets* that were used during emergencies, such as a cardiac arrest. With computer-based systems, documenting in these situations remains a challenge even with data auto entry systems. For some facilities, the decision is to convert to the original paper form during a code. Looking toward the future goal of having all documentation easily and appropriately entered into the EHR, it would be interesting to apply creative problem-solving strategies to address this issue. With current technology, there are defibrillators already on the market that will give voice prompts about the quality of cardiac compressions during a code, by interpreting data collected from the chest electrodes to sense chest movement of the patient during compressions. The defibrillator is able to instruct the rescuer to compress deeper or faster. Perhaps the EHR of the future could be triggered into a *code* mode and present a touch screen view similar to the original code sheets. The format could be modeled on the Basic Life Support and ACLS algorithms of the American Heart Association.

Similar to designing a code screen for a cardiac arrest, other scenarios could also have a specific screen designed for the data that are typically collected in such a situation. Examples of these types of scenarios could include an emergency department admission of a trauma patient, a burn unit admission of a critically burned patient, or an intensive care unit admission of a patient directly from the OR following customarily open heart surgery. By triggering an icon, the EHR would immediately present the screens for documenting these data. Data that could be automatically downloaded would begin to do so at the desired preset time interval. Assessments that need to be entered by the nurse would appear as a list of *tasks* visible on the side of the screen. Medications that are customarily administered would appear in a special location on the task bar so that the nurse would be reminded to go to the eMAR to see which medications were due or to document medications that had been given *stat*.

Improving communication between geographically separated care settings should be another priority. There should be a smooth transfer of information between the hospital, the physician or APN's office, the rehabilitation or long-term acute care centers, and home care services. The movement of a patient between the different settings should be seamless with the flow of information going easily from one location to another. Care should be taken so that the information is clearly delineated according to the setting where it is applicable, including separating different hospital admissions so that the information provided does not become overwhelming or confusing as to what is a current problem and what might have occurred and been treated and resolved on a previous hospital stay. However, in contrast, there should be a crossover feature that would allow any new information that is entered into the EHR, pertaining to the current hospital stay to trigger anything that is related in any of the communicating records from any other setting. This feature would address the issue of medication reconciliation, the challenge of keeping track of the medications that the patient was taking at home when being admitted to the hospital. Current practice is that the information on the medications that the patient is taking at home comes directly from the patient or family member when the patient is admitted to the hospital. It would be an added safety feature if this information could come directly from the EHR in the physician's office communicating with the EHR in the hospital.

The results of several studies support collaboration between designers and clinicians as being essential to creating the best EHR. But the best method to accomplish this goal has not been described. The question is raised as to whether discussion alone can accomplish this collaboration or whether more in-depth knowledge on the part of each discipline is required. Does there need to be more focus on nurses gaining a background in informatics and computer design so that they can communicate more clearly in the language that the coders will understand exactly what their priorities are, with a full understanding of what the capabilities of the hardware and software are and what it would take to take to program the desired options? Or should it be a requirement that anyone who will be involved in the design of an EHR in the application for hospital-based nursing practice or critical care nursing should spend time in an intensive care unit observing critical care nurses?

10.9 Critical Care Unit in 2025

If we fast forward to the year 2025 and take a look at the admission of an unstable, critically ill patient who has just undergone open heart surgery, it will be interesting to see how that scenario might unfold if all of the items on the *wish list* for the ideal EHR have been implemented.

The room in the cardiothoracic intensive care unit (CTICU) is ready for the patient who has already been placed on the bed in the OR. The patient will be transported to the unit by several members of the OR team, including the anesthesiologist, the nurse, the technician, and the surgeon. The CTICU nurse, who will be his primary nurse, received a report on the patient's status and the surgical procedure via her smart tablet, as well as a verbal confirmation from the OR nurse several minutes prior to the patient's arrival. In the room, all of the equipment that will be needed when the patient arrives is in place including the ventilator, the monitor for displaying his cardiac rhythm and pressure waves and pulse oximetry, SVO2, CO, and CI and core temperature. The portable computer is also in the room, and as the bed is being wheeled into the room by the OR team, the nurse scans the patient's ID bracelet, which activates the patient's EHR. He or she also scans his or her ID badge bar code, to indicate that he or she will be documenting on the patient and that the entries into the record are no longer taking place in the OR. The nurse's ID badge is matched to the CTICU and this will also trigger the time that the patient has arrived in the unit. The nurse also quickly scans the bar code on the ventilator and the monitor which will match them to the patient's EHR for wireless downloading of data.

In transit from the OR to the CTICU, the patient's ECG rhythm and arterial blood pressure were monitored via a transport monitor, which stored these data until the patient arrived in the unit and was in the proximity of the computer to transmit the data wirelessly for inclusion in the record as the final vital signs from the OR team. Once the patient's bed is in the room, the primary nurse begins to change the patient's ECG cable over from the transport monitor to the monitor in the room. When he or she has finished transferring all of the data cables to the monitor, the display will include a waveform of the ECG and a digital readout of the heart rate, an arterial waveform with a digital readout of the systolic pressure/diastolic pressure/MAP, a pulmonary artery waveform with a digital readout of the systolic pressure/diastolic pressure/mean PAPs, an SVO2, a CO, a CI, and a core temperature.

The nurse will also assess all aspects of the patient's status, utilizing a head-to-toe, system-by-system process. To enter these data into the EHR, the nurse has two choices. He or she can utilize the smart tablet where each system is displayed as part of a task list. Touching the system name will open a window with choices. The nurse will document the results of his or her assessment by touching as many of the descriptors that apply. He or she also has the ability to free-text if there is any information that he or she wants to add that does not fit into any of the available choices.

The other option for entering these data is to use the voice-recognition feature. There is a tiny, yet sensitive microphone embedded in the ID badge, with an icon that the nurse will touch to activate. As the nurse completes the assessment, he or she can simply speak the results aloud and it will be entered into the EHR. If he or she needs to begin another conversation, he or she can deactivate the microphone by again touching the icon. The microphone, while sensitive so that the nurse does not have to speak loudly, also has a very limited range, so as not to pick up room conversations. However, to also address this, as soon as the nurse is finished with his or her entry, he or she can quickly review the content for any extraneous items that were picked up but should not be included in the record. These can be deleted before being added as part of the permanent record.

The patient is also receiving four medications via continuous IV infusion. To document these medications in the EHR, the nurse scans the patient's ID, the bags, and the pumps which not only matches all of them to the orders in the electronic record to ensure that the correct medications are infusing but also signals the same information to the pharmacy for profiling and refilling purposes. By scanning, all of the medications populate into the eMAR and are already documented as being administered by the CTICU nurse. Each hour, the infusion pump will update the EHR with the dose as well as the volume being administered. The volume infused will also populate into the intake and output section of the EHR to be included with all other fluid that the patient has received that hour. If the nurse changes the dose and hourly rate of a particular medication, the pump will send the updated information to the EHR, so that it is documented at the time that it occurred. If the medication was changed because of a change in the patient's vital signs, the nurse needs to only touch an icon on the screen and the full data set will be sent to the EHR. This will allow for all aspects of the patient's status to be available for review and will make it possible to correlate any medication changes with the patient's physiological status at the time.

An unexpected, but very welcome, benefit is that since implementing the fully integrated EHR with complete bar-code scanning of the medications as well as the infusion pumps, with direct download, there has not been a single medication error involving a continuous IV infusion. The hospital's risk management department estimated that this has saved the hospital close to one million dollars, which justifies the initial financial investment that was required to implement this system.

For the first hour after the patient's arrival, the vital signs will be recorded every 15 min. The computer and the monitor have already been programmed with this frequency and will automatically download into the EHR at the specified interval. If the nurse notices something on the monitor that is unusual between these programmed downloads, he or she will touch an icon on the monitor screen and all data displayed at that moment will be downloaded. After an hour the monitor is programmed to decrease the downloading frequency to once every hour. The nurse confirms that the patient is stable enough for this by again touching an icon on the screen to reset the downloading interval to every hour. If the patient had been unstable and the nurse wished to continue recording the vital signs more frequently, he or she would have selected this frequency when the initial hour was over.

As the patient was being settled in the unit, there was a question about whether the patient was on medication for a thyroid condition prior to this hospitalization. It was not included in the admission assessment but one of the physicians thought that the patient might have been taking this medication at home. On the home screen of the EHR, there is an icon in the corner labeled, "Other Care Settings." Touching it opened a list that included other hospital stays as well as the physician's office records. Entering that portal and navigating to the section detailing the medication that had been prescribed for the patient, it was easily determined that the patient was in fact receiving thyroid replacement medication at home. This medication was then added to the medications that he or she would be receiving in the hospital. The entire process to obtain this information about the medications that he or she was on at home took a little less than 2 minutes.

Once the patient is settled, the nurse invites the patient's husband or wife and son or daughter to come and visit. This is the first time that they will be seeing the patient during the postoperative period and they are understandably anxious. The nurse is still completing the system assessment of his or her patient, but he or she is able to sit with the patient's family at the bedside to reassure them and explain what is happening. Since he or she is speaking with the family, he or she is using the smart tablet on his or her lap, rather than the voice recognition. Data entry is easy and the use of the tablet allows for more eye contact and a comfortable interaction with the family. The nurse was easily able to enter the data while still glancing at the monitor to view the patient's vital signs, as well as interacting with the family members. During the time that he or she was speaking with the family, the patient's vital signs were being entered automatically into the EHR every 15 min. The nurse was continuously watching the monitor to ensure that the vital signs were stable, but he or she did not have to record any of the information. Prior to the hospital's addition of the system for the monitor and other devices to communicate directly with the EHR, the nurse would have been typing all of the numbers displayed on the screen every 15 min, making a calm conversation with his or her patient's family virtually impossible. With the new system in place, the hospital has also seen HCAAPS scores rise dramatically, which has positively impacted Medicare and Medicaid reimbursement, by keeping the facility above all of the benchmarks set by CMS.

On top of the financial savings that occurred with the zero rate of IV medication errors and the increased reimbursement related to the higher HCAAPS scores, another benefit was a sharp decrease in HACs, such as falls and infections. It was determined that the reason for this was that the time that the nurses were not spending trying to document allowed them to spend more time providing high-quality nursing care for their patients and families. Finally, another benefit was a significant increase in employee satisfaction that resulted in a decreased turnover rate, thus decreasing orientation costs dramatically.

The tablet that the nurse was using, as he or she sat at the patient's bedside with the family, looked somewhat different than the tablets of 2015. It was thinner and, while it was much larger, it was also foldable. In its folded form, it fit easily in the pocket of a lab coat or in a side pocket on the computer used for the EHR. It could be used either folded or unfolded and will display the same data or allow for the same data entry in either state. The primary advantage of unfolding it to its full size is that it will display data in a size format that enables multiple categories of data to be displayed on the same sheet. This format was specifically designed to utilize the best features that the paper flow sheet had in previous years, while utilizing technology to take it to a whole new level. If the tablet is fully open, data will still be downloaded directly into it and the display will be updated as new data are entered. This design format was based on extensive neuroscience research into the optimum visual display of data to enable the viewer to accurately absorb complex information and use it to support critical-thinking processes.

Since the tablet is handled often and by different practitioners, at periodic intervals throughout the shift, the nurse places it in a specially designed sanitizing station that cleans it via controlled multispectral radiation. This process successfully eliminates even the superbugs of 2025. The same technology is also available as another option for hand hygiene in addition to the traditional soap and water and hand sanitizer. In fact, prior to the patient's admission to the room, the same multispectral radiation was used to sweep the room to create a clean environment.

The patient is also wearing a wristband with radio-frequency identification chips with a full record of past history. Any data that have been added during the hospital stay will be available for downloading, which includes not only data from the patient's history but the current data that have been added while the patient has been hospitalized. In the unlikely event that an evacuation is necessary if a power failure occurs, the information contained on the wristband is equivalent to having the full medical record. By 2025, the storage capability has increased dramatically.

Due to the patient's instability in the OR, an IABP was inserted into his or her descending aorta to serve as a support to his or her heart. That evening as his or her kidneys failed, the decision was made to start the patient on CRRT. At the start of therapy with both of these devices, the nurse scanned the bar code of each and scanned the patient's identification bracelet. This linked both devices with the EHR, and data from them were downloaded directly every hour, along with all of the other vital signs. The fact that the nurse did not have to type the numerous settings, pressures, alarm values, and parameters into the EHR meant that he or she was able to concentrate on his or her patient and instead of trying to keep up with recording the data, he or she was able to continuously observe and analyze it.

At 7 p.m., when the full set of vital signs and parameters needs to be entered into the computer, the nurse was busy suctioning the patient to maintain patency of his or her endotracheal tube, which had a large amount of secretions. He or she was also beginning to recover from the anesthesia and was responding to voice and following commands appropriately. The nurse reassured him or her that the surgery was over and that he or she would give him or her medication for pain, which he or she did.

During the time that the nurse was busy with the patient, the following data points were entered into the record: all information displayed on the monitor, including temperature, heart rate, rhythm, arterial BP, MAP, CVP, PAP, CO, CI, SVR, and SPO2; all respiratory parameters from the ventilator, including mode, set rate, actual rate, FIO2, TV, and PEEP; all IABP settings and pressures including ratio, systolic, augmented diastolic, and end diastolic; and all CRRT volumes and pressures including TMP, prefilter volume, postfilter volume, and access pressure.

Because the nurse was not busy typing, he or she was better able to observe and analyze all of the numbers and pressure waveforms. He or she was able to detect trends that indicated whether the patient was improving or deteriorating. He or she had time to spend with the patient. Part of this time was spent explaining to him or her and to his or her family members what was happening, while at the same time continuously observing the patient and all of the data displayed on the monitor and the support devices. He or she was also able to turn the patient to assess his or her skin integrity and to institute measures to prevent pressure ulcers. The hospital has seen a decrease in the incidence of facility-acquired pressure ulcers since implementing the fully integrated EHR system. This has improved reimbursement rates since they are in compliance with the CMS zero tolerance for pressure ulcer development. In addition, there have been no lawsuits relating to pressure ulcers. Additionally, there has been an improvement in other forms of documentation, such as patient and family education and compliance with core measures and patient safety goals. All of these have benefitted the hospital financially.

While the nurse is busy suctioning the patient and getting the pain medication, the surgeon comes to the bedside to see how the patient is doing. While he or she waits for the nurse to give him or her a verbal update on the patient's condition, he or she takes the tablet and opens it. He or she touches the appropriate icon and changes the view of the screen to the *flow sheet view* setting that displays of all of the vital signs along with the doses of all of IV medication infusions that he or she is receiving. This gives him or her a snapshot of the patient's overall condition. After he or she leaves, the nurse touches the microphone on his or her ID badge for voice entry and requests *events*. He or she states that the surgeon has just visited and is aware of all current vital signs and lab data. This information will be included in the EHR as a timed entry.

Shortly after the surgeon's visit, the patient's cardiologist views the EHR from home. He or she is also able to view the real-time data and waveforms on his or her computer screen at home. He or she is concerned about the patient and contacts the nurse via a tablet-to-tablet communication link. The nurse responds and in answer to the cardiologist's request, and he or she brings the tablet to the patient's bedside. It has viewing capability and the cardiologist can directly see the patient. He or she decides to change one of the IV medications to a different medication and he or she enters this order from home. Not only is the nurse able to see the medication order, but the pharmacist is able to see it too. He or she quickly profiles the medication and clears it so that the nurse can obtain it from the dispensing system on the unit. He or she scans the patient's ID band, scans the medication bag, and scans the bar code on the infusion pump. Since this is a new medication, the EHR searches for the physician's order in the record and will compare the details of the order to the concentration on the bag as well as cross-referencing this with the settings on the infusion pump. This will ensure that all details of the order are correctly carried out.

As the end of the shift approaches, the nurse quickly reviews the documents. He or she places the monitor in full-screen view that now organizes all of the current physiologic data onto the screen, arranged according to time. It also adds pertinent data regarding procedures that the patient has had done during the shift into a form that will be added to throughout the patient's hospital stay. With the touch of another icon, the data are displayed as a *shift report* view. The nursing staff has designed this view to use as a communication tool when they endorse to each other at the change of shift.

The reason that the hospital invested the initial capital to implement a fully functioning EHR system, with the ability to communicate with all monitors and devices, was that in 2018 the federal government selected *data entry* as the next meaningful use incentive. Hospitals had the same incentives for meeting benchmarks of data entry of physiologic parameters as they had in meeting the original meaningful use benchmarks that were the catalyst for the original explosion of EHR implementation.

10.10 Summary

If all of the desired features from the wish list of the EHR are incorporated, what will the EHR in a critical care unit look like in 2025? All devices that are capable of communicating with each other should do so. By 2025, there should be a body of research that demonstrates the positive effects of automatic data entry on an increased level of customer satisfaction because of the additional time spent by nurses with patients. There should also be a body of literature that begins to demonstrate the improved patient safety results. Any other data that do not download automatically should be easy to enter perhaps by a touch screen or voice recognition. Record retrieval will be easier as well. The research that supported the standardization of terminology also revealed that much of the entries that nurses made were into the narrative progress notes. The computer should be able to *read* or recognize certain key words. It should have the capability of looking anywhere in the record that the data are located. And, finally, it should be a priority that when hospitals make decisions about implementing and upgrading computer-based documentation systems, the frontline nurses have a strong voice in the selection process. The EHR needs to be a tool that utilizes the best features of computer-based technology so that it meets the needs of the frontline nursing staff, who are then freed up to spend their time doing what they do best, that is, providing expert care to critically ill patients and their families.

Questions

1. Discuss the documentation challenges that exist for nurses in the critical care setting.
2. Explain the legal requirements that govern documentation of the hospitalized patient.
3. Discuss three advantages to implementing an EHR that has full communication capability with monitors and other biomedical devices in the critical care setting.
4. Identify three potential research questions relating to the use of EHRs.
5. Discuss how the most effective qualities of a paper record could be incorporated and improved with the technology of a computer-based documentation system.

Glossary

Advanced cardiac life support (ACLS): The American Heart Association set of guidelines of clinical interventions for the urgent treatment of cardiac arrest, stroke, and other life-threatening medical emergencies, as well as the knowledge and skills to deploy those interventions. This content is also offered as a course comprised of lectures, hands-on practice, written test, and return demonstration.

Advanced practice registered nurse (APRN): An APRN is a registered professional nurse with an advanced degree, either masters or doctorate. There are four recognized APRN roles: certified registered nurse anesthetists, certified nurse midwives, clinical nurse specialists, and certified nurse practitioners.

Acute coronary syndrome (ACS): Refers to any group of symptoms attributed to the obstruction of the coronary arteries. The most common symptom prompting diagnosis of ACS is chest pain, often radiating to the left arm or angle of the jaw, pressure-like in character, and associated with nausea and sweating.

Augmented diastolic: An intra-aortic balloon pump (IABP) is positioned in the descending aorta. It inflates during diastole, displacing blood volume and increasing, or augmenting, the diastolic pressure in the aortic root.

Blood pressure: The pressure of the blood in the circulatory system, often measured for diagnosis, since it is closely related to the force and rate of the heartbeat and the diameter and elasticity of the arterial walls.

Blood products: Any component of the blood that is collected from a donor for use in a blood transfusion. Whole blood is rarely used; most blood products consist of specific processed components such as red blood cells, blood plasma, or platelets.

Blood type: Also referred to as "blood group." Any of various classes into which human blood can be divided according to immunological compatibility based on the presence or absence of specific antigens on red blood cells.

Braden Scale: An evidence-based method of determining a patient's risk of developing a pressure ulcer. The patient is assessed for the ability to move or the presence of moisture, among other items, each of which is scored. The total score indicates whether a patient is at high or low risk. This assessment is performed on admission and then either daily or every shift.

Cardiac arrest: The cessation of cardiac activity resulting in loss of an effective pulse. The treatment is immediate cardiopulmonary resuscitation.

Cardiac index (CI): The cardiac output (CO) corrected to reflect the size of the patient. It has the following formula: CO ÷ body surface area = CI. The body surface area is dependent on the patient's height and weight and is measured in liter/minute/square meter.

Normal value: 2.6 to 4.2 L/min/m2

Cardiac output (CO): The volume of blood pumped by the heart per minute, measured in liter per minute (L/min). Normal value, 5 to 6 L/min.

Cardiac rhythm: The electrical activity of the heart; the impulse starts at the sinus node, conducts through the atrial tracts into the atrioventricular node, and passes into the ventricles via the bundle of His, through the left and right bundle branches, and into the purkinje fibers in the ventricles.

Cardiogenic shock: Severely impaired circulation of blood and delivery of oxygen to the tissues secondary to failure of the heart as an effective pump.

Centers for Medicare and Medicaid Services (CMS): A federal agency within the U.S. Department of Health and Human Services that administers the Medicare program and works in partnership with state governments to administer Medicaid, the State Children's Health Insurance Program, and health insurance portability standards.

Central lines: An intravenous catheter that is passed through a vein and terminates in the right atrium of the heart.

Central venous pressure (CVP): The pressure measured in the right atrium of the heart. It serves as an estimate of blood volume, although it is not a direct measure of this parameter.

Chest tubes: A flexible plastic tube that is inserted through the chest wall into the pleural space or mediastinum. It is used to drain air, fluid, or blood from the thoracic or mediastinal cavities.

Clinical information system (CIS): A computer-based system that is designed for collecting, storing, manipulating, and making available clinical information for the healthcare delivery process.

Clinical nurse specialist (CNS): Licensed registered professional nurses with graduate preparation (either master's or doctorate). CNSs are clinical experts in the treatment of illness, and the delivery of evidence-based nursing interventions in a specialty population (e.g., critical illness, women's health, pediatrics, and geriatrics).

Continuous positive airway pressure: A technique of assisting breathing by maintaining the air pressure in the lungs and air passages constant and above the atmospheric pressure throughout the respiratory cycle.

Continuous renal replacement therapy (CRRT): An extracorporeal blood purification therapy intended to substitute for impaired renal function over an extended period of time.

Core measures: A set of quality indicators defined by the Centers for Medicare and Medicaid Services.

Critical care: The specialized care of patients whose conditions are life threatening and who require comprehensive care and constant monitoring, usually in intensive care units.

Cross match: In transfusion medicine, this refers to the testing that is performed prior to a blood transfusion in order to determine if the donor's blood is compatible with the blood of an intended recipient.

Diastolic: The lowest arterial blood pressure of a cardiac cycle occurring during diastole of the heart.

Electrolytes: Electrolytes are minerals in the blood and other body fluids that carry an electric charge. The primary electrolytes in the body are potassium, sodium, calcium, magnesium, chloride, and phosphorous.

Electronic medication administration record (eMAR): A method of listing the medications that are prescribed for a hospitalized patient and recording their administration.

End diastolic Pressure: The pressure in the ventricles at the end of diastole, when the ventricle is filled with blood, just prior to the systolic ejection.

Endotracheal tube: A hollow, flexible tube that is inserted via the mouth, through the vocal chords, and into the trachea. The purpose is to maintain a patent airway.

Foley catheter: A flexible catheter that is inserted through the urethra and into the bladder for the purpose of draining urine.

Fraction of inspired oxygen (FIO$_2$): The percentage of oxygen that a patient is inhaling. Room air is 21% oxygen. Therapeutic delivery systems can supply an FIO$_2$ up to 100%.

Heart failure: A clinical syndrome characterized by systemic perfusion inadequate to meet the body's metabolic demands as a result of impaired cardiac pump function.

Hemodialysis: Utilizing a device with a semipermeable membrane to filter wastes and fluids from the blood when the kidneys no longer function.

Hemodynamic monitoring: The expert collection and analysis of qualitative and quantitative data of cardiopulmonary function. Fluid-filled monitoring systems attach to intravascular catheters and are used for continuous invasive measurement of arterial and cardiac pressures.

Infusion pump: Medical devices that deliver fluids, including nutrients and medications such as antibiotics, chemotherapy drugs, and pain relievers, into a patient's body in controlled amounts.

Institute of Medicine (IOM): An independent, nonprofit organization that works outside of government to provide unbiased and authoritative advice to decision makers and the public. It was established in 1970 and is the health arm of the National Academy of Sciences, which was chartered under President Abraham Lincoln.

Interdisciplinary plan of care (IPOC): The goal of the IPOC is to support continuity, quality, and safe patient-centric care utilizing the expertise of the various members of the healthcare disciplinary team.

Interoperable: The ability of a system to work with or use the parts or equipment of another system.

Intra-aortic balloon pump (IABP): A mechanical device that is inserted via the femoral artery. It is comprised of a balloon that inflates with helium during diastole and deflates fight before systole. It increases myocardial oxygen perfusion and decreases the workload of the heart. It is used for patients with an acute myocardial infarction or cardiogenic shock.

The Joint Commission (TJC): An independent, not-for-profit organization, TJC accredits and certifies more than 20,500 healthcare organizations and programs in the United States.

Mean arterial pressure (MAP): The average pressure in a patient's arteries during one cardiac cycle. It is considered a better indicator of perfusion to vital organs than the systolic pressure. It is calculated with the following formula:

$$MAP = \frac{Systolic + 2(diastolic)}{3}$$

National Patient Safety Goals (NPSGs): In 2002, The Joint Commission established its NPSGs program. The NPSGs were established to help accredited organizations address specific areas of concern in regard to patient safety.

Never events: The National Quality Forum defines never events as errors in medical care that are of concern to both the public and healthcare professionals and providers, clearly identifiable and measurable, and of a nature such that the risk of occurrence is significantly influenced by the policies and procedures of the healthcare organization.

Oxygen saturation: Oxygen is carried in the blood attached to the hemoglobin molecules. Oxygen saturation is a measure of how much oxygen the blood is carrying as a percentage of the maximum that it could carry.

Peritoneal dialysis: A method of removing waste products and fluid from the blood in the setting of kidney failure. A fluid, dialysate, is instilled into the abdomen and the exchange takes place between the blood vessels in the peritoneum and the dialysate.

Positive end expiratory pressure (PEEP): A technique used with patients who are intubated and on a ventilator in which positive pressure is maintained in the airway throughout exhalation, so that the alveoli (air sacs in the lungs) do not deflate completely at the end of expiration. The objective is to increase the time for oxygen–carbon dioxide exchange as well as to facilitate reexpansion of the alveoli on the next inspiration.

Pressure ulcer: An injury to the skin and underlying tissue resulting from prolonged pressure, friction, or shearing forces.

Pulmonary artery pressure (PAP): A measure of the blood pressure found in the pulmonary artery measured by inserting a catheter into the right atrium and advancing it into the right ventricle and out into the pulmonary artery. The normal pressures are 9–18 mmHg/ 6–12 mmHg.

Pulse oximetry: A procedure used to measure the oxygen level (or oxygen saturation) in the blood. It is considered to be a noninvasive, painless, general indicator of oxygen delivery to the peripheral tissues, such as the finger or earlobe.

Radio-frequency identification: The wireless noncontact use of radio-frequency electromagnetic fields to transfer data, for the purposes of automatically identifying and tracking tags attached to objects.

Sepsis: A potentially life-threatening complication of an infection that occurs when chemicals released into the bloodstream to fight the infection trigger inflammatory responses throughout the body. This inflammation can trigger a cascade of changes that can damage multiple organ systems, causing them to fail.

STAT: A medical abbreviation for urgent or rush. Something ordered as STAT is to be done immediately.

Stroke: A stroke occurs when the blood supply to part of the brain is interrupted or severely reduced, depriving brain tissue of oxygen and nutrients. Within minutes, brain cells begin to die.

Systolic: The highest arterial blood pressure of a cardiac cycle occurring immediately after systole, or contraction, of the left ventricle of the heart.

SVO_2: Mixed venous oxygen saturation reflects the amount of oxygen consumed by the tissues. It measures the difference between the oxygen delivered by the arterial system and the amount of oxygen returned to the heart by the venous system. Normal SVO2 is between 60% and 80%.

Tidal volume: The volume of air inspired or expired in a single breath during regular breathing.

Tracheostomy: A surgical procedure to create an opening through the neck into the trachea. A tube is placed through this opening to provide an airway and to remove secretions from the lungs.

Ventilator: A device that supports breathing. It delivers oxygenated air to the lungs under positive pressure. The patient exhales passively.

Venous thromboembolism (VTE): A deep venous thrombosis is a blood clot that forms in a vein deep inside a part of the body. The most common site is in the large veins in the lower leg and thigh. The danger is that when a clot breaks off and moves through the bloodstream as an embolism, it can lodge in the lungs.

Ventricular assist device: A mechanical pump designed to support heart function and blood flow. Blood is taken from the ventricle and passes through the pump. It is then returned to the aorta for circulation throughout the body.

References

Collins, S.A., Cato, K., Albers, D., Scott, K., Stetson, P.D., Bakken, S., and Vawdrey, D.K. (2013). Relationship between nursing documentation and patients' mortality. *American Journal of Critical Care* 22(4), 306–313.

Englebright, J., Aldrich, K., and Taylor, C. (2013). Defining and incorporating basic nursing care actions into the electronic health record. *Journal of Nursing Scholarship* 46(1), 50–57.

Estrada, N. and Dunn, C. (June 2012). Standardized nursing diagnoses in an electronic health record: Nursing survey results. *International Journal of Nursing Knowledge* 23(2), 86–95.

Fleming, N.S., Becker, E.R., Culler, S.D., Cheng, D., McCorkle, R., da Graca, B., and Ballard, D.J. (2012). The impact of electronic health records on workflow and financial measures in primary care practices. *Health Services Research* 49 (1), Part II, 405–420.

Friedman, D.J., Parrish, G., and Ross, D.A. (2013). Electronic health records and US Public Health: Current realities and future promise. *American Journal of Public Health* 103(9), 1560–1569.

Fowler, S.A., Yaeger, L., Yu, F., Doerhoff, D., Schoening, P., and Kelly, B. (2014). Electronic health record: Integrating evidence-based information at the point of clinical decision making. *Journal of the Medical Library Association* 103(1), 52–55.

Galbraith, K. (2013). What's so meaningful about meaningful use? *Hastings Center Report* 43(2), 15–17.

Hamid, F. and Cline, T. (2013). Providers' acceptance factors and their perceived barriers to electronic health record (EHR) adoption. *Online Journal of Nursing Informatics* 17(3).

Harrington, L., Choromanski, L., Biddle, N., and Acosta, K. (2011). Documentation of others' work in the electronic health record. *Critical Care Nurse* 31(3) 84–86.

Keenan, G. (2014). Big data in health care: An urgent mandate to change nursing EHRs, *Online Journal of Nursing Informatics* 18(1). Available at http:/ojni.org/issues/?p=3081.

Keenan, G. et al. (2012). Maintaining a consistent big picture; Meaningful use of a web-based POC EHR system, *International Journal of Nursing Knowledge* 23(3), 119–133.

Kelly, P. (2011). The importance of documenting family history. *Critical Care Nurse* 31(4), 18.

Li, D. and Korniewicz, D. (2013). Determination of the effectiveness of electronic health records to document pressure ulcers. *Medical-surgical Nursing* January–February 22(1), 17–25.

McCullough, J. and Schell-Chaple, H. (2013). Maintaining patients' privacy and confidentiality with family communications in the intensive care unit. *Critical Care Nurse* 33(5), 77–79.

O'Mahony, D., Wright, G., Yogeswaran, P. and Govere, F. (2014). Knowledge and attitudes of nurses in community health centres about electronic medical records. *Curationis* 37(1), Art #1150 at http:// dx.doi.org/10.4102/curationis.v37i1.1150.

Pasek, T., Lefcakis, L., O'Malley, K., Licata, J., and Jackson, P. (2009). Power in documentation: An eProgress note for APNs. *Critical Care Nurse* 29(3), 102–104.

Penoyer, D.A., Cortelyou-Ward, K.H., Noblin, A.M., Bullard, T., Talbert, S., Wilson, J., Schafhauser, B., and Briscoe, J.G. (2014). Use of electronic health record documentation by healthcare workers in an acute care hospital system. *Journal of Healthcare Management* 59 (2), 130–144.

Savel, R.H. and Munro, C.L. (2013). Promise and pitfalls of the electronic health record. *American Journal of Critical Care* 22(6), 460–462.

Scherb, C., Maas, M.L., Head, B.J., Johnson, M.R., Kozel, M., Reed, D., Swanson, E., and Moorhead, S. (2013). Implications of electronic health record meaningful use legislation for nursing clinical information system development and refinement. *International Journal of Nursing Knowledge* 24(2), 93–100.

Silver, R.K. and Straub, H. (2014). What's missing from the electronic health record. *Contemporary OB/ GYN*. Published on January 1, 2014 on Contemporary OB/GYN (http:/contemporaryobgyn.modernmedicine.com.)

Staggers, N. (2011). The April 2011 hearing on EHR usability in crucial conversations about optimal design column. *Online Journal of Nursing Informatics* 15(2), Available at http://ojni.org/issues/?p=542.

Topaz, M. and Bowles, K.H. (2012). Electronic health records and quality of care: Mixed results and emerging debates in Achieving Meaningful Use in Research with Information Technology Column. *Online Journal of Nursing Informatics* 16(1), Available at http:ojni.org/issues/?p=1262.

11

Healthcare Management Information Technology in the Full Service Facility

Philomena Diquollo

Chapter goals: Explain various information technology (IT) roles and responsibilities in a healthcare setting; identify drivers for IT project decision making, discuss software implementation process.

11.1 Introduction

The evolution of technology use in patient care services has been fascinating. From the first "dumb" terminals and light pens at the nurse's stations to the use of sophisticated mobile devices at the point of care, the landscape and workflow have dramatically changed. Much like the dot.com phenomenon of days past, the healthcare market at the turn of the century was ripe for the introduction of ways to reduce the use of pen and paper in the acute care setting. Application development exploded. And, as in the dot.com era, those applications that were able to meet customer demands have survived and matured. Not only have applications matured but healthcare culture and behavior is changing as well. The expectation in these times is that hardcopy documentation is an exception rather than a rule and there should be easy ways to acquire data.

In this chapter, the focus will be on what it takes to support a healthcare organization, understanding the complexity of a heavily regulated, highly technical, and safety-conscious environment.

In the healthcare setting, the organizational role of the IT department is often that of "influencer" to support the mission and vision of the organization. The users of technology are the business owners directed and supported by the IT department. The domains IT supports are varied with necessary roles to manage operational and regulatory standards. Project selections and implementations are driven by infrastructure needs to stay technologically current and operational needs to support bedside and diagnostic departments. Management of projects is focused and uses industry standard practices to stay on time and on budget.

With the pervasive use of technology in healthcare, the role of the healthcare IT professional in organizations has evolved as well. Technology platforms themselves shape the skill set support of an environment. Mainframe programming and, operational and technical support require a very different skill set and team from a Cloud hosted thin client environment. Clinical support staff has emerged as a requirement to support system users.

A constant is changing technology needs in healthcare. Roles and responsibilities continually shift to meet the changing demands. The IT professional organization needs to be fluid and flexible to effectively lead and respond.

11.2 IT Sphere of Influence

Most people new to the healthcare IT field consider the job technical in nature with a focus on infrastructure. In fact, IT departments have a much wider sphere of influence in an organization.

11.2.1 Communicator

The hallmark of an effective IT department is the ability to communicate with all levels of the organization. Keeping the organization aware of the IT roadmap, timelines, changes, and updates builds trust and relationships. As in any facet of business, relationship is the key to accomplishing organizational goals. Walking rounds and face-to-face time demonstrate willingness to take customers' needs into consideration. Conversation, formal or informal, keeps a pulse on the organization and helps to anticipate a situation before it develops into a dissatisfied customer.

Communication can take many forms: face to face, meetings, policies and procedures, emails, blogs, newsletters, application messages, digital signage, and announcements. The important thing is to just do it. Keeping the intended audience in mind directs the method or methods that need to be employed.

11.2.2 Educator

Computers and software can still be foreign to many users in a healthcare organization. In spite of the pervasive use of technology in today's world, the workings of IT in the healthcare business world can be a mystery. Federal regulations, threats in the marketplace, correct use of the technology, and industry trends are areas in which the general user in healthcare needs guidance and assistance.

IT, like most industries, has its own language of acronyms and slang. The IT profession needs to be able to translate difficult concepts into terms the general user can understand. Often the general user does not understand why systems do not behave like personal devices. IT professionals are continually educating users on how and why things perform the way they do.

11.2.3 Decision Maker

IT professionals lead and direct choices related to technology and use of systems. There are factors to consider when choosing infrastructure and software for the organization: ease of use, flexibility, scalability, reputation, performance, support, to name a few. At the speed technology changes, the IT professional must be cognizant of trends and directions in the market place. Systematic methodology for making the right selections for the right reasons to sustain an organization for the long term is important. A choice for today will impact use for many years.

Technology decisions are best made with end user involvement. The best product in the world may never be embraced by users if they are not included in the process. Building the relationship to engage end user participation in decision making contributes to successful selections. A goal of the IT decision maker is to have the best information not only about a product but users' perceptions of the product usability in their workflow.

11.2.4 Change Agent

Technology change in an organization is an interesting phenomenon. Sometimes it is the clinicians who drive change because of a new procedure, piece of equipment, or regulatory requirement. Although the change may be biomedical in nature, today the line is blurred between pure biomedical engineering and computer technology. Most diagnostic and procedural equipment coming available has the means to capture and store data for viewing, reporting, and analytics. On the technology side, improvements in infrastructure, network, and desktop devices require changes to provide faster systems, storage capability, or bandwidth.

In either case, IT professionals are often the drivers of the change and as such an understanding of change theory, resistance to change, and communication effectiveness is valuable. Providing value to the end user when a new way of doing things is necessary supports culture change. Awareness that change is not easy prepares the IT professional to respond to users in a meaningful way.

11.2.5 Facilitator

There are times when a project may be contracted to third parties, or IT has been asked to participate in a demo or meeting for potential involvement. In these instances, it is important for the IT professional to facilitate communication and activities for the best interest of the organization. Regardless of who is performing functions of programming, installation, education, or support, the responsibility lies with the employed staff to ensure that all organization expectations and requirements are being met.

IT has a solid understanding of the way data move through the organization. Often IT is called upon to assist with linking fragments of data together, connecting the dots between systems to produce meaningful information or improved workflow. By facilitating communication in projects, IT can provide structure to non-IT projects in the organization.

11.2.6 Implementer

Technology staff is very accustomed to following project management methodology. Although a department may be the business owner of system, the IT organization is expected to provide structure and guidance to implementations. Members of the IT department are often called to participate as subject matter experts (SMEs) or as project leads in order to bring projects in on time and on budget.

11.2.7 Risk Taker

IT staff is constantly assessing risk to the organization. Evaluation of risk to end users related to business continuity, security, and malicious intent is weighing the potential for risk. And sometimes judgment calls must be made for the good of the many. It is difficult to deal in generalities when change is required. Assessment, coordination, and backup plans are a requirement to mitigate harm to the organization.

11.2.8 Listener

Users of IT may have difficulty articulating their needs. Especially when the request is for analytics, users may know the end result they are looking for but have difficulty explaining what they want. Often they need to be guided with specific questions to define what is needed. It is important that IT professionals listen without making assumptions. Time can be spent creating screens, forms, reports, outputs that are not what the user is requesting. Taking the time to listen and define saves time in the end.

Working with technology can be frustrating to users. It is important to have an environment where users can complain or criticize without judgment in order to fix a problem. As in most situations in life, sometimes it is important to just listen so that our customers feel that they are heard and then to be able to educate, repair, redesign, or think outside the box to achieve solutions to problems.

11.3 Information Technology Domains

Supporting healthcare environments requires groups of people whose function is devoted to particular aspects of the IT organization. To the casual observer, the "IT department" consists of staffs who manage desktops and printers. This perception cannot be further from the truth. Support of a complex healthcare environment requires teams of specialists who have specific areas of focus. Although the domains may vary from organization to organization, one will find typical types of specialties in any organization.

11.3.1 Strategic Planning

The IT executive team is the strategic planning unit for the technology direction of the organization. The executive team has the chief information officer who directs reports. This team directs the activities of the IT organization to support the mission and vision of the entity, whether it is a large multifacility healthcare system or a small local hospital. Planning is a necessity to being fiscally responsible and responsive to organizational needs.

Inputs to short- and long-term plans are provided by the organization stakeholders and from within the IT department itself. Together, plans or roadmaps are formulated to meet immediate needs and can extend out for several years.

11.3.2 Infrastructure

The infrastructure team is the foundation of the organization, which all other services build upon. The focus of the infrastructure team is obviously the building, maintenance, and support of networks, data centers, server rooms, Internet, RFID, WiFi, and devices that may be in use or connected to the network.

Without sound design and support, the performance of application tools and diagnostic equipment will be suboptimum. Poor performance leads to user dissatisfaction, which leads to underutilization of systems or constant complaints to and about the IT department. This team manages both hardware and the utility software required to run and monitor network infrastructures. Utility software such as asset management and device security software is managed by this group.

The implementation of superior networks brings satisfaction to the technology team; however, in the bigger picture a high performing infrastructure leads to greater employee satisfaction, supporting organizational change and acceptance.

11.3.3 Security

Healthcare organizations are highly regulated and audited by federal, state, and certifying organizations for quality and adherence to standards and best practice. Federal Health Information Technology for Economic and Clinical Health (HITECH) laws and the Health Insurance Portability and Accountability Act (HIPAA) drive security activities of the IT department. It is always a surprise to the newcomer to healthcare IT how threatened the IT environment has become. As a result of regulations and malicious intent, it is important to have a strong IT security department to provide direction, support, and monitoring of infrastructure and use of systems.

The IT or HIPAA Security Officer is a designated position in healthcare organizations. The responsibility includes responding to IT security incidents and breaches, educating employees on IT security policies and procedures, and working closely with the IT security department to protect the local entity or healthcare system from internal and external threats.

11.3.4 Clinical Applications

Clinical applications are those that are used by healthcare workers who provide direct patient care or systems in support of clinical care of the patient. Generally, doctors, nurses, therapists, medical technologists, assistants who treat and diagnose patients and document patient care are users of clinical applications. This is a very broad category that encompasses not only documentation systems such as an electronic medical record (EMR) but also "ancillary" systems such as the radiology, laboratory, pharmacy, perioperative, perinatal, and cardiology information systems, to name a few. The functions in this domain focus on support of the clinical user workflow, including data capture to meet documentation, regulatory and patient safety requirements, quality indicators, and report writing.

Applications in this domain can be as pervasive as an integrated physician order entry, documentation, charging and billing system such as an Epic, Cerner, Siemens, or McKesson product line, or a niche application that is used by a very specific subset of patient such as in an oncology center. Regardless of the type of application, the approach to implement and support the application follows similar paths.

11.3.5 Business (Nonclinical) Applications

Nonclinical applications support the operations of the organization: human resources, payroll, supply chain, registration, coding, billing, and decision support are examples in this domain. The support of these types of applications requires multiple teams that focus on the particular workflow of the respective departments.

11.3.6 Integration

Selections of software are shifting from the interfaced paradigm, or the "best of breed" implementations, to the integrated model, single-database structure for clinical and business applications. Even with this shift, legacy systems, niche software, and diagnostic modalities require some level of integration.

Whether HL7 or DICOM integration, this team's focus is on the transactions that move data from one system to another using these structure formats.

With the advent of accountable care organizations to manage population health and health information organizations to share regional and statewide patient data, the need to integrate will increase as time goes on.

11.3.7 Biomedical Engineering

As noted earlier, biomedical engineering and IT departments overlap more and more. Biomedical diagnostic and monitoring equipment relies heavily on IT infrastructure; IT is asked to facilitate and participate in biomedical equipment implementations.

The trend is to combine the departments. Combining the departments, or at least creating a dotted line connection, ensures communication. Biomedical companies have specifications to connect devices to the network; however, the infrastructure team has to review the technology to ensure that connections meet organization standards.

11.3.8 Telecommunications

Telecom, similar to biomedical engineering, has merged with IT due to overlapping infrastructure requirements. Many support devices for clinicians connect to networks, or run over IP networks in facilities. Smart phones, IP phones, IP voice badges require software management to program and connect devices, set up clinical groups, and activate features needed by clinicians to perform daily clinical and fast communication functions.

11.3.9 Clinical Leadership/Medical and Nursing Informatics

Physicians and nurses have had positions in the IT department in the past; however, with the surge of EMR implementations, the position has moved to the forefront as necessary for high performing healthcare organizations. EMR applications and clinical information systems have workflows that are physician centric. Evolving regulatory requirements and reimbursement models require that plans of care and orders are entered directly into applications by the physician. Nurses and therapists are required to respond to physician orders with electronic documentation and have their own sets of regulatory requirements to document standards of care.

To meet the needs of physicians, nurses, and therapists, informatics has developed into its own domain with expertise in clinical workflow, IT systems, and education of end users. Clinical practice has standards, yet it is not cookie cutter. Standards of care are the norm; however, applications must be flexible enough to account for the unusual or abnormal situation that may arise. Documentation and orders are still required, but understanding and responding to the needs of the clinicians require a team that understands the clinical workflow and speaks the same language as the customer base. Typically, physicians and nurses are the primary members of this team.

11.4 Healthcare IT Skill Sets

11.4.1 Project Management

The most successful installations are those managed by people with project management experience. IT installations are usually high-dollar, high-impact activities. To protect the organization by keeping projects well communicated, visible, structured, and moving forward, a certified project manager is necessary. In healthcare, there are typically two types of implementations: the purely technical implementation to support the infrastructure and the application implementation, which is an installation that ultimately impacts clinical and business applications users in their daily workflow.

Project managers may come from a variety of backgrounds; however, credentials from national certifying organizations such as the Project Management Institute or the American Society for Quality (6 and Lean Sigma) are the types of credentials a project management office (PMO) requires. Clinical or technical backgrounds may not be required but are preferred.

11.4.2 Hardware and Software

11.4.2.1 Technical Staff

Technical staff usually comes through certified agencies, for example, A+ training, technical schools, or degree programs. And some staff has come up through the ranks with on-the-job training. The trend today is to hire a college educated staff that comes to the job with an understanding of what the job entails or experience in the particular service line. Job opportunities are available in asset management, asset protection, network engineering, LAN administration, wireless infrastructure, data center operators, server room management, and desktop support.

11.4.2.2 Software Support

Software support staff in healthcare to date usually have come out of clinical areas when an opportunity to transition to an IT role has presented itself. Implementations in clinical settings have required IT staff that understand the jargon in the medical field and have an understanding of clinical workflow. Software support can be the EMR, ancillary systems such as the laboratory information system, niche software such as birth certificate reporting, or nonclinical applications used by the human resource and finance departments.

The term "out of clinical areas" does not necessarily mean a clinical provider. People exposed to clinical workflow and the terminology used, such as technicians, clerical staff, and technology staff, are examples of the types of staff that have typically transitioned into these types of roles. Logical thinking and an ability to pick up the clinical jargon are skill sets a person new to this role needs to possess.

With the emergence of degree programs, software support can be learned in the classroom setting but also needs to be paired with the skills described to be effective in a clinical setting. Software support positions through a vendor rather than a clinical setting employment allow for a longer learning curve to pick up workflow and unique medical terms, phrases, acronyms, and user needs.

These types of activities are implementations, maintenance of the application, end user support, workflow analysis, error resolution, and liaison between the clinical staff and the vendor.

11.4.2.3 Interfaces

Interface programming is a learned skill. HL7 and DICOM programming is typically not taught as a degree path of study but falls under the umbrella of application support. Interface programming is a path that is for the person who has the IT training and experience in a medical environment.

11.4.3 Biomedical Engineering

Biomed is an area of study that can stand on its own in a healthcare setting or combined with the IT department. Diagnostic and procedural equipment have been evolving with a heavy use of technology that now must conform to infrastructure and HIPAA standards established by the technology teams.

11.4.4 Telecommunications

Like biomed, telecom is its own field of study. Telecommunications management is heavily reliant on software not only in the switch room but also found in the tools used by telephone operators. Today operators use sophisticated keyboard consoles to manage incoming and outgoing calls, paging, IP phones, and other technologies used to notify or support healthcare staff, patients, families, visitors, and vendors.

11.4.5 Development/Programming

The development team consists of programming staff who are actual programmers. In a healthcare environment, generally third-party software from recognized vendors is installed. Sometimes a workflow or department is so unique that it needs "in-house" development. Development can be web based, use utility software for rapid development, SQL programming, or use traditional programming languages like C#. This team has to be versed in database management to manage size and space for developed apps.

11.4.6 Clinical Informatacists

The clinical voice drives the development and enhancements to applications used in healthcare settings. As a tool to document, collect, and present information, the inclusion of clinical technical leaders is necessary to add value to the electronic documentation system and promote the use of EMR. Physicians and nurses are valued and sought-after members of the team. Their input drives decisions on displays, input field layout, hard stops, warning, and language. Speaking the same language as the end users, the clinical informatacists bridge the gap between the technical teams and the providers.

11.4.7 Security and Asset Protection

The focus of these types of teams is protecting the assets of the organization, including hardware, software, and data. Hardware selection, software licensing and versions, tracking, disposal, network monitoring and protection, conformance with federal regulations regarding security, and asset protection fall into these categories. Staff typically have technical backgrounds. Activities revolve around threat surveillance, protection, and business continuity.

11.4.8 CIO and Leadership Team

The Chief Information Office and the management leadership team set the strategic and tactical IT goals of the organization. Leadership comes from a variety of educational and experiential backgrounds in IT, computer sciences, biomedical engineering, medical or nursing informatics, with a variety of experiences in healthcare, industry, or business. Hospital organization and operations knowledge makes for the most successful leaders in healthcare.

11.4.9 Competing Forces

Every physician and employee user of technology has an idea on how to improve services and workflow. Ideas and recommendations for improvements, enhancements, and new technology are discussed every day. Projects can be as simple as adding a data component to a screen or as complex as installing an application with hardware, network, interface, ongoing maintenance, and reporting requirements. Change is generally handled through a change control-management process, which requires business justification, analysis of the request, approval, and implantation. Simple requests generally are simple change control process; complex projects require more detailed justification.

The direction of clinical, business, and ancillary system implementations and change in hospitals takes into account different factors that drive decisions. IT expense is one of many competing demands on a healthcare facility where there are expenses related to physical plant, labor, supplies, and medical equipment. Several factors are considered when deciding on how dollars should be invested.

11.5 Stakeholder Analysis

11.5.1 Need

Three priorities that drive hospital expense decisions as to where dollars are best spent are patient safety, billing, and regulatory requirements. Keeping patients safe while maintaining high-quality care is of paramount importance in any healthcare organization. Safety is so important that healthcare has "National Patient Safety Goals," which hospitals must achieve to be considered a safe environment. Safety goals are nationally reported via scorecards and websites designed to keep the public aware of hospital performance. EMRs and department-specific applications support workflow to ensure that the right patient is receiving the right orders, right medications, and right procedures.

Revenue cycle applications manage the collection of patient information, both demographic and clinical, to produce an output of a clean bill to be sent to insurance companies for payment. Revenue cycle applications include but are not limited to registration systems, scheduling, forms printing, digital signature, and archiving of registration information, coding, billing, payments due, insurance verification, and medical necessity for procedures. Getting it right the first time to reach the ultimate goal of timely reimbursement back to the facility is what makes hospitals viable. Having applications that provide financial reporting and modeling assists executive and financial leadership in making informed decisions and strategic plans.

Healthcare is a heavily regulated industry. All aspects of healthcare business have some sort of best practice clinical care requirements, as well as monitoring or reporting requirements to the federal government, state, local, or certifying or monitoring agencies. Electronic systems support recording of documentation of care in formats that are legible and clear. Alerts and prompts can be added to applications to ensure data capture. Discrete data fields can be reported on with high reliability to normalize data and meet reporting requirements.

11.5.2 Stakeholders

Stakeholders help to guide decision makers. Having a business case to support funding, referencing the three drivers mentioned earlier, is how hard decisions are made on projects that move forward. The stakeholders must be able to justify how their requests for software and hardware fit into the organization's goals. Considering the breadth and depth of IT needs in an organization, there are many demands for funding. Stakeholders making their business case can be the most powerful influence in a decision to fund or not.

11.5.3 Politics

Political influences are both internal and external. Internally, hospitals are a business like any other business. Organizational relationships and culture factor into decisions on IT selections and implementations. External political influences are decisions by local, state, and federal administrations. As mentioned earlier, healthcare is a heavily regulated industry. All three branches of government collect data for public reporting and safety, provide payment for services, and guide relationships with healthcare entities through healthcare policy. Meeting regulations often involves IT solutions to capture, collate, and report necessary data elements such as lab results for public health surveillance, coding for billing, and clinical care outcomes for patient safety measurements.

11.5.4 Funding

There are four data streams for IT funding:

1. *Operating budgets for general day-to-day expenses*: Labor, supplies, contracts, repairs, licensing, training, and conferences generally fall into this category. Budgets are usually approved annually along with the rest of the hospital. The national benchmark for IT budgets is 4% to 7% of the total operating budget.
2. *Capital funding for high-dollar expenses on one-time purchases*: Generally, items greater than an organization threshold, such as $10 K, require additional approvals and are funded through capital dollars. Although the money comes from the same hospital revenue stream, these high-dollar investments for items such as initial implementations of hardware, software, or major upgrades are reported differently for acquisition and depreciation following accepted and regulated hospital accounting practices.
3. *Grant funding*: This type of funding is possible for IT projects as many support clinical care, research, or workflow improvement. Often IT is asked to provide detail on estimated expenses as part of a larger grant request. Grants are a valuable funding source to introduce new technology to the healthcare setting.
4. *Direct donations*: Usually provided by companies, individuals, or patients to support clinical initiatives, this type of funding is directed, meaning it is for a specific purpose, for example, a grateful family providing an electronic device to be used in a pediatric area or for patient teaching.

11.5.5 Executing the IT Project

Previously, factors that went into the selection process for IT projects were discussed: but how do we actually make it happen? This section examines the project lifecycle of a major implementation from the point of inception to the acceptance by the end user.

11.6 Managing IT Projects

11.6.1 Where Do We Begin?

11.6.1.1 Define Need

Many organizations use a PMO or steering committee to evaluate requests for IT implementations. Requests are submitted in writing and require specific information for assessment. Typical information gathered includes

- Project overview
- Business justification
- Procurement expense
- Ongoing licensing and maintenance fees
- Funding source
- Increase/decrease to labor expense, operating expense
- Project sponsor
- Project owner

11.6.1.2 Market Place Analysis

Departments or service lines may choose to arrange vendors themselves for demonstrations of the product and obtain proposals for implementations. Larger projects may require a request for information (RFI) asking specific questions on application functionality and/or a request for proposal (RFP), which includes both functionality and pricing. RFI and RFP returns from vendors are reviewed by a team of (SMEs) to accept or reject moving the vendor forward in the selection process.

11.6.1.3 Funding

Generally, for any project to move forward, funding has to be secured. As described earlier, one of the four funding sources will need to be defined and considered in the decision to execute.

11.6.1.4 Contracting and Security Review

Once proposal terms are negotiated, the agreement will move to the legal department for contract review of terms and conditions. Vendors doing business with a hospital are required to sign a Business Associate Agreement, which outlines guidelines for the two companies to work together ensuring confidential handling of sensitive information and generally accepted compliance practices.

Some organizations may require a simultaneous IT security review. Security assessments include generally accepted security or regulated topics such as HIPAA compliance related to password security, HIPAA audit and reporting tools, and encryption, to name a few. Remote hosted or Cloud solutions require a more in-depth analysis to confirm asset protection when data are stored offsite, including vendor privacy and security policies and procedures, disaster recovery, data backup, restore, and destruction practices, data center physical safeguards, to name few.

Whether initiated by a department or in partnership with IT, ultimately the request will go to the PMO for evaluation or assistance in the decision-making process and implementation process.

11.6.2 How Do We Do It?

11.6.2.1 Kickoff

The first meeting to take place is run by the project manager. This meeting includes the PMO, stakeholders, vendors, and the IT groups who will participate in the project. It reviews the contract for clarification for all parties, the project plan, milestone activities, and risks to the project.

11.6.2.2 Workflow Analysis

A work place assessment and analysis is scheduled with the stakeholders to understand current state, future state, and the gaps that need to be addressed. IT implementations change the way a department does business. As with any change process role definition, expectations, and concerns need to be addressed in advance of the implementation.

11.6.2.3 Environment Build

Based on the workflow analysis, the vendor and IT teams will begin the hardware and software configurations. Stakeholder SMEs will be called upon time to time for clarification and review.

11.6.2.4 Testing

One can never say enough about the need to test, test, and test. Testing follows a typical pattern of interface testing to ensure connectivity, then discrete data element testing to ensure each data component interfaces properly from one system to another and is displayed in the correct field with the correct value, followed by end-to-end or integrated testing. Integrated testing follows the workflow from the beginning of the process continuing all the way through to the last process. Many scenarios will be tested to insure that functionality is performing as expected. With a clinical system, integrated testing begins at the point of scheduling and continues through registration, clinical documentation, and coding until a bill is produced correctly.

11.6.2.5 Policy and Procedure Development

During the testing and training phase of the project, the stakeholders will review and edit or create policies to support use of the system. Policy and procedure may address day-to-day functionality and use as determined by the entity and will always include a policy specific to downtime and downtime recovery. At this time, it is recommended to develop a business continuity plan to address multiple types of outages or interruptions to system use, both short and long term.

11.6.2.6 Training

Training is the crux of a successful implementation. No matter how well a contract has been negotiated, a system has been built, or the testing is successful, an end user trained to navigate and use the system correctly is the key indicator of success of a project. Organizations may require a competency test to ensure end user readiness.

11.7 How Do We Know We Are Done?

11.7.1 Go-Live Decision

Prior to a go-live date, a "go–no go" meeting is held, chaired by the project manager and including the project team. System readiness is discussed as well as training status, hardware readiness, and training completed. The team will decide to proceed with the go-live or postpone if necessary. Generally, the live date is evaluated at milestones or when risk is identified to keep executive sponsors apprised of project progress and potential issues or concerns.

11.7.2 First Productive Use

Live dates require planning to support end users of software and hardware, command center space for project management, phone numbers or other contact information for immediate assistance, issues lists, and issues management plan. The scale of the implementation determines the space required for a command center and the personal for support. If departments are open 24 hours, round-the-clock coverage is arranged. Generally, go-live on site end user support lasts a few days or several weeks, depending on the implementation.

11.7.3 Acceptance

Most contracts include a period of acceptance, whereby the last payment due to the vendor per the contract is 30 days post live. Adding this clause to the payment terms ensures the vendor will meet its contracted deliverables. The project manager, in conjunction with the stakeholders, will determine if the vendor has met its deliverables satisfactorily and the issues that arose during the implementation are addressed to the stakeholder's satisfaction. At this time, the software/hardware is turned over to the support teams and the project is closed as completed.

11.8 Conclusion

Healthcare organizations are dynamic environments. As clinical and business needs drive the healthcare entity to change, the IT department has to be flexible and facile to respond. Medical informatacists are change agents who will lead and support organization demands.

12

Future Directions for Biomedical Informatics

Level I: Core Concepts

12.1 Introduction

Extrapolating future trends should be quantifiable if events followed linear causality, similar to a series of billiard balls. The superposition principle states that, for all linear systems, the net outcome caused by two or more stimuli can be calculated by the sum of the responses caused by each stimulus individually. Another example is wave interference; if two or more waves traverse the same space, the net amplitude at each point is the sum of the amplitudes of the individual waves. Even if the physics is more complex, we should be able to simulate possible outcomes. A classic example is the butterfly effect. If a butterfly flaps its wings thousands of miles away, we should be able to calculate the net effect on weather if our models are sophisticated enough to capture all variables.

The problem arises if the variables are nonlinear, "relating to a system of equations whose effects are not proportional to their causes." Such a set of equations can be chaotic. So if the effects—possible future technological outcomes—are not proportional to their causes, then we have to try our best guess. I will try to be more exact in the root causes and likely outcomes (Figure 12.1).

12.2 Predictions: A Cautionary Tale

Here is an allegory to illustrate how predictions can be wrong, that is, probable outcomes that resulted in unexpected results. The exponential growth of the US space programs in the 1960s led to the moon landing on July 20, 1969. The decision to expand our launch capabilities and land on the moon appears to have been motivated by military concerns during the Cold War—*controlling the high ground*. The cause and effect seems straightforward: Sputnik 1, a Russian satellite, was the first manmade satellite sent into orbit on October 4, 1957, beating US efforts. Then on April 12, 1961, Yuri Gagarin, a Russian, became the first human in space. Both the Americans and Russians captured Nazi rocket scientists after World War II who led their respective programs. One month later, on May 25, 1961, President Kennedy announced the intent to land on the moon by the end of 1960s. "We choose to go to the moon in this decade and do the other things, not because they are easy, but because they are hard, because that goal will serve to organize and measure the best of our energies and skills." "There is no strife, no prejudice, no national conflict in outer space as yet. Its hazards are hostile to us all. Its conquest deserves the best of all mankind, and its opportunity for peaceful cooperation may never come again." The space race began. National pride was the stated goal, probably used to sell the program to the public; sorry to be so cynical, but trying to extrapolate all contributing factors is the intent of this allegory. The underlined comment there is no conflict in outer space as yet seems clear. So far all straightforward cause and effect.

A sample of positive nonlinear factors: (1) The series *Star Trek* was televised from September 8, 1966, to June 3, 1969. It started off slowly but quickly became very popular; interest in space exploration grew. (2) In 1968, *2001 A space Odyssey* was another popular movie whose centerpiece was the space station, a stepping point to future space exploration. The enthusiasm for space was building. But moon landings were abruptly canceled a few years after the initial landing: what happened? Most predictions suggested an exponential growth in space exploration.

A few negative forces: (1) We beat the USSR to the moon, which (most likely) was the major driving factor for the space race, not future space exploration. (2) The Vietnam war was in progress and was enormously taxing on the American psyche and pocketbook. (3) The Watergate scandal (possibly) dominated our political discourse, and the impeachment of Nixon on August 9, 1974, dominated our political discourse. Political forces and budget priorities have complex origins.

The Soviet Union canceled its manned moon landing programs in 1970, that is, the Proton and Zond (Soyuz) programs, due to failures and the preceding Apollo 11 Mission success. The public assumption at

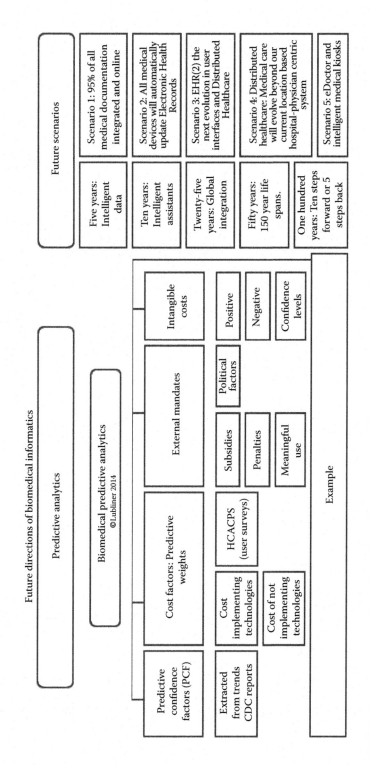

FIGURE 12.1 Future directions of biomedical informatics.

the time was that since they could not be first, they did not bother, or more likely the USSR was actually further behind then what they publicly admitted.

Apollo Missions 11–20 were planned, but the last three missions were canceled: Apollo 18 (scheduled for July 1973), Apollo 19, and 20. Written memos testify that Nixon, in August 1971, tried to cancel missions starting with Apollo 15. The stated intent was to focus resources on the Space Shuttle, one of whose missions was to launch satellites, including military satellites, and to use the Saturn V rockets for Skylab. Of the Saturn V rockets, Apollo-18-Saturn Rocket used for Apollo 17 moon mission, Apollo-19-Saturn Rocket on display in Houston Space Flight Center, and Apollo-20-Saturn Rocket were never built.

Why were the predictions about a continued space exploration at that time wrong? Could we have projected this retrenchment from moon and off-planet landings? Maybe. Was information on intent deducible? Yes, but a great deal was unavailable at that time. Could we have built a 2001 space station? Probably, if we started 30 years ago, but the will, at least funding, was unavailable. Very few scientists, maybe their wishful thinking, predicted the space retrenchment; maybe they were naive. Regardless of the public disappointment, future projections by a large part of the scientific community were wrong. We had beat the USSR to the moon; Vietnam and associated huge public military outlays were a factor, and maybe Nixon's Watergate deflected attention away, but that factor is a bigger stretch since that occurred 1 to 2 years later. Conclusion, projections are difficult, but if all components, including political factors, can be accounted for, a closer approximation of future trends can be obtained.

The purpose of this allegory was to illustrate that future projections, in this example space exploration, are composed of many complex factors. Even if they are based on sound technological grounds, they do not always come to fruition.

But that is not to say we should not try and project optimistic scenarios. We can improve our healthcare systems with access to all, beat disease, and improve longevity with the right combination of public and private support. Biomedical informatics (BMI) is at the forefront of healthcare and can influence the future of healthcare delivery. Dreams are the precursors of actions, the precursors of future utopias.

12.2.1 Metrics

In order to quantify the likelihood of any BMI trends, it is necessary to weigh the contributing factors and generate a predictive score that represents the likelihood of adoption and integration of future BMI initiatives.

Definition:

Predictive analytics is the practice of extracting information from existing data sets in order to determine patterns and predict future outcomes and trends. It does not tell you what will happen in the future. It forecasts what might happen in the future with an acceptable level of reliability and includes what-if scenarios and risk assessment.*

Predictive analytics mines data to predict trends. It is widely used in credit scoring to determine the future credit worthiness of individuals. It is a pattern of behavior and facts; that is, if that individual has paid his bills in the past, his job, income, and any criminal behavior are scored. In predictive analytics, the term of an explanatory variable is used, as opposed to independent variable, where the variables *may not be statistically independent.*

---

* www.webopedia.com

Definition:

An **independent variable** (explanatory variable), in mathematics, is a variable whose value determines the value of other variables.*

Definition:

The **dependent variable** (response variable) is a variable in a functional relation whose value is determined by the values assumed by other variables in the relation.

In psychology, the dependent variable is usually a measurement of some aspect of the participants' behavior. The independent variable is called *independent* because it is *free* to be varied by the experimenter. The dependent variable is called *dependent* because it is thought to *depend* (at least in part) on the manipulations of the independent variable (Weiten, 2013).

For example, the area of a circle is given by $A = \pi r^2$. Here, the independent variable is r, since its value determines the area (A). So the dependent variable is A.

12.2.2 Biomedical Predictive Analytics

Predicting any future technology or direction, especially for a particular discipline, has been an inexact science, no more than guesses. The goal of this section is to quantify predictive analytics for BMI. Similar results can be achieved for other disciplines by limiting the scope or independent variables and setting the limits of the nonlinear equations. Then combining these technological subsets into a unified field theory (UFT) of an entire field enhances the predictive accuracy (a lofty goal; in physics, UFT even eluded Einstein, but that too will eventually be realized).

Metrics that focus on specific factors unique to a field of study, that is, in this case the field of BMI, and incorporating into the predictive equation factors such as government mandates, reimbursement scales, user attitudes, and political support coefficients represented as probability coefficients, required HHS surveys HCAHPS that frame the scope of the predictive field will increase the accuracy of the prediction. Additional factors that enhance BMI predictive analytics are implementation and upgrade costs of electronic health records (EHRs), Health Information Technology for Economic and Clinical Health (HITECH) meaningful use criteria, etc. A metaphor for this approach would be predicting tree growth but starting at a particular branch and extrapolating growth patterns. The limbs and branches each have had contributing growth factors, and backtracking, we extrapolate future growth. Once each branch or subfield has been modeled, we can then backtrack and model the entire tree.

The BMI predictive equation will incorporate (Lubliner, 2015)

1. Predictive confidence factors (short, medium, long, and future-term coefficients)
2. Cost: predictive (factor) weights (implementing or not implementing new technology)
3. Government mandates (subsidies, penalties, meaningful use, and political factors)
4. Intangible costs (positive, negative, and confidence factors)

The rate of acceptance of a new technology or trend depends on cost, external mandates such as government regulations, and the will or wave of progress that moves technology to some degree of acceptance. Each of these factors is defined in the succeeding sections.

12.2.2.1 Predictive Confidence Factors

The predictive confidence factors (PCFs) are used to estimate the likelihood of an event occurring (Table 12.1). They are broken down into short-term predictions (in the next 5 years) that have a high probability of occurrence since they presuppose trends that are in the pipeline and extrapolate them to their

---

* http://www.sciencedictionary.com.

TABLE 12.1   Predictive Confidence Factor Coefficients (Multiplied by the Prediction to Indicate Predictive Likelihood or Divergence from Estimates)

Short Term: 5+ years (linear 3%/year)	Medium Term: 10+ years (linear 2%/year)	Long Term: 20+ years (nonlinear ±3%/year)	Future: 40+ years (nonlinear ±2%/year)
ST = 85%	MT = 70%	LT = 20%–40%	FT = 5%–20%
PCF = [ST, MT, LT, FT]			
= [3%, 2%, ±3%, ±2%]			

logical conclusions. Taking that into consideration, we need probability factors to reflect the likelihood based on the distance (time) to the predicted event, multiplied by the overall prediction for short term (5+ years), medium term (10+ years), long term (20+ years), and future (40+ years). The long-term prediction could be thought of as a nonlinear system "relating to a system of equations whose effects are not proportional to their causes." Examples are conflicts between nations, biological outbreaks, or some technological breakthrough, where the response has effects that are not proportional to the scale. Imagine a cure for some types of cancers. Attempting to calculate or predict future events has to include nonlinear factors. The longer the period, the higher the probability of nonproportional causes that may skew predictions.

The 3% rate for short- and medium-term trends was extrapolated from the January 2014 Center for Disease Control (CDC) report, indicating EHR adoption of 3.3% per year prior to the stimulus plan in 2009, HITECH Act (Figure 12.2). A PCF has to be extrapolated for each field based on representative trend data. Data were available for both 5- and 10-year periods (the 5-year EHR rate from 2001 to 2006

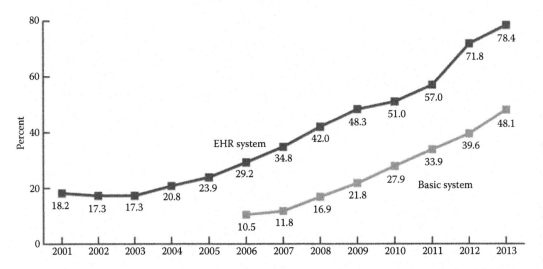

FIGURE 12.2   EHR implementation statistics as of January 2014. *Notes:* EHR is electronic health record. "Any EHR system" is a medical or health record system that is either all or partially electronic (excluding systems solely for billing). Data for 2001 to 2007 are from in-person National Ambulatory Medical Care Survey (NAMCS) interviews. Data for 2008 to 2010 are from combined files (in-person NAMCS and mail survey). Estimates for 2011–2013 data are based on the mail survey only. Estimates for basic system prior to 2006 could not be computed because some items were not collected in the survey. Data include nonfederal, office-based physicians and exclude radiologistis, anesthesiologists, and pathologists. (From CDC/NCHS, National Ambulatory Medical Care Survey and National Ambulatory Medical Care Survey, Electronic Health Records Survey. CDC https://www.google.com/url?sa=i&rct=j&q=&esrc=s&source=images&cd=&cad=rja&uact=8&docid=-Wg5J-nGEhQ6nM&tbnid=ZL5cFGMGhYbfKM:&ved=0CAUQjRw&url=http%3A%2F%2Fwww.cdc.gov%2Fnchs%2Fdata%2Fdatabriefs%2Fdb143.htm&ei=RwaeU9iYNq7jsATUyYDYCw&bvm=bv.68911936,d.cWc&psig=AFQjCNErUDWAq0Ky5ZuQKfNXsFQCleaoeg&ust=1402951600266245.)

was 2.2% per year, but there was an anomaly in 2002 and 2003 that skewed growth negative. Adjusting 5- and 10-year growth to 3% seems justifiable). After that in 2010, adoption doubled to 6.85%, the year after government mandates and cost sharing were contributing *cost factors*. These will be factored in Section 12.2.2.2. Nonlinear growth factors are based on external factors accelerating or decelerating predictive trends that have to be continuously recalculated for predictive accuracy. In this case, not only a stimulus plan that subsidized cost, but also government mandates, technological advancements, and the percentage increase in certain age populations (baby boomers) have changed the shape of the growth curve (Figure 12.2).

12.2.2.2 Cost Factors (Predictive Weights)

Predictive *cost factors* are broken down into several subfactors: cost of implementing new technologies, cost of lack of efficiency by not implementing a technology, and the intangible cost appearing to be falling behind the state of the art in that field (Table 12.2). This last factor, intangible costs, is a complex, nonlinear factor. If patients go to a hospital and find no EHRs, digital scheduling boards, Wi-Fi connectivity, or state-of-the-art technology, they may have a negative impression of the quality of the medical services.

The Health and Human Services (HHS) center for Medicare and Medicaid embeds the Hospital Consumer Assessment of Healthcare Providers and Systems (HCAHPS) survey under its Inpatient Prospective Payment System (IPPS) as one of the determining factors for reimbursement. Since patient satisfaction scores are required by HHS and penalties are assessed at 1%, 2%, and 3% per year progressively, they should be factored into cost predictions.

12.2.2.3 External Mandates

External mandates are government regulations and penalties that clearly rate high on any calculations to predict implementing technologies. These can take many forms: positive subsidies by government to offset costs, in particular the HITECH Act as part of the 2009 Stimulus Bill allocating $19.7 billion to help hospitals and physicians; penalties, where any Medicare or Medicaid bill, starting in 2015, will be reimbursed at a lower rate progressively, without electronic submission by physicians, not all medical practitioners as of 2015, or Hospital EHRs will incur a progressive 1%, 2%, and 3% penalty per year if bills are not submitted electronically. The meaningful use guidelines determine the integration level of the EHRs (Chapters 3 and 4). The last factor, *political factors*, influences funding levels. This is not a political statement, just an assessment of the role funding levels play in future predictions of BMI initiatives. Party A, as of 2014, voted 50+ times to repeal/replace the Affordable Care Act (ACA) (Obama Care) and did not support HITECH support to subsidize EHR implementation. Party B passed funding EHRs and the ACA and voted to increase funding in these areas. There are three values: a political party supportive

TABLE 12.2 Cost Factors, Predictive Weights

Implementing new technology (Cimp)	Not implementing new technology (CNimp)	Intangible costs
$Cimp = \dfrac{\text{Hardware and software outlays}}{\text{Avg.(net profits/year (s))}}$	Tyr = Revenues this year ex $150M$ Lyr = Revenues last year ex $175M$	Hospital Consumer Assessment of Healthcare Providers and Systems (HCAHPS)
Example $0.067 = Cimp = \dfrac{\$10 \text{ million (EHR Hosp.)}}{\$150 \text{ million net profit}}$	$CNimp = \dfrac{\Delta ABS[\text{avg.(revenues/years)}]}{\text{Avg.(net profits / year(s))}}$	Penalties 1%, 2%, and 3% (negative values) (publicly reported by HHS)
The average depends on length of projection; ST (2–4 years), MT (5 years), etc.	$CNimp = \dfrac{\$175M - \$150M}{\$150M} = 0.166$ Reduction in reimbursement 1%, 2%, and 3% after 2015	
If Cimp is below 10% (0.1) and reimbursement probability >90%, Cimp is not a factor.	This is a multiyear calculation If revenues have decreased for multiple years, one factor could be patient confidence. Should be correlated with HCAHPS score.	This is a patient satisfactory score that affects Medicare and Medicaid reimbursement. Hospitals must have 300+ completed surveys/year.

TABLE 12.3   BMI Prediction Calculation Factoring in Mandates

Mandates: Government or Professional			
(Relationship to Future Biomedical Informatics Predictions)			(Negative Value Disproportionally Affects BMI Predictions)
Subsidies	Penalties	Meaningful use (ranking the implementation quality)	Political factors
-HITECH subsides through end of 2015 value (1.0)	1%, 2%, and 3% reduction in Medicare and Medicaid reimbursement after 2015	Level 7=(1.0), Level 6 (0.9)	-Party supports healthcare (+1.0)
-After 2015 value (0.5) 50% future probability funding		Level 1=(0.3), no MU=(0.0)	-Party negative support (-1.0) (affect BMI funding levels)
			-Split congress (0.5) (funding could go either way)
MSi [1.0, 0.5]	MPi [0.1,.2,.3]	MUi [1,.9,.8..7.........0.0]	MPOLi [1.0, 0.5, −1.0]

TABLE 12.4   Intangible Factors

Intangible Costs (IC) (Positive or Negative Attitudes toward Biomedical Informatics Technologies Effecting Future Adoption)		
Positive (individual events) i.e., doctor, a procedure, etc.	Negative (individual events)	Confidence level (overall)
ICp confidence level from (0–0.9) (09. high confidence)	ICn same scale -ve(0–0.9)	ICo scale (0–1.0)
1.0 would be absolute certainly almost impossible to attain	A ICp=0.5 and ICn -0.5 cancel each other (i.e., no net effect)	This is an overall confidence of medicine related to doctor(s), pharmaceuticals research, etc.

of BMI (value 1.0); a spilt congress (value 0.5), in which case funding could go either way; and negative support (value −1.0). A negative mandate, no matter how compelling the scientific data, for example, climate change with a more than 98% global scientific community consensus, will influence funding and skew predictions accordingly. This may change in the future, and these coefficients should be adjusted accordingly (Table 12.3).

12.2.2.4 Intangible Costs

Intangible costs are the most difficult to assess. If patients/customers believe that a business or profession is not at an acceptable level of technology integration, they will be less confident of the skill level of the practitioners. Extreme examples might be a phone store selling flip phones or an electronics store selling cathode ray tube televisions or a doctor's office using a typewriter. As soon as you see stacks of paper records rather than EHRs, you predict that the physicians are not aware of the latest medical technologies (Table 12.4).

12.3 HCAHPS Score

A key metric is the HCAHPS survey of 21 questions measuring patient satisfaction required by the HHS, which will be publicly available and factored into Medicare and Medicaid reimbursement. The first public reporting of HCAHPS results in March 2008 included 2,521 hospitals and 1.1 million completed surveys; the Spring 2012 public reporting entailed 3,851 hospitals and 2.8 million completed surveys. Summary analyses of HCAHPS scores are available on the HCAHPS website www.hcahpsonline.org (Table 12.5).

Definition:

The intent of the HCAHPS initiative is "to provide a standardized survey instrument and data-collection methodology for measuring patients' perspectives on hospital care. HCAHPS survey

TABLE 12.5　HCAHAPS Patient Survey Categories

HCAHPS Cover Nine Topic Areas	
1	Communication with doctors
2	Communication with nurses
3	Responsiveness of hospital staff
4	Pain management
5	Communication about medicines
6	Discharge information
7	Cleanliness of the hospital environment
8	Quietness of the hospital environment
9	Transition of care
New	Overall rating of hospital

items complement the data hospitals currently collect to support improvements in internal customer services and quality related activities."*

Definition:

The Hospital Value-Based Purchasing (VBP) Program is an initiative of the Centers for Medicare and Medicaid Services (CMS) that rewards acute care hospitals with incentive payments for the quality of care they provide to people with Medicare.

The Hospital VBP Program was established by the 2010 ACA, which added Section 1886(o) to the Social Security Act. The law requires the Secretary of the Department of HHS to establish a VBP program for inpatient hospitals. To improve quality, the ACA builds on earlier legislation—the 2003 Medicare Prescription Drug, Improvement, and Modernization Act and the 2005 Deficit Reduction Act. These earlier laws established a way for Medicare to pay hospitals for reporting on quality measures, a necessary step in the process of paying for quality rather than quantity.†

Penalties‡:

- The Hospital Readmission Reduction Program imposes financial penalties on hospitals for "excess" readmissions compared to "expected" levels of readmissions. The penalty program began on October 1, 2012. The initial payment penalties are based on the 30-day readmission measures for heart attack, heart failure, and pneumonia that are currently part of the Medicare IQR.
- Reduce hospital base Medicare payments by up to 1% in FY 2013.
- The potential penalty increases to 2% of base payments in FY 2014.
- Three percent in FY 2015 and beyond.

The HHS center for Medicare and Medicaid embeds the HCAHPS survey under its IPPS as one of the determining factors for reimbursement. The complete title of the program is "Hospital Inpatient Prospective Payment Systems for Acute Care Hospitals and the Long-Term Care Hospital Prospective Payment System; Quality Reporting Requirements for Specific Providers; Hospital Conditions of Participation; Payment Policies Related to Patient Status."§

HHS requires that as part of its IPPS, the HCAHPS survey, hospitals must survey patients throughout each month of the year, and IPPS hospitals must achieve at least 300 completed surveys over four calendar quarters. HCAHPS is available in official English, Spanish, Chinese, Russian, and Vietnamese

---

* http://www.hcahpsonline.org/home.aspx.
† http://www.cms.gov/Medicare/Quality-Initiatives-Patient-Assessment-Instruments/hospital-value-based-purchasing/Downloads/FY-2013-Program-Frequently-Asked-Questions-about-Hospital-VBP-3-9-12.pdf.
‡ AHA.org.
§ http://www.gpo.gov/fdsys/pkg/FR-2013-08-19/pdf/2013-18956.pdf.

versions. *HCAHPS Quality Assurance Guidelines Manual* is available on the official HCAHPS website. Ten HCAHPS measures (six summary measures, two individual items, and two global items) are publicly reported on the Hospital Compare website* for each participating hospital.

HCAHPS Scoring[†]

1. Hospital VBP utilizes HCAHPS scores from two time periods: a baseline and a performance period. For FY 2013, the baseline period covers patients discharged from July 1, 2009, through March 31, 2010, and the performance period from July 1, 2011, through March 31, 2012.
2. The Patient Experience of Care Domain Score has two parts: the HCAHPS Base Score (maximum of 80 points) and the HCAHPS Consistency Points Score (maximum of 20 points).
3. The second part of the Patient Experience of Care Domain is the Consistency Points Score, which ranges from 0 to 20 points. Consistency Points are designed to target and further incentivize improvement in a hospital's lowest-performing HCAHPS dimension.
4. The Patient Experience of Care Domain Score is the sum of the HCAHPS Base Score (0–80 points) and HCAHPS Consistency Points Score (0–20 points), which ranges from 0 to 100 points and comprises 30% of the Hospital VBP Total Performance Score.

12.4 Center for Disease Control Data (Trends)

The CDC reported in January 2014 (Figure 12.2)[‡]

- 78% of office physicians had some form of basic EHR system (CDC data Table 12.2)
  - From 2001, where it stood at 18%, to 2010, where it was 51%
    - 51%–18% = 33% increase or 3.3% per year imp rate prior to stimulus incentives
  - From 51% in 2010 to 78.4% in 2013
    - 78.4–51 = 27.4% increase or 6.85% per year, doubled due to stimulus plan

12.5 Future Scenarios

The following are future BMI scenarios divided into several categories and time frames. They will be rated by time period (short, medium, long, and future); technological difficulty (easy, medium, and difficult); and the likelihood of occurring (low, medium, and high) in the indicated time frame and factors that may contribute positively or negatively. The scenarios proposed were chosen because they appear to be technologically feasible, following current trends; but feasibility can be trumped by other external forces. Each scenario will include a table entry summarizing parameters and predictions.

12.5.1 Scenario 1

Hypothesis: In the next five years, 95% of all medical documentation will be integrated and online; EHRs are just one of many components (Table 12.6).

Discussion

Data: As of 2013, the CDC data indicated that 78% of physicians use some form of EHR. Government mandates require EHRs by hospitals and physicians at the end of 2015 and subsequent penalties in Medicare and Medicaid reimbursement. By 2015, about 95% of physicians and hospitals will use EHRs. But what about dentists, optometrists, etc.?

---

* www.hospitalcompare.hhs.gov.
[†] http://www.hcahpsonline.org/files/HCAHPS%20Fact%20Sheet%20May%202012.pdf.
[‡] http://www.himss.org/News/NewsDetail.aspx?ItemNumber=27596.

TABLE 12.6 Scenario 1

Parameters	Time Period (Years) [ST, MT, LT, future] [5, 10, 20, 40+]	Technological Difficulty [easy, medium, difficult] [1, **2**, 3]	Likelihood of Occurring [low, medium, high, very high] [<25%, **50%,** 75%, 90+]
Predicted outcomes	Short term (5 years) (2015–19)	-Hospitals and physicians **1** -Dentists, optometrists, etc. **2**	-Very high 90%+ -Medium 50%

- By mid-2014, dentists do not have the regulatory requirements to convert to electronic dental records (EDRs).
- Minnesota is the only state that requires dentists to implement EHRs by the end of 2014, but there are currently no penalties.*
- Approximately 50% of dentists use digital x-rays as of June 2014.
- Electronic Dental Records (EDRs) have not yet reached the level of EHRs, and in general have not met the Health Insurance Portability and Accountability Act (HIPAA) and HITECH meaningful use criteria with associated supporting forms, labs, etc.
  - EDR pressures include
    - Safer record keeping during disaster recovery
    - Pressures from insurance companies to submit claims digitally
    - Drug interactions with other treatments
    - Linkages between dental disease and certain illnesses such as heart disease
    - Individual requests for copies of their dental records (currently physicians are required by HIPAA to supply copies of medical records)
- American Dental Association (ADA)†:
  - *ADA advice on the EHR incentive program (May 2013)*: "Theoretically, all dentists are eligible for both the Medicare and Medicaid EHR incentive programs since dentists were included in the provider categories established by the federal EHR incentive program statutes. Practically speaking, since Medicare pays for very little dental work the dentist's eligibility would depend on his/her work through the Medicaid program run by each state individually."
- The ADA has been working, since 2007, on Systemized Nomenclature of Dentistry (SNODENT) to standardize terminology in the dental field, similar to SNOMED (see Chapter 4)‡
  - To provide standardized terms for describing dental disease
  - To capture clinical detail and patient characteristics
  - To permit analysis of patient care services and outcomes
  - To be interoperable with EHRs and EDRs

Summary (Analysis)

The HHS mandates require all hospitals and physicians to convert to EHRs by 2015 or receive reimbursement penalties from Medicare and Medicaid if bills and data are not electronically submitted. The 2009 Stimulus Bill provided funding to help defray implementation cost not only for hospitals and physicians but other medical practitioners, including dentists, which will expire by 2015.

This combination of carrot and stick will ensure hospitals and physicians reach the 95%+ EHR implementation goal in the next 5 years. But additional funding beyond 2015 is not guaranteed. Political uncertainties in the next few elections will have a great deal of impact on EHR expansion for

---

* http://www.ihealthbeat.org/articles/2013/7/25/minnesota-requires-dental-care-providers-to-implement-ehrs.
† http://www.ada.org/en/member-center/member-benefits/practice-resources/dental-informatics/electronic-health-records.
‡ http://www.ada.org/en/member-center/member-benefits/practice-resources/dental-informatics/snodent.

TABLE 12.7   Scenario 2

Parameters	Time Period (Years) [ST, MT, LT, future] [**5**, **10**, 20, 40+]	Technological Difficulty [easy, medium, difficult] [**1**, 2, 3]	Likelihood of Occurring [low, medium, high, very high] [<25%, **50%,** 75%, 90+]
Predicted outcome	Short-medium (5–10 years) (2014–2023)	-Hospitals and physicians **1** -Wireless medical devices **1**	-Very high 90%+ -Medium 90+%

all other medical practitioners. Other medical specialties such as dentists, optometrists, mental health-care workers, etc., are estimated to be no better than 50/50 overall (physicians+dentists + other medical practitioners) whether they meet that 95%+ goal in the next 5 years.

12.5.2 Scenario 2

Hypothesis: In 5 to 10 years, all medical devices will automatically update EHRs directly. This will not only be in hospitals but will include wearable wireless medical devices (Table 12.7).

Discussion

In hospitals, this trend has already begun. Entering data by nurses is a tedious and time-consuming endeavor and prone to error. The primary factor is initial cost, upgrading EHRs and equipment, these minor impediments can be offset by the time saved by nurses and more accurate readings and seems to be a likely bet of occurring.

Nonhospital medical devices, that is, wireless wearable medical devices, equipment in physicians' offices, etc., will also have the ability to wirelessly update medical records. Data records may be kept by individuals, but this data will be accessible by physicians for a more longitudinal view of patients. Also at-home monitoring of critically ill patients will reduce hospital stays. This also seems highly likely especially for preventive care mandated in the 2010 ACA, Obama Care.

Summary

EHRs' aim is to provide a complete view of patient health data. Since most of this data are more relevant in everyday venues, not having this incorporated in EHRs seems counterproductive. So there is a high likelihood of automatic EHR integration.

12.5.3 Scenario 3

Hypothesis: EHR(2), defined as the next evolution in user interfaces and **distributed healthcare**. In the next 5 years, EHR user interfaces will be easily customizable to reflect the needs of each medical practitioner with little need for drop down menus and designed to reflect current phone and tablet user interfaces (Table 12.8).

Discussion

If current generation of EHRs follows past evolutionary designs, such as the Microsoft Office Suite or Windows 7-8 operating systems. Newer user interfaces Windows 10 and touch screen phones and tablets

TABLE 12.8   Scenario 3

Parameters	Time Period (Years) [ST, MT, LT, future] [**5**, 10, 20, 40+]	Technological Difficulty [easy, medium, difficult] [1, **2**, 3]	Likelihood of Occurring [low, medium, high, very high] [<25%, **50%,** 75%, 90+]
Predicted outcome	Short term (5 years) (2014–2018)	-Hospitals and physicians **1** -Dentists, optometrists, etc. **2** -**EHR(2)**	-Very high 75%+ -Very high 75% -Very high 50%–75%

will have intuitive user interfaces, either selecting an icon or gestures to expand the items with some series of gestures, etc.

A reasonable percentage of physicians access EHRs through their portable devices and some hospital staff also use tablets. The pressure to make screens more user friendly, enhancing efficiency, and leaving more time for medical care, as opposed to data entry, would seem to support EHR(2), the next evolution in EHR design. Predictive level is very high—75% for scenario 3.

12.5.4 Scenario 4

Hypothesis: Long term (20+ years) distributed healthcare: Medical care will evolve beyond our current location-based, hospital–physician office centric system. Wireless medical devices will be worn, or in more acute situations, pacemakers, defibrillators, cancer care, etc. devices will be implanted and connected wirelessly. Pill dispensers, as will most of devices, will be intelligently connected to the Cloud, to close the healthcare loop. Telemedicine be ubiquitous, communicating with either live or simulated health advisers. Proactive care will change the face of healthcare and reduce costs dramatically, since outpatient care is significantly less expensive (Table 12.9).

Discussion

The forces leading to a more distributed healthcare system are considerable. Hospitals are closing and being replaced by ambulatory emergency departments. Coverage for in-hospital stays is being reduced. Outpatient medical centers, both acute and nonacute, such as minute clinics are proliferating. Online apps that allow medical practitioners with Skype-like video interactions are already here. New certifications such as CCRN-E allow critical nurses to monitor patients in rural ICUs. Virtually everyone already has Smart phones and tablets that are increasing in capability; the computing power of Smart phones is comparable to PCs. In the near future, medical kiosks in malls and public spaces will allow the equivalent of a medical checkup in minutes automatically linked to EHRs and medical practitioners will immediately be notified to triage acute situations, possibly even to dispense drugs, with a wearable injection or patch. The systems may be able to detect pre-heart attack symptoms and dispense blood thinners connected to an eDoctor with embedded intelligence.

A new medical paradigm has to be designed as a real-time feedback system that integrates healthcare with the next generation of EHRs and real-time wireless medical equipment and communications.

Summary

All the factors leading to a distributed healthcare paradigm and EHR(2) seem inevitable. The technology is there, which will reduce the cost involved in outpatient care and facilities and will, in some respect, promote more personalized care through in-home doctor visits on demand through phone or tablet. Proactive healthcare with new wearable medical monitoring devices worn or through phones has already begun to appear. The only question is the speed at which this integrated system will be commonplace. The prediction is well above 50% in the next 20 years and even sooner.

TABLE 12.9 Scenario 4 Statistics

Parameters	Time Period (Years) [ST, MT, LT, future] [5, 10, **20**, 40+]	Technological Difficulty [easy, medium, difficult] [1, **2**, 3]	Likelihood of Occurring [low, medium, high, very high] [<25%, **50%**, 75%, 90+]
Predicted outcome	Long term (20+ years) (2014–2033)	-Distributed healthcare	-Medium 50%+
		-Intelligently web-based medical devices	-Medium 50+%

TABLE 12.10   Scenario 5 Statistics

Parameters	Time Period (Years) [ST, MT, LT, future] [5, 10, 20, **40+**]	Technological Difficulty [easy, medium, difficult] [1, **2**, 3]	Likelihood of Occurring [low, medium, high, very high] [<25%, **50%**, 75%, 90+]
Predicted outcome	Long term (40+ years) (2014–2053)	-eDoctor **2**	-Medium 25%–50%+
		-Intelligent kiosks 2	-Medium 25–50+%

12.5.5 Scenario 5

Hypothesis: **eDoctor** and **intelligent medical kiosks** that can diagnose and dispense drugs in the next 40 years (future), all linked to a global EHR network—**EHR(3)** (Table 12.10).

Discussion

We are moving toward intelligent self-driving cars. As of 2014, Google has prototypes that have driven over a million miles without an accident. There have been a few accidents, but currently with 50,000 driving deaths a year and hundreds of thousands of injuries and medical and repair costs into hundreds of billions a year, this would be a vast improvement. At the very least, the current cars that automatically stop before hitting the car in front will be commonplace shortly.

In 2014, the CDC reported that 600,000 people died of heart diseases per year in the United States. The cost is $108.9 billion annually.* Heart disease constitutes one in four deaths per year. There are 725,000 heart attacks each year, of which 525,000 are first heart attacks, and 92% first noticed chest pain as a symptom. Imagine if this happened in some public area or at work. A patient could walk to an intelligent kiosk or device; all public places could be mandated to have one, similar to defibrillators for airplanes. The device will do a quick diagnosis, and using its own software, eDoctor, or after an e-consult with an online doctor, will dispense an antiplatelet medication to prevent the formation of blood clots in the arteries. This could be true for asthma, allergic reactions, etc. If there were a predisposition to allergy or heart attack, it could be embedded into a wrist watch to dispense a life-saving drug. Wrist bands could also be available to dispense drugs while in sleep for individuals with a history of heart attacks.

Intelligent medical kiosks are similar. As computing speed and sensors increase, walking slowly through the entrance could generate a quick medical diagnostic evaluation. The third-generation **EHR(3)** would have a virtual doctor that could interact and recommend treatments and, by having your EHRs, could tell you to eat your vegetables, stop smoking, and more realistically monitor your exercise, possibly turning off the computer or TV until you complete your exercise regimen.

Summary

In 40+ years, it will be technologically feasible and could be incorporated into healthcare costs. EHR(3) and intelligent kiosks are feasible, but possible intrusion into people's lives might be a factor that can prevent adoption. It has a probability of 25% to 50%.

Level II: BMI Predictive Analytics Applied

12.6 Case Study: Scenario 1

The following calculates all factors in scenario 1 (utilizing predictive analytics equations)
Prediction: In the next 5 years, all (95%+) medical disciplines will ubiquitously incorporate EHRs.

- Predictive factors:
  - Cost: Reimbursement by Medicare, Medicaid, and prescriptions has mandated that after 2015, progressively 1%, 2%, and 3% will be subtracted from reimbursement if claims are not submitted electronically.

* http://www.cdc.gov/heartdisease/facts.htm.

- • Probability high.
- • Contributing factors:
  - • Cost of transitioning to EHRs will decrease.
- • This is a short-term prediction, occurring in the next 5 years, which usually has a high probability of occurrence since it presupposes trends that are in the pipeline and extrapolating to their logical conclusions.

12.6.1 BMI Predictive Equation Example

BMI Predictive Analysis: 2014–2019

1. Predictive Confidence Factor (PCF)
   i. Scenario A: **PCF**, Short Term = **0.3%**
      0.3% × 5 Years = 15%, implies starting with **85% probability** prediction is **accurate**

12.6.2 Cost Factors

2. Predictive Cost Factors

a. Cimp (cost of implementing new technology in physicians, office)			100,000 (software + hardware) cost 1,000,000 net income hospital =.1
2014, 2015	**0.9**	90% cost covered by Stimulus plan	
2016, 2017, 2018	**0.5**	Unclear 50/50 probability of	
Avg.	**0.7**	subsidized cost. New funding bills	
b. CNimp (cost not implementing new technology)			
	0.2% avg	Penalties: 1% 2016, 2% 2017, 3% 2018	
c. HCAHPS assume initial 10% impact			

Results		
Cimp (**0.7 factor × 0.1 EHR** compliance)	+ 0.2 (10% noncompliance by 2016; (i.e. CDC graph estimates 90% EHR implemented)	+0% HCAHPS
=(0.7 × 0.1)	+(0.2 × 0.1)	+0.0
=0.07	+.02	+0.0
=**0.09**	Means in 9% of physicians 2014–2019 cost may be an implementation issue	

Cost of implementation an issue for Adopting EHR (physicians) (**Only after 2016** when funding stops)		
0.09 or **9% of physicians** EHR implementation **costs will be an issue** (with CDC implementation curve 90% will have completed implementation, so this only **affects remaining 10%**)		Dependent on increase Funding after 2015

BMI Predictive Analysis	.85[CInt+Cnint+HCAPHPS)+(Mandates)+(Intangible costs)]
	=**0.85[0.09+(Mandated) + (Intangible costs)]**

12.6.3 Mandate Factors

3. Mandates: (Table 12.11)
   1. MSi (mandate compliance)
      from 2014 to 2019 (first 2 years reimbursement covered, last few years uncertain avg. value
      =(1.0 +.5 probability)/5 years
      =(1.0,1.0,0.5,0.5,0.5)/5= 3.5/5=0.7
   2. MPi (penalty): 1%, 2%, 3% reimbursement penalties for Medicare and Medicaid patients penalties for noncompliance start at end of 2015

TABLE 12.11 BMI Mandates

		Mandates: Government or Professional	
(Relationship to Future Biomedical Informatics Predictions)			(Negative Value Disproportionally Affects BMI Predictions)
Subsidies	Penalties	Meaningful use (MU) (ranking the implementation quality)	Political factors
-HITECH subsides through end of 2015 <u>value (1.0)</u>	1%, 2%, and 3% reduction in Medicare and	Level 7=(1.0), Level 6 (0.9)	-Party supports healthcare (**+1.0**)
-After 2015 <u>value (0.5)</u> 50% future prob. funding	Medicaid reimbursement after 2015	Level 1=(0.3), no MU=(0.0)	-Party negative support (**−1.0**) (affect BMI funding levels)
		Percentage have met MU	-Split congress (0.5) (funding could go either way)
MSi [1.0, 0.5] =**0.7**	MPi =**−0.112**	MUi [1,.9,.8..7.........0.0] **0.815**	MPOLi [1.0, 0.5, -1.0] **0.7**

3. 2014 to 2019

    When penalties start in 2016, the remaining outliers (no EHRs) will feel financial pressure to implement systems. EHR implementation (2014 = 78 + 3% = 81%, 2015 = 84%, 2016 = 87%, 2017 = 90%, 2018 = 93%)

    (100–81 = 19%, 100–84 = 16%, 13%, 10%, 7%) = 0.19 + 0.16 + 0.13 + 0.10 + 0.07)/5 = − 0.112

4. MUi (meaningful use)

    This is more difficult since there are seven levels of achievement and reimbursement percentages based on compliance levels that are in flux. Estimate in (compliant 1.0, partial 0.5, none −0.5) this last term reflects 5% do not implement EHR's,

    currently 78% have implemented EHRs (CDC data), and 22% remaining. If we predict 95% EHR compliance, 95%–78% = 17%.

    At an annual implementation rate of (3%–6.8%) per year, approximately avg. 5.0% = (1 × 0.78) + (0.5 × 0.17) − (0.5 × 5%) = 0.78 + 0.085 − 0.025 = 0.815

    (the political climate has an important effect on future funding)

5. From 2014 to 2016 president supportive of healthcare 1.0 in 2017, 2018 support could go either way 0.5 (1,1,0.5,0.5,0.5) per 5 years = 3.5/5 = 0.8

    The factors are multiplied by MPOLi since positive or negative support will determine funding or passing future initiates.

0.85	[0.09 + (Mandates)	+ (Intangible costs)]
0.85	[0.09 + ([**0.7 + 0.12**) × **0.815**] × **0.7**)	+ intangible costs]
0.85	[0.09 + (**.66178**) × **0.7**)	+ intangible costs]
0.85	0.09 + **.463246** + intangible costs]	+ intangible costs]
MPA = 0.85[.553246 + Intangible costs]		

12.6.4 Intangible Cost Factors

4. Intangible costs
    i. **ICp** (positive effects) (using 0.9 confidence level, best case, for EHR adoption)
        1. focusing on EHRs = (current EHRs 0.78 × 0.9) = 0.**702**
    ii. **ICn** (negative effects) (22% remaining (where 17% have upgraded 95% prediction)
        1. =(0.17 × 0.9) = **0.153**

TABLE 12.12 BMI Mandates

Intangible Costs (IC) (Positive Or Negative Attitudes toward Biomedical Informatics Technologies Affecting Future Adoption)		
Positive (individual events) i.e., doctor, a procedure, etc.	Negative (individual events)	Confidence level (Overall)
ICp confidence level from (**0–0.9**) (09. high confidence) 1.0 would be absolute certainly almost impossible to attain **=0.702**	ICn same scale -ve(**0–0.9**) A ICp=0.5 and ICn -0.5 cancel each other (i.e., no net effect) **0.153**	ICo scale (**0–1.0**) This is an overall confidence of medicine related to doctor(s), pharmaceuticals research, etc. **0.55**

iii. ICo (confidence level) this is difficult to assess, but in the United States, we have, as of 2013, 143 million Smart phones, which is about 45% of population. Let us assume 5% growth per year (2014–19). Overall confidence implies public support, which can influence public policies and future funding levels

    1. (0.45,0.5,0.55,0.60,0.65)/5 years **=0.55**

Caveat: If all the mandated factors indicated an absolute certainty of occurrence, that is, guaranteed future EHR funding, all users met optimum meaningful use goals, level 7, and political support was certain, the values could reach a probability exceeding 100%. These probability estimates generate reasonable results by balancing factors that represent historical results. Prior efforts by political parties for 50 years to pass healthcare reforms were without success. It is reasonable to assume there will be bumps in the road. Including factors that represent these historical norms may be more predictive of future realities (Table 12.12).

MPA = 0.85[.553246 + Intangible costs]
    = 0.85[.553246 + (0.702 – 0.1530) × 0.55]
    = 0.85[.553246 + (0.552) × 0.55]
    = 0.85[.553246 + 0.3036]
    = 0.85[0.856846]
    = 0.7283191 approximately 73%

Prediction there is a **73% probability** that 95% of all medical staff will have EHRs in 5 years.

12.6.5 Analysis of Results

At the start of this 5-year prediction, dentists, optometrists, dermatologists, mental healthcare workers, etc. are not required by law to implement EHRs and there is no government funding allocated for this purpose post-2015. There are pressures that will push medical practices in this direction, but this final group may move slower and take longer to implement EHRs saturation at the 95+% level.

Alternate Scenario:

If the political factors supported additional funding for EHR implementation through 2019, altering the MPOLi factors to (1: high probability of political support) for all 5 years, this would increase the predictive probability significantly, increasing the probability to 90% (Table 12.13).

TABLE 12.13 Altering Factors to Analyze Effect on Predictive Equations

Change Factors MPOLi (Implies Higher Probability of Expanded EHR Funder beyond 2015)	
Original MPA=	**New factors:** 0.5 is 1.0 (for 2016 – 2019)
MPOLi (1,1,0.5,0.5,0.5)/5 = **0.7**	MPOLi (1,1,1,1,1)/5 = **1.0**
= 0.85[0.09 + (**0.66178**) × 0.7 + 0.856846]	= 0.85[0.09 + (**0.66178**) × 1.0 + 0.3036]
= 0.85[0.856846]	= 0.85[1.05538]
= 0.7283191	= 0.8970
Probability approximately **73%**	Probability approximately **90%**

Level III: The Future of Biomedical Informatics

12.7 BMI Predictions

Where do we go from here, creating *meaning out of chaos*? In the second decade of the twenty-first century, we have already linked the planet into an integrated web that allows us to communicate virtually instantly. These early generations of Smart phones and tablets provide a glimpse of what is possible with intuitive user interfaces. We are poised at the threshold of the next evolutionary step.

In the next decade, technology will provide true symbiotic interaction between users and technology. Embedded sensors will provide real-time data to be collected in every sphere of science. The troika of computers, sensors, and intelligent energy monitors will reduce per capita energy usage and change the trajectory of our civilization. The only caveat is the unexpected: war, disease, religious strife, and maybe extraterrestrials, benevolent ones.

- In meteorology, satellites and ground-based sensors on land and in the oceans, with more accurate simulation software, will provide ever more detailed weather and climate projections.
- In transportation, sensors embedded in vehicles, roadways, and intelligent drones will dynamically adjust traffic patterns. Intelligent vehicles will reduce accidents, allow for smaller lighter vehicles, and immediately dispatch repair vehicles. Smaller lighter vehicles will also reduce overall energy consumption. The rate of 50,000 vehicle deaths per year may be reduced dramatically.
- More efficient intelligent buildings will reduce energy consumption. In 2012, about 461 billion kWh of electricity was used for lighting by the residential and commercial sectors. This was about 17% of the total electricity consumed by both these sectors and about 12% of total US electricity consumption.* Energy-efficient light bulbs use approximately 75% less energy than older light bulbs, so these energy consumption percentages will drop.† An example of a technology changing energy consumption is the intelligent web-controlled NEST Thermostat, which learns your personal patterns. As of 2013, it is estimated to have saved 30% of heating costs per year (https://community.nest.com/thread/1021). This trend of intelligent sensors will accelerate.

12.7.1 Five Years: Intelligent Data

These evolutionary technologies will also alter the face of healthcare. In the next 5 years, medical sensors will be ubiquitously embedded in all our devices, Smart phones, clothing, jewelry, etc., wirelessly linked through a newer more intelligent EHR. We may have to create a new term that represents real-time wireless integration of medical data linked into data accumulated in our daily lives, maybe a *"LIFE record"* (LIFEr). More than medical data will be accumulated; video clips, dietary choices, daily itineraries, website and reading preferences, medical records, etc. All these devices will be tied together with a personal digital assistant that learns your patterns and predicts your needs. For example, when you open your smart device, only news articles in your area of interest will be displayed first. Traffic patterns and alternate routes for your personal commute as well as shopping or sales items related to your past purchases will be displayed. Health-related data will also appear, suggesting exercise, dietary, and medical alerts.

---

* http://www.eia.gov/tools/faqs/faq.cfm?id=99&t=3.
† http://energy.gov/energysaver/articles/led-lighting.

12.7.2 Ten Years: Intelligent Assistants

Personal digital assistants will become relatively intelligent. You can have an intelligent dialog discussing specifically health and financial issues, and maybe these assistants will have the rudiments of a personal friend or therapist. They may also mine data from your LIFEr record, analyzing work frustrations and suggesting job changes, and the probability of success of landing that new position. They constantly inform you about available openings as well as education and training opportunities, a nagging mom. They can analyze job trends and suggest moving into related fields, both personal and financial. They can suggest available apartments that are more convenient to work. LIFEr would have access to your financial records and could suggest changes in your spending or investment strategies. With the ability to turn them off.

12.7.3 Twenty-Five Years: Global Integration

As communications are embedded in every device, including medicine, clothes, food items, etc., the world will truly be smaller. Food, medicine, or any commodity will be automatically tracked by every transaction and shipment or production adjusted automatically. This interdependence could be so great or the global scarcities of food and energy so acute that the borders will essentially dissolve. The other mitigating factor is military budgets that consume between 1% and 4.5% (the US budget was 4.5% of GDP in 2013) of world resources, which may be unsustainable. Other driving factors might be a global crises that could only be solved by global partnerships. At some point with the world population approaching 9 billion in 25 years, some global consolidation on a logical level seems probable.* (Though the world has surprised us before WWI, WWII, etc.)

12.7.4 Fifty Years: 150-Year Life Span

Information and research tools will allow intelligent software to share results in real time, and advancements will be fed directly into pharmaceutical or production facilities. This will include medical devices or embedded drug dispensers. Research equipment will be semi-intelligent in targeted areas to conduct research independently, thus speeding up medical discoveries. Since life expectancy doubled from 1900 (40 years) to 2000 (80 years), doubling again does not seem unreasonable in 50 years with the accelerated rate of technological and medical research.

12.7.5 One Hundred Years: Ten Steps Forward or Five Steps Back

This is a tough prediction. If we assume that technology continues to accelerate at the current pace, we could see advances that may be unrecognizable to scientists today. A hundred years ago, there were no computers, TV, Internet, and antibiotics, and medical scanners consisted of simple x-rays. How would we have described our current technology in early twentieth century terms? In the next 100 years, the lines between biology and technology will blur. Gene cell therapy will be adaptable to most diseases, and nano-robotics or intelligent microbes will traverse our system to augment our immune system. Stem cell research will generate or repair diseased organs, including our brains. These device-embedded biotechnologies will monitor and report to future EHRs. We too will have direct brain access to the global information web with technology. Education will transform to where we can close our eyes and join global virtual classrooms or interact with a virtual personal teacher. Since data or knowledge can be downloaded to an embedded storage device or instant access to global data stores, facts may not be as important as organizing and extracting meaning.

---

* http://data.worldbank.org/indicator/MS.MIL.XPND.GD.ZS.

Universal medical access will hopefully be available to all. Planetary resources should be adequate if global conflict and income inequalities are resolved and resources are equally shared. At the very least, some limit on resource allocation needs to be set. Nobody is so valuable that they are worth more than 10 or 100 times that of others. If an average salary in 2015 is $50,000, then 100 times that is $5 million. It is estimated currently that 100 families have the equivalent resources of 3 billion people. A future based on an individual's knowledge and contribution to society would benefit all.

Sociological advances seem to move more slowly. Many have the same prejudices their grandparents had. We could have the ability to start colonizing other planets, possibly driven by resource or overpopulation concerns, but if we bring our attitudes and prejudices with us, we remain stagnant and recreate the inequities of the past wherever we are. Will there be a rich–poor divide or will we evolve beyond our infancy. We have to be optimistic; we are the teachers, philosophers, gurus that will set the foundations of future societies. In 100 years from now, our future civilization will stand on our shoulders, a duty and privilege we do not always appreciate.

12.8 Summary

The science of BMI is in its infancy. The recent funding mandates that began in 2009 in the United States spurred adoption by hospitals and physicians. During this period of rapid expansion, physicians and nurses faced the challenge of navigating and entering data with relatively primitive user interfaces. Phase I involved the adoption of EHRs and the development of the support IT infrastructure. This next phase, beginning after 2015, will be to tailor the user interfaces to the needs of individual users and to provide sophisticated navigation capabilities that have been available to tablet and Smart phone users for the past decade. Auto data entry to EHRs has slowly begun, but this capability is critical in hospital settings where nurses have numerous monitoring devices, far too many to enter this data manually. Earlier in the book, consider the analogy to airplane pilots who might be similarly stressed if they had to fly the plane and simultaneously enter critical data on wind speed, direction, etc. Try this with five patients and the task is daunting.

This chapter proposes metrics to quantify predictive analytics for BMI. Any prediction is a complex combination of factors, but if most of the variables are provided, estimates can be reliable. Finally a series of possible evolutions to this science are discussed mostly to raise the concerns and hopes of professionals in the field regarding the future benefits that can be achieved. Proactive diagnosis and treatment can reduce the severity of most diseases, and with new treatment methodologies, these diseases can be cured. The adage "knowledge is power" should be the mantra of BMI.

Questions

Level I

1. Why extrapolate future trends in medical practice?
2. What is predictive analytics? Explain how independent and dependent variables are used in predictive analytics?
3. Explain what the author defines as the four components of medical predictive analytics.
   a. In your opinion what does each component add to the analysis of future trends?
   b. What are predictive confidence factors?
   c. What are cost: predictive (factor) weights?
   d. What are government mandates?
   e. What are intangible costs?

4. What are HCAHPS scores?
   a. Why are they included in the medical predictive analytics?
   b. What are the government penalties for low HCAHPS scores?
5. What do the CDC EHR trends imply for future EHR adoption? What do they include and exclude in their data?
6. In Section 12.5 (Scenario 2), do you agree or disagree with the prediction: "In 5–10 years all medical devices will automatically update Electronic Health Records directly. This will not only be in hospital but will include wearable wireless medical devices." Explain your analysis.

Level II

7. In Table 12.13, two alternative predictions are made concerning the "probability of expanded EHR funder beyond 2015": one prediction is 73% and another is 90%. Explain if you agree or disagree with higher mandates, government or professional, are reasonable. Explain your analysis.

Level III

8. In this section the author predicts a number of medical technologies for the next 5–100 years.
   a. Which one do you agree with and why?
   b. Which one do you disagree with and why?
9. Make your own prediction on future medical technologies or methods of medical practice, not discussed in the textbook. Provide some research data to support your hypothesis. As a class project, present your findings to the class.

Glossary

Dependent variable (response variable) is a variable in a functional relation whose value is determined by the values assumed by other variables in the relation.

Hospital Value-Based Purchasing Program is a Centers for Medicare and Medicaid Services initiative that rewards acute care hospitals with incentive payments for the quality of care they provide to people with Medicare.

HCAHPS initiative is "to provide a standardized survey instrument and data collection methodology for measuring patients' perspectives on hospital care. HCAHPS survey items complement the data hospitals currently collect to support improvements in internal customer services and quality related activities."

Hospital Readmission Reduction Program imposes financial penalties on hospitals for "excess" readmissions when compared to "expected" levels of readmissions.

Independent variable (explanatory variable), in mathematics, is a variable whose value determines the value of other variables.

Predictive analytics is the practice of extracting information from existing data sets in order to determine patterns and predict future outcomes and trends. It does not tell you what will happen in the future. It forecasts what might happen in the future with an acceptable level of reliability and includes what-if scenarios and risk assessment.*

---

* http://www.webopedia.com.

12.A Appendix: HCAHPS Survey*

HCAHPS Survey

SURVEY INSTRUCTIONS

- You should only fill out this survey if you were the patient during the hospital stay named in the cover letter. Do not fill out this survey if you were not the patient.
- Answer <u>all</u> the questions by checking the box to the left of your answer.
- You are sometimes told to skip over some questions in this survey. When this happens you will see an arrow with a note that tells you what question to answer next, like this:

  ☐ Yes
  ☑ No   ➔ *If No, Go to Question 1*

> *You may notice a number on the survey. This number is used to let us know if you returned your survey so we don't have to send you reminders.*
> *Please note: Questions 1-25 in this survey are part of a national initiative to measure the quality of care in hospitals. OMB #0938-0981*

Please answer the questions in this survey about your stay at the hospital named on the cover letter. Do not include any other hospital stays in your answers.

YOUR CARE FROM NURSES

1. During this hospital stay, how often did nurses treat you with <u>courtesy and respect</u>?
   - ¹☐ Never
   - ²☐ Sometimes
   - ³☐ Usually
   - ⁴☐ Always

2. During this hospital stay, how often did nurses <u>listen carefully to you</u>?
   - ¹☐ Never
   - ²☐ Sometimes
   - ³☐ Usually
   - ⁴☐ Always

3. During this hospital stay, how often did nurses <u>explain things</u> in a way you could understand?
   - ¹☐ Never
   - ²☐ Sometimes
   - ³☐ Usually
   - ⁴☐ Always

4. During this hospital stay, after you pressed the call button, how often did you get help as soon as you wanted it?
   - ¹☐ Never
   - ²☐ Sometimes
   - ³☐ Usually
   - ⁴☐ Always
   - ⁹☐ I never pressed the call button

July 2012   1

* http://www.hcahpsonline.org/Files/HCAHPS%20V7%200%20Appendix%20A1%20-%20HCAHPS%20Expanded%20 Mail%20Survey%20Materials%20(English)%20July%202012.pdf.

YOUR CARE FROM DOCTORS

5. During this hospital stay, how often did doctors treat you with <u>courtesy and respect</u>?

   ¹☐ Never
   ²☐ Sometimes
   ³☐ Usually
   ⁴☐ Always

6. During this hospital stay, how often did doctors <u>listen carefully to you</u>?

   ¹☐ Never
   ²☐ Sometimes
   ³☐ Usually
   ⁴☐ Always

7. During this hospital stay, how often did doctors <u>explain things</u> in a way you could understand?

   ¹☐ Never
   ²☐ Sometimes
   ³☐ Usually
   ⁴☐ Always

THE HOSPITAL ENVIRONMENT

8. During this hospital stay, how often were your room and bathroom kept clean?

   ¹☐ Never
   ²☐ Sometimes
   ³☐ Usually
   ⁴☐ Always

9. During this hospital stay, how often was the area around your room quiet at night?
   ¹☐ Never
   ²☐ Sometimes
   ³☐ Usually
   ⁴☐ Always

YOUR EXPERIENCES IN THIS HOSPITAL

10. During this hospital stay, did you need help from nurses or other hospital staff in getting to the bathroom or in using a bedpan?

    ¹☐ Yes
    ²☐ No ➔ If No, Go to Question 12

11. How often did you get help in getting to the bathroom or in using a bedpan as soon as you wanted?

    ¹☐ Never
    ²☐ Sometimes
    ³☐ Usually
    ⁴☐ Always

12. During this hospital stay, did you need medicine for pain?

    ¹☐ Yes
    ²☐ No ➔ If No, Go to Question 15

13. During this hospital stay, how often was your pain well controlled?

    ¹☐ Never
    ²☐ Sometimes
    ³☐ Usually
    ⁴☐ Always

14. During this hospital stay, how often did the hospital staff do everything they could to help you with your pain?

    ¹☐ Never
    ²☐ Sometimes
    ³☐ Usually
    ⁴☐ Always

15. During this hospital stay, were you given any medicine that you had not taken before?
 1☐ Yes
 2☐ No ➜ If No, Go to Question 18

16. Before giving you any new medicine, how often did hospital staff tell you what the medicine was for?
 1☐ Never
 2☐ Sometimes
 3☐ Usually
 4☐ Always

17. Before giving you any new medicine, how often did hospital staff describe possible side effects in a way you could understand?
 1☐ Never
 2☐ Sometimes
 3☐ Usually
 4☐ Always

WHEN YOU LEFT THE HOSPITAL

18. After you left the hospital, did you go directly to your own home, to someone else's home, or to another health facility?
 1☐ Own home
 2☐ Someone else's home
 3☐ Another health
   facility ➜ If Another, Go to Question 21

19. During this hospital stay, did doctors, nurses or other hospital staff talk with you about whether you would have the help you needed when you left the hospital?
 1☐ Yes
 2☐ No

20. During this hospital stay, did you get information in writing about what symptoms or health problems to look out for after you left the hospital?
 1☐ Yes
 2☐ No

OVERALL RATING OF HOSPITAL

Please answer the following questions about your stay at the hospital named on the cover letter. Do not include any other hospital stays in your answers.

21. Using any number from 0 to 10, where 0 is the worst hospital possible and 10 is the best hospital possible, what number would you use to rate this hospital during your stay?
 0☐ 0   Worst hospital possible
 1☐ 1
 2☐ 2
 3☐ 3
 4☐ 4
 5☐ 5
 6☐ 6
 7☐ 7
 8☐ 8
 9☐ 9
 10☐10   Best hospital possible

22. Would you recommend this hospital to your friends and family?

   1☐ Definitely no
   2☐ Probably no
   3☐ Probably yes
   4☐ Definitely yes

UNDERSTANDING YOUR CARE WHEN YOU LEFT THE HOSPITAL

23. During this hospital stay, staff took my preferences and those of my family or caregiver into account in deciding what my health care needs would be when I left.

   1☐ Strongly disagree
   2☐ Disagree
   3☐ Agree
   4☐ Strongly agree

24. When I left the hospital, I had a good understanding of the things I was responsible for in managing my health.

   1☐ Strongly disagree
   2☐ Disagree
   3☐ Agree
   4☐ Strongly agree

25. When I left the hospital, I clearly understood the purpose for taking each of my medications.

   1☐ Strongly disagree
   2☐ Disagree
   3☐ Agree
   4☐ Strongly agree
   5☐ I was not given any medication when I left the hospital

ABOUT YOU

There are only a few remaining items left.

26. During this hospital stay, were you admitted to this hospital through the Emergency Room?

   1☐ Yes
   2☐ No

27. In general, how would you rate your overall health?

   1☐ Excellent
   2☐ Very good
   3☐ Good
   4☐ Fair
   5☐ Poor

28. In general, how would you rate your overall mental or emotional health?

   1☐ Excellent
   2☐ Very good
   3☐ Good
   4☐ Fair
   5☐ Poor

29. What is the highest grade or level of school that you have completed?

   1☐ 8th grade or less
   2☐ Some high school, but did not graduate
   3☐ High school graduate or GED
   4☐ Some college or 2-year degree
   5☐ 4-year college graduate
   6☐ More than 4-year college degree

30. **Are you of Spanish, Hispanic or Latino origin or descent?**

    ¹☐ No, not Spanish/Hispanic/Latino

    ²☐ Yes, Puerto Rican

    ³☐ Yes, Mexican, Mexican American, Chicano

    ⁴☐ Yes, Cuban

    ⁵☐ Yes, other Spanish/Hispanic/Latino

31. **What is your race? Please choose one or more.**

    ¹☐ White

    ²☐ Black or African American

    ³☐ Asian

    ⁴☐ Native Hawaiian or other Pacific Islander

    ⁵☐ American Indian or Alaska Native

32. **What language do you mainly speak at home?**

    ¹☐ English

    ²☐ Spanish

    ³☐ Chinese

    ⁴☐ Russian

    ⁵☐ Vietnamese

    ⁶☐ Some other language (please print): _____

THANK YOU

Please return the completed survey in the postage-paid envelope.

[NAME OF SURVEY VENDOR OR SELF-ADMINISTERING HOSPITAL]

[RETURN ADDRESS OF SURVEY VENDOR OR SELF-ADMINISTERING HOSPITAL]

Sample Initial Cover Letter for the HCAHPS Survey
[HOSPITAL LETTERHEAD]

[SAMPLED PATIENT NAME]
[ADDRESS]
[CITY, STATE ZIP]

Dear [SAMPLED PATIENT NAME]:

Our records show that you were recently a patient at [NAME OF HOSPITAL] and discharged on [DISCHARGE DATE]. Because you had a recent hospital stay, we are asking for your help. This survey is part of an ongoing national effort to understand how patients view their hospital experience. Hospital results will be publicly reported and made available on the Internet at www.hospitalcompare.hhs.gov. These results will help consumers make important choices about their hospital care, and will help hospitals improve the care they provide.

Questions 1 to 25 in the enclosed survey are part of a national initiative sponsored by the United States Department of Health and Human Services to measure the quality of care in hospitals. Your participation is voluntary and will not affect your health benefits.

We hope that you will take the time to complete the survey. Your participation is greatly appreciated. After you have completed the survey, please return it in the pre-paid envelope. Your answers may be shared with the hospital for purposes of quality improvement. [*OPTIONAL*: You may notice a number on the survey. This number is used to let us know if you returned your survey so we don't have to send you reminders.]

If you have any questions about the enclosed survey, please call the toll-free number 1-800-xxx-xxxx. Thank you for helping to improve healthcare for all consumers.

Sincerely,

[HOSPITAL ADMINISTRATOR]
[HOSPITAL NAME]

Note: The OMB Paperwork Reduction Act language must be included in the mailing. This language can be either in the cover letter or on the front or back of the questionaire. The exact OMB Paperwork Reduction Act language is included in this appendix. Please refer to the Mail Only, and Mixed Mode sections, for specific letter guidelines.

Appendix A: Application Development for Electronic Health Records–Mobile Applications Development

Daniel Nasello

Brief synopsis of components available in all four appendices:

- Setting up a development environment
- Appeasing the Tiki gods
- Hello world
- Mobile app structure
- B: HTML
  - What is HTML?
  - HTML5 specification
  - Single-page applications
  - HTML tags: advanced
  - Creating an application wireframe
- C: What is CSS?
  - CSS3 specification
  - Applying styles to your wireframe
  - The human interaction
  - CSS advanced styles
  - Knowing your audience
  - Separating screens
- D: JavaScript
  - What is JavaScript?
  - Alert ("Hello world")
  - Some basic functions
  - Using libraries
  - Bringing your app to life
  - Applying functionality
- Wrapping up
  - Wrapping your application into PhoneGap
  - Deploying to Google Play

A.1 Introduction

These appendices, A1–A4, provide a brief tutorial on developing web applications. They are specifically targeted to biomedical informatics students who want to understand the core components used in creating both web and user apps for mobile devices. The components are HTML5, Cascading Style Sheets (CSS), JavaScript, and PhoneGap. PhoneGap (http://phonegap.com/) is a product from Adobe, which allows applications for mobile devices to be created from generic components such as HTML5 and JavaScript and translated so that they can be utilized by all mobile device operating systems such as iOS (Apple), Android, BlackBerry, and Windows devices.

A.2 What Is Covered?

The chapters of this book are structured around the various technologies necessary to build mobile applications using web-based technologies. We will review HTML (Hyper Text Markup Language), CSS, and JavaScript.

We will reinforce the theories presented in the chapters by building parts of a personal health records app by using the material presented throughout the chapters.

The first section is focused on getting familiar with the technologies used in mobile app development, along with the tools necessary to deploy our applications for production use.

The rest of the chapters are focused on covering "everyday use" HTML/CSS/JavaScript along with code examples, images, and step-by-step instructions in building and deploying a personal health records application.

A.3 Getting Started

Welcome to the rapidly expanding world of mobile app development using web technologies! Over the course of the next few chapters, we will walk through the process of creating App-Store ready mobile applications. Due to the high market share of Windows machines currently in circulation, we will focus on using the Android platform (you need a Mac and iPhone to develop iPhone applications). However, the beauty of using web technologies to create mobile applications is that we are easily able to reuse most, if not all codes for both platforms (one of the biggest benefits of using web technologies). The only requirement for the following code to run is a WebKit-based browser (Safari and Google Chrome at the time of writing this book).

A.3.1 Mobile Applications at a Glance

A.3.1.1 Using PhoneGap

Since most of our conversation throughout the book will be based upon using the technology "PhoneGap," I would like to give the technology its own introduction including its history and what it actually does so that we can jump into some of its amazing features.

PhoneGap is a program that allows web developers to use their preexisting web-based skills and create applications using HTML, CSS, and JavaScript rather than having to learn each platform's proprietary languages.

PhoneGap has created (and continues to create) APIs or modules for developers to access device-specific hardware using pure JavaScript, allowing the developer to have an almost native finished project.

By allowing the developer to develop in one language across all platforms, it allows developers to keep costs down and develop a larger quantity of apps in a shorter amount of time. PhoneGap is great for applications such as the following:

Informational applications
Directory applications (such as Yelp)
2D gaming
PHR/EHR applications
Enterprise business communication apps

PhoneGap does have its constraints, however. By developing in web languages, we sacrifice speed of creation with the power of UI animation and heavy computing. JavaScript is considerably slower (although there are major improvements with the language), it does not match each platform's native language in terms of computing power.

Also, since PhoneGap is essentially a webpage, we are limited to a single application view. In both iOS and Android, WebViews are allotted to use about 60% of the total memory allowed for the application, meaning we lose the ability to leverage 40% of the memory allotted for the application before the app launches.

Before developers use any technology, they should weigh the project at hand and use the appropriate technologies for the application that needs to be made.

A.3.1.2 Device Capabilities

Although we do not have enough time to go over most of the technologies that are available for developers to use when creating mobile applications, it is still worthwhile to mention what we can do briefly.

During the writing of the book, the following link: http://docs.phonegap.com/en/edge/guide_platforms_index.md.html will give you a full understanding of the hardware integration that PhoneGap has made available for us. Let us go over some of the main hardware APIs made available for us.

A.3.1.2.1 Touch

This is a phone-level API but one of the most important. JavaScript is able to log touch events such as touchstart, touchmove, and touchend. At the time of writing this book, all iOS devices and 99% of Android devices support both single and multiple touch events allowing the developer to allow for rich touch-based interaction with their applications.

A.3.1.2.2 Geolocation

Since the beginning of mobile app development, app developers have tried to integrate geolocation in as many apps as they can. The reason for this is because phones are mobile and developers want the user to be updated with correct geographical location. Whether it is to find restaurants around you, or get the local weather, the use of geolocation is a crucial aspect of most app developers' apps.

PhoneGap has created an easy way for us to access a user's initial geolocation and a way to update that geolocation as periodically as we want.

A.3.1.2.3 Hardware Sensors

Hardware sensors are standard in most phones, and developers have made use of these sensors to create rich applications for many uses.

Although there are many, PhoneGap currently has two readily available sensors for public use (although there are third-party plug-ins that are available for download and use).

A.3.1.2.4 *Accelerometer*

With the use of the accelerometer, we are able to capture device movement of the x, y, and z access of any device. This would be useful when creating an application that is "motion aware" such as a maze game where the ball or game piece moves based on the phone's current position in a user's hand.

A.3.1.2.5 *Gyroscope*

The gyroscope is generally used when a developer wants to capture and display the current heading (north, east, south, west) of a user. They are generally used for compasses and other applications that require the use of a compass or heading.

A.3.1.3 Device Connectivity

PhoneGap provides an interface for users to retrieve the current connectivity a user has at any given time. Suppose you are creating an application that requires the use of the Internet. If a user does not have an Internet connection, you could tell them that they need to have Internet connection to make use of the mobile application. As we will learn later on, making the life of your users as easy as possible is crucial to the commercial success of your application.

The current network statuses a phone could have are as follows:

- Connection: unknown
- Connection: Ethernet
- Connection: Wi-Fi
- Connection: Cell 2G
- Connection: Cell 3G
- Connection: Cell 4G
- Connection: Cell
- Connection: None

A.3.1.4 Camera

Multimedia such as photos and videos have become an intricate part of apps today (Instagram, Twitter, Facebook). With the use of PhoneGap, we are able to access a user's camera roll or give them the ability to take pictures in real time.

A.3.2 Preparing the Development Environment

In order to be successful in creating mobile applications, it is necessary to set up your computing environment to sustain the development of your applications.

1. Pick a text editor.
    a. I personally prefer Notepad++ (http://notepad-plus-plus.org/)
        i. Notepad++ is a very mature editor packaged with rich features.
            I. Color coding.
               Notepad++ detects what language you are writing and separates them with different colors and fonts.
            II. Line numbering.
               You can easily sift through your code and "bookmark" lines for later inspection.
            III. Notepad++ supports most major languages and is able to detect and separate them.
       However, every person has a preference. Please visit http://en.wikipedia.org/wiki/Comparison_of_text_editors for a larger list of text editors to compare and choose from.
2. Creating a folder structure to create an application.

Once you have chosen and downloaded a text editor of choice, it is time to set up our development directory.

On your desktop (or directory of choice), create a folder named PHR by right-clicking in the directory and navigating to the "new" option and selecting folder.

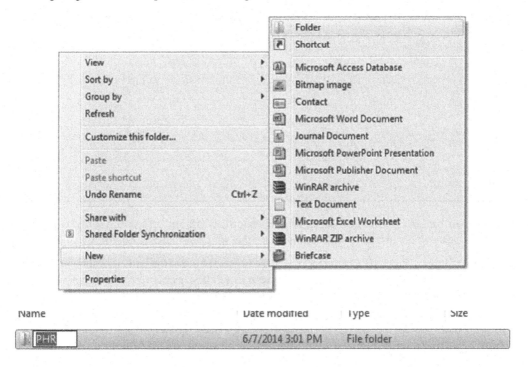

Once you have created the PHR directory, double-click it to enter the folder. Once inside, we need to create subdirectories to ensure we maintain an organized development directory (having files in one folder can make it hard to manage, especially larger projects).

As per the mentioned process create the following folders in the PHR folder:

- Images
- CSS
- Scripts

These folders will help us organize our projects and hold files based on their file extension to help us navigate through the project.

After you are finished, your folder structure should look like the following:

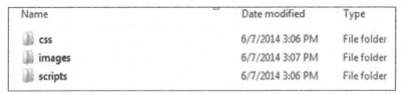

Next, open your text editor. We are going to create an HTML file that will serve as the "backbone" of our application.

To save an index.html file in your PHR directory from your text editor:

1. Go to File > New File.
2. Go to File > Save As.
3. Find the directory where you created the PHR folder and then enter the PHR folder.
4. Save the file as index.html.

Congratulations! You have now saved your first HTML document. If you double-click the document from the folder your default browser should open the document and you will see a blank screen.

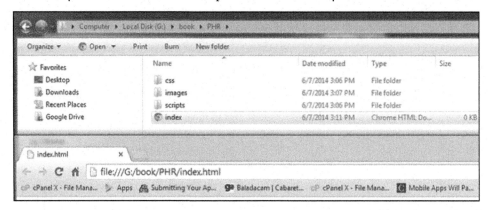

Now that we have our file structure set up, let us download, install, and set up our Android environment so that we have the ability to create and launch apps on either your Android device or the Android simulator.

1. Check for Java. The use of Eclipse for Android requires the use of the Java Development Kit, which is not standard on most computers. To update or install Java, please visit: http://www.oracle.com/technetwork/java/javase/downloads/jdk8-downloads-2133151.html

Java SE Development Kit 8u5

You must accept the Oracle Binary Code License Agreement for Java SE to download this software.

○ Accept License Agreement   ◉ Decline License Agreement

Product / File Description	File Size	Download
Linux x86	133.58 MB	⬇ jdk-8u5-linux-i586.rpm
Linux x86	152.5 MB	⬇ jdk-8u5-linux-i586.tar.gz
Linux x64	133.87 MB	⬇ jdk-8u5-linux-x64.rpm
Linux x64	151.64 MB	⬇ jdk-8u5-linux-x64.tar.gz
Mac OS X x64	207.79 MB	⬇ jdk-8u5-macosx-x64.dmg
Solaris SPARC 64-bit (SVR4 package)	135.68 MB	⬇ jdk-8u5-solaris-sparcv9.tar.Z
Solaris SPARC 64-bit	95.54 MB	⬇ jdk-8u5-solaris-sparcv9.tar.gz
Solaris x64 (SVR4 package)	135.9 MB	⬇ jdk-8u5-solaris-x64.tar.Z
Solaris x64	93.19 MB	⬇ jdk-8u5-solaris-x64.tar.gz
Windows x86	151.71 MB	⬇ jdk-8u5-windows-i586.exe
Windows x64	155.18 MB	⬇ jdk-8u5-windows-x64.exe

and download either the 64 bit or ×86 version (for 32-bit computers). Once downloaded and installed, we now can download Eclipse. Eclipse is a development environment used to create Java and Android projects. Android was generous enough to bundle Eclipse with all the necessary Android SDKs making it easy to start creating Android applications. Please follow the link http://developer.android.com/sdk/index.html and download and install the Eclipse ADT Bundle.

Once installed, place the resulting folder in a place where you will not need to move it (you will soon find out why).

The next step in setting up PhoneGap is adding variables to your Windows environment (PhoneGap is actually missing complete chunks of information, and it took hours to figure out on my own).

1. Go to your Start menu, navigate to the "Computer" tab, right-click it, and pick the Properties tab.

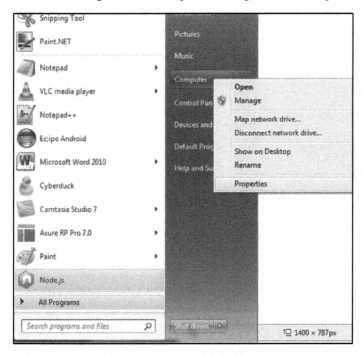

2. Once the Properties window appears, navigate to the left-hand pane and click the "Advanced System Settings" link. A "System Properties" window appears, click the button that says "Environment Variables."

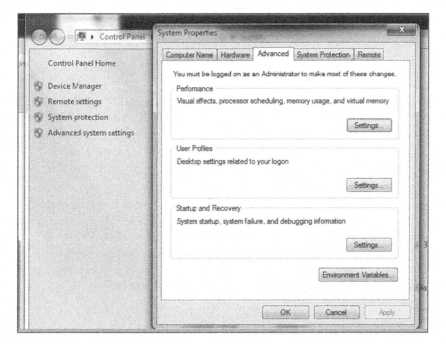

3. Once in your Environment Variables, navigate to the bottom half of the window "System Variables" and click the "New" button.

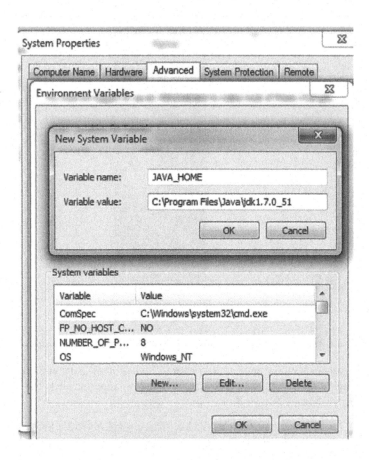

Type in "JAVA_HOME" (all capitals) for variable name and find the path where the Java JDK is in your system (should be in the program files folder in the C drive by default) and copy and paste that path into the variable value.

4. Press OK.
5. Press New once again.
   a. This time, type in ANT_HOME for the variable name.
   b. For the value, find the ANT_HOME folder in your system. It should be in the Eclipse folder we downloaded earlier (this is why you cannot move this folder, if you move it, you will need to update the system variables).
   c. Go to the adt-bundle folder > eclipse > plugins. You should see the org.apache. ant_1.8.4.v201303080030 folder. Double-click it. Copy the path name from the top window and make it the variable value for the ANT_HOME variable.

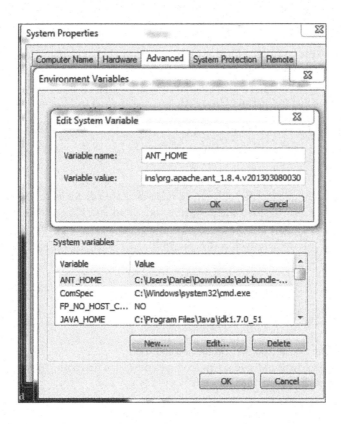

Press OK.

6. The environment we have to set up already exists, so all we have to do is to edit it.
   a. Find your way down to the PATH variable and click the Edit button.
7. Navigate back to the adt-bundle folder > eclipse > plugins on your system and take out a new notepad document.
   a. Double-click the Ant folder and then double-click the Bin folder that lies in the Ant folder.

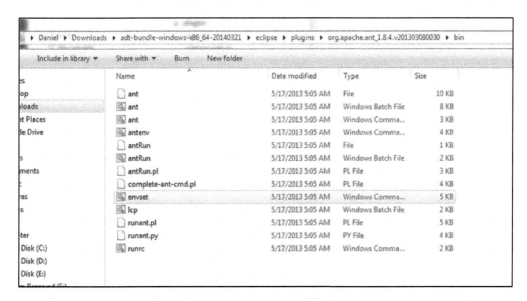

Copy the path at the top search bar into the notepad and then add a semi-colon ";".

8. Navigate back to the Java JDK folder in your C > program files folder and then double-click on the Bin folder within it.
   a. Copy the path at the top search bar and paste it after the semi-colon that follows the Ant path.
   b. Add a semi-colon to the end of that path.

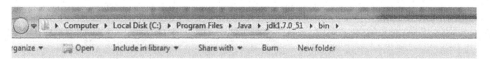

9. Navigate back to the **adt-bundle** folder and double-click the **sdk** folder this time. Double-click the **platforms** folder. Copy the path and paste it in your word doc. Place a semi-colon after the path.
10. Go back to the SDK folder and double-click on the **tools** folder. Copy the path and paste it in the word document. Place a semi-colon after the path.
11. Your word document should look like the following:

```
C:\Users\Daniel\Downloads\adt-bundle-windows-x86_64-20140321\eclipse\plugins\org.apache.ant_1.8.4.v201303080030\bin;
C:\Program Files\Java\jdk1.7.0_51\bin;
C:\Users\Daniel\Downloads\adt-bundle-windows-x86_64-20140321\sdk\platforms;
C:\Users\Daniel\Downloads\adt-bundle-windows-x86_64-20140321\sdk\tools;
```

Put all the paths on one line and copy them to the clip board.

Go back to the path variable and add a semi-colon to the last added path. Then paste all the paths we just created in the word document into the path.

Press OK.

Press OK to leave the environment variables. Press OK again to leave system properties.

Your paths should now be set and Cordova should be able to read them while trying to create an Android project.

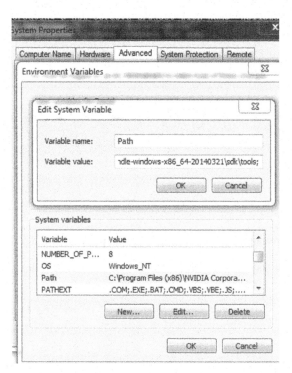

Great! Now let us set up PhoneGap! The PhoneGap setup takes a few steps. First, we will need to download a tool known as Node.js. Node is a command line tool that lets us download packages from the web. PhoneGap has adopted the use of Node.js in order to simplify and streamline the app creation process.

1. Download Node JS. Follow the link: http://nodejs.org/download/.
   a. Once downloaded and installed, we can test the install as follows. Go to your Start menu and type cmd in your search bar and press Enter to open the command prompt.
   b. To see if Node was properly installed, simply type npm and press Enter in the command prompt.
   c. You should see the following:

```
C:\Users\Daniel>npm

Usage: npm <command>

where <command> is one of:
    add-user, adduser, apihelp, author, bin, bugs, c, cache,
    completion, config, ddp, dedupe, deprecate, docs, edit,
    explore, faq, find, find-dupes, get, help, help-search,
    home, i, info, init, install, isntall, issues, la, link,
    list, ll, ln, login, ls, outdated, owner, pack, prefix,
    prune, publish, r, rb, rebuild, remove, repo, restart, rm,
    root, run-script, s, se, search, set, show, shrinkwrap,
    star, stars, start, stop, submodule, t, tag, test, tst, un,
    uninstall, unlink, unpublish, unstar, up, update, v,
    version, view, whoami

npm <cmd> -h     quick help on <cmd>
npm -l           display full usage info
npm faq          commonly asked questions
npm help <term>  search for help on <term>
npm help npm     involved overview

Specify configs in the ini-formatted file:
    C:\Users\Daniel\.npmrc
or on the command line via: npm <command> --key value
Config info can be viewed via: npm help config

npm@1.4.9 C:\Program Files (x86)\nodejs\node_modules\npm

C:\Users\Daniel>
```

If you did not see this, please try the installation of Node again.

A.3.2.1 Cordova

Once we know Node works we are going to follow the instructions at the following URL: http://docs.phonegap.com/en/3.4.0/guide_cli_index.md.html#The%20Command-Line%20Interface, which are instructions as to how to download and configure the Cordova command line tools for Android.

In your command prompt simply type npm install –gcordova

(Warning: If you are not the administrator on your computer this will not work. Make sure to gain administrator access to the computer you will be working on).

Node will then download the Cordova command line tools and you should now be able to create PhoneGap projects with ease.

(Note: The directory where you ran the install command is where the Cordova folder will be installed to, i.e., my Cordova folder is now installed in \Users\Daniel.)

Time to test our install! Let us type in a command to create our first Cordova project. Simply type the command Cordova create hello com.hello.hello HelloWorld.

If successful, you will receive a message like so:

```
C:\Users\Daniel>cordova create hello com.hello.hello HelloWorld
Creating a new cordova project with name "HelloWorld" and id "com.hello.hello" a
t location "C:\Users\Daniel\hello"
Downloading cordova library for www...
Download complete
```

There are four parts to the "Cordova" command to create an application:

1. Cordova create:
   a. Create is a command to run a batch file in the Cordova folder in which they compile the necessary files in order for you to be able to compile on an Android device.
2. Hello:
   a. Where we typed in hello is a friendly name where Cordova will create a folder so we can later find the project. When we navigate to the Cordova folder, you will see the folder named "hello."
3. com.hello.hello:
   a. We need not worry much about this except that we need one. This is a unique namespace that will uniquely identify itself on the Appstore. Google and Apple use it when you want to launch your app from an external website.
4. HelloWord:
   a. This is the last part of the command and certainly not the least important. This represents the actual project name.

If you do not type in the full command, the creation of the app will fail and you will need to try again.

We must now add the platforms we are going to make the application for. Currently, the two main competitors in the app world are Apple and Google so we will not bother with smaller markets such as Microsoft of Bada.

1. Change directory into the hello folder by typing cd hello in the command prompt.
2. Next, let us add the platforms we want to make the application for:
   a. Cordova platform add android
   b. Cordova platform add iOS
3. Then, let us build, prepare, and compile each platform so that they are ready to be used.
   a. Cordova build (press Enter)
   b. Cordova prepare android (press Enter)
   c. Cordova compile android (press Enter)

Great! You have now successfully built your first PhoneGap application for Android! Let us put this to the side for a bit as we will come back to it later as we learn some HTML skills and we want to test it on our emulator.

Examples:

Appendix A Example:

Now that we have Node JS and PhoneGap configured for our Windows environment, it is time to add the project to Eclipse and run it for the first time.

Step 1:

The first step in importing our PhoneGap project is to open Eclipse. Find the directory where you stored the adt-bundle download and double-click the Eclipse executable.

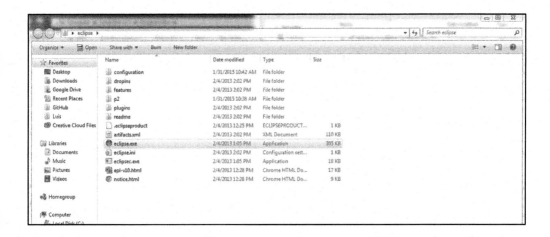

Once Eclipse is open, it is time to import the project for use. Importing a PhoneGap project is quite different than creating a new Android application from Eclipse. Traditionally Eclipse helps you create your Android application by "wrapping up" the necessary executable JAR files in order to run an Android project. However, Cordova does this for us when we create our application via the command line. They also include their own JAR files, which help us run applications using HTML, CSS, and JavaScript.

Step 2:

Now we have to import the project. We achieve this by doing the following:

1. Go to File > New > Project.

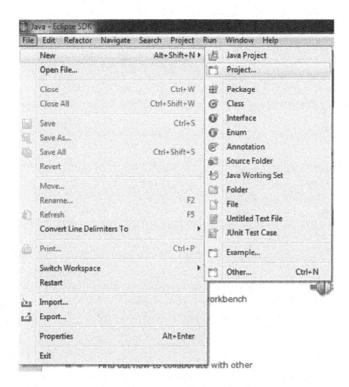

2. Select and expand the Android tab and select the "Android Project from Existing Code" Option.

3. Click on the Browse button

4. From here, search for the directory where we saved our "hello world" project. Once you find it, click on it, and press OK. You should now see the project (along with other Cordova files) in your package explorer located on the left-hand side of Eclipse.

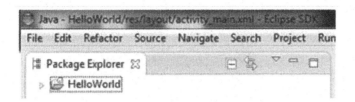

5. Now that the project is important, we need to set up our virtual Android device to allow us to run our projects on the Emulator. Note: If you have an Android device, you can compile directly on your device by connecting your phone via USB and installing the appropriate drivers from your manufacturer.
   a. We first need to go to the virtual device manager. On the main screen go to Window > Android Virtual Device Manager.
   b. Once in the AVD menu, click on the create button.

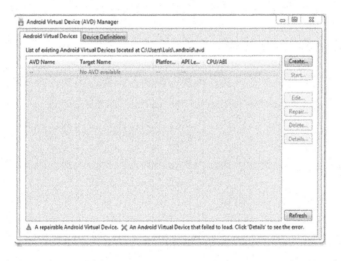

   c. Fill in the following information about your virtual device:
       i.   Device name
       ii. Device (you can choose from the drop down)
       iii. Target (operating system of the device)
       iv. CPU type
       v.   Memory options
            1. Note: set the RAM to 768 if you do not have at least 16GB of RAM installed on your computer, or your virtual device will not run.

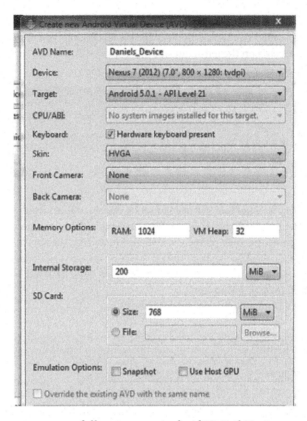

And press OK. We have now successfully set up our Android Virtual Device.

6. Our last step is to run the project. To do this, simply right-click the project, find Run As >, and select "Android Application."

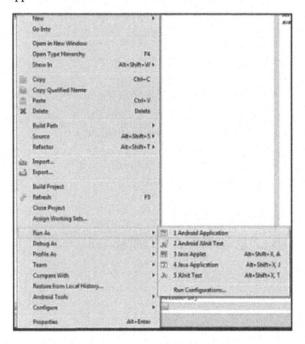

Your Android Virtual Device will now appear and the program will now run!

Appendix B: Mobile Applications Development

Daniel Nasello

B.1 HTML

HTML or Hypertext Markup Language will be the first skill we learn as it is the backbone and starting point to creating any web-based application.

B.2 What Is HTML?

HTML is a markup language that comprises a set of "tags" that allows developers to render text, images, video, audio, colors, shapes, and more on an HTML page. An HTML page is nothing more than a simple website on the Internet.

Go over HTML5 specification here.

B.3 What Are Tags?

Tags are nothing but separators in an HTML page that allow us to organize information in a meaningful way on an HTML page. In most cases, HTML tags have opening and closing tags and the information is enclosed within them. Let us take a look at some HTML tags. Open your text editor of choice and let us begin:

```
<! Doctype>
<html>
<head>
</head>
<body>
</body>
</html>
```

B.3.1 Let Us Break Each Tag Down

1. <!Doctype>
   a. The Doctype tag is a tag that is placed at the top of every HTML5 document. It simply tells the document to render HTML in the HTML5 specification. This tag is one of the very few that are self-closing.
2. <HTML>
   a. The HTML tag is a tag that encloses all HTML elements in a document. All HTML elements should be enclosed within this mandatory tag.

3. \<head>
   a. The Head tag is a tag that is used to link to external documents. It is not of much use now but it will be used to link external style sheets and JavaScripts.
4. \<body>
   a. The Body tag is a tag that encloses all "user facing" tags. Any tags that a user should see go between these tags.

Great! You now know the basic template for creating HTML web applications. Again these are guidelines, as if we put tags outside the body of a document they will still render. However, keeping the basic guidelines of HTML structure as important, as in most cases you will be working in teams and other developers will expect to see a "standard" of coding. Following this template also helps developers keep their code more "manageable" since most applications get quite big.

If you save and run your document, you will see that you will be viewing a blank page. HTML tags by default have no colors or size, so they will not appear unless explicitly told to. Let us start populating our document with tags that you will use when making web applications to make it a bit less boring.

Between the body tags, let us add a tag called a div(\<div>\</div>). Div tags stand for divider tag, which simply gives us a way of dividing information logically on a page. Think of a paragraph in a book. Each time you have a new thought or "section," we separate them by giving them a new paragraph. If the entire book was written in one big paragraph, the reader would not know where one thought stopped and a new thought began. This same concept goes into HTML documents.

B.3.2 Divs

1. Div is a nickname for "division."
2. You are "dividing" information.
3. Divs are block-level elements (we will come back to this).
4. Divs can hold the following:
   a. Text
   b. Images
   c. Video
   d. Audio
   e. Other tags

So, let us add a div with some content to our page:

By simply adding a divider to our document and inserting the words "Hello World" we tell the document to render these characters in the document. If we refresh, the page "Hello World" should appear in the top left corner.

The next tags we will go over are the UL tag and the LI tag. These tags are used in conjunction with each other, so it is worth going over both of them at the same time. ULs or unordered lists are used to encompass list items. In the past 10 years or so, web applications have gone from being "self-contained" applications to applications that are used by billions of people around the world. Organizing and displaying large sets of data has always been a challenge for developers and designers alike. On websites, the developers and designers have much larger screens to utilize for information display. However, since most phones are not much larger than 4 inches, we are faced with the challenges of displaying enormous data sets in small areas. The use of lists has been a best friend to mobile app developers.

B.3.3 UL

1. UL stands for unordered list.
2. Technically, it is no different than a div and renders the same.
3. We use them because as developers we expect to see a set of LIs or list items enclosed in unordered lists.
4. A block-level element.

LI or list items are exactly what they sound like, "list" "items." They are elements that are put into a list for the user to see. By default, <Li></li> tags are rendered with a bullet point (which we will later remove).

B.3.4 LI

1. Stands for list item.
2. Usually contains some sort of information that needs to be displayed as a list.
3. By default, most browsers render them with a bullet point.
4. They should be enclosed in ULs.

Now that we know what ULs and LIs are, we should now add them to our HTML document.

Notice that my LIs get rendered with bullet points. They are also on separate lines. This is called being a "block element." Block elements are tags or "elements" that have their own line space. After a tag is closed, HTML will automatically break the line and render the next element on the following line. Block-level elements are one of three types of elements. We will go over inline block and inline elements shortly.

Also note the indentation of elements when writing in my text editor. It is imperative that a developer writes codes in a way that is easy to read, for both yourself and other developers.

When an element is inside or a "child" of another element, it should be indented, so relationships between elements are easily recognized.

Writing comments is also a critical part of the application development life cycle. Since our document is now only 20 lines it does not help much; however, when our lines of HTML get to be thousands of lines, it helps to comment what elements do or what information they hold. This helps when having to update projects months later or when other developers help or collaborate in your project.

- Will finish HTML elements at a glance.

B.3.5 IMG

IMG tags allow developers to easily link images in an HTML document. Luckily for us, rendering images in HTML is as simple as including a link to the image resource and letting the browser handle the rest. In most programming languages, it is up to the developer to incorporate codes to render the image manually.

An image comprises two main (and mandatory) properties:

```
<div>
    <img src="url_to_image" alt="image_doesn't_work"/>
```

B.3.6 SRC Attribute

- This defines the actual source of the image in which the browser will try to render the image.

B.3.7 alt Attribute:

- If the browser cannot load the resource or the resource does not exist, the alt text will appear instead of an image.

Since we have no inner HTML in the IMG tag, the image tag need not be closed, thus making it a "self-closing" tag.

B.3.8 Inputs

Inputs are a very important part of HTML documents. Inputs allow interactivity between the program and the user. Without inputs, web applications are simply informational pages and they are quite boring.

Inputs can hold various amounts of information and perform different actions. On mobile devices, different kinds of inputs will trigger the phone to bring up different kinds of keyboards. Let us explore a few different kinds of inputs.

1. Input type of text

```
<div>
    <input type="text" placeholder="Name"/>
```

These inputs are meant to hold general text. This will trigger the general keyboard on a phone.

2. Input type of email

```
<div>
    <input type="email" placeholder="Name"/>
```

These inputs also hold general information. However, on mobile devices it will trigger the phone to use a keyboard that includes email characters such as the @ symbol as seen in the following:

3. Input type of tel

This input type is generally used for when you want the user to either enter a telephone number or be forced to use numeric keys. This input type will trigger the "number" pad and force the user to input numbers as seen in the following:

4. Input type of password

The input type of password will trigger the phone to raise a general keyboard; however, it will render all text as bullets instead of plain text to ensure privacy and keep a password private from others' eyes.

Important properties of inputs:

1. The type attribute:
   a. As we went over, inputs have a type attribute that will trigger different keyboards and trigger different behaviors in the document.

2. The placeholder attribute:
    a. The placeholder property allows us to tell the user what the input's purpose is without having to clutter the document with labels. This is especially useful since we have very limited spaces on mobile devices. The following example shows that the input is requesting for your email. Once the user starts typing, the browser automatically deletes the text and allows the user to type in their own value.

Open your HTML document and let us enter the following:

B.4 Application Skeleton

Writing a mobile application is comparable to building a house.

First, we build a structure, we add the walls and decorate, and finally, we move in. Mobile app development is similar. The first step in mobile application development is creating the app "skeleton," or the wireframe of the application. With a wireframe, we will create all HTML elements that will be used in the application.

B.5 Let Us Make a Wireframe

Enough with the theory, let us get to work! The first and probably hardest part in making any mobile applications is creating a "storyboard" for the application. When we make mobile applications, there are four questions we need to answer:

1. What are we making?
    Ans. For this particular book, we will be creating a mobile PHR application that allows us to enter personal health–related information to show, analyze, and keep track of our personal health history.
2. What information are we providing?
    Ans. In this case, we are providing our user with the ability to see their personal health history in an efficient manner.
3. Who is our audience?
    Ans. Usually, apps have a target audience (i.e., tinder for singles looking to date or open table for restaurant goers in their late 20s and early 30s). However, due to the rapid growth and awareness of the medical field in the past few years, our target audience has vastly increased. Our audience is now anyone from 12 years old to 99 years old that owns a smartphone.
4. How can we present the information to our audience?
    Ans. This question is really an accumulation of the past three questions. By answering the first three questions we can easily answer this question. However, we do need to make sure to create a sound HTML structure in order to be able to present our information to the public.

To see a full explanation of creating a preapplication checklist, please visit: <insert link with full explanation here>

Now that we have answered some preliminary questions, it is time for us to start coding! The first thing we are going to do is go into our PHR project folder and open our index.html file in your HTML editor (again, I use notepad++).

Let us start off by entering some of our basic tags.

```
<!doctype>
<!--Doctype declares an HTML5 document-->
<html>
<!--All HTML elements go inside the HTML tag-->

<head>
<!--We link Javascripts and Style Sheets in our head-->
</head>

<body>
<!--All publicly visible HTML elements go inside the body--

</body>
<!--End body-->

</html>
<!--End document-->
```

As you can see we are using the same tags as earlier. We need our Doctype to declare an HTML5 document, HTML tags to encompass all other HTML tags, our head tags to link JavaScripts and CSS, and our body that holds all visible HTML elements.

Our application consists of four pages:

1. Landing screen or "profile page."
2. Enter new data screen, where we will be able to fill in and store information about our medical history.
3. A list view of all past entries.
4. A settings page, where we can change personal information such as name and DOB.

In creating a wireframe, we need to create a "holder" or a division for each screen so that they have a place to "live" on the application. That being said, let us create an area for each screen to exist on the app.

```
<body>
<!--All publicly visible HTML elements go inside the body-->

    <div id="profile_screen" class="screen"></div>
    <!--this is where we are going to let the Profile Screen live-->

    <div id="add_item_screen" class="screen"></div>
    <!--this is where we are going to let the Add Items Screen live-->

    <div id="list_of_history_screen" class="screen"></div>
    <!--this is where we are going to let the History List Screen live-->

    <div id="settings_screen" class="screen"></div>
    <!--this is where we are going to be able to change our information such as name and age-->
</body>
<!--End body-->
```

All screens will have their own "containers," which will be represented by different divs. Notice all of the "screen divs" have the same class. We do this because we are going to later identify these screens with similar CSS in the next chapter. Also, clearly indenting children divs makes it easier to know that our screens are children of the body tag. Every child element should have one tab indent from its parent to help keep the document neat and organized while coding.

Since we now have the holder for our screens, it is time to decide and "code" the elements necessary to create each screen. Since this is an introductory book, let us keep each screen as simple as possible.

We allow the user to display their name on their profile along with their date of birth, weight, current age, a way to get to settings, and a way to see our current notes and add a note.

```
<div id="profile_screen" class="screen">
    <div id="information_holder">
    <!-- this div is the first top half of our screen,
    and will contain elements to hold name, age, etc-->
        <h1 id="my_name">Daniel Nasello</h1>
        <!--this H1 will contain our name, for now use
        your name as a placeholder so we can
        later style it with CSS-->
        <h2 id="date_of_birth">11/25/1986</h2>
        <!-- again, this will hold our date of birth.-->
        <h3 id="current_age">27 yrs old</h3>
        <!--will hold actual age-->
    </div>
</div>
```

Since the "profile" screen is our first screen, we will code all our HTML elements for this screen within the index.html page. Normally, each screen gets its own HTML page, which gets dynamically injected into the document. However, since HTML has some latency loading on phones, we want to ensure a "native" like experience for our users therefore having our first screen load as quickly as possible.

Daniel Nasello

11/25/1986

27 yrs old

If you run your HTML document, you will find that there are no styles associated with our elements. By default tags hold no styles (with the exception of ULs that have margins and LIs that have bullets).

Let us finish our profile page! We now should add a div to contain two buttons that will lead us to our health history or our settings page.

```
<div id="main_navigation_holder">
    <input type="button" id="settings_page_button" value="Settings"/>
    <input type="button" id="health_history_button" value="Health History"/>
</div>
```

Notice that inputs are self-closing tags. The reason that some elements are self-closing is because they have no "inner HTML" and only contain properties and values. All inputs (with the exception of the textarea tag) and IMG tags are self-closing tags.

And that is it! We have now successfully created the wireframe for the first page of our application!

Now since we have an idea of how we structure elements, I will briefly go over the structure to the rest of the pages so that we can then move on to CSS and styling our application.

Let us go back to the main folder of our PHR app on our computer and create a new file called "settings.html." Once it is created, open it in your HTML document.

Since they are actually just "fragments" of a bigger application, and not their own full page, we do not have to add the default Doctype and HTML tags that go on every HTML page. Rather, we will just add all the elements necessary to creating a page within the "settings_screen" div that lives in index.html.

```
<div id="settings_content_holder">
<!-- use this div to hold all of our settings content-->
  <div class="header">
        <!-- will contain title of page and some buttons-->
        <div class="back" id="settings_back">Back</div>
        <!-- will allow us to go back and exit screen-->
        <h1 class="page_title">Settings</h1>
        <div id="toggle_edit_info">-</div>
        <!--this will toggle input fields from being editable to non editable-->
  </div>
```

```
<form id="information_form">
<!--A form tag that allows us to
submit a form to either a server or to the phone-->
  <ul id="input_holder">
  <!-- we will put form items in a ul as list items to structure them-->
    <li class="settings_li settings_header">Name</li>
    <!--will contain the header for each field-->
    <li class="settings_li"><input type="text" id="person_name" name="name" placeholder="Name"/></li>
    <!--This input has a type of text and allows us to enter a person's name-->
    <li class="settings_li settings_header">Age</li>
    <li class="settings_li"><input type="date" id="age_picker"/></li>
    <!--The input type of date will trigger the native date picker
    allowing us to pick a date from the native calendar-->
    <li class="settings_li settings_header">Weight</li>
    <li class="settings_li"><input type="tel" id="person_weight" name="person_weight" placeholder="Weight"/></li>
    <!--this input is similar to the name field, however instead of
    using the "text" input type we will use tel. On phones, the input
    type of tel triggers the "numeric" keyboard, forcing the user to input
    numbers and minimizing the chances of the user inputting bad data.-->
    <li class="setings_li"><input type="submit" id="submit_settings" value="Submit"/></li>
  </ul>
</form>
</div>
```

Since this screen is packed with elements, we have to split them into two screen shots. On the top of the page, we are going to create a header, which holds the page title, a back button, and the "toggle edit" button. We will use the "toggle edit" button to enable or disable the ability for users to enter and edit information (so they do not do so by accident). We will encompass the inputs with in a form for later submission to either a phone or a server. Let us go over some new elements seen on the settings page.

When running the settings.html page, you should see all of your elements in a list view, with bullet points. Again, we will remove them later with the use of CSS. Congratulations, we have now wireframed the second screen in our application! Let us close settings.html and now open the editor and create a new file called "history.html."

This screen will provide us with a list view of all our current items we have entered in our PHR app to keep track of health changes over time. This list gets generated dependent on the user, so we cannot do much with it now except set it up for later use.

```
<div id="history_inner">
<!--will hold the UL for list view items-->
    <div class="header">
        <div id="history_back" class="back">back</div>
        <div id="add_new_item">+</div>
        <!-- will be the button that allows us to navigate to the add history item screen-->
    </div>
    <ul id="health_history_ul">
        <!-- we cannot do much with this screen because list items will be dynamically generated from a database.
        We will come back to this screen to style a "static" list item so we know how they will look in the future-->
    </ul>
</div>
```

And that is it! Our history.html is mostly generated LIs from a database so we do not have much static content to fill it with. However, we should note the "add_item" button. This button will allow us to get to the final screen, which will allow us to enter a new item in our personal health record history.

Let us move on to creating our add item screen. Close the history.html document and create a new html document called "additem.html."

This screen will not have many elements since it will simply contain a way for us to create a new item in our history list.

```
<link rel="stylesheet" type="text/css" href="css/add_item.css"/>
<div id="add_item_holder">
<!-- This div will allow us to hold all the elements to create a new item in our history-->
<div class="header">
    <div id="exit_add_item">Back</div>
</div>
<!--cancel adding a new item-->
<form id="add_history_item_form">
<!-- We use the form element to organize inputs we will use to capture input information and ultimately save to our local database-->
<!--Developers will expect to see "input information" when items are placed inside of a form. It is important to maintain standards
especially when working in a group environment-->
    <input class="add_new_item_input" placeholder="title"/>
    <!-- we can add a title for our history, so it is easily identifyable-->
    <textarea id="add_new_item_textarea" placeholder="Notes"></textarea>
    <!-- Let's add a multi line textarea so we are able to put some notes about our medical item-->
    <input type="submit" placeholder="Add Item" class="submit_button"/>
    <!-- allows us to submit our item-->
</form>
<!-- end form here-->
</div>
<!-- end fragment-->
```

First, we start with the "add_item_holder" which is just a way to organize all the other elements that belong within the add item "fragment." Again, when we run our application, we are going to load fragments of HTML to speed up initial load time and keep the html DOM light, preventing lag and decreased performance. Second, we add our back button that let us cancel creating a new item.

We then add our form. Our form contains most of the elements on this page, so let us go over them in detail.

1. The form element is used to logically hold inputs and textarea elements that allow for collaboration with other developers. Using HTML standards is important, especially in a collaboration environment.
2. We are going to use the input element to allow us to enter a title for our medical history item. We use "title" as the placeholder, eliminating the need for a traditional label to show the user the input's use.
3. We use a textarea to enter notes. A textarea allows the user to input multiline text that might be too long for an input. This is perfect for what we need it for, notes.
4. The last element is our Submit button. The input type of "submit" tells the HTML document that we want to perform an action with our form and usually will redirect us to another page. However, since this is a single-page application, we are going to use JavaScript to override the default behavior of our submit button and perform another action.

And we now have a complete skeleton of our application! It is now time to learn about CSS and start styling our application.

Html5 Language Reference (Source World Wide Web Consortium www.w3c.org)

HTML5 Markup Language (http://www.w3.org/TR/html-markup/elements.html) (Another HTML5 resource http://www.w3schools.com/tags/tag_menuitem.asp)	

Command	Example
Hyperlink	**Example: \<a href=".\/page.html" \</a\>**
	Basic html structure
\<!DOCTYPE html\>	
\<html\>	
\<head\>	
\<title\> my program\>/title\>	
\</head\>	
\<body\>	
\<h1\> start page LARGE FONT\></h1\>	
\<p\> this is a link < a href="test.html"> \</a\> \</p\>	
\<!-- a comment line --\>	
\<body\>	
\</html\>	
Address	address {display: block; } address {font-style: italic; }
Area	Area{display: none;}
The area element represents either a hyperlink with some text and a corresponding area on an image map	
Article	Article{display: block;}
The article element represents a section of content that forms an independent part of a document or site	
Audio	\<audio controls\>
An audio element represents an audio stream. Provides a standard for playing audio files.	\<source src="beatles.mp3" type="audio/mpeg"\> \</audio\>
B	b{font-weight:bold;}
Bold	
Base	
The base element specifies a document-wide base URL for the purposes of resolving relative URLs	Interface HTMLBaseElement :HTMLElement{attribute DOMString href; attribute DOMString target;};
Body	Body{display:block;margin:8px}
The body element represents the body of a document (as opposed to the document's metadata).	
Br	\<br\>
The br element represents a line break.	
Button	Button type=submit
The button element is a multipurpose element for representing buttons.	Button type=reset (resetting a from) Button type=button \<button type="button"\>Click Me!\</button\>
Canvas	\<script\>
which can be used for dynamically rendering of images such as game graphics, graphs, or other images.	var canvas=document.getElementById('myCanvas');

(Continued)

Html5 Language Reference (Source World Wide Web Consortium www.w3c.org)

HTML5 Markup Language	
(http://www.w3.org/TR/html-markup/elements.html)	
(Another HTML5 resource http://www.w3schools.com/tags/tag_menuitem.asp)	

Command	Example
	var ctx=canvas.getContext('2d');
	ctx.fillStyle='#FF0000';
	ctx.fillRect(0,0,80,80);
	</script>
Command type=radio	<input type="radio" name="your name" value= "choice"/>
The command element with a type attribute whose value is " radio" represents a selection of one item from a list of items.	
Form	Form{display: block; margin-top:0em;}
The form element represents a user-sub-mittable form.	<form>
	Password: <input type="password" name="pwd">
	</form>
Html	Html{display: block}
The html element represents the root of a document.	<!DOCTYPE HTML>
	<html>
	<head>
	<title> My test document </title>
	</head>
	</html>
H1-H6 font sizes	H1=24px
	H2=22px
	H3=18px
	H4=16px
	H5=12px
	H6=10px
Input	Input type ="text"
The input element is a multipurpose element for representing input controls.	Input type ="password"
	Input type ="checkbox"
	Input type =radio"
	Input type ="button"
	Input type ="submit"
	Input type ="reset"
	Input type="text"
	Input type ="file"
	Input type ="image"
	Input type ="date"
	Input type ="email"
	Input type ="search"
	Input type ="color"
	<form>
	First name: <input type="text"
	**Name="firstname"> **
	Last name:<input type="text"
	Name="lastname">
	</form>

(Continued)

Html5 Language Reference (Source World Wide Web Consortium www.w3c.org)

HTML5 Markup Language (http://www.w3.org/TR/html-markup/elements.html) (Another HTML5 resource http://www.w3schools.com/tags/tag_menuitem.asp)	
Command	Example
Link	<head>
The link element represents metadata that expresses inter-document relationships	<link rel="stylesheet" type="text/css" href="theme.css"> </head>
HTML5 video	<video width="320" height="240" controls>
Internet Explorer 9+, Firefox, Opera, Chrome, and Safari support the <video> element.	<source src="movie.mp4: type="video/mp4"> </video>

Appendix C: Cascading Style Sheets

Daniel Nasello

C.1 What Is It?

CSS or "Cascading Style sheet" is a markup language that allows us to style our HTML document. Without CSS, our HTML documents would be no more than simple text on the screen. With the use of CSS, we are able to create rich user interfaces that allow us to enhance the user experience by organizing and stylizing data. Through the use of CSS, we are able to render HTML tags with shapes, colors, sizes, positioning, borders, fonts, images, opacity, and more.

C.2 Why Do We Need It?

When creating an application, we are more than likely creating an app to appeal to a certain group of users. Through much trial and error, I have learned that certain groups of people need information displayed in a different manner. For example, when creating a medical-based application, I learned that medical professionals are used to looking at interfaces that had white and blue colors. Medical professionals are usually under high stress, and the use of bright colors such as orange or yellow make them feel like there is an emergency, while white and blue "calm" them. Also, displaying content is a challenge we face every day. In the medical field, doctors expect to read as little text as possible due to the fast-paced nature of the job. As app developers, we face this issue all the time.

C.3 Jumping Right in

Where do we put CSS? CSS has its own document type (.css) that gets linked in the head of our document. Let us go ahead and open our text editor. Create a new document and save it as index.css in the CSS folder of the PHR project we created earlier. Once saved, let us open our index.html document and link it in the head of the document.

```
<head>
<!--We link Javascripts and Style Sheets in our head-->
    <link rel="stylesheet" type="text/css" href="css/index.css"/>

</head>
```

As you can see, the stylesheet tag is linked in the head of the HTML document and contains three proprieties.

Rel: This tells the document that it is a style sheet.
Type: This also tells the document it is a text/CSS file.
Href: This can contain either a relative or an absolute path to a style sheet. Make sure you link the file correctly, or you will not see any styles.

Can styles not be placed directly in the document?
    Yes but, placing styles in separate sheets allow:

1. The developer to create a style sheet for every screen.
    a.   That is, one style sheet for the settings page, one for the main page, etc.
2. Easier to later identify and alter styles once you have created the application.
3. You can then make these style sheets templates that you can reuse in later applications.
4. You can dynamically load style sheets.
    a.   Larger or more files mean slower load times. If you import them as we use them (i.e., only load the settings CSS when we use the settings page), it helps keep the document lighter.

C.4 There Are Three Ways to Target Our Elements in CSS

C.4.1 We Are Able to Target Elements by Their ID

IDs are element identifiers used in the document to identify a unique element in the document. You should *not* use an ID more than once in the document. Doing this will "confuse the document" when applying styles and targeting elements in JavaScript.

```
#div_one{
      position:relative;
      }
```

We are able to target an element's ID in CSS by prefixing the ID with the # symbol.

C.4.2 We Are Able to Target Elements by Their Class Name

Classes are semi-unique identifiers meant to identify a group of "like" elements together. They can be used to apply similar styles to a set of HTML elements, or to apply a similar action to multiple HTML elements.

```
.list{
      position:relative;
      }
```

Targeting a class name requires the prefix of a period. I

C.4.3 We Are Able to Target Elements by Their HTML Tag Name

Each HTML element is associated with their own tag name. We are able to target elements by their tag name, i.e., we can target all divs with the div tag name or unordered lists with the UL tag.

```
div {
    position:relative;
}
```

The div tag requires no prefix.

C.5 Diving Right in

Due to the brevity of the book, I will not be able to go over all of the styles that CSS has to offer. To see a full list of styles along with their explanations, please visit: http://www.w3schools.com/css/default.asp.

Let us open our index.css document and our index.html document in our Word Editor. If you remember from the previous chapter, we made a few divs that were to be used as "screens" for our application. Each screen has their own ID. First, let us create a similar style for each that will act as the "template" for all screens. *Note, all images used in this sample app can be found at: http://combustioninnovation.com/PHR/img and may be used for this app.

Styles of note:

```
/*we make the body and the html elements the full height and width of our screen.
*since we do not know the height and width of the phone, we use percentages and let the browser
*do the math for us*/
body,html{
    height:100%;
    width:100%;
    position:absolute;
    padding:0;
    margin:0;
    overflow:hidden;
}
```

For every web application we create, we always set the body and HTML tags to full height and width of the screen by using percentages (since we do not know the height and width of the screen, we let the browser do the math for us), and we remove the 8px of margin that the browser inserts into the document by default.

```
/*all "screen" divideers in our app will always be height + width 100 percent as they should cover the
*view port
*/
#profile_screen{
    position:absolute;
    height:100%;
    width:100%;
}
```

Each screen should be the full height and width of the phone. We use percentages rather than a definite number of pixels because there are many different phone sizes. The web browser automatically does the math for us and will adjust the width and height of any element that has a percentage value.

C.6 Let Us Now Go Ahead and Finish Styling the Rest of the Profile Page. Put the Following Styles in Your Style Sheet

```
/*we make the body and the html elements the full height and width of our screen.
 *since we do not know the height and width of the phone, we use percentages and let the browser
 *do the math for us*/
body,html{
        height:100%;
        width:100%;
        position:absolute;
        padding:0;
        margin:0;
        overflow:hidden;
        background-color:#0c93b0;
}

/*screen one styles start*/

/*all "screen" divideers in our app will always be height + width 100 percent as they should cover the
 *view port
 */
#profile_screen{
        position:absolute;
        height:100%;
        width:100%;
}

/*holds our main information such as name,birthday, and age*/
#information_holder{
        position:absolute;
        top:0;
        left:0;
        width:100%;
        height:200px;
        background-color:#666666;
}

/*h1 for our name*/
#my_name{
        color:white;
        font-family:helvetica;
        text-align:center;
        font-weight:normal;
}

/*h2 for date of birth*/
#date_of_birth{
        color:white;
        text-align:center;
        font-family:helvetica;
        font-size:16px;
        font-weight:normal;
}

#current_age,#current_weight{
        color:white;
        text-align:center;
        font-family:helvetica;
        font-size:14px;
        font-weight:normal;
}


/*holds buttons at the bottom of screen to get to our settings + add item*/
/*since we do not know how high we can make our main nav div since we use 200px for the information
 *holder we will need to use math using javascript to set the height*/
#main_navigation_holder{
        position:absolute;
        top:200px;
        width:100%;
        min-height:200px;
}
```

```
/*holds buttons at the bottom of screen to get to our settings + add item*/
/*since we do not know how high we can make our main nav div since we use 200px for the information
 *holder we will need to use math using javascript to set the height*/
#main_navigation_holder{
        position:absolute;
        top:200px;
        width:100%;
        min-height:200px;
}
/* since we have buttons with the same class, we can set their "like" properties
 * to the class to write as litle styles as possible and keep our code more manageable*/
.main_button{
        width:50%;
        height:100%;
        -webkit-appearance:none;|
        background-color:transparent;
        outline:none;
        border:none;
        background-position:center center;
        background-size:85px;
        background-repeat:no-repeat;
}

/*we want to keep the settings button to the left hand side*/
#settings_page_button{
        position:absolute;
        left:0;
        background-image:url('../images/currentmedications@2x.png');

}
/* we want to put the health history button to the right*/
#health_history_button{
        position:absolute;
        right:0;
        background-image:url('../images/profile@2x.png');

}
/* end screen one styles*/


/*screen div, should be height with 100%
 *Since it isn't the first screen we see when we enter the app, we hide it by default*/
#add_item_screen{
        position:absolute;
        top:0;
        left:0;
        width:100%;
        height:100%;
        display:none;
}
```

Please visit http://combustioninnovation.com/PHR/img to download currentmedications@2x.png and profile@2x.png and place them into our images folder in our directory.

Notice that we have a class of "main_button" that defines base styles for both of our buttons in our style sheet. Go back to your index.html page and add the class of "main_button" to our profile and settings buttons and remove the "values" to allow there to be just a background image for both of the buttons.

```
<input class="main_button" type="button" id="settings_page_button" value=""/>
<input class="main_button" type="button" id="health_history_button" value=""/>
```

Our index.html page should now look like the following:

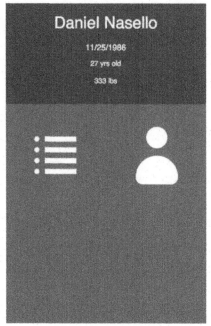

This completes our styles for our "main page." As mentioned earlier, we will dynamically load CSS into separate style sheets in order to maintain code and decrease loading times for our pages. Let us close index.html and index.css and open our settings.html page.

First, let us create the settings.css file in our CSS folder and link it on the top of our settings.html page. Traditionally, we would link CSS files in the head of our document, and this would be bad practice. However, to keep our page light, we are only going to link and load the settings.css file when we go to our settings page to compensate for phones and their limited processing power. The CSS file should be linked like the following:

```
<link rel="stylesheet" type="text/css" href="css/settings.css"/>
<div id="settings_content_holder">
<!-- use this div to hold all of our settings content-->
```

Now, let us style the page by applying the following styles in our settings.css page:

```
/*this is just so we can style each page separately so we can see what it would look like in the final product*/
body{
    margin:0;
    background-color:#0c93b0;
}

/*will hold all of the settings elements*/
#settings_content_holder{
    position:absolute;
    top:0;
    left:0;
    width:100%;
    height:100%;
    background-color:#0c93b0;
}

/*we make a top bar with a separate background color to logically separate back and save buttons*/
.header{
    background-color:#252525;
    position:relative;
    top:0;
    left:0;
    width:100%;
    height:45px;
    padding:0;
    margin:0;

}
```

```css
/*our page title. remove all default margin and padding and place in the header*/
.page_title {
    text-align: center;
    color: white;
    font-family: helvetica;
    font-weight:regular;
    font-size: 30px;
    position: absolute;
    width: 100%;
    top: 0;
    padding: 0;
    margin: 0;
    height: 45px;
    line-height: 45px;
}
/*back button to leave give z-index of 999 to make sure it is drawn above the header*/
.back{
    color:white;
    font-family:helvetica;
    height:100%;
    width:50px;
    text-align:center;
    line-height:45px;
    z-index:999;
}

/*this is a button that will allow us to make the settings fields disabled or not to disallow any editing by accident*/
#toggle_edit_info{
    color:white;
    font-size:22px;
    position:relative;
    left:15px;
    top:10px;
}

/*our form" does not need special styles*/
#information_form{
    width:100%;
    height:auto;
    position:relative;
    top:10px;
}
```

```css
/*our form" does not need special styles*/
#information_form{
    width:100%;
    height:auto;
    position:relative;
    top:10px;
}

/*lets remove the default margin and padding to make the elements flush to the left of the page*/
#input_holder{
    padding:0;
    margin:0;


}

/*our settings header, again these are all in a class so we can style them all at once instead of writing
*individual styles*/
.settings_header{
    width:100%;
    color:white;
    font-family:helvetica;
    text-align:center;

}

.settings_li{
    width:100%;
    position:relative;
    margin-top:5px;
}
```

```
/*this is a psuedo selector. We are targeting the "input" element inside of the settings_li element*/
.settings_li input{
    position:relative;
    width:90%;
    height:35px;
    border:0;
    outline:0;
    border-radius:0;
    margin-right:auto;
    margin-left:auto;
    display:block;

}


#submit_settings{
    width:90%;
    display:block;
    margin-left:auto;
    margin-right:auto;
    top:10px;
    background-color:#404040;
    color:white;
    font-family:helvetica;
    height:40px;
    font-size:20px;
    border:0;
    outline:0;
}
```

This page will allow us to update our personal information on the main page. As a refresher, the toggle_edit_info element will allow us to toggle our inputs disabled or enabled to ensure that we do not edit information by accident. After all styles are applied, our settings page should look like the following:

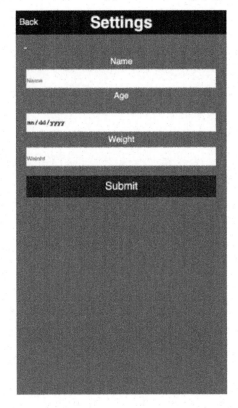

Please remove the body styles we applied in the settings.css, as it will conflict with our index.css style sheet when we dynamically load this page.

We can now close our settings.html and settings.css, as we will come back to it at a later time.

Next, let us open history.html. Just like the settings page, create history.css in the CSS folder and link it to the top of the history.html page. Once linked, let us apply the following styles:

```
/*this is just so we can style each page separately so we can see what it would look like in the final product*/
body{
    margin:0;
    background-color:#0c93b0;
}
/*we make a top bar with a separate background color to logically separate back and save buttons*/
.header{
    background-color:#252525;
    position:relative;
    top:0;
    left:0;
    width:100%;
    height:45px;
    padding:0;
    margin:0;

}

/*back button to leave give z-index of 999 to make sure it is drawn above the header*/
.back{
    color:white;
    font-family:helvetica;
    height:100%;
    width:50px;
    text-align:center;
    line-height:45px;
    z-index:999;
}

#add_new_item{
        position:absolute;
        right:0;
        width:50px;
        height:100%;
        color:white;
        text-align:center;
        font-family:helvetica;
        top:0;
        line-height:45px;
        font-size:22px;
}

/*the ul that will contain the history ul item*/
#health_history_ul{
    padding:0;
    margin:0;
    -webkit-overflow-scrolling:touch;
    position:absolute;
    top:0;
    left:0;
    width:100%;
    height:100%;
}
```

As you can see there is not much to style on this page at this point because most of the content on this page is dynamically generated as a list view of all of our medical items. We will come back and style our list items once we have an active list on the page. (Once we start using our local database.) For now, our history.html should look like the following:

We can now close history.html and history.css. Now open our add_item.html. Create the add_item. css in the CSS folder and link it on the top of the page. Let us apply styles based on the styles we have previously created for other elements in this app (we want to keep consistency in our styling throughout the app). Open add_item.css and add the following styles:

```css
body{
        position:absolute;
        top:0;
        left:0;
        height:100%;
        width:100%;
        padding:0;
        margin:0;
        background-color:#0c93b0;
}

/*we make a top bar with a separate background color to logically separate back and save buttons*/
.header{
        background-color:#252525;
        position:relative;
        top:0;
        left:0;
        width:100%;
        height:45px;
        padding:0;
        margin:0;

}
```

```
#exit_add_item{
        color:white;
    font-family:helvetica;
    height:100%;
    width:50px;
    text-align:center;
    line-height:45px;
    z-index:999;
}

#add_history_item_form{
        width:100%;
        height:auto;
        top:10px;
        position:relative;
}

#add_history_item_form input[type="text"] {
        margin-top:10px;
        margin-bottom:10px;
        display:block;
        width:90%;
        margin:auto;
        height:35px;
        border-radius:0;
        outline:none;
        position:relative;
}
```

```
#add_history_item_form textarea {
        top:10px;
        resize:none;
        outline:none;
        display:block;
        width:90%;
        margin:auto;
        height:105px;
        border-radius:0;
        outline:none;
        position:relative;
}

#add_history_item_form input[type="submit"] {

        position:relative;
        width:90%;
        display:block;
        margin-left:auto;
        margin-right:auto;
        top:25px;
        background-color:#404040;
        color:white;
        font-family:helvetica;
        height:40px;
        font-size:20px;
        border:0;
        outline:0;

}
```

After applying our styles, our add item HTML page should look like the following:

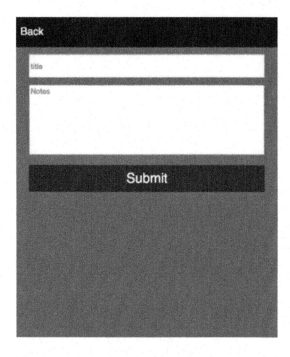

I have styled this page a little differently as I wanted to demonstrate some of the more "advanced" properties of CSS. Let us break down some of the differences in our styles:

1. #add_history_item_form input[type="text"]
   a. input[type="text"] is a CSS pseudo selector that allows us to only target inputs that have the type of text set as the "type" property. Also, since I am targeting #add_history_form as a prefix, it will only target inputs that are "children" elements of that element.
2. #add_history_item_form input[type="submit"]
   a. input[type="text"] is a CSS pseudo selector that allows us to only target inputs that have the type of submit set as the "type" property. Also, since I am targeting #add_history_form as a prefix, it will only target inputs that are "children" elements of that element.

We have now completed styling of our entire application! It is now time to use JavaScript to allow us to navigate through our app and fill it with data.

Additional information:

For additional information on CSS please visit the following:

List of CSS properties: http://www.w3schools.com/cssref/.

CSS pseudo selectors: http://www.w3schools.com/css/css_pseudo_classes.asp.

ID vs class selectors: http://css-tricks.com/the-difference-between-id-and-class/.

Appendix D: JavaScript

Daniel Nasello

D.1 What Is JavaScript?

JavaScript is an interpreted computer programming language. As part of web browsers, implementations allow client-side scripts to interact with the user, control the browser, communicate asynchronously, and alter the document content that is displayed. It has also become common in server-side programming, game development, and the creation of desktop applications. Interpreted programming languages get executed at runtime while compiled languages get precompiled and then run. The advantage to compiled languages is that they are more powerful and can do heavier calculations.

JavaScript does have its advantages, however. JavaScript has the ability to run on any device or platform that runs a web browser (which is pretty much any device with an Internet connection). JavaScript is almost standard across all platforms allowing developers to reuse the same code on any device rather than having to rewrite it when changing platforms.

By its nature, JavaScript is not an object-oriented language. JavaScript is a functional language with the ability to create objects. This allows developers to create a sequence of commands without the "steeper" learning curves of an object-oriented language and the overhead of creating objects in memory.

D.2 Where Do We Link Scripts?

Most developers link their scripts at the head of their document, while I prefer to link mine at the bottom of the body. The reason being (this holds true mostly for mobile), the loading of scripts may slow down the rendering of HTML elements because it is linked before HTML elements appear in the document (HTML documents read tags from the top of the document to the bottom). By linking scripts at the bottom of the page, we allow the page and its styles to load before we worry about loading the functionality of the page, ultimately enhancing the user experience.

D.3 Types of Variables

Variables
Variables are placeholders in memory that exist in every programming language. They give developers the ability to assign values to them dynamically without the developer knowing the actual value.

In JavaScript, we can easily assign data to variables.

```
function hello() {
    var firstvar = "hello";
    alert(firstvar);

}
```

In this case, we assign the first variable firstvar the string of "hello." Of course, this is not why we really use variables, especially if we know that we want to alert "hello." However, suppose we want to alert our user a value that we might not know.

For example, if we had an application where we wanted to display the users' date when they clicked a button, it would be impossible for us to know the current date for all users at any given time. How do we solve this? We assign a variable in which we know the "key" to, which would be a friendly name or address in which we can retrieve the value in storage, and then use it at a later time. Take a look at the following:

```
function hello() {
    var mydate = Date();
    alert(mydate);

}
```

As the developer, we know that we want to retrieve the date object for our user, but we do not know the actual time or value of that date. However, we do know that the variable "mydate" will represent the current date and time, so we can assign a date to it and use it in our function. If we alert mydate, it will tell us the current date and time.

D.3.1 Local Variables

Local variables are variables that are declared within a function and then "erased" from memory automatically when the function is complete. It is usually wise to declare a function locally because JavaScript deletes the function from memory and we no longer have to worry about it. However, the drawback of having our variables deleted is that sometimes we need variables to persist until the user has finished using the application. In this case, using a local variable will not suffice.

D.3.2 Global Variables

Global variables have an application-wide scope and are values that do not get deleted by JavaScript automatically (they must be manually removed from memory). However, unlike local variables, we only have to worry about assigning a value one time to our global variable.

For instance:

```
var myname = "dan";

function hello(){

    alert(myname);

}

function goodbye(){
    alert("Goodbye" + myname);

}
```

Since we know that our first name will always be the same, we should only have to declare that variable one time throughout our program. By doing this, we are able to allow multiple functions to utilize this variable without having to declare it again. Global variables do have drawbacks, however.

1. Any variable defined in the global name space owns that "location" in memory, so you will not be able to reuse the same variable name in memory again in any function.
2. JavaScript does not use garbage collection on global variables. If you have a lot of global variables, and do not manage your memory properly, your application starts to slow down noticeably.
3. The global variable is declared once, which is an issue for variables that need the most up-to-date information
   a. For instance:

```
var mydate = new Date();

function hello(){

```

If we declare mydate in the global namespace, it gets assigned the date from the second that the script is loaded into memory. Even though it may be more convenient for it to be declared once and reused, the date will remain the same even if we call the variable many hours later. If you want the value of the variable to update, you have to manually change the variable's values, as JavaScript will not do it for you. When using global variables, try to assign only values that will remain constant throughout your application, such as a name, age, or any other value that will probably not change throughout the user's session on the application.

What kinds of data have the ability to be assigned to variables?

Though this goes against most languages I believe that the following is one of JavaScript's biggest strengths. Developers have the ability to assign almost any kinds of data types to variables, as variables are data agnostic.

We are able to assign:

Strings: "Hello World";
Integers, Floats, Doubles: 1

Booleans: true
Objects: var person = {
"name":"dan",
"occupation", "rockstar",
}
Arrays: var array = ['one','two','three'];
Other functions: var dan = getName();

D.4 Making Our First Script

Let us create a new document called scripts.js and save it in the scripts folder we created previously.

```
<!--link our JavaScripts here-->
<script type="text/javascript" src="scripts/scripts.js"></script>
</body>
```

We have now linked our scripts to our HTML page and are able to perform any function that lies inside the scripts.js file.

D.5 Function Parameters

JavaScript, like most languages, has the ability to accept arguments or parameters in its functions to enable functions to by dynamic. Parameters are similar to variables, except that they are values usually passed from other functions, and do not have to be assigned a space in memory. It also gives the developer the ability to take one function's variables and pass it to another function to perform an action.

Parameter types:

Parameters can contain the same data as variables, which include

- Strings
- Integers
- Objects
- Arrays
- Other functions
- Booleans

Just like variables, parameters do not have to have a predefined data type, as they are read at runtime. As this is strength of JavaScript, this could also be a weakness if the developer abuses the "data type agnostic" methodology of JavaScript. Although a JavaScript error will not crash your application, it will cause your application to have a "dead end," which will result in a terrible user experience.

```
<body>
    <div onClick="age(3)">I am three years old</div>
    <div onClick="age(5)">I am five years old</div>

<script>
    function age(myage)
    {
        alert(myage);
    }
</script>
```

In the example given, we create a function that will alert the user's age. Between the function brackets, we place a parameter of my age that will be the variable when we alert a user's age. By using a function parameter, we have a way for multiple elements to call the function and change the variable value, with very little effort. This is one of the main advantages of passing parameters over using function variables.

Making our first script:

Let us create a new document called scripts.js and save it in the scripts folder we created previously.

```
<!--link our JavaScripts here-->
    <script type="text/javascript" src="scripts/scripts.js"></script>
</body>
```

We have now linked our scripts to our HTML page and are able to perform any function that lies inside the scripts.js file.

D.5.1 Creating Our First Function

In its most basic form, we create a function to perform an action. There are four parts to every function.

```
function helloWorld(){
    alert("Hello world");
}
```

1. Declaring the function with the word "function" tells the script we are going to declare a function.
2. "HelloWorld" is a friendly name created by us so we can later call that function.
   a. Preferably, it is much easier to name functions that have relevance to the function it will perform so we have better indication of what the function does.
3. () inside our brackets we are able to pass parameters to the function, which we will go over a little later.
4. {} Inside the curly braces is where we are able to tell the script what we want the function to do. Whether it has to have an alert box to say "Hello world" or change the font of a div, it will all go inside the curly braces.

Now since we know how to declare a function, we have to know how to trigger it. Just because it is linked, it does not mean we can use it yet. To use it in our document, we need to link it to an element.

Open your text editor and create a new HTML file called practice.html and enter the following:

```
<html>
    <head>

    </head>

<body>
    <input type="button" value="click" onClick="hello()"/>
    <script type="text/javascript" src="js/index.js"></script>
</body>

</html>
```

Then create a new file in your JS folder and call it index.js and enter the following:

```
function hello(){
    alert("Hello world");
}
```

Save it. Open your HTML page in chrome and press the button and you should see the following:

Congratulations, we have just created our first script!

D.6 Using a Library

JavaScript is great, and it is made even easier by using fantastic libraries that help us making syntax and mundane tasks easier and more efficient. When creating web and mobile applications, I usually use a library called JQuery (http://jquery.com). JQuery is a fantastic library that helps with many tasks such as attaching events to elements easily and efficiently.

JavaScript Language Reference

JavaScript Excellent source http://www.w3schools.com/	
Code	Example
JavaScript can be defined **before the HTML** code body	

```
<!Doctype html>
<html>
<head>
<script>                                                    //JavaScript
    Function getCELSIUS(farenheight) // converts farenheight to Celsius
    {
    return (5/9) * (farenheight - 32);
    }
</script>
</head>
<body>
<button type="button" onclick="getCELSIUS(72)"> </button> // calls function
</body>
</html>
```

JavaScript can be defined **in the HTML** code body

```
<!Doctype html>
<html>
<body>
<button type="button" onclick="getCELSIUS(72)"> </button>
<script> // defines JavaScript function
{
    Function getCELSIUS(farenheight) // converts farenheight to Celsius
    {return (5/9) * (farenheight - 32);
}
</script>
</body>
</html>
```

(Continued)

JavaScript Language Reference

JavaScript	
Excellent source http://www.w3schools.com/	
Code	Example
JavaScript can be defined **in an External Program**	

```
<!Doctype html>
<html>
<body>
<button type="button" onclick="getCELSIUS(72)"> </button>
// function is stored in an external file called DansScript.js
<script src="DansScript.js"></script>
</body>
```

Code	Example
Conditional Statements	If (x<10) {CODE;}
If	
Else	If (x<10) {CODE;}
Else if	Else {CODE2;}
Switch //use a number of alternative blocks. evaluates the variable or function, in this case variable x, if x=0 assigns result to xlow (something previous defined)	**Switch (x)** // some variable or function in parentheses
	{Case 0; xlow; break;
	Case 1: xmed; break; // assigns variable xmed if x=1;
	Case 2: xhigh; break;
	}
Function	Function **getCELSIUS**(farenheight)
JavaScript functions are objects	{return (5/9) * (farenheight - 32);
Return statement stops the execution of the function	}
	//to call the function in your html code
	Temp = getCELSIUS (75)
JavaScript **Loops**	For (i=0; i<10; i++)
	{some calculation;}
Math. Random();	//returns a random number
Math.min ()	//finds lowest number
	Math.max(5,10,15,20); returns value 5
Math.max()	Finds highest number
	Math.max (50,100,150) returns value 150

Glossary

Advanced cardiac life support (ACLS): The American Heart Association set of guidelines of clinical interventions for the urgent treatment of cardiac arrest, stroke, and other life-threatening medical emergencies, as well as the knowledge and skills to deploy those interventions. This content is also offered as a course comprised of lectures, hands-on practice, written tests, and return demonstration.

Advanced practice registered nurse (APRN): An APRN is a registered professional nurse with an advanced degree, either master's or doctorate. There are four recognized APRN roles: certified registered nurse anesthetists, certified nurse-midwives, clinical nurse specialists, and certified nurse practitioners.

Acute coronary syndrome (ACS): Refers to any group of symptoms attributed to the obstruction of the coronary arteries. The most common symptom prompting diagnosis of ACS is chest pain, often radiating to the left arm or angle of the jaw, pressure-like in character, and associated with nausea and sweating.

The Affordable Care Act (ACA): The act passed in March 2010 and upheld by the Supreme Court in June 2012, often referred to as Obama Care.

The American Medical Association (AMA) Ethics Group: sets guidance for physicians to pursue. The Ethics Group has three parts: Council on Ethical and Judicial Affairs, Ethics Resource Center, and Institute for Ethics.

American Reinvestment & Recovery Act (ARRA): Passed by the Congress in 2009 contained $782 billion to jumpstart the economy and $20 billion targeted at promoting EHRs.

Arterial blood gases (ABG): requires drawing blood from an artery. Often taken from the radial artery at the wrist or the femoral artery in the groin, but a number of other sites are also used. ABG provides more comprehensive information that simply pulse oximetry information, which is vital for critically ill patients in intensive care units (ICUs).

Augmented diastolic: An intra-aortic balloon pump (IABP) is positioned in the descending aorta. It inflates during diastole, displacing blood volume and increasing, or augmenting, the diastolic pressure in the aortic root.

Automaticity: AV cells can depolarize by themselves.

Batteries: provide electrical energy from chemical reactions, they incorporate electrochemical cells, which allow the flow of ions.

Beer–Lambert law: A law relating to the attenuation of light by a material passing through a substance.

Bioinformatics: research focus, analyzes datasets for genomics, proteins etc. "The branch of information science concerned with large databases of biochemical and pharmaceutical information" (world English Dictionary); it intersects with the field of computational biology.

Biomedical engineering: A field dealing with the application of engineering principles to medical practice. It also lies at the intersection of electrical engineering and the biological sciences.

Biomedical informatics: extrapolates meaning from diverse biological, medical, nursing, health, and clinical research sources and structures that data via intuitive interface with enhance healthcare and delivery. (Lubliner 2014)

Blood pressure: is the pressure on the walls of blood vessels exerted by circulating blood, which is measured by the force per unit area. Blood pressure is the brachial arterial pressure usually measured in the upper arm as blood moves away from the heart. The pressure of the blood in the circulatory system, often measured for diagnosis, since it is closely related to the force and rate of the heartbeat and the diameter and elasticity of the arterial walls.

Blood products: Any component of the blood that is collected from a donor for use in a blood transfusion. Whole blood is rarely used; most blood products consist of specific processed components such as red blood cells, blood plasma, or platelets

Blood type: Also referred to as "blood group." Any of various classes into which human blood can be divided according to immunological compatibility based on the presence or absence of specific antigens on red blood cells.

Bone marrow: The contents of the bone that contain stems cells that can develop into a variety of cell types, for example, neutrophils, eosinophils, basophils, monocytes, dendritic cells, and macrophages.

Braden scale: An evidence-based method for determining a patient's risk of developing a pressure ulcer. The patient is assessed for the ability to move or the presence of moisture, among other items, each of which is scored. The total score indicates whether a patient is at high or low risk. This assessment is performed on admission and then either daily or every shift.

Brain stem: Part of the brain that includes the midbrain, pons, and medulla oblongata. Functions include cardiac, respiratory, and autonomic (involuntary) functions; blood pressure; and heart rate.

Cardiac arrest: The cessation of cardiac activity resulting in loss of an effective pulse. The treatment is immediate cardiopulmonary resuscitation (CPR).

Cardiac index (CI): The cardiac output corrected to reflect the size of the patient. Formula: cardiac output ÷ body surface area = cardiac index. The body surface area is dependent on the patient's height and weight. Measured in liters/minute/square meter. Normal value: 2.6–4.2 L/min/m^2

Cardiac myocyte: A muscle cell that is 100 μ in length. It is composed of bundles of myofibrils that contain filaments. Myofibrils are tubelike structures that propagate signals inside muscles.

Cardiac output (CO): The volume of blood pumped by the heart per minute, measured in liters per minute (L/min). Normal value: 5–6 L/min.

Cardiac rhythm: The electrical activity of the heart; the impulse starts at the sinus node, conducts through the atrial tracts, into the atrioventricular (AV) node, passes into the ventricles via the bundle of His, through the left and right bundle branches, and into the purkinje fibers in the ventricles.

Cardiogenic shock: Severely impaired circulation of blood and delivery of oxygen to the tissues secondary to failure of the heart as an effective pump.

CCRN-E: An extension of the Critical Care Registered Nurse (CCRN) certification for RNs who monitor crucially ill patients remotely in a tele-ICU or an e-ICU.

Cells: The basic functional units of living organisms. They are the smallest units that can replicate. Humans contain approximately 100 trillion cells. Plants and animals are made up of eukaryote cells that contain compartmentalized areas, organelles, where metabolic activities take place.

Center for Medicare and Medicaid (CMS): A federal agency within the United States Department of Health and Human Services that administers the medicare program and works in partnership with state governments to administer Medicaid, the State Children's Health Insurance Program, and health insurance portability standards.

Central lines: An intravenous catheter that is passed through a vein and terminates in the right atrium of the heart.

Central venous pressure (CVP): The pressure measured in the right atrium of the heart. It serves as an estimate of blood volume, although it is not a direct measure of this parameter.

Cerebral cortex: The outer covering of the cerebrum in large mammals. Two thirds of its surface is embedded groves (valleys) called the "sulci." The ridges called "gyri."
It contains:

- Frontal lobe: voluntary movement, planning, thought
- Parietal lobe: includes the somatosensory cortex—touch
- Temporal lobe: hearing and comprehending speech
- Occipital lobe: visual processing center

Cerebellum: The part of the brain involved in motor control. Its functions include balance, voluntary movements, motor learning, and some cognitive functions (language) (10% volume, but contains 50% of the neurons in the brain).

Chest tubes: A flexible plastic tube that is inserted through the chest wall into the pleural space or mediastinum. It is used to drain air, fluid, or blood from the thoracic or mediastinal cavities.

Clinical Decision Support System (CDSS): A software that assists healthcare professionals in making diagnosis-, treatment-, and workflow-related decisions.

Clinical Document Architecture (CDA): The HL7 Version 3 Clinical Document Architecture (CDA®) is a document markup standard that specifies the structure and semantics of "clinical documents" for the purpose of exchange between healthcare providers and patients.

Clinical Information System (CIS): A computer-based system that is designed for collecting, storing, manipulating, and making available clinical information for the healthcare delivery process.

Clinical Nurse Specialist (CNS): Licensed registered professional nurses with graduate preparation (either master's or doctorate). CNSs are clinical experts in the treatment of illness, and the delivery of evidence-based nursing interventions in a specialty population (e.g., critical illness, women's health, pediatrics, geriatrics, etc.)

Clinical research informatics: The discovery and management of new knowledge relating to health and disease. It includes management of information related to clinical trials.

Computed tomography (CT or CAT): A technique that uses numerous 2D x-ray slices, to create a three-dimensional view of the body.

Cognitive systems: A series of artificial intelligence paradigms with "the ability to engage in abstract thought that goes beyond immediate perceptions and actions.

Combined DNA Index System (CODIS) program: The Federal DNA Identification Act in 1994, established this national identification index of DNA records.

Clinical Context Management Specifications (CCOW): CCOW is a standard for allowing independent systems to synchronize context on a single workstation, providing a seamless interface for the user of that workstation (ensuring consistent user authentication, display of the same patient, display of the same order, etc.)

Consumer Health Informatics: The field "devoted to informatics from multiple consumer or patient views. These include patient-focused informatics, health literacy and consumer education." The focus is on information structures and processes that empower consumers to manage their own health, for example, health information literacy, consumer-friendly language, personal health records, and Internet-based strategies and resources. The shift in this view of informatics analyzes consumers' need for information.

Continuity of Care Record (CCR): A subset of information focused on timely care of an individual either in an emergency situation or provided to another physician focusing on current health status, medications, and treatment.

Continuous positive airway pressure (CPAP): A technique for assisting breathing by maintaining the air pressure in the lungs and air passages constant and above atmospheric pressure throughout the respiratory cycle.

Continuous renal replacement therapy (CRRT): An extracorporeal blood purification therapy intended to substitute for impaired renal function over an extended period of time.

Core Measures: A set of quality indicators defined by the Centers for Medicare and Medicaid Services.

Critical Care: The specialized care of patients whose conditions are life-threatening and who require comprehensive care and constant monitoring, usually in intensive care units.

Cross Match: In transfusion medicine, refers to the testing that is performed prior to a blood transfusion in order to determine if the donor's blood is compatible with the blood of the intended recipient.

Council on Ethical and Judicial Affairs (CEJA): A council that focuses on periodic updates of the Code of Medical Ethics.

Data mining: The process of finding previously unknown patterns and trends in databases and using that information to build predictive models.

Defense in Depth: A security measure that involves layers, similar to an onion, of security to ensure any breach that occurs can be detected and repulsed.

Dependent variable: (response variable) A variable in a functional whose relation and value are *determined by the values assumed by other variables* in the relation.

Depolarization: Muscle cells, cardiac myocytes, are made up of negatively charged cells, when positive ions are pumped into the cell calcium (Ca^{2+}), sodium (Na^+), and potassium (K^+), the polarity of the cell becomes positive and the cell contract (negative to positive membrane potential).

Diastole: The *relaxation of the heart muscle,* accompanied by the filling of the chambers with blood. Initially both atria and ventricles are in diastole, and there is a period of rapid filling of the ventricles followed by a brief atrial systole. At the same time, there is a corresponding decrease in arterial blood pressure to its minimum, normally about 80 mm of mercury in humans.

Digital Communications and Communications in Medicine (DICOM): The DICOM standard facilitates interoperability of medical imaging equipment by specifying; *network communications,* a set of protocols to be followed by devices claiming conformance to the standard; the *syntax and semantics of commands* and associated information, which can be exchanged using these protocols; *media communication,* a set of media storage services to be followed by devices claiming conformance to the standard, as well as a file format and a medical directory structure to facilitate access to the images and related information stored on interchange media, information that must be supplied with an implementation for which conformance to the standard is claimed.

Digital radiography: A technique that replaces photographic film with x-ray sensors. It is used primarily by dentists.

Electrochemistry: "A science that deals with the relation of electricity to chemical changes and with the interconversion of chemical and electrical energy."

Electrocardiogram (EKG): A device that measures the electrical activity of the cardiac muscle of the heart.

Electrotonic spread: A change in membrane potential (e.g., a receptor potential or synaptic potential) originating in one region of a cell (ΔV_0) is associated with local transmembrane currents that distribute and flow intra- and extracellular to adjacent membrane regions (at distance d), where they in turn cause changes in membrane potential ($\Delta V(d)$). However, the underlying currents get progressively smaller with distance because fractions of them are diverted through transmembrane ion leak channels. Thereby, the elicited adjacent membrane potential changes ($\Delta V(d)$) are reduced in size and altered in shape (electro tonic decrement). http://www.springerreference.com/docs/html/chapterdbid/116505.html

Electrolytes: Minerals in the blood and other body fluids that carry an electric charge. The primary electrolytes in the body are potassium, sodium, calcium, magnesium, chloride, and phosphorous.

Electronic health record (EHR)*: A collection of health data from multiple sources. This is a *more expansive term,* versus EMR, and refers to all information of the health of the body. It is designed to share information among providers and includes all laboratory information and specialist data (used almost exclusively by the Office of the National Coordinator (ONC) for Health Information).

EHR-S: Functional Model (FM) Release 2 2014: "outlines important features and functions that should be contained in an EHR system." Through the creation of functional profiles, this model provides a standard description and common understanding of functions for healthcare settings.

Electronic medical record (EMR): Records used for diagnosis and treatment, refers to medical treatment and history and is a digital form of a medical chart and often refers to information gathered in a local practice. (It is often used, but EHR is the preferred term.)

Electronic Protected Health Information (ePHI): Guidelines to ensure patient confidentiality.

Electronic medication administration record (eMAR): A method of listing the medications that are prescribed for a hospitalized patient and recording their administration.

End diastolic pressure: The pressure in the ventricles at the end of diastole, when the ventricle is filled with blood, just prior to the systolic ejection.

Endotracheal tube: A hollow, flexible tube that is inserted via the mouth, through the vocal chords and into the trachea. The purpose is to maintain a patent airway.

Excitation-contraction coupling (ECC): The process whereby an action potential triggers a myocyte to contract.

Expert systems: Computerized applications that combine computer hardware, software, and specialized information to imitate expert human reasoning and advice.

Fast Health Interoperable Resources (FHIR): (hl7.org/fhir)—"is a next generation standards framework (2014) created by HL7. It combines the features of HL7's Version 2, Version 3 and CDA˙ product lines while leveraging the latest web standards and applying a tight focus on implementability for mobile phone apps, Cloud communications, EHR-based data sharing, server communications.

Foley catheter: A flexible catheter that is inserted through the urethra and into the bladder for the purpose of draining urine.

Fraction of inspired oxygen (FIO$_2$): The percentage of oxygen that a patient is inhaling. Room air is 21% oxygen. Therapeutic delivery systems can supply an FIO$_2$ up to 100%.

The Functional Magnetic Resonance Imager (fMRI) 1990s: measures brain activity and neural activity by alterations in blood flow.

GIFT (GNU image finding tool): is an open framework system. http://www.gnu.org/software/gift/ GNU (Gnu's Not Unix), a UNIX-like operating system, incorporates tools to query images. It allows you to create your own index of images.

HCAHPS: An initiative "to provide a standardized survey instrument and data collection methodology for measuring patients' perspectives on hospital care. HCAHPS survey items complement the data hospitals currently collect to support improvements in internal customer services and quality related activities."

Health informatics: Is "the interdisciplinary study of the design, development, adoption and application of IT-based innovations in healthcare services delivery, management and planning."

Heath Insurance Portability and Accountability Act (HIPAA): The Act of 1996 that required the Health and Human Services (HHS) to develop standards for Electronic health records, data interchange, security, and unique EHR identifies for records.

Health Information Technology for Economic and Clinical Health Act (HITECH): In 2009, the HITEC ACT, part of the ARRA, was adopted and provided almost $20 billion in funding to help hospitals and physicians make their transition to EHRs.

Heart failure: A clinical syndrome characterized by systemic perfusion inadequate to meet the body's metabolic demands as a result of impaired cardiac pump function.

Health information exchange (HIE): is the ability to share/exchange medical information across different medical records systems. http://www.healthit.gov/HIE

Health and Information Management Systems Organization (HIMSS): A global nonprofit organization focused on health IT.

Health Level 7 International (HL7): A standards organization that provides a framework for medical data exchange and sharing and standards that software organizations use to ensure for data interoperability. It is a nonprofit organization with members that represent a large percentage of all EHR development organizations. HL7 is an American National Standards International (ANSI) accredited standard for healthcare. The level 7 refers to the International Standards Organization (ISO) seventh level, the highest achievement of software integration and usability of the ISO seven layer models.

Hemoglobin: An iron-containing protein bound to red blood cells and makes up nearly all the oxygen present, with the exception of a small amount dissolved in the plasma. It is a metalloproteinase, a generic term for a protein that contains a metal ion cofactor.

HIPAA Title II: A standard that describes *security* and *privacy* that sets limits and conditions on the use and disclosure of medical information without patient authorization.

Hemodialysis: Utilizing a device with a semipermeable membrane to filter wastes and fluids from the blood when the kidneys no longer function.

Hemodynamic monitoring: The expert collection and analysis of qualitative and quantitative data of cardiopulmonary function. Fluid-filled monitoring systems are attached intravascular catheters and are used for continuous invasive measurement of arterial and cardiac pressures.

The HIPAA Privacy Rule: A rule that establishes national standards to protect individuals' medical records and other personal health information and applies to health plans, healthcare clearinghouses, and those healthcare providers that conduct certain healthcare transactions electronically.

The HIPAA Security Rule: A rule that establishes national standards to protect individuals' electronic personal health information that is created, received, used, or maintained by a covered entity.

The Hippocratic Oath: Dating back the fifth century BC, describes the responsibility of physicians to focus on the well-being of their patients.

The Immune System: "The immune system is a network of cells, tissues, and organs that work together to protect the body from infection." (NIH)

Immune System Response:

1. There are a number of triggers called danger-associated molecular patterns (DAMPs) that can differentiate between healthy and unhealthy cells.
   a. The innate immune system recognizes molecules via the innate immune system by pattern recognition receptors triggered by cell death or injury
   b. DAMPS are often derived from the plasma membrane, nucleus, endoplasmic reticulum, and cytosol and mitochondria.
1. Pathogen-associated molecular patterns (PAMPs) another set of triggers generated by bacteria and viruses.
   a. Delivery of PAMPs to their respective receptors constitute part of the initiated innate immune control.

Inference engines: Engines that determine which rules match those of the supplied data and match those with the highest probabilities.

Informatics: The "field of study to apply information technology to another field—from healthcare to journalism to biology to economics" (Indiana University).

The Hospital Value-Based Purchasing (VBP) Program: A Centers for Medicare & Medicaid Services (CMS) initiative that rewards acute-care hospitals with incentive payments for the quality of care they provide to people with Medicare.

Hospital Readmission Reduction Program (HRRP): The HRRP imposes financial penalties on hospitals for "excess" readmissions when compared to "expected" levels of readmissions.

Independent variable: (explanatory variable) In mathematics, is a variable whose value determines the value of other variables.

Infusion pump: A medical device that delivers fluids, including nutrients and medications such as antibiotics, chemotherapy drugs, and pain relievers, into a patient's body in controlled amounts.

Inductive charging: is a method by which a magnetic field transfers electricity from an external source to a mobile device without the use of standard wiring. It does this by generating a magnetic field and creating a current in the receiving device. Electricity can move through the air and recharge your device's battery.

Institutional Review Board (IRB) or Privacy Board

International Statistical Classification of Diseases and Related Health Problems (ICD9-10): Created by the World Health Organization (WHO), it provides a list of codes, symptoms, diseases, and social issues related to diseases. It has over 14,000 codes to ensure medical documents clearly refer to similar medical conditions to later be cross referenced to track epidemics and treatment. Example of some of the categories is A00-B99 Infectious and Parasitic Diseases, F00-F99 Mental and Behavioral Disorders, I00-I99 Diseases of the Circulatory System.

ICD Clinical Modification (CM): version 10 **(ICD 10 CM)** is maintained by the Center for Medicaid and Medicare Services (CMS) and is a U.S. national code, that provides more details than the WHO's ICD10, with 68,000 codes.

The Institute of Electrical and Electronics Engineers (IEEE) Standards Organization (SA): An organization that develops standards for the interoperability electronic of devices.

The international Health Terminology Standards Development Organization (IHTSDO): A nonprofit organization in Denmark. It owns SNOMED CT. http://www.ihtsdo.org/

The Integrating the Healthcare Enterprise IHE http://ihe.net/ A non-profit organization created by the U.S. Healthcare Industry and the Radiology Group of North America (RGNA) and supported by Health Information Management Systems Society (HIMSS).

The Institute of Medicine (IOM): An independent, nonprofit organization that works outside of government to provide unbiased and authoritative advice to decision makers and the public. It was established in 1970 and is the health arm of the National Academy of Sciences, which was chartered under President Abraham Lincoln.

Interdisciplinary Plan of Care (IPOC): The goal of IPOC is to support continuity, quality, and safe patient-centric care utilizing the expertise of the various members of the healthcare disciplinary team.

Interoperable: The ability of a system to work with or use the parts or equipment of another system.

Intra-Aortic balloon pump (IABP): A mechanical device that is inserted via the femoral artery. It is comprised of a balloon that inflates with helium during diastole and deflates fight before systole. It increases myocardial oxygen perfusion and decreases the workload of the heart. It is used for patients with an acute myocardial infarction or cardiogenic shock.

The Joint Commission (TJC): An independent, not-for-profit organization, TJC accredits and certifies more than 20,500 healthcare organizations and programs in the United States.

Korotkoff sounds: Sounds that medical personnel listen for when they are taking blood pressure using a noninvasive procedure. There are five Korotkoff sounds but only two are primarily used for blood pressure: systolic (first) and diastolic (fourth: within 10 mmHg above the diastolic blood pressure). Some devices also use the fifth. The other three are used to detect heart disease.

Logical Observation Identified Names and Codes (LOINC): Database used to identify medical laboratory observations.

Lymphocytes: Adaptive immune cells—B cells and T cells are responsible for mounting responses to specific microbes based on previous encounters (immunological memory).

Lymphatic system: A network of vessels and tissues composed of lymph, an extracellular fluid, and lymphoid organs, such as *lymph nodes*. Immune cells are carried through the lymphatic system and converge in lymph nodes, which are found throughout the body.

mHealth: Stands for mobile health. It is remote medical care supported by mobile devices.

Magnetic resonance image (MRI): or Nuclear MRI MRI's utilize non-ionizing absorption and emission in the Radio Frequency (RF) and is best suited for non-calcified i.e. soft tissue.

Mean arterial pressure (MAP): The average pressure in a patient's arteries during one cardiac cycle. It is considered a better indicator of perfusion to vital organs than the systolic pressure.

Meaningful use: Defined by the Center for Medicare and Medicaid Services (CMS) as a series of standards and incentive programs used as criteria for physician reimbursement.

Medical informatics: (Often used interchangeably with biomedical informatics but the term "biomedical" is currently the preferred term used by the leading informatics body in this field, the AMIA) "is the science and art of modeling and recording real-world clinical concepts and events into computable data used to derive actionable information, based on expertise in medicine, information science, information technology, and the scholarly study of issues that impact upon the productive use of information systems by clinical personnel." [S. Silverstein, MD].

Medical logic modules (MLMs): Modules containing knowledge for a single medical diagnosis decision.

Mini-clinics: are walk in clinics usually staffed by physicians assistants or registered nurses (RNs) to treat non-acute medical conditions.

Motor cortex: is the region of the cerebral cortex involved in the planning, control, and execution of voluntary movements.

The **primary motor cortex** generates neural impulses sent to the spinal cord that control the execution of movement.

The **supplementary motor area (SMA)**, involved in the planning of movement, planning of sequences of movement, and the coordination of the two sides of the body.

Nationwide Health Information Network (NHIN): Also called **eHealth Exchange** developed by the U.S. Office of the National Coordinator (ONC) for Health Information Technology, is a series of specifications to securely exchange health data. The goal of the ONC is to tie together HIEs to create a nationwide network.

National Patient Safety Goals: In 2002, The Joint Commission established its National Patient Safety Goals (NPSGs) program. The NPSGs were established to help accredited organizations address specific areas of concern in regard to patient safety.

Never events: The National Quality Forum defines never events as errors in medical care that are of concern to both the public and healthcare professionals and providers, clearly identifiable and measurable, and of a nature such that the risk of occurrence is significantly influenced by the policies and procedures of the healthcare organization.

Nursing informatics: The "science and practice (that) integrates nursing and implementation of communication and information technology" (AMIA).

Office of the National Coordinator (ONC) for Health Information Technology: The office at the forefront of the administration's health IT efforts and is a resource to the entire health system to support the adoption of health information technology and the promotion of nationwide health information exchange to improve healthcare. ONC is organizationally located within the Office of the Secretary for the U.S. Department of Health and Human Services (HHS)

Ohms law: $V = I \times R$ [Voltage = Current (I) (times) **R**esistance] describes the relationship between voltage, also called potential difference, which is the force that moves, or pulls, electrons through the wire.

Oxygen saturation: Oxygen is carried in the blood attached to the hemoglobin molecules. Oxygen saturation is a measure of how much oxygen the blood is carrying as a percentage of the maximum that it could carry.

Oxyhemoglobin: The oxygenated hemoglobin (HbO_2) saturation is the ratio, expressed as a percentage of the amount of oxyhemoglobin relative to the total amount of hemoglobin in blood.

Peritoneal dialysis: A method of removing waste products and fluid from the blood in the setting of kidney failure. A fluid, dialysate, is instilled into the abdomen and the exchange takes place between the blood vessels in the peritoneum and the dialysate.

Personal health records (PHR): is a personal copy of your health information so you can track, maintain, and make informed medical decisions. All doctors are required to provide this information upon request. It is a subset of the EHR and usually contains personal information, medical tests, diagnoses, medications, allergies, and family history.

Peukert's law: The efficiency factor for discharging a battery. Batteries ratings are quantified between the relationship between capacity, current, and discharge time. Qp = capacity when discharged at 1 amp/hr, I = amount of current drawn, k is a constant around 1.3: $t = Qp/I^k$

Pharmacy CDSS: A system in widespread use and is usually integrated with E-prescription systems. It checks drug interactions, contraindications, allergies, dosage levels, and reports possible side effects.

Picture archiving and retrieval system (PACS): A storage and retrieval system for medical images.

Positron emission tomography (PET): A nuclear medicine medical imaging technique that produces a three-dimensional image or map of functional processes or metabolic activities in the body.

Positive end expiratory pressure (PEEP): A technique used with patients who are intubated and on a ventilator in which positive pressure is maintained in the airway throughout exhalation, so that the alveoli (air sacs in the lungs) do not deflate completely at the end of expiration. The objective is to increase the time for oxygen-carbon dioxide exchange as well as to facilitate re-expansion of the alveoli on the next inspiration.

Predictive analytics: The practice of extracting information from existing data sets in order to determine patterns and predict future outcomes and trends. It does not tell you what will happen in the future. It forecasts what might happen in the future with an acceptable level of reliability, and includes what-if scenarios and risk assessment (www.webopedia.com).

Pressure ulcer: An injury to the skin and underlying tissue resulting from prolonged pressure, friction, or shearing forces.

Privacy rule: A rule that sets federal standards to protect individuals personal health information (PHI) and limits to disclosure without patient authorization: **Electronic Protected Health Information (ePHI)**.

Public key encryption systems (PKE): An asymmetric system that uses different keys to encrypt and decrypt.

Pulmonary artery pressure (PAP): A measure of the blood pressure found in the pulmonary artery measured by inserting a catheter into the right atrium and advancing it into the right ventricle and out into the pulmonary artery. Normal pressures are 9–18 mmHg/ 6–12 mmHg.

Pulse oximetry: A procedure used to measure the oxygen level (or oxygen saturation) in the blood. It is considered to be a noninvasive, painless, general indicator of oxygen delivery to the peripheral tissues, such as the finger or earlobe.

Radio Frequency Identification (RFD): The wireless noncontact use of radio frequency electromagnetic fields to transfer data, for the purposes of automatically identifying and tracking tags attached to objects.

Regional Health Information Organization (RHIO): often used interchangeably with an HIE, is a group of companies, hospitals or organizations that have developed a system for seamless exchange of health information.

Reference coordinate system (RCS): The RCS is the spatial coordinate system in a DICOM frame of reference.

HL7 Reference information model (RIM): is an object model that provides a pictorial representation of HL7 clinical data domains. It identifies the life cycle of message groups that are moved between domains of the model. It provides software developers with the architecture for information exchange between EHR in accordance with HL7 standards.

The Regenstrief Mapping Assistant (RELMA): is a search tool for the LOINC clinical database.

Retina: is a light-sensitive layer of tissue made up of photoreceptor cells located at the back of the eye. It is made up of rods that are used in peripheral vision, and cones, responsible for color vision.

Sepsis: A potentially life-threatening complication of an infection that occurs when chemicals released into the bloodstream to fight the infection trigger inflammatory responses throughout the body. This inflammation can trigger a cascade of changes that can damage multiple organ systems, causing them to fail.

Sinoatrial node (SA): is located in the right atrium where the superior vena cava joins the atrial tissue; the SA node acts as the main pacemaker in the heart.

Skin: Usually the first line of defense against microbes. Skin cells produce and secrete important anti-microbial proteins, and immune cells can be found in specific layers of the skin.

STAT: A medical abbreviation for urgent or rush. Something ordered as STAT must be done immediately.

Stroke: A stroke occurs when the blood supply to part of the brain is interrupted or severely reduced, depriving brain tissue of oxygen and nutrients. Within minutes, brain cells begin to die.

Symmetric key encryption (SKE): The technique that uses the same keys to encrypt and decrypt messages.

Systemized Nomenclature of Medicine (SNOMED) Clinical Terms (CT): The most comprehensive international medical classification available with 300,000 medical codes to support medical documentation, as of 2013.

Systole: is the period of contraction of the ventricles of the heart in a single heart beat. Systole causes the ejection of blood into the aorta (left) and lungs (right). During systole, arterial blood pressure reaches its peak, which is normally about 90–120 mm of mercury in humans.

SVO_2: Mixed venous oxygen saturation reflects the amount of oxygen consumed by the tissues. It measures the difference between the oxygen delivered by the arterial system and the amount of oxygen returned to the heart by the venous system. Normal SVO_2 is between 60% and 80%.

Telehealth: is an all-inclusive term encompassing remote healthcare and all its support.

Telemental health: Similar to the other "tele" definitions, it is defined as providing behavioral/mental health services, substance abuse, crisis intervention, and education remotely—services that are delivered using the Internet and wireless communications.

Telemedicine: is the use of medical information exchanged from one site to another via electronic communications to improve a patient's clinical health status. It is the technology used for the delivery of remote clinical services.

Telesurgery: A robotic system that can perform surgeries remotely, also referred to as telepresence, with higher accuracy and smaller incisions, that reduce the postoperative recovery period.

Thymus: T cells mature in the thymus, a small organ located in the upper chest.

Tidal volume: The volume of air inspired or expired in a single breath during regular breathing.

Tracheotomy: A surgical procedure to create an opening through the neck into the trachea. A tube is placed through this opening to provide an airway and to remove secretions from the lungs.

Transformer equation: An equation that relates to the turns of wire on the coil; that is, a coil is wire wrapped around a metal post a few thousand times. The equation relates the voltage between the first, primary coil, to the secondary coil: $V_p/V_s = N_p/N_s$.

Translational Bioinformatics: The development analytic methods to optimize the transformation of biomedical data, and genomic data, into proactive, predictive, preventive, and participatory health.

Unified Medical Language System (UMLS): A mapping system and toolset used to convert between different medical vocabularies. It is used by Medical Informatics developers. It contains approximately 5 million concepts names and 1 million concepts and relationships between names and terms.

Urgent care center: is a broad term that is defined as "the provision of immediate medical service offering outpatient care for the treatment of acute and chronic illness and injury."

Ventilator: A device that supports breathing. It delivers oxygenated air to the lungs under positive pressure. The patient exhales passively.

Venous oxygen saturation (SvO$_2$) (range 65%–75%): Percentage of oxygen bound to hemoglobin in blood returning to the right side of the heart.

Venous thromboembolism (VTE): A deep venous thrombosis is a blood clot that forms in a vein deep inside a part of the body. The most common sites are in the large veins in the lower leg and thigh. The danger is that when a clot breaks off and moves through the bloodstream as an embolism it can lodge in the lungs.

Ventricular assist device: A mechanical pump designed to support heart function and blood flow. Blood is taken from the ventricle and passes through the pump. It is then returned to the aorta for circulation throughout the body.

Virtual private network (VPN): allows you to send information securely over the internet as if it was your own private network. It sets up a virtual point to point connection, that is, a permanent link between two users, using either dedicated connections, encrypting the traffic or virtual tunneling protocols that appear as public messages.

Wireless medical devices: are defined as "any medical monitoring technology, worn or implanted, that gather physiological information."

Index